THE CAPITALIST SYSTEM

THIRD EDITION

THE CAPITALIST SYSTEM

A Radical Analysis of American Society

Written and Edited by

RICHARD C. EDWARDS
University of Massachusetts, Amherst

MICHAEL REICH
University of California, Berkeley

THOMAS E. WEISSKOPF
University of Michigan, Ann Arbor

PRENTICE-HALL, *Englewood Cliffs, New Jersey 07632*

Library of Congress Cataloging-in-Publication Data

Edwards, Richard
  The capitalist system.

  Bibliography: p.
  1. United States—Economic conditions—1945-
Addresses, essays, lectures. 2. United States—
Social conditions—1945   —Addresses, essays,
lectures. 3. Capitalism—United States—Addresses,
essays, lectures. 4. Socialism—United States—
Addresses, essays, lectures. I. Reich, Michael.
II. Weisskopf, Thomas E. III. Title.
HC106.5.E393 1986   330.973′092   85-25694
ISBN 0-13-113564-3

Editorial/production supervision and interior design: *Nancy G. Follender*
Cover design: *Lundgren Graphics*
Manufacturing buyer: *Ed O'Dougherty*

Printed in the United States of America

10 9 8 7 6 5 4 3 2 1

ISBN 0-13-113564-3   01

PRENTICE-HALL INTERNATIONAL (UK) LIMITED, *LONDON*
PRENTICE-HALL OF AUSTRALIA PTY. LIMITED, *SYDNEY*
PRENTICE-HALL CANADA INC., *TORONTO*
PRENTICE-HALL HISPANOAMERICANA, S.A., *MEXICO*
PRENTICE-HALL OF INDIA PRIVATE LIMITED, *NEW DELHI*
PRENTICE-HALL OF JAPAN, INC., *TOKYO*
PRENTICE-HALL OF SOUTHEAST ASIA PTE. LTD., *SINGAPORE*
EDITORA PRENTICE-HALL DO BRASIL, LTDA., *RIO DE JANEIRO*
WHITEHALL BOOKS LIMITED, *WELLINGTON, NEW ZEALAND*

CONTENTS

**PART FOUR
TOWARD AN ALTERNATIVE TO THE CAPITALIST SYSTEM**

PREFACE

This book analyzes modern capitalism from the perspective of radical political economy, with a primary focus on the experience of the United States. We have organized the book around a variety of different readings selected and edited from the work of many different authors. Our own contributions as author-editors include the choice and arrangement of readings, the authoring of several original articles, and the writing of extensive introductions to all the chapters and readings in order to bind the diverse materials into a coherent whole. Though we have conceived the book as the basis for an independent radical course in political economy, it can also serve as a useful collection of readings for other courses in the social sciences.

The last edition of this book was published in 1978. During the years since then, the issues and problems that we analyzed have continued to confront our society, and the world capitalist system as a whole has been subjected to new sources of stress and strain. At the same time, radical political economists in the United States and abroad have continued to develop and enrich their analyses of the operation and the contradictions of modern capitalism. It seemed to us important, then, that we revise our book so as to make it more relevant to present-day concerns and more representative of the current state of radical political economy.

In preparing this third edition, we have benefited from additional years of teaching and research and from the opportunity to draw on a great deal of new work by our colleagues in the Union for Radical Political Economics.[1] As a result, we have made many changes in the organization and content of the book; more than 50 percent of

[1]Founded in 1968 at the height of the radical political movement in the United States, URPE has continued to thrive through the 1980s, providing an organizational network for radical political economists engaged in teaching, research, communication, and political action. URPE publishes a quarterly *Review of Radical Political Economics*, sponsors a monthly bulletin of economic affairs, *Dollars and Sense*, and promotes sundry other activities; the URPE national office is located at 155 West 23rd St., 12th Floor, New York, New York, 10011.

this third edition is entirely new, and much of the rest has been modified or updated. We have thoroughly reorganized every chapter and rewritten all introductions. The major innovations include a greatly expanded treatment of the development and functioning of stages of capitalism in the United States and a new radical analysis of capitalist economic crises (Chapter 10).

We have edited judiciously most of the readings being reprinted. The editing, we trust, improves the clarity of exposition, avoids unnecessary repetition, and focuses on points that are most germane to our analysis. Deletions from the original text are indicated by ellipses. Each source is cited in full so that readers can consult the original text as desired. In excerpting readings, we removed footnotes that were not essential to the understanding or documentation of the piece and renumbered the footnotes and tables for continuity. Finally, we have included at the end of the book a bibliography of additional readings that we have found particularly useful.

As with previous editions, we communicated regularly and met often to plan this third edition. The resulting book thus represents a truly collective effort. Some division of labor was necessary for this edition: Michael Reich made the final selections of materials, wrote the chapter and section introductions, and edited the manuscript. S. William Segal provided excellent research assistance. Richard Edwards and Thomas E. Weisskopf reviewed the manuscript and improved the final product. Many other friends and colleagues, too numerous to identify here, helped during the course of work on this and the previous editions. To all we are profoundly grateful.

Richard C. Edwards,
University of Massachusetts, Amherst
Michael Reich,
University of California, Berkeley
Thomas E. Weisskopf,
University of Michigan, Ann Arbor

THE CAPITALIST SYSTEM

CHAPTER 1

Introduction

AMERICAN CAPITALISM HAS PRODUCED the most stupendous wealth any society has ever known. In the process, it has advertised its bright side and drummed into our heads its benefits. Its triumphs are shown to us in the happy faces of the Coca-Cola commercial, in the impressive technology of the space shuttles, in the endless procession of rising economic indexes. We know only too well how a poor farm boy named Henry Ford (or John D. Rockefeller or J. Paul Getty or H. Ross Perot or Edwin Land) was able to parlay "freedom of opportunity" into a billion-dollar fortune. We see pictures of vast piles of wheat and soybeans being loaded for export to countries that cannot feed themselves. We are dazzled, especially at Christmas-time, by the new toys, the newly essential "feminine hygiene" products, new recreation vehicles, pocket calculators, cameras, clothes fashions, "natural" foods. We observe the tide of state lotteries and TV game shows in which the process of becoming rich is telescoped from a "lifetime of sacrifice" to a convenient half-hour. Life is increasingly pictured for us through the carefully nurtured images of "celebrities"—those affluent, happy, witty, and active personalities who people the movies, professional sports, TV's situation comedies, rock music, and politics. American capitalism's wealth has produced much that glitters.

Yet as we proceed through the closing decades of the twentieth century, we hardly need to be told that American capitalism has another side as well, a less affluent, less eternally happy, less secure, less sensible, and less decent side: there is a seamy side to its advertised froth. After all, situation comedies alternate with shows of crime and violence. Henry Ford's fortune (now Henry Ford II's) stands in stark contrast to the underpaid auto workers' plight. The space shuttle has proved unsuited for mass transit. Rising economic indexes can measure rising prices, unemployment, and misery as well as increasing output. And what are we to make of the booming sales of Valium and other drugs that seem to be necessary to keep masses of Americans from being chronically overanxious or depressed? Or of the continued massive scarring of Appalachia and, increasingly, Montana, Wyoming, Arizona, and elsewhere as strip-mining literally eats up the land? Or of the startling but repeated reports of children's malnutrition at home as the food stamp program is unable to service all those who need aid? Or of the visible deterioration in urban housing? Or of the race riots that erupt from the attempts to desegregate Boston and Louisville? Or of the disclosures of a far-reaching domestic spying apparatus run by the federal government to disrupt political opposition and prepare for "emergency detention" of opponents? Or of the CIA's assistance to the fascist generals or corrupt politicians in South Africa, El Salvador, and Chile? These are also very much a part of modern American capitalism.

American troops and bombers are no longer decimating the people of Indochina, but we keep learning about new parts of the world where well-funded American agents are fighting against movements of popular liberation.

2

The U.S. government ignores pressing needs for health care and environmental protection while facilitating the growth of the military-industrial complex and serving the interests of giant multinational corporations. Most people's jobs are alienating; wealth and power are concentrated in the hands of a privileged elite; poverty, racism, and sexism persist despite highly publicized efforts to diminish them. Perhaps the most important new development in recent years has been the failure of our economic system to do one thing it had done tolerably well since World War II: maintain a fairly low level of unemployment with a reasonable degree of price stability. In the 1970s and 1980s we have experienced rates of unemployment and inflation unprecedented in the last three decades, and we have learned that in spite of the best efforts of sophisticated economists our capitalist society is not immune to economic crises.

Despite its wealth and democratic promise, our society continues to be afflicted with such problems. Are they simply the modern equivalents of age-old forms of oppression, to be expected in any society because people are inherently greedy, selfish, and power-seeking? Or, formidable as they may seem, are they merely aberrations of a basically just and humane society, problems that can be solved with enough intelligence and determination on the part of our leaders?

We reject both of these explanations. We believe, instead, that human behavior is significantly shaped by the socioeconomic environment within which people work and live. Oppression has its roots in the basic economic institutions of a society, and the various forms of oppression we observe in our own society today derive in large part from its capitalist institutions.

The perspective we bring to this book is that of radical political economy, which draws its inspiration and its basic analytic framework from the Marxist tradition of critical theory, interdisciplinary analysis, and struggle for change. We do not find everything that Marx or his followers have written to be useful, or even relevant or correct. On the contrary, readers familiar with the Marxist literature will notice (and may complain) that many strands of Marxist thought are not represented in this book. Nonetheless, our approach is fundamentally Marxist and our primary intellectual debt is to Karl Marx.

The following quotation from Ernesto (Che) Guevara describes well our position.[1]

> The merit of Marx is that he suddenly produces a qualitative change in the history of social thought. He interprets history, understands its dynamic, predicts the future, but in addition to predicting it (which would satisfy his scientific obligation), he expresses a revolutionary concept: the world must not only be interpreted, it must be transformed.

Explanation alone is not enough. The purpose of social and economic analysis should be to help eradicate the current sources of oppression rather than merely describe them, or—still worse—to obscure them. We want to place our analysis squarely on the side of progressive movements for radical social change. For, as a result of our studies and our association with these movements in the United States, it has become clear to us that to achieve a better society the capitalist system must and can be challenged.

We do not imply that *all* forms of oppression can be attributed *solely* to capitalism, nor that they will automatically disappear when capitalism is replaced by a new social order. We have respect for the tenacity of such phenomena as sexism and military expansion, which predate the rise of capitalism and are not unique to capitalist societies today. Yet we do believe that most often capitalism makes use of and reinforces these forms of oppression. To eradicate them it is therefore necessary, but not sufficient, to transform the basic institutions of the capitalist system itself. To achieve a truly humane society, the struggle against capitalism must be intimately linked with struggles against all forms of oppression.

[1]"Notes for the Study of the Ideology of the Cuban Revolution," *Studies on the Left,* 1, no. 3, 1960.

The purpose of this book is to contribute to these struggles by analyzing the structure and the dynamics of the capitalist system in the United States. In so doing, we seek to illuminate the relationships between capitalist institutions and the various forms of oppression discussed above, and we seek to identify those forces in the development of American capitalism that create the potential for a radical transformation of the social order.

CAPITALISM AND SOCIALISM

Throughout this book we will be criticizing the capitalist system that dominates the Western world today. In chapter 2 we define quite explicitly what we mean by the capitalist mode of production and how it is to be distinguished from alternative modes. But it will be useful at the outset to clarify our understanding of the differences between capitalism and socialism, since the meaning of both terms has been subject to much confusion.

A common view, which we find inappropriate, is that the difference between capitalism and socialism depends solely upon the legal relations of ownership of the means of production. Capitalism is often equated with private ownership of capital, while socialism is equated with public or state ownership of capital.

In many advanced capitalist countries—such as England, France, or Sweden—the state-owned branches of production have grown in importance in recent decades, and the state has taken on the responsibility of regulating and managing the entire economy. These countries are often said to be examples of mixed systems, in that they embody elements of both capitalism and socialism. However, the state-owned production sectors in these countries tend to differ only marginally, if at all, from the private sectors of the economy, inasmuch as the state employs capitalist-oriented criteria in organizing its activities. These countries are examples of what we would call *state capitalism*.

At the same time, in the Soviet Union and the Eastern European countries, virtually the entire economy is run by a centralized state apparatus. This system has resulted in a stratified, bureaucratic, and hierarchical society in which the maximization of material goods production—subject to the constraint of preserving hierarchical control—is a primary objective. Such a society might best be called *state socialism*. In Serge Mallet's apt analogy, the state socialist societies of the Soviet Union and Eastern Europe are to true socialism what "the monsters of the paleolithic era are to present animal species: clumsy, abortive, prototypes."[2] It would be incorrect to equate mechanically state socialism and state capitalism, for the two systems do differ in significant respects. For example, the state socialist societies have gone much further toward equalizing the distribution of essential goods and services such as food, housing, medical care, and transportation. Yet state socialism and state capitalism are akin in many respects: neither are model societies of socialism to be emulated.

For us, socialism is more than a juridical change in the legal relations of ownership. Socialism means democratic, decentralized, and *participatory* control for the individual: it means having a say in the decisions that affect one's life. Such a participatory form of socialism certainly requires equal access for all to material and cultural resources, which in turn requires the abolition of private ownership of capital and the redistribution of wealth. But it also calls for socialist men and women to eliminate alienating, destructive forms of production, consumption, education, and community and family life. Participatory socialism requires the elimination of corporate bureaucracies and all such hierarchical forms, and their replacement, not by new state or party bureaucracies but by a self-governing and self-managing people with directly chosen repre-

[2]Serge Mallet, "Bureaucracy and Technology in the Socialist Countries," *Socialist Revolution*, 1, no. 3 (May/June 1970), p. 45.

sentatives subject to recall and replacement. Participatory socialism entails a sense of egalitarian cooperation, of solidarity of people with one another; but at the same time it respects individual and group differences and guarantees individual rights. It affords to all individuals the freedom to exercise human rights and civil liberties that are not mere abstractions but have concrete day-to-day meaning.[3]

Our vision of a radical social transformation of the United States clearly involves far more than formal changes in political and economic institutions. Such changes must be part of an ongoing process of change in social and cultural consciousness that will constitute a revolution of social relations among people.

[3]We pursue further our conception of socialism in Chapter 11, where it is described in greatest detail by Lerner, Section 11.3, p. 414. By our criteria, no existing country has as yet achieved full participatory socialism.

CHAPTER 2

THE CAPITALIST ECONOMY: STRUCTURE AND CHANGE

"EVERY CHILD KNOWS," Karl Marx once wrote, "that a country that ceased to work would die."[1] Every society must organize the production, distribution, and consumption of the necessities of life if it is simply to survive. Every society must, moreover, organize its own reproduction if it is not to disappear. There must be some particular social arrangement for these tasks to be achieved; in fact, there are a dazzling variety of ways in which different human societies have organized and divided these tasks in the course of human history. *Why* is any particular society organized the way it is, how did it come to be that way, and what makes it change? Is there any logic to the complex patterns of development of different societies? What is the relationship between the "economic" and the "noneconomic" spheres of a society?

This chapter presents one approach to these questions: the conceptual approach to history developed by Marx and known as historical materialism. We shall use this approach to analyze the structure and dynamics of capitalism, to ask such questions as: How did the social system that we call capitalism, with its particular way of organizing production, distribution, consumption, and reproduction, come into being? What are the essential features of the capitalist mode of production? How has it changed over time?

I: Historical Materialism

The materialist approach to history begins its analysis of any society by examining the particular social arrangement of production. The act of production always has two main aspects. First, people produce by transforming an object, a raw material of the physical world, into another object, using some sorts of tools or means of production. Second, while engaging in this production process, people simultaneously enter into particular social relationships with one another. These relationships can take a variety of forms. In a rural patriarchal farm family, for example, the hierarchical kinship relations of age and sex in the family determine the way the labor of the family is carried out, the way tasks are divided, and the specific tasks assigned to each family member. In an egalitarian cooperative farm, by contrast, the organization and allocation of tasks will be determined quite differently. Marx argues that people's social relations, their ideas about themselves and their social world (their consciousness), as well as their laws, morality, ethics, and religion, can only be understood in relation to the way they organize their productive and reproductive activity.

We begin the presentation of historical materialism by introducing the important concepts that we need to analyze the dominant mode of production in any society: forces of production, surplus product, social class, relations of production, mode of production, base, and superstructure. The *forces of production* con-

[1]Marx, Letter to Dr. Kugelmann, July 1868.

7

sist of the raw materials, tools, instruments, machines, buildings, and equipment used in the process of production as well as the state of science and technology, the organizational techniques of production, and most importantly, the abilities, skills, and knowledge of people themselves. The degree of development of the productive forces measures a society's capacity to produce.

The *surplus product* is that part of a society's total potential product remaining beyond those used to reproduce both the means of production (at their current level) and the producers (at a consumption level equal to current norms).

In all but the most primitive societies, the productive forces have developed beyond a rudimentary level, and a surplus is or potentially could be produced. It is then generally possible to identify two different groups: those who *produce* the surplus, or the producing class, and those who, through some form of direct or indirect coercion, *appropriate* the surplus, or the appropriating class. A *social class* is thus defined as a group of people who have a common relation to the production and appropriation of the surplus. The appropriating class dominates the producing class by capturing the surplus. The process of domination usually includes the appropriating class using its power to organize the production process in a hierarchical manner and organizing exchange in markets in an advantageous manner. Because the two classes have antagonistic interests, *class struggle* is an inherent element of any class society.

The *social relations of production* are defined by the specific manner in which the surplus is produced and then appropriated from the direct producers. The relations of production can be described by answering four questions: (1) Who possesses the instruments or means of production? (2) What are the direct social relations in the production process between the producers and appropriators of surplus? (3) By what manner does the appropriating class arrange to appropriate the surplus? (4) Are things produced for direct use or for exchange on a market?

We define the *mode of production* as the combination of the existing forces of production and the existing relations of production. This mode of production provides us with a way to periodize history, for every society can be characterized by its particular dominant mode of production. At any given time an actual society will contain a variety of modes of production within it, but one of them can usually be identified as dominant.

An elaboration of slave, feudal, petty commodity, and capitalist social relations of production will help to clarify the concept of a mode of production. In each example, we will address the four questions that were just listed. In slave societies, the producers (the slaves) do not own or control the instruments or means of production. The slaves are owned by the master as pieces of property that he or she is legally free to sell. The slave is supervised in the process of production by the master or his or her assistant, who organizes in detail the tasks and process of production. The master through direct coercive force appropriates the total product of the slaves' labor, using some of the products to provide the slaves' subsistence. Slave production can be either for use or for exchange; on the slave plantations of the pre–Civil War South cotton was grown not for internal consumption but for external sale on a world market.

In feudal societies, the most important means of production, the land, cannot be sold by either lords or serfs and so is not subject to private ownership. The producers (the serfs) possess the instruments of production and work on allocated plots of land. They organize the production process themselves and are responsible for providing for their own subsistence. The serfs are tied to the land and cannot be removed by the lord. The lord extracts surplus from the serf through traditional obligations on the serf to perform certain annual economic services; the lord provides in return basic military protection. Most production is for internal consumption by the serfs and the lord of the manor, with little being exchanged on a market.

A petty commodity mode of production is

characterized by a class of free, independent small producers, usually artisans (crafts people) and small farmers. These producers own the means of production, the craft tools, and the land. They organize and control their own production process and sell their products on a market, thereby obtaining funds to purchase other commodities for their needs. Petty commodity production is thus for exchange rather than for use. There is no apparent appropriating class here. The petty commodity mode is an example of an incomplete or transitional mode. It often exists in a relation to another predominant mode or tends to become fairly quickly transformed into another mode as some of the producers begin to accumulate their surplus and develop into an appropriating class.

Capitalist relations of production are characterized by the complete separation of the producers (wageworkers) from the means of production. Capitalists as a class have a monopoly on the means of production while workers have only their labor-power, which they must sell to the capitalists for a wage if they are to subsist. The capitalist directly organizes the labor process, so that workers labor under the supervision of capitalists or their managers. In respect to control of the work process and ownership of the means of production, capitalism resembles slavery and differs from feudalism and petty commodity production. The objective of the capitalists is to expand their initial capital by combining labor and means of production and selling the resultant commodities, which are their property, for a profit. Hence, capitalist production is for exchange, not for use. Workers are free to change employers, while capitalists are free to hire and fire workers as needed. Capitalist relations of production thus differ from slavery and feudalism in that the relationship between the worker and the owner of the means of production is purely contractual, with no direct coercion involved. The appropriation of the surplus occurs by means of a market exchange.

As we have just seen, each of these four types of class societies are characterized by

profoundly different relations of production; they provide our starting point for analyzing these societies. For example, by examining capitalist relations of production we shall see not only the role of class struggle between workers and capitalists but also the constant need of capitalism to expand.

Each of the four different relations of production is associated with a particular set of property laws, or concepts of property and possession. These in turn necessitate legal and juridical institutions and some sort of political structure or state to articulate and enforce those laws. In addition, each mode of production will also have a corresponding ideology and institutions to promote that ideology. An ideology is a set of commonly held values that contributes to the stability and cohesion of a given society by legitimizing the position of the dominant class that appropriates the surplus. The legal, political, and ideological institutions form part of the *superstructure* of a society; this superstructure rests upon and is also essential for the maintenance of the social relations of production that constitute the economic *base*. The legal, political, and ideological functions of the superstructure may be carried out directly by the appropriating class, or by social groups dependent upon it—for example, a state bureaucracy.

The social relations of production are in these ways crucial to understanding the general character of a society. But the connection between the base and the superstructure of the society is not simple. A purely unidirectional analysis of base and superstructure would be grossly inadequate, for social custom, tradition, culture, ideology, philosophical views, kinship and family relations, religion, politics, judicial forms, and the like all certainly have a historical dynamic of their own and to some extent condition the base. The economic factors are themselves constituted in part by these superstructural relationships.

The relationship between the base and the superstructure may be different in societies based on different modes of production. When the appropriation of the surplus involves transparent coercion, as in a feudal society, the superstructure takes on a more important role, as religion did in feudal times. Serfs accepted the appropriation of the surplus they produced as a part of their station in a religious order created by God. In a capitalist society, the appropriation of surplus is indirect, obscured by market relations, and the base plays a particularly dominant role. Instead of society controlling material life, the economic base dominates much more of social life, and more of the social product takes the form of commodities.

Surplus product, social class, mode of production, base and superstructure: these concepts describe a society from an objective structural viewpoint. But societies consist of people. An adequate understanding of a society requires a theory of how people act as well, how human activity is situated in, and in turn shapes, these objective structures. Class struggle, for example, emerges from the recognition by members of a class of their common interests and opposition to another class.

A consideration of human activity in a structural context enables us to understand historical change, how societies are transformed from one dominant mode of production to another, from one class structure to another. The key to historical change is the unfolding contradiction within a mode of production between the forces of production and the relations of production. The forces of production develop and grow over the long run, although in a manner and rate that depend on the given social relations of production. But the social relations of production tend to be much less dynamic than the forces of production because of the vested interests of the dominant class in preserving the social status quo. The contradiction between the forces and the relations of production provides the evolving context in which struggle between opposing classes occurs and develops.

The contradiction is likely to intensify as the social relations of production become a fetter on the further development of the forces of production. For example, in England, traditional feudal ties and monopolistic charters granted by the crown inhibited the develop-

ment of productive possibilities that could only be realized with free markets in land, labor, and other commodities—that is, with capitalist social relations. An emergent capitalist class thus found itself in direct conflict with the feudal landed aristocracy and the crown. But a dominant class is unlikely to give up its privileged status peacefully. The contradiction between the forces of production (represented in England by the rising capitalists) and the social relations of production (represented by the ruling feudalists) grows in intensity and is expressed in cultural, ideological, and political as well as economic forms, producing a generalized social and political crisis. The crisis is resolvable only by a decisive and often violent rupture with the status quo that transforms the existing class structure. Historical examples of such ruptures include the English Revolution with its beheading of King Charles in 1649 (in large part, a capitalist rebellion against the absolutist monarchy and feudalism); the French Revolution in 1789 (a revolt against the feudal nobility and clergy); the American Civil War in 1861–65 (the destruction of slavery allowed the full development of capitalist relations of production); the Russian Revolution in 1917; and the Chinese Revolution in 1949.

II: The Capitalist Mode of Production

Earlier we defined a mode of production in terms of both "forces of production" and "relations of production" and analyzed the historical emergence of the capitalist mode of production. We shall continue our theoretical inquiry into the capitalist system by examining in greater detail the essential features of the capitalist mode of production. In so doing we shall be abstracting for the moment from many of the realities of our society, such as its complex class structure, international relations, production within the home, and so on in order to focus more clearly on the most important characteristics of the capitalist mode of production itself. We shall then, in the next parts of this book, become much more concrete and apply the theoretical analysis of the capitalist mode of production developed here to present-day capitalism in the United States.

The relations of production under capitalism define the distinguishing characteristics of a capitalist society: the basic economic structures or institutions by which the production, distribution, and consumption of goods and services are organized. These structures are "basic" in a triple sense. First, as Dobb argues in this chapter, the emergence of these institutions defines the *historical* period of capitalism, providing us with a historical delineation of the capitalist epoch. Second, they are basic in a *logical* sense in that they define what we mean by the capitalist mode of production. Third, they are basic in an *empirical* sense; as we argue through the rest of this book, these institutions are the most important for understanding the nature of capitalist society.

Let us review the basic characteristics that distinguish the capitalist mode of production. First of all, the production of goods and services takes the form of production of commodities; that is, goods and services are produced for sale on a market rather than for direct use by the producer. But the prevalence of market exchange does not by itself signify the existence of a capitalist mode of production, for we could imagine a society of independent artisans and small farmers who produced for a market. Such a society, which existed, for example, in New England about 1600 to 1750, tends to be transitional because its relatively egalitarian class structure is unstable. Sooner or later, significant inequalities in wealth and power are bound to emerge.

Distinguishing the capitalist mode of production from the "petty commodity production" of independent market-oriented artisans and farmers, the second basic characteristic of capitalism is the existence of two classes: a class of *capitalists* who among themselves have a class monopoly over the means of production, and a class of propertyless *wage-workers* who sell their capacity to work, or labor-power, to capitalists in exchange for a wage or salary. The vast majority of people own very little or no property, aside from personal property such as their clothes, cars, homes, and household items. More precisely, most people own very little *income-earning* property, and they therefore can obtain the income they need to maintain themselves and their families only by selling their labor-power on a labor market to the highest bidder. Hence under capitalism labor-power is a commodity, subject to the fluctuations of "supply and demand" in the market for labor. The capitalist mode of production therefore presupposes both the existence of commodity production in general and the transformation of labor-power itself into a commodity in particular.

A third basic characteristic of the capitalist mode of production is that capitalists and not workers control the process of production itself. As part of the wage bargain, workers relinquish control over their labor during the stipulated working day and have no say in the disposition of the things the workers produce, the product. Hence workers are deprived of control over both their work activities and the work product. The decisions about what to produce, how to organize the production process, what technology to use, and so forth are made by capitalists. As the forces of production develop over time, capitalists tend to organize the production process along increasingly hierarchical lines, creating many different levels of employment, from production and clerical workers on the bottom to "middle management" to high-level managers and executives. Capitalists organize production hierarchically in order to maintain their control over the production process and to further the productivity of their workers. Thus the social relations of production take hierarchical forms under capitalism.

Certain particular legal relations of ownership, or private property rules, derive from these basic characteristics of the capitalist mode of production. These rules, whose enforcement is the primary responsibility of the state, establish that the owner of a piece of property has the exclusive right to the use of that property, to enjoy the benefits from it, to consume it, to dispose of it, to sell it, and so forth. For personal items, such as household articles, these rules usually just reflect patterns of use: the "ownership" of beds or tooth-brushes among people in a family only identi-fies the ways in which the beds or toothbrushes will be used. However, for *social objects*, such as factories, offices, schools, recreation areas, land in a community, and labor services, these property rules also signify and reflect relations among people in different classes. No matter how social in character "private" property may be, the vesting of ownership of society's economic apparatus in the hands of capitalists gives capitalists the legal right to control that property's use and disposition. Our legal sys-tem does not make this distinction between personal possessions and income-producing property, but the distinction is important nonetheless in understanding capitalism.

In this chapter we shall investigate the im-portant features of a society dominated by these capitalist relations of production: the re-ality of exploitation underlying legal forms of equality and freedom; the hierarchical nature of the capitalist mode of production, apparent once we leave the realm of markets and ex-change and enter factories and offices to ex-amine production and the labor process directly; the ceaseless drive to expand that is inherent in the process of capital accumula-tion; the cyclical economic crises of capitalism that are generated both by the basic class con-flicts between capitalists and workers and by the competition among the capitalists as they attempt to *sell* the commodities they produce; and finally, the ways in which the capitalist mode of production reproduces not only capi-tal but also capitalist social relations.

EXPLOITATION

Unlike societies characterized by slavery and serfdom, capitalist societies such as the United States guarantee to each individual freedom and equality before the law. That means that no one is directly compelled to work for some-one else or to enter into any sort of contract or exchange. On the contrary, each of us has the freedom to enter into contracts as we desire

and to own property without interference. This apparent freedom and equality to carry on our private affairs have led many defenders of capitalism to laud the operations of the competitive market. As Milton Friedman has put it, with a free market everybody gains be-cause "no exchange will take place unless both parties benefit from it";[2] otherwise they would not enter into the transaction.

How, then, is it possible to speak of ex-ploitation under capitalism, of the reproduc-tion of a class division between those who have to work for a living and those who can live, without needing to work, off the fruits of other people's labor? The answer is that although the basic transaction between capitalists and workers appears on the surface to be a volun-tary contractual exchange between equals, it is in reality a coercive exchange between une-quals. Workers do not have to sell their labor services to any individual capitalist, but they must work for some capitalist in order to ob-tain the income they need to buy the com-modities necessary to maintain themselves and their families. The wage or salary income that workers receive is necessary for their immedi-ate survival. Capitalists, with their accumu-lated wealth arising from ownership of the means of production, are not so immediately vulnerable. They enter as buyers into the mar-ket for labor with the great advantage of being able to wait, if necessary, until the terms are favorable to them, and being able to influence those terms with the wealth at their disposal. The result is unequal: the working class as a whole produces commodities whose total mon-etary value is much greater than the value of their wage and salary income. The difference is captured by the capitalist class in the form of profits, interest, and rent.

Think of the economy as a way of organiz-ing and dividing the total labor time available to society for the production of valuable com-modities (including the production of ma-chines, buildings, and so on that are used as inputs in the production of other commodi-

[2]Milton Friedman, *Capitalism and Freedom* (Chicago: Uni-versity of Chicago Press, 1963), p. 13.

ties). Each person's income represents his or her share of that total product. Then we see that capitalists and workers receive shares of the *product* of all social labor that do not correspond to the shares of labor time actually worked, as is evident from the fact that an owner of a factory need not put in any labor time to receive a share of the product. The commodities the workers can buy with their wages and salaries embody less social labor time than they themselves put in. The basically unequal and coercive nature of the capital-labor relationship is thus obscured by the existence of markets. This exploitation of labor occurs even in a competitive capitalist economy.

AUTHORITARIANISM IN PRODUCTION

The lack of freedom and equality that characterizes the capitalist mode of production becomes much clearer once we leave the sphere where commodities are exchanged (i.e., markets) and investigate directly the organization of production in capitalist factories, offices, farms, and mines. In any capitalist firm the organization of production is authoritarian in that the basic decisions are made by capitalists and executed by workers. The right to participate in decision making defines, in the political sphere, what we mean by a democracy. This basic democratic right is relinquished by workers when they sell the disposition of their labor-power to capitalists for a stipulated time period.

However, the workers are not mere pawns; they are also actors in their own right. As a result, the relationship between capitalists and workers is one of conflict. Capitalists want to get as much work as possible out of workers, to turn their potential to work, or labor-power, into maximum labor actually done. Capitalists expend a great deal of energy trying to increase the productivity of workers, using the threat of firing them, the incentives of promotions, bonuses, and so on. Workers, on the other hand, are active human beings who

want to minimize the unpleasantness of the time they must spend working, and they certainly do not want to work so hard as to increase the work demanded of them; so they spend much energy trying to circumvent the aims of the capitalists. The conflict between workers and capitalists is thus one that involves not only bargaining over wage rates but also the very organization of production itself. It is out of this basic struggle that the capitalists' problem of managing labor arises, and this is a problem that gets more complex as firms get larger; organizing production on an authoritarian and increasingly hierarchical model has historically been the capitalists' solution. Despite the *appearance* of equality and freedom in the marketplace, capitalist production is premised on inequality and coercion.

ACCUMULATION OF CAPITAL AND CRISES

The reason that capitalists are in business is in order to make profits and thereby expand their capital. It is not merely a matter of greed on the part of individual capitalists, but the inexorable pressure to make profits that is created and enforced by the competitive structure of the capitalist mode of production. To meet the competition and stay in business, each individual capitalist must look continuously for ways to protect or increase profits by expanding sales, cutting costs, and finding new markets and new products. This in turn is likely to require an increasing *scale* of production—hence the drive to accumulate capital by reinvesting profits. The class struggle between workers and capitalists also forces capitalists to accumulate capital. When labor costs rise too high and begin to encroach on profits, capitalists must invest in new technologies that can displace workers and they search for new areas to relocate their capital. Capitalism is thus by its very nature a system that is constantly striving to expand. As a result, capitalism spreads its geographic net and also transforms more and more areas of social life into profit-making activities.

The accumulation process can be described as a circuit or series of steps in which a capitalist starts with a certain amount of money or capital and seeks to complete the circuit with more capital. The process begins when a capitalist *invests* money in raw materials and labor-power and also buys or rents the tools, machines, and buildings needed in production. In the second part of the circuit, the *labor process,* the capitalist brings together the means of production and the workers, who, under the direction and supervision of the capitalist and/or the capitalist's managers, labor to produce commodities. This step involves the authoritarian organization of work just discussed above. To complete the circuit successfully, the commodities must then be circulated or sold on a market, for it is only when the receipts are safely in from the buyers that the capitalist will actually *realize* the profits and be able to increase the capital. The circuit can then be repeated with still greater amounts of capital involved.

The *rate* at which the accumulation of capital takes place in the economy will in general be uneven; periodically *economic crises* will break out, characterized by falling production and increased unemployment. This *cyclical* nature of capitalist expansion is due, among other things, to conflicts that occur between workers and capitalists in the realm of production and to a recurrent tendency for capitalists as a whole to produce more than can be sold.[3] The long-term rate at which accumulation takes place depends on the level of profits in the economy, as well as the rate at which capitalists reinvest their profits. The level of profits in turn depends on several factors: the ability of capitalists to increase worker productivity, especially by introducing more and improved machines or other innovations in production; the amount of wage costs, as determined by a bargaining process that takes place between capitalists and workers within a given labor market environment (i.e., conditions of labor shortage or conditions of labor surplus); and the intensity with which workers work and the

number of hours they work. The rate at which capitalists reinvest their profits depends upon their *expectations* of being successful in making profits in the future. All these factors are shaped by the class struggle between workers and capitalists.

SOCIAL REPRODUCTION

As a result of the accumulation of capital, capitalism reproduces itself over time on an expanded scale. The accumulation of capital means that production is taking place on a larger scale. To achieve this growth in production, capitalists on the whole need to hire more workers, even though the introduction of new technologies displaces workers in some sectors. So capitalists need to draw more and more people into the labor market as wage-workers who will work under capitalist relations of production. The result is that capitalist production reproduces not only capital but also labor and the capitalist relations of production.

The expansion of the wage-labor force, or *proletariat,* occurs as capital re-creates the conditions that require more people to sell their labor-power. First of all, almost all of those people who are already workers must continue to sell their labor-power. Their wages and salaries enable them and their families to purchase the commodities they need for their material reproduction, but very few are able to save a sufficient amount out of their earnings to go into business for themselves. Second, given population growth, the number of young people who enter the labor market each year more than replaces older retiring workers. Third, as the expansion of large-scale capital increasingly drives small capitalists (including many small farmers, merchants, and professionals) out of business, these formerly independent small capitalists are drawn into the labor market as workers. Fourth, more women enter the labor market as more areas of production are removed from the home to capitalist enterprises. Finally, immigration from other countries provides an addi-

---

[3]We analyze the sources of economic crises in Chapter 10.

tional important source of labor supply, particularly during periods when the demand for labor is growing rapidly. These various means of replenishing and expanding the supply of labor-power tend to meet the growing demand for labor-power by capitalists. The increasing supply ensures that competition among capitalists for workers will not go so far as to upset the unequal class relationship between the capitalists and the workers.

What if the demand for workers nonetheless far outruns the growth in the supply of workers, so that the wages paid to workers rise to such an extent that they begin to cut into the profits of the capitalists? Capitalists can then respond by introducing machinery that increases the productivity of their workers and

"frees" some of them for work elsewhere, and/or by reducing the rate of reinvestment of their profits, thereby throwing many people out of work and setting off an economic crisis. This crisis then re-creates the conditions necessary for a new round of capital accumulation. We thus see that "the capitalist production process reproduces ... the conditions which force the laborers to sell themselves in order to live, and enables the capitalist to purchase them in order that he may enrich himself. It is no longer a mere accident that capitalist and laborer confront each other in the market as buyer and seller."[4]

[4]Karl Marx, *Capital,* vol. I (New York: International Publishers, 1967), p. 577

2.1 *The Essence of Capitalism*

How should we define capitalism? What are its distinguishing features? In the following reading Maurice Dobb argues from a historical materialist perspective that capitalism can be characterized as a system of production for the market in which labor-power itself has become a commodity like any other article of exchange. With this definition, capitalism can be identified as a distinct historical epoch. The prerequisite for the capitalist mode of production was the creation of a class of producers separated from the means of production and the concentration of those means of production in the hands of another class, the capitalists. Thus, for capitalism to exist, there must be two types of people, capitalists and workers, who come together and meet in a market. Dobb divides history into periods, each characterized by a different mode of production; the antagonistic social classes of each period are defined by the manner in which surplus product is produced and appropriated.

I

It is perhaps not altogether surprising that the term Capitalism, which in recent years has enjoyed so wide a currency alike in popular talk and in historical writing, should have been used so variously, and that there should have

been no common measure of agreement in its use. What is more remarkable is that in economic theory, as this has been expounded by the traditional schools, the term should have appeared so rarely, if at all. There is even a school of thought, numbering its adherents both among economists and historians, which has refused to recognize that Capitalism as a title for a determinate economic system can be given an exact meaning. . . .

To-day, after half a century of intensive research in economic history, this attitude is rarely regarded by economic historians as tenable, even if they may still hold the origin of the term to be suspect. . . . But if to-day Capitalism has received authoritative recognition as an historical category, this affords no assurance that those who claim to study this system are talking about the same thing . . . If it is the pattern which historical events force upon us, and not our own predilections, that is decisive in our use of the term Capitalism, there must then be one definition that accords with the actual shape which historical development possesses, and others which, by contrast with it, are wrong. Even a believer in historical relativism must, surely, believe that there is one picture that is right from the standpoint of any given homogeneous set of historical observations.

. . .

We [accept] the meaning originally given by Marx, who sought the essence of Capitalism neither in a spirit of enterprise nor in the use of money to finance a series of exchange transactions with the object of gain, but in a particular mode of production. By mode of production he did not refer merely to the state of technique—to what he termed the state of the productive forces—but to the way in which the means of production were owned and to the social relations between men which resulted from their connections with the process of production. Thus Capitalism was not simply a system of production for the market—a system of commodity-production as Marx termed it—but a system under which labour-power had "itself become a commodity" and was bought and sold on the market like any other object of exchange. Its historical prerequisite was the concentration of ownership of the means of production in the hands of a class, consisting of only a minor section of society, and the consequential emergence of a propertyless class for whom the sale of their labour-power was their only source of liveli-

hood. Productive activity was furnished, accordingly, by the latter, not by virtue of legal compulsion, but on the basis of a wage-contract. It is clear that such a definition excludes the system of independent handicraft production where the craftsman owned his own petty implements of production and undertook the sale of his own wares. Here there was no divorce between ownership and work; and except where he relied to any extent on the employment of journeymen, it was the purchase and sale of inanimate wares and not of human labour-power that was his primary concern. What differentiates the use of this definition from others is that the existence of trade and of money-lending and the presence of a specialized class of merchants or financiers, even though they be men of substance, does not suffice to constitute a capitalist society. Men of capital, however acquisitive, are not enough: their capital must be used to yoke labour to the creation of surplus-value in production.

. . .

II

If it be right to maintain that the conception of socio-economic systems, marking distinct stages in historical development, is not merely a matter of convenience but an obligation—not a matter of suitable chapter-headings but something that concerns the essential construction of the story if the story is to be true—then this must be because there is a quality in historical situations which both makes for homogeneity of pattern at any given time and renders periods of transition, when there is an even balance of discrete elements, inherently unstable. It must be because society is so constituted that conflict and interaction of its leading elements, rather than the simple growth of some single element, form the principal agency of movement and change, at least so far as major transformations are concerned. If such be the case, once development has reached a certain level and the various elements which constitute that society are poised in a certain way, events are likely to move with unusual rapidity, not merely in the sense of quantitative growth, but in the sense of a change of balance of the constituent elements, resulting in the appearance of novel compositions and more or less abrupt changes in the texture of society. To use a topical analogy: it is as though at certain levels of development something like a chain-reaction is set in motion.

Clearly the feature of economic society which produces this result, and is accordingly fundamental to our conception of Capitalism as a distinctive economic order, characteristic of a distinctive period of history, is that history has been to-date the history of *class societies:* namely, of societies divided into classes, in which either one class, or else a coalition of classes with some common interest, constitutes the dominant class, and stands in partial or complete antagonism to another class or classes. The fact that this is so tends to impose on any given historical period a certain qualitative uniformity; since the class that is socially and politically dominant at the time will naturally use its power to preserve and to extend that particular mode of production—that particular form of relationship between classes—on which its income depends. If change within that society should reach a point where the continued hegemony of this dominant class is seriously called in question, and the old stable balance of forces shows signs of being disturbed, development will have reached a critical stage, where either the change that has been proceeding hitherto must somehow be halted, or if it should continue the dominant class can be dominant no longer and the new and growing one must take its place. Once this shift in the balance of power has occurred, the interest of the class which now occupies the strategic positions will clearly lie in accelerating the transition, in breaking up the strongholds of its rival and predecessor and in extending its own. The old mode of production will not necessarily be eliminated entirely; but it will quickly be reduced in scale until it is no longer a serious competitor to the new.[1] For a period the new mode of production, associated with new pro-

ductive forces and novel economic potentialities, is likely to expand far beyond the limits within which the old system was destined to move; until in turn the particular class relations and the political forms in which the new ruling class asserts its power come into conflict with some further development of the productive forces, and the struggle between the two is fought to a climax once again.

The common interest which constitutes a certain social grouping, a class in the sense of which we have been speaking, does not derive from a quantitative similarity of income, as is sometimes supposed: a class does not necessarily consist of people on the same income level, nor are people at, or near, a given income level necessarily united by identity of aims. Nor is it sufficient to say simply that a class consists of those who derive their income from a common source; although it is source rather than size of income that is here important. In this context one must be referring to something quite fundamental concerning the roots which a social group has in a particular society: namely to the relationship in which the group as a whole stands to the process of production and hence to other sections of society. In other words, the relationship from which in one case a common interest in preserving and extending a particular economic system, and in the other case, an antagonism of interest on this issue can alone derive, must be a relationship with a particular mode of extracting and distributing the fruits of surplus labour, over and above the labour which goes to supply the consumption of the actual producer. Since this surplus labour constitutes its life-blood, any ruling class will of necessity treat its particular relationship to the labour process as crucial to its own survival; and any rising class that aspires to live without labour is bound to regard its own future career, prosperity and influence

[1] It is not necessary to assume that this is done as part of a conscious long-term plan; although, in so far as the dominant class pursues a definite political policy, this will be so. But it assumes at least that members of a class take common action over particular questions (e.g., access to land or markets or labour), and that greater strength enables them to oust their rivals.

as dependent on the acquisition of some claim upon the surplus labour of others. "A surplus of the product of labour over and above the costs of maintenance of the labour," said Friedrich Engels, "and the formation and enlargement, by means of this suplus, of a social production and reserve fund, was and is the basis of all social, political and intellectual progress. In history up to the present, this fund has been the possession of a privileged class, on which also devolved, along with this possession, political supremacy and intellectual leadership."[2]

The form in which surplus labour has been appropriated has differed at different stages of society; and these varieties of form have been associated with the use of various methods and instruments of production and with different levels of productivity. Marx spoke of Capitalism itself as being, "like any other definite mode of production, conditioned upon a certain stage of social productivity and upon the historically developed form of the productive forces. This historical prerequisite is itself the historical result and product of a preceding process, from which the new mode of production takes its departure as from its given foundation. The conditions of production corresponding to this specific, historically determined, mode of production have a specific, historical passing character."[3] At a stage of social development when the productivity of labour is very low, any substantial and regular income for a leisured class, living on production but not contributing thereto, will be inconceivable unless it is grounded in the rigorous compulsion of producers; and in this sense, as Engels remarked, the division into classes at a primitive stage of economic development "has a certain historical justification."[4] In a predominantly agricultural society the crucial relationships will be connected with the holding of land; and since the division of labour and exchange are likely to be little developed, surplus labour will tend to be performed directly as a personal obligation or to take the form of the delivery of a certain quota of his produce by the cultivator as tribute in natural form to an overlord. The growth of industry, which implies the invention of new and varied instruments of production, will beget new classes and by creating new economic problems will require new forms of appropriating surplus labour for the benefit of the owners of the new instruments of production. Mediaeval society was characterized by the compulsory performance of surplus labour by producers: producers who were in possession of their own primitive instruments of cultivation and were attached to the land. Modern society, by contrast, is characterized, as we have seen, by a relationship between worker and capitalist which takes a purely contractual form, and which is indistinguishable in appearance from any of the other manifold free-market transactions of an exchange society. The transformation from the mediaeval form of exploitation of surplus labour to the modern was no simple process that can be depicted as some genealogical table of direct descent. Yet among the eddies of this movement it is possible for the eye to discern certain lines of direction of the flow. These include, not only changes in technique and the appearance of new instruments of production, which greatly enhanced the productivity of labour, but a growing division of labour and consequently the development of exchange, and also a growing separation of the producer from the land and from the means of production and his appearance as a proletarian. Of these guiding tendencies in the history of the past five centuries a special significance attaches to the latter; not only because it has been traditionally glossed over and decently veiled behind formulas about the passage from status to contract, but because into the centre of the historical stage it has brought a form of compulsion to labour for another that is purely economic and "objective"; thus laying a basis for that peculiar and mystifying form whereby a leisured class can exploit the surplus labour of others which is the essence of the modern system that we call Capitalism.

[2]*Anti-Dühring,* 221.

[3]*Capital,* vol. III, 1023–24.

[4]*Anti-Dühring,* 316.

III

The development of Capitalism falls into a number of stages, characterized by different levels of maturity and each of them recognizable by fairly distinctive traits. But when we seek to trace these stages and to select one of them as marking the opening stage of Capitalism, there is an immediate consideration about which it is of some importance that there should be no confusion. If we are speaking of Capitalism as a specific mode of production, then it follows that we cannot date the dawn of this system from the first signs of the appearance of large-scale trading and of a merchant class, and we cannot speak of a special period of "Merchant Capitalism," as many have done. We must look for the opening of the capitalist period only when changes in the mode of production occur, in the sense of a direct subordination of the producer to a capitalist. This is not just a point of terminology, but of substance; since it means that, if we are right, the appearance of a purely trading class will have of itself no revolutionary significance; that its rise will exert a much less fundamental influence on the economic pattern of society than will the appearance of a class of capitalists whose fortunes are intimately linked with industry; and that, while a ruling class, whether of slaveowners or feudal lords, may take to trading or enter into a close alliance with traders, a merchant class, whose activities are essentially those of an intermediary between producer and consumer, is unlikely to strive to become a dominant class in quite that radical and exclusive sense of which we were speaking a moment ago. Since its fortunes will tend to be bound up with the existing mode of production, it is more likely to be under an inducement to preserve that mode of production than to transform it. It is likely to struggle to "muscle in" upon an existing form of appropriating surplus labour; but it is unlikely to try to change this form.

When we look at the history of Capitalism, conceived in this way, it becomes clear that we must date its opening phase in England, not in the twelfth century as does Pirenne (who is thinking primarily of the Netherlands) nor even in the fourteenth century with its urban trade and guild handicrafts as others have done, but in the latter half of the sixteenth and the early seventeenth century when capital began to penetrate production on a considerable scale, either in the form of a fairly matured relationship between capitalist and hired wage-earners or in the less developed form of the subordination of domestic handicraftsmen, working in their own homes, to a capitalist on the so-called "putting-out system." It is true that already prior to this, fairly numerous examples are to be found of a transitional situation where the craftsman had lost much of his independence, through debt or in face of the monopoly of wholesale traders, and already stood in relations of some dependence on a merchant, who was a man of capital. It is also true that in the fourteenth century or even earlier there was a good deal of what one may call (to use modern terminology) *kulak* types of enterprise—the well-to-do peasant in the village or the local trader or worker-owner in town handicrafts, employing hired labour. But these seem to have been too small in scale and insufficiently matured to be regarded as much more than adolescent Capitalism, and scarcely justify one in dating Capitalism as a new mode of production, sufficiently clear-cut and extensive to constitute any serious challenge to an older one, as early as this. At any rate, one can say with considerable assurance that a capitalist mode of production, and a special class of capitalists specifically associated with it, did not attain to any decisive significance as an influence on social and economic development until the closing decades of the Tudor era.

In the career of Capitalism since this date it is evident that there are two decisive moments. One of them resides in the seventeenth century: in the political and social transformations of that decisive period, including the struggle within the chartered corporations, which the researches of Unwin have brought to light, and the Parliamentary struggle against monopoly, reaching its apex in the Cromwellian revolution, the results of which were very far from being submerged, despite a certain measure of compromise and reaction at the Restoration. The second consists of the industrial revolution of the late eighteenth and earlier half of the nineteenth century, which was primarily of economic significance; it had a less dramatic, but far from unimportant, reflection in the political sphere. So decisive was it for the whole future of capitalist economy, so radical a transformation of the structure and organization of industry did it represent, as to have caused some to regard it as the birth pangs of modern Capitalism, and hence as the most decisive moment in economic and social development since the Middle Ages. Maturer knowledge and judgment today clearly indicate, however, that what the industrial revolution represented was a transition from an early and still immature stage of Capitalism, where the pre-capitalist petty mode of production had been penetrated by the influence of capital, subordinated to capital, robbed of its independence as an economic form but not yet completely transformed, to a stage where Capitalism, on the basis of technical change, had achieved its own specific production process resting on the collective large-scale production unit of the factory, thereby effecting a final divorce of the producer from his remaining hold on the means of production and establishing a simple and direct relationship between capitalist and wage-earners.

2.2   The Rise of the Bourgeoisie

The capitalist class, having stripped away the restrictions of feudalism and having created a working class, was able to achieve tremendous advances in the development of the material forces of production. There are few paeans so eloquently appreciative of capitalism's accomplishments as the following reading from Karl Marx and Friedrich Engels' *Communist Manifesto* of 1848. The bourgeoisie dominates an ever-increasing proportion of social activity and draws into itself an ever-increasing proportion of the globe. In the process it not only creates a proletariat but it also constantly expands that proletariat and begins to draw it together. The dynamic of capitalism contains an internal contradiction between (1) the increasing centralization of the means of production under continuing private control, on the one hand, and (2) the increasingly social character of production, on the other.

> Excerpted from *The Communist Manifesto* by KARL MARX and FRIEDRICH ENGELS (first published in 1848).

The history of all hitherto existing society is the history of class struggles.

Freeman and slave, patrician and plebeian, lord and serf, guild-master and journeyman, in a word; oppressor and oppressed, stood in constant opposition to one another, carried on an uninterrupted, now hidden, now open fight, a fight that each time ended, either in a revolutionary re-constitution of society at large, or in the common ruin of the contending classes.

In the early epochs of history, we find almost everywhere a complicated arrangement of society into various orders, a manifold graduation of social rank. In ancient Rome we have patricians, knights, plebeians, slaves; in the Middle Ages, feudal lords, vassals, guild-masters, journeymen, apprentices, serfs; in almost all of these classes, again, subordinate gradations.

The modern bourgeois society that has sprouted from the ruins of feudal society, has not done away with class antagonisms. It has but established new classes, new conditions of oppression, new forms of struggle in place of the old ones.

Our epoch, the epoch of the bourgeoisie, possesses, however, the distinctive feature; it has simplified the class antagonisms. Society as a whole is more and more splitting up into two great hostile camps, into two great classes directly facing each other: Bourgeoisie and Proletariat.

From the serfs of the Middle Ages sprang the chartered burghers of the earliest towns. From these burgesses the first elements of the bourgeoisie were developed.

The discovery of America, the rounding of the Cape, opened up fresh ground for the rising bourgeoisie. The East-Indian and Chinese markets, the colonization of America, trade with the colonies, the increase in the means of exchange and in commodities, generally, gave to commerce, to navigation, to industry, an impulse never before known, and thereby, to the revolutionary element in the tottering feudal society, a rapid development.

The feudal system of industry, under which industrial production was monopolized by closed guilds, now no longer sufficed for the growing wants of the markets. The manufacturing system took its place. The guild-masters were pushed on one side by the manufacturing middle-class; division of labor between the different corporate guilds vanished in the face of division of labor in each single workshop.

Meantime the markets kept ever growing, the demand, ever rising. Even manufacturing no longer sufficed. Thereupon, steam and machinery revolutionized industrial production. The place of manufacture was taken by the giant, Modern Industry, the place of the industrial middle-class, by industrial millionaires, the leaders of whole industrial armies, the modern bourgeoisie.

Modern Industry has established the world-market, for which the discovery of America paved the way. This market has given an immense development to commerce, to navigation, to communication by land. This development has, in its turn, reacted on the extension of industry; and in proportion as industry, commerce, navigation, railways extended in the same proportion the bourgeoisie developed, increased its capital, and pushed into the background every class handed down from the Middle Ages.

We see, therefore, how the modern bourgeoisie is itself the product of a long course of development, of a series of revolutions in the modes of production and of exchange.

Each step in the development of the bourgeoisie was accompanied by a corresponding political advance of that class. An oppressed class under the sway of the feudal nobility, an armed and self-governing association in the medieval commune, here independent urban republic (as in Italy and Germany), there taxable "third estate" of the monarchy (as in France), afterwards, in the period of manufacturing proper, serving either the semi-feudal or the absolute monarchy as a counterpoise against the nobility, and in fact, cornerstone of the great monarchies in general, the bourgeoisie has at last, since the establishment of Modern Industry and of the world-market, conquered for itself, in the modern representative State, exclusive political sway. The executive of the modern State is but a committee for managing the common affairs of the whole bourgeoisie.

The bourgeoisie, historically, has played a most revolutionary part.

The bourgeoisie, wherever it has got the upper hand, has put an end to all feudal, patriarchal, idyllic relations. It has pitilessly torn asunder the motley feudal ties that bound man to his "natural superiors," and has left remaining no other nexus between man and man than naked self-interest, than callous "cash payment." It has drowned the most heavenly ecstasies of religious fervor, of chivalrous enthusiasm, of philistine sentimentalism, in the icy water of egotistical calculation. It has resolved personal worth into exchange value, and in place of the numberless indefeasible chartered freedoms, has set up that single, unconscionable freedom—Free Trade. In one word, for exploitation, veiled by religious and political illusions, it has substituted naked, shameless, direct, brutal exploitation.

The bourgeoisie has stripped of its halo every occupation hitherto honored and looked up to with reverent awe. It has converted the physician, the lawyer, the priest, the poet, the man of science, into its paid wage-laborers.

The bourgeoisie has torn away from the family its sentimental veil, and has reduced the family relation to a mere money relation.

The bourgeoisie has disclosed how it came to pass that the brutal display of vigor in the Middle Ages, which Reactionists so much admire, found its fitting complement in the most slothful indolence. It has been the first to show what man's activity can bring about. It has accomplished wonders far surpassing Egyptian pyramids, Roman aqueducts, and Gothic cathedrals; it has conducted expeditions that put in the shade all former Exoduses of nations and crusades.

The bourgeoisie cannot exist without constantly revolutionizing the instruments of production, and thereby the relations of production, and with them the whole relations of society. Conservation of the old modes of production in unaltered form, was, on the contrary, the first condition of existence for all earlier industrial classes. Constant revolutionizing of production, uninterrupted disturbance of all social conditions, everlasting uncertainty and agitation distinguish the bourgeois epoch from all earlier ones. All fixed, fast-frozen relations, with their train of ancient and venerable prejudices and opinions, are swept away, all newly-formed ones become antiquated before they can ossify. All that is solid melts into air, all that is holy is profaned, and man is at last compelled to face with sober senses, his real conditions of life, and his relations with his kind.

The need of a constantly expanding market for its products chases the bourgeoisie over the whole surface of the globe. It must nestle everywhere, settle everywhere, establish connections everywhere.

The bourgeoisie has through its exploitation of the world-market given a cosmopolitan character to production and consumption in every country. To the great chagrin of Reactionists, it has drawn from under the feet of industry the national ground on which it stood. All old-established national industries have been destroyed or are daily being destroyed. They are dislodged by new industries, whose introduction becomes a life and death question for all civilized nations, by industries that no longer work up indigenous raw material, but raw material drawn from the remotest zones; industries whose products are consumed, not only at home, but in every quarter of the globe. In place of the old wants, satisfied by the productions of the country, we find new wants, requiring for their satisfaction the products of distant lands and climes. In place of the old local and national seclusion and self-sufficiency, we have intercourse in every direction, universal interdependence of nations. And as in material, so also in intellectual production. The intellectual creations of individual nations become common property. National one-sidedness and narrow-mindedness become more and more impossible, and from the numerous national and local literatures there arises a world-literature.

The bourgeoisie, by the rapid improvement of all instruments of production, by the immensely facilitated means of communication, draws all, even the most barbarian, nations into civilization. The cheap prices of its commodities are the heavy artillery with which it batters down all Chinese walls, with which it forces the barbarians' intensely obstinate hatred of foreigners to capitulate. It compels all nations, on pain of extinction, to adopt the bourgeois mode of production; it compels them to introduce what it calls civilization into their midst, i.e., to become bourgeois themselves. In a word, it creates a world after its own image.

The bourgeoisie has subjected the country to the rule of the towns. It has created enormous cities, has greatly increased the urban population as compared with the rural, and has thus rescued a considerable part of the population from the idiocy of rural life. Just as it has made the country dependent on the towns, so it has made barbarian and semi-barbarian countries dependent on the civilized ones, nations of peasants on nations of bourgeois, the East on the West.

The bourgeoisie keeps more and more doing away with the scattered state of the population, of the means of production, and of property. It has agglomerated population, centralized means of production, and has concentrated property in a few hands. The necessary consequence of this was political centralization. Independent, or but loosely connected provinces, with separate interests, laws, governments and systems of taxation, became lumped together in one nation, with one government, one code of laws, one national class-interest, one frontier and one customs-tariff.

The bourgeoisie, during its rule of scarce one hundred years, has created more massive and more colossal productive forces than have all preceding generations together. Subjection of Nature's forces to man, machinery, application of chemistry to industry and agriculture, steam-navigation, railways, electric telegraphs, clearing of whole continents for cultivation, canalization of rivers, whole populations conjured out of the ground—what earlier century had even a presentiment that such productive forces slumbered in the lap of social labor?

We see then: the means of production and of exchange on whose foundations the bourgeoisie built itself up, were generated in feudal society. At a certain stage in the development of these means of production and of exchange, the conditions under which feudal society produced and exchanged, the feudal organization of agriculture and manufacturing industry, in one word, the feudal relations of property became no longer compatible with the already developed productive forces; they became so many fetters. They had to be burst asunder; they were burst asunder.

Into their places stepped free competition, accompanied by a social and political constitution adapted to it, and by the economical

and political sway of the bourgeois class.

A similar movement is going on before our own eyes. Modern bourgeois society with its relations of production, of exchange and of property, a society that has conjured up such gigantic means of production and of exchange, is like the sorcerer, who is no longer able to control the power of the nether world whom he has called up by his spells. For many a decade past the history of industry and commerce is but the history of the revolt of modern productive forces against modern conditions of production, against the property relations that are the condition for the existence of the bourgeoisie and of its rule. It is enough to mention the commercial crises that by their periodical return put on trial, each time more threateningly, the existence of the entire bourgeois society. In these crises a great part not only of the existing products, but also of the previously created productive forces, are periodically destroyed. In these crises there breaks out an epidemic that, in all earlier epochs, would have seemed an absurdity—the epidemic of over-production. Society suddenly finds itself put back into a state of momentary barbarism; it appears as if a famine, a universal war of devastation had cut off the supply of every means of subsistence; industry and commerce seem to be destroyed; and why? Because there is too much civilization, too much means of subsistence, too much industry, too much commerce. The productive forces at the disposal of society no longer tend to further the development of the conditions of bourgeois property; on the contrary, they have become too powerful for these conditions, by which they are fettered, and so soon as they overcome these fetters, they bring disorder into the whole of bourgeois society, endangering the existence of bourgeois property. The conditions of bourgeois society are too narrow to comprise the wealth created by them. And how does the bourgeoisie get over these crises? On the one hand by enforced destruction of a mass of productive forces; on the other, by the conquest of new markets, and by the more thorough exploitation of the old ones. That is to say, by paving the way for more extensive and more destructive crises, and by diminishing the means whereby crises are prevented.

The weapons with which the bourgeoisie felled feudalism to the ground are now turned against the bourgeoisie itself.

But not only has the bourgeoisie forged the weapons that bring death to itself; it has also called into existence the men who are to wield those weapons—the modern working-class—the proletarians.

In proportion as the bourgeoisie, i.e., capital, is developed, in the same proportion is the proletariat, the modern working-class, developed, a class of laborers, who live only so long as they find work, and who find work only so long as their labor increases capital. These laborers, who must sell themselves piecemeal, are a commodity, like every other article of commerce, and are consequently exposed to all the vicissitudes of competition, to all the fluctuations of the market.

Owing to the extensive use of machinery and to division of labor, the work of the proletarians has lost all individual character, and, consequently, all charm for the workman. He becomes an appendage of the machine, and it is only the most simple, most monotonous, and most easily acquired knack that is required of him. Hence, the cost of production of a workman is restricted, almost entirely, to the means of subsistence that he requires for his maintenance, and for the propagation of his race. But the price of a commodity, and also of labor, is equal to its cost of production. In proportion, therefore, as the repulsiveness of the work increases, the wage decreases. Nay more, in proportion as the use of machinery and division of labor increases, in the same proportion the burden of toil also increases, whether by prolongation of the working hours, by increase of the work enacted in a given time, or by increased speed of the machinery, etc.

Modern Industry has converted the little workshop of the patriarchal master into the great factory of the industrial capitalist. Masses of laborers, crowded into the factory, are organized like soldiers. As privates of the industrial army they are placed under the command of a perfect hierarchy of officers and sergeants. Not only are they the slaves of the bourgeois class, and of the bourgeois State, they are daily and hourly enslaved by the machine, by the over-looker, and, above all, by the individual bourgeois manufacturer himself. The more openly this despotism proclaims gain to be its end and aim, the more petty, the more hateful and the more embittering it is.

The less the skill and exertion or strength implied in manual labor, in other words, the more modern industry becomes developed, the more is the labor of men superseded by that of women. Differences of age and sex have no longer any distinctive social validity for the working-class. All are instruments of labor, more or less expensive to use, according to their age and sex.

No sooner is the exploitation of the laborer by the manufacturer so far at an end, that he receives his wages in cash, than he is set upon by the other portions of the bourgeoisie, the landlord, the shopkeeper, the pawnbroker, etc.

The low strata of the middle-class—the small tradespeople, shopkeepers, and retired tradesmen generally, the handicraftsmen and peasants—all these sink gradually into the proletariat, partly because their diminutive capital does not suffice for the scale on which Modern Industry is carried on, and is swamped in the competition with the large capitalists, partly because their specialized skill is rendered worthless by new methods of production. Thus the proletariat is recruited from all classes of the population.

The proletariat goes through various stages of development. With its birth begins its struggle with the bourgeoisie. At first the contest is carried on by individual laborers, then by the workpeople of a factory, then by the operatives of one trade, in one locality, against the individual bourgeois who directly exploits them. They direct their attacks not against the bourgeois conditions of production, but against the instruments of production themselves; they destroy imported wares that compete with their labor, they smash to pieces machinery, they set factories ablaze, they seek to restore by force the vanished status of the workman of the Middle Ages.

At this stage the laborers still form an incoherent mass scattered over the whole country, and broken up by their mutual competition. If anywhere they unite to form more compact bodies, this is not yet the consequence of their own active union, but of the union of bourgeoisie, which class, in order to attain its own political ends, is compelled to set the whole proletariat in motion, and is moreover yet, for a time, able to do so. At this stage, therefore, the proletarians do not fight their enemies, but the enemies of their enemies, the remnants of absolute monarchy, the landowners, the nonindustrial bourgeoisie, the petty bourgeoisie. Thus the whole historical movement is concentrated in the hands of the bourgeoisie; every victory so obtained is a victory for the bourgeoisie.

2.3   *Capitalism and Class Conflict*

How can we understand the central role of class inequality and class conflict in capitalist economies? Modern neoclassical economic analysis characterizes economic relations in market economies as voluntary choices made by free individuals acting under conditions of equality. In the following reading Michael Reich articulates an alternative conception of the structural relations among the principal economic agents in capitalist economies. This alternative conception shows how inequality and conflict between labor and capital coexist with competition among individuals in capitalist markets.

Excerpted from *Racial Inequality: A Political-Economic Analysis* by MICHAEL REICH. © 1981 by Princeton University Press. Reprinted by permission of the author and Princeton University Press.

The capitalist class and the working class, the two great classes whose relation Marx persistently examined, now, more than ever, dominate the economic life of advanced capitalist countries. Ownership of capital assets has become increasingly more concentrated than in the nineteenth century, or even in the first third of the twentieth century, while the growth in the proportion of the population whose livelihood depends exclusively or almost exclusively on the sale of labor power has been equally spectacular.[1] In the model of a perfectly competitive market economy, these two classes meet in the marketplace as atomistic individuals with different initial endowments, some holding only labor and others with capital. How does this meeting differ from the neoclassical tale of the equal relations that are inherent in a free market?

One difference concerns the market outcomes resulting from the initial unequal endowment distribution. The initial lack of assets among workers other than their labor power insures that worker households have no choice but to supply their capacity to labor to the market. Wages are determined by supply of and demand for labor power. For a capitalist-type market economy to exist, labor must be supplied with sufficient elasticity to meet the condition that the market-determined wage rate is significantly less than the average product of labor. This condition is usually met through a variety of mechanisms: periodic economic downturns limit the demand for labor, new groups join the wage-labor population, labor productivity rises, and so forth. The elas-

[1]See Reich, Section 4.1, p. 122.

ticity of the labor supply guarantees that, whatever the demand for labor, capitalists can appropriate a share of the total product.

Competition among firms in the labor market insures that firms pay a wage equal to a worker's marginal product, as neoclassical theory suggests. The difference between the marginal product received by labor and the larger average product produced by labor constitutes the return to capital (profits). With the condition that wages (expressed in money terms using ruling prices) are strictly less than the average product of labor (expressed also in ruling prices), the equilibrium rate of profit will be strictly positive.[2]

Capitalists then reinvest their profits (or at least the proportion they do not expend on consumption), thereby setting in motion on an expanded scale another cycle of production, exchange, distribution, consumption, and investment. Competition among capitalists necessitates the expansion of capital in order to reduce average and marginal costs. Over time the stock of accumulated capital does expand. The supply and the productivity of labor also grow, thereby continuing to insure a positive return to capital. The market meeting between workers and capitalists therefore permits capitalists to expand their capital.

The results for workers are quite different. Although real wages may rise substantially above the socially determined level of subsistence, which also tends to rise over time, most workers' income levels permit a very small amount of personal household savings over their life cycle. Moreover, the greatest part of these savings is reserved for illness, retirement, children's education, and other specific activities. That is, these savings constitute a reallocation of expenditures over the life cycle rather than a sustained accumulation of assets. Since these life-cycle oriented savings do not result in the accumulation of financial assets,

they do not change the worker's financial dependence on labor earnings. And it takes a substantial accumulation of financial assets to permit long-term independence from labor market earnings. Consequently, the market reproduces the workers' necessity to sell their labor power, thus reproducing the unequal class relation between workers and capitalists. Perfectly competitive markets are consistent with the reproduction of classes, with immobility, that is, between classes.

This immobility is relative rather than absolute. For example, some workers are able to save sufficiently to start their own small businesses. Such businesses usually depend on large inputs of the owners' labor as well as their capital. Most of these small businesses fail in their first few years of operation. A minority succeed, however, and together with the short-lived failures, they constantly replenish the ranks of small capitalists, one of the middle groupings between the capitalist class and the working class.

A very low percentage of small businesses are much more successful and expand to the point where the owner-entrepreneurs not only employ wageworkers, but also hire managers. Once they no longer need to mix their own labor with their newly accumulated capital in order to make profits, these small capitalists rise in status to capitalists proper. Such Horatio Algers are exceedingly few in number in relation to the size of both the working class and small capitalists, but they may play a significant role in replenishing the ranks of the capitalist class. Moreover, they generate powerful aspirations for upward mobility among the remainder of the population and sustain the hope among many workers that hard work and initiative will result in such economic success.

The small business class always exists in a capitalist economy, although its relative size is much smaller today than in the beginning of the nineteenth century. This intermediate class between workers and capitalists blurs the line that demarcates one class from another. It also makes the capitalist class a heterogeneous category.

[2]For a more rigorous statement of this proposition, see Michio Morishima, *Marx's Economics* (New York: Cambridge University Press, 1973); or Donald Harris, *Capital Accumulation and Income Distribution* (Stanford University Press, 1978).

A capitalist economy also contains another group whose economic position lies somewhere between workers and capitalists: managers and professionals. Managers themselves form a spectrum from first-line supervisors, who are entirely subordinate to capitalists, to presidents of large corporations. The class position of presidents merges with that of the capitalist owners. Professionals are more difficult to categorize, since they perform a variety of tasks in widely varying conditions of supervision and autonomy. They occupy a contradictory position that incorporates attributes of both workers and capitalists.[3] These groups have grown markedly in size in this century.

Finally, we can also discern significant differences within the working class itself. Three main working-class segments are identifiable. Some workers are artisans, possessing considerable skills in their crafts; this group has much in common with many professionals and low-level managers. A second group works at more routinized jobs requiring little skill; these workers constitute the traditionally identified working class. Other workers are employed irregularly; they are rarely unionized and often depend on welfare, unemployment insurance, and other transfer payments for their survival.

The structural class position model presented here more powerfully explains the distribution of earnings than the usual human capital model of neoclassical theory. Both the level of income and the returns to skill investments of individuals are significantly affected by their position in the class structure. A model that highlights these structural relations thus turns out to be superior to a model that obscures them.[4]

The structural conditions that give rise to the contemporary organization of classes and to conflict between classes are better understood with a more articulated analysis of the modern capitalist firm. This analysis of the capitalist firm constitutes the second main characteristic distinguishing the class conflict theory from the neoclassical approach.

A CLASS CONFLICT THEORY OF THE CAPITALIST FIRM

Class conflict theory views the worker-capitalist employment relation in the firm as follows. Workers sell their labor time to capitalists in exchange for a wage or salary. The worker gets a specified amount of money, the capitalist gets control over the worker's labor capacities for a specified time period. Capitalists, usually together with their managers, decide what products will be produced and how the work will be organized. Capitalists legally own the product that the workers produce, and they attempt to sell this product at a price that generates profits to them.

By entering the employment relation, workers surrender to capitalists not only authority over the tasks they will perform, but also most of the political and civil rights they enjoy as citizens of the state. When they walk into the factory or office, they are on the private property of the capitalist, where the guarantees provided by the Bill of Rights do not apply. Freedom of speech and assembly, the presumption of innocence until proven guilty, due process, equality before the law, and other rights protect citizens from action by the state. Except for a limited number of government incursions into the employment relation, workers have no analogous legal protections from the actions of employers at the place of employment.

Some rights have been won by workers and are recorded in collective bargaining agreements or in Federal law. For example, the grievance filing procedures contained in virtually all collective bargaining agreements give unionized workers some due process rights, and Federal legislation gives workers the right to bargain collectively, to "engage in concerted activity for mutual aid and protection,"

[3]For more detailed discussions of these intermediate strata, see Erik Wright, *Class, Crisis and the State* (London: New Left Books, 1978), chapter 2; and Richard Edwards, *Contested Terrain: The Transformation of the Workplace in the Twentieth Century* (New York: Basic Books, 1979).

[4]See Erik Wright, *Class Structure and Income Determination* (New York: Academic Press, 1979).

some limited free-speech rights, the right not to be discriminated against because of race, sex, religion, or national origin, and the right to submit without penalty complaints concerning safety and health conditions to the Federal Occupational Safety and Health Administration.[5]

The law leaves most rights in the hands of employers. They can legally fire workers for any reason, except a few that are forbidden by law.[6] Whatever other rights workers have at their jobs must be obtained through the collective bargaining process, and less than a quarter of the United States work force is covered by collective bargaining agreements.

In any case, virtually all collective bargaining agreements leave in management's hands the power to decide what will be produced and how, where plants will be located, and who will be hired. For example, paragraph 8 of the General Motors contract with the United Auto Workers contains a long-standing clause spelling out management prerogatives: "The right to hire, promote, discharge, or discipline for cause; and to maintain discipline and efficiency of employees, is the sole responsibility of the Corporation except that Union members shall not be discriminated against as such. In addition, the products to be manufactured, the location of plants, the schedule of productions, the methods, processes and means of manufacturing are solely and exclusively the responsibility of the Corporation."[7] Similarly, although many collective bargaining agreements contain dozens of pages spelling out work rules, almost all of the important decisions concerning the organization of production remain under the control of management. Employers and unions frequently do clash over such issues as the rate at which work is to be performed. But despite the efforts of unions, few labor-management contracts have treaded significantly on management prerogatives.

What exactly does the capitalist purchase by hiring workers? The purchase and sale of labor power by a capitalist differs fundamentally from the purchase and sale of products, raw materials, capital goods, money, land, buildings, and other exchanges in a market economy. When capitalists purchase a machine or a certain quantity of raw material, they are able to determine with considerable precision the place of these inputs in the production process. Similarly, when capitalists hire an independent contractor, they are exchanging a definite sum of money (the agreed-upon price of the product or service) for a rather definite product or service. Typically, a written or an implied contract specifies in great detail what the purchaser is buying from the seller.

The labor contract is different. By hiring an employee, the capitalist does not purchase a specific and agreed-upon set of services to be performed, but rather disposition over the worker's capacity to labor for an agreed-upon amount of time. Why emphasize this point? Because unlike the case with other inputs, how much work the worker actually performs for the capitalist is problematic in a central sense. The amount of work to be performed is not expressed contractually, regardless of whether the pay system is organized according to time or piece rates. Instead, the quantity of work performed and its cost depend on how successfully capitalists are able to elicit work from their workers.

The workers want to obtain the maximum wage for the minimum amount of alienating effort and, insofar as possible, to make the work creative and satisfying rather than alienating. The employers' desire to maximize worker productivity and minimize labor costs is inconsistent with these goals. The United States Supreme Court has on occasion voiced a similar analysis. In *Holden* v. *Hardy* (1898), the Court noted

---

[5]The phrase in quotes comes from the key section of the National Labor Relations Act. The limited free-speech rights provided by the NLRA are discussed in Staughton Lynd, "Employee Speech in the Private Workplace: Two Doctrines or One?" *Industrial Relations Law Journal* (1977).

[6]The rights protected in the law (not always enforced) are mentioned in the previous paragraph.

[7]See Staughton Lynd, "Workers' Control and Workers' Rights," *Radical America* (September–October 1976).

that the proprietors of . . . establishments and their operatives do not stand upon an equality, and that their interests are, to a certain extent, conflicting. The former naturally desire to obtain as much labor as possible from their employees, while the latter are often induced by the fear of discharge to conform to regulations which their judgment, fairly exercised, would pronounce to be detrimental. . . . In other words, the proprietors lay down the rules and the laborers are practically constrained to obey them.[8]

Greater worker productivity and cost minimization requires that capitalists manage the workers to exert greater effort without thereby raising labor costs. The conflict between workers and employers on both the individual and class levels rests ultimately on this antagonistic set of interests.

The central point of this argument can be restated as follows. The workplace is not simply a place of technical production where inputs are combined according to engineering and economic principles in such a fashion as to minimize costs. The workplace also constitutes a social system, where the quantity of work performed and the wage paid for the work are variables determined by the interaction of the different actors in the system.

If the employment relation poses such headaches for employers, why do they not simply substitute sales contracts for services performed, acting as traders or contractors who mediate between direct producers and market for the final assembled product? Why doesn't the firm simply concentrate on marketing its products and refrain from playing a very large role in organizing production itself?

Such a view of the firm and employer indeed resembles that found in neoclassical economic theory. This view of the firm had some relevance to eighteenth- and nineteenth-century factory conditions. For example, during the early stage of the Industrial Revolution,

the "putting-out" contractors provided or "put out" raw materials to workers producing in their homes and purchased the manufactured product from them. This description of the firm also fits the reality inside many nineteenth-century United States enterprises, where one found considerable "inside contracting"; skilled workers contracted with capitalists to provide a service for a price rather than for a wage. The hiring of unskilled helpers and the organization of tasks was controlled by the skilled crafts contractor, while the raw materials, tools, machinery, and other equipment were provided by the capitalist. By the twentieth century, however, such production relations were becoming increasingly rare.

In modern capitalism, most corporations have elaborate labor management structures constructed primarily to extract greater productivity from the employees while at the same time blocking worker coalitions that would give workers greater power and increased wages. These management systems typically take the form of bureaucratic and hierarchical structures of authority at the workplace, and include direct supervision, the use of machine-paced technologies (assembly lines), elaborate promotion ladders, and performance evaluation techniques. Such organizational forms turn out to be more profitable than the earlier model where capitalists played little direct role in organizing the work process.

It is elementary that the likelihood of solidarity among workers depends on the extent of common interests, the benefits any individual obtains by exiting from the collectivity, and the extent of the sanctions the collectivity can enforce on noncooperative individuals. In order to minimize the threat of collective behavior by employees, employers frequently have moved to fragment work groups in order to reduce the common interests of employees. Many employers have chosen to pay wage rates higher than the "market" level to some of their workers in order to elicit loyalty from these workers and make more forceful the

[8]*Holden* v. *Hardy*, 169 U.S. 366 (1898), quoted in Glenn Miller, *Government Policy Toward Labor: An Introduction to Labor Law* (Columbus, Ohio: GRID, 1975), p. 112.

threat of dismissal. They also have used the prospect of employee promotion and advancement to secure their loyalty. And they have attempted to structure the allocation of tasks and decision-making in a vertical hierarchical manner in order to minimize the sanctions that a group of workers can impose upon one of their coworkers.[9] The creation of incentive schemes and "internal labor markets" therefore involve more than attempts to pay individual workers according to their actual productivity.

At the same time, using informal methods as well as formal organizations, workers have attempted to enhance solidarity-enhancing goals and to maximize the leverage they have over other workers and over managers. Although unionization significantly increases worker power in this regard, it is important to stress that unorganized workers also can make significant efforts to the same end.[10] The model of the firm proposed here therefore presents the firm not as a location controlled exclusively by managers and capitalists, but as a contested terrain in which capitalists and managers have predominant but not total power.

If profitability rather than efficiency determines the organization of work in capitalist firms, it would seem to follow that cooperatively run enterprises could prove more efficient. Workers who could borrow sufficient capital could presumably set up their own firms and outcompete their capitalist counterparts. But greater static efficiency does not by itself imply greater long-run competitiveness. The outcome depends on a number of additional variables: the rate of effort and number of work hours that cooperative members would desire to maintain; the wages these workers would pay themselves; the rate of technical change they could sustain; the rate at which they would choose to reinvest their profits in their own enterprise; their flexibility in adjusting to short-term fluctuations in demand; and their capacity and desire to retool their skills and capital goods as demand for their product changes over the long run. A summation of the comparisons between capitalist and cooperative firms on most of these variables would no doubt yield ambiguous results.

However, on one of these variables the capitalist firm maintains a decisive edge. It can use layoffs to shift the burden of recessions and other sources of economic risk onto workers. Capitalists can spread their risk by investing in a variety of industries, but workers invest all their labor power in a particular firm. Moreover, cooperative members invest much of their capital in a single enterprise. These considerations make cooperatives less likely to be competitive with capitalist firms in the long run, and they explain the difficulties facing individual workers' cooperatives when they operate in an environment of mainly capitalist firms.

WORKER CAPITALIST RELATIONS AND THE STATE

The modern worker-capitalist relation inside the workplace is not worked out solely between workers and capitalists. Typically a third party, the state, also plays an important role. Federal statutes have defined the rights of workers to organize into unions and bargain collectively, and an elaborate bureaucratic and judicial structure has been constructed to administer this legislation. Other Federal legislation sets standards for minimum-wage levels, maximum hours, administration of pension funds, and internal governance of unions. Some states have "right to work" laws that prohibit the "closed union shop." The conflict between workers and capitalists is therefore

[9]See Herbert Gintis, "The Nature of the Labor Exchange: Toward a Radical Theory of the Firm," *Review of Radical Political Economics* (Summer 1976).

[10]See, for example, Stanley Mathewson, *The Restriction of Output Among Unorganized Workers* (Carbondale, Ill.: Southern Illinois University Press, 1969) (originally published in 1931); Donald Roy, "Quota Restrictions and Goldbricking in a Machine Shop," *American Journal of Sociology* (March 1952); Donald Roy, "Efficiency and the 'Fix': Informal Intergroup Relations in a Piecework Machine Shop," *American Journal of Sociology* (1954–1955).

not limited to struggles of individual employers with their workers, but also takes place on the political terrain of the state.[11]

The evolution of labor legislation reflects the growth of collective worker power in the 1930s and 1940s, as well as the continuing predominance of capitalist power. Unions per se have not been illegal in the United States since the landmark case of *Commonwealth* v. *Hunt* in 1842. But until the 1930s the power of the state was used almost exclusively against unions and strikers. Courts issued injunctions and other judicial decisions against strikers, while the legitimate violence of the state—Federal troops, the National Guard, and local police—was deployed frequently against striking workers. The passage of the National Labor Relations Act of 1935 (known popularly as "the Wagner Act") required employers to bargain with worker organizations, specified a series of unfair employer labor practices, and established a National Labor Relations Board (NLRB) to administer this legislation. State power now also protects some worker rights.

The reforms of the New Deal era substantially advanced and consolidated the political influence of the organized labor union movement. Workers now advance their interests through economic bargaining with employers and through political activity and influence. As a result, the employment relation today is much less of a private contract than it was before the 1930s, and the collective organization and activity of workers in the political arena significantly affects the terms of the worker capital relation within the firm.

While these changes tip the scales of state justice in labor's direction, capitalists continue to retain the advantage. The Wagner Act and its successors contain numerous loopholes and inadequate enforcement provisions.[12] . . . A long lag, often lasting for several years, can separate the initial filing of a complaint with the National Labor Relations Board against an employer's unfair practices and an ultimate NLRB decision. Most individual workers and unions cannot afford to rely on this recourse against employer intimidation. Even if the NLRB rules against an employer, the low penalties that the NLRB can impose frequently do not constitute a sufficient deterrent to employers.

Labor law developments in the post–New Deal era eroded many of the reforms of the 1930s and regulated industrial conflict in order to limit class-wide action by workers. The most significant legislation of this type, the 1948 Taft-Hartley Act, forbade secondary boycotts and otherwise limited solidaristic activity by one section of labor for another. The 1955 Landrum-Griffin Act forbade Communists from holding union office. These and other details of state involvement in the worker-capitalist relation indicate the limitations of the gains won by workers through state activity and illustrate how capitalists have used the state to divide and weaken workers.

The relation between workers and capitalists is also shaped outside of the workplace, notably in the state and the market itself. The active part each group takes in attempting to influence state activities indicates how collective political struggles influence economic variables. These state activities include the macroeconomic policy determining the overall level of economic activity (and therefore the state of the labor market), the structure and incidence of taxation, the level and composition of expenditures (both purchases and transfer payments), and pay and working conditions for public employees. Macroeconomic

---

[11]See Michael Reich and Richard Edwards, Section 5.5, p. 200, for a more detailed discussion of the role of the state in the process of class conflict.

[12]Many employers refused to abide by the Wagner Act and did not recognize unions in the years after its passage in 1935. It took massive and sustained strikes and factory occupations, such as the 1936–1937 sit-down strikes in auto, rubber, and other major industries to bring many employers into compliance. These labor actions undoubtedly influenced the Supreme Court to validate the law in April 1937. Nonetheless, many employers continued to withhold compliance. See Sidney Fine, *Sit-Down* (Ann Arbor: University of Michigan Press, 1976).

policy is especially significant, since a high rate of unemployment will weaken workers' bargaining position while strengthening the position of employers. Economists traditionally recognize the importance of nonmarket political variables in the setting of tariffs, agricultural subsidies, and other government policies that affect the composition of final demand and the distribution of income. More recently, there has been some recognition of the important distributive effects of various government expenditures, from schooling and military spending to river valley development and power projects. These activities constitute important centers of conflict between classes, for class power significantly influences the distribution of gains and losses from state action. These conflicts therefore call forth collective behavior by both sides.

2.4   *The Logic of Capital Accumulation*

The capitalist mode of production has proven to be a powerful mechanism for developing and expanding the forces of production. Despite periodic economic crises, capitalism has produced ever-greater quantities of commodities. The following essay by Richard C. Edwards shows how the basic institutions of the capitalist mode of production generate an inexorable systemic pressure to expand the scale of production.

Several qualifications should be kept in mind in this discussion of the "productivity" of the capitalist mode of production. First, the growth process described below does not necessarily apply to capitalist countries in the underdeveloped part of the worldwide capitalist system. Second, every item produced for the market is counted as "productive" economic output, whether or not it increases the "standard of living"—nuclear weapons, moon rockets, and television commercials are included, for example. Many things important to the quality of life are excluded—wisdom, community, justice, the opportunity for friendship. Third, the benefits from increased production are very unequally distributed. Finally, market measures of economic output do not take account of the widespread pollution, exhaustion of natural resources, and ecological damage resulting from capitalist production. Hence, while a greater quantity of production *may* contribute to a higher "standard of living," by no means does it necessarily do so.

The capitalist period as an historical epoch has been characterized by a rapid expansion of production in the advanced countries.[1] The material productiveness of advanced capitalist societies was noted by Marx and Engels, writing in 1848:[2]

---

[1] Note that we are talking only about the *advanced* countries; the *failure* to generate such growth in the outlying areas is one of the aspects of this growth in advanced countries.

[2] The quote is from *The Communist Manifesto*, excerpted in Section 2.2, p. 20.

The bourgeoisie, during its rule of scarce one hundred years, has created more massive and more colossal productive forces than have all preceding generations together. Subjection of nature's forces to man, machinery, application of chemistry to industry and agriculture, steam navigation, railways, electric telegraphs, clearing of whole populations conjured out of the ground—what earlier century had even a presentiment that such productive forces slumbered in the lap of social labor?

If the statement seemed true in 1848, how much truer it appears from the affluent perspective of another hundred years.

The purpose of this essay is to show how the basic capitalist institutions described at the beginning of this chapter have fostered such a tremendous expansion of economic capacity. How has capitalism led to the development of what Marx and Engels called "colossal productive forces"?

The argument presented below is divided into two parts. The first section deals with those motivations and pressures which induce capitalists to strive to expand output; we note both "internal" motivations (the capitalist's own desire to accumulate) and "market pressures" (the necessity for the capitalist to maintain a competitive market position). The second section outlines the way in which workers enter the production process under capitalism, leading to the market allocation of labor resources according to profit criteria.

THE CAPITALIST AS OWNER

The capitalist mode of production is historically unique in that it concentrates the means of production in the hands of a few people—capitalists—whose *only* role in the society is to make profits; they stand to gain personally, directly, and in large measure from the expansion of profits. Their interest in production, then, is not in the social merit or intrinsic value of what they produce, but only in their product's potential profitability.

This social justification places the capitalist in contrast to the feudal lord, the ancient slave-owner, or the eastern potentate, all of whom controlled the production process as firmly as the capitalist does today. However, these earlier dominant classes rested their ideological superiority and their right to rule on claims other than economic prowess. Some classes had religious claims (the Hebrew priests, the medieval church, "divinely" appointed kings); others had military claims (medieval lords, Roman emperors, Indian war chiefs); still others had political, cultural, or other claims. Only the capitalist class bases its claim to dominance and privilege directly on its ability to make profits by selling goods on the market.

Hence it is understandable that previous dominant classes should have had less interest in expanding production, and that the capitalist class, whose single rationale is making and accumulating profits, should have been the historical agent for creating growth in material production.

The fundamental characteristic of capitalist production is that it is organized, controlled, and motivated by capitalists and their firms to make profits. The capitalist firm *realizes* profits only by producing goods and selling them on the market. Firms therefore attempt to sell as much as possible at as high a price as possible. The motivation to capture profits leads the capitalist firm to produce huge quantities of goods for sale on the market if it thinks it can sell them.

The question, then, is what motivates the capitalist to strive so diligently to make and accumulate profits? First, of course, the profits which are generated in a firm *belong* to the owner-capitalist. So undoubtedly the primary motivation is simply the *personal* one: the capitalist, by increasing profits, increases his own wealth and ability to consume, expands his own power and sphere of control, and enhances his own privileges and status. In capitalist society, power and status are gained primarily through one's control over commodities, especially ownership of wealth; so the incentive to accumulate is correspondingly stronger. Furthermore, these attributes are measured *relative* to other people's situations, so the desire to expand profits (and hence increase one's wealth, power and status) continues indefinitely.

Second, we have already noted the ideological basis for capitalists' need to maximize profits. The social rationale for putting capitalists in charge (rather than, say, running firms democratically or letting communities operate local firms) is that capitalists *own* as private property the means of production, and therefore they have the *right* to determine its use.

But the efficacy of this claim for *private* control of what is after all the *social* means of production, while it rests in the first instance on the inviolability of private property, ultimately reflects a deeper ideological assertion: that the whole society benefits by granting capitalists the right to control production. Everyone benefits, the argument goes, because property-owning capitalists organize society's production efficiently. The magnitude of his profits provides the evidence demonstrating the capitalist's social usefulness; for he realizes profits only to the extent that he efficiently produces what people want and need. This reasoning thus transforms the capitalist's act of making profits for himself into a socially essential and useful act. The *raison d'être* of the capitalist is his ability to expand production for the good of all. This ideological justification reinforces the capitalists' personal stake in expanding profits.

Capitalists' personal and ideological interest in expanding profits would by itself lead us to expect a powerful dynamic within capitalism for expansion of output. But they are driven to expand profits not only because they *want* to, but also because if they are to remain capitalists, the market *forces* them to do so. Capitalists do not operate independently; they sell goods in a market and buy labor and raw materials in other markets and must therefore face the constraints of supply and demand and market competition.

The choice of technology, the need to expand production, and the organization of the work process are determined primarily by the structure of the market system, and only in small part by the particular characteristics of individual capitalists. A particularly greedy or insensitive capitalist may exacerbate the oppressive conditions of the workplace, for example, but he cannot alter the basic situation. Neither can a particularly kind and humane capitalist change matters. *Capitalists act as capitalists because, if they are to survive as capitalists, the market forces them to act that way.* For example, suppose a certain capitalist decided on his own to pay higher wages, not to introduce oppressive kinds of new technology, and to distribute the product to the community at a lower price. He would be successful for a while, making smaller profits than other capitalists, but nonetheless remaining in business.

But sooner or later other capitalists would enter the scene. They would realize that they could make higher profits if they simply paid the market wage rate, not the higher rate that our "humane" capitalist voluntarily decided to pay. They would also realize that they could make higher profits if they were unafraid to introduce more efficient technology, which our "humane capitalist" refused to do because of the alienating characteristics of that technology. Finally, with the savings gained by paying lower wages and using more efficient technology, these new capitalists would realize that they could reduce the price even a bit further than the humane capitalist did, and still make profits. By doing so, they would underprice the "humane capitalist's" profits and drive his goods from the market.

Since he can no longer sell his products, the "humane capitalist" is now faced with a dilemma: either emulate the other capitalists, reduce wages, and introduce the new technology—in short, act as a "nonhumane" capitalist—or quit being a capitalist altogether. The conclusion is that no matter how much he might wish to act differently, if he is to remain a capitalist, he must act within the constraints set by competition in the market.[3] Marx described this process as follows:[4]

> The method of production and the means of production are constantly enlarged, revolutionized, division of labor necessarily draws after it greater division of labor, the employment of machinery greater employment of machinery, work upon a large scale work upon a still

greater scale. This is the law that continually throws capitalist production out of its old ruts and compels capital to strain ever more the productive forces of labor for the very reason that it has already strained them—the law that grants it no respite, and constantly shouts in its ear, March! March! . . .

No matter how powerful the means of production which a capitalist may bring into the field, competition will make their adoption general; and from the moment that they have been generally adopted; the sole result of the greater productiveness of his capital will be that he must furnish *at the same price,* ten, twenty, one hundred times as much as before. But since he must find a market for, perhaps, a thousand times as much, in order to outweigh the lower selling price by the greater quantity of the sales; since now a more extensive sale is necessary not only to gain a greater profit, but also in order to replace the cost of production (the instrument of production itself grows always more costly, as we have seen), and since this more extensive sale has become a question of life and death not only for him, but also for his rivals, the old struggle must begin again, and it is all the more violent the more powerful the means of production already invented are. *The division of labor and the application of machinery will therefore take a fresh start, and upon an even greater scale.*

Whatever be the power of the means of production which are employed, competition seeks to rob capital of the golden fruits of this power by reducing the price of commodities to the cost of production; in the same measure in which production is cheapened, i.e., in the same measure in which more can be produced with the same amount of labor, it compels by a law which is irresistible a still greater cheapening of production, the sale of ever greater masses of product for smaller prices. Thus the capitalist will have gained nothing more by his efforts than the obligation to furnish a greater product in the same labor time; in a word, more difficult conditions for the profitable employment of his capital. While competition, therefore, constantly pursues him with its law of the cost of production and turns against himself every weapon that he forges against his rivals, the capitalist continually seeks to get the best of competition by restlessly introducing further subdivision of labor and new machines, which, though more expensive, enable him to produce more cheaply, instead of waiting until the new machines shall have been rendered obsolete by competition.

If we now conceive this feverish agitation as it operates in the *market of the whole world,* we shall be in a position to comprehend how the growth, accumulation, and concentration of capital bring in their train an ever more detailed subdivision of labor, an ever greater improvement of old machines, and a constant application of new machines—a process which goes on uninterruptedly, with feverish haste, and upon an ever more gigantic scale.

Thus, not only does the capitalist firm *want* to expand production and profits, it is *forced* to expand production and cut costs to *retain* profits. The firm cannot stand still. It must push on.

This pressure to keep up with the market and to maintain one's competitive position also induces firms to seek new products, entirely new markets, and new technologies. Often this search for new sources of profits is carried on within the domestic economy as new products are promoted by advertising, or old markets are entered by new firms. But since the motivation is simply realization of profits, capitalist firms have increasingly turned to the cultivation of foreign markets. So a powerful tendency towards geographic expansion and extension of market control on an international scale has likewise characterized capitalism.[5]

This dynamic competition, in addition to the more routine price competition Marx described, poses both opportunities and con-

---

[3]Notice that only certain decisions are made by the market and that there is tremendous scope left in capitalists' hands for control of work. The capitalist decides what products to produce, who shall work for him, where and at what hours work shall be performed, when new factories shall be built, what the authority relations among the workers shall be, and so forth. The market merely places *constraints* on his options, requiring him, for example, to pay the market wage, to avoid inefficient technologies, to ignore ecological damage, etc. For an excellent historical discussion, see S. A. Marglin, "What Do Bosses Do? The Origins and Function of Hierarchy in Capitalist Production," *Review of Radical Political Economics,* July 1974.

[4]Karl Marx, *Wage Labour and Capital.*

[5]See MacEwan, Section 3.6, p. 107.

stant threats to all firms. According to Schumpeter:[6]

> The essential point to grasp is that in dealing with capitalism we are dealing with an evolutionary process.... Capitalism is by nature a form or method of economic change and not only never is, but never can be stationary. And this evolutionary character of the capitalist process is not merely due to the fact that economic life goes on in a social and natural environment which changes and by its change alters the data of economic action; this fact is important and these changes (wars, revolutions, and so on) often condition industrial changes, but they are not its prime movers. Nor is this evolutionary character due to a quasi-automatic increase in population and capital or to the vagaries of monetary systems of which exactly the same thing holds true. The fundamental impulse that sets and keeps the capitalist engine in motion comes from the new consumer goods, the new methods of production or transportation, the new markets, the new forms of industrial organization that capitalist enterprise creates.... In capitalist reality as distinguished from its textbook picture, it is not price competition or a small cost advantage which counts but the competition from the new commodity, the new technology, the new source of supply, the new type of organization (the largest-scale unit of control for instance)—competition which commands a decisive cost or quality advantage and which strikes not at the margins of the profits and the outputs of the existing firms but at their foundations and their very lives.
>
> It is hardly necessary to point out that competition of the kind we now have in mind acts not only when in being but also when it is merely an ever-present threat. It disciplines before it attacks. The businessman feels himself to be in a competitive situation even if he is alone in his field or if, though not alone, he holds a position such that investigating government experts fail to see any effective competition between him and any other firms in the same or a neighboring field and in consequence conclude that his talk, under examination, about his competitive sorrows is all make-believe. In many cases, though not in all, this will in the long run enforce behavior very similar to the perfectly competitive pattern.

Most industries have become so concentrated that one or a few firms dominate the entire national industry. In the United States a few firms in each industry account for most of the market in automobile, steel, food processing, computers, oil, drugs, aviation, chemicals, and most other goods. In these industries collusion and price agreements among the large firms have largely eliminated price competition. But even the largest firms do not escape the market pressure for reducing costs, introducing more productive technologies, expanding one's market, increasing profits, and repeating the whole cycle. Large firms face *international* competition from similarly large firms in other advanced countries. Likewise *nonprice* competition continues in both domestic and foreign markets.[7]

As we noted earlier, the firm only *realizes* profits by *selling* its products in a market. So the drive for greater profits leads inevitably to the drive to expand marketed output. In many industries, especially the more monopolistic ones, unlimited expansion of sales (and profits) may be ruled out, because demand has been satisfied as much as the profit criterion allows. However, if sales cannot be expanded, profits can nonetheless be increased by reducing costs; that is, by reducing the amount of labor and other inputs which the firm must buy. The resources released by reducing inputs are then available for production elsewhere. Likewise, if output cannot be profitably expanded in one's own market, this simply increases the incentive for the firm to enter new markets—either markets in different goods or geographically new markets. In ei-

[6]Joseph Schumpeter, *Capitalism, Socialism and Democracy* (New York: Harper & Row, 1950), pp. 82–85.

[7]See Baran and Sweezy, Section 3.3, p. 78.

ther event, the result is the same: expanding profits directly or indirectly require and hence lead to the expansion of production.[8]

But output (and hence profits) are expanded only by reinvesting previous profits to make more profits. To this end, the firm will attempt to expand its factory or build a new one, buy new and better machines, or do whatever it thinks best to increase output, capture a price advantage from its competitors, develop new markets, or invade new industries—all in the pursuit of turning its previously earned profits into more profits.

Now of course the capitalist firm will reinvest its profits only if it expects to get in return not only the amount reinvested but also a dividend, the interest on the capital, or put simply, more profits than it invested. Otherwise, there would be no reason for it to invest—it could as well put the money in a safe mattress.

Hence there is an ever expanding volume of profits seeking opportunities for reinvestment. Every time profits are created, they must be reinvested. And reinvestment means precisely creating more output, reducing costs (thus freeing resources for employment elsewhere), and expanding profits. Then the cycle is repeated. This expanding volume of profits therefore impels the firm to look for new markets, search for new products to be produced, and create more output to sell.

This process ensures that production will become increasingly efficient or market-rationalized; i.e., the capitalists will produce whatever brings the highest market value using resources for which the capitalist had to pay the least. Hence a new technology is in-

troduced, people are thrown out of work, transferred, etc. when the savings of inputs from the new method promises higher profits.

Both "internal" motivations and competitive market pressures drive the capitalist toward more profits. Capitalists therefore have the *motivation* to expand profits. With ownership and legal control of the means of production, they have the *power* required to institute and carry out this drive for expanded profits. Finally, their accumulated profits, their control over the social surplus, provides them with the material *resources* needed to expand production. *The capitalist has therefore gathered into his own hands all of the elements required for him, in his social role as production organizer, to structure and restructure the workplace to suit his drive for profits.*

THE WORKER AS COMMODITY

The market in labor is an important link in this process of market-rationalizing production. The wage contract is viewed as a voluntary exchange of labor services for wages. The capitalist is then free to hire, fire, and reemploy workers at will and without regard for the social consequences. In medieval society, production was carried out with the work force on the manor. The entire work force—serfs, artisans, bailiffs, and lord—all shared the vicissitudes of the crops. They shared unequally, of course, the lord getting many times the portion due the serf. Yet no one was fired in bad times; each person had a claim to his "just" part of the product, and everyone had a right to participate in the tradition-determined organization of work.

In a labor market, however, the capitalist firm makes its decisions about whom to hire and how many to hire strictly on the basis of profitability. Labor is treated as a commodity like any other raw material required for production. The capitalist firm is not tied to its workers by traditional obligations, as the feudal lord was to his serf. The capitalist need not consider workers' lives or rights when choosing a work force. Hence the allocation of people

---

[8]In industries where only a few firms dominate the market, the prices are presumably set by an agreement among the firms at the level which they think will yield the greatest profits. Further expansion of sales would require reduction of the artificially high monopoly price, and if the price decline was large enough, would reduce profits. It is sometimes claimed that since in this case firms *restrict* output, the existence of monopoly refutes the tendency described in the text for capitalism to generate ever-greater output. But it should be clear that while output may be restricted in particular industries, the continuing incentive to reduce costs simply requires the expansion mechanism to operate indirectly and does not change the result.

among various jobs is determined by the market criterion of profitability. Each worker, as the commodity "labor," is assigned to that job where he has the highest productivity, for that employment will produce the greatest profit for the capitalist.

The size of the wage which a capitalist is willing to pay depends on how valuable a worker is to the firm—or more precisely, how much his work adds to the profits of the firm. For example, a skilled worker is more valuable than an unskilled worker. Consequently, when a skilled worker enters the labor market, capitalist firms will compete to hire him and will be willing to pay a higher wage.

Capitalists will bid against each other for workers, and will quit bidding when they perceive that the wage they pay the worker would be greater than the additional profits realized from his being hired. The winner in the bidding will be that capitalist who has organized production in the most profitable manner, hence who can offer the most "productive" (i.e., profitable) employment. Labor therefore tends to be "efficiently" allocated among various uses.

The individual worker is given tremendous incentive to obtain those skills which make him valuable to the production process. Most people own no wealth assets which could provide a large enough income to support them without working. Consequently, for survival, they must sell their labor power in the market. Since a worker's labor power will be more highly valued in the market if he has productive skills, the incentive is created for him to obtain those skills. The worker goes to school, learns vocational skills, learns to be a "respectful" and disciplined worker, and so forth, in the hopes that he can earn a higher wage.

The market allocation of labor thus directly reinforces the tendency towards expansion of output under capitalism. Greater production occurs because workers are assigned to their most productive employments and because workers themselves strive to become more productive to gain higher wages.

The major theme of this essay is perhaps best restated by Baran and Sweezy.[9]

We have come a long way since the historical dawn of capitalist production and even since Karl Marx wrote *Das Capital*. Nowadays the avaricious capitalist, grasping for every penny and anxiously watching over his growing fortune, seems like a stereotype out of a nineteenth-century novel. The company man of today has a different attitude. To be sure, he likes to make as much money as he can, but he spends it freely, and the retirement benefits and other perquisites which he gets from his company enable him to take a rather casual attitude towards his personal savings. Noting the contrast between the modern businessman and his earlier counterpart, one might jump to the conclusion that the old drive has gone out of the system, that the classical picture of capitalism, restlessly propelled forward by the engine of accumulation is simply inappropriate to the conditions of today.

This is a superficial view. The real capitalist today is not the individual businessman but the corporation. What the businessman does in his private life, his attitude toward the getting and spending of his personal income—these are essentially irrelevant to the functioning of the system. What counts is what he does in his company life and his attitude toward the getting and spending of the company's income. And here there can be no doubt that the making and accumulating of profits hold as dominant a position today as they ever did. Over the portals of the magnificent office building of today, as on the wall of the modest counting house of a century or two ago, it would be equally appropriate to find engraved the motto: "Accumulate! Accumulate! That is Moses and the Prophets!"

[9]Paul Baran and Paul Sweezy, *Monopoly Capital* (Monthly Review Press, New York, 1966), pp. 43–44.

2.5   *Accumulation and Stages of Capitalism*

The readings thus far in this chapter have examined the essential structural features that characterize all capitalist economies. Yet these economies have changed profoundly since the birth of capitalism. Indeed, capitalism's several decisive qualitative transformations, described in the next reading, suggest that capitalism has passed through successive stages of development. In order to understand these changes, David M. Gordon, Richard Edwards, and Michael Reich present a theory of the stages of capitalist development that emphasizes the broader environment within which accumulation and change take place.

Excerpted from *Segmented Work, Divided Workers: The Historical Transformation of Labor in the United States* by DAVID M. GORDON, RICHARD EDWARDS, and MICHAEL REICH. © 1982 by Cambridge University Press. Reprinted by permission of the authors and Cambridge University Press.

Capitalist economies do not stand still, but continually change and develop, driven constantly by the dual dynamic forces of inter-capitalist competition and capital–labor conflict. Indeed, a principal strength of the historical materialist framework has been its ability to illuminate some of the most important historical developments in capitalist societies. More specifically, the version of the historical materialist perspective that we use illuminates five principal tendencies that have dominated the trajectory of capitalist development. . . .

1. Capitalist accumulation continually attempts to *expand* the boundaries of the capitalist system. Seeking to increase their sales and profits, capitalists continually seek to expand the geographical limits of their markets and try to transform more areas of social life into profit-making activities. This expanding nature results both from the necessity for each capitalist to meet the competition of other capitalists and from the cost pressures created by worker–capitalist conflict.

2. Capitalist accumulation persistently increases the size of large corporations and *concentrates* the control and ownership of capital in proportionately fewer hands. This tendency

is also produced by competition among capitalists and by capital–labor conflict. Bigger firms are better able to capture economies of scale, where present. Large firms are also better able to find new supplies of labor and to develop successful means of labor management; the cost of these activities gives large firms definite advantages over smaller ones.

3. The accumulation of capital *spreads wage labor* as the prevalent system of production, draws a larger proportion of the population into wage-labor status, and *replenishes the reserve pool of labor*. The expansion of large-scale capital continually drives out small businesses (including merchants, professionals, and farmers); these previously independent groups must then work for another capitalist. The continuing quest for new supplies of labor brings additional workers into the labor market from outside the traditional boundaries of the capitalist economy, while labor-saving innovations replenish the supply of labor from inside the wage-labor economy. The relative power of capitalists and workers is mediated by the rate at which this replenishment proceeds.

4. Capitalist accumulation continually *changes the labor process*, both through employ-

ers' introduction of improved technologies and new machines and through the imposition of increasingly intensive labor–management systems upon workers. A replenished reserve pool of labor–tendency (3) above—simply ensures that capitalists can find workers who are required to submit to capitalist authority in the workplace. The extraction of effort from the workers does not necessarily follow; it requires the development of labor–management techniques. These techniques have become more complex as firms have grown larger and as worker organizations have gained in power.

5. In order to defend themselves against the effects of capitalist accumulation, workers have responded with their own activities and struggles. Atomized through labor market competition and faced with the continual threat of surplus labor supplies, workers are driven to strengthen their connections with other workers in order to protect their wages, jobs, and working conditions and in order to advance their own interests. This tendency toward *collective working-class activity* leads not only to labor unions but also to informal resistance on the job and more organized forms of political activity and self-defense off the job. Consequently, capitalist development has led to the progressive development of more formal, better organized, and more extensive expressions of collective working-class strength.

Each of these five tendencies has developed unevenly, and it would take us too far afield to recount the details for each case. To give one example, the tendency toward concentration of capital may be periodically arrested and even turned back by the appearance of new technologies, the opening of new markets or sources of raw materials supply, or the entrance of new firms seeking to expand from successful operations in other industries. The pace of concentration may also vary considerably among economic sectors. Yet, for the economy as a whole over long time periods, capitalist development has produced the domination of the economy by progressively larger corporations.

These five dynamic tendencies, framed even within a relatively traditional Marxian analy-

sis, account for a great deal of the concrete history of capitalist societies. However, several considerations have led us and many others to move beyond this perspective in order to correct some of its weaknesses and to add additional tools with which to understand the history of capitalist development.

First, many traditional Marxists have used this dynamic analysis to generate mechanical theories of historical inevitability in which the emergence of a class-conscious proletariat always lurks around the next corner. In recent decades many Marxists have corrected this mechanical determinism by adding to the traditional analysis a variety of complicating factors and insights. This recent literature has featured the role of intermediate strata and classes and the resulting variety of possible multiclass alliances, the relative autonomy of political and ideological forces, an emphasis on human agency rather than abstract laws in historical change, an emphasis on the influence of production relations upon the evolution of production forces, the importance of historical contingency in shaping the responses of different groups to capitalist development, and the diverse spatial and temporal paths of capitalist development. These additions permit a more creative approach to the study of historical change, moving beyond kismetic views of inevitable historical evolution.

Second, the Marxian analysis of capitalist dynamics, no matter how subtly one pursues its modern reformulation, remains indeterminate when it is pursued *only* on this abstract level. For our purposes here, the most important instance of this indeterminacy arises in the analysis of the labor process and labor markets.

While the dynamic tendencies outlined above help shape the organization of capitalist production in general, the specific evolution of production relations also depends on the changing relative power of the opposing classes and their respective instruments of struggle. These depend most importantly, but not exclusively, on the character of the production relations. This interdependence between production organization and the shape of the capital–labor conflict means that a final specification of the character of production at any point and time cannot depend solely on analysis at an abstract level but must also focus on more concrete determinations.

Similar caution should inform analyses of the labor market. Here, employers and workers bargain over the effective wage rate, the hours of work, and other elements of the wage-labor contract. The outcome of this bargaining reflects an extraordinarily wide range of forces: the extent to which workers are unified or divided, the intervention of the state, the ability of capitalists to develop new wage-laboring populations, the availability of new labor-saving technologies, the elements of race and ethnicity, the pace of accumulation and hence the strength of the macroeconomy. Noting the extent of development of the five major dynamic tendencies of capitalist economies is not sufficient.

ACCUMULATION AND STAGES OF CAPITALISM

The abstract analysis outlined above must be complemented by an analysis of long swings and stages of capitalism. In this section we review the most important theoretical building blocks for this theory of stages of capitalism. We begin with a review of the requirements of capital accumulation, turn next to an analysis of the relation between long swings and social structures of accumulation, and close with a more formal theoretical discussion of this view of institutional change.

The Social Structure of Accumulation

The accumulation of capital through capitalist production cannot take place either in a vacuum or in chaos. Capitalists cannot and will not invest in production unless they are able to make reasonably determinate calculations about their expected rates of return. Both the Marxian and mainstream traditions of economics have recognized this relation between investment and expectations. Unfortunately,

however, both traditions have tended either to elude the importance of the external environment in the formation of expectations about the rate of profit or to fail to provide a substantive account of that environment. Although many economists may recognize the importance of external factors, most have nonetheless left the investigation of those factors to sociologists and political scientists.

We argue, in sharp contrast, that macrodynamic analyses should begin with the political-economic environment affecting individual capitalists' possibilities for capital accumulation. Without a stable and favorable external environment, capitalist investment in production will not proceed. We refer to this external environment as the social structure of accumulation. Its elements derive from the specific set of requirements, neither unlimited nor indeterminate, that must be satisfied for capital accumulation to take place. . . .

The process of capital accumulation contains three major steps. Capitalists, in business to make profits, begin by investing their funds (money capital) in the raw materials, labor power, machinery, buildings, and other commodities needed for production. Next, they organize the labor process, whereby the constituents of production are set in motion to produce useful products or services—the input commodities are transmuted through production into output commodities. Finally, by selling the products of labor, capitalists reconvert their property back to money capital. These funds then become the basis for the next round of capital accumulation.

The social structure of accumulation consists of all the institutions that impinge upon the accumulation process. Some institutions have a general impact; others relate primarily to one specific step in the process. We discuss each in turn.

As capitalists push their capital through each step of the accumulation process, they are touched by some general institutional features of their environment. Among the most important institutions are the system ensuring money and credit, the pattern of state involvement in the economy, and the structure of class struggle. Money and credit are essential at every step because money is required for exchange or credit is needed until the exchange can take place. The pattern of state involvement in the economy likewise affects all the steps of capital accumulation because the state can enhance the profitability of investment (through subsidies, enforcement of regulations, greater commodity purchases, and so forth) or diminish it (through taxation, regulation, legitimizing unions, and so forth). Finally, the structure of class struggle, whether conducted through unions, in political parties, sporadically by spontaneous outburst, or through the electoral system, conditions the expectations of capitalists at every stage.

The first step in the capital accumulation process, the collection of the necessary inputs, relies more particularly on systems of natural resource supply, intermediate (produced goods) supply, and labor supply. The structure of natural supply will determine the extent to which capitalists can secure access to needed quantities of raw materials and energy at predictable prices. The supply of intermediate goods determines access to produced goods used in production. Labor supply, the most problematical of the three, involves both the structure of the labor market, determining the immediate supply of labor, and the social institutions (family, schools, etc.) that reproduce the labor force generationally.

The process of production, the second step in the capital accumulation process, takes place inside the capitalist enterprise itself, an institution under the capitalist's own control. The enterprise consists of two related parts; the top management structure and the organization of the actual labor process.

The final step in capital accumulation, the selling process, involves at least three institutional features. First, the capitalists' success in realizing their profits depends upon the structure of final demand, including consumer purchases, government expenditures, export markets, and so forth. Second, the pace of capital accumulation is conditioned by the structure of intercapitalist competition, namely, the degree to which elements of competition and

monopoly are present and the various forms of that competition. Third, this step relies upon sales and marketing systems, including distribution networks and advertising.

The construct of the social structure of accumulation, comprising a specific set of institutions, has both an inner and an outer boundary. Its inner boundary demarcates the institutional environment for capital accumulation (that is, the "social structure") from the capital accumulation process itself. Its outer boundary distinguishes this social structure from other social structures in the rest of a society.

We understand the capital accumulation process to be the microeconomic activity of profit making and reinvestment. This activity is carried on by individual capitalists (or firms) employing specific workforces and operating within a given institutional environment. We wish to separate that process from its environment. This separation is obvious in the case of such institutions as markets, including labor markets, since they exist externally to the firm.

The separation between capital accumulation and its institutional environment is less obvious but no less important in the case of our other main focus of interest, the organization of the labor process. Here, how each individual capitalist goes about organizing the labor process in his or her firm is properly considered an aspect of the accumulation process itself. However, each capitalist organizes the labor process within a specific social context, which contains a socially "representative," customary, or expected organization of the labor process. We stipulate that this latter element in the organization of the labor process constitutes a component of the social structure of accumulation.

The inner boundary of the social structure of accumulation, then, divides the capital accumulation process itself (the profit-making activities of individual capitalists) from the institutional (social, political, legal, cultural, and market) context within which it occurs.

In the other direction we specify the outer boundary so that the social structure of accumulation is not simply a shorthand for "the rest of a society." We do not deny that *any* aspect or relationship in society potentially and perhaps actually impinges to *some* degree upon the accumulation process; nonetheless, it is not unreasonable to distinguish between those institutions that directly and demonstrably condition capital accumulation and those that touch it only tangentially. Thus, for example, the financial system bears a direct relation whereas the character of sports activity does not.

In our judgment, the imprecise and hence inevitably arguable nature of this outer boundary does not reduce the usefulness of the concept of a social structure of accumulation. Moreover, we recognize that different social structures of accumulation may incorporate (or exclude) differing sets of social institutions. Indeed, it would be possible to argue (although we have not done so below) that successive social structures of accumulation have incorporated increasing aspects of social life, thus making, for example, the post-1945 structure the most complex and societally far-reaching.

Based on this analysis of the process of capitalist accumulation, we further propose that a social structure of accumulation alternately stimulates and constrains the pace of capital accumulation. If the constituent institutions of the social structure of accumulation are stable, working smoothly and without challenge, capitalists are likely to feel secure about investing in the expansion of productive capacity. But if the social structure of accumulation begins to become shaky, if class conflict or past capital accumulation have pressed the institutions to their limits and they begin to lose their legitimacy, capitalists will be more disposed to put their money in financial rather than direct investments, earning a financial rate of return whose security compensates for its lower average expected levels.

Because capital accumulation depends on disconnected investment decisions by individual firms, it appears that one can understand those decisions through models of individual behavior. Investment in capitalist economies is mediated fundamentally by social (or institutional) forces, however—that is, by factors external to individual capitalists that are determined by collective social activities. Macrodynamic analyses of growth and disequilibria must take the structure and contradictions of this conditioning environment into account. The social structure of accumulation, in short, is external to the decisions of individual capitalists, but it is internal to the macrodynamics of capitalist economies.

Long Swings and Social Structures of Accumulation

Both mainstream and Marxist economists have tended to agree that capitalist economies are likely to experience periodic short-term and self-correcting business cycles. Many economists within both traditions have also suggested that capitalist economies may be prone to disequilibria, leading at least potentially to crisis tendencies or stagnation from which the economy is incapable of recovering without external assistance. Our model of stages of capitalism goes beyond both traditions, suggesting not only that capitalist economies are prone to longer-term fluctuations in the pace of capital accumulation but also that these fluctuations are mediated by a determinate institutional structure, the social structure of accumulation, which cannot be analyzed separately from (and therefore is not exogenous to) the capitalist economy itself.

· · ·

We propose an alternative model that views long swings as in large part the product of the success or failure of successive social structures of accumulation in facilitating capital accumulation. Although we do not wish to deny the important consequences of largely exogenous events in producing long swings, we note that such forces as demographic trends and technological innovation are heavily influenced by endogenous economic conditions, particularly when we concentrate on the world (as opposed to national or regional) capitalist system. Our institutional analysis suggests that the conditions creating a period of prosperity contain endogenous contradictions that ultimately bring the prosperity to an end. But the manner in which the ensuing crisis is resolved is not fully endogenous, for the crisis exacerbates conflict over the structural reforms that are necessary for a recovery, and the resolution of this conflict involves unpredictable political elements. The periods of boom and stagnation alternate, then, partly in response to exogenous events but more importantly in response to endogenous changes in the institutional context.

We develop our model here by tracing the connections between the social structure of accumulation and the pace of accumulation through a single stage of capitalist development. We then consider some theoretical issues that arise in this model.

Our scenario begins at the onset of a period of expansion in a capitalist economy (such as the late 1840s, late 1890s, or early 1940s in the United States). We have already noted that rapid economic growth depends upon the existence of a favorable social structure of accumulation. We are therefore presupposing that a previous crisis has somehow been resolved through the construction of a new social structure of accumulation. In particular, given the importance of production for capital accumulation, we are specifically presupposing a stabilization of conditions of production and, therefore, a moderation of whatever class struggle has intensified during the previous period of crisis.

Once begun, the expansion is likely for several reasons to continue for many years. First, the previous crisis is likely to have restored many of the conditions of profitability in the economy, for example, through depreciation or abandonment of less productive capital or through the stimulation of new technological and managerial innovations. Second, the initial investments necessary to form the social structure of accumulation are likely to provide a large (multiplier/accelerator) stimulus at the beginning of this period of expansion. Most importantly, the boom period is long because favorable conditions for capital accumulation have become institutionalized. In other

words, these conditions become established not just as the current policy of the current dominant political party; rather, they become embedded in the society's institutional structure.

It seems just as likely, however, that the expansion will not continue at a rapid pace indefinitely. (We discuss this problem more formally in the following section.) First, as we have already noted, the growth process in capitalist economies is prone to a variety of disequilibria that can choke the boom; the Great Depression of the 1930s was set off by such a development. Second, and more important for our purposes, the expansion itself is likely to set off forces that undermine the institutional basis of the expansion. At first, short-term business cycles appear and act as self-correcting economic adjustment mechanisms. Such corrections take place within the context of the established institutions, which are slow to change and remain relatively unaffected by the short-term cyclical fluctuations. But at some point barriers to accumulation begin to appear that persist through the short-term business cycle.

These barriers develop because successful capital accumulation ultimately either runs up against limits imposed by the existing institutional structure or begins to destabilize that structure. In the first case, the institutions themselves produce the constraints; in the second case, the disruption of the institutions produces the constraints. In either case, further rapid capital accumulation becomes more problematic within the existing set of institutions.

Although the development of these barriers in each of our three periods is discussed in detail in subsequent chapters, it will be useful to provide some illustrations here. The initial proletarianization and the homogenization periods provide examples of how the prevalent organization of work could begin to limit the profitability of production. In the late nineteenth century the artisans' control over the production process limited further advances in productivity in many industries. In the 1930s the homogenization of labor produced the conditions under which mass-production workers could successfully organize unions, thereby undermining the profitability of the homogenization system. The segmentation period provides an example of how a long boom period can upset its own institutional bases. The prosperity of the 1960s undermined the postwar capital–labor accord by giving labor and other noncapitalist groups greater economic and political power, thereby destabilizing one of the principal institutional arrangements that had made the long boom possible. In each case, prevailing institutions no longer worked favorably for rapid capital accumulation.

As the economy begins to stagnate, the institutions of the social structure of accumulation are further disrupted, complicating the process of recovery. Institutional destabilization may occur either because the resources that are required for the maintenance of the institutions themselves are becoming scarcer or because those institutions presuppose a smoothly functioning economy. Class conflict may intensify during this phase, as it did in the 1870s or 1890s and again in the 1930s. Given the stagnation, there is less chance for a labor peace purchased out of the (reduced) growth dividend.

Individual capitalists are then unlikely to engage in productive investment until a new and reliable environment emerges. Consequently, the resolution of a period of economic instability will depend upon the reconstruction of a social structure of accumulation. Indeed, we can define an economic crisis as a period of economic instability that requires institutional reconstruction for renewed stability and growth. For capitalists seeking such reconstruction the process is difficult and unpredictable, because it requires some collective action and the creation of a political consensus. Individual capitalists acting in isolation cannot restore prosperity.

As economic crisis deepens and the social structure of accumulation begins to become unfavorable, capitalists are in ever greater need of collective strategies capable of restoring the rate of profit. At first they may not engage in self-conscious collective action, for the early phases of crisis are likely to generate virulent intercapitalist competition. In those instances reforms may be forced upon them by the state or by noncapitalist groups. Even if capitalists are able to overcome their differences, their collective actions are likely to coexist with efforts by other classes and groups that seek to protect their working and living conditions. As a result, the resolution of an economic crisis is likely to be shaped by the relative power and the respective objectives of capitalists, workers, and other economic groups.

This point is illustrated in the United States by the responses to the economic crises of the late nineteenth century and the 1930s. In each case, major structural changes were required to create the basis for a subsequent long swing of prosperity; but the character of the outcomes differed substantially in the two cases.

The economic crisis at the end of the nineteenth century was resolved by institutional changes in the form of intercapitalist competition, in the role of government, and in the organization of the labor process. The merger movement produced oligopolies in most major industries, but a split between small and large capitalists prevented the immediate consolidation of a new social structure. Only the war provided the context for building a political constituency that could stifle antibusiness reform and establish a favorable regime. By the 1920s large capitalists were relatively united and labor had been defeated. Management had succeeded in capturing greater control over the organization of work in reducing the effectiveness of labor resistance.

The crisis of the 1930s was also ultimately resolved on the basis of a greater role for the state, this time involving Keynesian demand management and changes in capital–labor relations. The state now regulated capital–labor relations directly, both at the workplace (through the machinery set up by the Wagner Act and its successors) and through the provision of a variety of social welfare programs. Although employers were relatively divided during this period, workers were better organized, and they were able to influence the outcome on terms that were substantially more favorable than in the previous crisis period.

Both of these examples indicate that the onset of a stagnation phase marks the beginning of increasing pressure on all classes to maintain their positions. As stagnation tips into crisis, all classes must maneuver to restructure economic relations so as to protect and advance their own interests–some, of course, with more power and self-consciousness than others. Although there is no guarantee that a successful new social structure will emerge, if one does it will reflect the alignment of class forces (and other social influences) that produce it. Thus, the rise of a new social structure of accumulation depends upon the previous downswing and more specifically on the concrete historical conditions that the period of the downswing bequeathes to the major classes.

In this respect, "exogenous" forces may be very important. For example, the war devastation elsewhere in the world during World War II left the United States in an overwhelmingly powerful economic and political position, and the nuclear monopoly created an awesome military advantage, all of which may be considered at least partly exogenous. In this context, it was possible to create a new social structure of accumulation based in part on steadily rising real wages for American workers.

Regardless of the importance of exogenous forces, it is significant that the old institutions are not restored intact once the crisis has been resolved. This pattern results from systematic factors. Because collective actors are seeking solutions to their problems within a context of institutional instability, their struggles during crisis are likely to make problematic the reestablishment of the previously existing social structure of accumulation. For example, after U.S. workers had organized industrial unions in the late 1930s, it was virtually inconceivable that a resolution of the economic crisis of the 1930s could build upon old labor process and labor market structures from the 1910s and 1920s. The restoration of favorable conditions for capital accumulation after an economic crisis usually requires the shaping of a

new social structure of accumulation, whose character is formed in large part by the nature of capitalists' and workers' collective struggles during the previous period of economic crisis.

We thus have the likelihood of a *succession* of social structures of accumulation within the capitalist epoch. We refer to the periods featuring these respective social structures of accumulation as *stages of capitalism*.

This scenario, focusing on the connections between long swings and social structures of accumulation, can be summarized in a series of discrete propositions:

1. A period of expansion is built upon the construction and stabilization of a favorable social structure of accumulation.

2. The favorable institutional context for capital accumulation generates a boom of investment and rapid economic activity.

3. The success of the capital accumulation process pushes investment to the limits that are possible within the social structure of accumulation. Continued rapid capital accumulation requires (among other changes) either a reproduction of the conditions existing at the beginning of the boom or a transition to a new organization of the labor process and labor markets. The initial conditions are difficult to reproduce, and needed reforms are not easily achieved.

4. Accumulation slows and the period of stagnation is entered. Attempts to alter the institutional structure are met with opposition, especially in a stagnationary context.

5. Economic stagnation promotes the further dissolution of the existing social structure of accumulation.

6. The restoration of the possibility of rapid capital accumulation during an economic crisis depends on the construction of a new institutional structure.

7. The internal content of this institutional structure is profoundly but not exclusively shaped by the character of the class struggle during the preceding period of economic crisis.

8. The new social structure of accumulation is virtually certain to differ from its predecessor, thereby generating a succession of stages of capitalism.

9. Each stage of capitalism is likely to feature a long period of expansion, then a subsequent long period of stagnation.

In presenting this theoretical approach to long swings and stages of capitalism, we do not mean to imply that this dynamic constitutes the only structural and conflictual force affecting social and economic change in capitalist societies. Structural conflicts arising from relations among races, genders, and nations, for example, are also likely to have their own relatively independent logic and dynamics. Such forces are not unimportant or even necessarily less important than those that we address in our analysis. We have simply concentrated on one important dimension of our social and economic history; these other critical dimensions are not our main focus in this work.

2.6   The Emergence of Capitalism in the United States

Cross-national comparisons tell us that capitalism can develop in a variety of ways. The specific process that created a central capitalist institution in the United States—production based on wage labor—is discussed in the next reading.

Excerpted from *Segmented Work, Divided Workers: The Historical Transformation of Labor in the United States* by DAVID M. GORDON, RICHARD EDWARDS, and MICHAEL REICH. © 1982 by Cambridge University Press. Reprinted by permission of the authors and Cambridge University Press.

The United States was born as a child of emergent British capitalism, yet its parentage did not immediately stamp it as capitalist itself. Indeed, at the beginning of the nineteenth century the capitalist organization of production—that is to say, production carried on for profit by means of wage labor—constituted an insignificant proportion of the total economic life of the nation. The United States *developed* into a capitalist country; it was not born as such.

In North America, as elsewhere in the empire, the imperial needs of British capitalism had spawned nearly all modes of production except the capitalist mode. After independence as well as before it, agriculture was the predominant sector of production (and remained so throughout the nineteenth century), and wage labor was little used anywhere in farming. Slaves produced the most important crops, tobacco being in decline but cotton ascendant. Among the free labor force, independent farmers constituted by far the largest group. The arrangement closest to wage labor was bonded labor, a condition in which people were bound for a period of some years in repayment of a trans-Atlantic passage or other debt; in practice, however, the redemptioners moved on to independent farming, rarely accepting permanent wage-labor status.

Even in the small nonagricultural sectors, use of wage labor was spotty and irregular. Most craft and artisan production was carried on by independent producers, perhaps with the aid of family members, apprentices, and others, including journeymen sharing in the proceeds. Most of the textile products and even many other manufactured goods that found their way into the domestic and export trade were in fact produced on the farm; household manufacturing supplied country folk with employment during slack seasons, and some family members, especially adolescent girls, worked their spinning wheels and looms pretty much throughout the year, providing the family with hard-earned money income for their essential purchases. Part-time manufacture blended gradually into full-time cottage industry, as some families specialized—at least to the extent of making their gardens, livestock, fishing, and other sources of income secondary. In the cities, the extensive commercial and trading activities tended to be conducted by family businesses, and the porters, clerks, and others who worked for wages supplemented rather than supplanted this principal labor force. These diverse alternatives to wage work created the widely observed "scarcity of labor" in the colonies and young nation.

Wage workers found their employment primarily in the major cities, where port activities drew most workers. David Montgomery has provided the most insightful view of the early nineteenth-century urban working classes, and he reports that "it was the demand for seamen, longshoremen, carters, and domestic servants which absorbed unskilled wage laborers already in the eighteenth century." By the 1820s and 1830s, two other sources of demand opened up: work building the roads and canals and work in the construction trades (including shipbuilding) within the cities.

Yet even as these activities came to depend upon wage employment, workers in these areas still constituted a tiny fraction of the productive labor force. Statistics on this point are virtually nonexistent, but perhaps the orders of magnitude can be suggested by the following. In 1800, Stanley Lebergott estimates, wage earners in cotton textiles and iron manufacture amounted to a mere 2,000 persons, between 0.1 and 0.2 percent of the nonslave labor force. Michael Reich, lumping together indentured servants with wage workers, suggests that such labor in all occupations accounted for not more than 20 percent of the nonslave workforce in 1780.

Thus, although wage labor was not unknown, it was far from being a prevalent or even common way of organizing production. Slave production, independent farming, craft and artisan production, household manufacture, trade and commerce, indentured servitude, family work, petty commodity production—these were the chief relations of production within which the early-nineteenth-century labor force operated. Although they lived in a capitalist world, productive Americans were not for the most part themselves subjected to capitalist relations of production. Capitalism was a revolution yet to come.

The construction of this first social structure of capitalist accumulation in the United States can be understood without much simplification as a process dependent upon the creation of a wage-labor supply. Other elements were also involved, to be sure: the property issues resolved in the Constitution, the establishment of the Bank of the United States as the basis for a credit and monetary system, tariff protection from British goods, and the extension of political sovereignty in the West, among others.

With these developments as background, we are concerned with two great changes that transformed the American labor force between the 1820s and the 1890s.

First, the release of the slaves from their servitude freed them legally to choose any economic pursuits they wished. But before blacks entered the wage-labor force, they had to pass through several decades of brutality and poverty in the quasi-feudal system of sharecropping or tenant farming. Finally, having survived this system and been driven from it, they began, some fifty years after their emancipation, to "choose" wage labor. The integration of blacks into the modern working class, made possible by the demise of chattel slavery in the nineteenth century, thus properly belongs to the history of the twentieth century.

The other great transformation also involved an emancipation, a "freeing," but it effected a different change in economic relations as it proceeded. Out of the diverse working population of noncapitalist production—that is to say, out of the independent craftsmen, farmers, household producers, and others who constituted the precapitalist population—a working class of laborers dependent upon their wages for survival was created. The process by which this came about, despite all of its enormous diversity in detail, was in essence uniformly simple. Those who became wage workers had first been stripped of their means of production—freed or deprived, that is, of all alternate ways of supporting themselves. They were driven to wage labor.

This process involved much more than slowly adding to the pool of available wage workers; wage labor, as we have already seen, can be traced to the earliest settlers. (By the end of the eighteenth century, it was possible to point to the young women in the Boston sail duck factory visited by George Washington in 1789; to the forge workers, at least those who were not slaves, at the Baltimore Iron Works; to the carters and stevedores on the Philadelphia and New York docks; to the families employed by General Humphrey, Moses Brown, and other pioneer mill owners; and to others who had become entirely dependent on wages). More fundamentally, the new groups that entered the labor force after the turn of the century, and especially in the 1820s and 1830s, came to constitute the first phalanx of a permanent and sizable working class. Whereas the earlier wage workers had been exceptional, noteworthy for their very peculiarity, the new groups of wage workers soon made wage labor legitimate.

Capitalists, the eventual employers of these new workers, provided the chief dynamic force, their goods competing with, eroding, undermining, pushing in at the boundaries of traditional production until it was finally overwhelmed. At each small advance, some producers rooted in and sustained by a precapitalist mode of production suffered a loss, either being entirely "released" from such production to find their duty in wage labor or, at a minimum, discovering a heightened dependence upon that portion of their activities that involved a capitalist as middleman or part-time employer. This competition between emergent capitalist and stagnant noncapitalist production operated all the way up from the village level, where "capitalist" master shoemakers hired more than their share of *jours* (or journeymen) and extended their operations at the expense of the independent cordwainers,

to the international level, where the new spinning and weaving mills in Lancashire displaced both British cottage weavers and spinners on New England farms. In this important sense capitalism developed from the bottom up, following Marx's "really revolutionary road," and constituted an impersonal social force, a revolutionary movement nearly without names or leaders or important personages except those humble entrepreneurs who saved and reinvested and saw their businesses grow.

Capitalist producers put their products into direct competition with the handiwork of craftsmen, and here they had certain inherent advantages. Unlike the conservative, slow-to-change craftsmen, the new capitalists were intent upon exploiting the possibilities opened up by social change. They tended to be oriented more to the developing market, in the case of the merchants qua capitalists, because their previous experience was in marketing and because, having been relieved of the necessity of devoting full attention to production (they hired workers to produce), they could turn their energies in part to working the market. For example, in shoemaking, it was the capitalists who saw the possibilities in producing heavy boots for the western miners and cheaper shoes for the Southern market, and their control over these markets gave them much leverage to force journeymen shoemakers to accept their terms.

The capitalists also introduced technical change in the production process, although here, except for textiles, their advantage did not lie primarily in making use of "modern" technology (that came somewhat later). Their edge here resulted from their willingness to ignore the craft traditions. The crafts, organized to protect the collective interests of its members, stressed control of supply and quality of workmanship. But the capitalists cared little for either, and although they by necessity adopted the technology of the crafts, they soon introduced changes: They were less finicky about standards, and they used cheaper labor—poorly trained jours or would-be apprentices—wherever possible.

The biggest advantage enjoyed by the capitalists, however, was the cheapening and regularizing of production they could achieve through control of the labor process. Blanche Hazard's observation about the making of boots and shoes was also true for weaving, cooperage, and the other crafts: The factory was profitable because it permitted effective supervision. The workers, brought together under the foreman's watchful eye, had to work steadily and submit to the discipline of an industrial rhythm. Craftsmen had been accustomed to following their own work patterns, working hard during some parts of the day and easing up during other times, observing "Blue Monday" but banging away the rest of the week, keeping up the pace during some seasons and slacking off in others. Then, too, when every shoemaker worked in his own "ten-footer" or a weaver kept his own loom, each could knock off when the garden needed tending or the fishing was good or a neighbor needed help in building a fence. Such casualness gave the craftsmen much freedom, but it understandably did not provide for regular or stable production. It also made it difficult to expand production when new markets opened.

When capitalists stepped in to hire the jours themselves, they began to organize the production process directly. They could now require steady work and put overseers on the job to ensure that the production pace was maintained. As Moses Brown, of the firm of Almy and Brown, put it, "We have 100 people now at weaving, but 100 looms in families will not weave so much cloth as 30, at least, constantly employed under the immediate inspection of a workman." Such supervision did not change the production technique at all, but it certainly reduced production costs. Wastage and spoilage were reduced, product uniformity improved, and the effective labor input of the workforce vastly increased. Although craftsmen did not quickly yield either their casual pace or their old work habits, they were now literally forced to defend themselves, as Herbert Gutman has so convincingly argued, on the capitalists' turf rather than on their own. Eventually this change would spell the demise of the crafts, as, for example, when Andrew Carnegie and the other steel masters waged their epic battle later in the century with the iron crafts for exactly the reasons cited by Moses Brown. Yet even in the more immediate situation, control over the labor process benefited capitalist producers in their struggle with the independent craftsmen. Thus, in addition to having a more acute sense of the market, the capitalists brought to market goods that were cheaper in quality and almost always cheaper in price. When it came to relatively unfettered market competition, they simply outclassed the craftsmen.

Yet the social context within which these pioneer capitalists had to operate was usually ungiving and sometimes openly hostile to their efforts. Labor—that is, workers for hire more or less permanently on a full-time, year-round basis—was scarce, costly, and in many cases just unavailable. Traditional society resented and often resisted the investors' efforts to create a labor supply. In this sense, initial proletarianization required more than the independent and uncoordinated actions of humble entrepreneurs; it required more dedicated and class-conscious action to establish a social structure of accumulation. Whole populations rooted in noncapitalist ways of producing were released from traditional employments through this broader process.

The story is complicated in another sense by the qualifications necessarily introduced through the special circumstances surrounding U.S. proletarianization. Throughout most of the proletarianization phase, for example, farmland at the frontier could be obtained by adventurous and optimistic souls. Those willing to settle—the people who moved to the railroad lands were a case in point—could usually obtain some credit, so even the start-up costs did not need to be accumulated in full beforehand. But if land was available, how is it possible to say that alternate means of survival were unavailable? Here we must rely on less than absolutes. As the century wore on, of course, the frontier moved west, and the costs of getting to the frontier, not to mention land

and equipment costs, increased. Although mortgages were available, loans for equipment and seed were more difficult to obtain. Moreover, the farmers' periodic protests throughout the century reinforced the easterner's well-founded suspicion that making a go of farming was more difficult than simply moving to the frontier.

In addition, farming required certain skills and even an agricultural temperament, and many ruined craftsmen or destitute immigrants undoubtedly (and no doubt correctly) perceived that they would make poor farmers. Knowledge of when and what to plant, how to handle livestock, what to do about drought or plant disease or pests, and how to market a crop eluded many workers not brought up in farm families. And of course, women, especially single women, who were most in need of an income, were essentially precluded from the chance to set up as independent farmers in the West.

Thus, though land was theoretically available (and a real avenue of escape for many who did have some resources), it was of little practical significance to the people most threatened by the advance of capitalism. Moving west to farm was costly, risky, full of unknown dangers, and often impossible. Young men without families could take the chance, just as they could scramble for gold in California, but for most people the great escape valve was shut.

So, as conditions in their traditional callings deteriorated, usually as a result of competition from capitalists entering the same line of endeavor, these household producers and craftsmen and others suffered real declines in their living standards. When their situations became desperate, they saw little alternative. Freed of their traditional livelihoods, they "chose" wage labor.

The story was also complicated because people in very different circumstances came to be freed for wage labor, and their stories are not the same. . . . The four main groups who entered wage employment in the early- and mid-nineteenth century were native-born white males, craft workers, native-born white women and children, and immigrants. These overlapping groups held distinctive places in the precapitalist systems of production, and the burgeoning capitalist sector touched each of them in diverse ways.

. . .

By the early 1840s, then, when business activity began slowly recovering from the severe depression of the preceding few years, employers had experimented with and explored these four pools of wage labor. They had tested the water and found that while it was chilly, it was by no means unbearable. To an extent that would have seemed unbelievable to even a perceptive observer like Tench Coxe a generation earlier, the dearth and dearness of American labor no longer presented an insurmountable obstacle to a growing capitalist sector. No more was an employer restricted to hiring apprentices and journeymen, with their cantankerous and contentious craft demands, or widows, orphans, and poorhouse inmates, with their own peculiar liabilities. Employers too had been "freed," or had freed themselves, to exploit the possibilities inherent in social production and wage labor on a mass scale.

As these accounts indicate, the labor force recruited in the nineteenth century was marked by great diversity. There was, first of all, the division between the artisans and skilled workers and the unskilled. Although both were now subject to the discipline of the capitalist, they brought to that relationship very different expectations and traditions. For the craft workers, capitalist rule in the workplace seemed demeaning and illegitimate, a usurpation of the craft workers' rightful prerogative to work for themselves. They opposed any further intrusions, especially when the bosses sought to reorder the labor process itself, and they used the control inherent in their skills to defend their privileges.

The unskilled workers, and especially the Irish and other foreign-born, had, by contrast, little conception of an alternate organization of production, little relevant experience to draw upon, and little power to bargain with or resist the capitalists. They were more helpless in the face of the forces swirling around them. They did not come unmarked by their pasts, as though they were clean slates for the capitalists to draw upon. With their primarily rural origins they, too, were unused to the rhythms and disciplines of capitalist production; and for some, like the Irish, religious and ethnic allegiances provided a source of identity that they used to resist the capitalists' efforts to remold them. Still, their position was weaker, which showed in how little they could wring from the system.

Then there was the sexual and age division, between men in most lines of work and women and children concentrated in the textile industry and parts of the needle trades. Women workers were like the unskilled in that they had no useful tradition of an alternate production system—the patriarchal relations within the household could hardly serve. On the other hand, their class origins were mostly different from those of the unskilled, and in this respect they were more like the craft workers. But mainly the women workers were just different—different from men, to whom the patriarchal society delegated the task of providing for their families, and different even from most women, who remained in the home (as wife, spinster in-law, domestic servant, daughter, or whatever). Few male workers and even few of the female workers themselves—if we can accept the evidence of such sources as Harriet Martineau and the *Lowell Offering* or the staunchly prolabor *Voice of Industry*—accepted that they, as wage workers, shared much with other workers.

Then there were the ethnic divisions—"ethnic" standing as shorthand for that whole complex of religious, cultural, psychological, familial, and other differences that marked the way men and women went about their work, built their communities, lived and died and even sent off their dead. Scottish weavers, German tradesmen, Jewish tailors, Italian, Irish, and Lettish peasants, Poles, Dalmatians, Greeks, French-Canadians, and Bohemians all brought distinct traditions and attempted to adjust to their new circumstances in unique ways.

Little wonder, then, that the American working class would have so little conception of itself *as a class*. Indeed, David Montgomery reminds us that contemporary accounts were accurate when they almost invariably spoke of the working *classes*. Change had come quickly, in the span of one or two generations, and the differences between workers loomed larger than their commonalities. This is not to say that they never took joint action; occasionally they did, as, for example, when Philadelphia workers staged a general strike in the mid-1830s or when both men (mainly mechanics) and women (mainly textile operatives) joined in the 1840s to press for the ten-hour day. Still, though capitalist organization had subjected them all to the insecurity of the labor market and to the discipline of the workplace boss, and in this sense had brought them objectively to wage-labor status, it remained for subsequent capitalist development to bring their common status to the fore.

The Period of Consolidation: 1840s to 1870s

The new labor situation provided the basis for a highly successful social structure of accumulation and hence for the long boom that extended from the 1840s until the mid-1870s. Other elements within the institutional environment—notably political support for roads, canals, and other internal improvements; the rapidly developing domestic market based on shipping goods to the South and West; and, of course, the tremendous boost to industry from the Civil War—all contributed to facilitating the accumulation process. There can be little doubt, however, that the solution of the labor problem provided the key to the construction of a viable social structure of accumulation.

This "solution" contained limits and constraints, and the limits helped shape the kind of development that would take place. (Moreover, while capitalists would reap big profits within the system, they would ultimately run up against the constraints as well.) Most fundamentally, capital accumulation was to be based on proletarianized but largely *untransformed* labor. Capitalists hired labor but relied on traditional techniques of production. They organized the production process in the social sense, gathering together labor, materials, tools, and other essential ingredients of production and disposing of the output. Yet, except where there was no preexisting organization of production to draw upon, they did not organize or transform the labor process in detail. Instead, they adopted existing (precapitalist) methods, including major reliance on the workers' own knowledge of production. Although producers lost their tools and independence when they became wage workers, large numbers of them retained their skills and control over their work processes.

The use of proletarianized but untransformed labor implied two important consequences for the succeeding decades of development. First, it meant that the capital accumulation process would be marked by tremendous diversity, as the array of noncapitalist methods of production were transferred wholesale into the capitalist sector and these, plus some new ones introduced by the capitalists, were operated side by side. Later in the century, the pressure of intense competition would begin to generate an evenness, pushing all producers to adopt the same techniques, as the slackness that permitted alternate methods was wrung out of the system. But here, in the middle decades of the century, diversity prevailed.

Second, development and growth in the labor process itself came primarily in the form of extension rather than qualitative change. Operations grew bigger, employment increased, capitalization soared, and output steadily mounted, but the nature of the production process itself changed slowly. Even where change was the most impressive, where new machinery and new power sources necessarily disrupted old ways, they tended to be used to extend and multiply traditional techniques rather than introduce qualitatively new methods.

Both of these points, the second one especially, run counter to much received wisdom among economic historians, and we must be clear not to weaken the argument by over-

statement. In some whole industries and in some operations within other industries, particularly in those lines of production for which the antecedents were limited or lacking altogether, qualitatively new methods appeared. This, too, was part of the diversity of development. Yet it would be a mistake to characterize the period as an industrial revolution in which technical change provided the overpowering catalytic impetus to growth. Capitalist accumulation required a new social organization of producers: proletarianized but not necessarily transformed labor. Within this cleared field, technical change could be harnessed and made to work for employers, improving the harvest, but hardly causing it.

The rapid development made possible by the new social structure of accumulation was apparent throughout the emerging industrial economy. Real output and employment increased dramatically in all the leading industries. In cotton goods, which had already achieved substantial growth by 1840, real output more than tripled and employment doubled by 1870. In boot and shoe manufacture, real output nearly quadrupled, and the 1870 labor force was five times the size of the 1840 staff. And although capitalist production expanded most dramatically in manufacturing, the highly favorable accumulation context was evident elsewhere as well. In railroads, employment (not counting clerks and officials) had jumped from a few thousand in 1840 to 154,000 in 1870, and throughout the transportation, communications, and extraction sectors, employment soared. Even in agriculture, particularly in the harvesting of the corn and wheat crops in the midwestern farm belt, wage labor became an increasingly important feature of farm operations.

.   .   .

The Period of Decay: 1870s to 1890s

In September 1873, the financial house of Jay Cooke and Company went bankrupt, throwing the entire financial and credit system into panic. Just as, a half-century later, a stock market crash would destroy business confidence and thereby emphatically punctuate the onset of a depression that was already being generated by other forces, so now the financial panic triggered the Long Depression of the 1870s and signaled the beginning of the long downswing that would persist until the end of the century. The seventies and the nineties would see terrible depressions, and the mid-eighties could only be characterized as hard times indeed. The long boom was clearly over.

The social structure of accumulation based on proletarianized but untransformed labor, which had provided the context for the long boom, became the focus of increasing attack and conflict after the mid-1870s. The inadequacy of this structure accounts for the long downturn, which in part reflected the growing tensions and in turn contributed to the crisis and collapse of this social structure.

The attacks came from two directions at once. On one side, capitalists responded to the growing competitiveness in the economy at large by attempting ever-deeper intrusions in the labor process to revolutionize it and transform labor itself. On the other side, and in substantial response to these employers' efforts, workers of all sorts, but especially craft workers, struggled to defend their status and advance their interests.

The result was a period of prolonged, intense, bitter, and spreading class conflict. The conflict culminated in the economic and social crisis of the 1890s, during which the labor challenge was decisively defeated. On the basis of its victory, the capitalist class was able to construct a new social structure of accumulation, one based on the homogenization of labor.

The very success of accumulation during the long boom generated the increasingly severe competition of the last three decades of the century. One significant effect on the rapid accumulation was to encourage and provide the resources for capitalists to attempt to extend their operations into new markets for their products. Everywhere local producers sought to expand into city-wide or regional markets, bringing them into competition with other producers. Simultaneously, the heavy investments in transportation and communications, especially railroads, battered down the cost advantages that protected local producers from wider competition. Long-haul and (less so) short-haul freight rates dropped precipitously, and previously isolated local product markets came more and more to be connected into regional or even national markets. Individual capitalists experienced this phenomenon both as an expanding set of opportunities and as rapidly intensifying competition.

As intercapitalist competition and economic instability intensified during the 1870s and 1880s, the effects were quickly transported to capital–labor relations. Prices began to fall rapidly from the mid-1870s, in particular, and capitalists felt mounting pressure to reduce costs in order to preserve their margins. Although they sought wherever possible to reduce wages, capitalists faced increasingly militant workers who frequently made it impossible to reduce workers' wages as rapidly as final product prices were falling. . . . This situation placed growing pressure on the production process itself, both toward cost reduction and greater intensification of labor.

The traditional systems of labor management did not readily provide opportunities for either cost reduction or labor intensification. Two critical weaknesses in these systems of control soon became apparent. First, craft workers continued to exercise vast influence over the pace and character of production. Because so many production processes still depended upon the special skills and knowledge of experienced craft workers, employers were perpetually vulnerable to their power to slow down production and to bargain effectively over their wages. . . .

Second, even where craft workers had relatively little influence, there were problems with the intensity and reliability of labor control over production. The pace of production was often irregular. The authority of employers and foremen was problematic, depending heavily on the particularities of an industry's craft traditions, its technology, and its system of direct worker supervision. Management in general had relatively little control over the pace at which the labor power it had hired was transformed into directly productive labor activity. This kind of unpredictability prompted Frederick Taylor's first studies of new management techniques. As Taylor observed about his experiences as a foreman in the 1880s, "As was usual then . . . in most of the shops in this country, the shop was really run by the workmen and not by the bosses. The workmen together had carefully planned just how fast each job should be done." In those industries where a substantial degree of craft control had been eliminated, such as boot and shoe and agricultural implements, "internal management techniques, particularly those involving relations between the factory managers and workers, were not fundamentally different from what they had been in the craftman's shop. "In this respect," Nelson continues, "the factory . . . remained a congeries of craftmen's shops rather than an integrated plant."

The successful accumulation of the boom years had also generated a rapid expansion in plant size. . . . This rapid increase in factory size had a corresponding effect on the social relations of the factory. Work that had been organized by relatively particularistic relations between supervisor and supervisee was transferred to the larger factories, where personal relationships were much more difficult to sustain and authority became more impersonal. Reliance on hired officials introduced an unstable and often dysfunctional element into the firm's management.

Finally, capitalists were stymied in their efforts to reduce costs by the growing ability of important elements of the emerging labor movement to limit further increases in the length of the working day. Millis and Montgomery document this trend in a summary of surveys of twenty-one industries, which suggests that a gradual reduction in average hours of labor per day began after the Civil War.

Hemmed in by these constraints, yet driven by the intensifying intercapitalist competition, employers began attacking the basic foundations of the social structure of accumulation:

the untransformed character of proletarianized labor, the diverse and intractable systems for controlling the labor process, and the splintered (and in that sense noncompetitive) structure of labor markets. . . .

Workers no less than capitalists arrayed themselves against the prevailing arrangements, as intensifying class conflict signaled the growing inadequacy of the system. Whereas earlier the social structure had created a terrain that limited the effectiveness of the workers' movement, the very success of the accumulation process, by intensifying competition among firms, eroded the conditions underlying that structure.

The workers' challenge did not lag much behind the onset of hard times. Although high unemployment and severe downward pressure on wages after 1873 destroyed many craft unions, they activated industrial workers. The miners' "Long Strike" in the summer of 1875 (and the associated "Molly Maguire" incidents) and a major walkout by textile operatives in the fall of that year marked the prelude to this new class warfare. Then, in 1877, what Jeremy Brecher has aptly described as the "great upheavel" began: the first national railroad strike and, with it, strikes spreading to associated industries and general strikes in Pittsburgh, St. Louis, and elsewhere. This first American experience with the *mass* strike was defeated in the end only by the intervention of military and police force.

Through the 1880s and early 1890s, working-class unrest spread more and more widely among industrial wage earners. Historians have richly described the working-class upheavals of these years, and we will not recount that history here. We should note, however, that the character of the struggles themselves changed. Haymarket, Homestead, and Pullman, like the great upheaval of 1877, were not simply isolated conflicts affecting one industry or region; rather, they essentially became class battles, seizing the nation's attention, integrally involving state and federal governments, and having crucial class-wide consequences.

Moreover, the available evidence documents the widening dimensions of this protest.

According to reasonably comprehensive figures collected by the federal government, workers waged strikes with mounting frequency from the early 1880s.

· · ·

Under the twin pressures of growing competitiveness (and hence declining profit margins) and rising class conflict, the old social structure of accumulation, like a horse-drawn dray in the railway age, could no longer carry the load. A new vehicle was needed, and its design was already faintly discernible amid the attempts to patch up the decrepit and obsolete structure.

CHAPTER 3

CAPITAL ACCUMULATION AND THE CAPITALIST CLASS

IN CHAPTER 2 WE presented a general theory of the capitalist economy and introduced the relation between accumulation and stages of capitalist development. In this and the next two chapters we concentrate on the present stage of U.S. capitalism, which we term "contemporary capitalism."

In the past 150 years, U.S. capitalism has undergone three major historical changes, each involving a new stage of development. The first stage, competitive capitalism, lasted until the 1890s. In this stage, capitalist institutions spread throughout the U.S. economy, slavery was abolished, and the capitalist form of organizing production emerged dominant over production by independent artisans. We call this stage *competitive capitalism* because it was during this period that competition among capitalists became increasingly prevalent in most industries.

Competitive capitalism gave way to the second stage—monopoly capitalism—about the turn of the century, when huge concentrations of capital emerged. These immense concentrations took various forms as corporations, trusts, cartels, financial groups, conglomerates, and multinationals. The large capitalists now became dominant not only over artisans but also over small capitalists and industrial workers. This dominance was challenged during the Great Depression of the 1930s, and a new stage of capitalism then followed.

The third stage of U.S. capitalism is contemporary capitalism. In this chapter we analyze the accumulation process in contemporary capitalism and its relation to the U.S. capital-ist class. We trace the evolution and growth of corporations as institutional mechanisms for accumulation, the evolution of competition and monopoly, the difficulty capitalists as a group sometimes have in finding sufficient markets for their goods, the impact of accumulation on the formation and reproduction of capitalists as a class, the international character of capital accumulation, and the consequences of the accumulation process for the structure of international relations among the capitalist countries.

CORPORATIONS IN THE ACCUMULATION PROCESS

The conditions under which capital accumulation occurs have in some ways changed greatly since the nineteenth century. Then, production typically took place in small family businesses. But the period since the turn of the century has been characterized by the rise of giant corporations—firms like General Motors, IBM, AT&T, General Electric, and so on. The necessary complement to their growth, less apparent to us now because they no longer exist, was the failure of millions of unsuccessful smaller firms. In most major industries, a few huge firms by themselves account for the bulk of economic activity. The large corporations as a group dominate the American economy and are rapidly expanding, alongside giant European and Japanese firms, in the world capitalist economy. This increase in the size of firms and the increasing power of the surviving giants is a systematic consequence of the capitalist accumulation process.

In place of the individual capitalist tycoons who dominated the nineteenth century, in our own time big corporations reign supreme as the chief "capital-accumulators." As Paul Baran and Paul Sweezy have pointed out,

> The real capitalist today is not the individual businessman but the corporation. . . . The giant corporation of today is an engine for maximizing profits and accumulating capital to at least as great an extent as the individual enterprise of an earlier period. But it is not merely an enlarged and institutionalized version of the personal capitalist. There are major differences between these types of business enterprise, and at least two of them are of key importance to a general theory of monopoly capitalism: the corporation has a longer time horizon than the individual capitalist, and it is a more rational calculator.[1]

Even the giant corporations themselves sometimes turn out to be but building blocks in still more colossal units of capital. Bankers and other capitalists operating through financial institutions are often able to gain control over several corporations, creating a "financial group." In these cases the resources centralized into one still privately owned "interest" are truly fantastic.

At the same time that successful corporations have grown large, they have succeeded in eliminating much of the competition they had earlier faced in the markets for their commodities. For example, General Motors, Ford, and Chrysler were able to drive Studebaker, Packard, Kaiser, and hundreds of other firms out of the automobile business. The result is a situation in which the predominant market structure is not competitive but rather monopolistic—or what might more accurately be described as monopolistically competitive: that is, competition continues, but it is competition only among the few remaining giant firms and

it is restricted to certain forms of competitive behavior.

Declining competition in product markets creates a greater chance for large firms to achieve higher profit rates than they would otherwise have. If firms can use their monopoly power to raise prices higher than would have existed if the industry had been competitive, they can earn "monopoly profits." Large firms are thus likely to have not only larger profits than smaller firms, but profits that are more than proportionately larger. These higher profit *rates* then become the basis for the large firms' more rapid growth, and the disparity between them and smaller firms increases.

The declining competition in product markets also has implications beyond the particular industries involved. A firm in any industry may find new customers either because industrywide demand grows or because the firm is able to lure buyers away from other firms. Where many firms populate an industry, each firm tries to grow not only as the industry's market grows but perhaps more importantly, given the market, by underpricing other firms. Because each firm is a small part of a large market, it assumes that its behavior will have little effect on the overall market; in this case, the market itself determines the outcome. But where only a few firms coexist in an industry, they all realize that a price war would likely result in lower prices and profits for everyone. In part this obvious interdependence among firms reinforces for each firm the incentive to advertise in order to boost demand for the industry's product; in part it increases the pressure for each firm to advertise so as to defend or expand its sales relative to the other firms.

Monopolistic competition thereby circumscribes the role of the market in establishing the price and simultaneously introduces new costs (the costs of an expanded sales effort) into the firm's operations. More importantly, monopolistic competition typically limits each firm's growth to its share of the growth in the industry's overall market. While these firms are thereby inhibited from expanding rapidly in their own industries, their high profits impel

[1]Paul Baran and Paul Sweezy, *Monopoly Capital* (New York: Monthly Review Press, 1966), p. 47.

them to seek new areas for profitable reinvestment. The result is a strong impulse on the part of large firms to enter different industries, to develop new products, and to invade foreign markets.[2]

Nonetheless, while big business dominates American production, it does not exhaust it. Typically each industry contains, along with a few large, expanding firms, some small, economically insecure firms which survive only in a subservient role to the big firms. Suppliers of parts to the big automobile manufacturers and makers of specialty tools for industry are typical cases of small firms dependent on large ones. Small, competitive firms also retain their importance in wholesale and retail trade, in the provision of most services, in agriculture, and in certain other industries. Since smaller firms usually cannot afford large amounts of capital per worker, productivity in the competitive sector lags behind the monopoly sector. As a result, competitive firms are more important in the economy as employers than would be suggested by their percentage of total production. Table 3-A gives a rough estimate of the relative sizes of the two sectors. Our analysis of the accumulation process in

[2]This point is further developed in MacEwan, Section 3.6., p. 107.

present-day United States must also include, then, an understanding of the relations *between* big and small business.

American corporations must also operate in the context of the world economy. During most of the post–World War II period these firms have been able to expand in their overseas markets rapidly while facing little threat to their home markets from foreign producers. Foreign profits became an increasingly important part of U.S. corporate earnings. But beginning with the invasion of Volkswagens and Japanese transistor radios in the late 1950s, large European and Japanese corporations have not only competed vigorously for their home markets but have increasingly challenged American firms in U.S. markets. In textiles, chemicals, oil, steel, autos, and countless other products foreign capitalists have either greatly increased their exports to the United States or have gone a step farther and opened up production facilities in the United States. Especially since the early 1970s this rising international competition has tended to diminish the market power of domestic monopolistic corporations in the United States at the same time that the multinationals—both American and foreign—have increased their market power in the world economy.

TABLE 3-A   NATIONAL INCOME AND EMPLOYEES BY SECTOR, 1977

	Value Added During Production (billions of dollars)	Percent of National Income	Millions of Workers	Percent of Total Workers
Monopolistic industries	$ 484	31%	21	21%
Competitive industries	837	54	54	54
Government	230	15	18	18
Unemployed	—	—	7	7
	$1551	100%	100	100%

Sources: Industries classified according to William Shepherd, *Market Power and Economic Welfare* (New York: Random House, 1970), appendix 14; data calculated from *1977 Economic Censuses; Statistical Abstract of the United States, 1982–83; Employment and Earnings,* March 1978; *Survey of Current Business,* July 1982.

CAPITALISTS AND THE ACCUMULATION PROCESS

While large corporations have become the chief institutional mechanisms for accumulation in monopoly capitalism, behind them stand people—the owners. These are the people who benefit from corporate activities, and it is to them that we now turn our attention. After all, corporations and markets are merely ways of organizing particular social relationships, and these relationships ultimately exist between people, not institutions. For example, the accumulation process results in the payment of wages, profits, rent, and so on, thereby laying the basis for the different levels of consumption that are available to various classes in society.

Moreover, an emphasis on institutions obscures the fact that from time to time continued accumulation requires that more conscious and coordinated action be taken. For example, the Great Depression made "business as usual" impossible, and to resuscitate the system, the functions of government had to be greatly expanded; in the 1930s major reforms necessary for continued accumulation emerged (in part) out of collective action by capitalists. Similarly, in the opening decades of this century an emerging anticapitalist movement among workers challenged the system itself; to defend capitalism, employers worked out a coordinated policy stressing repression, union busting, and welfare policies. More recently, the partial nationalization of the railroads reflects a third case in which collective action was required, that is, where the interests of individual railroad capitalists had to yield to those of the capitalist class as a whole.

In all these cases, the normal operation of corporations and markets was seen as insufficient to reproduce the conditions for accumulation. Instead, capitalists as a group took more coordinated action in defense of their shared interests; that is, they acted as a *class*, defending their class interests.

On the other hand, as we shall see in the next chapter, accumulation has reduced most other people in society to wage-labor (employee) status. The capitalist class has thereby created a far larger class, antagonistic in its interests and potentially more powerful as an adversary. In Chapter 5 we will investigate the clash of these conflicting classes.

3.1 *The Evolution of the Corporation*

In every stage of capitalism there have been some small, some medium-sized, and some large firms. Moreover, there are always more small firms than big ones; in the United States, in 1980, there were nearly 17 million firms, but only about 3000 of these had assets in excess of $250 million.[1]

On the other hand, the kind of firm in which the bulk of economic activity occurs—the "representative" firm—has changed over time. In the nineteenth century, most production took place in quite small firms—what in the following reading are termed "Marshallian" firms (after the famous economist Alfred Marshall, who made this type of firm the basic unit of his theory). But with the transition to monopoly capitalism, the giant corporation has come to dominate the U.S. economy. Small firms have either been relegated to a strictly subsidiary role as "satellites" to big firms (e.g., auto parts suppliers at the mercy of the big auto companies) or continue only in relatively unimportant or stagnant industries.

[1]*Statistical Abstract of the United States, 1984,* pp. 532, 539.

In the following reading Stephen Hymer traces the evolution of the representative firm from its beginnings as a small workshop to its current status as an international corporation.

Excerpted from "The Multinational Corporation and the Law of Uneven Development" by STEPHEN HYMER. From *Economics and World Order,* edited by Jagdish Bhagwati. Copyright © 1972 by the Macmillan Company. Reprinted by permission of the Macmillan Company.

Since the beginning of the Industrial Revolution, there has been a tendency for the representative firm to increase in size from the *workshop* to the *factory* to the *national corporation* to the *multidivisional corporation* and now to the *multinational corporation.* This growth has been qualitative as well as quantitative. With each step business enterprise acquired a more complex administrative structure to coordinate its activities and a larger brain to plan for its survival and growth.... This essay traces the evolution of the corporation, stressing the development of a hierarchical system of authority and control.

.   .   .

THE MARSHALLIAN FIRM AND THE MARKET ECONOMY

Giant organizations are nothing new in international trade. They were a characteristic form of the mercantilist period when large joint-stock companies, e.g., The Hudson's Bay Co., The Royal African Co., The East India Co., to name the major English merchant firms, organized long-distance trade with America, Africa and Asia. But neither these firms, nor the large mining and plantation enterprises in the production sector, were the forerunners of the multinational corporation. They were like dinosaurs, large in bulk, but small in brain, feeding on the lush vegetation of the new worlds (the planters and miners in America were literally *Tyrannosaurus rex*).

The merchants, planters and miners laid the groundwork for the Industrial Revolution, but the driving force came from the small-scale capitalist enterprises in manufacturing, operating at first in the interstices of the feudalist economic structure, but gradually emerging into the open and finally gaining predominance. It is in the small workshops, organized by the newly emerging capitalist class, that the forerunners of the modern corporation are to be found.

The strength of this new form of business enterprise lay in its power and ability to reap the benefits of division of labor. Without the capitalist, economic activity was individualistic, small-scale, scattered and unproductive. But a man with capital, i.e., with sufficent funds to buy raw materials and advance wages, could gather a number of people into a single shop and obtain as his reward the increased productivity that resulted from specialization and cooperation. The reinvestment of these profits led to a steady increase in the size of capital, making further division of labor possible, and creating an opportunity for using machinery in production. A phenomenal increase in productivity and production resulted from this process, and entirely new dimensions of human existence were opened. The growth of capital revolutionized the entire world and, figuratively speaking, even battered down the Great Walls of China.

The hallmarks of the new system were *the market* and *the factory*, representing the two different methods of coordinating the division of labor. In the factory, entrepreneurs consciously plan and organize cooperation, and the relationships are hierarchical and authoritarian; in the market, coordination is achieved through a decentralized, unconscious, competitive process.

To understand the significance of this distinction, the new system should be compared to the structure it replaced. In the pre-capitalist system of production, the division of labor was hierarchically structured at the *macro* level, i.e., for society as a whole, but unconsciously structured at the *micro* level, i.e., the actual process of production. Society as a whole was partitioned into various castes, classes and guilds, on a rigid and authoritarian basis so that political and social stability could be maintained and adequate numbers assured for each industry and occupation. Within each sphere of production, however, individuals by and large were independent and their activities only loosely coordinated, if at all. In essence, a guild was composed of a large number of similar individuals, each performing the same task in roughly the same way with little cooperation or division of labor. This type of organization could produce high standards of quality and workmanship but was limited quantitatively to low levels of output per head.

The capitalist system of production turned this structure on its head. The macro system became unconsciously structured, while the micro system became hierarchically structured. The market emerged as a self-regulating coordinator of business units as restrictions on capital markets and labor mobility were removed. (Of course the state remained above the market as a conscious coordinator to maintain the system and ensure the growth of capital.) At the micro level, that is, the level of production, labor was gathered under the authority of the entrepreneur capitalist.

Marshall, like Marx, stressed that the internal division of labor within the factory, between those who planned and those who worked (between "undertakers" and laborers), was "the chief fact in the form of modern civilization, the 'kernel' of the modern economic problem."[1] Marx, however, stressed the authoritarian and unequal nature of this relationship based on the coercive power of property and its anti-social characteristics. He focused on the irony that concentration of wealth in the hands of a few and its ruthless use were necessary historically to demonstrate the value of cooperation and the social nature of production.[2]

. . .

THE CORPORATE ECONOMY

The evolution of business enterprise from the small workshop (Adam Smith's pin factory) to the Marshallian family firm represented only the first step in the development of business organization. As total capital accumulated, the size of the individual concentrations composing it increased continuously, and the vertical division of labor grew accordingly.

It is best to study the evolution of the corporate form in the United States environment, where it has reached its highest stage. In the 1870s, the United States industrial structure consisted largely of Marshallian type, single-function firms, scattered over the country. Business firms were typically tightly controlled by a single entrepreneur or small family group who, as it were, saw everything, knew everything, and decided everything. By the early twentieth century, the rapid growth of the economy and the great merger movement had consolidated many small enterprises into large national corporations engaged in many functions over many regions. To meet this new strategy of continent-wide, vertically integrated production and marketing, a new administrative structure evolved. The family firm, tightly controlled by a few men in close touch with all its aspects, gave way to the administrative pyramid of the corporation. Capital obtained new powers and new horizons. The domain of conscious coordination widened, and that of market-directed division of labor contracted.

According to Chandler[3] the railroad, which played so important a role in creating the national market, also offered a model for new forms of business organization. The need to administer geographically dispersed opera-

---

[1] Alfred Marshall, *Principles of Economics,* 8th ed. (London: Macmillan, 1920), p. 75.

[2] Karl Marx, *Capital,* vol. I (Moscow: Foreign Language Publishing House, 1961), p. 356.

[3] Alfred D. Chandler, *Strategy and Structure* (New York: Doubleday & Co., 1961).

tions led railway companies to create an administrative structure which distinguished field offices from head offices. The field offices managed local operations; the head office supervised the field offices. According to Chandler and Redlich, this distinction is important because "it implies that the executive responsible for a firm's affairs had, for the first time, to supervise the work of other executives."[4]

This first step towards increased vertical division of labor within the management function was quickly copied by the recently formed national corporations, which faced the same problems of coordinating widely scattered plants. Business developed an organ system of administration, and the modern corporation was born. The functions of business administration were subdivided into *departments* (organs)—finance, personnel, purchasing, engineering, and sales—to deal with capital, labor, purchasing, manufacturing, etc. This horizontal division of labor opened up new possibilities for rationalizing production and for incorporating the advances of physical and social sciences into economic activity on a systematic basis. At the same time a brain and nervous system, i.e., a vertical system of control, had to be devised to connect and coordinate departments. This was a major advance in decision-making capabilities. It meant that a special group, the Head Office, was created whose particular function was to coordinate, appraise, and plan for the survival and growth of the organism as a whole. The organization became conscious of itself as organization and gained a certain measure of control over its own evolution and development.

The corporation soon underwent further evolution. To understand this next step we must briefly discuss the development of the United States market. At the risk of great oversimplification we might say that by the first decade of the twentieth century, the problem of production had essentially been solved. By the end of the nineteenth century, scientists

[4]Alfred D. Chandler and Fritz Redlich, "Recent Developments in American Business Administration and Their Conceptualization," *Business History Review*, Spring 1961, pp. 103–28.

and engineers had developed most of the inventions needed for mass producing at low cost nearly all the main items of basic consumption. In the language of systems analysis, the problem became one of putting together the available components in an organized fashion. The national corporation provided *one* organizational solution, and by the 1920s it had demonstrated its great power to increase material production.

. . .

[But] the uneven growth of per capita income [that characterized economic development under capitalism] implied unbalanced growth and the need on the part of business to adapt to a constantly changing composition of output. Firms in the producers' goods sectors had continuously to innovate labor-saving machinery because the capital/output ratio was increasing steadily. In the consumption goods sector, firms had to continuously introduce new products since, according to Engel's Law, people do not generally consume proportionately more of the same things as they get richer, but rather reallocate their consumption away from old goods and towards new goods. This nonproportional growth of demand implied that goods would tend to go through a life-cycle, growing rapidly when they were first introduced and more slowly later. If a particular firm were tied to only one product, its growth rate would follow this ame life-cycle pattern and would eventually slow down and perhaps even come to a halt. If the corporation was to grow steadily at a rapid rate, it had continuously to introduce new products.

Thus, product development and marketing replaced production as a dominant problem of business enterprise. To meet the challenge of a constantly changing market, business enterprise evolved the multidivisional structure. The new form was originated by General Motors and DuPont shortly after World War I, followed by a few others during the 1920s and 1930s, and was widely adopted by most of the giant U.S. corporations in the great boom following World War II. As with the previous stages, evolution involved a process of both differentiation and integration. Corporations were decentralized into several *divisions*, each concerned with one product line and organized with its own head office. At a higher level, a *general office* was created to coordinate the divisions and to plan for the enterprise as a whole.

The new corporate form has great flexibility. Because of its decentralized structure, a multidivisional corporation can enter a new market by adding a new division while leaving the old divisions undisturbed. (And to a lesser extent it can leave the market by dropping a division without disturbing the rest of its structure.) It can also create competing product-lines in the same industry, thus increasing its market share while maintaining the illusion of competition. Most important of all, because it has a cortex specializing in strategy, it can plan on a much wider scale than before and allocate capital with more precision.

The modern corporation is a far cry from the small workshop, or even from the Marshallian firm. The Marshallian capitalist ruled his factory from an office on the second floor. At the turn of the century, the president of a large national corporation was lodged in a higher building, perhaps on the seventh floor, with greater perspective and power. In today's giant corporation, managers rule from the top of skyscrapers; on a clear day, they can almost see the world.

U.S. corporations began to move to foreign countries almost as soon as they had completed their continent-wide integration. For one thing, their new administrative structure and great financial strength gave them the power to go abroad. In becoming national firms, U.S. corporations learned how to become international. Also, their large size and oligopolistic position gave them an incentive. Direct investment became a new weapon in their arsenal of oligopolistic rivalry. Instead of joining a cartel (prohibited under U.S. law), they invested in foreign customers, suppliers and competitors. For example, some firms found they were oligopolistic buyers of raw materials produced in foreign countries and feared a monopolization of the sources of supply. By investing directly in foreign producing enterprises, they could gain the security implicit in control over their raw material requirements. Other firms invested abroad to control marketing outlets and thus maximize quasi rents on their technological discoveries and differentiated products. Some went abroad simply to forestall competition.

The first wave of U.S. direct foreign capital investment occurred around the turn of the century, followed by a second wave during the 1920s. The outward migration slowed down during the depression but resumed after World War II and soon accelerated rapidly. Between 1950 and 1969, direct foreign investment by U.S. firms expanded at a rate of about 10 percent per annum. At this rate it would double in less than 10 years, and even at a much slower rate of growth, foreign operations will reach enormous proportions over the next 30 years.

Several important factors account for this rush of foreign investment in the 1950s and the 1960s. First, the large size of the U.S. corporations and their new multidivisional structure gave them wider horizons and a global outlook. Secondly, technological developments in communications created a new awareness of the global challenge and threatened established institutions by opening up new sources of competition. For reasons noted above, business enterprises were the first to recognize the potentialities and dangers of the new environment and to take active steps to cope with it.

A third factor in the outward migration of U.S. capital was the rapid growth of Europe and Japan. This, combined with the slow growth of the United States economy in the 1950s, threatened the dominant position of American corporations. Firms confined to the U.S. market found themselves falling behind in the competitive race and losing ground to European and Japanese firms, which were growing rapidly because of the expansion of their markets. Thus, in the late 1950s, United States corporations faced a serious "non-American" challenge. Their answer was an outward thrust to establish sales production and bases in foreign territories. This strategy was possible in Europe, since governments there provided an open door for United States investment, but was blocked in Japan, where the government adopted a highly restrictive policy. To a large extent, United States business was thus able to redress the imbalances caused by the Common Market, but Japan remained a source of tension to oligopoly equilibrium.

What about the future? The present trend indicates further multinationalization of all giant firms, European as well as American. In the first place, European firms, partly as a reaction to the United States penetration of their markets, and partly as a natural result of their own growth, have begun to invest abroad on an expanded scale and will probably continue to do so in the future, and even to enter the United States market. This process is already well underway and may be expected to accelerate as time goes on. The reaction of United States business will most likely be to meet foreign investment at home with more foreign investment abroad. They, too, will scramble for market positions in underdeveloped countries and attempt to get an even larger share of the European market, as a reaction to European investment in the United States. Since they are large and powerful, they will on balance succeed in maintaining their relative standing in the world as a whole—as their losses in some markets are offset by gains in others.

3.2   *The Centralization of Economic Power*

Larger firms have generally been able to produce commodities at lower cost than smaller firms, and indeed this advantage has often been a cause for their growth. In part these "economies of scale" no doubt reflect more efficient technologies: as more is produced, the firm can institute a greater division of labor; it can have machines designed for more specific uses; it can profitably introduce techniques such as moving assembly lines. Probably more importantly, size yields economies of scale in market transactions as well: the larger firm can demand lower prices when buying raw materials in volume; it can better predict and coordinate production and demand; it can usually obtain credit more cheaply; it can better exploit the possibilities for "vertical integration," where it buys up sources of essential raw material supplies or gains control of the distribution and retailing network; and so on. These advantages reduce the per-unit costs of production and permit the firm profitably to underprice smaller competitors. Eventually the higher-priced producers are driven out of the market.

As accumulation proceeds, the growth of some firms and the parallel demise of many more tend to create the conditions for monopolistic market structure. Historically, as surviving firms grew larger and progressed from the workshop to the factory and then to the national corporation, they grew so big that in each industry just a few of them could produce enough to satisfy the entire national market.

But the internal growth of the firm was not the only way capitalists attained the advantages of size. They also combined or merged their firms. In some cases inefficient-sized plants were shut down. In more cases the new combinations took advantage of their size to exploit market economies of scale. Even in cases in which no economies of scale were realized, the benefits of monopoly power could be. Where previously, with many small firms, there had been many capitalists to include in the "deal," now it was possible for just a few large capitalists to organize pricing for the entire industry. Instead of competition driving prices (and profits) down, monopoly power could maintain or even raise prices (and profits).

The following reading by Richard Edwards describes the centralization of economic power that characterizes contemporary American capitalism.

Excerpted from *Contested Terrain: The Transformation of the Workplace in the Twentieth Century* by RICHARD EDWARDS. © 1979 by Basic Books. Reprinted by permission of the author and Basic Books.

A few hundred corporations with extensive market power and tens or hundreds of thousands of employees exist at the center of the economy. These firms—collectively termed the economy's "core"—control the major portion of the economy's production, profit making, and accumulation.

Around them, in industries or branches of industry that the big corporations have not yet invaded, nearly 12 million small and medium-sized firms—the economy's "periphery"—continue to survive. These firms represent a continuation of nineteenth-century capitalism. Only in one important respect have things changed: small firms now exist in a system dominated by big business. Where nineteenth-century firms were powerless in the face of the impersonal mechanisms of the competitive market, their small-fry counterparts today must also cope with the power of big firms. Thus, while small firms have many competing sellers in their own product markets, they face great monopoly power everywhere else. They may be able to sell to only one or a few firms, a situation auto parts suppliers well understand; they may use raw materials or finished products available from only one or a few manufacturers, as McDonald's franchises do; they may depend on the big capitalists for financing, for retailing their products, or for granting subcontract work. And even where small businesses are relatively independent of these pressures, they always face the chance, usually the disaster, of having a giant invade their market. Small firms today exist under either the actual dominance or the long shadow of the big firms.

The change has altered the small firms' environment and reduced their prospects. Yet it has not fundamentally altered the way they operate. Generally they must compete in markets with few barriers to the entry of other firms. Their labor forces tend to be small and quite informally organized. . . . Small firms bear a high chance of failure, and, especially during the recession phase of the business cycle, bankruptcies are frequent. The success or failure of such firms rides heavily on the owning family's ability to produce competent leadership for the firm.

Core firms, on the other hand, have developed into mechanisms for accumulation quite different from their nineteenth-century predecessors. . . .

CENTRALIZATION IN THE CORE CORPORATION

Archimedes claimed that, given a lever and a place to stand, he could move the earth. Corporate capitalists, unwittingly manipulating the twin levers of competition and credit, hastened the process of centralization and thereby moved the world of the corporation.

It is possible for firms to grow without expanding their market power, as happens, for example, when all firms in an industry grow at a rate equal to or less than their industry's rate of growth. Similarly, it is possible for monopoly power to increase without any corresponding growth in firm size; firms can expand their market power by simply agreeing to collude, regardless of whether or not they are growing. But this is not what usually happens.

It is the linking of monopolization and growth in firm size that generates the dramatic transforming effect of centralization. As centralization occurred within the basic industries, it tended to produce monopoly. As it occurred within the context of an expanding national (and international) economy, it tended to produce firms of enormous size. The combination of monopolization and growth proved to be highly profitable. And as the core firms reaped enormous profits, they experienced inexorable pressures to spill over into new markets—through vertical integration, diversification, and multinationalism. The end results of this process of centralization have been, for the largest firms, an enduring state of high profitability and a low risk of failure. The corporation has become, in Robert Averitt's phrase, "eternal."

The core firm's ability to survive and prosper grows out of its success in combining two quite different (and, in the peripheral firm, especially antagonistic) elements of investment: high return and low risk. Investment always carries with it the promise of return but also the risk of loss. Small-business owners and corporate capitalists alike seek to gain the return and avoid the risk. But small businesses usually can obtain the promise of high return only at the cost of bearing exceptional risk. A few small firms may succeed, winning at the long odds and thereby growing rapidly, but most small businesses realize low profit rates or failure, or both.

Core firms, in contrast, have been able to improve the trade-off significantly, getting, as it were, the promise of high returns with relatively low risk of loss. The success of the large firm, then, must be understood as deriving from its ability to influence both these aspects of investment.

Monopolization

The core economy is in part defined by the presence of monopoly power. The growing domination of the monopoly firms in the economy as a whole is apparent in several ways. If we look at individual industries, we find that in old industries, monopoly has remained; in new industries, monopoly has emerged. If we look at all industries together, the global estimates show slowly but steadily increasing market power.

Consider first the old industries. By the 1920s, consolidation had taken place in industries producing goods such as dairy products, grain mill products, meat, bakery products, refined sugar, tobacco, soaps and toilet articles, chemicals, petroleum, tires and rubber, shoes, shoe machinery, steel, aluminum, copper, fabricated metal, electrical products, household appliances, communications equipment, motor vehicles, railroad equipment, photographic equipment, telephones, and gas and electricity, and services such as life insurance and commercial banking. Note that these early-established oligopolies continue to exist today. The persistence in oligopoly is quite remarkable considering the tremendous changes, technological and social, that fifty years of rapid accumulation have wrought.

William Shepherd's sample of thirty-five "consensus" oligopolies—industries he asserted would be widely accepted as true oligopolies—provides another indication of the persistence of shared monopoly once it has been established. Comparing industrial concentration in 1947 and 1966

> yield[ed] a fairly definite answer—oligopoly concentration persists. There was no "significant" change for twenty-nine of thirty-five industries. There were four significant rises [in industrial concentration] as against two declines, and these rises were generally bigger than the declines. Of the two declines, one (electric motors and generators) at least partly reflected antitrust action. The other one (aircraft engines) reflects a statistical quirk, since in fact the industry is approaching a duopoly condition.[1]

Based on this and other evidence, Shepherd concluded that "the main body of evidence

[1]William G. Shepherd, *Market Power and Economic Welfare* (New York: Random House, 1970), p. 118, appendix table 9.

suggests that tight oligopoly and near-monopoly, once attained, tend to persist." If we extend Shepherd's analysis to the 1972 data, we find that seven of thirty-three industries showed declines in the four-firm concentration ratio of ten points or more during the twenty-five-year period. Eight oligopolies increased their market power, while most (eighteen) simply persisted.

Moreover, dominant firms have appeared in new industries that have developed since the 1920s, such as computer and aircraft manufacture, air transportation, television broadcasting, photocopying, and miniaturized electronics. The trend is also unmistakable in some older industries that had not "matured" by the 1920s, including grocery retailing, lumber and newsprint manufacture, dry-goods merchandising, grain exporting, and fast-food service.

The trend towards monopolization has not been uniform, of course, and some change has occurred. Over very long periods, major technical innovations or changes in demand have undermined old markets, forcing firms either to enter entirely new markets (witness Pullman's entry into engineering and construction) or to suffer decline (as has happened to companies in railroad equipment manufacturing, leather goods production, and—until recently—coal mining). Also, some dominant firms have been unable or unwilling to increase market shares: U.S. Steel has suffered a consistent decline in its market share, and General Motors until very recently was unwilling to allow its share to go much over 50 percent. Given the antitrust constraints and other options for investment, these firms have sought oligopoly rather than monopoly. In some industries, one or two new firms have pushed their way into oligopoly, as the Kaiser and Reynolds companies did in joining Alcoa in the aluminum industry. In a very few instances (for example, Cuba Cane Sugar), big firms have failed because of poor management, despite a continued strong demand for their industry's product. Nonetheless, in the vast majority of cases, relatively tight oligopoly has continued to be the rule.

The result has been increasing market concentration in the economy.

.   .   .

Growth in Firm Size

Even in a stationary economy, the centralization of capital would imply growth in the size of the largest firms. In the expanding United States economy in the 1920s and again after 1940, centralization produced colossal aggregations.

.   .   .

Absolute size confers important benefits on a firm. Any remaining technical economies of scale—whether efficiencies at the plant level or marketing or transactions economies at the firm level—now become realizable. More importantly, projects once too large to be considered become serious investment candidates for the firm. One illustration is the franchising of fast-food outlets. These outlets sell much the same product as small nonfranchised restaurants, so their success owes little to new products or new technology. While initially they may attract customers through their low prices and convenience, increasingly the value of the franchises depends on regional or nationwide advertising that differentiates the product in the consumer's mind. The entry of firms with sufficient size to undertake large-scale advertising makes franchising profitable. Size, then, expands the range of profitable investments available to the firm.

Even so, the essence of centralization is the growth in the size of the firm *relative* to the size of other economic or political entities. And here the process is equally visible. The top 100 manufacturing firms have increased their share of total manufacturing assets from approximately a third in 1925 to roughly half today. Sales of the 500 largest industrial corporations as a percentage of the gross national product have grown from 40 percent in 1955 to 57 percent in 1975—increasing by nearly half in a span of just twenty years.

The increasing relative and absolute size of the typical core firm equips it with many advantages. One of the most important is the ability to capture the benefits of new technology. Innovation may come either from within the core sector's own research labs or from outside (small businesses or individual inventors). But generally such technology can only be profitably *exploited* by firms of sufficient scale to produce, market, and advertise for the national market, leaving no uncontested markets to potential competitors. Even outside innovation, once it has been proven, typically winds up being sold out to core firms. In the context of a system of big firms, bigness is a prerequisite to joining the game.

Another crucial advantage conferred by size is access to political power, an important resource with the increasing government role in the accumulation process. Government contracts have become an important source of corporate sales; regulatory agencies play a bigger part in setting prices, defining fair business practices, allocating markets, and setting product or work safety standards; and government policies concerning collective bargaining, interest rates, depreciation and tax schedules, pollution standards, export promotion, energy use, and a host of other issues have come to impinge directly on the prospects for corporate profit making. Bigness yields political influence for corporations, permitting them to avoid damaging legislation, to shape regulatory rulings to their own needs, to enforce claims for protection of foreign investments, to undertake costly and lengthy litigation, and to demand their "rightful" share of lucrative government contracts. In an increasingly politicized economy, the ability to lobby effectively has a direct impact on the profitability of "private" investments.

Other Aspects of Centralization

If it is confined to one industry, the growing firm will sooner or later reach the limits of its growth. As it reaches a position of (shared or single) monopoly, the firm can only grow as fast as the industry's market. But usually when this happens, the firm's accumulating profits push it to expand its horizons and find a bigger world in which to operate.

Vertical integration, diversification, and multinationalization are alternate paths of growth. They can all be thought of as different ways for the firm to redefine its own industry by expanding it. The limits imposed on the firm's growth by shared monopoly in the original market are now thrown off. And the tendency toward monopolization now reappears within this new and larger sphere of operation.

Vertical integration involves expansion to include more stages of production in the firm's own operations. Most large industrial firms began by manufacturing some product. Typically they purchased their raw materials from other businesses and sold their products through independent wholesalers and retailers. Seeking new areas of investment, big firms began to encroach upon the businesses of their suppliers and distributors. Thus, big firms purchased outright or gained a significant ownership position in the extractive industries, parts manufacturing, or other sources of critical raw materials. Similarly, they moved downstream to achieve more control over distribution and sales. Where products once passed through many stages of production, from farm or mine to basic processor to parts maker to assembler to wholesaler to retailer, with each stage being performed by a separate firm, now with vertical integration their manufacture was increasingly centralized within one corporation.

. . .

Vertically integrated firms gain the possibility of capturing their suppliers' or distributors' profits to supplement earnings from their original industry. Whether this strategy is attractive or not depends on the investment possibilities available elsewhere. In some cases higher profits have undoubtedly been the lure, but in most cases it appears that vertical integration was primarily intended for defensive purposes, that is, to reduce the risk associated with the primary line of business.

Diversification—spreading the company's activities to unrelated or only marginally related products—is another manifestation of the centralization of capital in big corporations. In contrast to earlier periods, the 1960s saw an extremely high proportion of business mergers between firms that were neither competitors nor buyers or sellers of each others' products. Yet diversification has a much longer history than the recent merger wave; for example, the Federal Trade Commission (FTC) found extensive diversification as early as 1950. After studying 926 product classes to determine how frequently the one thousand largest firms were leading producers in industries *other* than their own, the FTC found that at least one of the big firms was among the leading four producers in over 28 percent of the industries studied (264 product classes). No comparable study has been undertaken since, but few observers doubt that diversification has increased substantially.[2]

Large companies have diversified their operations primarily through acquisitions and mergers rather than by simply opening new lines of business. Slightly over two-thirds of the growth in the two hundred largest corporations' share of total manufacturing assets between 1948 and 1967 resulted from acquisitions. Since the largest corporations tend to acquire firms with well-established operations—generally those with assets between $10 million and $100 million—the impact on medium-sized firms has been devastating. One study calculated that in the absence of mergers there would have been at least 40 percent more medium-sized firms.

As a rule, when large firms diversify, they tend to enter industries that are competitive. There have, of course, been some notable exceptions, as when Kaiser Industries tried to break into the auto industry, when RCA and GE tried to invade IBM's computer preserve, or when Howard Hughes attempted to develop a fourth television network. Yet these attempts have been noteworthy largely for their failure and for the impressive power of the entrenched firms that they reveal.

Given that it is more profitable to create a monopoly than to fight one's way into a pre-existing one, firms wishing to diversify have moved into the periphery. William Shepherd

calculated how frequently large firms entered major industries between 1960 and 1965 and compared his "entry index" for each industry with the existing degree of market concentration. The resulting correlation was highly negative, lending strong support to the proposition that large firms have tended to enter relatively competitive industries.[3] These findings reinforce the general point that the centralization process tends to proceed from the large corporations outward toward the competitive periphery.

Diversification not only provides the firm with new areas of potentially profitable investment, but, even more important, it also tends to reduce corporate risks by spreading investment over a greater number of industries. Fluctuations in trade, changes in consumers' preferences, or technological obsolescence that adversely affects one industry will affect only a part of the diversified firm's operations.

Geographical extension represents another, and historically the most important, path for corporate expansion; in the present period such extension is necessarily multinational. United States business began producing for foreign markets as far back as the cod trade in the seventeenth century, but the distinctive feature of multinationalism—the establishment of production facilities abroad—awaited the rise of the large firms. Even then, the full flowering of multinational operations occurred only after the Second World War, when a combination of several factors—favorable monetary arrangements under the Bretton Woods agreement, devastated economies in the other advanced capitalist countries, the military and political hegemony of the United States, and, of course, the core firms' need to find new areas to reinvest their huge domestic profits—established exceptionally favorable circumstances for foreign investment.

The total foreign assets of United States investors (primarily corporations) grew from $19 billion in 1950 to nearly $200 billion in 1974. In relative terms, corporations nearly doubled their foreign investment, from 5 per-

[2]Ibid., p. 141.

[3]Ibid., pp. 142–143.

cent of total invested capital in 1950 to nearly 10 percent by 1972. The role of multinationalism is also evident in the rising share of profits that firms derive from foreign operations: foreign profits increased from 7 percent of total corporate profits in 1950 to nearly 25 percent in 1972.[4]

Multinationalism, like vertical integration and diversification, is directly linked to the centralization of capital in core firms. On the one hand, core firms' market power in their home markets leads them to invest abroad. They may enter foreign markets to forestall potential competition and to prevent foreign rivals from growing large enough to threaten the firms' original sphere of operations. Also, while competitive firms always have the option of expanding in their home markets, core firms find that extensive expansion at home spoils their market; hence they are more likely to seek expansion abroad. On the other hand, core firms' size seems to be an essential precondition to investment abroad. One study found that, after accounting for interindustry differences, the only factor statistically associated with whether or not firms went abroad was firm scale. Small or medium-sized firms may trade in world markets, but they rarely produce abroad.

Since core firms are more attracted to foreign investment and have the resources to undertake it, it is not surprising to find that core firms account for almost all American investment abroad. In 1967 and 1968, for example, some 561 companies were responsible for 90 percent of all United States foreign investment.[5]

Multinational operations provide the core firm with several new possibilities. In some cases, the multinational enterprise may capture benefits from traditional economies of scale or comparative advantage. Also, the multinational firm can draw on capital sources in other countries; it can exploit its wider markets to even out lags or excesses in production; it can use the threat or fact of the runaway shop to discipline labor in its home operations; it can play rival governments off against each other to gain important concessions and subsidies; and it can, by rigging internal prices, avoid or largely escape taxes. But at the top of this long list of advantages is the simple fact that new markets and new sources of labor provide the essential preconditions for expanded accumulation.

The primary result of these advantages of investing abroad is a higher profit rate. The higher profit rate explains why the share of a firm's profits coming from abroad typically exceeds the share of its assets invested abroad. In 1971, for example, GE's foreign profits came to 20 percent of total GE profits, while its foreign investment was only 15 percent of its total investment; similarly, IBM gained 54 percent of its profits on foreign operations while having invested only 34 percent of its capital abroad. For all corporations, the 9.8 percent foreign share of their total invested capital earned them 24.4 percent of their overall profits.

More directly, between 1950 and 1972 the average profit rate on the foreign operations of corporations ranged from 12 to 17 percent, compared to an average profit rate for all their operations of between 5 and 11 percent. Multinationalism has thus raised the core firms' profit rate.[6]

To a lesser extent, multinationalism has also reduced the risks associated with core firms' investments. By concentrating on production and sales elsewhere, the multinational firm can weather depressions or waves of labor militance in any one country. Of course, this advantage does not extend to those times, like the 1930s or middle 1970s, when the crisis is worldwide.

Once a multinational has entered a foreign market, the forces pushing toward centraliza-

[4]See Section 3.5, p. 98.

[5]Raymond Vernon, *Sovereignty at Bay* (New York: Basic Books, 1971).

[6]See Section 3.5, p. 98.

tion also emerge in that market. But there is a difference. The new firm is not a small competitor, requiring decades of growth to be able to dominate the market; rather, it is a huge firm with vast resources that can move quickly to capture a significant share of it.

Appendix to 3.2 (by the editors)

To get a concrete sense of the significance of the giant corporation in the U.S. economy, let us turn to some figures on assets, sales, employment, and profits of the largest firms.[1]

In 1981, the 500 largest industrial (mining and manufacturing) corporations controlled 82 percent of the *sales* of all industrial corporations, 78 percent of their total *profits*, and 68 percent of total industrial *employment*. If we include the "Second 500", we find that in 1981 the top 1000 industrial corporations accounted for 87 percent of industrial *sales*, 84 percent of industrial *profits*, and about 75 percent of industrial *employment*. In other words, the "Second 500" controlled about 5 percent of sales, 6 percent of profits, and 7 percent of industrial jobs—a small fraction of the business done by the top 500, leaving very little indeed for the remaining hundreds of thousands of industrial corporations.[2]

The industrial corporation with the greatest assets is Exxon; in 1981 its assets stood at $62.9 billion. The company with the smallest assets of the top 500 was Rath Packing, with $67 million. Exxon's sales in 1981 were $108 billion; Rath Packing's, $465 million.

The top 500 industrial corporations had sales totaling $1773 billion in 1981; gross national product—the total money value of all goods and services produced during the year—was $2938 billion. Sales of the Second 500 were $121 billion. The largest ten corporations, ranked by asset size—Exxon, Mobil, GM, Texaco, Standard Oil of California, Ford, Standard Oil of Indiana, IBM, Gulf Oil, and Atlantic Richfield—had sales of $490 billion. That is, the top 500 companies controlled well over half of the nation's GNP; the top ten corporations more than 15 percent of GNP (and about 28 percent of the top 500 and more than four times the sales of the entire Second 500). The top twenty-five of the 500 did 41 percent of the business of the 500. In short, the concentration of the economy is continued within the top 500, where the bulk of power is centralized in the hands of a small percentage.

In 1981 the top 500 industrial companies had assets of $1283 billion. For the Second 500, the figure was $91 billion. The assets of the top ten corporations alone came to $304 billion, more than three times that of the entire Second 500.

---

[1]Most of the figures in the following discussion are from *Fortune*, "The Fortune Directory of the Largest U.S. Industrial Corporations," May 1982, and "The Fortune Directory of the Largest Non-Industrial Companies," July 1982.

[2]Federal Trade Commission, *Quarterly Financial Reports for Manufacturing, Mining and Trade Corporations*, 1981:2 and 1981:4; *Statistical Abstract of the United States, 1982–83*, p. 390.

The profits of the largest ten nonfinancial corporations (industrial and non-industrial)—AT&T, Exxon, Mobil, GM, Texaco, Standard Oil of California, Ford Motor, Sears Roebuck, Standard Oil of Indiana, and IBM—were $26.8 billion *after* taxes in 1981. The two largest, AT&T and Exxon, raked in $6.9 billion and $5.6 billion, respectively. Total nonfinancial corporate profits in 1981 were $117.5 billion after taxes. That is, the top ten corporations gained more than 20 percent of *all* corporate profits.

Table 3-B and Figures 3-A, 3-B, and 3-C present some further evidence on the significance of the giant corporation in the U.S. economy. Table 3-B lists the twenty-five largest industrial corporations and their total sales, profits, and assets; the bottom rows in the table show data for the largest 100 and 500 firms as well. Note that these are the largest *industrial* (mining and manufacturing) firms only.

TABLE 3-B   THE LARGEST INDUSTRIAL FIRMS, 1984

1. Exxon	14. Chrysler
2. General Motors	15. U.S. Steel
3. Mobil	16. United Technologies
4. Ford Motor	17. Phillips Petroleum
5. Texaco	18. Occidental Petroleum
6. IBM	19. Tenneco
7. E. I. du Pont de Nemours	20. Sun
8. American Telephone and Telegraph	21. ITT
9. General Electric	22. Procter & Gamble
10. Standard Oil (Indiana)	23. R. J. Reynolds Industries
11. Chevron	24. Standard Oil (Ohio)
12. Atlantic Richfield	25. Dow Chemical
13. Shell Oil	

		Sales	Assets	Profits
		(in millions of dollars)		
TOTAL	top 25	$ 748,904	$ 620,429	$ 42,931
	top 100	1,223,009	985,502	72,236
	top 500	1,758,700	1,409,400	86,400
Top 25 as percent of total economy		20.8%[a]	12.9%[b]	21.9%[c]
Top 100 as percent of total economy		33.9[a]	20.5[b]	36.8[c]
Top 500 as percent of total economy		48.8[a]	29.3[b]	44.1[c]

[a]Corporate sales as percent of total final sales.

[b]Corporate assets as percent of total nonfinancial corporate assets.

[c]Corporate profits as percent of nonfinancial corporate profits, after taxes and with inventory valuation and capital consumption adjustments (closest to reported profits in corporations' own books).

Sources: "The Fortune Directory of the Largest U.S. Industrial Corporations," *Fortune,* April 29, 1985; *Statistical Abstract of the United States, 1985,* p. 522; *Economic Report of the President 1985,* pp. 240, 268, 275, 328; Board of Governors of the Federal Reserve System, *Balance Sheets for the U.S. Economy* (1985).

FIGURE 3-A   PERCENT OF ALL MANUFACTURING ASSETS HELD BY TOP
MANUFACTURING CORPORATIONS

Notes: These asset data, collected by the U.S. Federal Trade Commission (FTC), do not fully reflect joint ventures among firms, investments, or only partly consolidated subsidiaries. Consequently, they understate the extent of aggregate concentration. The first break in the figures results from the unavailability of data for World War II years. The second break results from a change in methodology; beginning in 1974, the FTC excluded foreign assets, which are disproportionately concentrated among the largest firms, from the series.

Sources: U.S. Federal Trade Commission, Staff Report, *The Economics of Corporate Mergers* (1969); Bureau of the Census, *Statistical Abstract of the United States, 1975*, p. 502; David W. Penn, "Aggregate Concentration: A Statistical Note," *Anti-Trust Bulletin*, 21, 1976; *Statistical Abstract of the United States*, 1985, p. 522.

Figures 3-A to 3-C chart the importance of big industrial firms in the U.S. economy. Figure 3-A shows the increasing concentration of assets among the top manufacturing companies. Figure 3-B shows, for selected industries, the controlling position of the few big producers.

Figure 3-C shows the concentration of sales and profits among the largest industrial firms relative to the economy as a whole. Until the mid-1970s, economy-wide sales and profits were becoming even *more* concentrated among the largest industrial firms, even as services were growing faster than industry. Since 1981, sales and profits of the industrial giants have plummeted relative

FIGURE 3-B   ECONOMIC CONCENTRATION IN SELECTED MARKETS, 1983.

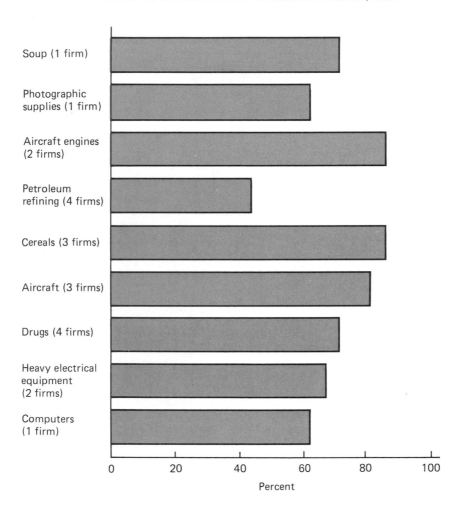

The degree of concentration is measured by the percent of total sales of all U.S. firms done by the largest firms in the market.

Source: William G. Shepherd, *Market Power and Economic Welfare* (New York: Random House, 1970), pp. 152–154, updated by the editors.

FIGURE 3-C   PERCENT OF FINAL SALES, PROFITS, AND EMPLOYMENT ACCOUNTED FOR BY 500 LARGEST INDUSTRIAL CORPORATIONS.

Note: Sales as percent of final sales (sales of top 500 include intermediate and foreign sales)); profits as percent of all nonfinancial corporate profits; employment as percent of civilian private employment.

Sources: "The Fortune Directory of the 500 Largest U.S. Industrial Corporations," *Fortune*, July 1956, August 1961, October 1966, April 1985. *Statistical Abstract of the United States*, 1957, 1962, 1971, 1975, 1977, 1978, 1979, 1982–83, 1985. *Economic Report of the President, 1982, 1984, 1985.*

to the economy-wide figures, suggesting unevenness in the economic recovery of the mid-1980s.[1]

[1]Note that the sales and employment of large firms, when expressed as a percentage of the total economy's sales and employment, tend to be overstated: their sales are overstated because intermediate *and* final sales are included for corporations but just final sales for the economy; employment is overstated because in some cases firms report both domestic and foreign employment, whereas only domestic employees are included in the economy figures. (These problems do not affect the profits data.) The percentages reported nonetheless provide a useful basis for comparison, and the trends are likely to be valid since we have no reason to believe that the data limitations affect different years differently.

3.3   *Competition among Monopoly Capitalists*

The giant corporations' rise to industrial dominance has transformed the nature of competition and the role of markets. We now turn to the question of the relations among large firms (relations we have characterized as "monopolistic competition") and to the impact of these relations on the accumulation process. In the following essay Paul Baran and Paul Sweezy argue that while price competition has been largely eliminated, other forms of competition continue.

Monopoly capitalism is a system made up of giant corporations. This is not to say that there are no other elements in the system or that it is useful to study monopoly capitalism by abstracting from everything except giant corporations. It is both more realistic and more enlightening to proceed from the outset by including, alongside the corporate-monopoly sector, a more or less extensive smaller-business sector, the reason being that smaller business enters in many ways into the calculations and strategies of Big Business. To abstract from smaller business would be to exclude from the field of investigation some of the determinants of Big Business behavior.

One must, however, be careful not to fall into the trap of assuming that Big Business and smaller business are qualitatively equal or of coordinate importance for the *modus operandi* of the system. The dominant element, the prime mover, is Big Business organized in giant corporations. These corporations are profit maximizers and capital accumulators. They are managed by company men whose fortunes are identified with the corporations' success or failure.

.   .   .

Overall, monopoly capitalism is as unplanned as its competitive predecessor. The big corporations relate to each other, to consumers, to labor, to smaller business primarily through the market. The way the system works is still the unintended outcome of the self-regarding actions of the numerous units that compose it. And since market relations are essentially price relations, the study of monopoly capitalism, like that of competitive capitalism, must begin with the workings of the price mechanism.

The crucial difference between the two is well known and can be summed up in the proposition that under competitive capitalism the individual enterprise is a "price taker," while under monopoly capitalism the big corporation is a "price maker."

.   .   .

When we say that giant corporations are price makers, we mean that they can and do choose what prices to charge for their products. There are of course limits to their freedom of choice: above and below certain prices it would be preferable to discontinue production altogether. But typically the range of choice is wide. What determines which prices will be charged within this range?

The typical giant corporation . . . is one of several corporations producing commodities which are more or less adequate substitutes for each other. When one of them varies its price, the effect will immediately be felt by the others. If firm A lowers its price, some new demand may be tapped, but the main effect will be to attract customers away from firms B, C, and D. The latter, not willing to give up their business to A, will retaliate by lowering their prices, perhaps even undercutting A. While

A's original move was made in the expectation of increasing its profit, the net result may be to leave all the firms in a worse position.

Under these circumstances it is impossible for a single corporation, even if it has the fullest information about the demand for the products of the industry as a whole and about its own costs, to tell what price would maximize its profits. What it can sell depends not only on its own price but also on the prices charged by its rivals, and these it cannot know in advance. A firm may thus make ever so careful an estimate of the profit-maximizing price, but in the absence of knowledge about rivals' reactions it will be right only by accident. A wrong guess about rivals' reactions would throw the whole calculation off and necessitate readjustments which in turn would provoke further moves by rivals, and so on, the whole process quite possibly degenerating into mutually destructive price warfare.

Unstable market situations of this sort were very common in the earlier phases of monopoly capitalism, and still occur from time to time, but they are not typical of present-day monopoly capitalism. And clearly they are anathema to the big corporations with their penchant for looking ahead, planning carefully, and betting only on the sure thing. To avoid such situations therefore becomes the first concern of corporate policy, the *sine qua non* of orderly and profitable business operations.

This objective is achieved by the simple expedient of banning price cutting as a legitimate weapon of economic warfare. Naturally this has not happened all at once or as a conscious decision. Like other powerful taboos, that against price cutting has grown up gradually out of long and often bitter experience, and it derives its strength from the fact that it serves the interests of powerful forces in society. As long as it is accepted and observed, the dangerous uncertainties are removed from the rationalized pursuit of maximum profits.

With price competition banned, sellers of a given commodity or of close substitutes have an interest in seeing that the price or prices established are such as to maximize the profits of the group as a whole. They may fight over the division of these profits—a subject to which we return presently—but none can wish that the total to be fought over should be smaller rather than larger. This is the decisive fact in determining the price policies and strategies of the typical large corporation. . . .

If maximization of the profits of the group constitutes the content of the pricing process under monopoly capitalism, its form can differ widely according to specific historical and legal conditions. In some countries, sellers are permitted or even encouraged to get together for the purpose of coordinating their policies. Resulting arrangements can vary all the way from tight cartels regulating both prices and outputs (a close approach to the pure monopoly case) to informal agreements to abide by certain price schedules (as exemplified by the famous "Gary dinners" in the American steel industry in the early years of the century). In the United States, where for historical reasons the ideology of competition has remained strong in spite of the facts of monopolization, antitrust laws effectively prevent such open collusion among sellers. Secret collusion is undoubtedly common, but it has its drawbacks and risks, and can hardly be described as the norm toward which a typical oligopolistic industry tends. That norm, it seems clear, is a kind of tacit collusion which reaches its most developed form in what is known as "price leadership."

As defined by Burns, "price leadership exists when the price at which most of the units in an industry offer to sell is determined by adopting the price announced by one of their number."[1] The leader is normally the largest and most powerful firm in the industry—such as U.S. Steel or General Motors—and the others accept its dominant role not only because it profits them to do so but also because they know that if it should come to price warfare the leader would be able to stand the gaff better than they could.

[1]Arthur R. Burns, *The Decline of Competition: A Study of the Evolution of American Industry*, New York, 1936, p. 76.

Price leadership in this strict sense is only the leading species of a much larger genus. In the cigarette industry, for example, the big companies take turns in initiating price changes; and in the petroleum industry different companies take the lead in different regional markets and to a certain extent at different times. So long as some fairly regular pattern is maintained such cases may be described as modified forms of price leadership. But there are many other situations in which no such regularity is discernible: which firm initiates price changes seems to be arbitrary. This does not mean that the essential ingredient of tacit collusion is absent. The initiating firm may simply be announcing to the rest of the industry, "We think the time has come to raise (or lower) price in the interest of all of us." If the others agree, they will follow. If they do not, they will stand pat, and the firm that made the first move will rescind its initial price change. It is this willingness to rescind if an initial change is not followed which distinguishes the tacit-collusion situation from a price-war situation. So long as all firms accept this convention—and it is really nothing but a corollary of the ban on price competition—it becomes relatively easy for the group as a whole to feel its way toward the price which maximizes the industry's profit. What is required is simply that the initiator of change should act with the group interest as well as its own interest in mind and that the others should be ready to signal their agreement or disagreement by following or standing pat. If these conditions are satisfied, we can safely assume that the price established at any time is a reasonable approximation to the theoretical monopoly price.

What differentiates this case from the strict price leadership case is that there all the firms are in effect committed in advance to accept the judgment of one of their number, while here they all make up their minds each time a change is in question. To borrow an analogy from politics, we might say that in the one case we have a "dictatorship" and in the other a "democracy." But the purpose in both cases is the same—to maximize the profits of the group as a whole. The "dictatorships" of course tend to occur in those industries where one firm is much bigger and stronger than the others, like steel and autos; while the "democracies" are likely to be industries in which the dominant firms are more nearly equal in size and strength.

A qualification of the foregoing analysis seems called for. In the "pure" monopoly case, prices move upward or downward with equal ease, in response to changing conditions, depending entirely on whether a hike or a cut will improve the profit position. In oligopoly this is no longer quite the case. If one seller raises his price, this cannot possibly be interpreted as an aggressive move. The worst that can happen to him is that the others will stand pat and he will have to rescind (or accept a smaller share of the market). In the case of a price cut, on the other hand, there is always the possibility that aggression is intended, that the cutter is trying to increase his share of the market by violating the taboo on price competition. If rivals do interpret the initial move in this way, a price war with losses to all may result. Hence everyone concerned is likely to be more circumspect about lowering than raising prices. Under oligopoly, in other words, prices tend to be stickier on the downward side than on the upward side, and this fact introduces a significant upward bias into the general price level in a monopoly capitalist economy. There is truth in *Business Week*'s dictum that in the United States today the price system is one that "works only one way—up."[2]

One further qualification: while price competition is normally taboo in oligopolistic situations, this does not mean that it is totally excluded or that it never plays an important role. Any company or group of companies that believes it can permanently benefit from aggressive price tactics will not hesitate to use them. Such a situation is particularly likely to arise in a new industry where all firms are jockeying for position and no reasonably stable pattern of market sharing has yet taken shape (all industries, of course, have to go

[2]*Business Week,* June 15, 1957.

through this phase). In these circumstances, lower-cost producers may sacrifice immediately attainable profits to the goal of increasing their share of the market. Higher-cost producers, unable to stand the pace, may be forced into mergers on unfavorable terms or squeezed out of the market altogether. In this fashion, the industry goes through a shakedown process at the end of which a certain number of firms have firmly entrenched themselves and demonstrated their capacity to survive a tough struggle. When this stage is reached, the remaining firms find that aggressive price tactics no longer promise long-run benefits to offset short-term sacrifices. They therefore follow the example of older industries in abandoning price as a competitive weapon and developing a system of tacit collusion that is suited to their new circumstances.

. . .

The abandonment of price competition does not mean the end of all competition: it takes new forms and rages on with ever increasing intensity. Most of these new forms of competition come under the heading of what we call the sales effort. . . .

There are, it seems to us, two aspects of non-price competition which are of decisive importance here. The first has to do with what may be called the dynamics of market sharing. The second has to do with the particular form which the sales effort assumes in the producer goods industries.

To begin with, the firm with lower costs and higher profits enjoys a variety of advantages over higher-cost rivals in the struggle for market shares. . . . The firm with the lowest costs holds the whip hand; it can afford to be aggressive even to the point of threatening, and in the limiting case precipitating, a price war. It can get away with tactics (special discounts, favorable credit terms, etc.) which if adopted by a weak firm would provoke retaliation. It can afford the advertising, research, development of new product varieties, extra services, and so on, which are the usual means of fighting for market shares and which tend to yield results in proportion to the amounts spent on

them. Other less tangible factors are involved which tend to elude the economist's net but which play an important part in the business world. The lower-cost, higher-profit company acquires a special reputation which enables it to attract and hold customers, bid promising executive personnel away from rival firms, and recruit the ablest graduates of engineering and business schools. For all these reasons, there is a strong positive incentive for the large corporation in an oligopolistic industry not only to seek continuously to cut its costs but to do so faster than its rivals.

There is an additional reason, in our judgment as important as it is neglected, why a tendency for costs of production to fall is endemic to the entire monopoly capitalist economy, even including those areas which if left to themselves would stagnate technologically. It stems from the exigencies of non-price competition in the producer goods industries. Here, as in industries producing consumer goods, sellers must be forever seeking to put something new on the market. But they are not dealing with buyers whose primary interest is the latest fashion or keeping up with the Joneses. They are dealing with sophisticated buyers whose concern is to increase profits. Hence the new products offered to the prospective buyers must be designed to help them increase their profits, which in general means to help them reduce their costs. If the manufacturer can convince his customers that his new instrument or material or machine will save them money, the sale will follow almost automatically.

Probably the clearest example of the cost-reducing effects of the innovating activity of manufacturers of producer goods is to be found in agriculture. As Galbraith has pointed out, "there would be little technical development and not much progress in agriculture were it not for government-supported research supplemented by the research of the corporations which devise and sell products to the farmer."[3] No doubt, as this statement implies,

[3] J. K. Galbraith, *American Capitalism*, Boston, 1952, pp. 95–96.

government research has been the main factor behind the spectacular reduction in agricultural costs during the last two decades, but the sales-hungry manufacturers of farm machinery, fertilizers, pesticides, etc., have also played an important part in the process. Similarly, producers of machine tools, computers and computer systems, business machines, automatic control equipment, loading and transfer machinery, new plastics and metal alloys, and a thousand and one other kinds of producer goods are busy developing new products which will enable their customer—comprising literally the entire business world—to produce more cheaply and hence to make more profits. In a word: producers of producer goods make more profits by helping others to make more profits. The process is self-reinforcing and cumulative, and goes far toward explaining the extraordinarily rapid advance of technology and labor productivity which characterizes the developed monopoly capitalist economy.

. . .

The whole motivation of cost reduction is to increase profits, and the monopolistic structure of markets enables the corporations to appropriate the lion's share of the fruits of increasing productivity directly in the form of higher profits.

. . .

Price competition has largely receded as a means of attracting buyers, and has yielded to new ways of sales promotion: advertising, variation of the products' appearance and packaging, "planned obsolescence," model changes, credit schemes, and the like.

. . .

Advertising expenditures in the American economy have experienced a truly spectacular rise. A century ago, before the wave of concentration and trustification which ushered in the monopolistic phase of capitalism, advertising played very little part in the process of distribution of products and the influencing of consumer attitudes and habits. Such advertising as did exist was carried on mainly by retailers, and even they did not attempt to promote distinctive brands or labeled articles. The manufacturers themselves had not yet begun to exploit advertising as a means of securing ultimate consumer demand for their products. By the 1890's, however, both the volume and the tone of advertising changed. Expenditures on advertising in 1890 amounted to $360 million, some seven times more than in 1867. By 1929, this figure had been multiplied by nearly 10, reaching $3,426 million.

Thus as monopoly capitalism reached maturity, advertising entered "the state of persuasion, as distinct from proclamation or iteration."

Accordingly, the advertising business has grown astronomically, with its expansion and success being continually promoted by the growing monopolization of the economy and by the effectiveness of the media which have been pressed into its service—especially radio, and now above all television. Total spending on advertising media rose to $10.3 billion in 1957, and amounted to over [$26.5] billion in [1974]. Outlays on market research, public relations, commercial design, and similar services carried out by advertising agencies and other specialized firms add more billions. And this does not include the cost of market research, advertising work, designing, etc., carried on within the producing corporations themselves.

This truly fantastic outpouring of resources does not reflect some frivolous irrationality in corporate managements or some peculiar predilection of the American people for singing commercials, garish billboards, and magazines and newspapers flooded with advertising copy. What has actually happened is that advertising has turned into an indispensable tool for a large sector of corporate business. Competitively employed, it has become an integral part of the corporations' profit maximization policy and serves at the same time as a formidable wall protecting monopolistic positions. Although advertising at first appeared to corporate managements as a deplorable cost to be held down as much as possible, before long it turned into what one advertising agency has rightly called "a must for survival" for many a corporate enterprise.

The strategy of the advertiser is to hammer into the heads of people the unquestioned desirability, indeed the imperative necessity, of owning the newest product that comes on the market. For this strategy to work, however, producers have to pour on the market a steady stream of "new" products, with none daring to lag behind for fear his customers will turn to his rivals for their newness.

Genuinely new or different products, however, are not easy to come by, even in our age of rapid scientific and technological advance. Hence much of the newness with which the consumer is systematically bombarded is either fraudulent or related trivially and in many cases even negatively to the function and serviceability of the product.

It is entirely different with the second kind of newness. Here we have to do with products which are indeed new in design and appearance but which serve essentially the same purposes as old products they are intended to replace. The extent of the difference can vary all the way from a simple change in packaging to the far-reaching and enormously expensive annual changes in automobile models.

· · ·

The emergence of a condition in which the sales and production efforts interpenetrate to such an extent as to become virtually indistinguishable entails a profound change in what constitutes socially necessary costs of production as well as in the nature of the social product itself. In the competitive model, given all the assumptions upon which it rests, only the minimum costs of production (as determined by prevailing technology), combined with the minimum costs of packaging, transportation, and distribution (as called for by existing customs), could be recognized by the market—and by economic theory—as socially necessary costs of purveying a product to its buyer.

· · ·

Matters are very different under the reign of oligopoly and monopoly. Veblen, who was the first economist to recognize and analyze many aspects of monopoly capitalism, put his finger on the crucial point at a relatively early stage:

> The producers have been giving continually more attention to the salability of their product, so that much of what appears on the books as production-cost should properly be charged to the production of salable appearances. The distinction between workmanship and salesmanship has been blurred in this way, until it will doubtless hold true now that the shop-cost of many articles produced for the market is mainly chargeable to the production of salable appearances, ordinarily meretricious.[4]

[4]Thorstein Veblen, *Absentee Ownership and Business Enterprise in Recent Times*, New York, 1923, p. 300.

Afterword to 3.3 (by the editors)

Does a more monopolistic market structure tend to enhance or inhibit the accumulation of capital? The answer to this question involves a great many considerations, a few of which will be explored here. In particular, we shall first consider this question at the microeconomic level; that is, are monopolistic firms more profitable than competitive firms and hence better able to invest and accumulate capital? Then we will consider the question at the macroeconomic level; that is, what is the impact of monopoly on accumulation in the economy as a whole? We will explore this second question further in Chapter 10.

The erosion of competition has equipped the monopoly corporations with greatly enhanced power compared to competitive firms. One significant power big firms enjoy is the ability to raise prices beyond what would exist under competitive conditions. Since increasing the price of commodities by itself generally entails no additional costs, higher prices mean higher profits.

At this point we might ask: What prevents the big firms from using their power to raise their prices *indefinitely?* After all, if high prices are good, are not higher prices always better? Indeed, they are, *as long as those higher prices actually result in sales.* But higher prices might reduce a firm's sales, and this limits the extent to which monopoly firms can raise prices. Customers may not be able or willing to pay the higher prices, so firms must balance the extra profits gained on each unit sold as a consequence of higher price against the loss in profits from selling fewer units of the good.

Moreover, if monopoly firms raise their prices too high, other large corporations may try to enter the market to capture some of the high profits. Indeed, the firm can raise its prices only to a level that will be still sufficiently unremunerative for other firms so as not to attract them. This level may be relatively high, especially where large amounts of capital are required to join the industry or where other barriers exist to inhibit firms from entering the market. Nonetheless, the firm's prices must remain within the limits imposed by these considerations.

Two factors not mentioned by Baran and Sweezy further limit the ability of monopoly firms to raise prices. One is competition from foreign firms. As European and Japanese capitalists seek out new markets, they upset old, established pricing policies and agreements on market sharing. They may attempt to establish market positions precisely by reintroducing price competition. Another factor is product substitutability: if steel firms raise prices too high, for example, their customers may try to substitute aluminum, glass, or plastic for steel. As all these limitations show, monopoly power is relative; the ability of firms to raise prices depends on their degree of monopoly power.

Let us next investigate the monopoly firms' costs. The large scale of most monopolistic corporations often permits them to reduce per-unit costs compared to smaller firms. Large corporations are able to reduce costs both because they are more rational calculators of profit opportunities (using sophisticated market research, cost accounting, etc.) and because their longer time horizons permit them to engage in extremely long-run planning. In part these economies result from being able to employ technologies that are more efficient when larger quantities are produced. More significantly, the large firm can realize savings from volume buying, manipulation of product markets, better coordination of production and demand, vertical integration, and other market economies of scale.

But monopolistic competition may also bring into play new or additional costs. The most important of these is the cost of expanded sales efforts: advertising, redesigning products for fashion or style, market research, sales staff, and so on. Each firm finds these costs necessary when all firms in an industry agree to avoid price competition, since with prices fixed, expanding sales is the only way to increase revenues. If any one firm did not engage in such advertising, it would lose its share of the market.

Whether or not monopolistic competition results in higher profits depends on the interplay of these forces. Prices are likely to be higher than if purely competitive conditions obtained, resulting in higher per-sale revenues but perhaps somewhat reduced sales. Whether costs are higher or lower depends on (1) the ability of the large firm to reduce costs—that is, whether new costs outweigh economies of scale—and (2) given the large firm's ability to reduce costs, the extent to which it desires or is forced to do so. On the first point,

Baran and Sweezy argue that despite the rising costs of the sales efforts, technical change in the capital goods industry plus the corporation's own efforts will lead to a persistent possibility for total per-unit costs to fall. On the second point, while monopoly firms may have less incentive to reduce costs because they are not so hard-pressed by competition, Baran and Sweezy argue that the "dynamics of market sharing" will reinforce the firms' resolve to cut costs wherever possible. We might note that this pressure is likely to be most strongly felt during times of business depression and crisis.

If we look at what has actually happened, the data suggest that on balance monopoly-sector firms have earned persistently higher profit rates than other firms. First, large firms seem to have earned higher profit rates than have smaller ones, even though the business cycle caused the profit rates of all firms to fluctuate. Table 3-C presents the results of one study relating corporate size and profitability.[1] Other studies have reported that the profits of big firms tend to be less risky as well, in the sense that there is less variability than in smaller-firm profits. Second, profits tend to be higher in industries where one

TABLE 3-C   THE LONG-RUN RELATION BETWEEN CORPORATE ASSET SIZE AND RATE OF RETURN[a]

Size (by assets)	Profit Rate[b]
$ 0–1 million	3.7%
1–5 million	5.3
5–10 million	6.7
10–50 million	7.4
100–250 million	8.1
150 million–1 billion	8.8
1 billion and over	11.7

[a]All U.S. manufacturing corporations, 1956–1975.

[b]Profit before taxes divided by stockholders' capital.

Source: U.S. Federal Trade Commission, *Quarterly Reports of U.S. Manufacturing Corporations* (Washington, D.C.: GPO 1956–1975), as cited in Howard Sherman and Gary Evans, *Macroeconomics* (New York: Harper & Row, 1984), p. 373.

or a few firms account for the bulk of the industry's sales than in more competitive industries; Figure 3-D illustrates this relation.[2] Profits are particularly high where "barriers to entry" prevent outside firms from easily entering the market.[3] Finally, a third set of studies (see Figure 3-E) points out that the correlation between concentration and higher profits exists only for *large* firms. Apparently it is only the combination of size *and* market power characteristic of monopoly-sector firms which ensures higher profit rates.[4]

[1]See also William G. Shepherd, *Market Power and Economic Welfare* (New York: Random House, 1970), pp. 187–188.

[2]Many studies have replicated this result; for a review, see L. Weiss, "Quantitative Studies in Industrial Organization," in M. Intriligator, *Frontiers in Quantitative Economics* (Amsterdam: North Holland Publishing, 1971).

[3]See Joe S. Bain, *Industrial Organization* (New York: Wiley, 1968).

[4]H. Demsetz, *The Market Concentration Doctrine* (Washington, D.C.: American Enterprise Institute, 1973).

FIGURE 3-D   THE RELATION BETWEEN MONOPOLY POWER AND RATE OF RETURN.

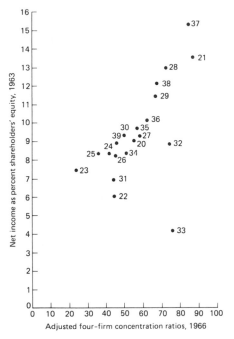

Note: Each dot represents one two-digit SIC industry.

Source: William G. Shepherd, *Market Power and Economic Welfare* (New York: Random House, 1970), p. 191.

Does a more monopolistic market structure tend to enhance or inhibit the accumulation of capital? We can now give, for the microeconomic level, a fairly definite answer: monopoly increases accumulation. Monopoly-sector firms on average are more profitable than competitive-sector firms, and hence better able to accumulate.

One final implication: under competitive conditions, the rate of profit on all units of capital will tend to be the same. Inequalities will be evened out by the flow of capital from low-profit to high-profit industries. In monopoly capitalism, however, barriers to entry prevent capital from flowing into the monopolistic industries, which as we have seen will ordinarily be the areas of higher profits. Monopoly capitalism introduces the likelihood of different rates of profit, then, not only between sectors but also between industries within the monopoly sector.

Let us now return to the question, to be considered in broader context in Chapter 10, of the effect of monopolistic competition on the general level of economic activity and on capital accumulation in the society as a whole.

To answer this question we must raise another first: Will there be sufficient demand for the output of the economy to employ both the means of production and the labor force at their full or near-full capacity? Or will the level of "aggregate demand" be insufficient, resulting in idle factories and unemployed workers? If the former is true, boom conditions will result, profits will

FIGURE 3-E   PROFIT RATES OF CORE AND NONCORE FIRMS, 1958–1971.

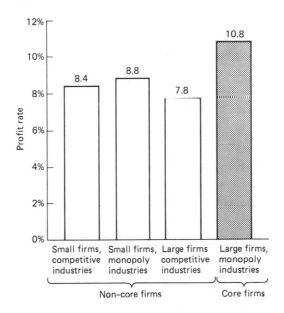

Source: Richard Edwards, *Contested Terrain* (New York: Basic Books, 1979), p. 83.

be high, and accumulation will tend to proceed rapidly. If the latter holds, depression conditions will emerge, accumulation will be slow, and "stagnation" will result.

Capitalists sell various types of output. They sell consumption goods to consumers, capital goods to investors (other capitalists), military hardware and other items to government, and exports to foreign buyers. Despite increasing world trade, exports remain a relatively small part of the U.S. national economy and are largely offset by imports anyway; we can safely ignore them as a major source of sales and employment. Sales to governments are considerably larger, and we shall consider them in a moment.

Consumption goods are by far the largest category of aggregate sales, and the level of consumer buying is an important determinant of the level of economic activity. Nonetheless, consumers by and large spend most of their incomes (primarily wages), so consumer spending tends itself to be determined by the level of economic activity. Therefore, while consumer spending is one of the elements that affects whether or not stagnation occurs, it is not an important *independent cause* of prosperity or depression.

Investment, on the other hand, *is* a significant and relatively independent determinant of the level of economic activity. As capitalists earn profits, whether or not they reinvest their income becomes crucial.[5] If they do, the

[5]We ignore here capitalists' consumption out of profits (which would have the same effect as reinvestment) on the grounds that it is neither very large nor very volatile compared to other components in aggregate demand.

demand for investment goods will increase; rising demand will lead to more employment and higher wages; and rising wage incomes will tend to increase consumer spending, producing relatively full employment and high output. If capitalists do not reinvest their profits, demand for investment goods will fall, wage incomes will tend to sink, consumers will have less income to spend on consumer goods, output will fall, and stagnation will result. Hence, the rate of investment in the economy plays a critical role in determing the overall level of economic activity.

Capitalists choose to reinvest or not depending on how profitable potential investments appear to be. If there is a strong likelihood of large profits, they will be eager to reinvest; if future profits seem meager, they will be more reluctant to do so.

The question of the impact of monopoly on aggregate accumulation and on the overall level of economic activity can now be rephrased as follows: *Does monopolistic competition tend to reduce the capitalist's incentive to invest?* If it does, monopoly will tend to lead to stagnation.

Paul Baran, among others, has argued that monopolistic competition reduces the incentive for each firm to reinvest in its own industry.[6] Baran suggested two arguments. First, competitive firms are often compelled to invest in new technology while monopolistic firms can choose when to invest. Every competitive firm *must* invest in any newly discovered device or technique which reduces the cost of production, even if its preexisting machines are not yet worn out; if it doesn't invest, its competitors will invest and will be able to underprice and drive out of business the noninvesting firm. But monopolistic firms are not threatened by such competition, so they can include other considerations in deciding whether or when to invest in new technologies. For example, although new machines might reduce costs, existing machines may have considerable life left; monopolistic firms might decide to work their old machines until they wear out before buying new ones. Or, they might delay buying new ones because they expect further improvements shortly and want to wait for even more advanced technology. Thus, for a variety of reasons investment in monopolistic industries might be slower (and in any given period, less) than in competitive industries.

Second, Baran suggested that many new investments are feasible or profitable only if production is expanded. But in a monopolistic industry, extra output can be sold only if the industry's market expands or if the investing firm captures the customers of the other giant firms in the industry. The former rarely offers much opportunity, and the latter may provoke a ruinous fight. Thus monopolistic firms tend to be less willing to invest in new output-expanding technology than competitive firms.

Moreover, market barriers to entry restrict the profitability of investment in other monopolistic industries. The possibilities for new investment outlets are increasingly limited to the competitive industries; but these industries, suffering the continuing invasion by monopolistic firms, are themselves shrinking. Other things being equal, the result is a tendency within capitalism toward growing stagnation.

[6]Paul Baran, *The Political Economy of Growth* (New York: Monthly Review Press, 1957), chapter 3.

Note that this argument considers long-run trends in monopoly capitalism. The economy actually rides the roller coaster of the business cycle, in which boom years alternate with ones of bust. But the argument implies that aside from these *cyclical* ups and downs, there exists a long-term *secular* trend toward stagnation. In any short period this long-term movement may be offset by the prosperity of the cyclical boom, but over the longer period, the secular forces will reassert themselves.

The actual experience of the economy—whether or not stagnation occurs—depends on factors other than the negative impact of monopoly on the incentive to invest. Technical change, product innovation, the appearance of new industries, investment in foreign markets, and the like would tend to offset the impact of monopoly. Most importantly, if private consumption and investment should prove insufficient to avoid depression, public expenditures may take up the slack. Indeed, such "Keynesian spending" has assumed increasing proportions in monopoly capitalism, especially since the 1930s.[7] Nevertheless, the structure of monopoly capitalism greatly intensified the pressures toward stagnation.

[7]But as we note below, both international competition and the interests of individual capitalists increasingly place constraints on the goverment's ability to pump up the economy.

3.4   *Competitive Capital and Monopoly Capital*

As we have seen, large corporations have come to dominate the economy, but they have not entirely swallowed it up. Small businesses, and associated with them a diminishing but still significant class of small business owners, remain an important feature of the American business landscape.

In these parts of the economy the conditions under which accumulation occurs are somewhat different. One important difference involves technical change. In the competitive sector, technological changes that reduce the costs of production tend, through competition, to get widely introduced and then to result in product price declines. In this case the users of the product obtain most of the benefit from the discovery or invention. In the monopoly sector, when technical change occurs, the monopoly power of large corporations permits them to maintain prices. In this case the new technique results in higher profits, since prices have been maintained while costs were reduced.

To understand the dynamics of accumulation, we must investigate the specific conditions existing in each sector, and then attempt to understand how they interact. This is what James O'Connor does in the following reading.[1]

As O'Connor points out, the monopolistic firms are more significant than their percentages of employment or sales might suggest because they are the most *dynamic* sector. The huge, concentrated profits of monopoly corporations, when reinvested, create enormous change—change in the technologies used in

[1]In the book from which this reading is taken, O'Connor treats the state as a third sector. The public sector accounts for more than 20 percent of toal purchases of goods and services but only 16 percent of total employment. We defer consideration of the public sector until Chapter 5.

production, change in the type of products offered for sale, change in where jobs are available and what skills they require, change in what markets big firms operate in, and so on. Competitive firms, having smaller and more scattered profits to reinvest, tend to be more stagnant, surviving in those markets left by the big firms. Moreover, many competitive firms are totally dependent on monopolistic firms, either as chief suppliers or as chief customers. Hence the development of the economy as a whole is much more heavily influenced by the investment decisions of the monopoly corporations than by those of the competitive firms.

Finally, the higher profit *rate* in monopoly firms speeds up the process of centralization of capital. Monopoly firms have more than proportionately larger earnings to reinvest (as well as greater access to credit from finance capitalists), producing unequal growth in the two sectors. Because they accumulate more rapidly, monopoly firms tend to expand into remaining competitive industries, and the monopoly sector as a whole grows at the expense of the competitive sector.

Production and distribution in the private sector fall into two subgroups: competitive industries organized by small business and monopolistic industries organized by large-scale capital.

THE COMPETITIVE SECTOR

In the competitive sector the physical capital-to-labor ratio and output per worker, or productivity, are low, and growth of production depends less on physical capital investment and technical progress than on growth of employment. Production is typically small scale, and markets are normally local or regional in scope. Familiar examples include restaurants, drug and grocery stores, service stations, and other branches of trade; garages, appliance repair shops, and other services; clothing and accessories, commercial displays, and other manufacturing industries. Competitive industries employ roughly one-third of the U.S. labor force, with the largest proportion in services and distribution.

What is the significance of low ratios of capital to labor and low productivity? First, competitive sector wages are relatively low, and second, there is a tendency toward overcrowd-ing because it is relatively easy to set up business. Further, many competitive industries produce for (or sell in) markets that are seasonal, subject to sudden change in fashion or style, or otherwise irregular or unstable. Small businessmen whose product markets are irregular have little opportunity to stablize production and employment. Nor is there much incentive to do so even when the opportunity arises: they have invested very little capital per worker and thus business losses from excess physical capacity and time in set-up and shut-down operations are relatively small.

Unstable and irregular product markets and unstable and irregular labor markets go together in competitive industries. Employment in the competitive sector tends to be relatively low paid and casual, temporary, or seasonal. Workers who want and are unable to find full-time, year-round, well-paid work in the monopolistic or state sectors will accept employment in the competitive sector on almost any terms. In the United States the chief examples are black and other minority workers who are cut off from "mainstream" opportunities by racism and discrimination, women who are excluded by sexism from good jobs and good pay, and older workers who are retired involuntarily from high-wage industries (which dictate most compulsory retirement rules). The supply of labor in competitive industries is further inflated by workers (e.g., married women, students, retired workers) who want, and will accept lower wages to obtain, irregular work; they make up about one-half of the nonagricultural labor force working less than thirty-five hours weekly. It has been estimated that about 45 percent of the U.S. work force is "peripheral," or marginal, either by choice or necessity.

The labor movement in the competitive sector is relatively underdeveloped, in part because the social characteristics of the work force, the multitude of firms in a particular industry, and the small-scale, localized nature of production obstruct the organization of strong unions. Further, highly competitive product markets, rapid business turnover, and small profit margins make it costly for employers to recognize unions. Thus it is not unusual for union negotiators to sign "sweetheart" contracts, and established unions often are unable to influence wage rates significantly. There are partial or full exceptions—for example, the foundry industry, with about 5000 small plants, where the trend is toward industry-wide bargaining; and branches of the garment industry concentrated in a few square blocks of mid-Manhattan, where unions and contractors have enormous influence in local and state government, and which employ skilled workers.

Still, the dominant feature of the competitive sector is that workers are condemned to relative material impoverishment. In 1968, over 10 million workers earned less than $1.60 per hour, including 3.5 million paid less than $1.00 per hour. Two-thirds of these workers were employed in retail trade and service industries, and more than one-tenth were employed in agriculture, forestry, and fishing—all highly competitive and relatively low-wage industries.

Working conditions in competitive industries tend to be poor and unemployment and underemployment high. Normally, workers do not earn enough to save for times of unemployment, indebtedness, sickness, or death. Weak or corrupt labor organizations do not secure adequate company-paid health, retirement, and other fringe benefits.

Historically, incomes have been supplemented in this sector by subsistence production, extended family systems, and community-help programs (e.g., "mom and pop" grocery stores, small-scale manufacturing and related facilities which provide employment for family members independent of their productivity, subsistence farming, artisan labor, "taking in the neighbor's wash," etc.). However, in modern capitalism the increasing "proletarianization" (or increase in percent of work force with nothing to sell but labor power) of the entire population, the decline in subsistence and artisan production, and the weakening and destruction of traditional community bonds increasingly compel workers to look to the state for means of subsistence. Thus they are condemned to be full or partial dependents of the state, the recipients of income supplements in the form of public hospital services and health care, subsidized housing, welfare and relief, old age assistance, food stamps, transportation subsidies, and the like.

THE MONOPOLY SECTOR

At one time most if not all industries now in the monopoly sector were organized along competitive lines. The process of monopolization involved a rapid growth in the physical capital-to-labor ratio and output per worker (physical productivity). Today, the growth of production depends less on growth of employment than on increases in physical capital per worker and technical progress. Production is typically large scale and markets are normally national or international in scope—for example, capital goods such as steel, copper, aluminum, and electrical equipment; consumer goods such as automobiles, appliances, soap products, and various food products; transportation industries such as railroads, airlines, and branches of shipping. About one-third of the U.S. work force is employed in monopolistic industries, the largest proportion in manufacturing and mining.

Wages are relatively high, even in the smaller "fringe" firms that coexist with the giants in some monopoly industries. However, low-seniority workers and many in unskilled and semi-skilled jobs are frequently little better off than their counterparts in competitive industries. For example, steelworkers with less than two years' service are ineligible for supplementary unemployment benefits, and a 1971 Equal Employment Opportunity Commission report condemned "Ma Bell" for confining women workers to "the most stifling and repetitive (and low-paid) jobs."

Barriers to the entry of new capital in monopoly industries (e.g., state regulatory agencies, high capital requirements, high overhead costs, advertising and brand loyalty, and product differentiation) create relatively stable industrial structures. Moreover, the large amounts of fixed capital invested per worker compel management to regularize production and employment to avoid losses attributable to unused productive capacity. The complexity of modern technology and work processes and the enormous task of coordinating disparate elements in the production process also compel management to minimize arbitrary or unexpected elements in production and distribution. Planning is extended downward to insure the availability of raw materials and other supplies at stable prices and upward into wholesale and retail operations in order to control demand.

For these reasons, the demand for labor is relatively stable and work is available on a full-time, year-round basis. There are two broad layers of workers in the monopoly sector (in addition to the bottom layer mentioned previously): (1) blue-collar production, maintenance, and similar workers and (2) a so-called middle class of white-collar, technical, administrative workers (the great majority white adult males, excluding women who hold typing, filing, and other unskilled and semi-skilled white-collar jobs). The typical competitive firm is small and its technology is less complex; thus the demand for bureaucratic-administrative and technical-scientific workers in this sector is relatively low.

The social makeup of the work force, the relatively inelastic demand for labor, and the physical and geographic concentration of production units facilitate the growth of powerful labor unions in monopolistic industries. And monopolistic product markets, stable industrial structures, and large profit margins make it comparatively inexpensive for corporations to recognize unions. Thus since the 1930s and early 1940s, when workers in most monopolistic industries forced employers to recognize and bargain with their unions, the labor movement in this sector has been relatively well developed.

. . .

WAGE AND PRICE DETERMINATION

Competitive sector wages, prices, and profits are determined chiefly by market forces. The essence of the competitive market mechanism is the process by which productivity increases are transformed into higher standards of living via changes in prices and profits. Assume, for example, that a group of farmers introduces hybrid corn that doubles land yields and hence (ignoring other costs) reduces costs by one-half. Clearly, given the market price of corn, they will make a profit over and above the usual margin in the industry. Three consequences are likely: first, the innovating farmers will be tempted to expand production to make even greater profits; second, other corn farmers will be compelled to introduce the hybrid, or risk being driven out of business; third, farmers growing other crops will be tempted to plant corn. In any (or all) of these events, total corn production and supply increase, and more corn is sold, but at lower prices. With demand constant, the expansion of supply will drive down prices and sooner or later eliminate the original larger-than-normal profit margins. The final effect is that the consumer (i.e., society as a whole) benefits from the innovation and cost reductions in the form of lower prices for things needed for survival.

If consumers buy the entire crop for immediate use, there is a direct link between the technical innovation (hybrid corn) and a higher material standard of life (lower prices). If manufacturers buy the corn to process it, the effect on material well-being is indirect: Fresh corn prices fall, pushing down production costs in the canneries, thus increasing profits in this branch of industry. In turn, a mechanism similar to the one just described is touched off. Cannery owners will expand production to take advantage of higher profit margins, and other businessmen will enter the corn-canning industry to make a higher return on their capital. The effect will be to increase the supply of processed corn, lower prices, eliminate excessive profits, and indirectly spread the gains from technical progress to society.

To summarize: All other things being equal, prices in competitive industries fall more or less in proportion to increases in productivity. The gains from technical progress are not monopolized by any one group of capitalists and workers in the form of permanently higher prices, profits, and wages, but rather are distributed more or less evenly among the population as a whole. "The basic principle of the market system," Joan Robinson writes, summarizing the whole issue, "is that the benefits of progress are passed on to the community as a whole, not bottled up in the industries where they happen to arise."[1]

If prices are determined by productivity in the competitive sector, what determines wages? Total demand in the economy as a whole. Upward surges of competitive-sector money wages are attributable to inflation, not to technical progress and improvements in productivity. During periods of high labor demand and general inflation, wages in unorganized industries (mainly competitive industries) increase faster than wages in organized industries (mainly monopoly industries). During periods of sluggish labor demand, union-nonunion wage differentials shift in favor of organized workers.

[1]Joan Robinson, *Economics: An Awkward Corner* (New York: 1968), p. 14.

In the monopoly sector market forces are not the main determinants of wages, prices, and profits. Monopolistic corporations have substantial market power. Prices are administered, and in comparative terms price movements are sealed off from market forces. Most corporations operate on the basis of an after-tax profit target (normally between 10 and 15 percent). If labor costs rise, monopolistic corporations will attempt to protect planned profit targets by increasing prices. Assuming that labor productivity remains unchanged, money wages are thus the main determinants of monopoly sector prices.

What forces determine the level of money wages? The process of wage determination in the monopoly sector will be simplified in order to highlight its essential features. First assume that the economy is expanding. In an economic boom the demand for labor increases (as well as demand for nearly everything else) in both competitive and monopoly sectors.

The supply of labor available to competitive industries is relatively inelastic and hence a sizable increase in demand will raise wages in this sector. If businessmen fail to raise wages they will not be able to attract enough workers to expand production and fill orders, nor will they be able to retain some workers already employed in competitive industry. Workers in the competitive sector (and the unemployed, as well) will seek employment in the generally more desirable monopoly sectors. Will monopoly capital be forced to offer higher wages to attract the workers it requires to expand production in the short run and meet the higher level of demand? Except during periods of extreme boom (e.g., the peak years of the Korean War), the supply of labor available to monopoly capital is relatively elastic. Thus it can attract all the workers it needs from the competitive sector at the going wage rate. Put another way, monopoly capital is able to draw on the pool of underemployed competitive sector labor (or the "invisible" reserve army of the unemployed).

Although the market forces tending to drive up monopoly sector wages normally are relatively weak, the political forces at work are very powerful. In a nutshell, during a boom the production relations alter in favor of labor. Profit margins grow at precisely the same time that unemployment falls, and union bargaining strength is enhanced at the same time that there is a larger surplus (profits) to bargain over. In the last analysis it is the collective power of organized labor that wrests higher wages from monopolistic corporations, not the normal forces of supply and demand.

What are the specific principles governing the administration of wages in monopoly industries? First, labor productivity; second, cost of living. Again the process will be simplified in order to focus on basic elements. The sequence of wage changes starts in monopoly sector industries in which productivity is advancing most rapidly. Unions bargain for wage increases at least commensurate with productivity increases. Subsequently, unions representing workers in other monopolistic industries seek wage increases as great as those won by their brethren in the high-productivity industries. This is called *pattern bargaining*. One of its results is that average wages tend to rise somewhat faster than average productivity (and of course, considerably faster than productivity throughout the economy).

Several empirical studies support these theses. According to one of the most thorough, "productivity gains are more likely to go to the workers the more unionized and concentrated [i.e., monopolized] the industry, although the union elasticity carries the greater weight."[2] Another scholar concludes that wage increases in one monopoly sector industry spill over to others.[3] However, pattern bargaining and uniformity of wage increases do not "trickle down" into the competitive sector. "Changes in the union-nonunion [wage] differential," Livernash writes, summing up available evidence, "and changes in relative earnings among industries do not support the existence of strong pattern influences operat-

ing broadly across industry lines throughout the economy as a whole."[4]

The final result of the process of administered prices and wages, productivity wage increases, and pattern bargaining is that many or most gains from productivity increases arising from technical progress (and other factors such as scale of production and degree of capacity utilization) are not distributed evenly throughout the population, but rather are "bottled up" in the monopoly sector by corporations and organized labor. One side-effect is the drift toward permanent inflation—that is, the continuous upward movement of wages and prices. In effect, the classic competitive market mechanism breaks down and the dominant production relations (monopoly capital and organized labor), not impersonal market forces, determine the allocation of economic resources, the wage structure and distribution of income within the working class and capitalist class.

At this point, an anomaly in the political economy of modern America must be emphasized. The determination of wages and prices in the competitive sector was analyzed without reference to the actual production or power relationships because wages and prices in these industries are determined by market forces—that is, they are determined independently of the intentions of businessmen and workers. For example, as indicated above, capitalists attempting to increase profits by expanding production lower prices and thus reduce all capitalists' profits—clearly an unintended effect.

Comparatively speaking, the situation is different in the monopoly sector: Production is planned and wages and prices are administered. Because there is more conscious human control over income and income distribution, market theory per se can throw only a limited light on the determinants of wages, prices, and profits. Precisely because wages are relatively insensitive to changes in the demand for labor and because productivity gains tend to be monopolized, we must look behind the market categories and discover the historical, social,

[2]Sara Behman, "Wage Changes, Institutions, and Relative Factor Prices in Manufacturing," *Review of Economics and Statistics,* 51 (August 1969), p. 236.

[3]E. Robert Livernash, "Wages and Benefits," in *A Review of Industrial Relations Research,* pp. 110–12.

[4]Livernash, "Wages and Benefits," p. 100.

and political forces shaping wages, prices, and income distribution.

This excursion into history begins at the close of World War II. The inseparable link between productivity and cost of living and wages in the monopoly sector and the bifurcation of wage-price determination in the monopoly and competitive sectors is rooted in an agreement imposed on organized labor during the last half of the 1940s. At the end of the war the large industrial unions entered into permanent collective bargaining relationships (for the first time under normal conditions) with large corporations that exercised monopolistic control over prices. The unions could win higher wages in two ways. The first was to demand higher wages at the expense of profits. However, because the corporations controlled prices, they could (and can) easily raise prices and pass on wage increases not "justified" by rising productivity to consumers—and thus protect their profit margins. The unions could have countered this move only by adopting a working-class perspective (in contrast to an industrial-union perspective) and agitating politically for a return to price controls without a revival of wage controls. Obviously, such a course would have been unrealistic in the context of early cold war America.

The alternative for the industrial unions was to demand that the workers share in the benefits accruing from increased productivity. In theory, two courses were available to union leaders. First, they could try to force the monopolistic corporations to lower prices when increased productivity led to lower production costs. Thus the benefits of technical progress would have been distributed more or less evenly among all consumers. But the unions recognized that they had (and have) no control over prices and chose the second course: They demanded that wages increase with productivity (and demanded cost-of-living wage adjustments, as well), with the inevitable (and clearly unintended) effect of bifurcating the working class still further. Competitive sector workers suffered. On the one hand, their wages were (and are) relatively low; on the other, they had (and have) to buy at relatively high monopolistic prices.

Needless to say, big business did not begin to grant annual wage increases, cost-of-living adjustments, additional fringe benefits, and so on without a quid pro quo. In return for wage scales pegged to productivity plus, the unions agreed not only to abstain from fighting mechanization but also to collaborate actively when major innovations required large-scale reorganization of the work process. There have been exceptions, mainly in declining industries such as railroading where featherbedding has been a major issue. From the standpoint of monopoly capital the main function of unions was (and is) to inhibit disruptive, spontaneous rank-and-file activity (e.g., wildcat strikes and slowdowns) and to maintain labor discipline in general. In other words, unions were (and are) the guarantors of "managerial prerogatives." Union leaders have long recognized that demands for both increased wages and more control over production are contradictory because wage demands are based on rising productivity which requires that management be free to fire redundant workers. At times, union leaders have been hard pressed to maintain labor discipline, especially over the issue of labor-saving technological changes. As will be seen, the number of jobs (and employed workers) in the monopoly sector tends to rise slowly, in some cases to decrease absolutely. Hence unions are one agent of technical progress and rational (in terms of profits) labor-power planning by monopoly capital.

THE EXPANSION OF THE MONOPOLY SECTOR

. . . [There is a] tendency for monopoly capital to take over and dominate competitive capital. The extensive (as contrasted with intensive) character of monopoly capital growth not only generates more unemployment in competitive industries (surplus labor) but also liquidates large numbers of small businessmen (surplus capitalists). Consider U.S. agricultural production, for example. Farming is increasingly dominated by large-scale capital employing modern technology. Thus farm output expanded by 45 percent between 1950 and 1965, whereas farm employment (workers and owners) fell by 45 percent. In the mid-1960s, almost 30 percent of the farm population (3.9 million people; an unknown number were previously farm owners) and over 23 percent of the rural nonfarm population (almost 10 million people) lived in poverty. This high incidence of poverty is attributable more to unemployment (unemployment and under-employment rates in the mid-1960s were about 20 and 40 percent, respectively) and the displacement of the small farm operator than to low wages.

The take-over by monopoly capital of traditional competitive industries such as agriculture, construction, trade, and services, together with the long-run expansion of labor supply, tends to depress profits of competitive capital. Profits also are depressed when small business must compete with large-scale capital and when a superabundance of cheap labor encourages the setting up of small business, and thus produces "overcrowding" in the competitive sector. Moreover, the relative decline in wages in competitive industries that have resisted union organization tends to keep prices down, and under certain circumstances can decrease profits. Finally, because of the economically depressed condition of competitive industries, small businessmen and farmers (as well as workers) are forced to depend more and more on the state for material survival, indirectly in the form of fair-trade laws and similar protective legislation, directly in the form of loan guarantees, farm subsidies, and similar programs.

Afterword to 3.4 (by the editors) "The Capitalist Class"

This chapter has focused on capital accumulation and the rise of the giant corporations. Because capitalists organize production through such firms, the behavior of these firms, taken together and understood as a system, is relevant for analyzing the workings of the American economy. Now, however, it is time to turn our attention to the capitalists who own these firms and to the class that benefits from this system.

A class is a group of people sharing a common position in the mode of production.[1] Workers have in common the condition that they must sell their labor-power to "earn" their "living." Similarly, capitalists share a common situation: they own capital, which they lend or use to purchase the labor-power of workers (and other things required in production) in order to produce and sell commodities and realize profits; their income thus accrues in the form of profits and interest.

Included in this category of "capitalists" are individuals as different in their situations as small businesses are different from big business: some capitalists employ few workers, face great competition, have insecure business prospects, and achieve relatively modest profits, whereas at the other extreme exist the Rockefellers, the Mellons, and the Fords. Numerically, the capitalist class is small—only 10 percent or less of the population could in any sense be categorized as capitalists. Yet in terms of their ownership of wealth, this small group is very important: in 1962 the richest 6.7 percent of the population owned 56.3 percent of all wealth in the country, and their control of corporate assets was even higher: 77.7 percent; a 1983 survey found a similar pattern.[2]

---

[1] See introduction to Chapter 2.

[2] See Tables 4-D and 6-F.

With the rise of monopoly capitalism a tiny segment of super-rich capitalists emerged within the capitalist class. (For the most notable examples, see Tables 3-D and 3-E.) In 1969, 1 percent of the population owned more than half of all corporate stock.[3] One study has estimated that the extraction of monopoly profits since the turn of the century has benefited this group almost exclusively, allowing it to more than double its share of wealth compared to what its share would have been if no monopoly profits had existed.[4] But a large part of the profits from monopoly capitalism have probably been concentrated in an even tinier, more privileged group, the few thousand super-rich families.

TABLE 3-D   SUPER-RICH INDIVIDUALS AND THEIR WEALTH, 1983

Name	Source of Wealth	Residence	Age	Wealth ($ billion)
1. Gordon P. Getty	Inherited (oil)	San Francisco	49	2.2
2. Sam M. Walton	Discount stores	Bentonville, Ark.	65	2.2
3. Daniel K. Ludwig	Shipping, real estate	New York City	86	2.0
4. David Packard	Hewlett-Packard Company	Los Altos Hill, Calif.	71	1.9
5. An Wang	Wang Laboratories	Lincoln, Mass.	63	1.6
6. Nelson Bunker Hunt	Inherited (oil)	Dallas	57	1.4
7. Caroline Hunt Schoellkopf	Inherited (oil)	Dallas	60	1.3
8. H. Ross Perot	Computers	Dallas	53	1.0
9. Margaret Hunt Hill	Inherited (oil)	Dallas	68	1.0
10. George P. Mitchell	Oil, real estate	Houston	64	1.0
11. Forrest E. Mars, Jr.	Candy	Las Vegas	79	1.0
12. David Rockefeller	Inherited, banking, real estate	New York City	68	1.0
13. Philip F. Anschutz	Oil	Denver	44	1.0
14. William H. Hunt	Inherited (oil)	Dallas	54	1.0
15. Marvin Davis	Oil	Denver	57	1.0

Source: "The Forbes Four Hundred," *Forbes* (Fall 1983), pp. 71-159.

In 1979, 3,600 families (0.004% of all families) reported gross incomes of $1 million or more to the Internal Revenue Service (see Table 6-J, p. 227). The combined income of these super-rich families totaled over $8.1 billion that year. Although many of these families contained highly paid corporate executives, most of their income—over four-fifths—derived not from work but from the ownership of property.

Careful and complete data on the holdings of the super-rich are extremely difficult to obtain. Some incomplete estimates of the personal fortunes of the most prominent members suggest their immense wealth. (See Tables 3-D and 3-E.) These tables show that most of the richest Americans inherited all or a major part of their fortunes. Many of these fortunes are connected to real estate and oil. The fastest way to multiply one's wealth may be through mergers: Gordon Getty's holdings increased from $2.2 billion in 1983 to $4.1 billion in 1984 through this route.[5]

[3]J. D. Smith and S. D. Franklin, "The Concentration of Personal Wealth, 1922–1969," *American Economic Review* (May 1974), table 1, p. 166.

[4]W. Comanor and R. Smiley, "Monopoly and the Distribution of Wealth," *Quarterly Journal of Economics,* 1975.

[5]*Forbes Magazine,* 1 October 1984.

TABLE 3-E   SOME LARGE FAMILY FORTUNES, 1983

Name	Source of Wealth	Wealth ($ billion)
1. du Pont	Inherited (Du Pont Company)	$10.0
2. Hunt	Inherited (oil)	6.4
3. Rockefeller	Inherited (oil, banking)	3.6
4. Bass	Oil	2.5
5. Mellon	Inherited (banking)	2.2
6. Cullen	Inherited (oil)	2.0
7. Koch	Oil	1.5
8. Phipps	Inherited	1.3
9. Hearst	Inherited (publishing)	1.3
10. Annenberg	Inherited (publishing)	1.1

Source: "The Forbes Four Hundred," *Forbes* (Fall 1983), pp. 71-159.

The combined wealth and power of these super-rich is indeed awesome. The total personal net worth of Forbes' 482 individuals and families amounted in 1984 to over $166 billion, equal to half the value of all nonresidential fixed investment in that year and comparable to the $175 billion of total U.S. coins and currency in circulation.

But the $166 billion figure massively understates the control and power exercised by this wealth. Most of the richest families have created giant foundations (Ford, Rockefeller, Getty and so forth) and continue to control the extensive assets of these institutions. The Pew family, for example, with a net worth of $350 million in 1983 and ownership of 6% of Sun Oil Company, also controlled seven family foundations with $1.8 billion in assets (not counted by Forbes), amounting to another 25% of Sun stock.

Recognizing as well that effective control does not require 100 percent ownership, MIT economist Lester Thurow has calculated that the assets held by the members of the Forbes lists alone leads to control over about 40% of all fixed nonresidential private capital in the United States.[6] The super-rich capitalists associated with the giant corporations constitute the most privileged and politically powerful part of the capitalist class.

[6.]Lester Thurow, "The People Who Own America," *San Francisco Chronicle,* 21 October 1984.

3.5   *Capital Accumulation on a World Scale*

Since its beginnings, capitalism has evolved as an international system with unequally developed parts. To complete our analysis of the capital accumulation process, we focus next on capitalism as an international system, and we investigate the processes that have produced inequality among the capitalist countries.

Written by the editors for this book.

Capitalism, by its very nature, cannot be contained within national boundaries. Since its origin, the rise of capitalism has been associated with the displacement of relatively self-contained local economies by an increasingly international network of social and economic relations. And the more that the capitalist system has developed over time, the greater the extent to which market relations and capital movements have eroded national boundaries and linked distant areas together within one and the same world capitalist economy.

Not only has the capitalist system always been essentially *international* in character but it also has always been characterized by *unequal* international relations. Capitalism is a system built upon hierarchy and inequality, and this applies at the international level as well as at the level of the nation or the firm. It is for this reason that the term "imperialism" is used to characterize international relations within the world capitalist system. Imperialism connotes a relationship of dominance/subordination between a stronger and a weaker nation or people. In the context of the capitalist system, imperialism refers to the dominant relationship of the most powerful nations within the world capitalist economy to other nations and territories with which they enter into social, political, and economic relations.[1]

At any given time one can (at least roughly) divide the capitalist world into a "center" and a "periphery." The center includes those nations from which capital accumulation is propelled—the major sources of economic management, financial control, and technological progress. The periphery refers to those countries and territories that are linked to the center in an economically subordinate manner. Today, for example, the capitalist center includes the rich and industrialized nations of North America, Western Europe, and Japan, while the periphery includes much, but not all, of Asia, Africa, and Latin America.

With the passage of time and the evolution of the world capitalist system, both the nature of the basic imperialist relationship and the delineation of the center and the periphery have been changing. In the following paragraphs we review briefly the way in which imperialism has changed as the capitalist system has developed since its origin.

THREE STAGES OF IMPERIALISM

The capitalist world system has evolved through three broad stages of imperialism in which first plunder, then trade, and finally direct investment have been most representative of the economic relations between the center and the periphery. In each stage of imperialism the periphery has played an important role in contributing to the growth of the capitalist economies in the center. But the effect of the imperialist relationship on the periphery has varied from one stage to another.

The capitalist mode of production arose initially from the interstices of feudal society in Western Europe; it developed most rapidly in England, where it became the dominant form of socioeconomic organization by the eighteenth century. To a significant extent the rise of capitalism in England and elsewhere in Western Europe was predicated upon the overseas exploits of explorers and traders. The European explorations of the fifteenth, sixteenth, and seventeenth centuries were motivated largely by a spirit of adventure, acquisition, and plunder rather than by any desire for capital accumulation. Nonetheless, they did serve as an important source of "primitive accumulation" (i.e., original capital accumulation) as the profits from foreign ventures returned home and ultimately helped to stimulate the rise of the new capitalist class.

Marx described this early phase of capitalist history as follows:

[1] The dominance of weaker nations by a stronger nation is of course not unique to the capitalist system. A reading of world history suggests that empire-building has been the rule rather than the exception for human societies. The point of this essay is not to argue that imperialist drives arise only out of a capitalist society but to examine the particular form that imperialism takes under capitalism. This concern is warranted both by the dominant position of capitalism in the modern world and by the particularly tenacious character of imperialism within the world capitalist system.

The discovery of gold and silver in America, the extirpation, enslavement and entombment in mines of the aboriginal population, the beginning of the conquest and looting of the East Indies, the turning of Africa into a warren for the commercial hunting of black-skins, signalized the rosy dawn of the era of capitalist production. These idyllic proceedings are the chief momenta of primitive accumulation.

. . .

The treasures captured outside Europe by undisguised looting, enslavement, and murder, floated back to the mother-country and were there turned into capital.[2]

In this first stage of imperialism, the capitalist center (which then included England and a few coastal regions of continental Europe) made use of the periphery (Asia, Africa, and the Americas) primarily as an object of plunder or a source of exotic products and slaves. This predatory relationship between the center and the periphery was dominant for several centuries following the initial overseas explorations of the late fifteenth century. By the beginning of the nineteenth century, changes in the character and the needs of capitalism in the center were leading to changes in the nature of imperialism in many parts of the world. There ensued a second broad stage of imperialism in which the increasingly capitalist nations of Western Europe began to industrialize on a significant scale and became interested in the periphery primarily as a partner in trade, supplying food and raw materials in exchange for industrial manufactures.

By this second stage many of the American territories previously colonized by the European powers had become politically independent nations. But in the Caribbean, in Asia, and (by the end of the nineteenth century) in Africa the Europeans strengthened their political control, establishing direct rule over their overseas territories and forming a worldwide system of rival colonial empires.

In spite of the differences in political status of different parts of the periphery, the economic relations between center and periphery were quite similar throughout the world. Each major European power sought to preserve for its own capitalists the economic gains accruing from trade with those parts of the periphery which it dominated, either as colonial ruler (e.g., England in India, France in Indochina) or as principal trader (e.g., England in South America). In the process of promoting a rapid growth of world trade, capitalists from the center exported increasing amounts of capital to the periphery. With the aid and protection of their national governments they invested in mines, plantations, and related infrastructural facilities designed to improve access to needed raw materials and to create expanded markets for the export of manufactured goods from the center. In this way the peripheral economies were shaped to meet the needs of the center.

Marx expected that when the center began to take an active interest in promoting productive enterprise in the periphery (rather than simply plundering it or trading with it), the imperialist relationship would favor the extension of the capitalist mode of production and the promotion of economic growth in the periphery. Impressed with British plans for the development of Indian railways, he wrote:

England has to fulfill a double mission in India: one destructive, the other regenerating—the annihilation of old Asiatic society, and the laying of the material foundations of Western society in Asia.

. . .

I know that the English millocracy intend to endow India with railways with the exclusive view of extracting at diminished expenses, the cotton and other raw materials for their manufactures. . . . [But] you cannot maintain a net of railways over an immense country without introducing all those industrial processes necessary to meet the immediate and current wants of railway locomotion, and out of which there must grow the application of machinery to those branches of industry not immediately connected with railways. The railway system will therefore become, in India, truly the forerunner of modern industry.

. . .

---

[2]Karl Marx, *Capital,* vol. I, pt. VIII, chapter 31.

All the English bourgeoisie may be forced to do will neither emancipate nor materially mend the social condition of the mass of the people, depending not only on the development of the productive powers, but of their appropriation by the people. But what they will not fail to do is lay down the material premises for both. Has the bourgeoisie ever done more? Has it ever effected a progress without dragging individuals and peoples through blood and dirt, through misery and degradation?[3]

Thus Marx viewed capitalist penetration of the periphery as an unambiguously progressive force: at a high cost in human misery, to be sure, imperialism would lay the basis for the capitalist development of the periphery.

As it turned out, however, Marx's expectations were not realized in most of the periphery during the second stage of imperialism. Only in a few areas of European settlement—the United States, Canada, Australia, and New Zealand—and in Japan did the capitalist mode of production begin to flourish and promote a process of sustained capital accumulation and rapid economic growth. Moreover, these parts of the periphery were unusual in several respects. In the first place, they were among the countries that had become politically independent well before the twentieth century. In the four countries of European settlement the settlers virtually destroyed the preexisting native peoples rather than ruling over them, as they did elsewhere in Asia, Africa, and Latin America. And Japan was unique in the third world in having resisted altogether any form of colonial domination by the Western powers. Thus it was only under exceptional circumstances that a few nations emerged from the periphery to form part of the capitalist center, which consisted by the early part of the twentieth century of Western Europe, North America, Australia, New Zealand, and Japan.

At the same time, the rest of Asia, Africa, Latin America, and southern and Eastern Europe remained in the periphery. Throughout these peripheral areas, imperialism in its second stage had the effect of inhibiting the development of the capitalist mode of production and blocking industrialization. This regressive effect was due largely to the fact that capitalists and their governments in the center found it advantageous to maintain the local power of traditional elites in the periphery and to promote production based on precapitalist social relations rather than wage-labor.

The second stage of imperialism was characterized by intense rivalries among the major capitalist powers. In seeking to facilitate their own economic and political expansion, they competed with one another to carve up the rest of the world into their respective colonial empires or spheres of influence. This competition contributed greatly to the tensions that led to World Wars I and II and ultimately resulted in a major transformation of the world capitalist system.

A third stage of imperialism has emerged in the second half of the twentieth century, following the disruptions of the two world wars and the rise of state socialist rule in most of Eastern Europe and mainland East Asia. The weakening of the European colonial powers led to the dissolution of their colonial empires; within a few decades of World War II almost all of the former colonial territories had gained their political independence. Imperialist relations between the center and the periphery are no longer mediated by colonial rule; instead, they operate in a "neocolonial" manner between formally independent nation-states. Moreover, the emergence of the state socialist nations has removed a substantial part of the world from the capitalist orbit. Thus the periphery is now confined to Latin America, southern Europe, Africa, and Asia, exclusive of Japan, China, and the adjacent smaller state socialist nations.[4]

[3]Karl Marx, "The Future Results of British Rule in India," reprinted in Shlomo Avineri, ed., *Karl Marx on Colonialism and Modernization* (New York, Doubleday, 1968), pp. 132–139.

[4]It is difficult to draw a precise line between the center and the periphery, for there are always some nations that may be in transition from a subordinate to a more independent status within the world capitalist system. Countries such as Israel and South Africa share some of the attributes of both the center and the periphery and could be classified either way.

The period since World War II has been characterized by a rapidly increasing integration of the world capitalist economy. With the erosion of colonial barriers and the establishment of a new international economic framework under the leadership of the United States,[5] economic relations among the nations of the capitalist center and between the center and the periphery have developed on an unprecedented scale. This increasing integration has involved a great expansion of foreign trade, but it is most dramatically manifested in the rapid growth of direct foreign private investment. Rather than simply exporting their products to foreign markets, capitalist firms have found it increasingly profitable to set up or buy out production facilities in foreign countries and territories. Thus the "multinational corporation" has become the hallmark of modern capitalism and the primary vehicle of imperialist relations between the metropolis and the periphery.

The dominance of the center over the periphery in the contemporary stage of imperialism has been maintained not by direct political control but by virtue of the economic power of the center nations and their multinational corporations. Virtually all of the foreign investment within the world capitalist economy has been undertaken by corporations based in the center nations; it has been directed both to other center nations and to the periphery. As the dominant capitalist power in the postwar period, the United States has accounted for the lion's share of the foreign investment since World War II. Of a total value of direct foreign private investment assets estimated (conservatively) at $165 billion in 1971, slightly over 50 percent was owned by U.S.–based multinational corporations.[6] British firms held roughly 15 percent of the total, and

no other country accounted for more than 6 percent. In a statistical appendix following this essay, we present a series of tables designed to document the growth and nature of U.S. private investment in foreign countries.

The rapid growth of direct foreign private investment in the world capitalist economy since World War II was facilitated by the economic, political, and military hegemony of the United States. Diplomatic pressures, economic sanctions, covert operations, and military interventions have all played a role in the process whereby the U.S. government has sought to maintain a favorable international climate for capitalist activity in the periphery without a system of formal colonies. Yet the economic recovery of the rival capitalist powers of Western Europe and Japan, and the growing success of anti-imperialist movements (most notably in Indochina), have weakened considerably the dominant position of the United States. Today the center continues to subordinate much of the periphery, but rivalries among center powers and challenges from some of the peripheral nations—e.g., the oil-exporting countries—are beginning to change some of the characteristics of this third stage of imperialism.

STATISTICAL APPENDIX: THE GROWTH OF U.S. PRIVATE INVESTMENT ABROAD

Table 3-F presents data on the growth of U.S. private investment assets in foreign countries from 1950 to 1980. The total value of foreign private investment includes not only direct investment assets (equity capital invested in enterprises located abroad) but also other long-term assets (loans for a year or more) and short-term assets (loans for less than a year). Long-term assets account for the bulk of the total value of U.S. private investment abroad, and direct investment represents more than 60 percent of the total. Total assets, long-term assets, and direct investment abroad have all multiplied by roughly ten times in the thirty-

---

[5]See MacEwan, Section 3.6, p. 107, for a discussion of the international economic framework that emerged within the capitalist system following World War II.

[6]Estimates of the distribution of direct foreign private investment by source country in 1967 and 1971 are given in United Nations, Department of Economic and Social Affairs, *Multinational Corporations in World Development* (New York, United Nations, 1973), table 5.

year period, growing at average rates of more than 10 percent per year.[1]

Table 3-F also lists the annual value of capital outflow and the corresponding balance of payments inflow associated with U.S. direct private investment abroad. A major share of this investment is financed in foreign countries, both from local sources and from reinvested earnings of the foreign affiliates of American enterprises. Thus the annual outflow of direct investment capital from the United States is much less than the corresponding annual increase in the value of U.S. direct investment assets abroad. The return flow from abroad includes both investment income (that part of the income from existing foreign investment that is repatriated back to the United States) and royalties and fees (the various payments for licenses, technological know-how, managerial services, etc., made by foreign affiliates to their American parent companies). As shown in Table 3-F, both the outflow of new investment capital and the in-

flow of investment income plus royalties and fees have increased greatly from 1950 to 1980, but the latter has been consistently higher than the former. There has thus been a continuous (and indeed steadily increasing) net capital inflow associated with U.S. direct private investment abroad.[2]

With the recovery of the West European and Japanese economies from the devastation of World War II, the primacy of the United States in the world capitalist economy has come increasingly under challenge. The decline in U.S. hegemony has become quite evident since the 1970s, and is reflected in, among other things, a growth of direct investment by foreign corporations in the United

[1]All the data presented in this reading are based on dollar values at current prices. Thus real rates of growth are overstated by the amount of price inflation that took place in the period under consideration.

[2]This net capital inflow belies the notion that private capital from the United States adds directly to the capital resources available to the rest of the world. In fact the return flow of profits exceeds the outflow of new capital. But foreign private investment has indirect as well as direct effects on the availability of capital in foreign countries. An estimate of the overall impact of U.S. private investment abroad would have to take account of its net contribution to domestic income, the extent to which it displaces or inhibits domestic capital formation, and other such variables that affect the availability of capital in foreign countries.

TABLE 3-F   THE GROWTH OF U.S. PRIVATE INVESTMENT ABROAD, 1950–1980

	Value of Assets (year-end) ($ billions)		Direct Investment Flows (during year) ($ billions)	
	Total U.S. Private Assets Abroad	U.S. Direct Investment Position Abroad[a]	Capital Outflow[b]	Capital Inflow[c]
1950	19.0	11.8	1.1	2.0
1955	29.1	19.4	1.8	3.1
1960	49.4	31.9	2.0	4.2
1965	81.5	49.5	5.0	6.7
1970	116.4	75.5	7.4	11.1
1975	208.3	124.1	14.0	20.1
1980	516.4	215.4	27.7	42.9

[a]Book value of U.S. direct investors' equity in, and net outstanding loans to, their foreign affiliates (i.e., net claims of U.S. parents on their affiliates, not the total assets of these affiliates).

[b]Additions to the U.S. direct investment position abroad—the sum of (a) equity and intercompany account outflows, (b) reinvested earnings of incorporated affiliates, and (c) valuation adjustments.

[c]The sum of (a) interest, dividends, and earnings of unincorporated affiliates, (b) reinvested earnings of incorporated affiliates, and (c) royalties and fees.

Sources: *Survey of Current Business*, annual articles on "U.S. Direct Investment Abroad" and "The International Investment Position of the United States."

States. By 1983 the value of foreign direct investment assets in the United States had become nearly equal to three-fifths of the value of the corresponding U.S. assets abroad.[3]

Table 3-G attempts to place the postwar growth of U.S. direct private investment abroad into an appropriate perspective by comparing it with the growth of total corporate business activity in the United States. The figures show that investment abroad not only has grown rapidly in absolute terms but also has grown substantially in relative terms. Between 1950 and 1980 the value of U.S. direct private investment assets abroad doubled from 5 percent to roughly 10 percent of total corporate investment assets (at home and abroad). The rise in the share of foreign profits[4] in total

after-tax corporate profits was even more dramatic, from roughly 7 percent in 1950 to more than 25 percent in 1980. The fact that the foreign share of profits was substantially higher than the foreign share of invested capital throughout the period reflects the consistently higher average profitability of foreign as compared to total (and *a fortiori* domestic) business activity. The average foreign profit rate ranged between 13 and 20 percent from 1950 to 1980, while the corresponding average overall profit rate ranged between 5 and 11 percent. Indeed, the relative profitability differential in favor of foreign investment seems to have increased during the postwar years.

The remaining two tables are intended to illustrate the extraordinary power of leading

[3]U.S. Department of Commerce, *Survey of Current Business* (August 1984, October 1984).

[4]As Frank Ackerman has pointed out in his review of Harry Magdoff's *Age of Imperialism* (*Public Policy*, 19, no. 3 [Summer 1971]), it is necessary to make some adjustments on the reported data on foreign earnings in order to make them comparable with domestic after-tax profits. The

data available from the Department of Commerce show foreign earnings after foreign taxes but before U.S. taxes. Because U.S. tax laws allow firms to deduct from their U.S. taxes an amount equal to foreign taxes paid on repatriated income (provided foreign tax rates do not exceed the U.S. tax rates), the effective U.S. tax rate on foreign earnings is much lower than the rate (about 50 percent) that applies to domestic profits.

TABLE 3-G   THE RELATIVE SIZE AND PROFITABILITY OF U.S. DIRECT PRIVATE INVESTMENT ABROAD, 1950–1980

	Total Investment			Investment Abroad			Foreign/Total Ratios	
Year	After-tax Profits ($ billions)	Invested Capital ($ billions)	Profit Rate (%)	After-tax Profits ($ billions)	Invested Capital ($ billions)	Profit Rate (%)	After-tax Profits (%)	Invested Capital (%)
1950	25.0	224	11.1	1.9	11.2	17.0	7.6	5.0
1955	27.2	344	7.9	2.9	18.5	15.7	10.7	5.4
1960	27.1	409	6.6	4.0	30.8	13.0	14.8	7.5
1965	46.3	536	8.6	6.3	47.0	13.4	13.6	8.8
1970	41.3	752	5.5	10.4	71.8	14.5	25.2	9.6
1975	81.5	1095	7.4	18.9	116.1	16.3	23.6	10.6
1980	149.8	1944	7.7	40.3	201.7	20.0	26.9	10.4

Sources: Corporate after-tax profits, U.S. Department of Commerce, *National Income and Product Accounts* (published annually in July issue of *Survey of Current Business*), table 6.23B.

Corporate invested capital, U.S. Internal Revenue Service, *Statistics of Income: Corporate Income Tax Returns* (annually), data on net worth of corporations.

After-tax profits from foreign private investment, calculated by multiplying before-tax profits by 94 percent for reasons explained in footnote 4. Before-tax profits obtained by adding together repatriated investment income, royalties and fees, and undistributed profits (reinvested earnings), as reported in the "capital inflow" column of Table 3-F.

Foreign private invested capital, figures for each year represent the average of the year-end book value of direct investment assets for the preceding and given years, as reported in the sources for Table 3-F.

Profit rate and foreign/total ratios: calculated directly from the corresponding values in the table.

TABLE 3-H   RANKING OF NATIONS AND CORPORATIONS BY SIZE OF ANNUAL PRODUCT, 1976

Rank	Economic Entity	Product[a] ($ billion)	Rank	Economic Entity	Product[a] ($ billion)
1	United States	1694.9	31	Indonesia	36.0
2	USSR	717.5	32	South Africa	33.7
3	Japan	513.5	33	Norway	32.0
4	West Germany	461.8	34	Venezuela	31.3
5	France	355.9	35	Nigeria	30.9
6	China	307.1	36	Rumania	30.0
7	United Kingdom	233.5	37	*Ford Motor*	28.9
8	Italy	183.0	38	Finland	27.9
9	Canada	182.5	39	*Texaco*	26.4
10	Brazil	143.0	40	*Mobil Oil*	26.1
11	Spain	107.2	41	South Korea	25.3
12	Poland	99.0	42	Hungary	24.8
13	Australia	97.3	43	Greece	23.6
14	Netherlands	91.6	44	Bulgaria	21.6
15	India	87.9	45	*Standard Oil (California)*	19.4
16	East Germany	75.8	46	*British Petroleum*[b]	19.1
17	Sweden	74.2	47	Taiwan	17.1
18	Iran	69.1	48	*Gulf Oil*	16.4
19	Belgium	68.9	49	*IBM*	16.3
20	Mexico	65.5	50	Thailand	16.2
21	Switzerland	58.1	51	Portugal	16.1
22	Czechoslovakia	56.5	52	*Unilever*[b]	15.7
23	*Exxon*	48.6	53	*General Electric*	15.7
24	*General Motors*	47.2	54	Colombia	15.6
25	Austria	42.2	55	*Chrysler*	15.5
26	Turkey	41.2	56	Peru	13.5
27	Argentina	40.7	57	Pakistan	13.1
28	Denmark	39.0	58	*ITT*	11.8
29	Yugoslavia	37.7	59	*Standard Oil (Indiana)*	11.6
30	*Royal Dutch/Shell*[b]	36.1	60	*Phillips Petroleum*[b]	11.5
				All other developing countries	less than 11.5

[a]Gross national product for countries and gross sales for corporations.

[b]Corporations based outside the United States, in the United Kingdom or the Netherlands.

Sources: Gross national product figures from the *World Bank Atlas* (Washington, D.C., World Bank, 1978). Corporate sales figures from United Nations, Department of Economics and Social Affairs. *Transnational Corporations in World Development, A Re-Examination* (New York: United Nations, 1978), table IV-1.

(footnote 4 continued)

According to table 4 in "The Multinational Corporation and the World Economy" (a staff report published in *Hearings before the Subcommittee on International Trade of the Committee on Finance, U.S. Senate, 93rd Congress, 1st Session* [February/March 1973]), the taxes paid to the U.S. government on income from foreign investment averaged approximately 6 percent of that income in 1968 and 1970. Using this figure, after-tax profits from U.S. foreign private investment have been calculated in Table 3-G by multiplying the available data on profits (before U.S. taxes) by 94 percent in all years.

multinational corporations within the world economy. Table 3-H ranks the top sixty nations and corporations together according to the size of their respective gross national product (GNP) or gross annual sales in 1976. Such figures do not measure precisely the relative economic strength of the different entities, for national governments control only a part of the income from their country's GNP and corporate directors control only a part of the revenues from their company's gross sales.

TABLE 3-I   FOREIGN OPERATIONS OF THE TOP TWENTY-FIVE INDUSTRIAL CORPORATIONS, 1981

				Foreign Content as Percent of			
Rank	Corporation	Home Country	Sales ($ billion)	Sales[a]	Assets	Profits	Employment
1	Exxon	United States	113.2	74	62	53	66[c]
2	Royal Dutch/Shell	Netherlands/United Kingdom	82.3	60	64	67	66
3	Mobil Oil	United States	68.6	65	52	60	—
4	General Motors	United States	62.7	25	30	119[b]	29
5	Texaco	United States	57.6	67	55	60	—
6	British Petroleum	United Kingdom	52.2	63	80	86	73
7	Standard Oil (California)	United States	45.2	53	47	40	27[c]
8	Ford Motor	United States	38.2	49	48	13	58
9	Standard Oil (Indiana)	United States	31.3	18	29	35	11
10	ENI	Italy	30.9	19	—	—	16[c]
11	Gulf Oil	United States	30.0	38	40	46	40
12	IBM	United States	29.1	38	47	37	42
13	Atlantic Richfield	United States	28.2	9	5	11	—
14	General Electric	United States	27.9	23	25	18	29
15	Unilever	Netherlands/United Kingdom	24.1	39	40	56	55
16	Du Pont	United States	22.8	17	26	17	20
17	TOTAL	France	22.6	59	71	—	43
18	VEBA	West Germany	22.0	7[c]	—	—	8[c]
19	Fiat	Italy	19.4	—	—	—	20
20	Elf Aquitaine	France	19.2	26	70	41	36
21	Renault	France	19.0	45	—	—	25
22	B.A.T.	United Kingdom	18.8	78	80	93	73
23	International Telephone and Telegraph	United States	17.3	47	37	59	—
24	Nissan	Japan	17.1	—	—	—	—
25	Phillips Petroleum	Netherlands	17.0	93	70	95	78

[a]Sales of overseas subsidiaries as percent of worldwide sales.

[b]Net loss in home country.

[c]1978 figure.

Source: John M. Stopford and John M. Dunning, *The World Directory of Multinational Enterprises 1982–83: Company Performance and Global Trends* (Detroit: Gale Research, 1983), p. 113.

Nonetheless, the table does convey a rough idea of the comparative power of nation-states and corporations.

Table 3-H indicates that in 1976 the top six industrial corporations (five of them based in the United States) ranked among the top thirty-five nations whose GNP exceeded $25 billion. Among the top sixty economic entities in the rank-ordering by GNP or sales are six-teen corporations and forty-four nations. Thus a substantial majority of the hundred-odd peripheral nations and territories (those not listed in the table) ranked behind the largest sixteen corporations in economic power.

Table 3-I presents detailed information on the extent to which the twenty-five largest industrial corporations in the world (ranked by gross sales in 1981) are involved in foreign op-

---

It should be noted that even these adjusted figures tend to understate the profitability of foreign investment. On the one hand, profits made by overseas affiliates can be disguised by artificially high prices charged for the supply of inputs imported from the parent company. Such over-invoicing has the effect of transferring the profits from the accounts of the overseas affiliate to the accounts of the parent company in the United States. On the other hand, the reported value of foreign assets may well overstate the true value of the invested capital because of overpricing of the capital equipment and/or capitalization of costless assets such as brand names.

erations. Thirteen of these twenty-five corporations are based in the United States. The available data on the foreign share of total sales, assets, earnings, and employment show varying degrees of foreign involvement for these corporations. It is clear, however, that the foreign share of total economic activity is higher for most of the U.S. corporations on the list than it is for the U.S. economy as a whole. It follows that foreign economic activity is highly concentrated among a relatively small number of major corporations in the United States.[5]

3.6   *Capitalist Expansion and the Sources of Imperialism*

In the following essay Arthur MacEwan argues that imperialism necessarily arises in a capitalist system. MacEwan shows first that the logic of capitalist expansion leads inevitably to the flow of capital across national boundaries and that large monopolistic firms tend to dominate the expansionary process. He then goes on to discuss the role of the state in the expansion of capitalism, and he illustrates this role with a brief look at the history of U.S. foreign policy since the turn of the century. Finally, he examines modern imperialism, emphasizing the critical role of capitalist ideology in supporting an imperialist foreign policy.

In developing his argument, MacEwan identifies three stages of expansionary activity during the process of the internationalization of capital, the development of national economies, the formation of colonies and spheres of influence, and the integration of the world capitalist economy. These three stages correspond to the three stages of imperialist relations between the center and periphery discussed in the previous essay.

The Vietnam War, its profound impact on U.S. society, and the final defeat of the United States in Vietnam have led us all to ask many questions about the foreign policy of the United States. Such an inquiry reveals that the United States has a long history of intervening—militarily, politically, economically—in the affairs of other nations. The intervention in Vietnam was unusual only in that it developed into a full-scale war which the United States lost.

In order to understand the origins of the Vietnam War, it would thus be an error to confine oneself to the history and immediate bases of that particular *military* intervention. The Vietnam War should be examined in the context of the entire history of U.S. foreign involvement. This history reveals the extent to which U.S. business and the U.S. government have extended control over other nations. It is this extension of control, in all its aspects, that I shall describe by the term "imperialism."

While U.S. imperialism operates in many spheres—political, economic, cultural—it is in

[5]It has been estimated that in 1970 the income derived from foreign operations by the top ten U.S. industrial corporations (ranked by foreign sales) represented 30 percent of the total foreign earnings of all U.S. industrial corporations, and the income derived by the top fifty accounted for roughly half of the total. For documentation, see Thomas E. Weisskopf, "American Economic Interests in Foreign Countries, An Empirical Survey," Discussion Paper no. 35, Center for Research on Economic Development, University of Michigan (April 1974), p. 16.

its most fundamental sense an economic phenomenon. That is, this international extension of control has its basis in the economic organization of American society. Within a capitalist economic system—and the United States is the most advanced capitalist system in history—there are basic forces that push that system toward expansion. This expansion carries with it an extension of control; hence, a capitalist system necessarily develops into an imperialist system.

THE EXPANSION OF CAPITAL

The fundamental principle of operation for the capitalist firm is the search for profits.[1] This search takes on many forms. One form is the introduction of new techniques of production and organization which allow cost reductions. The introduction of new techniques is often associated with a dependence upon expansion in the size of the enterprise's operation. For example, an extension of the division of labor—that hallmark of capitalist efficiency—is almost always dependent upon an expansion of sales. In this manner, technical change in the production process is often intricately bound up with another form of the search for profits—namely, the search for new markets. Whether or not cost-cutting innovations are introduced, the opening of new markets allows an expansion of sales without a corresponding decline in price. In the absence of increasing costs, new markets thus provide a basis for expanding profits.

Particularly important for the purposes of this essay is that the search for markets will often involve an expansion of the geographic sphere of operations. Geographic expansion has many advantages. For a firm operating in a competitive industry, geographic expansion allows the exploitation of markets where the downward pressure on prices is not so severe. For firms selling a relatively new product, the size of the local market may not be sufficient to take advantage of economies of scale, and international sales are necessary if production is to be profitable. In each case profitability is, of course, the criterion of geographic expansion, but profitability is often limited by uncertainty, lack of information, and political or economic instability. These factors can be significant barriers to the geographic expansion of the small firm.

For the large monopolistic firm, such matters of information, uncertainty, and instability are of less importance. In confronting each of these problems, the large firm has a natural advantage. It has the facilities to gain knowledge and gauge the possibility for profits, and it can help ensure its investments against instability. There are additional reasons why the monopolistic firm is apt to place particular importance upon international expansion of its markets.[2] First, simply in order to maintain its monopolistic position, it must control markets outside its original sphere of operation. Otherwise new firms may develop in those areas and eventually threaten the original base of operation. The consequences of a failure to control new markets are clear from the development of the European and Japanese automobile industries and their subsequent inroads on U.S. markets. While U.S. firms did attempt to control through the purchase of some European firms (e.g., Opel) they were unable to halt the European competition.[3]

Second, in the same manner that it will search for new products rather than expand its own product line, the monopolistic firm will seek to expand in new markets rather than expand and cut profits (through a lowering of

---

[1]For an analysis of the profit-making drive of the capitalist firm, see Edwards, Section 2.4, p. 32.

[2]The argument presented here and in the next paragraph is developed more fully, in the context of a "product-cycle" model by T. Moran, "Foreign Expansion as an 'Institutional Necessity' for U.S. Corporate Capitalism," *World Politics,* 25, no. 3 (April 1973).

[3]Ernest Mandel, in *Europe vs. America* (New York: Monthly Review Press, 1970), provides much information and an analysis of the competition for markets among enterprises from advanced capitalist nations.

the price) in its basic market. This is exemplified by the pharmaceuticals industry, which is notorious for its monopolistic practices in the United States and which has become a leader in the development of international markets.[4]

In addition to the search for new markets, there are other forms of the international search for profits. The availability of raw materials has always drawn capitalist enterprises throughout the world. While a firm of any size may be attracted by the profitability of obtaining raw materials, it is the large monopolistic firm that is particularly active and successful. In the first place, the exploitation of raw materials often requires large capital resources. Second, the large firm that is vertically integrated (e.g., the bauxite-aluminum-aluminum products companies) and thus uses the raw materials and sells the final product often has a special advantage. Third, and perhaps most important, the monopolistic firm is concerned about control. Whatever the narrow profitability of obtaining particular raw materials, controlling their supply is often important to the large firm which must continue to ensure that other firms do not make inroads on its realm. The petroleum industry is the most prominent example of an international exploiter of raw materials, and it exhibits each of these advantages of monopolistic operation. Aluminum, copper, and other mineral industries also provide good examples.[5]

Another form which the internationalization of business takes is the extension to new areas of the production process itself. On the one hand, the establishment of production operations in new areas is a means to exploit the markets of those areas. Sometimes the nature of the product is such that it is necessary or desirable to undertake production, or at least the final stages of production, close to the market in which it is sold. The refining of oil, the processing or packaging of food products (Coca-Cola!), the provision of a service, and construction projects all provide examples. Sometimes legal restrictions of the host country—tariffs, for example—require that a product be produced in the area where it is to be sold. This is true of the automobile industry in Mexico and in several other Latin American countries. Insofar as the establishment of production operations in a new area is based on such motives, it often involves not a complete operation but only the final assembly of a product.

On the other hand, production activities are frequently established in a new area in order to exploit the relatively low-cost labor in that area. The assembly of electronic components in Taiwan, punching IBM cards in Hong Kong, making shoes in Italy, and hand typesetting in several countries have all been developed by U.S. industries to avoid the relatively high labor costs at home. As with other types of international expansion, we can expect the monopolistic enterprise to take the lead in the international exploitation of labor. In terms of its ability to control and to transfer technology, its ability to secure sufficient demand for the new production enterprise, and its political ability to cope with the local population as a work force, the large firm has marked advantages.

In summary, the basic method of operation of the capitalist firm leads to international expansion in several ways. While the overall motivation is always profit, the particular medium through which the profits are gained can be the extension of markets, the obtaining of raw materials, or the exploitation of new sources of labor. In general, monopolistic enterprises can be expected to take the leading role in the internationalization of capital.

The internationalization of capital is a process that does not take place in a political vacuum. Capital requires direct protection and the institutions through which it operates must

[4]Michael Kidron, in *Foreign Investments in India* (New York, Oxford University Press, 1965), chapter 4, section 5, provides a particularly interesting description of the inroads of Western pharmaceutical firms into the Indian market.

[5]For accounts of the operations of the petroleum industry that develop these points see M. Tanzer, *The Political Economy of International Oil and the Underdeveloped Countries* (Boston: Beacon Press, 1969); R. Engler, *The Politics of Oil* (New York: Macmillan, 1961); and H. O'Connor, *World Crisis in Oil* (New York: Monthly Review Press, 1962).

be protected. Thus the expansion of the area of operation of capital is always associated with an expansion of the political influence of the state with which that capital is associated. In the following section I shall examine the historical operation of state and capital in the expansionary process.

THE ROLE OF THE STATE

In the history of capitalist development, we may distinguish three broad stages of expansionary activity. These stages, while they do not conform in a precise way to historical eras, are useful analytical tools for examining the internationalization of capital. In each of the stages the state can be seen providing the essential framework for expansion.

First is the stage of creating *national economies* in which the locus of economic activity moves from cities or small regions toward a national framework. Second is the stage of *colonialism and spheres of influence* in which the business interests of advanced nations extend their control beyond their own boundaries but with each nation operating in separate geographic areas. Third is the stage of *international capitalist integration,* in which barriers to economic activity among capitalist countries tend to be eliminated and firms from each nation have access to the economies of all of the geographic areas within the world capitalist orbit. In this third stage it is possible for a single dominant capitalist power to exercise economic hegemony over the entire capitalist world, as the United States did for the first few decades after World War II. But in more recent times several European nations as well as Japan have gained enough strength to challenge U.S. hegemony, so the third stage of international capitalist integration is now increasingly characterized by a new form of competition among rival capitalist powers.

The First Stage: The Development of National Economies

The early development of capitalism required the expansion of the size of the capital-

ist economic unit. In this expansion the state played a crucial role.

The key aspect of capitalist production is that the worker must be separated from the control of any productive factors other than his or her own labor and that the production process must be controlled by the owner of capital.[6] The process of separating workers from their means of production, and thus forcing them into the labor market and into capitalist production relationships, was facilitated by the power of the state. The state was instrumental in the development of capitalism in England, for example, through promotion of the enclosure movement in the eighteenth century and through legislation forcing the poor to enter the work force in the nineteenth century. It played a similar role in other parts of Western Europe and in Japan (after the Meiji Restoration in 1868), where the persistence of feudal institutions threatened to impede the growth of capitalism.

The profitable use of a developing labor force by the capitalist firm depends upon an expansion in the size of the unit of production. The division of labor that provides the basis for capitalist efficiency could not take place in a small craft shop of the precapitalist era. However, an enterprise could be profitably expanded only to the extent that there was a market for increased output. (This was true, for example, of the development of textile mills in England: a national market was necessary to support these harbingers of the factory system.) Thus it was necessary for capitalist development that local restrictions on trade be broken down, that means of transportation and communication be developed, that a uniform system of law and order be established over a wide area—in short, it was necessary that national economic units be developed and strengthened.

---

[6]See Chapter 2, and especially the introduction, p. 7, for a more detailed description of the capitalist mode of production.

The Second Stage: Colonies and Spheres

The stage in capitalist development that followed the political and economic development of the nation was characterized by colonial expansion and the creation of spheres of influence. As in the preceding stage, the economic integration of a larger geographic area was the key to the expansion process. However, while the need for markets and labor played some role, the effort to develop sources of supply for important foodstuffs and raw materials became particularly important in the second stage. The role of the state remained as before: to break down local restrictions on economic activity; to create a labor force; to create means of transportation and communication; to ensure stability through the imposition of law and order.

Britain, for example, united the regional economies of India and opened the whole subcontinent to penetration by British capital. Each colonial power established its own currency as the medium of exchange throughout its realm. The European colonial powers in Africa imposed monetary taxes on the indigenous people, forcing them to leave the traditional economy and enter the capitalist labor force to earn cash incomes to pay the taxes. Throughout the colonial world, railways directed toward import-export activity were given priority. Britain, France, Germany, and all of the colonial powers backed up their economic decisions in the most direct manner—with armed force.

In organizing trade within its particular sphere, each nation reserved for its own capitalist class special economic privileges—with respect to both the subordinate areas in its control and other leading capitalist powers. Thus, for example, Portugal prohibited the development of manufacturing in Brazil, reserving the market for goods produced in the parent country, and England restricted the trade of its North American colonies with other European powers.

The Third Stage: International Capitalist Integration and the Role of the United States

It is not surprising that the United States was a latecomer in building spheres of influence and establishing colonies. First, the United States itself had been under the control of Britain and became a nation only when many European nations were well established as international powers. Second, as long as the United States was able to expand westward within the North American continent, there was little pressure for the more typical overseas expansion.

As continental boundaries were reached, the United States began to enter seriously the competition among the big powers for new areas of exploitation. Around the turn of the last century, the United States and Britain were instrumental in ushering in a new era of capitalist international relations. The policies of the new era were typified by the U.S. demand for an "open door" in the Far East. With several European powers scrambling to establish control in China, the United States in 1899 demanded that all countries be allowed commercial access to this area—that the door be left open to all. This policy signified a movement away from national spheres of influence toward a single integrated international capitalist economy. Two world wars were to be fought, however, before this final stage would be firmly established.

Part of the reason that the U.S. government took a diplomatic lead in altering the relations of international capitalism was that U.S. business interests were latecomers to international activity. Thus, short of all-out war with other imperialist powers, the government had no way other than diplomatic initiative to gain access to many areas for U.S. business. More important, the government's demand for open access and equal terms was natural since the nation was rapidly becoming the world's greatest economic power. Under conditions of open access, the emerging political and eco-

nomic strength of the United States would ensure that its interests would prevail more often
than not.

Coincidentally with the rising international
power of U.S. business, the U.S. government
engaged in numerous military interventions
around the beginning of the century. The
Spanish-American War led to the establishment of formal U.S. colonies in Puerto Rico
and in the Philippines (an important stepping
stone for establishing influence in China) and
virtual colonial control over Cuba (only nominally independent). In each of these areas, the
extension of U.S. political control was followed by a rapid increase of U.S. economic interests.[7]

In 1912 the United States intervened militarily in Nicaragua in order to ensure that the
interests of U.S. banks financing a railway
were not interfered with. In 1915 the United
States occupied Haiti in order to ensure that
the Haitian government "honor" its obligations to U.S. bankers. In 1916, the U.S.
Marines were sent to Santo Domingo and
seized control of the customs and treasury of
that nation in order to ensure that obligations
to American companies would be fulfilled.
And again in 1916, when U.S. oil interests
were threatened in Mexico, the marines were
sent to the scene. While the majority of U.S.
military interventions in this period were in
the Caribbean, they were by no means limited
exclusively to that area. In 1911 and 1912,
and later in 1924 and 1926, U.S. armed forces
made their presence felt in China in order to
protect U.S. private property during civil disturbances there; these military actions provided the backdrop for the growth of U.S.
trade and financial interests in China.[8]

Military interventions, however, should not
necessarily be taken as typical of the operation
of U.S. imperialism. More often than not, control has been exercised through economic
power or through nonmilitary political pressure.

MODERN IMPERIALISM

Economic power provides the basis for control
in a modern imperialist system. Imperialism
results from the internationalization of capitalist economic relations, and it involves the internationalization of capitalist power relations.
In the first place, the rationale of commodity
markets is that those who can sell products the
cheapest will hold the dominant position.
Thus, important sectors of the economies of
secondary capitalist countries are dominated
by the more advanced enterprises of the pri-

I spent thirty-three years and four months in active service as a member of our country's most agile
military force—the Marine Corps. I served in all commissioned ranks from a second lieutenant to major-
general. And during that period I spent most of my
time being a high-class muscle man for Big Business,
for Wall Street, and for the bankers. In short, I was a
racketeer for capitalism. . . .

Thus I helped make Mexico and especially Tam-
pico safe for American oil interests in 1914. I helped
make Haiti and Cuba a decent place for the National
City Bank boys to collect revenues in. . . . I helped pu-
rify Nicaragua for the international banking house of
Brown Brothers in 1909–1912. I brought light to the
Dominican Republic for American sugar interests in
1916. I helped make Honduras "right" for American
fruit companies in 1903. In China in 1927 I helped see
to it that Standard Oil went its way unmolested.

During those years I had, as the boys in the back
room would say, a swell racket. I was rewarded with
honors, medals, promotion. Looking back on it, I feel I
might have given Al Capone a few hints. The best he
could do was operate his racket in three city districts.
We Marines operated on three *continents*.

Major-General Smedley D. Butler, *Common Sense* (Novem-
ber 1935), as quoted by L. Huberman and P. Sweezy in
Cuba: Anatomy of a Revolution (New York: Monthly Review
Press, 1960).

---

[7]See S. Nearing and J. Freeman, *Dollar Diplomacy* (New
York: Monthly Review Press, 1966), for the details of the
early period of U.S. military interventions.

[8]This era is summed up in the following statement by a
retired marine commander:

mary imperialist nations. While such domination has an impact at all levels of the international system, it takes on its most overt form in the poor countries.

Second, international capitalism tends to develop or reinforce a class structure in poor countries that serves its interests. Classes in subservience to and alliance with international capital tend to control the political apparatus; their power derives directly from their association with international capital. Both directly through the market and indirectly through the class structure, the economic power of the capitalist elite in the advanced capitalist nations enables them to dominate the economies of the poor countries.

The rapid growth in recent years of multinational corporations has greatly enhanced this economic power. The multinational corporations have a great deal of bargaining power in setting the terms on which their capital will be deployed in host countries simply because they have numerous options. They control technology and can regulate its dissemination according to their own priorities. They have the power, through internal pricing and bookkeeping adjustments, to artificially adjust the international location of their revenues and outlays and thereby affect the finances and balance of payments of host countries. The international capitalist market is like any national capitalist market: those who dominate the control of the means of production dominate the economy.

Imperialist control operates through political as well as economic channels. First, day-to-day control operates through normal diplomatic channels. The role of U.S. diplomatic missions throughout the world is defined as looking after the interests of its nationals, and this means in practice looking after the interests of U.S. business. Second, long-run control operates through the determination of the institutions of the international capitalist economy. Good examples are the negotiation of trade agreements favorable to U.S. capital and the establishment of an international monetary system in which the dollar is key. Such operations serve to maintain the long-run international hegemony of U.S. capital.[9]

Finally, the dominance of the world capitalist economy by the United States is backed up by tremendous military strength. Modern imperialist operations depend on the actual deployment of the military only when problems arise which economic power and quiet political dealings cannot handle. But today imperialism is being presented with serious challenges, and as these challenges become a threat to the entire system, military responses become increasingly necessary.

The Socialist Challenge

With the Russian Revolution in 1917—but more clearly following World War II when the Soviet Union emerged as a major world power, socialism "spread" to Eastern Europe, and successful socialist revolutions occurred in China, Korea, Vietnam—the political position of international capitalism has been severely altered. The system has been forced to move from a purely offensive political strategy toward a defensive posture.

In the early part of this century the state functioned to establish and to ensure the operation of capitalist relationships in areas where those relationships had not been fully established or were unstable. This was true of the numerous Caribbean military interventions cited above. Failures by foreign governments to honor contractual commitments with U.S. business, an elementary condition of capitalism, brought on the U.S. military. In the post–World War II era, however, the dominant concern of U.S. foreign policy has been the prevention of moves toward socialism by countries within the capitalist system. Thus, the interventions in Iran in 1953, in Guatemala in 1954, in Cuba in 1961, and in the Dominican Republic in 1965 should be seen primarily as defensive efforts against the threat—real or perceived—that the nations in

[9]For elaboration and substantiation of the assertions of this paragraph see Harry Magdoff, *The Age of Imperialism* (New York: Monthly Review Press, 1969), Chapters 3 and 4.

question would opt out of the international capitalist system. The same is true of the long and ultimately unsuccessful U.S. military involvement in Indochina, and the intervention of the CIA in Chile which helped to overthrow the leftist government of Salvador Allende in 1973.

As the major capitalist power emerging from the debacle of World War II, the United States assumed most of the burden of protecting the world capitalist empire. But the preservation of international capitalism is a goal in which not every American citizen has an equal interest. On a direct and material level, the income returned to the United States from direct foreign investment amounts to roughly one percent of national income.[10] In terms of its direct contribution to overall employment or its contribution to individual income, this figure would indicate that the international involvement of U.S. business is not very important. However, this income from international activity goes predominantly to those who obtain their income from profits. As a share of after-tax corporate profits, income from direct foreign investment has been growing rapidly and exceeded 25 percent by the early 1970s.[11] If one examines the very large corporations, the importance of the international economy becomes even more apparent. Exxon, Mobil Oil, Texaco, General Motors, and many other major corporations derive more than 50 percent of their earnings from overseas.[12] In 1972, the First National City Bank, the first bank to earn more than $200 million in a single year, earned $109 million abroad.[13]

[10]Table 3-F, p. 103, presents figures on the inflow of income from abroad associated with direct private foreign investment. Comparing these figures with the corresponding levels of GNP in current dollars published in table B-1 of the *Economic Report of the President, 1976,* one can see that 1974 was the first year that the ratio of foreign investment income to GNP exceeded 1 percent.

[11]See Table 3-G, p. 104.

[12]See Table 3-I, p. 106, and the sources cited therein.

[13]See R.J. Barnet and R.E. Müller, *Global Reach* (New York: Simon & Schuster, 1975), p. 28.

These data support two points. First, U.S. business in general, and large firms in particular, have a very real interest in international operations taken as a whole. They clearly benefit from the foreign policy described above. Second, people who earn their income from sources other than capital, and even a good deal of the business community, do not significantly depend directly on the preservation of international capitalism. This mass of the population should not find such great appeal in a foreign policy explicitly based on the concept that the government must protect and facilitate the search for profits overseas. Where economic interest is lacking, however, a popular form of the ideology of capitalist expansion provides the domestic support for the U.S. government's foreign policy.

The Role of Ideology

The ideology of capitalist expansion—the set of ideas that justify and support the system—has developed out of the needs of the expansionary process. In providing support for the system, one of its most important functions is to establish criteria for judging political activities. Thus, growing out of an economic process, the capitalist ideology provides a basis for unifying the economic and political realms of the system and for facilitating their joint operation.

The expansionist ideology is based on the functioning of the capitalist enterprise, and its primary element is simply the belief that the function of economic enterprise is the pursuit of profit. As was argued in the first part of this article, acceptance of the pursuit of profit as a guiding principle means that the behavior of capitalist firms will be expansionary. In order for capitalist expansion to be successful, it is necessary that basic capitalist institutions be created and maintained: the labor market and other basic factor and commodity markets; private property; legal sanction for economic contracts; control of the work process by the owners of capital. According to the ideology of capitalism, these institutions promote "economic freedom." Actions taken by the state that preserve this "freedom" or that facilitate its operation become synonymous with actions that preserve a decent society.

Translated into the realm of foreign policy, the task of the capitalist state then becomes that of facilitating and protecting the international business activities of its nationals. On the level of particular interests, for example: the U.S. diplomatic mission in India sees to it that U.S. pharmaceutical companies are allowed to produce and sell under "reasonable" conditions; in Bolivia and Peru, when U.S.-owned oil companies are nationalized, it is the business of the U.S. government; when Brazilian coffee producers begin to sell instant coffee below the price at which U.S. companies can produce, the U.S. government "encourages" the Brazilian government to impose an export duty.[14] On a broader level, the government provides mechanisms for the general expansion of U.S. interests abroad: the U.S. government encourages foreign governments to lower tariffs for U.S. goods and to enter reciprocity arrangements with the United States; the U.S. government provides insurance against nationalization or other political "disasters" in unstable areas; the international sections of various government departments—for example, commerce, labor—devote themselves to providing U.S. business with investment and trade information on countries throughout the world. Finally, on the broadest level, the role of the U.S. government in protecting the international business interests of its citizens is the protection of the system that allows those interests to operate—that is, the protection of international capitalism.

The keystone of the ideology of capitalist expansion during the post–World War II period has been anticommunism. Communism has been presented to the American people as an international conspiracy which has as its design the enslavement of all the peoples of the world and the consequent destruction of everything that they are taught to hold dear, from the private family and religion to freedom of speech and the two-party system. Such a threat must be fought at every step of the way, partly to protect those immediately in danger, but ultimately to protect the American people themselves. The fact that communism presents a systematic threat to the uninhibited operation of international capital is not emphasized in the popular form of the ideology.

Anticommunism is not the only form in which the ideology of expansionist policy has been popularized. At an earlier time, Christianity, manifest destiny, and the "white man's burden" have all done service to imperialist strategy. Indeed, today, as the force of anticommunism has begun to wane, a new set of popular justifications for U.S. interventions is taking form under the heading of "modern liberalism." At its base lies the sentiment that it is the task of the rich, powerful United States to help the poor, backward countries of the world in their quest for development. Economic advisory missions, foreign investment, the Peace Corps, and ultimately military involvement can all be justified on this basis.

In any society, over time the dominant class molds ideology in terms of its own interests. We need only mention various ways in which the U.S. business community shapes ideas about foreign affairs to indicate how all-pervasive is its influence. First, the individuals who hold foreign policy positions in the U.S. government are drawn heavily from the business community. The point here is not the importance of these individuals in making particular decisions but rather their role over a long period in shaping the institutions and developing the criteria by which decisions are made.[15] Second, by its control over resources,

---

[14]The Indian example is discussed by Kidron in the book cited above in footnote 4. The Brazilian example is from *The Economist*, February 24, 1968, and is cited by Harry Magdoff in *The Age of Imperialism* (New York: Monthly Review Press, 1969), p. 163. The Bolivian and Peruvian cases are well known.

[15]See Domhoff, Section 5.4, p. 191, or, for a more detailed study, G. William Domhoff, "Who Made American Foreign Policy, 1945–1963?", in *Corporations and the Cold War*, ed. David Horowitz (New York: Monthly Review Press, 1969).

directly or through foundations, the business community sponsors in conjunction with the government virtually all of the writing, research, and teaching that is done in the area of foreign affairs. Here, the concept of "a marketplace of ideas" is truly apt. As in any commodity market, the goods demanded by those who control resources and who have purchasing power are the ones that continue to be produced. By this process, not only are the dominant ideas reinforced and strategy and apologia developed for actions, but the growth of any ideological counterforce is severely limited. Other means by which the business community can shape concepts of foreign policy include its control over the media, its sponsorship of the Council on Foreign Relations and lesser organizations of policy consideration, and its extensive lobbying practices. In each case, power rests not on any formal arrangements but on the control over resources and on a common objective interest in the general design of policy.

Having established the conceptual framework for U.S. foreign policy, the U.S. business community can expect relatively little difficulty in having its way in most cases. Thus, to explain the U.S. government's actions, from aid giving to military intervention, we need not argue that any particular interests are being served, nor even that business interests have been directly involved in the development of policy. A powerful ideology provides a guide to action, the link between economic interests and political policy. When the integrity of the world capitalist system is threatened and the rules of international capitalist operation are in jeopardy, the ideology of capitalist expansion propels the U.S. government into action to preserve international capitalism.

The Case of Vietnam

So it was with Vietnam. Prior to the late 1960s, U.S. business had relatively few direct economic interests in Vietnam, or even in the rest of Indochina. While one could point to its economic potential or argue that Vietnam was the key to a much larger economic realm, an argument that explains U.S. intervention in Vietnam in terms of particular economic interests is clearly inadequate. There was simply not very much at stake for U.S. business in Vietnam. However, in terms of the general interest of maintaining the integrity of the international capitalist system, of which South Vietnam was a small but recognized part, there was very much at stake. The United States, as the dominant capitalist power, had to make every possible effort to prevent the rise in South Vietnam of a government and social system that would break all the rules of international capitalism.

The fact that the United States was ultimately unsuccessful in defending the capitalist empire in Vietnam does not detract from the cogency of the above argument. The loss of South Vietnam to capitalist enterprise has not caused any fatal damage to those firms whose assets were lost; much less has the loss of these assets had a serious direct impact on the U.S. economy as a whole. However, the impact of the loss of South Vietnam on the integrity of the international capitalist system has in fact been quite profound. For one thing, the neighboring countries of Laos and Cambodia quickly followed South Vietnam out of the capitalist orbit. And throughout Asia and the rest of the third world, antiimperialist forces gained in strength.

The point is that what was at stake in Vietnam was *not just some business assets or a piece of capitalist territory, but a set of rules and the integrity of an international system.* A violation of the system is a serious threat in and of itself. In order to function effectively, a social system must be supported by a set of beliefs regarding its legitimacy and its durability. These beliefs constitute the ideological support for the system. If violation or destruction of any part of the system occurs, then those beliefs are called into question and the whole system is in danger.[16]

[16]An analogy may be useful. Suppose that the Cincinnati Reds are playing the San Diego Padres in the last game of the regular season. Cincinnati has already secured the pennant by twenty-five games and the Padres are in last place by an equal margin. Cincinnati is ahead by a score

CONCLUSION

The explanation of imperialist state activity that has been offered in this essay is, of course, an economic explanation. It is not economic in the simple sense that immediate economic interests directly determine state policy. The argument has been the somewhat more complex one that the economic organization of a capitalist society generates an ideology which, in turn, provides the framework for state action. The state thus responds indirectly to the needs—both immediate and general—of the capitalist class.

The whole process of international capitalist expansion and its associated state intervention reveals some fundamental contradictions of capitalism. A successful capitalism is a geographically expanding capitalism. But the process of geographic expansion generates resistance in the form of conflicts among advanced powers and, as in Vietnam, conflicts with indigenous liberation movements. While these conflicts can often be contained, they will at times develop into major military engagements. In those cases, they can threaten the basic stability of the system.

The dependence of the expansionary process on an ideological link between economic interests and state action can exacerbate the contradictions of expansion. Were interventions to be carried out on a hard-nosed, carefully calculated basis, the related directly to economic interests, it would then be conceivable for a government to disengage when a venture became too costly. For example, when in Vietnam the United States found itself unable to win and the domestic costs of the war—both social and economic—became extremely burdensome, we might have expected a "rational" disengagement. Because the policy was based on an ideological link, however, "rational" disengagement proved difficult. The *immediate* basis of action was ideological, not economic, and military setbacks and domestic difficulties could not easily or quickly alter that ideological basis.

In the wake of the U.S. defeat in Vietnam, we may now begin to appraise the implications of the whole experience. At first, it might appear that in spite of military defeat, the contradictions contained in the conflict were overcome; the world capitalist system still stands. However, U.S. capitalism and the international empire which it dominated have been profoundly altered. Partly as a result of events set in motion by the Vietnam War, the U.S. government no longer has a free hand to suppress rebellions abroad (as recent events in Angola have illustrated); the oil-producing nations wield a new power in world affairs and have imposed severe constraints on the economies of the metropolitan capitalist powers; the international monetary system was disrupted and weakened; and world capitalism entered into its most serious economic crisis since the 1930s. In short, the era of international capitalist integration under U.S. hegemony has come to an end. World capitalism has entered a new period of instability, in which rival capitalist powers are competing with one another for economic influence and the future of the international capitalist system is clouded with uncertainties.

---

of 31 to 2; there are two outs and no men on in the last of the ninth. The Padre at bat, who is batting .208 for the season, has two strikes. He swings and misses a third pitch. But instead of walking off, the batter turns to the umpire and says, "How about a fourth strike?" He alludes to the above-mentioned facts, and he points out that no one's interests can possibly be seriously jeopardized by giving him a fourth strike. No immediate interests are at stake, but is it conceivable that such a violation of the rules of the game, a violation of the system, would be allowed?

CHAPTER 4

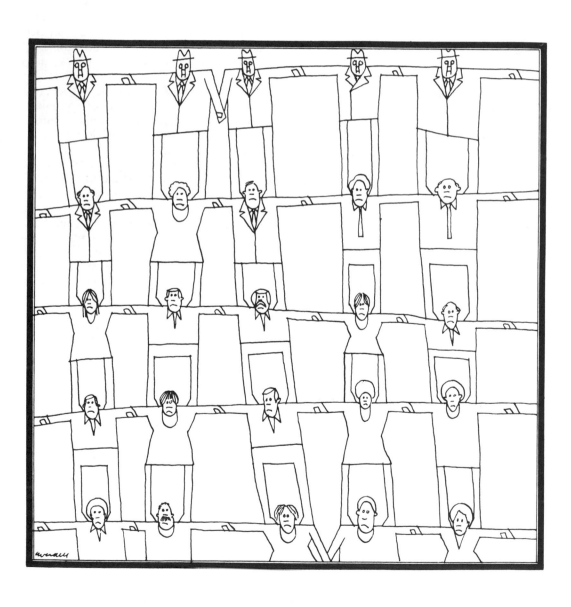

THE LABOR PROCESS
AND THE WORKING CLASS

IN THE LAST CHAPTER we saw how the small family-operated enterprises of the early nineteenth century have given way to the giant multinational corporations and banks that dominate American capitalism today. The tremendous concentration, centralization, and expansion of capital that has characterized the era of contemporary capitalism has simultaneously generated a major expansion of wage-labor and the working class and significantly changed the conditions of U.S. workers. In this chapter we will investigate the development of the working class in the period of contemporary capitalism. We will look at the evolution of the wage-labor force, the continuing transformation of the labor process, the diversity of the working class, the struggles by workers to form unions and other organizations to advance their interests, and the role that labor unions have played in contemporary capitalism.

THE GROWTH OF WAGE-LABOR

During the last century there has been a significant decline in the number of small property holders—farmers, merchants, independent professionals, and small business people—in the United States. At the same time there has been an equally significant growth in the number of people who must and do sell their labor-power for a wage or salary and who thereby surrender control over their labor-power, their authority over their work process, and their right to the final product. This group of people, whom we call wage-workers, includes not only blue-collar factory workers paid on an hourly basis but also many white-collar and service employees in offices, hospitals, schools, restaurants, government agencies, and so on. The expansion of wage-labor (and the simultaneous diminution of the old middle strata) is one of the most striking and important features of capitalist development in the United States.

The evolution of the class structure results directly from the requirements of the capitalist accumulation process. As capitalists seek to expand their profits, they employ more workers. This tendency to require more wage-labor is reinforced by the victories of hard-fought labor struggles to limit the legal length of the working day, to restrict the use of child labor, to set minimum health and safety conditions, and to otherwise limit exploitation of workers. In addition to employing more wage-workers, capitalists have also expanded surplus value by using their economic power to appropriate and incorporate into capitalist production noncapitalist activities that are capable of producing a surplus, by increasing the productivity of their workers and by expanding their efforts to sell the commodities produced. The growth in the demand for wage-labor and the progressive elimination of noncapitalist producers have each contributed to the expansion of the working class in the United States. The growth of worker productivity and the sales effort by capitalists have involved substantial changes in the nature of work in capitalist enterprises.

The supply of wage-labor in the United States has been expanded from several different sources. These include the natural growth of the population, immigration from foreign countries, and the recruitment of people previously outside the sphere of capitalist production. Generally, only a small percentage of workers are able to accumulate sufficient savings to go successfully into business on their own. The natural growth of the population and increases in years of life expectancy then expands the numbers of wage-workers more than enough to compensate for the increase in the age at which people leave school and the reduction in the average retirement age. This source of expansion has been supplemented through most of U.S. history by successive groups of foreign immigrants, most recently from Mexico, Asia, and the Caribbean. Finally, as large capitalists have replaced independent producers in the home, on the farm, and in the small store and workshop, they have set "free" new sources of labor supply for capitalist production. This category includes women, who had formerly worked only in the home, and such people as displaced farmers and small capitalists. After World War II, for example, capital-intensive farming by agribusiness corporations displaced millions of farm people, who were then absorbed on urban payrolls. As the remaining number of people engaged in farming dwindled by the 1960s and 1970s, an increasing number of women joined the wage-labor force.

In addition to increasing the employment of wage-labor, capitalists have expanded surplus value by increasing the productivity of that labor. In the monopoly and contemporary capitalist periods, this growth in the productivity of labor has been impressive; it has derived from several sources. The most important sources are the systematic reorganization by capitalists of the labor process itself, increases in the general skills and training of workers, increased mechanization as more capital goods are used in production, advances in the technology of production, the reallocation of labor from low-productivity to high-productivity industries, and the reduction in unit costs achieved by producing on a larger scale. All told, the rate of increase of worker productivity (or output per worker) in the United States has been estimated to be about 3 percent per year during the twentieth century.

Of course, this increase in productivity would not result in increased profits for capitalists if workers were able to capture the full benefits of their increased capacity to produce goods and services. On the other hand, any reduction in real wages paid by capitalists would increase profits even if productivity did not rise. In general, the movement of wages depends upon a number of factors: the degree of competition among capitalists for wageworkers, the success of capitalists in expanding the supply of labor, the cost of reproducing workers, and a bargaining power struggle between capitalists and workers over wages, the outcome of which depends on the factors just mentioned and the degree of organization and militancy on each side. As it has turned out, the growth in the real wage rate in the long run has just about matched the increase in worker productivity, leaving both capitalists and workers with the same share of total income they each previously received, while increasing the absolute amount of profit for capitalists and wages for workers.

ABSTRACT LABOR, HIERARCHY, AND SYSTEMS OF CONTROL

The expansion of capital through the continual revolutionizing of the labor process itself has produced far-reaching changes in the way that work is organized in modern capitalist enterprises. The skilled craftsperson of an earlier era has increasingly been replaced by a mass production worker who carries out only a small number of repetitive operations. The earlier artisans had specific knowledge and skills that were applied to a specific product in a self-controlled labor process. The modern capitalist firm, seeking to minimize its costs and to extract more work from its workers, organizes the labor process so as to standardize and routinize as much as possible the tasks and motions of workers, to render these workers into "interchangeable parts" abstracted from the specific product or process of production.

The result is the creation of what Marx called the "abstract worker," with the progressive removal of control and knowledge of the production process from the workers themselves to their "managers." As a consequence, although workers today have more years of general schooling than ever before, only a small proportion of many workers' skills are utilized in capitalist production. The process of breaking down tasks, of systematizing and rationalizing the labor process, goes on constantly, and extends today not only throughout production jobs in manufacturing, construction, and transportation but also to services and much white-collar work.

At the same time that much artisan work has become degraded, new skilled and unskilled occupations are also being created and expanded. The skilled jobs have much less routinized work and are often associated with new products or new technologies. A cycle then sets in, as capitalists attempt to expand and appropriate surplus produced in these jobs by reorganizing the labor process, breaking down the tasks, and again initiating a process of routinization and abstraction of labor. In some instances this process may not be very practicable, as when the product and therefore the labor process is not easily standardized (e.g., for repair services, gourmet restaurants, or in many aspects of medical and legal practice). In these cases the creation of abstract labor is much less marked, and the prevalence of thousands of small entrepreneurs is very noticeable.

As capitalist firms have grown larger and more complex in their organizational structure, they have systematized and made more sophisticated the organizational techniques they use to control the labor process. In place of just a boss and a few managers or supervisors who personally oversee the production process, exercising arbitrary and discretionary power over workers, the modern giant corporations have added a bureaucratic system of rules, sanctions, incentives, formal grievance procedures, hiring, promotion, and firing policies, and so on. This more formally structured organization of the labor process institutionalizes the exercise of capitalist power within the firm, making it seem less arbitrary and personal, and more fair and rational.

The bureaucratic hierarchy at the workplace is often presented as a necessary product of advanced technology, unavoidable in a complex industrial society. In fact, the content and hierarchical arrangement of most jobs has very little to do with the nature of the technological processes being used. The hierarchy must be seen primarily as a *system of control*, instituted to stratify workers, to get them to compete against each other, and thereby to elicit more work from them. The very successes of workers' struggles to limit their employers' power by organizing unions and developing solidarity among themselves has posed for capitalists the problem of finding new means of controlling workers, since the traditional means—such as firing rebellious workers and bringing in a reserve army of labor—could no longer work as well. One solution has been the institution of hierarchical job structures.

DIVISIONS AND UNIONS AMONG WORKERS

In addition to the hierarchical system of control at the workplace, continuing differences in working conditions between monopoly and competitive capitalist firms have provided a material basis for persistent divisions in the working class in the United States. Small competitive firms, often on the edge of survival, cannot afford the same wage rates, pensions, and health plans, or promises of long job tenure and promotion, as large monopolistic corporations. Often these differences correspond to divisions between unionized and nonunionized workers and add to existing racial, sexual, and ethnic differences among workers. Other important sources of divisions are between "abstract workers" and the remaining craft workers, such as plumbers and carpenters who belong to their own separate craft unions; and divisions between workers employed directly by capitalists and those paid by the state out of tax revenues. These divisions produce a working class that is still diversified in both its objective conditions and its subjective consciousness.

What role do labor unions play as workers' organizations in the period of monopoly capitalism? As we have already indicated, the struggles of workers against capitalists arise from the antagonistic nature of the relationship between capitalist and workers in the capitalist mode of production. The rights that many (but by no means all) American workers have today to organize collectively, to form unions, and to require employers to recognize those unions as the legitimate bargaining agents of the workers are rights wrested from capitalists in major labor struggles, particularly in the 1930s. Many capitalists actively resisted those organizing efforts, and militancy and active struggle on the part of workers were necessary to gain some minimal rights at the workplace.

Despite this history of struggle, the post–World War II role of the labor unions has been much more conservative. The once radical stance of many unions was curbed in the years after World War II as left-wing militant unionists were expelled from unions and legislation limiting unions' right to strike was passed by the federal government. More importantly, the economic prosperity of the postwar era provided an opportunity for capitalists to come to a more or less implicit accommodation with the nonradical leaders of the organized labor unions. The basis of this "social contract" between capital and labor was that capital would accept the legitimacy of the unions and be willing to negotiate real wage increases in line with increases in labor productivity, while unions would limit their demands to such wage increases and discipline their own members who violated labor-management negotiated contracts.

Capitalists thus tended to channel unions into "economism," the concentration on negotiable quantitative wage demands, with less emphasis placed on qualitative demands relating to working conditions, particularly issues of control. This arrangement promoted stability in the work force, permitted greater scope for long-range corporate planning, and co-opted the radical anticapitalist thrust of unionism. Liberal capitalists believed that these benefits would far outweigh the costs of granting wage increases and relinquishing some managerial prerogatives.

By the 1980s, however, the social contract had seriously decayed. A fundamental problem was the much reduced ability of U.S. capitalism to provide increasing real wages to its workers. Anti-union offensives by employers reduced both the extent and strength of unions. The war between labor and capital continues.

4.1   *The Proletarianization of the Labor Force*

The structure of the labor force has undergone profound changes since the early days of capitalism in the United States. In the following reading Michael Reich documents the changing occupational structure of the American population and the changing character of the labor force. The proportion of wage and salary workers in the labor force has steadily and markedly increased since the American Revolution, and in recent decades white-collar workers have become more important than blue-collar workers as a proportion of wage and salary earners. Although the latter trend might suggest that the proletarian character of the labor force is weakening, Reich argues that the nature of much modern white-collar work is increasingly indistinguishable from blue-collar work. Despite the changing conditions of work, most workers have no choice but to sell their labor power in the marketplace and to surrender control over their own work.

Written by MICHAEL REICH for this book. Copyright © 1986 by Michael Reich.

Capitalism comes into full being when a large number of propertyless individuals come to a labor market to sell their labor-power to a much smaller number of proper-tied capitalists; these capitalists combine the means of production they own with the la-bor-power they purchase and direct the pro-duction of commodities which they sell on a market. When the United States began its existence as an independent nation in 1776 it was not yet by these criteria a fully developed capitalist society. There was, to be sure, pro-duction of goods that were sold as commodi-ties and also significant class inequalities; wealth was concentrated among a small number of large landowners, slaveholders, and urban merchants. But about four-fifths of the nonslave labor force were themselves property owners and professionals—farmers, merchants, traders, artisans, small manufac-turers, lawyers, ministers, and doctors—who derived their income from their own property and labor.[1] Of those who did hire themselves out as workers, many raised their own food on small plots of land and also carried on their own business, as blacksmiths, tailors, carpenters, etc.[2] Most of the population lived in rural areas; in 1810, 80 percent of the labor force worked in agriculture.

This society of wealthy merchants, inde-pendent commodity producers, slaveholders, and slaves became dramatically transformed in the succeeding two centuries as a capitalist class structure developed in the United States. In the early nineteenth century, capi-talist relations of production began first in the manufacturing of textiles, with a labor supply recruited initially from the surround-ing agricultural population but subsequently expanded mainly by European immigration. By 1890, after slavery was abolished and as the United States was rapidly industrializing, less than two-fifths of the adult work force was classified by the census takers in the cate-gory of "independent enterprisers."

With the further advance of large-scale in-dustry and the emergence of monopoly capi-talism in the twentieth century, the proportion of small independent producers continued to decline, as did even the absolute number of petty manufacturers and merchants, shop-keepers, small-scale family farms, and arti-sans. Since 1930, more than three-fourths of all adults in the labor force have been nonmanagerial wage and salary employees, sellers of their labor-power on a labor market.[3] This process of proletarianization, or transfor-mation of the labor force into mere sellers of labor-power, is summarized statistically in Ta-ble 4-A.

Table 4-A exhibits another significant pat-tern: a steady rise in the proportion of salaried managerial and supervisory workers. This in-crease is related to the decline in the propor-tion of self-employed. As more of the labor force works in large organizations, an increas-ing number of bureaucratic personnel are

---

[1] Slaves totaled 20 percent of the population. An extended examination of the class structure in this period is con-tained in Jackson T. Main, *The Social Structure of Revolution-ary America* (Princeton, N.J.: Princeton University Press, 1965).

[2] Ibid., p. 271.

[3] I have excluded salaried managers from the proletariat because many of them supervise large numbers of workers and are highly paid executives who have more in common with capitalist owners. Some of these "managers," how-ever, are low-level administrators, as the quotation on p. 127 from Braverman indicates.

TABLE 4-A   THE PROLETARIANIZATION OF THE U.S. LABOR FORCE[a]

Year	Wage and Salary Employees[b]	Self-Employed[c]	Salaried Managers and Administrators	Total
1780[d]	20.0	80.0	—	100.0
1800	17.4	82.6	—	100.0
1860	48.0	52.0	—	100.0
1880[e]	59.8	39.1	1.1	100.0
1890	60.7	38.1	1.2	100.0
1900	63.3	35.4	1.3	100.0
1910	69.2	29.0	1.8	100.0
1920	72.6	24.8	2.6	100.0
1930	74.8	22.3	2.9	100.0
1940	75.6	21.4	3.0	100.0
1950	79.1	16.5	4.4	100.0
1960	81.1	13.6	5.3	100.0
1970[f]	83.5	10.4	6.1	100.0
1980[f]	81.4	10.8	8.6	100.0

[a]Percentage distribution of the employed, excluding unpaid family workers. Figures in this table differ from those in previous editions of this book because of refinements in sources, concepts, and estimating methods.

[b]Excluding salaried managers and administrators.

[c]Business proprietors, professional practitioners, independent artisans, and farm owners.

[d]Figures for 1780–1860 are rough estimates, excluding slaves (who comprised between 20 and 30 percent of the total labor force); white indentured servants are included among wage and salary employees.

[e]Self-employment figures for 1880 on exclude southern tenant farmers; their businesses were directly managed by moneylenders and landowners.

[f]Figures for self-employed in 1970 and 1980 have been adjusted to include owners receiving salaries from their own corporations; this adjustment was not possible for 1950 and 1960 and not necessary or significant for 1940 and previous years.

Sources: 1780: Jackson T. Main, *The Social Structure of Revolutionary America* (Princeton, N.J.: Princeton University Press, 1965), pp. 270–277. 1800–1860: Stanley Lebergott, "The Pattern of Employment Since 1800," in *American Economic History*, ed. Seymour E. Harris (New York: McGraw-Hill, 1961), p. 292. 1880–1890: Spurgeon Bell, *Productivity, Wages, and National Income* (Washington, D.C.: Brookings Institution, 1940), p. 10, with adjustments from Lebergott estimates for 1900. 1900–1970: Stanley Lebergott, *Manpower in Economic Growth* (New York: McGraw-Hill, 1964), tables A-3, A-4. 1950–1980: *Employment and Training Report of the President, 1982* (Washington, D.C.: U.S. Government Printing Office, 1982), table A-23; *Census of Population, 1950, 1960, and 1970*; and T. Scott Fain, "Self-Employed Americans: Their Number Has Increased," *Monthly Labor Review*, November 1980, p. 7. Data on southern tenant farmers from U.S. Bureau of the Census, *Historical Statistics of the United States, Colonial Times to 1970*, Series K-128. On the allocation of southern tenant farmers, see Joseph D. Phillips. *The Self-Employed in the United States* (Urbana: University of Illinois Press, 1962), pp. 13–15, 20; and Roger Ranson and Richard Sutch, *One Kind of Freedom* (New York: Cambridge University Press, 1977).

needed to manage and monitor these employees.[4]

[4]Table 4-A also shows a small increase from 1970 to 1980 in the percentage of self-employed, an apparent, but not real reversal of the long-term downward trend. The apparent increase in the self-employed in the 1970s largely reflects the rapid growth of business franchising, most visible in but not limited to fast-service restaurants. It is questionable whether franchise holders should be counted together with the other self-employed. Although the

To some degree, the proletarianization shown in Table 4-A reflects the changing

franchised owners of McDonald's and Burger King outlets provide much of the capital and day-to-day management of their restaurants, they are themselves closely supervised by the parent company and they are not free to expand or innovate. Since they do not keep all the profits and their decision-making power is mainly limited to management of their employees, their role more resembles shareholding managers than independent owners.

TABLE 4-B   SECTORAL DISTRIBUTION OF EMPLOYEES AND SELF-EMPLOYED, 1900–1980[a]

Year	Total (1)	Farm			Nonfarm				
		(2) Self-Employed[b]	(3) Employees[c]	(4) Total (2+3)	(5) Self-Employed	(6) Business	(7) Employees[d] in Households (domestics)	(8) Government	(9) Total (5+6+7+8)
1900	100.0	19.3	15.0	34.3	16.1	37.4	7.5	4.6	65.6
1910	100.0	14.6	13.4	28.0	14.4	46.0	6.5	5.1	72.0
1920	100.0	13.2	10.5	23.7	11.6	53.9	4.4	6.3	76.2
1930	100.0	10.3	10.6	20.9	12.0	54.3	5.4	7.4	79.1
1940	100.0	9.6	8.6	18.2	11.8	56.5	5.0	9.2	82.5
1950	100.0	6.0	4.4	10.4	10.5	65.8	3.3	10.1	89.7
1960	100.0	3.8	3.3	7.1	9.8	67.4	3.4	12.3	92.9
1970[e]	100.0	2.2	1.6	3.8	8.2	69.7	2.3	16.0	96.0
1980[e]	100.0	1.6	1.6	3.2	9.2	70.3	1.2	16.1	96.8

[a]Excluding unpaid family workers.

[b]Excluding southern tenant farmers. See Table 4-A, note e.

[c]Including southern tenant farmers.

[d]Including salaried managers (because of data limitations).

[e]1970 and 1980 census data have been corrected to include employees of own corporations in the self-employed category.

Sources: 1900–1940: S. Lebergott, *Manpower in Economic Growth* (New York: McGraw-Hill, 1964), tables A-3, A-4, and A-8. 1950–1980: U.S. Department of Labor, *Employment and Training Report of the President, 1982* (Washington, D.C.: U.S. Government Printing Office, 1982), p. 183, table A-23; U.S. Bureau of the Census, *Census of Population, 1970,* vol. 3, *Occupational Characteristics,* table 43; T. Scott Fain, "Self-Employed Americans: Their Number Has Increased," *Monthly Labor Review,* November 1980, p. 7.

sectoral composition of the economy. Both the decline of agriculture, with its large proportion of self-employed family farmers, and the growth of government employment, which by definition does not contain a self-employed group, have contributed to the decline in the overall percentage of the self-employed in the labor force. But these trends, which are documented in Table 4-B (columns 4 and 9), account for only one of the sources of proletarianization.

Another source of proletarianization is visible when we look at self-employment trends within either the entire nonfarm sector or within just the nonfarm business sector (the latter excludes government employment and paid household workers—mainly domestics). These patterns are evident in Tables 4-B and 4-C, which present the trends since 1900, the earliest year for which the disaggregated data are available. Columns 2 and 4 of Table 4-B

TABLE 4-C   DEGREE OF PROLETARIANIZATION BY SECTOR, 1900–1980

Year	(1) Farm	(2) Nonfarm	(3) Nonfarm Business
1900	44.0	75.5	60.9
1910	44.4	80.0	76.2
1920	44.1	84.8	82.3
1930	50.8	84.8	81.9
1940	49.4	85.7	82.7
1950	42.5	88.5	86.2
1960	46.7	89.5	87.3
1970	42.3	91.5	88.3
1980	49.2	90.5	88.4

Note: Degree of proletarianization equals ratio of employees to sum of self-employed and employees.

Col. 1 = Table 4-B col. 3/col. 4
Col. 2 = Table 4-B cols. (6 + 7 + 8) col. 9
Col. 3 = Table 4-B col. 6/cols. (5 + 6)

show that farm self-employment fell from 19.3 percent of total employment in 1900 to 1.6

percent in 1980.[5] The weight of nonfarm self-employment also fell, from 16.1 percent in 1900 to 9.2 percent in 1980. Table 4-C shows that while the degree of proletarianization within the farm sector has not exhibited a consistent trend up or down, the degree of proletarianization within the nonfarm and nonfarm business sectors has shown a definite upward trend. Thus, proletarianization has resulted both from intersectoral shifts in the economy and changes within the nonfarm sector.

This growth of the wage and salary proletariat is even more remarkable when one examines the transformed role of women and blacks in the economy. Although women have always participated significantly in home production and in agriculture, the growth of capitalism in the twentieth century has dramatically increased in the proportion of women who work outside the home as wage and salary earners, many of them on a full-time and year-round basis. In 1890, only 18 percent of adult women worked at paid jobs outside the home. Most of these women were single, under 25, and tended to leave employment when they married; most older women were married and worked primarily at home. By contrast, in 1930, 51.5 percent of adult women were in the paid labor force, most of them wage and salary employees; and more than 50 percent of married women living with their husbands and over more than half of all mothers with children under the age of eighteen were active members of the paid labor force in 1930. As these data suggest, women are in the wage labor force on a more permanent basis: if past trends continue, women born in 1960 will spend an average of twenty years of their life as wage or salary workers.[6]

The most dramatic transformation of working status has occurred among blacks. After the Civil War some ex-slaves became artisans, some became wage earners in urban areas or on reorganized plantations, and a few obtained land of their own to farm. But most ex-slaves eked out an existence as farm tenants or sharecroppers, dependent on the white landlord for credit, tools, work animals, and feed. Beginning about the turn of the century, however, and particularly since 1940, blacks have left agriculture and sharecropping in large numbers and joined the wage and salary proletariat. By 1980, less than 15 percent of blacks were living in rural areas, and more than 98 percent of employed blacks were working outside agriculture, almost all as nonmanagerial wage and salary workers.[7]

Most wage and salary employees in the United States depend upon their jobs for their livelihood. Many may own a car, a house, household possessions, and a small amount of savings. But setting aside savings just for retirement needs and medical emergencies, very few workers have been able to accumulate financial wealth in sufficient amounts to provide more than several months of subsistence income (without a job).

A special 1983 government survey of consumer finances determined that 50 percent of all families had less than $2000 in liquid assets (defined as checking accounts, savings accounts, money market accounts, certificates of deposit, personal retirement accounts, and savings bonds), 74 percent had less than $10,000 in such holdings, and only 8 percent held liquid assets of $40,000 or more.[8] Total financial assets (defined as liquid assets plus stocks, other bonds, and trusts) were also unequally distributed (see Table 4-D): 48 per-

---

[5]This finding for the farm sector, it should be noted, results in part from treating southern tenant farmers—many of them sharecroppers—as not self-employed. The number of tenant farms fell even faster than the number of owned farms.

[6]U.S. Bureau of the Census, *Historical Statistics of the United States, from Colonial Times to 1957* (Washington, D.C.: U.S. Government Printing Office, 1960); *Statistical Abstract of the United States, 1982-83*, pp. 382–383. See also V. Perella, "Women and the Labor Force," *Monthly Labor Review*, February 1968, p. 2.

[7]U.S. Department of Commerce, Census Bureau, *Census of Population,* 1980.

[8]"Survey of Consumer Finances, 1983," *Federal Reserve Bulletin,* September 1984, p. 685, table 9. Some of these families were receiving nonwage income from farm programs, educational grants, pension funds, unemployment compensation, medicare, welfare, or other government-provided income security programs; but only a tiny percentage of able labor-force–aged individuals receive the bulk of their income over time from such sources. See Section 6.1, p. 217.

cent of families had total holdings of less than $2000, 83 percent held less than $25,000, and 90 percent had holdings of less than $50,000. (With a rate of return of 8 percent, assets worth $50,000 bring $4000 per year in income.)

At the same time, in the words of the Federal Reserve Board (which sponsored and analyzed the survey): "The concentration of nonliquid financial assets in a small number of families with very high incomes is apparent. . . . More than 70 percent of the dollar holdings of nontaxable bonds, 50 percent of the stockholdings, and 39 percent of the other bonds are held by the 2 percent of families with [yearly] incomes that exceed $100,000."[9]

In short, the United States has become a nation of wage and salary employees who have virtually no access to income from property or control over the production process and whose economic welfare is determined by the vicissitudes of the labor market. The process by which capitalist development progressively reduces more adults to the status of seller of labor-power has taken place in all capitalist countries; for example, data for France and Germany also indicate a steadily increasing proportion of wage and salary earners.[10]

At the same time, the old capitalist class has also been changing. While the traditional image of a leisure class of rentiers who live by clipping coupons of stocks and bonds was never very accurate, it has become particularly obsolete under modern capitalism. More common today is the large capital owner who also participates in production, for a high salary, as director, manager, trustee, or executive. A large proportion of high-level managers and executives in the largest corporations and banking institutions has substantial personal holdings in the stocks and bonds of those companies.[11]

[9]Ibid., p. 689.

[10]Data for France and Germany are reported in E. Mandel, *Marxist Economic Theory* (New York: Monthly Review Press, 1968), pp. 164–165.

[11]See Robert J. Larner, "The Effect of Management-Control on the Profits of Large Corporations," in *American Society, Inc.,* ed. Maurice Zeitlin (Chicago: Markham, 1970).

TABLE 4-D   DISTRIBUTION OF TOTAL FINANCIAL ASSETS, 1983

Size of Holding ($ thousands)	Percent of Families
None	12
0–1	27
1–2	9
2–5	13
5–10	10
10–25	12
25–50	7
50–100	5
100 and more	5
Total	100

Source: "Survey of Consumer Finances, 1983," *Federal Reserve Bulletin*, September 1984.

With the increasing complexity of modern corporate organizations and bureaucracies, managers have become increasingly numerous (see Table 4-E). As Harry Braverman has pointed out, however, the Census Bureau's classification of managers can be quite misleading. The 6.5 million persons classified as "managers, administrators and proprietors, except farm" in 1970 "included perhaps a million managers of retail and service outlets, and as much as another million self-employed petty proprietors in these same fields. It included buyers and purchasing agents, officials and administrators at the various levels of government, school administration, hospitals and other such institutions; postmasters and mail superintendents; ships' officers, pilots, and pursers; building managers and superintendents; railroad conductors; union officials; and funeral directors. Since such categories consume almost half of the entire classification, it is clear without further analysis of the rest that the managerial stratum of true operating executives of the corporate world is quite a small group."[12]

THE STRUCTURE OF THE PROLETARIAT

The growth of capitalist production on a large scale and the extension of capitalist produc-

[12]Harry Braverman, *Labor and Monopoly Capital* (New York: Monthly Review Press, 1974), p. 259.

tion into new areas have led to significant structural changes within the wage and salary labor force. Along with a growing hierarchy in the production process, a pyramidal social structure has developed as white-collar workers, many of whom occupy intermediate positions in the occupational structure, have grown in number. C. Wright Mills was fond of referring to such workers as the *new middle class*, since, unlike the small farmers and shopkeepers of the old middle class, most of these white-collar workers do not own property, which is significant in the production process. In what follows we trace the changing composition of the labor force and indicate how the character of white-collar jobs is being transformed.

The importance in the economy of blue-collar labor in industry (mining, manufacturing, and construction) increased continuously in the United States until about the 1930s, as in-

dustry displaced the family farm and the farm laborer. Since the 1930s, however, white-collar and service employment have replaced industrial blue-collar employment as the most rapidly expanding occupations in the economy. The proportion of nonmanagerial white-collar workers in the labor force grew from about 6.7 percent in 1870 to 24 percent in 1940 and 42 percent in 1982. By contrast, blue-collar employees in mining, manufacturing, and construction accounted for 37 percent of the total labor force in 1940 and have remained near this proportion since. At the same time, the proportion of service workers (excluding maids and other private household workers) in the labor force has grown from less than 5 percent in 1910 to 15 percent today (see Table 4-E).

These long-run changes in the occupational structure reflect advances in the technology of production, changes associated with the

TABLE 4-E   THE CHANGING OCCUPATIONAL STRUCTURE OF THE LABOR FORCE

Occupational Group	1910	1940	1960	1982[a]	1995[a, b]
Managers, administrators, and proprietors (except farm)	6.6%	7.3%	8.5%	9.3%	9.6%
White-collar workers	14.7	23.8	33.8	42.0	42.9
Professional and technical	4.7	7.5	11.4	16.3	17.1
Clerical	5.3	9.6	15.0	18.8	18.9
Sales	4.7	6.7	7.4	6.9	6.9
Blue-collar workers	38.2	39.8	39.5	30.0	29.2
Craft workers and supervisors	11.6	12.0	14.3	11.4	11.6
Operatives	14.6	18.4	19.7	12.8	12.1
Nonfarm laborers	12.0	9.4	5.5	5.8	5.5
Service workers	9.6	11.8	11.7	16.0	16.3
Private household workers (e.g., maids)	5.0	4.7	2.8	1.0	0.7
Other services	4.6	7.1	8.9	15.0	15.6
Agriculture	30.9	17.4	6.3	2.6	1.9
Farmers and farm managers	16.5	10.4	3.9	1.4	1.1
Farm laborers and supervisors	14.4	7.0	2.4	1.2	0.8
Total[c]	100.0	100.0	100.0	100.0	100.0

[a]Data for 1982 and 1995 refer to employed persons only.

[b]Projections

[c]Individual items are rounded separately and therefore may not add up to totals.

Sources: 1910–1940: U.S. Department of Commerce, Bureau of the Census, *Historical Statistics of the United States, Colonial Times to 1957*, table D72-122. 1960: U.S. Department of Commerce, Bureau of the Census, *U.S. Census of Population, 1960*, table 201. 1982 and 1995: George Silvestri, John Lukasiewicz, and Marcus Finstein, "Occupational Employment Projections through 1995," *Monthly Labor Review*, November 1983, table 1, pp. 38–43.

growth of corporate bureaucracies, and shifts in the sectoral composition of goods and services produced in the economy.

With technical improvements related primarily to mechanization and automation, fewer industrial workers are needed to produce increasing quantities of output. For example, in manufacturing, total output increased 233 percent between 1950 and 1981, with only an 18 percent increase in production workers.[13]

In the same period, white-collar nonproduction employment increased by 150 percent in manufacturing. As Stephen Hymer has pointed out, modern corporate enterprises have become increasingly complex in their organizational structure.[14] The modern giant corporation has far-flung sales and distribution networks and specialized divisions for research and development, product design and styling, cost accounting, personnel management, sales, marketing, finance, and over-all corporate coordination. As a result, more white-collar workers—managerial, professional, technical, clerical, and sales—are needed. Research and development activities have become particularly important in many military-related sectors in American industry. These high-technology industries, such as electronics, telecommunications, and missile guidance systems, employ large numbers of scientists, engineers, designers, and technicians.

Thus, white-collar workers are becoming an increasing proportion of the total labor force within the manufacturing sector of the economy (see Table 4-F). We can expect this trend to continue; nonmanagerial white-collar workers comprised less than 10 percent of employment in manufacturing in 1899, 20 percent of total manufacturing employment in 1952, and 27 percent in 1981.[15]

The changes in the sectoral composition of goods and services produced in the economy have also contributed to the growth of white-collar and service employment. The service sectors—wholesale and retail trade; finance, insurance, and real estate; professional, business, and personal and repair services; institutions (private hospitals, universities, foundations, etc.); and government—become increasingly important at higher levels of gross national product. These service sectors tend to employ a high percentage of white-collar workers.

On the other hand, many workers in the service occupations—such as restaurant labor, laundry and dry-cleaning workers, chambermaids, janitors, nursing aides, porters, barbers and hairdressers, and guards and police officers—fill positions that are by no means traditional white-collar office jobs. The same could be said of workers in automobile or machine repair shops, who are classified *occupationally* as blue-collar workers, but classified *industrially* in service industries. Overall, the *rate*

[13]*Statistical Abstract of the United States, 1984* (Washington, D.C.: U.S. Government Printing Office, 1984), pp. 764–765; *Historical Statistics of the United States from Colonial Times to 1970*, pp. 666–667.

[14]See Hymer, Section 3.1, p. 61.

[15]The 1899 estimate is cited in Eli Chinoy, *Automobile Workers and the American Dream* (Boston: Beacon Press, 1963), p. 5; 1952 figure is from Bureau of Labor Statistics Bulletin 1599; 1981 figure is from *Employment and Earnings*, January 1982.

TABLE 4-F   SELECTED WHITE-COLLAR OCCUPATIONS AS A PERCENT OF TOTAL MANUFACTURING EMPLOYMENT

	1940	1952	1963	1975	1981
Professional and technical	3.0	5.3	9.3	11.2	11.6
Clerical	14.1	11.8	12.2	12.2	12.4
Sales		2.8	3.3	3.6	2.5
Total	17.1	19.9	24.8	27.0	26.5

Source: U.S. Census of Population, 1940; Bureau of Labor Statistics, *Bulletin 1599*; unpublished BLS data presented in E. Kassalow, "White Collar Unionism in the United States," in *White Collar Trade Unions of Urbana*, ed. A. Sturmthal (Urbana: University of Illinois Press, 1966), p. 318; *Employment and Earnings*, January 1982, p. 167.

of increase in employment in service *occupations* has matched the increase in white-collar occupations.

The increased employment in the service sector is underscored by comparisons to industrial employment trends. For example, "the *increase* in employment in eating and drinking establishments between 1970 and 1980 was greater than the total number employed in the steel, copper, and aluminum industries in either year. The *increase* in employment in the field of health between 1950 and 1960 was greater than the total number employed in automobile manufacturing in either year."[16]

THE NATURE OF WHITE-COLLAR EMPLOYMENT

As the number of white-collar jobs has grown, the character of these jobs has been transformed. First, the greatest increases (in absolute numbers) in white-collar jobs have occurred in the low-level clerical and sales categories. Second, the growth of bureaucracies and the increasing importance of machinery of various types in modern offices—copying machines, new varieties of dictating equipment, improved typewriters, keypunch machines, and other accessories to electronic data and word processing—have made much work in the modern office resemble factory and assembly-line labor. The work of a telephone operator or of a secretary in a typing pool is similar in many ways to the work of a machine operator in a textile factory. Hierarchy, barriers to advancement, extreme specialization, and lack of control more and more characterize many white-collar jobs. Several recent national surveys have pointed to increasing job dissatisfaction among white-collar workers as a result of such changes.[17]

Furthermore, the independent status of many once elite professional white-collar jobs has been steadily eroded. Scientists, engineers, architects, teachers, nurses, university professors, technicians, and others find that they work in ever-larger organizations in which the content of their jobs, as well as their working conditions, are more narrowly defined and set down from above. In recent years many professional and technical white-collar workers have become subject to layoffs, a long-time hallmark of blue-collar employment.

Even doctors and lawyers have not escaped some loss of independence. For example, an increasing percentage of all doctors are employed on a salary basis in the large, urban, often university-connected hospitals, clinics, and research institutes. Fewer lawyers are engaged primarily in their own practice; many now work for large law firms or are employed directly by corporations and governments on an annual salary basis.

Finally, the salaries of white-collar workers have not risen as fast as those of blue-collar workers. In 1890, white-collar workers received on the average about double the average wage of the blue-collar manufacturing worker.[18] Today most white-collar clerical and sales workers earn less than many blue-collar workers. While female clerical and sales workers receive the lowest pay, the average income of male clerical and sales workers alone is below the average income of skilled blue-collar workers.

The relative position on the income scale of professional white-collar workers has also fallen. For example, in 1904 high school teachers in large cities earned nearly three times the wage of an average manufacturing production worker.[19] Today, high school

[16]*Employment and Earnings,* January 1971, pp. 53, 58; *Employment and Earnings,* June 1982 (supplement), pp. 34, 201.

[17]For a summary of some recent studies, see *Work in America,* Report of a Special Task Force to the Secretary of Health, Education and Welfare (Cambridge, MA.: MIT Press, 1973).

[18]In 1890, average annual earnings for clerical workers in manufacturing and steam railroads were $848, compared to $439 for blue-collar wage earners in manufacturing; see *Historical Statistics,* p. 92. In 1969, the average weekly pay of clerical workers was $105, compared to $130 for blue-collar production workers.

[19]P. G. Keat, "Long-Run Changes in the Occupational Wage Structure," *Journal of Political Economy,* 58, no. 6 (December 1960).

teachers earn only about 50 percent more than the average manufacturing wage earner.

In short, the expansion of the wage-labor force has occurred simultaneously with a breaking down of the old sharp distinctions between blue-collar, white-collar, and service work. Although important differences among workers still remain, as we shall see later in this chapter, there is no doubt that an increasing proportion of the total labor force falls into the category that we call the working class.

4.2   *Conflict and Control in the Workplace*

For capitalists to make profits, the inherent capital-labor conflict at the workplace must be resolved on terms that permit capitalists to obtain desired work behavior from their workers. The existence of a pool of unemployed workers, eager to replace those already hired, provides one classic lever of such control. Capitalists have also developed other modes of regulation of labor. In the following reading Richard Edwards shows how three different types of social organization of the workplace constitute systems of control over workers.

Excerpted from *Contested Terrain: The Transformation of the Workplace in the Twentieth Century* by RICHARD EDWARDS. © 1979 by Basic Books. Reprinted by permission of the author and Basic Books.

Capitalism itself came into being when labor power (as opposed to merely labor's products) became a commodity, that is, a thing bought and sold in the market. Employers, in business to make profits, begin by investing their funds (money capital) in the raw materials, labor power, machinery, and other commodities needed for production; they then organize the labor process itself, whereby the constituents of production are set in motion to produce useful products or services; and finally, by selling the products of labor, capitalists reconvert their property back to money. If the money capital obtained at the end of this cycle exceeds that invested initially, the capitalists have earned a profit.

Focusing on the central role of the labor process in this sequence, Karl Marx noted that:

The money-owner buys everything necessary for [production], such as raw material [and labor power], in the market, and pays for it at its full value. . . . The consumption of labor power is completed, as in the case of every other commodity, outside the limits of the market. . . . Accompanied by Mr. Moneybags and by the possessor of labor power, we therefore take leave for a time of this noisy sphere, where everything takes place on the surface and in view of all men, and follow them both into the hidden abode of production, on whose threshold there stares us in the face, "No admittance except on business." Here we shall see, not only how capital produces, but how capital is produced. We shall at last force the secret of profit making.

On leaving this sphere of [the market], . . . we think we can perceive a change in the physiognomy of our dramatis personae. He, who before was the money-owner, now strides in front as capitalist; the possessor of labor power follows as his laborer. The one with an air of importance, smirking, intent on business; the other, timid and holding back, like one who is bringing his own hide to market and has nothing to expect but—a hiding.[1]

[1]*Capital*, vol. I (New York: International Publishers, 1967), pp. 175–176.

The market equality between buyer and seller of the commodity labor power disappears in this "hidden abode," and the capitalist takes charge. No wonder the capitalist strides ahead, "intent on business," for it turns out that the commodity he has purchased is not what is useful to him. What the capitalist buys in the labor market is the right to a certain quantity of what Marx has called *labor power*, that is, the worker's capacity to do work. Labor power can be thought of as being measured in time units (hours, days) and it may be improved or expanded by any skills, education, or other attributes that make it more productive than "simple" labor power. Thus, the capitalist, in hiring a carpenter for a day, buys one day's quantity of carpenter labor power.

But the capacity to do work is useful to the capitalist only if the work actually gets done. Work, or what Marx called *labor*, is the actual human effort in the process of production. If labor power remains merely a potentiality or capacity, no goods get produced and the capitalist has no products to sell for profit. Once the wages-for-time exchange has been made, the capitalist cannot rest content. He has purchased a given quantity of labor power, but he must now "stride ahead" and strive to extract actual labor from the labor power he now legally owns.

Workers must provide labor power in order to receive their wages, that is, they must show up for work; but they need not necessarily provide *labor*, much less the amount of labor that the capitalist desires to extract from the labor power they have sold. In a situation where workers do not control their own labor process and cannot make their work a creative experience, any exertion beyond the minimum needed to avert boredom will not be in the workers' interest. On the other side, for the capitalist it is true *without limit* that the more work he can wring out of the labor power he has purchased, the more goods will be produced; and they will be produced without any increased wage costs. It is this discrepancy between what the capitalist can buy in the market and what he needs for production that

makes it imperative for him to control the labor process and the workers' activities. The capitalist need not be motivated to control things by an obsession for power; a simple desire for profit will do.

These basic relationships in production reveal both the basis for conflict and the problem of control at the workplace.[2] Conflict exists because the interests of workers and those of employers collide, and what is good for one is frequently costly for the other. Control is rendered problematic because, unlike the other commodities involved in production, labor power is always embodied in people who have their own interests and needs and who retain their power to resist being treated like a commodity. Indeed, today's most important employers, the large corporations, have so many employees that to keep them working diligently is itself a major task, employing a vast workforce of its own. From the capitalist's perspective, this is seen as the problem of management, and it is often analyzed simply in terms of the techniques of administration and business "leadership." But employment creates a two-sided relationship, with workers contributing as much to its final form as managers or capitalists.

In some cases, the management task may be trivial. Employers may, for example, contract for particular labor services when workers are hired; if the exact nature of the duties can be spelled out beforehand, competition among job applicants—i.e., the labor market—effectively enforces the contract. Similarly, employers may pay only for work actually done;

---

[2]Of course, this conflict is only superficially confronted with regard to an individual worker. Any worker who, once on the job, refuses to work or who even works less than the most eager job-seeking unemployed person will simply be fired. Individual resistance by a worker, if it is detected, is easily dealt with, so long as a replacement is standing by in the unemployment line. Meaningful conflict arises, then, with regard to groups of workers or an employer's or an entire industry's workforce. The amount of labor that can be extracted from the purchased labor power depends on the workforce's willingness to perform useful work and enterprise's ability to compel or evoke such work.

if each worker's output is independent, piece-rate pay compels adequate production. Other workplace schemes may be directed toward the same end.

In general, however, capitalists have found it neither practical nor profitable to rely on such devices. Complete market contracting (by exhaustively specifying the worker's duties before hire) is usually impossible and almost always too expensive. Piece-rate pay has limited application and frequently engenders conflict over the rates themselves. In both cases, evaluation of the contracted work raises further problems. Other schemes—profit sharing, the distributing of company stock to workers, and more elaborate incentive schemes—also fail. Most importantly, all these devices founder because their targets, the workers, retain their ability to resist. Typically, then, the task of extracting labor from workers who have no direct stake in profits remains to be carried out in the workplace itself. Conflict arises over how work shall be organized, what work pace shall be established, what conditions producers must labor under, what rights workers shall enjoy, and how the various employees of the enterprise shall relate to each other. The workplace becomes a battleground, as employers attempt to extract the maximum effort from workers and workers necessarily resist their bosses' impositions.

.   .   .

These . . . basic relations exist in all workplaces; indeed, the shop floor, the office, the drafting room, the warehouse, the hospital ward, the construction site, and the hotel kitchen all become places of continuing conflict. Workers resist the discipline and the pace that employers try to impose. At most times the workers' efforts are solitary and hidden; individual workers find relief from oppressive work schedules by doing what their bosses perceive as slacking off or intentionally sabotaging work. At other times resistance is more conspiratorial; informal work groups agree on how fast they will work and combine to discipline rate-busters; or technicians work to rules, sticking to the letter of the production manual and thereby slowing work to a fraction of normal efficiency. More openly, workers or even union locals (often against the commands of their leaders) walk off the job to protest firings, arbitrary discipline, unsafe working conditions, or other grievances. More public still, established unions or groups seeking to achieve bargaining rights strike in order to shut down production entirely.

The struggle in the workplace has a closely intertwined parallel in the bargaining that goes on in the marketplace. Here conflict concerns wages, as labor and capital contend over the reward for the laborer's time. Sometimes this bargaining occurs collectively; sometimes it takes an individual form. At times wage bargaining creates a crisis; at other times it assumes an entirely pacific form. But here, too, the clash of interests persists.

Thus, in the slogan, "A fair day's work for a fair day's pay," *both* elements become matters of conflict. "A fair day's work" is as much an issue for bargaining, resistance, and struggle as is the "fair day's pay." The old Wobbly[3] demand—"Good Pay or Bum Work!"—expressed one connection. But especially in times (such as the 1910s and 1930s) when self-consciously anticapitalist groups have appeared, these two conflicts merge to challenge the very basis of capitalist production itself.

Conflict in the labor process occurs under definite historical circumstances, or, what is the same, within a specific economic and social context. Most importantly, production is part of the larger process of capital accumulation, that is, the cycle of investment of prior profits, organization of production, sale of produced commodities, realization of profits (or loss), and reinvestment of new profits. This process constitutes the fundamental dynamic of a capitalist economy. But capital accumulation, while it remains the basic theme, is played out with substantial variations, and a whole set of factors—the degree of competition among capitalists, the size of corporations, the

---

[3]A member of the radical Industrial Workers of the World (IWW), a labor organization that was a strong force between 1905 and 1920.

extent of trade union organization, the level of class consciousness among workers, the impact of governmental policies, the speed of technological change, and so on—influence the nature and shape and pace of accumulation. Taken together, these various forces provide both possibilities for and constraints on what can occur within the workplace. What was possible or successful in one era may be impossible or disastrous in another. Conflict at work, then, must be understood as a product of both the strategies or wills of the combatants and definite conditions not wholly within the grasp of either workers or capitalists. As Marx put it,

> People make their own history, but they do not make it just as they please; they do not make it under circumstances chosen by themselves, but under circumstances directly found, given, and transmitted from the past.[4]

Conflict occurs within definite limits imposed by a social and historical context, yet this context rarely determines everything about work organization. After technological constraints, the discipline of the market, and other forces have been taken into account, there remains a certain indeterminacy to the labor process. This space for the working out of workplace conflict is particularly evident within the large corporation, where external constraints have been reduced to a minimum. Here especially, the essential question remains: how shall work be organized?

The labor process becomes an arena of class conflict, and the workplace becomes a contested terrain. Faced with chronic resistance to their effort to compel production, employers over the years have attempted to resolve the matter by reorganizing, indeed revolutionizing, the labor process itself. Their goal remains profits; their strategies aim at establishing structures of control at work. That is, capitalists have attempted to organize production in such a way as to minimize workers' op-

portunities for resistance and even alter workers' perceptions of the desirability of opposition. Work has been organized, then, to contain conflict. In this endeavor employers have sometimes been successful.

THE DIMENSIONS OF CONTROL

How much work gets done every hour or every day emerges as a result of the struggle between workers and capitalists. . . . Each side seeks to tip the balance and influence or determine the outcome with the weapons at its disposal. On one side, the workers use hidden or open resistance to protect themselves against the constant pressure for speed-up; on the other side, capitalists employ a variety of sophisticated or brutal devices for tipping the balance their way. But this is not exactly an equal fight, for employers retain their power to hire and fire, and on this foundation they have developed various methods of control by which to organize, shape, and affect the workers' exertions.

Control in this sense differs from coordination, a term that appears more frequently in popular literature describing what managers do, and it may be useful at the outset to distinguish the two. Coordination is required, of course in all social production, since the product of such production is by definition the result of labor by many persons. Hence, whether a pair of shoes is produced in a Moroccan cobbler's shop, a Chinese commune, or an American factory, it is an inherent technical characteristic of the production process that the persons cutting and tanning the leather must mesh their efforts with those who sew the leather, those who attach the heels, and others. Without such coordination, production would be haphazard, wasteful, and—where products more complex than shoes are involved—probably impossible as well. Hence, coordination of social production is essential.

Coordination may be achieved in a variety of ways, however, and the differences are crucial. Coordination may be achieved by tradition—through long-established ways of doing

4"The Eighteenth Brumaire of Louis Bonaparte," in *The Marx-Engels Reader*, ed. Robert C. Tucker (New York: W. W. Norton, 1972), p. 457.

the work and the passing on of these trade secrets from master to apprentices. Or it may be achieved directly by the producers themselves, as occurs when the members of a cooperative or commune discuss their parts in the production process to ensure that their tasks are harmonized. As the scale of production increases, workers may designate one member (or even choose someone from the outside) to act as a full-time coordinator of their interests, thus establishing a manager. As long as the managerial staff, no matter how large, remains accountable to the producers themselves, we may properly speak of their efforts as "coordination" or "administration."

A different type of coordination characterizes capitalist workplaces, however; in capitalist production, labor power is purchased, and with that purchase—as with the purchase of every commodity in a capitalist economy—goes the right to designate the use (consumption) of the object bought. Hence there is a presumption, indeed a contractual right backed by legal force, for the capitalist, as owner of the purchased labor power, to direct its use. A corollary presumption (again backed by legal force) follows: that the workers whose labor power has been purchased have no right to participate in the conception and planning of production. Coordination occurs in capitalist production as it must inevitably occur in all social production, but it necessarily takes the specific form of top-down coordination, for the exercise of which the top (capitalists) must be able to control the bottom (workers). In analyzing capitalist production, then, it is more appropriate to speak of control than of coordination, although of course, control is a means of coordination.[5]

"Control" is here defined as the ability of capitalists and/or managers to obtain desired work behavior from workers. Such ability exists in greater or lesser degrees, depending upon the relative strength of workers and their bosses. As long as capitalist production continues, control exists to some degree, and the crucial questions are: To what degree? How is control obtained? and How does control lead to or inhibit resistance on a wider scale? At one extreme, capitalists try to avoid strikes, sitdowns, and other militant actions that stop production; but equally important to their success, they attempt to extract, day by day, greater amounts of labor for a given amount of labor power.

In what follows, the *system of control* (in other words, the social relations of production within the firm) are thought of as a way in which three elements are coordinated:

1. Direction, or a mechanism or method by which the employer directs work tasks, specifying what needs to be done, in what order, with what degree of precision or accuracy, and in what period of time.

2. Evaluation, or a procedure whereby the employer supervises and evaluates to correct mistakes or other failures in production, to assess each worker's performance, and to identify individual workers or groups of workers who are not performing work tasks adequately.

3. Discipline, or an apparatus that the employer uses to discipline and reward workers, in order to elicit cooperation and enforce compliance with the capitalist's direction of the labor process.

THE TYPES OF CONTROL

Systems of control in the firm have undergone dramatic changes in response to changes in

---

[5]As this implies, control is thus not a form of coordination unique to capitalism, since it obtains, for example, in slave societies and in socialist societies like the U.S.S.R., where democratic coordination over the labor process has not been established. Coercive coordination is required in all class-based social systems.

Even where workers and capitalists enjoyed precisely the same objective interests in the efficiency or productivity of production—as would be true, for example, where each worker's wage was simply a fixed percentage of the firm's "profits"— coordination would take the form of control. Imagine that the capitalist and workers of a firm disagreed on how best to pursue maximum profits; as long as the capitalist has the final say, rather than being accountable to the workers, management must be able to force the workers to follow the capitalist's program rather than the workers'. As this example illustrates, coordination need not involve coercion, but control does.

the firm's size, operations, and environment and in the workers' success in imposing their own goals at the workplace. The new forms did not emerge as sharp, discrete discontinuities in historical evolution, but neither were they simply points in a smooth and inevitable evolution. Rather, each transformation occurred as a resolution of intensifying conflict and contradiction in the firm's operations. Pressures built up, making the old forms of control untenable. The period of increasing tension was followed by a relatively rapid process of discovery, experimentation, and implementation, in which new systems of control were substituted for the older, more primitive ones. Once instituted, these new relations tend to persist until they no longer effectively contain worker resistance or until further changes occur in the firm's operations.

In the nineteenth century, most businesses were small and were subject to the relatively tight discipline of substantial competition in product markets. The typical firm had few resources and little energy to invest in creating more sophisticated management structures. A single entrepreneur, usually flanked by a small coterie of foremen and managers, ruled the firm. These bosses exercised power personally, intervening in the labor process often to exhort workers, bully and threaten them, reward good performance, hire and fire on the spot, favor loyal workers, and generally act as despots, benevolent or otherwise. They had a direct stake in translating labor power into labor, and they combined both incentives and sanctions in an idiosyncratic and unsystematic mix. There was little structure to the way power was exercised, and workers were often treated arbitrarily. Since workforces were small and the boss was both close and powerful, workers had limited success when they tried to oppose his rule. This system of "simple" control survives today in the small-business sector of the American economy, where it has necessarily been amended by the passage of time and by the borrowings of management practices from the more advanced corporate

sector, but it retains its essential principles and mode of operation. . . .

Near the end of the nineteenth century, the tendencies toward concentration of economic resources undermined simple control; while firms' needs for control increased, the efficacy of simple control declined. The need for coordination appeared to increase not only with the complexity of the product but also with the scale of production. By bringing under one corporate roof what were formerly small independent groups linked through the market, the corporation more than proportionately raised the degree of coordination needed. Production assumed an increasingly social character, requiring greater "social" planning and implying an increased need for control. But as firms began to employ thousands of workers, the distance between capitalists and workers expanded, and the intervening space was filled by growing numbers of foremen, general foremen, supervisors, superintendents, and other minor officials. Whereas petty tyranny had been more or less successful when conducted by entrepreneurs (or foremen close to them), the system did not work well when staffed by hired bosses. The foremen came into increasingly severe conflict with both their bosses and their workers.

The workers themselves resisted speed-up and arbitrary rule more successfully, since they were now concentrated by the very growth of the enterprise. From the Homestead and Pullman strikes to the great 1919–1920 steel strike, workers fought with their bosses over control of the actual process of production. The maturing labor movement and an emergent Socialist Party organized the first serious challenge to capitalist rule. Intensifying conflict in society at large and the specific contradictions of simple control in the workplace combined to produce an acute crisis of control on the shop floor.

The large corporations fashioned the most far-reaching response to this crisis. During the conflict, big employers joined small ones in supporting direct repression of their adversaries. But the large corporations also began to move in systematic ways to reorganize work. They confronted the most serious problems of control, but they also commanded the greatest resources with which to attack the problems. Their size and their substantial market power released them from the tight grip of short-run market discipline and made possible for the first time planning in the service of long-term profits. The initial steps taken by large companies—welfare capitalism, scientific management, and company unions—constituted experiments, trials with serious inherent errors, but useful learning experiences nonetheless. In retrospect, these efforts appear as beginnings in the corporations' larger project of establishing more secure control over the labor process.

Large firms developed methods of organization that are more formalized and more consciously contrived than simple control; they are "structural" forms of control. Two possibilities existed: more formal, consciously contrived controls could be embedded in either the physical structure of the labor process (producing "technical" control) or in its social structure (producing "bureaucratic" control). In time, employers used both, for they found that the new systems made control more institutional and hence less visible to workers, and they also provided a means for capitalists to control the "intermediate layers," those extended lines of supervision and power.

Technical control emerged from employers' experiences in attempting to control the production (or blue-collar) operations of the firm. The assembly line came to be the classic image, but the actual application of technical control was much broader. Machinery itself directed the labor process and set the pace. For a time, employers had the best of two worlds. Inside the firm, technical control turned the tide of conflict in their favor, reducing workers to attendants of prepaced machinery; externally, the system strengthened the employer's hands by expanding the number of potential substitute workers. But as factory workers in the late 1930s struck back with sit-downs, their action exposed the deep dangers to employers in thus linking all workers' labor together in one technical apparatus. The conflict at the workplace propelled labor into its "giant step," the CIO.

These forces have produced today a second type of work organization. Whereas simple control persists in the small firms of the industrial periphery, in large firms, especially those in the mass-production industries, work is subject to technical control. The system is mutually administered by management and (as a junior partner) unions. . . .

There exists a third method for organizing work, and it too appeared in the large firms. This system, bureaucratic control, rests on the principle of embedding control in the social structure or the social relations of the workplace. The defining feature of bureaucratic control is the institutionalization of hierarchical power. "Rule of law"—the firm's law—replaces "rule by supervisor command" in the direction of work, the procedures for evaluating workers' performance, and the exercise of the firm's sanctions and rewards; supervisors and workers alike become subject to the dictates of "company policy." Work becomes highly stratified; each job is given its distinct title and description; and impersonal rules govern promotion. "Stick with the corporation," the worker is told, "and you can ascend up the ladder." The company promises the workers a *career*.

Bureaucratic control originated in employers' attempts to subject nonproduction workers to more strict control, but its success impelled firms to apply the system more broadly than just to the white-collar staff. Especially in the last three decades, bureaucratic control has appeared as the organizing principle in both production and nonproduction jobs in many large firms, and not least of its attractions is that the system has proven especially effective in forestalling unionism. . . .

Continuing conflict in the workplace and employers' attempts to contain it have thus brought the modern American working class under the sway of three quite different systems for organizing and controlling their work: simple control, technical control (with union participation), and bureaucratic control. . . .

The typology of control embodies both the pattern of historical evolution and the array of contemporary methods of organizing work. On the one hand, each form of control corresponds to a definite stage in the development of the representative or most important firms; in this sense structural control succeeded simple control and bureaucratic control succeeded technical control, and the systems of control correspond to or characterize stages of capitalism. On the other hand, capitalist production has developed unevenly, with some sectors pushing far in advance of other sectors, and so each type of control represents an alternate method of organizing work; so long as uneven development produces disparate circumstances, alternate methods will coexist.

4.3   *Alienation and Labor*

Asked if he liked his job, one of John Updike's characters replied, "Hell, it wouldn't be a job if I liked it." But why do most jobs seem so onerous? Is this inevitable in any modern industrial society? Or does it have something to do with the capitalist mode of production? The following two readings seek to answer these questions by investigating further the way in which work is organized and shaped in a capitalist society.

Written by the editors for this book. © 1978, 1986 by RICHARD C. EDWARDS, MICHAEL REICH, and THOMAS E. WEISSKOPF.

The stultifying character of factory work has been a major theme in descriptions of capitalist societies since the rise of industrial capitalism. Adam Smith, considered the founder of modern (bourgeois) economics, wrote in 1776 that "in the progress of the division of labor, the employment of the far greater part of those who live by labor . . . comes to be confined to a few very simple operations. . . . But the understandings of the greater part of men are necessarily formed by their ordinary employments. . . . [A man so employed] generally becomes as stupid and ignorant as it is possible for a human creature to become."[1]

But it is Karl Marx who is rightly associated with the most penetrating descriptions and analyses of the condition of labor under capitalism. In his *Economic and Philosophical Manuscripts of 1844*, Marx introduced the concept of alienation to analyze the situation of workers in a capitalist enterprise.[2] For Marx, alienation does not describe a subjective feeling on the part of workers; rather, it refers to an objective situation in which they find themselves under the capitalist mode of production.

Today we tend to think of alienation as a psychological state of mind involving elements of dissatisfaction with the world and isolation from others. An alienated worker doesn't like his or her job; an alienated student can't get along with his or her teachers; an alienated person is simply "turned off" by the society in which he or she lives. In this way we use the

[1]Adam Smith, *The Wealth of Nations* (New York: Modern Library, 1937), p. 734.

[2]The discussion of Marx's concept of alienation in the following paragraphs is based on the section on "Alienated Labor" in Marx's *Economic and Philosophical Manuscripts*, published in *Karl Marx Early Writings*, trans. and ed. T. B. Bottomore (New York: McGraw-Hill, 1963), pp. 120–134.

term "alienation" in its subjective sense to describe something that people experience and feel. It is important to distinguish clearly between this *subjective* concept of alienation and the *objective* concept which Marx used in his analysis of capitalism. In its objective sense, alienation means powerlessness or lack of control; a person is alienated from something (e.g., a job) if he or she has no control over it. Clearly, an objective situation of alienation can give rise to a subjective feeling of alienation; but it need not necessarily do so.

Marx characterized workers under capitalism as "alienated labor" because their position as a class in the social relations of production is subject to three kinds of objective alienation. First, workers are alienated from the *product* of their work. Because the capitalist owns the means of production and the output of the production process, workers have no control over what is produced and how it is used. Second, workers are alienated from the *process* of work. It is the capitalist (and/or his hired managers) who determine how the process of production takes place and what the worker must do during his or her working hours. Finally, workers are alienated from their "species being"—that is, from their own essence as human beings. Here Marx reasons from the premise that the distinguishing feature of human life is that work is undertaken not just in order to permit physical survival (as in the case of animals); most importantly, work is undertaken as a purposefully creative act that gives meaning to life. Under capitalism, work becomes essentially a means for maintaining the worker's physical existence and it ceases to be in any relevant sense a life-fulfilling activity. Thus workers are alienated from themselves because they have no control over their own humanness—that is, their potential for creative work.

To understand the way in which objective alienation is bound up with the capitalist mode of production, one need only compare the position of a worker in a capitalist enterprise (e.g., a textile mill worker) with that of an independent craftsperson (e.g., a handloom weaver). The mill worker has no influence on what kind of cloth is produced, nor on how it is produced, nor on when it is produced; indeed, he or she may never even see the final product and has no reason to take any interest in it. On the other hand, the weaver makes many decisions about the production of his or her fabric and can take pride in the final product. For the mill worker the only reason to work is to earn a wage on which to live. The weaver must also work for a living, but the weaver's greater degree of control over the work product and process generates opportunities for creativity and fulfillment that give the work a very different and more fundamentally human character.

Although the contrast between textile mill workers and handloom weavers was a very important one in the nineteenth century, during Marx's lifetime, such examples may seem somewhat irrelevant in the late twentieth century. One might well question whether Marx's characterization of alienated labor still applies to contemporary advanced capitalist societies. And one might ask whether there exist alternative, nonalienated forms of labor that are feasible in a modern industrial society.

There is indeed a great deal of job dissatisfaction in the United States today.[3] Alienation among workers has become a frequent subject of newspaper reports, magazine articles, and books. But this refers to alienation in its subjective sense. Does alienation in Marx's objective sense exist too, and is it responsible for the subjective alienation we hear so much about?

We argue that most of the American working class is indeed alienated in the Marxist sense, in spite of all of the technological change that has taken place during more than a century of capital accumulation. We find that it is this objective state of alienation that is responsible for much of the dissatisfaction with work that we observe in the United States. Since the objective alienation of workers is inherent in capitalist social relations of

[3]For a more thorough discussion of this issue, see Report of the Special Task Force to the Secretary of Health, Education and Welfare, *Work in America* (Cambridge, Mass.: MIT Press, 1973), chapter 3.

production, it follows that the subjective alienation of workers can be attributed in large part to our capitalist institutions. As long as work is organized along capitalist lines, dissatisfaction with work is bound to be a continuing problem.

Job dissatisfaction is not only a serious concern in its own right; it often has even more serious consequences. Tedious and unrewarding work threatens both the physical and the mental health of the worker. Alcoholism and drug addiction are not uncommon responses to working conditions in American factories. Even more common is the general state of passivity outside the workplace. The effects of a deadening job carry over into the home and community life of the workers, resulting in a subjective feeling of alienation not only from work but from family, community, and the society at large.

Moreover, the objective situation of alienation at the workplace also has deleterious consequences for other spheres of life. The worker who is denied participation and control over the work situation is unlikely to be able to participate effectively in community or national decision making, even if there are formal opportunities to do so. This is because effective participation in decision making requires certain skills (keeping oneself informed, understanding the issues, presenting one's viewpoint clearly and forcefully) and certain attitudes (a motivation to participate, and the self-confidence to do so) which a worker shut off from decision making at work has little opportunity to develop. In other words, participatory democracy at the workplace appears to be an essential prerequisite for meaningful democracy in community and national affairs.[4]

For all the problems associated with alienated labor, the question remains: Is there any alternative? Many people believe that alienated labor (in both senses) is not merely characteristic of capitalist social relations but is inextricably rooted in the nature of complex technology in a modern industrial society. In this "technologically determinist" view, alienated labor is necessary for the efficient operation of large-scale modern enterprises, and such enterprises are in turn necessary to maintain a high and growing standard of living. The experience of the Soviet Union, where workers appear to be just as alienated as in the United States, is often cited to support the technologically determinist view of alienation.

We believe that alienation is *not* the inevitable product of technological advance. The character of technological change itself has been shaped by capitalists in their own interest; what appears as the inevitably alienating nature of work in a modern enterprise is in fact largely the result of deliberate choice by the dominant capitalist class. This implies that alternative social relations of production might well give rise to different forms of technological change and work organization. In particular, we would expect that a society controlled by the working class in its collective interest would develop nonalienated forms of labor, thereby minimizing alienation in its subjective as well as its objective sense. It is of course unrealistic to imagine a nation of craftspeople in the United States today. But worker control of even large-scale and complex modern enterprise can generate opportunities for pride and fulfillment arising out of participation in a common endeavor whose social purpose is understood and valued by the whole community. Thus, we believe that truly democratic control of the workplace can go a long way to reduce alienation and all of its harmful consequences.

But is this likely to happen in the United States? Even if there are more desirable forms of work organization than the authoritarian and alienating structure imposed by capitalists, what prospects are there for any real change in the current situation? Like so many aspects of our capitalist society, the organization of work is not stable: it gives rise to certain contradictions which are likely to intensify over time. For example, increasing worker consciousness of alienation and dissatisfaction

<hr>

[4]This point is very persuasively developed in Carole Pateman, *Participation and Democratic Theory* (London: Cambridge University Press, 1970).

with work may well lead to reduced motivation and initiative, higher absenteeism, production slowdowns, and even sabotage, all of which threaten the profitability of the enterprise for the capitalist. Such contradictions in turn offer opportunities for significant change, provided that workers can organize effectively to challenge some of the basic elements of capitalist control over the workplace.

One final note: it should be apparent from the discussion that our analysis of the capitalist enterprise applies not only to privately owned firms but also to state-run enterprises insofar as these are organized along authoritarian and hierarchical lines. For some purposes the distinction between private and public ownership is in itself significant—for example, for a discussion of the distribution of income. But for the questions raised here, it is the distinction between authoritarian and democratic forms of work organization that is paramount. Authoritarian enterprises are found in both the private and public sectors of capitalist societies and also in the public sector of many "state socialist" societies such as the Soviet Union. Truly democratic enterprises are much rarer in the contemporary world, but, in certain ways, producers' cooperatives in the United States, the kibbutzim of Israel, and the worker-managed enterprises of Yugoslavia come close to the democratic ideal.

4.4   *Alienation and Capitalism*

Worker alienation is now widely recognized as a serious problem in the United States and, indeed, in all advanced capitalist societies. There remains considerable confusion, however, about what is meant by the term "alienation." And there is much disagreement about its causes.

In this reading Herbert Gintis and Samuel Bowles seek to clarify the concept of alienation and the relationship between capitalism and alienation. Part I (drawn from an article by Gintis) analyzes the meaning of alienation, making the important distinction between its subjective and its objective senses. Part II (drawn from an article by Bowles and Gintis) makes a powerful case that the roots of alienated labor lie in the social relations of capitalist production rather than in the nature of technology itself.

Part I:
The Meaning of Alienation

THE EXPERIENCE OF ALIENATION

As Robert Blauner explains in his book *Alienation and Freedom,*[1] the worker experiences alienation from work in the form of powerlessness, meaninglessness, isolation, and self-estrangement. He or she is *powerless* because bureaucratic organization is ruled from the top, through lines of hierarchical authority treating

[1]Robert Blauner, *Alienation and Freedom* (Chicago: University of Chicago Press, 1964), especially Chapter 1.

the worker as just another piece of machinery, more or less delicate and subject to break-down, to be directed and dominated.

Work seems *meaningless* because it is divided into numberless fragmented tasks, and the worker has some expertise over only one of these tasks; consequently, his contribution to the final product is minimal, impersonal, and standardized. Work also seems meaningless because most workers realize only too well the limited extent to which their activities contribute to perceived social welfare. If he produces steel, his factory pollutes atmosphere and streams. If he makes automobiles, his product congests, smogs, kills, and, finally, after thirty months of "service," falls apart. If he processes cost accounts or his secretary types the corporation's plan to avoid paying taxes, they know their work is unrelated to satisfying anyone's real needs. If he sells insurance, he understands that his success depends only on his relative cunning and talent in duping his customer.

Moreover, the worker is supremely and uniquely *isolated* in work: fragmentation of tasks precludes true solidarity and cooperation; hierarchical authority lines effectively pit workers on different "levels" against one another; and since workers do not come together to determine through their social interaction the important decisions governing production, no true work community develops. Lastly, the powerless, meaningless, and isolated position of the worker leads him to treat work merely as an *instrument*, as a *means* toward the end of material security, rather than an end in itself. But work is so important to a person's self-definition and self-concept, that he then comes to view *himself* as an instrument, as a means, to some ulterior end. Hence develops his *self-es-trangement.*

That a person may be self-estranged—alienated from himself, his essence, and his psyche—has been characterized as the focal point of the industrial worker's self-concept, be he blue-collar or white-collar. As Erich Fromm notes:[2]

[2]Erich Fromm, *The Sane Society* (New York: Rinehart and Winston, Inc., 1955), p. 142.

[A person] does not experience himself as an active agent, as the bearer of human powers. He is alienated from these powers, his aim is to sell himself successfully on the market. His sense of self does not stem from his activity as a loving and thinking individual, but from his socio-economic role. . . . He experiences himself not as a man, with love, fear, convictions, doubts, but as that abstraction, alienated from his real nature, which fulfills a certain function in the social system. His sense of value depends on his success: on whether he can make more of himself than he started out with, whether he is a success. His body, his mind, and his soul are his capital, and his task in life is to invest it favorably, to make a profit of himself. Human qualities like friendliness, courtesy, kindness, are transformed into commodities, into assets of the "personality package" conducive to a higher price on the personality market.

A PROBLEM POSED

That capitalist society is alienating is a central element in the radical critique of capitalism, and the term has even attained general public acknowledgement—bemoaned by politicians everywhere, trotted out as a catch-all explanation of "youth unrest" by television commentators, and generally seen by youth themselves as characterizing their own condition. But exactly what alienation *is*, and the nature of its *causes,* remains shrouded in uncertainty and confusion.

The difficulty surrounding the concept of alienation arises from the fact that it comprises both subjective, psychological elements and objective, social elements. Before the rise of the New Left in the decade of the 1960s, alienation was treated as a purely subjective phenomenon, essentially independent of the structure of society. In the Silent Decades following World War II, alienation was proposed as a part of the "human condition" by noted French philosophers, among whom Sartre, Camus, and Beckett are the most widely read in the U.S. We personally encounter the phenomenon on this subjective level, and we respond most immediately to its manifestations in our own lives, in the Beatles' "Nowhere Man," Nichols' *The Graduate,* and Phillip

Roth's *Portnoy's Complaint*. Yet the sources of alienation inhere in the social system itself. Alienation as a general phenomenon coincides with the rise of capitalism.

We now see the treatment of alienation as an element of human nature as merely symptomatic of the political quiescence of the Silent Decades. Indeed, the very *appearance* of the concept of alienation coincides with the breakdown of feudal society and the rise of capitalism, in the works of Hegel and Marx, and the literary works of Kafka and Dostoevsky.

Yet the growing awareness of the social basis of alienation—an awareness of quite recent vintage—still fails to achieve the proper analytical depth. This is due in part to the particular *form* in which this awareness is couched. Alienation is seen to arise directly from the nature of technology in "modern industrial society" and, hence, to remain independent of any particular set of economic institutions. This view is reinforced through our understanding of the historical development of capitalism's main competitor, state socialism in the Soviet Union and Eastern Europe. So-called "socialist man" seems to differ little from his capitalist counterpart, and so-called "socialist society" seems little better equipped to avoid the problems of Alienated Man and Alienated Woman than its avowed adversary.

This paper will try to show not only that alienation is a social rather than a psychological problem at its root but that it results from the structure of technology only in the most immediate and superficial sense, because the form that technological development takes is itself strongly influenced by the structure of economic institutions and their day-to-day operations. If capitalist and [state] socialist economies experience these same problems, it is due to some essential similarities of their basic economic institutions.

AN ANALYSIS

The root meaning of the verb "to alienate" is "to render alien" or, more concretely, "to separate from" (e.g., "She alienated my husband's affections" means "She separated my husband's affections from me"). We can use this root meaning to motivate a social definition of alienation: when your pocket is picked, you are "alienated" from your wallet; similarly, when the structure of society denies you access to life-giving and personally rewarding activities and relationships, you are alienated from your life. Alienation, on the subjective level, means that elements of personal and social life that should be meaningful and integral, become meaningless, fragmented, out of reach, and—if one has an existentialist bent—absurd. The alienated individual is powerless to control central aspects of his life, just as he cannot "control" the wallet snatched from him.

Alienation appears on many levels. Most of these can be explained in terms of *social roles*. A social role is a "slot" that people fit into, carrying with it characteristic duties and obligations, and defined by what other people expect of the person in that role. These expectations become institutionalized, so the same behavior is expected of any individual who occupies a particular role. For example, take the role of foreman. A foreman, no matter what particular individual happens to occupy the position, is expected to supervise his workers, remain somewhat aloof and above them, and in general be more responsive than are the workers to the company's interests in getting the work done. Butcher, baker, worker, soldier, capitalist, lover, husband, community member—all these are social roles.

The nature of these roles and their availability to the individual are quite as important as the distribution of material goods and power in assessing the value of a social system. Alienation occurs because the roles open to individuals do not satisfy their immediate needs in terms of their interpersonal activities in family, community, and work, and their requirements for healthy personal psychic development. Thus, we center on the role concept to emphasize the inherently *social* nature of alienation. To be alienated is to be separated in concrete and specific ways from "things" important to well-being; however, these "things" are not physical objects or natural resources but are types of collaboration with others, with society, and with nature. These "things" are social roles.

The structure of roles at a point in time, and the way they change and develop over time, depends on criteria and priorities laid down by basic social and economic institutions.... [A]lienation arises when the social criteria determining the structure and development of important social roles are *essentially independent of individual needs*. These conditions are precisely what occur under capitalism: the social roles involving participation in work process and community (and to a lesser extent family life) develop in accordance with market criteria and are essentially independent of individual needs. The result is alienation.

·   ·   ·

ALIENATION OF WORK PROCESS

To illustrate the alienating consequences of capitalist institutions, consider the organization of work activities. An individual's work is of utmost importance for his personal life. Work directly engages nearly half of one's active life and is potentially the single major outlet for initiative, creativity, and craft. Moreover, work roles are basic and formative in individual personality development. But are these considerations reflected in the actual social decisions determining the structure of work roles? For instance, is the factory worker's welfare considered when the capitalist decides to produce automobiles by routine and monotonous assembly line operations? Are the secretary's needs considered when she is reduced to the full-time subservient role of typing, stenography, and stamp licking? The structure of work roles is essentially determined by a set of basic economic institutions that operate on quite different criteria. The market in labor means that the worker sells his services to the capitalist firm and essentially agrees to relinquish total control over his work activities, thus leaving the determination of work roles to those who control capital and technology. Both technology and work roles are essentially determined by the dictates of

profit maximization or output maximization and maintenance of hierarchy.

Control of work activities through alienating institutions has implications on both subjective and objective levels. Subjectively, workers mostly experience their work activities as "alien"—as opposing rather than contributing to their personal well-being and psychic growth. This is understandable in that their own needs were peripheral in the decision process determining the nature of work roles—their work activities have been snatched from them.

Objectively, alienating control leads to predictable consequences. In the early stages of the Industrial Revolution, this control resulted in work activities that were brutal, unhealthy, boring and repetitive, and required long hours. More recently, it has taken the form of bureaucratic organization of production, where individual work roles are so fragmented and formalized that the worker finds his initiative and autonomy totally muffled by and subordinated to a mass of regulations and "operating procedures." Also, hierarchical stratification of workers along lines of status and authority subjugates some workers to the personal control of others, subjects all workers to the control of managers and capitalists, and precludes cooperation and equality as a condition of production. Hence, bureaucratic organization and hierarchical control are the concrete modern manifestations of the worker's alienation from his [or her] work activities.

Part II: The Source of Alienation

MARKETS, TECHNOLOGY, AND ALIENATED WORK

Few readers will question [the alienated character] of work in the corporate capitalist economy. But have we correctly identified capitalism as the source of the problem? If the historical development of the structure and content of jobs is responsive to the wills and needs of workers to the extent feasible, given the technological alternatives, our indictment of capitalism must be tempered; for in this case alienated labor would assume the status of a condition of humankind, an externally imposed technological imperative.

What are the determinants of jobs in U.S. capitalism? The private ownership of the means of production and the operation of the market in labor, or more broadly the social relations of capitalist production, act to place the determination of the organization of production—and hence the content of the job—in the hands of a small group of employers, while compelling most individuals to relinquish disposition over their productive activities to these employers in return for a wage or salary. Moreover, employers determine the content of work-activities, as well as the direction of technological and organizational innovation, according to criteria manifestly tangential if not inimical to the concerns of workers: profitability and the maintenance of the employers' own elevated economic positions. Lastly, the product of labor is not owned by the worker; nor does the worker have a voice in determining what commodities the enterprise will produce.

The *prima facie* case, that the roots of alienated labor lie in the social relations of capitalist production, is thus quite strong. The needs and wishes of workers will be embodied in employers' decisions only to the extent that they further the latter's goals. The social relations of the corporate capitalist enterprise are organized to reflect the interests of capitalists and directors, to whom all other groups are subservient and even pitted against one another. However, the issue is really considerably more complex. For workers can express their needs, not directly through control within the enterprise, but indirectly through their personal discretion as to which jobs they will or will not accept. Indeed, the standard argument in liberal economic theory is an attempt to prove the following assertion. When firms maximize profits, and when labor and all other factors of production are bought and sold on markets where prices and wages are determined by supply and demand, then the

structure of jobs will reflect workers' preferences, subject only to the availability of natural resources and known technologies of production. Thus the sphere of work is integrated, in the sense that workers essentially choose their job structures within the limits imposed by nature and the level of scientific knowledge.

Let us consider the argument in more detail. Suppose that workers are faced with a job structure characterized by repressive and routine jobs subject to hierarchical authority, and they decide they would prefer more satisfying work. How do they express this preference? Clearly by offering their services at a lower wage or salary to an employer who provides the kind of work they desire. Thus some enterprising employer will note that he can obtain cheaper labor than his competitors if he provides these jobs, and will look around for a production technique compatible with them, the (ostensibly lower) efficiency of which is more than counter-balanced by the lower wage bill. If he discovers such a profitable organizational or technical alternative, then the workers will get the jobs they prefer and his competitors will be forced to adopt the same production technique in order to hold their workers. So the story goes.

In this view, if jobs are unrewarding it must be due to either the nature of technology or the preference of workers for higher incomes as opposed to desirable jobs. The desirability of jobs is reflected in the wage at which the worker is willing to accept the job, or what economists call the supply price of labor. Indeed, most of us, in deciding our life's work, make some trade-offs between income and job desirability. The employer does have some incentive to make work attractive, hence lowering his labor costs. But does this mechanism render work responsive to the needs or wills of workers? We believe not.

First, there is ample evidence, to be reviewed shortly, that even within the confines of existing technologies work could be organized so as to be more productive and more satisfying to workers. That these opportunities exist and are resisted by employers points to the unresponsiveness of job structure and content to worker needs. Second, technology itself is not the result of the inexorable and unidimensional advance of knowledge. Rather, it reflects the monopolization of control over new investment and effective control over technical information by capitalists and their representatives. The history of technology thus represents an accumulation of past choices made for the most part by and in the interests of employers. Hence even the limits of present technologies cannot be exempted from analysis. We must ask, "Was the process determining the path of technological change responsive to the needs of workers?" Lastly, there is ample evidence that the choices made by workers facing a trade-off between higher incomes and more participatory workplaces (or other work objectives) are systematically biased by the compulsory forms of socialization—especially schooling—imposed on young people.

We conclude that work is a social phenomenon which under capitalism follows a logic of its own, apart from the wills of the mass of individuals affected by it. Thus alienated labor is a condition of capitalist society. It is neither a psychological condition of workers nor a product of modern "mass-production technology."

That the hierarchical division of labor is not necessarily efficient contradicts many deeply held, but empirically unsubstantiated, opinions. We shall discuss three of these. The first such opinion is that the productivity of capitalist enterprise and its victory over traditional work-forms during the Industrial Revolution demonstrate the unique compatibility of the hierarchical division of labor with advanced technology. The second opinion is that the fragmentation and routinization of jobs leads, in itself, to increased productivity, despite its deleterious effect on worker satisfaction. The third, and most important, is that no other known form of work organization is more productive than the hierarchical division of labor. We believe all three are incorrect.

Rather we believe that the success of the factory system in the early stages of the Indus-

trial Revolution was due primarily to the tapping of cheap labor supplies, the extension of the hours of work, and the forced increase in the pace of work; that job fragmentation is a means of reducing the solidarity and power of workers; and that democratic participation in production tends to increase productivity.

The inability of new technologies to account for the emergence of the capitalist factory system in Great Britain has been documented by Stephen Marglin[3] . . . He argues that the success of the capitalist production unit must be attributed to its efficacy as a means of economic and social control. First, if all workers could perform all tasks, their knowledge of the production process would allow them to band together and go into production for themselves. In the guild system this was prevented by legal restrictions—the guild masters had control over the number of new masters admitted, and all production had to be under the direction of a legal guild-approved master. In "free enterprise" this form of control was interdicted.

Second, even within the capitalist firm, the boss's control depended on the lack of control of each worker. To allow all workers the capacity to deal knowledgeably and powerfully with all parts of the production process both increases their sense of control and autonomy and undercuts the boss's legitimacy as the coordinator of production. Yet it is this legitimacy which maintains his position of financial controller and intermediary between direct producers and consumers. Job enlargement and democratic worker control would soon threaten the political stability of the firm. That this policy of "divide and conquer" through task-fragmentation was central in the minds of bosses is amply illustrated in Marglin's cited essay.

But if early factories used technologies apparently similar to the contemporary worker-controlled operations, why were the former

[3]Stephen Marglin, "What Do Bosses Do? The Origins and Functions of Hierarchy in Capitalist Production," *The Review of Radical Political Economics,* Vol. 6, No. 2 (Summer 1974).

able to undersell and eventually displace their more traditional competitors? To what was the increase in per capita productivity in the early Industrial Revolution due? The answer seems to lie in the system of hierarchical control as a direct means of increasing the employers' power over workers. Having all workers under one roof allowed the capitalist to increase drastically the length of the work week. Instead of making his or her own work-leisure choice, the worker was forced to accept a 12- to 15-hour work day, or have no work at all. Since all workers were paid more or less subsistence wages independent of the length of the work-day, the factory system drastically reduced labor costs. Moreover, the system of direct supervision in the factory allowed the capitalist to increase the pace of work and the exertion of the worker. Lastly, the factory system used pools of pauper, female, and child labor at much lower cost than that of able-bodied men.

As a result, the capitalist was able to pay generally higher weekly wages to the male labor force, while reducing the cost of output and appropriating huge profits. It was their greater capacity to accumulate capital, to reinvest and expand, which tipped the balance in favor of capitalist enterprise. But this was due to increased exertion of labor, not to the technical efficiency of the factory system. This situation forced the independent producers to increase their own work-day to meet their subsistence needs, given the falling prices of their product. In this way these producers maintained their position alongside the factory for over a quarter century.

Eventually, however, the factory system did win out on technical grounds. The reasons are interesting in light of our discussion of technological determinism. First, because only the capitalist producers had the financial resources to invest heavily in new machinery, inventors sought to meet their needs. They thus geared their innovations to types compatible with the social relations of factory production. Second, because of the large number of independent producers, it would have been impossible for them to protect patent rights, whereas

the large size of the capitalist firm provided a stable and conspicuous market for the inventor. Third, most inventors aimed at allying with capitalist partners and going into production for themselves. All these factors lend to the pattern of technical innovation a strong bias toward the hierarchical, fragmented production relations of the capitalist firm.

The tremendous pace of technological change in the nineteenth century was of course a major factor in the success of the capitalist class and in the rapid international expansion of capitalism. And the development of new techniques, as well as the pressure for product standardization and rigid production scheduling, no doubt brought about changes in the social relations of production. Yet, our analysis, which draws heavily on Stephen Marglin's "What Do Bosses Do?" indicates that the division of labor and the power relations of the capitalist enterprise cannot be explained by technological necessity. In a path-breaking study of the development of the U.S. steel industry, Katherine Stone has documented that the social organization of work did not arise from technological necessity at all, but from the needs of management to *control* the process of production.[4] In the period from 1890 to 1910, steel came of age in the United States. Spurred by the merger activities of Andrew Carnegie, U.S. Steel became the world's first billion-dollar corporation, which, by 1901, controlled 80 percent of the U.S. market. This phenomenal growth, which involved large-scale introduction of new techniques and machine processes in production, was securely founded on the hierarchical division of labor. Yet the evidence clearly shows that the new social relations of steel production were *not* technologically determined.

Prior to 1890, steel production was characterized by a great degree of worker control over production. The group of skilled workers contracted with management, receiving a price per ton of steel based on a sliding scale

[4]Katherine Stone, "The Origins of Job Structures in the Steel Industry," *The Review of Radical Political Economics*, Vol. 6, No. 2 (Summer 1974).

which reflected the current market price. The skilled workers then hired other workers ("unskilled") whom they paid out of their pockets, and agreed on a division of receipts among themselves. Because of their knowledge and control of the work process, and through the power of their union (the Amalgamated Association of Iron, Steel and Tin Workers), the skilled workers had veto power over any management-proposed changes in the work process, including technical innovation.

This situation posed a crucial dilemma for the early steel magnates: How could technical innovation be introduced without the benefits accruing to the workers themselves? Clearly only by breaking the power of workers to control the process of production. In 1892, Henry Clay Frick was called on to do the job. Workers were locked out of the Homestead Mill, Pinkerton men were called in to enforce company decisions, and a "non-union shop" was declared. The Amalgamated Steel Workers Union was smashed, hierarchical procedures instituted, innovation proceeded apace, and the future of a high-growth and high-profit steel industry was assured. As David Brody concludes: "In the two decades after 1890, the furnace worker's productivity tripled in exchange for an income rise of one half; the steel worker's output doubled in exchange for an income rise of one fifth. . . . The accomplishment was possible only with a labor force powerless to oppose the decisions of the steel men."[5]

Here we have a clear case of profit rather than efficiency determining the social division of labor. But once centralized control is imposed, it does seem to follow that efficiency dictates fragmented and routinized jobs. Indeed, this is the converse of a general proposition deduced from many laboratory experiments in organizational efficiency. Vroom has summed up the results of these laboratory exercises in his masterful survey of experimental literature in industrial social psychology. The evidence indicates, he writes, that "decentralized structures have an advantage for tasks which are difficult, complex, or unusual, while centralized structures are more effective for those which are simple and routinized."[6] Turning this proposition around, we find that, given that the corporate unit is based on centralized control, the most efficient technologies will be those involving routinized, dull, and repetitive tasks. In a decentralized environment, the reverse would be true. This shows that the common opinion as to the superior productivity of fragmentation, as based on the observed operation of centralized corporate enterprise, entails a false inference from the facts.

Finally, the opinion that there is no known organizational technique superior to hierarchical control, seems also to be controverted by the extensive evidence on the efficiency of worker participation. The results of dozens of studies indicate that when workers are given control over decisions and goal-setting, productivity rises dramatically. The recent HEW study, *Work in America*, records 34 cases of the reorganization of production toward greater worker participation which simultaneously raised productivity and worker satisfaction.[7] Also Blumberg concludes:

> There is scarcely a study in the entire literature which fails to demonstrate that satisfaction in work is enhanced or . . . productivity increases accrue from a genuine increase in workers' decision-making power. Findings of such consistency, I submit, are rare in social research . . . the participative worker is an involved worker, for his job becomes an extension of himself and by his decisions he is creating his work, modifying and regulating it.[8]

[5]David Brody, *The Steel Workers in America: The Non-Union Era* (New York: Harper & Row, 1970).

[6]Victor H. Vroom, "Industrial Social Psychology," in G. Lindsey and E. Aaronsen (eds.), *The Handbook of Social Psychology* (Reading, Mass.: Addison-Wesley, 1969), p. 242.

[7]*Work in America*, Report of a Special Task Force to the Secretary of Health, Education and Welfare (Cambridge, Mass.: M.I.T. Press, 1973).

[8]Paul Blumberg, *Industrial Democracy* (New York: Schocken Books, 1969), p. 123.

But such instances of even moderate worker control are instituted only in marginal areas and in isolated firms fighting for survival. When the crisis is over, there is usually a return to "normal operating procedure." The threat of workers' escalating their demand for control is simply too great, and the usurpation of the prerogatives of hierarchical authority is quickly quashed. Efficiency in the broader sense is subordinated to the needs of bureaucratic control.

The lower productivity of the hierarchical division of labor must be ascribed directly to worker alienation. In a situation where workers lack control over both the process and product of their productive activities, their major preoccupation is to protect themselves from the arbitrary dictates of management. Their concern for the efficiency goals of management is at best perfunctory, and usually these goals are actively opposed as contrary to their interests. Significantly, many unions oppose current work reorganization schemes— even those allowing token worker participation—because workers have little defense against being displaced by productivity increases, and do not stand to share in whatever profit increases result. But this should not be allowed to obscure the fact that workers normally harbor a tremendous "reserve power" of effectiveness and inventiveness, awaiting only the proper conditions of control and integration to be liberated. The burden of proof has shifted markedly to those who contend that hierarchical forms of production are the necessary price of ever-increasing affluence. Work is for the most part "meaningless" and repressive not because of the nature of technology and the division of labor, but because of the nature of the class structure and the social relations of production.

.   .   .

CONCLUSION

To locate the source of alienated labor in the social relations of capitalist production, and to understand the roots of these social relations in the class structure of society, is of fundamental importance. For social relations can be changed, and such changes in the past have been the major historical markers of progress toward civilization.

We propose a goal for the transformation of work, i.e., work as an *integrated process* wherein the dialectic relating our social being to our social becoming is strengthened rather than fragmented through the structure of the production unit. Integrated work means that jobs develop over time in keeping with our needs, to limits imposed by productive technology—a technology which, through democratic control, itself moves toward liberated embodied forms. The various experiments in worker control—however limited their extent—show the viability of this vision.

A thoroughgoing industrial democracy must be a cornerstone of a socialist program in the contemporary capitalist world. Yet control over the immediate work process by producers themselves, essential as it may be in the revolutionizing of society, is certainly no panacea, and may have little meaning if isolated from other fundamental issues. Workers' control, by itself, does not provide answers to questions such as: What will be produced, how much power will individual productive units have in allocating resources, where will production be located, where will people live, what will be the approach to leisure and culture, the role of work and creativity? If our ultimate aim is human liberation, we must tackle much more than the workplace, and our analysis of alienated work must be part of a more general program of socialist transformation.

4.5   *Labor Unions: Context and Crisis*

Although the first workers' organizations in the United States were formed before 1800 (Philadelphia printers conducted a strike in 1786), as late as 1933 fewer than 3 million workers—about 5 percent of the total labor force—were organized into unions.[1] These unions were predominantly structured along craft lines—that is only skilled craftworkers were eligible for membership. Very few semiskilled or unskilled workers, and few blacks or women, belonged to these craft unions.

Before the 1930s, ethnic and racial antagonisms, an open frontier, and above all, organized employer resistance (often violent and repressive and backed by the military and police power of the state) combined in blocking numerous attempts to organize industrywide unions. But during the decade of the 1930s, industrial unionism became a mass movement: 4 million workers, many of them semiskilled or unskilled, were organized into the Congress of Industrial Organization (CIO) between 1934 and 1938 alone. The movement reached a crescendo in the massive sit-down strikes of 1936–1937, when tens of thousands of workers successfully occupied factories, often for weeks, until their unions were recognized as legitimate bargaining agents by the employers. The CIO solidified its success during World War II when it organized an additional 4 million workers into unions. By 1947, union membership had reached 14.8 million, or about 24 percent of the total labor force, and about 34 percent of the nonfarm labor force.

More than 17 million American workers were members of labor unions in 1984. About half of all blue-collar workers are members of unions and 70 percent of all union members are in mining, manufacturing, construction, and transportation. By contrast, a much smaller percentage of service and white-collar workers are unionized. Thus the decline in blue-collar production employment and the rise of white-collar and service occupations have contributed, together with employer resistance, to a decline in the proportion of the nonfarm labor force that is unionized: 34 percent in 1947 versus less than 20 percent in 1984.

The degree of unionization varies considerably by industry, region, sex, and race. Approximately one-quarter of all manufacturing workers and two-fifths of government workers are organized. As for regional differences, union organization tends to be less extensive in the South. Women and blacks are underrepresented in the unions: about 34 percent of union members are women, although they comprise 46 percent of the labor force; similarly, blacks comprise only 14 percent of all union members, although they are one-fifth of the highly organized blue-collar occupations. Recently, unions have become smaller and less powerful in basic industry, and have not grown further among white-collar public employees—clerks, teachers, social workers, and so on. Unions, in short, face a crisis.

What has been the impact of the unions? To what extent have the unions modified traditional employer control over the process of production and the conditions surrounding the workers' sale of their labor-power? Why are they in a state of crisis in the 1980s? Richard Edwards and Michael Podgursky address these questions in the following reading.

Written by RICHARD EDWARDS and MICHAEL PODGURSKY for this book. © 1986 by Richard Edwards and Michael Podgursky.

[1]For data on unionization cited in this and the following paragraphs, see U.S. Department of Labor, Bureau of Labor Statistics Bulletin, *Directory of National Unions and Employee Associations* (Washington, D.C.: U.S. Government Printing Office, 1973) and *Employment and Earnings*, January 1985, Table 5.2, p. 208.

Modern American unionism has its roots in a set of institutional, economic, legal, and political relationships that solidified in the decade following the end of World War II. These relationships are here termed the "labor accord." The labor accord was an implicit, moatly unwritten *modus vivendi* between unions and large employers. Important aspects of this relationship were governed by federal (and state) labor laws, which structured the central element in the labor accord, the process of collective bargaining. The accord constituted the "rules of the game" in industrial relations, so that the contention, bargaining, and conflict that occurred between employers and workers were laid out within thesc rules.

The accord created the conditions necessary for integrating "responsible" unionism into the postwar American political economy. In this sense the accord constituted "corporate liberalism's" program for managing American capitalism, and it came to bc seen, even by corporate leaders, as a positive element in the "modern" corporate industrial system. It established the basis for an industrial partnership of capital and labor, and in this wider sense the accord provided an ideological as well as institutional framework within which the unions operated in the postwar era.

We argue in the next section that the present dilemma of American unions results not just from the decline in union bargaining power or loss of members but also from the erosion or undermining of the labor accord itself. Most importantly, the accord required a certain degree of cooperation—cooperation rooted in the fact that both employers and workers saw the advantages of the accord as outweighing its disadvantages. It is this condition, we argue, which has changed; specifically, management has shown an increasing willingness to abandon the accord—it has instituted a retreat from collective bargaining. What, then, exactly was this labor accord?

ORIGINS OF THE LABOR ACCORD

The labor accord emerged from the period of intense class conflict between roughly 1934

and 1950. During the first half-dozen of these years, workers had successfully established industrial unions in the mass production industries, and the labor movement had achieved legal recognition and protection in federal law. The war years saw a consolidation of this position, during which there were no major organizing breakthroughs but there was a massive increase in membership. During the late 1940's, however, employer and conservative counter-attacks successfully limited or rolled back some of what had been achieved. The Cold War and its domestic legacy left the union movement fragmented and divided, fighting against itself and weekened vis-a-vis its external opponents. Employer and conservative political groups were able to rewrite federal labor law, drastically restricting union activities.

The result of this 15-year development was an accommodation in which employers were forced to accept unions but the unions' power and activities were highly restricted by federal labor law. This relationship was most clearly articulated in large-scale industry, between large corporate employers and the unions. The arrangements were extensively supervised and mediated by federal law and the federal regulatory mechanism, and the state became, as it were, a third party to the accord. For example, the state often intervened to force recalcitrant employers to bargain with recognized unions. Moreover, the development of the accord was heavily shaped by the larger political forces operating in American society, and indeed, both employers and unions turned frequently to the state to achieve ends they could not attain in industrial negotiations.

The legal basis of the accord was the National Labor Relations Act (NLRA) and a patchwork of state and other federal laws. The NLRA covers most non-supervisory private-sector workers, whereas other laws cover many, but by no means all, public employees and a portion of those private-sector workers not covered by the NLRA.

The NLRA, enacted in 1935 and amended several times in the subsequent decades, ostensibly guaranteed workers the right to join or organize unions and bargain collectively with their employers. It also required that employers bargain "in good faith" with these freely-chosen worker associations. In order to protect these rights, it proscribed a variety of employer behaviors; as a result of the 1947 Taft-Hartley amendments, it also included a list of proscribed union behaviors.

The NLRA also established a labor court system—the National Labor Relations Board—to conduct "certification" elections whereby workers choose or reject union representation, and which investigates and prosecutes violations of worker rights under the act by employers or unions. In practice, the vast majority of NLRA cases concern employer violations of the act.

Successful operation of this system was premised on the general acceptance of collective bargaining by management, so federal labor law is *remedial* rather than *punitive* in nature. The NLRB cannot fine or imprison an employer who willfully violates the act, but is limited to providing remedial relief to workers or unions. For example, a worker (illegally) discharged for union activity may receive reinstatement with partial or total back pay. An employer engaging in threats or other illegal activity will be required to "cease and desist" and perhaps be compelled to post a statement to that effect on a bulletin board. The NLRA might therefore be compared to an anti-shop-lifting law which only requires that a shoplifter who is caught return what he has taken—less what he has already consumed. Such a law has force only in a context where the violator is perceived to be an "outlaw" and suffers social reprobation as a result.

In practice, the labor accord covered a portion, only, of the entire labor force. It was limited in two ways. On the one hand, unionized workers represented, at the peak, no more than one-third of postwar non-agricultural wage employment. Even making allowances for those workers who were not union members but who were effectively covered by union provisions—non-union workers in union-organized plants or firms, for example, and

workers in firms seeking to forestall unionism by preemptively granting union-like wages and working conditions—the accord still could be said to incorporate only half or so of the wage-labor force. These workers were mainly employed in the "core" sector of the economy—the arena of large corporations with substantial market power and the regulated industries. Only here were unions regularly able to achieve the relationships outlined below. Unions elsewhere (in the garment industry and retail trade, for instance, and in some service occupations) typically experienced quite different conditions from those established under the accord.

Unions achieved more in the core economy because the employers in the core each manifested some combination of three attributes. First, oligopoly market power (combined with size) raised profit rates, and so unions here confronted employers who could be forced to, in effect, share some of their monopoly rent with their workers.

Second, some corporations in the core had their prices and/or profit rates set administratively through government regulation. Regulation restrained competition among public utility companies, communications firms, airline, trucking, railroad, and bus companies, and broadcasting firms, among others. In other cases (e.g., construction under the Davis-Bacon Act), particular laws shielded a union position. Regulation meant that the cost of union gains in those industries could more likely be passed along to consumers without cutting into profits. Thus, even if regulation did not raise profit rates in each of these industries (in some cases it undoubtedly did), it nevertheless tended to compensate the companies for any union gains. If, as frequently happened, these industries captured the regulators, unions captured some of the benefits of regulation.

Third, some employers were tied to particular locations, thereby strengthening the unions' power. New entering firms no less than existing employers were locationally constrained in coal mining (before the opening of western strip mines), industrial and public works construction, longshoring, and many services (e.g., those provided by airport and railroad workers): and locational constraints implied more limited labor relations alternatives for employers. In order to mine central states coal, for instance, new (or old) employers had to enter the mineworkers' "territory."

The set of relationships and arrangements which developed reflected the compromise on which it was based. Most fundamentally, employers were obliged by law and in practice to recognize and bargain with unions where they existed. Unions became an accepted and legitimate part of the system of industrial relations. Unions, on the other hand, were brought into a collective bargaining arrangement in which they were stripped of their most powerful and disruptive weapons (such as sit-down strikes, secondary boycotts, and the general strike) and confronted with numerous sanctions and incentives for "responsible" behavior. These elements were the basis for "modern collective bargaining."

COLLECTIVE BARGAINING UNDER THE ACCORD

At the center of the accord was the system of collective bargaining. In the United States, collective bargaining centers on the negotiation and administration of collective bargaining agreements covering members of the bargaining unit. Naturally, unions seek to influence the level and structure of wages and benefits. Since social insurance and labor market regulation are less extensive in the United States than in many other industrial nations, the scope of bargaining on these matters is somewhat broader. Since there are no minimum national standards for sick pay, national health insurance, shift differentials, or weekend and holiday pay, unions must secure these benefits through collective bargaining. Similarly unions also seek contractual language concerning dismissal, advance notification of redundancies, layoff procedures, and recall rights, since legislation in these areas is virtually nonexistent. Unions also use the collective bargaining mechanism to secure greater control over the labor process.

Collective bargaining in the United States is very decentralized as compared to most other industrial nations. It is estimated that there are over 150,000 collective bargaining agreements covering the roughly 20 million workers in the United States. Data are available only on contracts covering 1,000 or more workers (6.6 million workers in 1980). Nearly one-fifth of these workers are covered by single plant agreements, and three fifths by single-employer agreements. Within manufacturing the shares are even higher: one-third are in single plant units, and over four-fifths in single employer units.

Even where workers are covered by central agreements, unions will frequently negotiate local supplemental agreements covering shop-floor issues of job control. For example, the United Auto Workers negotiates national "master" agreements with the major auto companies covering wages and benefits and a variety of job rights covering thousands of workers in scores of plants. At the same time local unions negotiate supplemental plant-level agreements covering very specific shop-floor issues of job description, assignment, and job rights.

The typical U.S. collective bargaining agreement is three years in length, and usually contains a "no strike" provision for the term of the contract. Workers who are aggrieved during this period must rely on the grievance-arbitration procedure laid out in the contract to deal with their concerns. Most contracts lay out a multi-step grievance procedure whereby disputes over the contract may be resolved at successive levels of management and union hierarchies. Most contracts also provide for binding arbitration as a final step in this process. The elaborate grievance-arbitration process in private-sector industrial relations operates outside of the formal judicial system, and relies on private arbitration services.

Despite decentralized bargaining, the actual wage determination process has until recently approximated a more centralized system through "pattern bargaining." A complex pattern of custom based "wage contours" existed such that "key settlements" influenced bargaining outcomes in many other workplaces. For example, in many industries characterized by company-by-company bargaining such as autos, earlier settlements set a strong pattern for subsequent contracts. In other industries, joint settlements with major "core" companies defined the proposals unions would take to independents or smaller companies. Similar patterns operated across industries. A loose three-year bargaining cycle was defined by the contemporaneous expiration of major contracts in auto, steel, meatpacking, trucking, chemicals, and several other major industries. Commentators as well as participants regularly acknowledged the pressure exerted by prior settlements.

Under the accord, management rights to "run the business" remained intact except where specifically limited by contract. This meant that in practice management retained many powers, including typically the right to hire whom it pleased, to determine the size of the labor force needed, to choose the technology of production, to decide the location of production, to control all decisions relating to new investment (and disinvestment), and to otherwise take the initiating role in all matters relating to the organization of the labor process.

Employer rights to shop-floor management were in fact limited by union contract, and with respect to certain aspects, these limitations were extensive. The right to dismiss workers, for instance, was limited by procedures or protections requiring "just cause." Layoffs were generally required to occur in reverse order of seniority (within the job class or the enterprise), and call backs from layoffs in order of seniority. Changes in jobs or production methods were often subject to new bargaining to establish appropriate new wage levels, work standards, and so on.

Real wages in accord-organized industries rose regularly, justified by and tied loosely to productivity gains. . . . Rising real wages were not automatic, since wages were established only through bargaining and the collective bargaining framework offered no guarantees as to the size of union wage gains. Moreover,

union contracts set money wages, and, with three-year contracts being the norm, unions (and employers) had to estimate future inflation in order to predict how money wages would be translated into real wages. Inflation between 1950 and 1968 was quite low and stable, making the distinction between money wages and real wages easier to project. By the time inflation began to make this distinction central to contract terms, that is, beginning in the late 1960's, many unions were able to gain cost-of-living adjustments (COLA's) in contracts to reduce or eliminate the gap.

Despite these problems, the productivity dividend often became the "conspicuous bargaining point" around which wage negotiations centered. The Kennedy "wage-price guidelines" raised this connection between wage increases and productivity growth to the level of national policy, and while as a national policy it was not notably successful, the guidelines did express a relationship that had already emerged in practice within the accord. This system resulted in a substantial premium of union wages over non-union wages, and union wages especially in the concentrated industries tended to drift upwards relative to the unorganized sectors of the economy.

Technical change under the labor accord tended to be both rapid and continual. Both employers and unions (in different ways) gained from technical change. Employers enjoyed substantial freedom to introduce technical change and perceived it as one of the best methods (the other being product price increases) for recouping whatever wage concessions they were forced to make during contract bargaining; in this sense, high wages in the accord created a strong incentive for employers to discover ways to raise productivity enough to make such jobs profitable. For workers and unions, the linkage of real wage increases to productivity gains gave them a substantial incentive to accommodate productivity-enhancing technical change.

The workplace came to be governed under the labor accord by a set of rules established by contract and collective-bargaining-derived custom. Grievance procedures, careful definitions of "grievable" issues, seniority protections in job assignments, job bidding rights based at least in part on seniority, written job descriptions, explicit or customary standards for work pace, standardized procedures for disciplining, and other rules tended to limit the arbitrary application of supervisors' power. These governance rules, except in those cases of the most rigid application, tended not to interfere with the management's efforts to organize production so much as they brought order and a sense of legitimacy to the shop floor. Some observers have described this function of unions as providing workers with a "voice" option (in addition to the "exit" option of strikes and turnover) in registering their complaints.

The labor accord helped integrate the top AFL-CIO leadership into a set of political and institutional relationships with the leaders of the Federal Government, large corporations, and elite policy groups (such as the Council on Foreign Relations and the Brookings Institution). Top leaders, George Meany in particular, became regular visitors to the White House. Union efforts to merge were encouraged (which the AFL and CIO did in 1955), reflecting a government desire to have a dominant, "responsible" House of Labor. Union leaders were solicited and heavily supported in government-stimulated efforts to rebuild the European labor movements along American lines, and both Democratic and Republican administrations worked hard to ensure AFL-CIO support for the "bipartisan" (Cold War)) American foreign policy.

The union movement was placed in a legal and administrative context under the accord which, as was to become apparent perhaps only in retrospect, made it extremely difficult to organize non-union workers outside of the existing union sector. The accord represented, as it were, a "cease-fire in place." Although unions had gained legal and substantive recognition where they already existed, and while growth in membership in the *already*-unionized industries would occur, new advances were effectively undercut. The only major exception to this rule was the growth of unionism in the public sector. In the South and Southwest, the dominant political forces were very hostile to unions, and the region constituted for employers a large and inviting non-union enclave inside the borders of the United States. The restrictions on union activities imposed by the Taft Hartley law, and particularly its "right to work" provision which came to have especial impact in the South, made union organizing much more difficult. Union expansion did occur in some sectors: among governmental employees (such as police, firefighters, guards, and social service personnel); in professional occupations (teachers, nurses, professors); and among some clerical and service workers. Nonetheless, the South and Southwest and private-sector industries not already unionized at the beginning of the accord period remained largely non-union.

The accord depended upon the state to provide close regulation and scrutiny to police the "rules of the game." The emphasis in state intervention changed over time and depending upon which party was in power, but in the three decades following 1950 there was an underlying consistency in support of the central processes of collective bargaining. The state also consistently disciplined or constrained the extremes: on the one hand, the government investigated and prosecuted both militant (especially Communist) union leaders and those unions thought to have corrupt connections (e.g., with organized crime); on the other hand, pressure was brought to bear, especially early in the period, on employers who flouted the labor laws. This close state intervention in and regulation of collective bargaining gave the state considerable power in industrial relations: it meant that a decisive turn away from the accord by a new administration could be felt very quickly in the actual practices of collective bargaining.

If these various aspects constituted the principal operational elements of the labor accord, there was another overriding dimension, an ideological framework, which encased them all. It was this: The accord represented, for broad sections of American ruling circles, a program for orderly industrial government and for avoiding class confrontations. "Moderate" (Eisenhower) Republicans as well as mainstream Democrats, and many of the most important corporate leaders, supported reliance on collective bargaining, "responsible" unionism, and the integration of the union movement into the legitimized institutional structure of American society as a means for achieving these goals. In this sense, the labor accord came to represent "corporate liberalism's" program for managing American capitalism. The accord itself came to be seen by employers as not just an unfortunate and undesirable element forced upon American business by workers, but rather as a positive element in the "modern" way of doing business. . . .

Corporate interest in such a vision was stimulated by memories of the militant class struggle of the 1930's. So, too, the continuing success of socialist and communist elements in the European labor movements inspired American business leaders to search for ways of effecting an "American compromise." And the emerging notion of "modern industrial relations" paralleled other business-inspired developments—the corporation as a "corporate citizen," the "soulful" corporation, corporate "social accountability," the notion of corporations as having several constituencies (workers, consumers, local communities, and managers as well as shareholders)—attempted to provide the corporation with a sense of legitimacy and higher purpose than profit maximization alone offered.

In this more ideological sense, the accord was not simply an arrangement to be evaluated by the calculus of short-run profits and losses. Neither was it to be abandoned at the first sign that employers could make more money elsewhere. While it is important not to overemphasize the corporate commitment to the accord, neither should it be overlooked that the accord represented for the business community a long-run strategy in pursuit of

larger and more overreaching goals than the simple short-run pursuit of profits.

THE EROSION OF THE LABOR ACCORD

The labor movement which entered the 1970's was one equipped organizationally, ideologically, and psychologically to succeed within the terms of the labor accord. Collective bargaining strategies, for example, aimed at completing the roster of benefits that could be obtained under existing relations rather then (e.g.) organizing non-union workers, confronting union-threatening technical and market changes, or addressing the dangers to unions in corporate multi-nationalism. The prior two decades had been a time of flattering and highly seductive tri-partitism for union leaders in Washington.

At the same time, however, the mid-1970's brought a variety of institutional, economic, and political changes that dramatically altered—and worsened—the context within which unions operated. Indeed, these changes fundamentally eroded the labor accord: although many individual features remain (e.g., the NLRA as the basic labor law), these changes have in fact mostly destroyed the logic of the old system in which unions had a recognized place in the political economy.

One set of changes derived from the alteration of those particular micro-economic features that underlay the accord. That combination of core employers' market attributes—oligopoly market power, government regulation, and locational immobilities—which had shielded unions and the accord were progressively eroded.

Import penetration, especially into the markets of those industries subject to the labor accord, increased substantially during the 1970's and dramatically undercut market power. As product markets became increasingly exposed to international competition, workers whose wages had previously been sheltered came under increasing wage pressure.

The deregulation movement, begun under President Carter and continued during the Reagan years, exposed many industries to wider market competition. In the transportation and communications industries, de-regulation has led to the proliferation of non-union companies paying significantly less than the union scale wage. In the construction industry, attempts to weaken the Davis Bacon Act, in concert with other developments, have led to a growing market share for large non-union contractors such as Bechtel and Brown and Root.

And technical change, changes in law or its administration, and changing relative energy prices eroded some important locational immobilities for employers. In communications new technologies have weakened the unions' control over critical skills. Previously, skilled union switchmen, for example, played a strategic role in keeping the large electro-magnetic switching devices operating; with the introduction of progressively more sophisticated computerized switching devices, machines which diagnose their own problems, union bargaining power has been considerably reduced. While the overall skill requirements in the industry may not have fallen, due to new skills needed to run the new technology, the union has had difficulty keeping the new jobs in the bargaining unit. In the retail sector, changes in the technology of beef processing—less captivating, perhaps, than the computer chip, but no less revolutionary—have all but eliminated the skills of grocery butchers, and in so doing, greatly weakened the bargaining power of their union, the United Food and Commercial Workers (UFCW). The last decade has seen the rise of large meatpacking plants in the West which now ship pre-processed vacuum-wrapped boxed meat products directly to grocers; these companies have eliminated most of the former work of the grocery butcher.

One result of these micro-economic changes is that increasingly the same company may operate union and non-union facilities, thereby internalizing the competition. In the trucking industry, for instance, many large trucking firms (e.g., Roadway) established or acquired non-union subsidiaries in the wake of deregulation. In manufacturing, the phenomenon of "parallel production" of similar products in both union and non-union plants, often with the former in the "frostbelt" and the latter in the "sunbelt," has become common. These processess have undermined many of the micro-economic conditions upon which the accord was based.

Equally important were the macro-economic forces. Beginning in the 1970's, the American economy, like those of the other advanced capitalist countries, experienced a marked slowdown in growth and deteriorating overall performance. Whereas the American GNP had grown, on average, by 3.7 percent annually between 1941 and 1973, growth slumped to 2.1 percent annually between 1973 and 1983. Inflation was higher, unemployment grew, real wages stagnated, and major industries and industrial regions declined.

Economic stagnation and higher unemployment could have been expected to, and did, weaken the labor movement's bargaining power. The length of the stagnation, as a long-swing downturn rather than just the usual business cycle recession, meant that it had an especially detrimental impact on labor's position. The stagnation intensified the impact of the micro-economic changes to erode the very underpinnings of the accord itself.

The stagnation grew out of the long-term decline in the profit rate between 1966 and 1983. As the profit rate fell, employers were pressed to search out new cost-cutting strategies and began exploring new ways of organizing production and their relations with their workers. . . .

This change in employer attitudes has been accompanied by larger labor market developments which also affect the labor movement's fortunes. On the supply side, U.S. labor force growth has been considerably more rapid than most other industrial nations. From 1970 to 1980, the civilian labor force grew at a compound annual average rate of 2.2%. The Bureau of Labor Statistics projects that this growth rate has declined to 1.8% for 1980–1985 and will decline further to 1.2% for 1985–1990, largely due to the maturation of the "baby boom" generation.

Another source of labor force growth is female labor force participation. The labor force participation of women rose from 43.3% in 1970 to 51.7% in 1980. The Bureau of Labor Statistics projects further increases in female labor force participation in the remainder of the decade, albeit at a slower rate than the 1960's and '70's.

This growing labor force is increasingly college-educated. In 1970, 27.5% of workers in the labor force completed at least one year of college, and 13.6% had completed four or more years. By 1982 these shares rose to 38.0% and 20.0%, respectively, Moreover, since the educational attainment of each successive cohort exceeds that of earlier cohorts, the labor force average will continue to rise over time.

In sum, the labor force which the labor movement seeks to inspire, organize, and represent in the coming decade will be older, more educated, and decidedly more female.

On the demand side, the shift away from manual, blue-collar work to white-collar and service jobs associated with the relative decline in goods-producing industry has been very pronounced in the United States, and it is expected to continue and perhaps accelerate in the coming decade. In 1970, blue-collar jobs accounted for 35.3% of total employment. By 1982 the blue-collar share shrank to 29.7%. In 1970, manufacturing accounted for 27.3% of nonagricultural wage and salary employment; by 1984, it had declined to 20.7%.

There is little doubt that the United States is losing employment in traditional industries, and this has been particularly wrenching for the labor movement, for this is where the bulk of its membership is to be found. In 1980, blue-collar and manufacturing workers comprised 55.2% and 33.7% of union membership.

Finally, it should be noted that labor supply has generally outstripped labor demand, and as a consequence, the average unemployment rate has drifted upward. This has contributed

to a harsher economic environment within which unions must operate and has eroded their relative bargaining power.

Much has been made of the United States employment "miracle": 27.1 million jobs created since 1970 and 6.5 million since 1980. In fact, while employment has grown briskly, the labor force has grown faster; the result is a secular rise in the unemployment rate. If we skip the "mini-recession" of 1980, we find that the unemployment rate at expansion peaks has increased:

Expansion Peak Quarter	Unemployment Rate
1969: III	3.6%
1973: III	4.8%
1979: IV	6.0%

The labor force which makes up this rising noncyclical pool of unemployed is primarily experienced adult workers, and is disproportionately blue-collar.

In short, a more educated and more female labor force is entering occupations and industries with a weaker tradition of collective bargaining. So union fortunes do not look bright either in the old traditionally unionized industries, where employers are increasingly anti-union, or in the newer growth industries, where unions have for the most part been unsuccessful in attracting workers to the union standard.

THE RETREAT FROM COLLECTIVE BARGAINING

In the face of new pressures and new opportunities, American employers have taken an aggressive stance against unions. Where unions exist, they find themselves facing very serious challenges, with traditional bargaining patterns eroding and new opportunities limited. Where unions do not exist, employers have redoubled their efforts to keep them out. The larger structure of industrial relations that we have called the labor accord is being undermined and transformed. This process is visible in the changes occurring in a variety of industries.

Automobiles

The auto industry represented the classic and most explicitly articulated expression of the labor accord. The bargaining structure in the auto industry by the early 1970's had come to be characterized by company-by-company bargaining with virtual compensation parity across companies. This centralized bargaining structure was achieved only after interplant and inter-regional wage gaps were gradually eliminated over a series of many early contracts. In each bargaining round the UAW would target a particular company to set the industry standard. If negotiations with this company reached an impasse, only this company would be struck. The resulting settlement was carried to the other companies in the industry.

Company-wide "master" agreements establish wages and fringe benefits, grievance procedures, job security provisions, and other matters pertaining to wages and working conditions. These master agreements are supplemented with local plant agreements which deal with specific plant-level issues, including work rules. Finally, of course, there is *de facto* day-to-day bargaining between union representatives and management over grievances, on various joint committees, and other personnel matters.

Bargaining settlements in the auto industry set an important pattern, not only for companies organized by the UAW, but also for unions in other industries. The 1948 GM settlement set a particularly important standard in the auto industry, when GM unilaterally established a guaranteed annual improvement factor reflecting economy-wide productivity, and a cost-of-living adjustment provision. This became a *de facto* standard for settlements in many other unionized industries.

The crisis in the U.S. automobile industry in the late 1970's shattered this bargaining structure. Concession bargaining began when American Motors, facing bankruptcy, broke away from the "big four" settlement in 1977. It continued when Volkswagen opened its assembly plant in Pennsylvania in 1979 with wages and benefits considerably below the "big 3" rate. The "big 3" became the "big 2" when Chrysler and the United States Congress sought and obtained concessions from the union in 1979 and 1980. As the recession deepened and more auto plants closed, the UAW was forced to accept poorer contracts even at GM and Ford.

The concessions included a number of substantial and long-term changes as well as temporary give-backs. One example is the introduction of a lower wage rate for new hires. At GM and Ford, new hires begin at 85% of the normal rate, gradually rising to the standard rate over 18 months. In terms of management flexibility, the union agreed to the elimination of a contract provision which had allowed members to refuse overtime. As a consequence, workers at a number of UAW plants may now work long work-weeks while other workers remain on layoff. Undoubtedly management received both contractual and non-contractual concessions on work rules and other personnel matters in local supplemental agreements, but no systematic public information is available at this time on the extent or economic value of such concessions.

The UAW sought to use the concessions as leverage to obtain substantial qualitative gains, such as job security. This effort, though born of weakness, was not entirely unsuccessful. Some agreements were obtained that included temporary moratoria on plant closings, a plan for a "guaranteed income stream" for workers with at least 15 years of seniority, pilot "life-time job security" projects at a few select plants, employee stock ownership plans, profit-sharing plans, and union membership on the Chrysler Board of Directors.

A new round of contracts were negotiated during the fall, 1984. With industry profits at record levels and million-dollar-plus bonuses for company executives, the stage seemed set for substantial union gains and perhaps a return to the old accord arrangements. Nonetheless, the union was unable to obtain major breakthroughs. It chose to make job security its chief priority, and did obtain a job retraining program as well as some plant closing protections. The wage settlement was exceptionally modest, on the scale of 2 percent per year. Although no longer making direct concessions, the union in this round of bargaining continued to suffer from its weakened position.

These various changes have virtually eliminated the old system of pattern bargaining, as the contracts at each company (and increasingly, each plant) have come to be tailored for specific conditions. Moreover, a growing part of the industry—so far limited to "peripheral" operations like auto parts, and motorcycles—has become non-union.

Communications

The communications industry illustrates the combined effects of deregulation and the sweeping implementation of new microelectronics technologies on the labor accord and traditional collective bargaining relationships. Until recently, telecommunications was a regulated industry dominated by the American Telephone and Telegraph Company (ATT), the largest U.S. corporation. The major telecommunications union, the Communications Workers of America (CWA) thrived in this regulated environment. Indeed, the growth of the CWA is a good illustration of the efforts of a union to "take wages out of competition" by consolidating and centralizing the collective bargaining structure.

While the furious winds of competition and technological change swept through the largely non-union computer and data-processing industries during the 1970's, the CWA remained safe and secure behind a regulatory barrier. Regulatory restrictions prevented ATT from entering the computer and data-processing industries and kept non-union high-technology juggernauts such as IBM and Xerox out of telecommunications.

This arrangement ended in 1982, when a divestiture agreement was announced between the Federal Government and ATT; the divest-

iture set in motion not only a major restructuring of the company but also a sweeping deregulation of the telecommunications industry. Under this agreement, the 22 ATT subsidiaries that provided local service have been reorganized into seven independent regional companies; these firms will be free to compete in all facets of data-processing services and equipment. ATT will retain other subsidiaries (Western Electric Company, Long Lines, and Bell Labs), but it will face much greater competition in their respective markets. Conversely, ATT will no longer be prevented from entering expanding new fields of information technology and services.

This transformation presents both a peril and an opportunity for the CWA. The peril is clear. Virtually overnight, the CWA has been thrust from a unionized telephone industry into a non-union information industry. Non-union competition, with the advantage of lower wages and benefits, is placing pressure on unionized workers in many segments of the industry. Moreover, ATT and the seven regional telephone companies are attempting to keep the union out of new subsidiaries and attempting to shift union work to non-union subsidiaries.

On the other hand, the transformation is also an opportunity. Unlike many industrial unions, such as those in autos and steel, which face bleak futures in their industries, the *potential* jurisdiction of the CWA is growing rapidly; and it will continue to grow in the foreseeable future. The challenge for the union is to develop new organizing strategies to reach these information workers.

The union has responded to these changes mainly by stressing job (or income) security. Beginning in 1977, a Supplemental Income Protection Plan was established to provide supplemental pay to workers faced with layoff who qualified for pensions and who chose early retirement or downgrading. CWA won agreements from ATT providing job and benefit security and moving expenses for transferred employees, and preferential rehire for laid-off employees in the reorganization. In addition, the union made progress in establishing: joint labor-management technology committees, which examine and discuss the effect of new technology and work redesign; quality of worklife programs, which focus on job content and other worker concerns; and employer-funded training and career development programs.

Collective bargaining in the telecommunications industry is in a state of flux, and it is too early to discern the new bargaining relationships that will emerge in this rapidly changing industry. Nonetheless, it is clear that many of the old arrangements from the days when ATT was unified and regulated have been washed away.

Coal

The United Mine Workers (UMW) signed its first national agreement with the industry association, the Bituminous Coal Operator's Association (BCOA), in 1950. This agreement ushered in the labor accord in coal mining, based on consolidated national bargaining. The accord lasted from early 1950 until the mid-1960's. The coal companies looked upon the UMW as a stabilizing factor in a highly competitive and unstable industry. During this period, the strike rate fell sharply and collective bargaining proceeded smoothly. Under the accord, employment in the industry fell sharply, due to mechanization and a lagging demand for coal caused by the general substitution of cheap oil for coal.

These patterns began to break up in the late 1960's. Coal production shifted from high-sulphur, high BTU underground coal in the east to low-sulphur, low-BTU, surface coal in the west. More subtly, the ownership structure of the industry shifted away from small independent operators toward concentrated utilities and oil-based energy conglomerates. Many of the new owners, especially the oil companies, brought non-union attitudes with them when they entered the industry. In consequence, coal employers, especially the managements of large energy corporations, have intensified their opposition to the UMW. In this new stage, UMW's share of coal produc-

tion has declined from 74% in the late 1960's to just 44% in the early 1980's.

The UMW has made very little headway in organizing the western surface mines. Moreover, non-union underground mines, many owned by companies operating union mines, are also being opened in previous union strongholds in the east. . . .

In coal mining, the accord relationships have been largely vitiated. Many coal managements no longer want to deal with the UMW and the UMW is in an increasingly weak position to force them to do so. Coal, once an exemplar of the accord, is rapidly becoming an example of its demise.

Transportation

Deregulation has shattered the accord-based bargaining structure of the airline, trucking, and intercity bus industries. In each case, intensified competition produced by deregulation has spilled over to the labor market. Industry-wide pattern bargaining has yielded to company-by-company concession bargaining. Changes in the product market have brought about fundamental structural changes in the collective bargaining process.

The transportation deregulation process began in airlines in 1977, and set off intense rate competition as well as a major restructuring of the industry. This has led to bankruptcies at two major carriers, Braniff and Continental, although both are now operating more limited systems on a non-union basis. In addition, other carriers have established "double-breasted" subsidiaries to compete in highly competitive markets. These new subsidiaries may or may not operate under union contract, but in either case, they operate at compensation rates well below the union scale in the rest of the company.

This restructuring has had drastic consequences for the collective bargaining process. In return for concessions, the unions have sometimes gained substantial new opportunities. The process has gone farthest at Eastern Airlines. Unions at Eastern gained a 25% ownership share of the company's stock through an Employee Stock Ownership Plan in return for temporary wage reductions, work rule concessions, and a "stretch out" for pilots and stewardesses. The concessions have also given the Eastern unions more input into management, since Eastern granted the unions four seats on the 21-member board of directors. Eastern has also agreed to "open the books" to the unions and has given the union consultation rights regarding business plans.

The deregulation of the trucking industry in 1980, which had been under way administratively for several years prior to 1980, has also accelerated the fragmentation and decline of the collective bargaining structure in the industry. The historic victory of the International Brotherhood of Teamsters (IBT) had been the National Master Freight Agreement which permitted the union to organize over-the-road operators and transform a casual, "secondary" labor market into a "primary" one providing regular employment, wages and benefits, job safety, and improved working conditions. Unionized company drivers, having regular schedules, could approximate the work schedule and family life of any other blue-collar worker. While overnight trips might be required, they would be predictable, and the union contract would provide *per diem* costs for meals and lodging.

Regulation and the Master Freight Agreement created uniform rates, wages, and working conditions among the thousands of trucking firms; deregulation has undone this. The unionized company driver has been replaced in much of the over-the-road segment of the industry by non-union company drivers, or frequently, owner-operators who contract their services and equipment to large carriers. Owner-operators must bear the market risk and keep their equipment in continuous operation or risk not making their payments. Commonly, they submit themselves to very long and gruelling hours of work. . . . To a considerable extent, deregulation in the trucking industry has provided the trucking companies with the ultimate flexibility in the form of owner-operators, who stand ready to move freight anywhere at any time at a flat fee.

The IBT may now represent no more than a fifth of over-the-road drivers. No precise figures are available on the number of owner-operators, but they now dominate the over-the-road shipment of agricultural commodities and truck-load general freight in the United States.

In 1982, the inter-city bus industry was also deregulated. Unlike the airline and trucking industries, however, the inter-city bus industry is highly concentrated, dominated by Greyhound and Trailways, both of which are diversified conglomerates. Deregulation allowed these carriers to drop many unprofitable routes from their system. The combination of the recession, increased flexibility to drop routes, and the generally aggressive business mood emboldened Greyhound, the industry wage leader, unilaterally to gut the prior collective bargaining arrangements. After a bitter and sometimes violent strike, the Amalgamated Transit Union accepted a large cut in wages and fringe benefits, increased employee contributions for pensions and medical care, and a two-tiered system in which new employees will earn lower rates; the union made no gains on job security, stock ownership or control over management authority as compensation for these concessions.

The transportation sector, particularly airlines, over-the-road trucking and inter-city busing, has experienced a dramatic erosion of union bargaining strength and substantial disruption of established bargaining patterns.

Retail

Retail trade is an industry that has been largely outside the labor accord. Unions have never had a strong presence in the retail industry; in 1980, the latest year for which comprehensive statistics are available, the unionization rate in retail was just 10.5 percent. Although unions have operated in parts of the industry, they have never achieved long-term relationships like unions operating under the accord.

The one segment of the retail industry in which unions have traditionally maintained a substantial presence is retail grocery. Unionization in grocery retailing grew out of the employment of formerly highly skilled butchers, who had a strong union tradition; the butchers no doubt contributed to the unionization and bargaining leverage of retail clerks as well. This link was strengthened when the retail clerks and butchers and meatcutters unions merged in 1979 to form the United Food and Commercial Workers Union (UFCW). The structure of bargaining in this industry is decentralized, with negotiations between one or more local or regional chains and the UFCW.

The last decade has witnessed a growing level of market concentration in the industry and the expansion of large chains in the non-union fringe of the industry. In many cases, companies own both union and non-union chains. In some cases, union chains have been acquired by anti-union companies which then proceed to eliminate the unions. At the same time technological changes such as scanners at checkout counters and preprocessed beef products have reduced the bargaining leverage of both clerks and butchers, making both groups of workers easier to replace in the event of a strike.

This environment has led union employers to seek significant concessions from the unionized labor force, and several major strikes have resulted. The union presence in the general retail trade industry was never sufficient to permit an accord to develop. In that segment of retail trade where unions have been strongest, namely grocery retailing, the non-union sector is expanding and traditional union relationships have weakened.

Health

Unlike the other industries considered thus far, unionism has made significant gains during the 1970's and early 1980's in the health care industry in the United States, and will likely continue to do so albeit at a slower pace. Is it the case that union losses and erosion of the labor accord in other sectors will be offset by gains in service industries such as health care?

Health care is a rapidly expanding industry, consuming an ever-increasing share of GNP. Between 1950 and 1981, health care expenditures rose from 4.5% to 9.8% of GNP. It is also a very labor-intensive industry, with employment growing by 5.2% annually between 1970 and 1981, and a total employment of 7.5 million in 1981.

We will only consider hospitals, which account for two-thirds of health care employment, and currently represent the major center of collective bargaining activity in the health care industry. As with health care generally, hospital employment has also grown rapidly—3.8% per year between 1970 and 1981. Union advances in hospital organizing during the 1970's were facilitated by changes in the laws covering this industry, and a significant increase in union penetration occurred. In 1967, only 7.7 percent of U.S. hospitals had one or more collective bargaining agreements with their staff; by 1981, this figure had risen to 27.4 percent.

The labor force in the hospital industry has been described as an "hour-glass," with skilled professionals and technicians at the top of the earnings structure, a large group of unskilled and low-wage service and maintenance workers at the bottom, and relatively few in-between. As a result of specialized training and extensive professional certification, the skilled trades are highly segmented. Given this hierarchical and highly segmented labor force, it is not surprising that unions have had different rates of penetration among the work groups. The structure of collective bargaining is segmented as well, with physicians, registered nurses, other professionals, technical employees, service and maintenance personnel, and clerical workers typically in different bargaining units, and, if organized, in different unions.

No one union in the American labor movement has jurisdiction over the hospital industry. Consequently, many unions or employee associations have organized selected groups of hospital workers. Unions seem to have made fewer contractual inroads into management rights in the hospital industry, particularly in the areas of union and job security, at least as compared to unions in other industries. . . .

In sum, the health care industry is expanding rapidly, and a number of unions, some of whom face declining membership in their own jurisdictions, are seeking to organize the health care labor force. Changes in the legal environment during the late 1960's and early 1970's for the first time extended collective bargaining rights to workers in much of this industry. As a result, the unionization rate in health care rose sharply during the 1970's. While unions now have gained a firm foothold in the industry, the available evidence suggests that their bargaining position remains relatively weak and they have not made major inroads into management control over the workplace, at least as compared to unions in other industries. If the experience of unions in other industries serves as a guide, health care unions will continue to make incremental gains in these areas.

Public Employees

While the unionization rate among private-sector workers fell sharply from the mid-1960's to the present, unionization among public sector workers increased sharply, and has helped to sustain and transform the U.S. labor movement. Unionization among public employees was facilitated by a number of changes in the legal environment during this period. As noted above, public employees are not covered by the NLRA. Bargaining rights were extended to Federal employees by several Presidential orders, and a 1978 Congressional revision of the Civil Service Act. Unlike their private-sector peers, however, Federal employees cannot bargain over compensation, nor can they legally strike. In spite of these restrictions, unionization among Federal employees has flourished.

The legal environment for state and local government employees is more complex. There are no Federal requirements or standards governing state and local industrial re-

lations; indeed, such standards would likely be viewed in the courts as an unconstitutional extension of Federal power. Only the states may regulate their public employee industrial relations.

In response to pressure from public employees and the labor movement, states began to pass collective bargaining laws for their employees during the late 1960's and 1970's. As late as 1962, no state had collective bargaining legislation for state employees. By 1980, 13 states had legislation extending bargaining rights to all state and local employees and 23 other states extended these rights to some workers.

The most highly unionized occupational groups among state and local workers are blue-collar workers such as sanitation (44%), highway (44%), policemen (53%) and firefighters (71%), and more recently school teachers (65%). These rates of unionization are high compared to the private sector.

Like Federal workers, state and local employees generally do not have the right to strike. In spite of this fact, strikes by state and local workers were very common during the 1970's, prompted in part by layoffs and wage freezes carried out by state and local governments facing fiscal difficulties. In 1965, there were just 42 strikes among state and local workers involving fewer than 23,000 workers. Ten years later this had risen to 478 strikes involving 318,000 workers. In 1980, there were 538 strikes involving just over 247,000 workers. While the strike rate among private-sector workers fell sharply during the 1970's, militancy among state and local workers has remained high.

Strikes among Federal employees remain rare. The largest strike by Federal employees was that by 156,000 postal workers in 1970. The most recent and significant Federal employee strike occurred in August, 1981, when 12,000 air traffic controllers walked off their jobs. When its order to return to work was met by mass refusal, the newly-inaugurated Reagan administration showed its support for the new employer militancy and signalled a new pattern for national industrial relations by firing all striking controllers. The destruction of the air controller's union (PATCO) was accomplished by an accelerated training program for new controllers; use of military personnel, supervisors, and strike-breakers; an emergency re-regulation of landing rights and entry into key routes; and a notable lack of solidarity on the part of other airline unions or public support for PATCO. The Reagan administration has continued its aggressive industrial relations policy with other Federal employee unions.

LABOR'S CURRENT SITUATION

Are we in a new stage of industrial relations? Certainly union bargaining strength is less now than it was, say, in 1973, at the beginning of the period of long stagnation and higher unemployment. While this is not uniformly true (cf., the health care industry), the overall trend seems unmistakable.

Many unions have, in the past few years, made economic concessions to management. Nowhere is the gravity of these concessions more apparent than in the widespread introduction of "two-tier" wage structures, under which unions agree to allow new hires to enter the enterprise at a lower rate than current union employees. In some cases, as in the auto industry, the division is temporary; by stages, new hires reach the union scale in 18 months. In many others cases, however, the division is permanent. Such systems represent a major retreat from union's traditional commitment to horizontal wage equity and the "standard rate." This segmentation of the union workforce may further weaken unions if the economic separation of old and new employees produces a political separation within the union.

But if it is apparent that the anti-union effects of the complex of forces we have described have sapped union bargaining strength, does the evidence also support a stronger conclusion, namely that the collective bargaining framework, the labor accord itself is being transformed? The industrial relations experience in our panel of industries suggests that it is. A central feature of the old accord was a stable structure of collective bargaining characterized by strong pattern bargaining, or what some have termed "orbits of coercive comparisons." These structures were built up gradually as unions attempted to "take wages out of competition" in their relevant labor market and establish a wage norm for their respective trade or industry.

In most of the industries discussed above, the bargaining structures built up over many years are crumbling and collapsing. Inter-industry bargaining has given way to industry-by-industry crisis bargaining. Industry-wide agreements are yielding to company-by-company bargaining. And in the face of plant closure threats, company-wide agreements have been superseded or supplemented by plant-level concessions. Unions now find themselves negotiating with increasingly centralized corporations at an increasingly decentralized level.

Rising product market competition, deregulation, and technological changes; adverse labor force dynamics; worsening public policy; and the legacy of the long stagnation have thrust the labor movement into a qualitatively new stage. This new period is characterized, among other aspects, by: (a) greater corporate mobility, power, and militance; (b) ineffective labor law and a growing indifference, and in some cases, outright opposition of the government towards organized labor and collective bargaining; and (c) a waning belief in unions as the agents of working class interests. In these hostile circumstances, American unions face a difficult and troubling future.

CHAPTER 5

CLASS CONFLICT AND THE STATE

THIS CHAPTER ANALYZES the relationship between class conflict and the state. For the United States during the period of contemporary capitalism, we investigate both the state's role in class struggle and the impact of class forces on the evolution of government.

Conflict in capitalist society results most fundamentally from antagonism between the interests of the capitalist class and those of the working class.[1] On one side stands the capitalist class, seeking to maintain its position and privileges. To do so, capitalists must ensure the continuation of the chief prerequisite of their existence, capitalist social organization itself: markets, property relations, and capitalist control over the means of production. Capitalists survive as a class only if from generation to generation they can *reproduce* capitalist social relations and hence capitalist society. More immediately, capitalists also have a collective interest in attempting to create conditions favorable to profits and their ability to *accumulate*. Each firm's profits depend to some extent on environmental conditions which it shares with other firms (e.g., the aggregate level of economic activity and the tax rate on profits). Capitalists have a class interest in seeing that conditions are favorable to accumulation. Their most serious concern is the degree of organization and militancy of the working class.

On the other side stand the workers. Within individual firms, workers resist the conditions that produce high profits, since those same conditions typically tend to reduce workers to a more degraded, dependent, and insecure status. Other things being equal, each firm can make higher profits when its own workers earn lower wages and when its workers, afraid of losing their jobs, cannot challenge the power of bosses. The labor movement at large, by effectively challenging work rules and, dur-

---

[1]The class nature of social conflict is quite apparent when workers clash with their employers over conditions at the workplace: the level of wages, the pace of work, job safety, or control over production decisions. Here capitalists directly confront workers. So too class interests are visible when, for example, union organizing is met with restrictive labor legislation or when national economic policy to regulate the level of unemployment or set the tax rate on profits is established. Here as well classes have directly opposing interests.

Class antagonisms are less obvious but equally fundamental to other forms of conflict. Capitalists (as sellers) and workers (as consumers) struggle in the marketplace—and increasingly through government agencies—over the price, safety, and quality of consumer goods and services. In their communities, workers (as residents) resist capitalist efforts to raise rents or to introduce "commercial devel-

opment" (which may erode home property values); they oppose the pollution from neighboring plants and regressive taxation which restricts the quality and character of schooling available to their children. In the realm of electoral politics, groups based in the working class have opposed sending their taxes and sons to protect the foreign investments of U.S. corporations, and they push for improved health care, more jobs, and unemployment benefits. Although not always identified as class battles, these conflicts as well derive fundamentally from class differences.

In some cases conflict may cut across class lines, pitting multiclass interest groups against each other; however, as we argue in this chapter, such conflict tends to be less important than class-rooted conflict.

ing periods of prosperity, by demanding higher wages, tends to undermine the social conditions that produce high profits. Similarly, working-class groups oppose capitalists when capitalists try to increase their profits by reducing the taxes they pay, by cheapening the products they sell, by ignoring the costs of pollution or the dangers from unsafe technology, or by exacerbating racial and other differences among their workers. As workers struggle to defend and improve their living conditions, in all these areas, they are naturally led to oppose capitalist interests.

The struggles of working people to improve their situations are crucial for defending their wages and living standards and for extracting from capitalists important reforms—for example, unemployment compensation and the social security system. During most periods these efforts to defend their interests are carried on through less than classwide groups—through individual unions, consumer groups, minority organizations, environmental groups, veterans' associations, feminist groups, student organizations, tax-reform associations, blue-collar groups, welfare rights groups, and so forth.[2] These groups attempt to combat particular symptoms or manifestations of class oppression.

Workers' struggles do not automatically threaten capitalism itself. While each working-class group poses a threat to some capitalist interests, collectively their very diversity undermines their challenge to the system, by creating the possibility for capitalists to play off some groups against others.

Social conflict, then, though it derives most fundamentally from the class divisions of society, rarely takes the form of an actual confrontation between classes. Such a confrontation inherently involves the possibility of revolution, and "normally" the power of the capitalist class is sufficient to forestall such challenges. But separate struggles may be transformed into class confrontation during periods when the contradictions within capitalism are most intense; that is, when the systemic origins of the various manifestations of class oppression are clearest.

Because of their class origins, challenges to individual capitalists are closely related to challenges to capitalists as a class. Sometimes capitalists respond to these challenges individually. At other times they act more collectively, through such organizations as the National Association of Manufacturers, chambers of commerce, employers' organizations, industry or trade associations, and the major foundations. But in general capitalists have responded collectively to class conflict through the mechanism of the state.[3]

In this chapter we analyze the role of the state in this process of class conflict. First, however, we must consider how the capitalist class is able to dominate the activities of the state.[4]

CAPITALIST RULE OF DEMOCRATIC GOVERNMENT

The organization of the present state grew out of the struggle between capitalists and the feudal aristocracy. As capitalist property relations replaced feudal relations, the feudal bases for the legitimacy of state power (the hereditary rights of nobility and monarchy) were replaced by a capitalist (especially *laissez-faire*) foundation. The state, reflecting the interests of the new dominant class, came to take the form of a separate public sector or government. Still, the form of the state,

---

[2]There are of course many other so-called "interest groups" which represent capitalist rather than working-class interests and attempt to promote particular interests within the capitalist class.

[3]The state is the agent or institution in society which has the legitimate monopoly on the use of violence. That is, the state can pass laws that people either must follow or suffer the consequences of punishment, and the state can call upon police, the military, and others to force people to obey the law. Coercion and even violence to enforce compliance with laws is "legal": a policeman who shoots a bank robber faces no punishment, whereas a bank robber who shoots a policeman does. Power and force are the essential underpinnings of the state.

[4]See Domhoff, Section 5.4, p. 191, and Reich and Edwards, Section 5.5, p. 200.

whether authoritarian or democratic, was not settled.

In the advanced capitalist countries, the state came to be democratic in form, while in the undeveloped capitalist nations the state tends to be authoritarian. Yet in each case the state has acted primarily on behalf of capitalists. Here we investigate the role of the state in the advanced countries, especially the United States, and ask the question: how was it possible for capitalists, who constituted an insignificant minority of the voting public, to get the state to act on their behalf?

The democratic organization of the state inherently creates a potential source of serious challenge to the capitalist class's rule. The extent to which this potential threat can be transformed into an actual challenge is limited, however, by the larger capitalist context in which the democratic state operates.

In three distinct but mutually reinforcing ways this context strengthens the capitalist class's grip on state power. First, the capitalist organization of the economy means that state activities that impede the accumulation process will create economic problems in society. Most importantly, as long as the primary responsibility for organizing production and distribution remains with the capitalist class, the state must carry out policies acceptable to capitalists. If policies are pursued which cause the profitability of new investments to decline substantially, capitalists go "on strike" by refusing to invest any further, thereby precipitating a general economic crisis. In the absence of a major and imminent alternative to capitalism, the state (no matter what party or person has been elected to power) can resolve the crisis only by taking back its anti-capitalist policies. These restrictions on what the state can do derive from the capitalists' domination of the system of production and are independent of their voting strength.[5]

Second, the capitalist class can draw upon its vast financial resources to manipulate the electoral process, and the efforts by capitalists directly to control state policies lead the modern state to be much less democratic in practice than in theory. The American political system incorporates persistent and pervasive antidemocratic practices: capitalist domination of election financing, bureaucratic government decision making, "checks and balances" to reduce government accountability to the people, corporate corruption and bribery of officials, discriminatory administration of justice, unequal access to the media, unequal lobbying efforts, and more. These abuses of democracy in practice greatly enhance the capitalist class's power.

Third, the wider capitalist context within which the state operates provides a powerful ideology supporting capitalist rule. This ideology inhibits challengers to the capitalist class from mounting an attack on the state's commitment to defend private property. The capitalist class, through its control over the media, its influence in school curricula, and its control over other "ideological resources," attempts to prevent anticapitalist or socialist ideas from being accepted by large parts of the population. The capitalist class's ability to perpetuate capitalism through the "consent of the governed" thus depends crucially on the strength of capitalist ideology: the hegemony of this ideology acts to forestall challenges to capitalist property relations.

In large part this ideology is powerful because capitalist interests are served by formal equality in the political system. For example, the Constitution requires that the state, regardless of which groups are "in power" at the moment, enforce contracts and defend private property. Even if its actions are applied equally to all citizens (an ideal frequently violated in practice), the state's defense of property will necessarily perpetuate capitalism— that is, the state will wind up acting on behalf of those with the most property to protect.[6] The state in this sense acts as umpire to en-

[5]See Reich and Edwards, Section 5.5, p. 200.

[6]This is the point of Anatole France's famous remark that "the law in its majesty prohibits both the rich man and the beggar from sleeping under the bridge."

force a set of rules—the laws surrounding property rights—which in principle and to a considerable extent in fact are applied equally to everyone but, nonetheless, systematically benefit capitalists. Just as in the economic sphere where equal exchange among unequally endowed individuals permits capitalists to exploit workers, so in the political sphere, where the law presupposes the rights of private property, "equality before the law" works to the benefit of capitalists.

The state's activity, including its use of force against particular working-class movements or communities, thus achieves widespread legitimacy because, *acting within the context of capitalist property relations*, the state appears to be (and often is) fair-minded and neutral in the antagonistic relationship between classes. The state guarantees legal rights to people in all economic classes; all citizens have equal rights to the protection of their persons and equal freedom to dispose of their property as they choose; in elections and juries, each citizen has one vote. The state thus appears to be "above" class or other divisions, representing instead the "public" or "national" interest.

But if capitalists have used democratic forms to perpetuate their privileges, their commitment to democracy ends at the point where genuine popular rule threatens property relations. As demonstrated by the Palmer Raids of 1919–1920, or the illegal suppression of the Black Panthers, or the decades-long unconstitutional and violent FBI and CIA campaigns against American socialists, or alternatively, the subversion of the democratically elected government of Chile in 1973, capitalists abandon democracy when "national security" or "the free world" or "the free enterprise system"—that is, capitalist property relations—are at stake. In these cases capitalist ideology has failed to prevent serious challenges to capitalists' rule from appearing, and capitalists, like other dominant classes before them, have demonstrated that they were not willing to give up their privileges without a fight.

Because (democratic) governments must operate within a larger capitalist context, and because the class relations of capitalist society

greatly limit what those governments can do, the state is properly referred to as a "capitalist" state, successor to the "feudal" state, despite its democratic form.

THE FUNCTIONS OF THE STATE: REPRODUCTION AND ACCUMULATION

The highest priority of capitalists operating through the state, as Paul Sweezy has noted, is the defense of capitalist property relations. This role of the state in perpetuating capitalism we can identify as its *reproduction function*. In the United States, the government's efforts to maintain the system have taken various forms, depending on circumstances. The most extensive activities have involved legitimation, or fostering capitalist ideology. In part, the state legitimates capitalist rule through "fair-handed" administration of (property-based) laws and through the (largely illusory) appearance of democratic control of government; the state has taken a more direct hand as well in fostering capitalist ideology through schooling, direct propaganda, the media, the sponsorship of research, campaigns to purge "communist" influences from libraries and motion pictures, and so on. But the state's efforts to perpetuate the system have also taken on a variety of forms in addition to legitimation. In particular, the state has violently repressed anticapitalist threats, as in the attacks on strikers during and after World War I and the suppression of the Black Panthers in the late 1960s. The state has also been used by capitalists to grant reforms and concessions to undermine growing dissent, as during the New Deal era of the 1930s and the War on Poverty of the 1960s.

A second important role of the state is its *accumulation function*. Although in general the state does not itself accumulate capital, its activities directly aid private accumulation. State revenues and expenditures have contributed to accumulation. To provide benefits either to particular groups of capitalists or to the class as a whole, the state has granted subsidies (in the form of tax credits, direct payments, or favorable "regulation") to countless industries, paid for costly research programs, supported vocational training and other educational efforts to develop the labor force, and so on. To counteract stagnation, the state has undertaken massive military expenditures and other spending programs which increase aggregate demand. Laws and administrative policies have also aided accumulation. To ensure an adequate labor supply, the state has placed restrictions on welfare, minimum wage, and unemployment compensation to prevent these programs from interfering with the replenishment of the reserve army of the unemployed. To restrain trade union power, the Taft-Hartley Act and other labor laws have outlawed certain union activities and weakened workers vis-à-vis their employers. These state activities have been directly aimed at assisting accumulation.

But capitalist society is not a harmonious world. The capitalist state, attempting to carry out its dual functions, has continuously faced conflict. One historically important source of conflict has resulted from the accumulation needs of one group of capitalists coming into opposition with the class's need to reproduce the system. For example, the Vietnam War directly benefited the capitalists who profited from war spending; these capitalists came into conflict with other capitalists who perceived the antiwar movement as a growing threat to capitalism itself. Similarly, at the turn of the century the profits of the newly formed trusts brought finance capitalists into conflict with other members of the capitalist class who feared both individual ruin and the rising tide of antibusiness opposition.

As conflict emerged among capitalists seeking to shape state policies to serve their class needs, the state developed a certain *relative autonomy* from the influence of individual capitalists. Conflicts within the class have blocked efforts by particular factions of capitalists to dominate governmental policies, and capitalist influence on the state has come to serve the more collective interests of the class. For ex-

ample, for reproduction capitalists have understood that the state must appear to act on behalf of the public interest; for accumulation, some autonomy is needed to resolve conflicts among competing capitalists or groups of capitalists. Capitalist domination of the state must therefore be understood as class domination (based on the constraints imposed on the state by its capitalist context and operating through the whole range of capitalists' associations, interest groups, and political parties) rather than as control by particular individuals.

In attempting to carry out its dual functions the capitalist state has faced a second source of conflict. The working class and other dispossessed groups have from time to time directly opposed the state, creating a class confrontation. Even short of such conflict, however, workers' opposition creates a contradiction between those state activities needed for reproduction and those required for accumulation. In the late 1960s and early 1970s, an era of riots and protest, increasing public services were conceded in order to defuse dissent; these concessions in combination with Vietnam War expenses enlarged the state budget and enhanced the bargaining strength of workers. Intensifying international competition, on the other hand, pushed capitalists to demand lower taxes and cheaper unit labor costs in order to maintain their profit rates. This conflict contributed to creating the economic crisis of the 1970s.[7] The crisis was rendered more severe because previous working-class struggles, particularly those in the 1930s and 1940s in trade unions, political parties, and, at times, openly anti-capitalist organizations, had the effect of restricting the policy alternatives available to the state. For example, during the recessions of the 1970s and 1980s, in part because of the power of organized labor, the disastrously high unemployment which the state had permitted in the 1930s was no longer a viable option for the state. Instead the state was forced to institute haphazard policies of wage and price controls, the extension of government planning, and so on.

[7]See Chapter 10, p. 359.

Thus, not only has the state been a crucial element in class relations, thereby affecting the course of class struggle, but class struggle in turn has shaped and stimulated the evolution of the state. Such conflict is not the only factor influencing the state's development: later in the chapter we argue, for example, that the continuing concentration and centralization of capital have also placed new demands upon the state. Yet even here class conflict has played a part: the government's increased intervention in the economy was due in part to the struggle between corporate capitalists and small business people and in part to the effort by workers to establish industrial unions in response to the rise of giant corporations. Thus, the state itself is subject to a development process, being transformed at the same time that it is used to suppress opposition to the system.

We turn now to a historical sketch of the relation between class conflict and the evolution of government in the United States.

CLASS CONFLICT AND THE EARLY EVOLUTION OF THE AMERICAN STATE

The earliest form of the state in North America was merely an extension of European imperial government. In the English colonies, colonial government grew out of the royal charters and other legal relations emanating from the British state. Local governors and other officials enforced decrees promulgated by the British cabinet or crown. Colonial laws were primarily those received from the British common law or passed by Parliament. And taxes, trade regulations, immigration policies, and the like were primarily designed to foster British trade and economic dominance and to enrich the crown treasury.

The growing economic importance of the colonies tended to create conflicts between British imperial needs and the interests of colonial merchants, manufacturers, planters, and others. For example, trade laws required colonial imports from the European continent

to pass through London—the British entrepôt. Other laws called for all colonial exports to be transported in British ships and for some exports destined for European consumption to be marketed through England. While such laws ensured that British merchants would control colonial commerce, they simultaneously placed a fetter on the colonial economy: they prevented development of an internal market, and merchants desiring to participate in worldwide trade and planters wanting to sell tobacco in non-British markets were excluded from these profits. And in order both to capture the benefits from land speculation and to make Indian allies useful in its imperial rivalry with France, British policy placed restrictions on the settling of western lands; these limits produced resentment among poorer farmers eager to escape the coast and exploit the rich interior farmlands.

Such restrictions led ultimately to the American Revolution, which established the United States as an independent nation. The achievement of independence had the important effect of freeing an incipient American capitalism from the fetters of British imperial policy. It established the necessary conditions for the development of an indigenous American capitalist class, just as the British capitalists' successful struggle against the feudal state led to the expansion of British capitalism.

In part, the independence struggle awakened new and liberating forces within American society. Several of the new state constitutions abandoned British precedent by dropping property qualifications for the franchise and by providing civil rights and personal liberties previously lacking—though these gains were still restricted to white males. A large segment of the richest colonists (the Loyalists) departed, while poorer groups such as farmers and artisans formed political groups and actively engaged in political life. Ideas of social equality and popular rule, best expressed in Tom Paine's writings, gained widespread currency.

But the new state that emerged from this period reflected more the interests of the coalition of dominant classes upon which the society continued to be based: the southern slave-owning planters and northern merchants, landowners, and manufacturers. The new constitution accepted slavery, placed restrictions on who could vote, strictly limited the powers of the federal government, protected property, insulated executive and judicial power from the "passions" of the people, and so forth.[8] Thus, the U.S. Constitution, while a product of more than capitalist interests, was effectively shaped by the property-owning elements of the population.

Between the Revolution and the Civil War, the American state made a long transition from its pre-Revolution colonial status to a more fully capitalist form. During this period the national government was controlled by an alliance of southern planters and northern merchants and industrial capitalists; the representatives of western farming and land interests acted as junior partners. The coalition was based on a common need to defend property, yet the alliance was by no means solid. These groups' antagonistic interests intensified as the nineteenth century proceeded. The inability of any group to dominate the national government meant that no group was willing to grant it broad powers, with the result that it remained relatively weak.

Nonetheless, the state even during this period played a crucial role in establishing the conditions necessary for capitalist production. First, it actively aided the process of primary accumulation. The national government's purchases and extension of territorial rights to the West proved to be the first "gold mine" for land speculators, promoters, and developers. The military campaigns to dispossess Indians of their traditional homelands reproduced in more genocidal fashion the eviction of serfs from manors in Europe. The concentration of assets was more directly aided by subsidies, in the form of cash grants, exclusive franchise

rights, and land grants, for canals, roads, and railroads; by the establishment of a National Bank and other credit institutions to mobilize profits from the southern cotton trade and foreign commerce; and by state governments' bond issues and other efforts to accumulate funds.[9]

Second, the new state also carried out its reproduction function, suppressing challenges to its authority and to property rights in general. George Washington's suppression of the Whiskey Rebellion—a protest by Pennsylvania farmers against new whiskey taxes—was an early example; but state and national governments also dissipated or suppressed other challenges: the New York tenant farmers' refusal to pay rents to landlords, the Massachusetts revolt known as Shays' Rebellion, slaves' resistance to their bondage, artisans' attempts to organize trade unions, and textile workers' strikes for better conditions.

The governing alliance increasingly came apart over two issues: that of tariffs, which were designed by industrialists to protect them from foreign competition in the American markets, but which raised the cotton planters' and western farmers' costs; and the extension of slavery to new areas, demanded by planters to secure their continuing economic and political position. The final break in the alliance came with the Civil War, in which the increasingly powerful northern bourgeoisie asserted its dominance and smashed the southern slavocracy as a contender for power.

---

[8]The legislative branch was partially isolated as well: senators were originally elected by state legislatures rather than directly by voters; appointed judges and selection of the president through the electoral college were similar restraints.

[9]Primary accumulation took a different path in the United States than in Europe, where it simultaneously concentrated assets and "freed" the peasants for wage labor. In the United States the growth of capitalist production continued to be hindered by the deficiency of the wage-labor pool, a problem that was solved only by the massive Irish immigrations of the 1840s and subsequent immigrations. In this area, the state appears to have taken little action, except inadvertently: the construction of canals and roads to the West and the resulting movement of foodstuffs to the East ruined many New England farmers. While in general the farmers did not enter the factories, their financial straits encouraged their daughters to. The famous "Yankee farm girls" constituted the first large labor supply for the textile mills.

The American state emerged from the Civil War firmly in capitalist hands. With the end of Reconstruction in 1877, the radical Republicans were purged from positions of power and white southern property owners were readmitted to the governing alliance. Now, however, they were junior partners, representatives of a "New South" cleared of precapitalist obstacles and open to capitalist penetration. Elsewhere, massive western land grants to railroad promoters hastened the primary accumulation process. Increasingly in the northern industrial areas, state governments and eventually the national government began intervening on the side of employers to suppress militant workers. Most importantly, the state during this period simply allowed the expansion of capitalist production to proceed on its own momentum.

THE CONTEMPORARY AMERICAN STATE

The readings in this chapter investigate the role and activities of government in the United States in this century. During this period the state has continued to be guided by the dual needs of reproduction and accumulation. But the structure of capitalism and the needs of capitalists have changed, and so also have the demands upon and the programs of the state.

The most significant change is the vastly expanded role of the state. In part, new state activities have emerged in direct response to capitalists' demands. Capitalists have increasingly sought to have the state stimulate, regulate, and coordinate the accumulation process as production has become increasingly social in character. Government planning and administration are needed to develop and operate transportation systems, to train the labor force, to regulate the international monetary system, and so forth.

At the same time small capitalists have continued to decline as a class while the working class has grown both numerically and as an organized economic and political power. In part this increased power has meant that the working class has been able to gain more access to the state and to obtain some reforms. Thus in part new activities have been forced upon the state by workers' demands: the social dislocation created by the Great Depression required the state to assume responsibility for the stability of the macroeconomy; the working class's fight for some economic security required the state to undertake social security, welfare, medicare, and other income maintenance programs.

Such new demands upon the state have propelled it and the political system into a position that is central to both the long-term reproduction and the day-to-day functioning of American capitalism. For example, ensuring long-run energy supplies and assessing long-run capital needs have increasingly become subjects for governmental planning; wage bargaining and product pricing for the major industries increasingly involve governmental supervision; the macro trade-offs between inflation and unemployment increasingly become issues of state policy; the access to jobs and seniority rights for minority and female workers increasingly become matters for the courts and public commissions. In all these ways, the accumulation process in contemporary capitalism has become increasingly *politicized*, and as a consequence, class conflict has increasingly tended to take place around state policies and to occur through the institutions of the state. Attempts by conservatives in the 1980s to reduce the role of the state make sense in this historical context.

5.1 *The Capitalist State*

What is the relationship of the state to the capitalist mode of production? What makes the state a capitalist state? Ian Gough provides some introductory answers to these questions in the following reading.

Excerpted from IAN GOUGH, *The Political Economy of the Welfare State* ©1979 (London: Macmillan). Reprinted by permission of Macmillan and Humanities Press International (Atlantic Highlands, New Jersey).

What is the nature of the state in capitalist society? Is it a neutral mechanism for reconciling conflicting interests and for representing the 'common interest' of the nation, as pluralist political theory would have it? Or is it, in the famous phrase of *The Communist Manifesto,* 'but a committee for managing the common affairs of the whole bourgeoisie'? The common element in all Marxist theories of the state, which distinguishes them from all other theories, is the subordination of the state to the particular mode of production and to the dominant class or classes within that mode. In other words, the *economically* dominant class is also the *politically* dominant or *ruling* class. Nevertheless, reality is a good deal more complicated than this bald phrase of Marx and Engels would suggest. In particular there is in Marx's writings, in contrast to those of Engels and Lenin for example, a much richer analysis of just what is specific about the *capitalist* state, which is after all the object of our study here.

The analysis of capitalism developed . . . uncovered two specific features not found in previous modes of production. First, exploitation takes place automatically within the economic system; that is, the extraction of surplus labour does not require the political coercion, open or latent, of feudalism or slavery. The generation of surplus value is secured without conscious control by means of the market. Second, and due to this, the capitalist economy has a momentum or dynamic of its own which is again basically outside the control of any agent or class. Together these indicate that under capitalism the 'economy' becomes separated from politics, the 'private' sphere from the 'public'. The notion of a distinct political sphere is, therefore, peculiar to capitalism. The very individualism of capitalism, the fact that all subjects are formally free and equal to pursue their own ends, requires a separate structure, the state, to represent their 'common interest'. What results are the separate institutions of the modern

state and their apparent automomy from the relations of exploitation. It is this appearance which permits most students of the welfare state to counterpose the rights of citizens or the needs of people, as mediated by the state, to the requirements of the market. This appearance is not entirely false, but it only a partial truth.

What Marx demonstrates in this way is that the very existence of political freedom is a necessary condition for exploitation to take place. The latter is based on the free sale and purchase of labour power as a commodity. For exploitation to take place all that is necessary is that capitalists (who own the means of production) and workers (who do not) should be treated identically before the law as free and equal partners. Any feudal or other ties on the free sale of labour power are anathema to capitalism and must be removed for capitalist relations to be established and reproduce themselves. Paradoxically, the capitalist system demands freedom and equality before the law in order for exploitation to take place. In Marshall's words, the growth of citizenship provides 'the foundations of equality on which the structure of inequality could be built'. Rather, we would say that capitalist exploitation and inequality provided the foundation on which the structure of political 'freedom' and 'equality' can be built.

This also helps us understand the persistence of representative democracy and modern Parliaments within the advanced capitalist world this century, despite intervening periods of fascism and military dictatorship in certain countries. One reason for this is that representative democracy corresponds particularly well to the 'free' and 'equal' treatment of individuals as individuals which is necessary for capitalist exploitation to take place.

In its turn, representative democracy becomes a most powerful ideology (grounded in reality), consisting of a belief by the population that they 'exercise ultimate self-determination' through the state. The reasons for the spread of liberal democracy in the Western World lie beyond its functional congruence with capitalism . . . Nevertheless, modern legislatures are specific to the capitalist mode of production.

Ultimately, however, this requirement of political equality and freedom is a paradox, for ultimately the rule of any class rests on force. This means that a distinct instrument of coercion is also required. Alongside the legislature we find the armed forces, the police force and the judicial systems of modern states. It is true that since all class societies rest on some form of coercion, these 'repressive state apparatuses' are common to all, but only under capitalism do they become separated from the economically dominant classes and centralised in the separate institutions of the state. Lastly, for reasons discussed in subsequent chapters, the executive and administrative branches of the state have grown tremendously in recent years. Their power has increased not only absolutely but also relative to that of the legislature. Parliament is but one part of the ramifying state system of modern times.

To summarise, the capitalist state takes the form of a set of institutions, consisting of the repressive apparatus, the judiciary, the legislature, the executive and the administrative branches, together with local and regional organs of government and increasingly a range of *ad hoc* semi-public bodies. These all have in common their separation and relative autonomy from the economic 'base'—the capitalist economy. But we now appear to have moved a long way from our starting point—that this self-same state acts to secure the political domination of one class by another. By what means does this state apparatus serve the interests of the dominant capitalist class and secure the conditions for the reproduction and accumulation of capital? This is still the subject of considerable debate, . . . and only a

brief answer to this important question can be given here.

The first point to note is that the state requires a degree of autonomy from the economically dominant class(es) in order adequately to represent their interests. As Miliband points out, 'the *common* affairs of the *whole* bourgeoisie'[1] implies that there are different and potentially conflicting elements within this class, and that they have sectional as well as common interests. If the state is to act as more than a sounding board for these various pressures, if it is to act in the long-term political interests of the capitalist class a a whole, then it must clearly be distinct and possess a degree of autonomy from this class. Only in this way can it perform such a reconciling and mediating function. It is not the only institution performing this function—the political parties based on the capitalist class, independent foundations and 'think-tanks' and so forth also play their role—but it is by far the most important institution today.

However, this still leaves open the question why the state *should* act in this way, rather than reflect impartially the interests of all groups in society as pluralist theories of the political process would have it. In answer to this question, Miliband puts forward three distinct explanations. The first concerns the personnel of the state:

> The people who are located in the commanding heights of the state, in the executive, administrative, judicial, repressive and legislative branches, have tended to belong to the same class or classes which have dominated the other strategic heights of the society, notably the economic and the cultural ones.[2]

They therefore share certain common ideological and political positions, values and perspectives. The second answer concerns the power which the capitalist class can wield over the state

---

[1]R. Miliband, *The State in Capitalist Society* (Weidenfeld and Nicolson, 1969).

[2]R. Miliband, *Marxism and Politics* (Oxford University Press, 1977), p. 68

by virtue of its ownership and control of economic resources and of its strength and influence as a pressure group, in a broad meaning of the term.[3]

This focuses on the imbalance of class power in capitalist society. The third explanation is in terms of the 'structural constraints' which its insertion within the capitalist mode of production imposes on the state. Whatever the class background of state personnel, or the pressures exerted on the state from outside, the capitalist economy

> has its own rationality to which any government or state must sooner or later submit, and usually sooner.[4]

These are all important factors, but it may be deduced from the foregoing that in my view the third is the most important. The class background of state personnel can change. The class power of capital can be partially countered by the class power of labour. Yet in a country like Britain, where both these factors are important, there is little indication of any fundamental change in the state, or of the welfare state for that matter.

But the third explanation is relatively empty if the nature of these 'structural constraints' cannot be specified. Here it is crucial to remember that we are dealing not with one all-powerful world state, but with a system of nation states of varying power. The historic origins of this go back to the era of absolutist states within Europe, a product of the long decline of feudalism. But once capitalism became established on a world scale, the sovereign nation state became generalised as the norm. At the same time, as we have seen, capitalism continued, and continues, to develop an ever more integrated world economic system. The 'law of value' or market pressures now operate on a global scale: the rise of multi-national corporations is a reflection rather than a cause of this movement. It follows that any

single nation state cannot entirely ignore the requirements of capital accumulation and reproduction. To do so would invite the flight of capital to other, more promising, centres of accumulation. This is one major reason why the nation state, short of a revolutionary change, will not contravene the long-run imperatives of capital accumulation.

But this requires in turn that the majority of the population accept this domination of capital, and here the ideology of the modern state is all-important. The state is regarded as the respresentative of the common interests of 'a people', precisely because it is premised on the individual interest of capitalist society. Because the general or social will is abstracted from the genuine interests of individuals, the state paradoxically sanctions or legitimises the latter.

> In the name of a universal principle (the obligatory aspect of 'law' as expression of a general or social will) it consecrates private property, or the right of individuals to pursue their own exclusive interests independently of, and sometimes *against*, society itself.[5]

This process in capitalist societies provides a powerful ideology buttressing every operation of the capitalist state. Its relevance to an understanding of the emergence of citizenship and the welfare state is obvious, but unfortunately we cannot pursue this any further here.

So for these reasons the autonomy and independence of the capitalist state, and *ipso facto* of the welfare state, is only apparent. What distinguishes Marxist theory is not the view that a particular class dominates the institution of the state (though this is the normal state of affairs), but that whoever occupies these positions is constrained by the imperatives of the capital accumulation process. But at the same time the separation and relative autonomy of the state permits numerous reforms to be won, and it in no way acts as the passive tool of one class. Within these constraints there is room for manoeuvre, for com-

---

[3]Ibid. p. 71.

[4]Ibid., p. 72.

[5]L. Colletti, in K. Marx, *Early Writings* (Penguin, 1975), p. 37

peting strategies and policies. There is scope for the various organs of the state to initiate policies, to reverse them, to make choices and to make mistakes. So we reject here both the pluralist view of the state, that it is a neutral arbiter between competing groups in society; and the crude economistic view, that it is but an instrument of the dominant class in society. An analysis based on the *relative* autonomy of the capitalist state avoids both these pitfalls and permits what is hopefully a fruitful understanding of the modern welfare state.

5.2   *Soldiers and Strikers: Class Repression as State Policy*

Class conflict takes many forms, but the sharpest struggles have frequently occurred during industrial strikes. Indeed, American history is peppered with massive, often bloody, battles between workers and capitalists: the B&O strike (railroads, 1877), Homestead (steel, 1892), Pullman (rail cars, 1894), Cripple Creek (coal, 1903), Lawrence (textiles, 1912), Ludlow (coal, 1914), U.S. Steel and the Seattle general strike (1919), Gastonia (textiles, 1929), the sit-downs (rubber, auto, and electric industries, 1930s), and GE, GM, and the great postwar strike wave (1946). In the present period farm workers, state and municipal workers, hospital employees, clerical workers, southern textile employees, and others continue this tradition of struggle.

Throughout this history the state has frequently used physical force to suppress capitalists' working-class opponents. In this reading, Vincent Pinto traces the history of police and military intervention in several labor struggles. The instances he describes are illustrative of a much more extensive pattern of government actions on behalf of employers. Often these interventions have merely enforced statutes (or court injunctions) which favored employers' interests, because of capitalists' control over the political system; the postal strike of 1970, for example, was declared illegal under the provisions of the Taft-Hartley Act. In other cases, as at Cripple Creek, official actions were clearly illegal, yet such niceties did not prevent public officials from smashing labor militance. In still other cases (the IWW in the early 1900s and the Black Panthers in the 1960s) legal harassment and false arrests, even though eventually overturned, nonetheless crippled the organizations by tying up their resources and immobilizing their leadership. In all these ways, the state has employed legal, extralegal, and illegal violence to curb working-class resistance.

Excerpted from *Soldiers and Strikers: Counterinsurgency on the Labor Front, 1877–1970* by VINCENT PINTO (1972). Reprinted by permission of United Front Press.

The history of common people in America is one of struggle and insurrection based in the labor movement and extending in time from about the close of the Civil War to World War II. Not all of our grandparents accepted the poverty of their lot meekly. They fought back, at first in thousands and then in millions and left as their legacy the only institution in the country created by the working class: the labor unions.

On the whole, labor unions are now safely tucked away inside the system, another bureaucracy with which the worker must come to terms. By acting as the gatekeepers to every significant blue collar job, union bosses have entrenched themselves as political powers in the land. In exchange for "labor cooperation" they accept social legislation piecemeal from Congress and wage increases from corporations which are taken right back again by war taxes and profits. Now that the government is trying to blame unions for inflation, labor is rediscovering some old antagonisms.

.   .   .

But there was a time when a lot more was expected from unions, when the rank and file and many of its leaders were in a life and death struggle and were of a mind to seize the means for a decent living.

The right of workers to organize was not even recognized by law until 1935. Up until that time the courts could, and frequently did, declare unions "illegal conspiracies" and jail anyone they could get their hands on. The laws and powers of the state were wholly on the side of the owners.

Despite the forces arrayed against them the workers did win victories. The victories came because the workers at times were able to make a greater show of power. It was open warfare, and everyone recognized it as such.

The following recounts briefly some of the most famous and inglorious battles in our nation's history, instances in which uniformed American troops were used to smash strikes or break up labor demonstrations. These examples show us that armies exist for more than just fighting other armies. They also show that Vietnam [was] not a new war, but a type of war which the state and the people who control it have fought before: a war in which an insurgent civilian population is the target and the suppression of the people the only objective.

THE RAILROAD STRIKE OF 1877

It began on the B&O line near Martinsburg, West Virginia, on July 16. The firemen and brakemen quit first. Of all the back-breaking jobs, theirs were the worst. The immediate cause was a pay cut, but another in a long series of pay cuts which workers all over the

country had been suffering in the wake of a depression that began in 1873.

Business was bad so unemployment was high, and resentful people roamed around in gloom. The average weekly wage for up to eighty hours' work on the railroads was $5 to $10, and that was good money. Then the B&O and other major lines gave out the news: anybody making more than a dollar a day would take home 10 percent less from now on. Since labor was getting plentiful it was also getting cheaper, and railroad bosses together decided to adjust to the change in value.

The workers, of course, saw it differently, and they too combined for concerted action. On the morning of the 16th of July a force of 1,200 brakemen and firemen seized the depot at Martinsburg and stopped all freight traffic. That was the spark. With nothing but local leadership, a spontaneous workers' insurrection erupted during the rest of July in 14 of the 38 states. The cities of Baltimore, Pittsburgh and Chicago passed out from under the powers of government, and for a time were governed by tinsmiths and mill hands—until the soldiers came.

When news spread about what the railroaders had done at Martinsburg, miners came down from the hills and black workers off the farms to help out. The mayor tried to head things off by arresting what leaders he could find, but this only focused attention on the town jail. When the workers prepared to storm it, he ordered the prisoners released. Governor Matthews then decided to restore calm with a portion of the West Virginia state militia, but the troops only fraternized and joked with the workers. State power was slipping away as fast as the strike was growing, and the Governor telegraphed the President for federal troops.

In the following few days the strike spread to every major railroad center in the East and Midwest. Led by the railway workers, employees in other industries struck for higher pay, and the unemployed also joined the struggle.

In Baltimore, two regiments of troops were called out for use against strikers outside the city. A crowd of several thousand of the city's workers tried to prevent them from boarding trains, and twelve were killed.

In Pittsburgh, even some businessmen favored the strike. The Pennsylvania Railroad, they felt, had been charging them outrageous freight rates. The sheriff of Pittsburgh lost control of the situation and the local militia was called out, but they, too, went over to the workers' side.

From all over the country, reports were telegraphed to Washington that the state militias were unreliable. President Hayes was kept informed by the Army's Signal Service.

The militia garrison at Philadelphia was called on to remedy the situation in Pittsburgh. When they arrived they found the city in the hands of the workers. The depot had been burned to the ground, and the freight yards were a shambles. Twenty-six workers were killed as the troops were driven into a roundhouse and held captive all night.

At Reading, Pennsylvania, the militia shot down more than a dozen strikers.

The Governor wired the President that Pennsylvania was in a state of "domestic insurrection" which he could not control, and warned that if action were not taken soon the whole country would be in "anarchy and revolution." Certainly the nervous clatter of telegraph keys all around the country made such doom-saying credible; Red flags were decorating the Bowery in New York City; in Kansas City there was a general strike; in St. Louis there were preparations for one. The atmosphere in Philadelphia, Buffalo, Cincinnati, Indianapolis was described as "menacing." From far-off San Francisco came reports that the town was being run by workers. General Phil Sheridan had already been recalled from putting down Sioux Indians and his cavalry was thrown against workers in Chicago. In Indiana, future President Benjamin Harrison was leading the militia personally.

President Rutherford B. Hayes and his Administration have vanished from history almost without a trace. On this occasion, however, he and his cabinet were called upon to make their mark. On Tuesday, July 24, the cabinet met to consider the use of federal troops—the first time ever against strikers. The Secretary of the Navy wanted to send some gunboats to New York "to clear the streets around the Custom House," but the Secretary of the Treasury told him the streets were too crooked in that part of the city.

The Navy stayed home, but the Army was called out. Sheridan was ordered to go to Chicago with his cavalry. On Wednesday federal troops were ordered to open up communication with Pittsburgh. Two-thirds of all United States troops in the Military District of the Atlantic were sent to Pennsylvania alone. Six companies of the 23rd U.S. Infantry arrived at Union Depot in St. Louis after being sidetracked for awhile by strikers at Sedalia, Mo., but their bayonets could not prevent a socialist-led general strike from developing. At Albany, New York, General Carr said he would, regardless of bloodshed, open the blockade on the New York Central; and the next day he did. Eventually, with the overwhelming force of the military, local authorities were able to restore their control. The cost was high in human lives, but the established government, knocked off balance, had reasserted itself. By August all pockets of resistance had been cleared out.

In the wake of the insurrection, authorities had a new appreciation of the worker. They recruited larger numbers for the military, built fortress-like armories in the middle of large cities, and developed a service of secret detectives to spy on the activities of labor unions.

Many men lost their jobs as a result of that summer's strike; the railroads blacklisted anyone who had struck, and others were sent to jail. Whole families migrated to places where chances for a new life seemed better.

During the next two decades the bitter struggles of the workers continued. In 1885, General Sherman, then head of the army, predicted that "there will soon come an armed contest between capital and labor. They will oppose each other not with words and arguments and ballots, but with shot and shell, gunpowder and cannon. The better classes are tired of the insane howlings of the lower strata, and they mean to stop them."

ACTION—REACTION

In the 1930's the labor movement in the United States made spectacular gains, advancing during a depression decade, when labor was cheap and plentiful, and working people felt even more the need to organize to survive. Not since 1910 and before had collective action of the workers been so persistent and widespread.

Though many of the nation's mines and railroads had been organized for years, and though much craft work was done under contract, most industrial production, especially in the giant basic industries of steel, auto, and rubber, was still on the so-called "American Plan," that is, not unionized. This was in part due to the single-minded life-long policy of the bureaucrats within the American Federation of Labor who stubbornly clung to "trade unionism, pure and simple," confining themselves to organizing only the better-paid craft workers. The rest, the unskilled blanket stiffs and mill hands, were ignored.

Many, including Socialists and Communists, within the AFL agitated to include these workers within the ranks of organized labor, enventually forming, in the late 1935, the independent CIO (Committee for Industrial Organization, later called the Congress of Industrial Organizations). One labor historian wrote of this event: "It was as if the entire history of the American labor movement had been only a mere introduction to the great crusade that was the CIO. . . . It was a revolutionary, apocalyptic time. What generations had battled in vain to accomplish was accomplished now in a matter of weeks or days. The impossible was achieved daily. Of a sudden, or so it seemed, labor could not lose."

Strikes, show-downs, sabotage, and mass picketing were daily events as the CIO swept the country like a summer storm. Then a new tactic, the sit-down was used with success by the rubber workers of Akron, Ohio, in January, 1936. But it was not until almost a year later, when national attention was focused on Flint, Michigan, that the sitdown strike became a fine-edged weapon in the hands of the United Automobile Workers. The National Guard was called out in this strike, too, but although there were several pitched battles between strikers and troops, a Governor sympathetic to the workers held the troops in check. After occupying the plants for forty-five days the workers won recognition for their union from General Motors.

It was one of the first big breakthroughs in big industry. The United Electrical, Radio and Machine Workers swept through the General Electric, Westinghouse and Philco plants signing up workers for the CIO. In the summer of 1936 the UE won a hard-fought strike at the RCA plant in Camden, New Jersey. National Guard troops were used in 1938 against the UE employees in the Maytag plant at Newton, Iowa, where a 10 percent wage cut was being resisted.

The CIO grew from 1,000,000 members in 1936 to over 4,000,000 in 1940. The entire labor movement advanced in this period, taking advantage of the policies of Franklin D. Roosevelt, who saw it in the interest of government and business to make some compromises and concessions to labor.

During the Second World War organized labor rallied behind the effort to defeat fascism. It pledged itself to a "no strike" policy and voluntarily abandoned double pay for Sunday and holiday work, even though the war economy soon produced a 29 percent increase in the cost of living. In 1943 Congress limited union wage increases to 15 percent. Some small, short-lived local strikes broke out as a result, and the press treated them with extreme hostility. One large strike did take place, however. The United Mine Workers called a halt to work in April, 1943 under the leadership of John L. Lewis, who felt that Congressional wage controls required the working man to make sacrifices of a type not required of the businessman. The Federal Government seized the mines, and Lewis was forced to bargain a partial victory with the Secretary of the Interior, Harold Ickes.

LABOR'S POST-WAR STRUGGLES

The specter of the military on the labor scene appeared again after 1945, when labor initiated a large number of strikes to regain the purchasing power lost during the war.

In 1946, during a national railroad strike, President Truman seized the affected lines. He went before Congress to ask for emergency power to break strikes in any industry controlled by the government. These powers included a provision to draft strikers into the Army and then put them back to work, and imprisonment of union officers. The rail strike was settled minutes before the President delivered his message, but the House passed the measure anyway. As the strike's effects faded, so did support for the bill, and it was allowed to die.

Repressive labor legislation did pass the Congress, however, in the form of the infamous Taft-Hartley Act of 1947. Although passed by Congress, this act was drawn up by the National Association of Manufacturers. It was business's gun to take back what labor had won in the past 30 years. It's intent was to cripple the growing power of working people and their unions.

Provisions of the Taft-Hartley Act reinstituted injunctions, gave courts the power to fine for alleged violations. It established a sixty day cooling off period in which strikes could not be declared. It outlawed mass picketing . . . denied trade unions the right to contribute to political campaigns. It abolished the closed shop (where all workers had to be in the union). . . . It authorized employer interference in attempts of his employees to organize a union. It prohibited secondary boycotts. It authorized and encouraged the passage of state anti-union, "right to work" laws.

The Taft-Hartley Act gave business another weapon against labor, and several more justifications for the government to intervene directly on the side of business to crush strikes, including military intervention.

·   ·   ·

POSTAL STRIKE—1970

When the postal workers went on strike in 1970 they violated Taft-Hartley, which outlawed strikes by Federal employees.

It was the first postal strike in the history of the United States, and there was an air of insubordination about it; not only was the law against it, but so was the opinion of most of the unions' national leadership. Nevertheless, the first picket line appeared shortly after midnight Tuesday morning, March 17, on the 45th Street side of the Grand Central Post Office in New York City.

The nation's 600,000 postal workers were divided into seven different unions, and Branch 36 of the Letter Carriers, which set up the first picket line, was one of the more militant locals among a group of unions not especially militant. The postal employees had been bargaining with the government since September, 1969, and now came word that the Nixon Administration wanted to postpone a pay raise another half-year, and make it conditional on Congressional approval of a semi-private postal corporation. The starting salary for a carrier was $6,100 a year and after 21 years of service rose to only $8,442. It was no wonder, said the union, that 7 percent of the postal workers in New York City were on welfare.

By Wednesday night it was clear the strike was going to be a big one. Members of the Manhattan and Bronx Postal Union, representing 25,000 clerks and handlers, held a stormy meeting in the Statler Hilton Hotel and demanded that their officials call a sympathy strike with the carriers. Amid shouts of "Strike! Strike! Strike!" union members took over the speaker's platform and forced the local's president to flee through the kitchen.

Most mail in New York City had come to standstill earlier in the day, and the government put an embargo on letters and packages destined for the financial capital. Officials of the Stock Exchange, banks, insurance companies and department stores publicly wrung their hands over what a long strike would mean.

According to the United States Code, each striking worker could be fined up to a thousand dollars or sent to prison up to one year, or both, but it was not clear at this time how hard a line the government was going to take against the strike.

Over Wednesday night and into Thursday other cities began walking out, first in the suburbs of New York, then Akron, Ohio, St. Paul, Minnesota, Buffalo, Philadelphia, New Haven and others. It was a ragged action, not well coordinated or nationally led because the unions' top officers didn't want it. Three hundred local officials were summoned to union headquarters in Washington to attempt to get things back under control. They met privately on Thursday and on Friday negotiated a deal with the government: Union leaders would urge the men to go back to work armed with a promise from the government to take up their grievances "shortly." The rank and file met this with a chorus of boos, and promptly Chicago, Denver, Pittsburgh, Cleveland and every other major city outside the South walked out, too.

Saturday had the air of a crisis about it. Story after story filled the media about what hardship, real and imagined, the strike was causing. In Washington, there were some unusual Saturday comings and goings reported at the Pentagon involving the National Guard commander. When on the same day the President said, "On Monday, I will meet my obligation to see to it that the mails go through," rumors that troops would be used seemed confirmed.

By Sunday it was obvious the national union officials could not get the men back. James Rademacher, national president of the Letter Carriers, asked the Post Office Department to investigate his contention that radical agitators from SDS had infiltrated the union. Though this remark made headlines it did not strike a responsive chord in the rank and file, who continued to blast Rademacher from the steps of the General Post Office in New York City, and within range of TV network microphones.

Monday the strike reached full steam, with 300,000 estimated participants. Then the President went on a national television hookup and struck a law-and-order stance: "What is at issue [he said] is the survival of a government based upon law." A national emergency existed by his own proclamation and, by further proclamation, certain National Guard and Reserve units of all services were mustered for duty in New York. "New York City is where the current illegal stoppages began. It is where the mail has been halted the longest." He might have added that New York was the center of most of the resistance, also.

By nightfall, buses and truck loads of troops began arriving in the city from Fort Dix and McGuire AFB in New Jersey, and other locations. There was some grumbling among the soldiers about strikebreaking, but mostly there was indifference. The biggest concern was over possible violence, because they were unarmed.

"You've heard of the Boston massacre and the My Lai massacre," a 22-year-old soldier told a reporter as he bedded down at Fort Hamilton in Brooklyn, "tomorrow you're going to see the New York mail massacre. It's going to be a farce. I'm a medic. I don't know a thing about the Post Office Department. Nobody knows what they're supposed to do."

The Pentagon called it Operation Graphic Hand. What it came down to for the soldier was to sort each letter on the first three digits of the zip code. There were reports of sabotage, that some soldiers were deliberately tossing letters into the wrong slots, but this was never confirmed. The striking postal employees, many of them ex-servicemen, were not especially hostile to the troops, who were thought of as conscripted labor rather than willing strikebreakers.

But Washington's action did have its designed effect. Ever since the President's announcement morale among the strikers had been slipping fast. Though the workers in New York put up a brave front at first, there was the threat of still more troops and reports that strikers in other cities were returning to the job. Only a small proportion of the total volume of backed-up mail was moving, but every official was acting as if the strike were over.

By Wednesday, the strike everywhere had crumbled, though pockets of resistance continued in New York for the rest of the week. The last troops were withdrawn from the city on Monday, March 30.

Afterword: Corporate Liberalism and the Monopoly Capitalist State

Although officially sanctioned violence suppresses challengers in the short run, as the preceding reading suggested, it is an extreme act which in the longer term may *expose* class relations and *foster* more opposition. Consequently, the more secure and forward-looking segments of the capitalist class have often advocated state programs involving accommodation, reform, and ideological efforts to legitimize the state and capitalist society.

The Progressive Era—those critical opening decades of this century when the economy moved from its competitive to its monopolistic phase—was one of the periods during which such policies were most vigorously promoted. In The Corporate Ideal and the Liberal State (Boston: Beacon Press, 1968) James Weinstein argues that although the reforms of this period were originally inspired by "those at or near the bottom of the American social structure," the actual policies instituted were shaped by capitalists associated with the large corporations. The aim of these capitalists, in addition to deflecting dissent, was to reshape the state so that it could more appropriately respond to the new needs of the emerging monopoly sector. It is revealing that this campaign was carried forward by the agents of monopoly capital, sometimes even against the interests and over the protests of smaller capitalists, for it was during this period that the corporate capitalists achieved a dominant position within the capitalist class.

Just as the rise of competitive capitalism produced a laissez-faire ideology, so the evolution to monopoly capitalism resulted in a more interventionist state. The sources and rationale for this change have been obscured, as Weinstein notes, by a historical confusion about the meaning of the term "liberalism." In both periods, the rising group has advocated its reforms under the "liberal" banner and has been opposed by the "conservative" defenders of the status quo. Both early capitalists proclaiming laissez faire against precapitalist restrictions and, in turn, corporate capitalists advocating an expanded state against laissez-faire proscriptions did so as "liberals." The current distinction between "conservatives" and "liberals" continues to reflect in part the dichotomy between the relatively more parochial and backward-looking capitalist elements based in the competitive sector and the more economically secure, "progressive," and forward-looking capitalists in the corporate sector.

5.3   *The Expanding Role of the State*

The transition to monopoly capitalism produced a vastly greater role for government than under competitive capitalism. As James O'Connor argues in the next reading, this increasing role of the state resulted in part from the increasingly social character of production.

The state's new and more extensive activities serve the capitalist needs of reproduction and accumulation within the changed economic and social context. As O'Connor notes, larger state expenditures for military forces, welfare, social security, pollution control, and so on are required to stabilize the capitalist social order, both at home and abroad. While some of these costs of reproducing capitalist society may also contribute to accumulation, others constitute a drag on it. The state budget also expands to finance programs aimed directly at fostering accumulation: highway construction, basic research to develop new technologies, job training, subsidies to maintain essential rail service, and so forth. The result is a growing public sector, both at the federal and at the state and local levels.

Excerpted from "The Fiscal Crisis of the State" by JAMES O'CONNOR. From *Socialist Revolution*, nos. 1 and 2 January/February and March/April 1970). Reprinted by permission of *Socialist Revolution*.

In general, the state budget continuously expands owing to the intensification of economic integration. Social production has advanced so rapidly and along so many fronts that it has pressed hard upon and finally spilled over the boundaries of immediate private property relations. [The result is] a higher and more general form of social integration rendered necessary by the advanced character of social production.

. . .

The first major category of [state] expenditures consists of facilities which are valuable to a specific industry, or group of related industries. These are projects which are useful to specific interests and whose financial needs are so large that they exceed the resources of the interests affected. They also consist of projects in which the financial outcome is subject to so much uncertainty that they exceed the risk-taking propensities of the interests involved. Finally, these are projects which realize external economies and economies of large-scale production for the particular industries.

. . .

[One] important state investment serving the interests of specific industries [is] highway expenditures.[1] Domestic economic growth since World War II has been led by automobile production and suburban residential construction, which requires an enormous network of complementary highways, roads, and ancillary facilities. Rejecting public transportation, on the one hand, and toll highways, on the other, the state has "socialized intercity highway systems paid for by the taxpayer—not without great encouragement from the rubber, petroleum, and auto industries.[2]

. . .

[1]Weapon expenditures fall partly into this category, but since their ultimate determinant lies elsewhere, discussion of military spending is postponed until later.

[2]Payntz Taylor, *Outlook for the Railroads*, New York, 1960, p. 91.

II

The second major determinant of state expenditures stems from the immediate economic interests of corporate capital as a whole. The budgetary expression of these interests takes many forms—economic infrastructure investments, expenditures on education, general business subsidies, credit guarantees and insurance, social consumption, and so on. In the United States, most of these forms appeared or developed fully only in the twentieth century, although in Europe [these governmental responsibilities] emerged in an earlier period—in France, during the First Empire, generalized state promotion buoyed the private economy; in Germany, state economic policy received great impetus from political unification and war; in Italy, laissez-faire principles did not prevent the state from actively financing and promoting accumulation in the major spheres of heavy industry; and everywhere liberal notions of small, balanced budgets and indirect taxation came face to face with the fiscal realities of wartime economies.

In the United States, the budget remained small throughout the nineteenth century; transportation investments were chiefly private, and natural resource, convervation, public health, education and related outlays were insignificant. The state served the economic needs of capital as a whole mainly in non-fiscal ways—land tenure, monetary, immigration, tariff, and patent policies all "represented and strengthened the particular legal framework within which private business was organized."[3] State subsidies to capital as a whole were confined to the State government and local levels and were largely the product of mercantile, rather than industrial capital, impulses.[4]

[3]Henry W. Broude, "The Role of the State in American Economic Development, 1820–1890," in Harry N. Scheiber, Ed., *United States Economic History: Selected Readings,* New York, 1964.

[4]Louis Hartz, *Economic Policy and Democratic Thought: Pennsylvania, 1776–1860,* Cambridge, Mass., 1948, pp. 290–91.

In the twentieth century, however, corporate capital . . . rooted in the development of the productive forces and the concentration and centralization of capital [has produced new needs.] More specifically, the rapid advance of technology has increased the pace of general economic change, the risk of capital investments, and the amount of uncontrollable overhead costs. Further, capital equipment is subject to more rapid obsolescence, and there exists a longer lead time before the typical investment is in full operation and thus is able to pay for itself. The development of the production relations has also compelled corporate capital to employ state power in its economic interests as a whole, and socialize production costs. . . .

The most expensive economic needs of corporate capital as a whole are the costs of research, development of new products, new production processes, and so on, and, above all, the costs of training and retraining the labor force, in particular, technical, administrative, and non-manual workers. Preliminary to an investigation of the process of the socialization of these costs, a brief review of the relationships between technology, on the one hand, and the production relations, on the other, is required.

The forces of production include available land, constant capital, labor skills, methods of work organization, and last but not least, technology, which is a part of, but not totally identified with, the social productive forces. The advance of technology, the uses of technology, and its distribution between the various branches of the economy are all determined in the last analysis by the relations of production. The transformation from a labor-using to a labor-saving technology in mid-nineteenth century Europe was ultimately caused by the disappearance of opportunities for industrial capitalists to recruit labor "extensively" from the artisan and peasant classes at the given wage rate. During the last half of the nineteenth century, the established industrial proletariat faced less competition, their organizations were strengthened, and they were better able to win wage advances. Thus, it was the class struggle that compelled capital to introduce labor-saving innovations.

Despite the rapid advance of technology during the first half of the twentieth century, until World War II the industrial corporations trained the largest part of their labor force, excluding basic skills such as literacy. In the context of the further technological possibilities latent in the scientific discoveries of the nineteenth and twentieth centuries, this was a profoundly irrational mode of social organization.

The reason is that knowledge, unlike other forms of capital, cannot be monopolized by one or a few industrial-finance interests. Capital-as-knowledge resides in the skills and abilities of the working class itself. In the context of a free labor market—that is, in the absence of a feudal-like industrial state which prohibits labor mobility, a flat impossibility in the capitalist mode of production—no one industrial-finance interest can afford to train its own labor force or channel profits into the requisite amount of research and development. The reason is that, apart from the patent system, there is absolutely no guarantee that their "investments" will not seek employment in other corporations or industries. The cost of losing trained manpower is especially high in those industries which employ technical workers with skills which are specific to a particular industrial process.

World War II provided the opportunity to rationalize the entire organization of technology in the United States. As Dobb writes, "a modern war is of such a kind as to require all-out mobilization of economic resources, rapidly executed decisions about transfer of labor and productive equipment, and the growth of war industry, which ordinary market-mechanisms would be powerless to achieve. Consequently, it occasions a considerable growth of state[-directed] capitalism. . . ."[5] The intervention of the state through government grants to finance research programs, develop new technical processes, and construct new facilities and the forced mobilization of resources converted production to a more social process. The division of labor and specialization of work functions intensified, industrial plants were diversified, the technical requirements of employment became more complex, and, in some cases, more advanced. The end result was a startling acceleration of technology.

At the end of the war, corporate capital was once again faced with the necessity of financing its own research and training its own technical work force. The continued rationalization of the work process required new forms of social integration which would enable social production to advance still further. The first step was the introduction of the GI Bill, which socialized the costs of training (including the living expenses of labor trainees) and eventually helped to create a labor force which could exploit the stockpile of technology created during the war. The second step was the creation of a vast system of lower and higher technical education at the local and state level, the transformation of private universities into Federal universities through research grants, and the creation of a system to exploit technology in a systematic, organized way which included not only the education system, but also the foundations, private research organizations, the Pentagon, and countless other Federal government agencies. This system required enormous capital outlays, a large expansion of teaching and administrative personnel, an upgrading of teachers at all levels, together with programs of specialized teaching training, scholarships, libraries—in short, vast new burdens on the state budget. In turn, this reorganization of the labor process, and, in particular, the free availability of masses of technical-scientific workers, made possible the rapid acceleration of technology. With the new, rationalized social organization of technology and the labor process completed, technical knowledge became the main form of labor power and capital. There occurred a decline in the relative importance of living labor, and an increase in the importance of dead labor in the production process. Thus, statistical studies, beginning in the mid-1950's and multiplying rapidly since then, indicate that the

[5]Maurice Dobb, *Capitalism Yesterday and Today*, New York, 1962, p. 75.

growth of aggregate production is caused increasingly less by an expansion in labor "inputs" and the stock of physical assets, and more by upgrading labor skills, improvements in the quality of physical assets, and better organization of work. One famous study demonstrated that increased education accounted for over three-fifths of the growth of output per man-hour in the United States from 1929–1957.[6]

．．．

The uncontrolled expansion of production by corporate capital as a whole creates still another fiscal burden on the state in the form of outlays required to meet the *social costs of private production* (as contrasted with the socialization of private costs of production, which we have discussed above). Motor transportation is an important source of social costs in the consumption of oxygen, the production of crop- and animal-destroying smog, the pollution of rivers and oceans by lead additives to gasoline, the construction of freeways that foul the land, and the generation of urban sprawl. These costs do not enter into the accounts of the automobile industry, which is compelled to minimize its own costs and maximize production and sales. Corporate capital is unwilling to treat toxic chemical waste or to develop substitute sources of energy for fossil-fuels that pollute the air. (There are exceptions to this general rule. In Pittsburgh, for example, the Mellon interests reduced air pollution produced by its steel mills in order to preserve the values of its downtown real estate.) And corporate farming—the production of agricultural commodities for exchange alone—generates still more social costs by minimizing crop losses (and thus costs) through the unlimited use of DDT and other chemicals that are harmful to crops, animals, water purity, and human life itself.

By and large, private capital refuses to bear the costs of reducing or eliminating air and water pollution, lowering highway and air accidents, easing traffic jams, preserving forests, wilderness areas, and wildlife sanctuaries, and

conserving the soils. In the past these costs were largely ignored. Today, owing to the increasingly social character of production, these costs are damaging not only the ecological structure, but also profitable accumulation itself, particularly in real estate, recreation, agriculture, and other branches of the economy in which land, water, and air are valuable resources to capital. The portion of the state budget devoted to reducing social costs has therefore begun to mount. In the future, the automobile industry can be expected to receive large-scale subsidies to help finance the transition to the electric or fuel-cell car. Capital as a whole will receive more subsidies in the form of new public transportation systems. Subsidies to public utilities to finance the transition to solar, nuclear, or sea energy will expand. Corporate farmers will insist on being "compensated" for crop losses arising from bans on the use of DDT and other harmful chemicals. And more Federal funds will be poured into the states to help regulate outdoor advertising, alleviate conditions in recreational areas, finance the costs of land purchase or condemnation, and landscaping and roadside development, and otherwise meet the costs of "aesthetic pollution."

．．．

III

The third major category of state expenditures consists of the expenses of stabilizing the world capitalist social order: the costs of creating a safe political environment for profitable investment and trade. These expenditures include the costs of politically containing the proletariat at home and abroad, the costs of keeping small-scale, local, and regional capital at home, safely within the ruling corporate liberal consensus, and the costs of maintaining the comprador ruling classes abroad.

These political expenses take the form of income transfers and direct or indirect subsidies, and are attributable fundamentally to the unplanned and anarchic character of capitalist development. Unrestrained capital accumulation and technological change create three

---

[6]E. F. Denison, *The Sources of Economic Growth in the U.S. and the Alternatives Before Us,* New York, 1962, p. 148.

broad, related economic and social imbalances. First, capitalist development forces great stresses and strains on local and regional economies; second, capitalist growth generates imbalances between various industries and sectors of the economy; third, accumulation and technical change reproduce inequalities in the distribution of wealth and income and generate poverty. The imbalances—described by Eric Hobsbawm as "the rhythm of social disruption"—not only are integral to capitalist development, but also are considered by the ruling class to be a sign of "healthy growth and change." What is more, the forces of the marketplace, far from ameliorating the imbalances, in fact magnify them by the multiplier effects of changes in demand on production. The decline of coal mining in Appalachia, for example, compelled other businesses and able-bodied workers to abandon the region, reinforcing tendencies toward economic stagnation and social impoverishment.

These imbalances are present in both the competitive and monopoly phases of capitalism. Both systems are unplanned and anarchic as a whole. But monopoly capitalism is different from competitive capitalism in two fundamental respects that explain why political subsidies are budgetary phenomena mainly associated with monopoly capitalism.

First, an economy dominated by giant corporations operating in oligopolistic industries tends to be more unstable and to generate more inequalities than a competitive economy. The source of both instability and inequality is oligopolistic price-fixing, since the interplay of supply and demand that clears specific commodity markets is no longer present. Shortages and surpluses of individual commodities now manifest themselves in the form of social imbalances. In addition, the national (and, increasingly, the international) character of markets means that economic and social instability and imbalances are no longer confined to a particular region, industry, or occupation, but rather tend to spread through the economy as a whole. Finally, Federal government policies for economic stability and growth soften the effects of economic re-

cessions, lead to the survival of inefficient businesses, and hence, in the long-run to the need for more subsidies.

The second difference between competitive and monopoly capitalism concerns the way in which economic and social imbalances are perceived by capital and wage-labor. In a regime of competitive capitalism, businessmen exercise relatively little control over prices, production and distribution. Unemployment, regional underdevelopment, and industrial bankruptcy appear to be "natural" concomitants of "free markets." Moreover, the level and structure of wages are determined competitively, individual capitals are not able to develop and implement a wage policy, and, thus, the impact of wage changes on the volume and composition of production, the deployment of technology, and unemployment, appears to be the consequence of impersonal forces beyond human control. Because imbalances of all kinds are accepted by capital as natural and even desirable, and because the ideology of capital is the ruling ideology, the inevitability and permanence of imbalances and transitory crises tend to be accepted by society as a whole.

With the evolution of monopoly capitalism and the growth of the proletariat as a whole, this fatalistic attitude undergoes profound changes. Business enterprise gradually develops economic and political techniques of production and market control. Gradually, oligopolistic corporations adopt what Baran and Sweezy have termed a "live-and-let-live attitude" toward each other. In this setting, the imbalances generated by capitalist development begin to be attributed to the conscious policies of large corporations and big unions, rather than to the impersonal forces of the market. Corporate capital, small-scale capital, and the working class alike begin to fix responsibility for the specific policies on particular human agents. Only in this context can the proletariat, local and regional capital, and the comprador classes be contained and accommodated by corporate capital.

The political containment of the proletariat requires the expense of maintaining corporate liberal ideological hegemony, and, where that fails, the cost of physically repressing populations in revolt. In the first category are the expenses of medicare, unemployment, old age, and other social insurance, a portion of education expenditures, the welfare budget, the anti-poverty programs, non-military "foreign aid," and the administrative costs of maintaining corporate liberalism at home and the imperialist system abroad—the expenses incurred by the National Labor Relations Board, Office of Economic Opportunity, Agency for International Development, and similar organizations. The rising flow of these expenditures has two major tributaries.

In point of time, the first is the development of the corporate liberal political consensus between large-scale capital and organized labor. Through the 19th century, private charity remained the chief form of economic relief for unemployed, retired, and physically disabled workers, even though some state and local governments occasionally allocated funds for unemployed workers in times of severe crisis. It was not until the eve of the 20th century that state and local governments introduced regular relief and pension programs. Until the Great Depression, however, welfare programs organized by the corporations themselves were more significant than government programs. Economic prosperity and the extension of "welfare capitalism" throughout the 1920s made it unnecessary for the Federal government to make funds available (in the form of loans to the state) for economic relief until 1932.[7]

The onset of the Great Depression, the labor struggles that ensued, and the need to consolidate the corporate liberal consensus in order to contain these struggles, all led finally to state guarantees of high levels of employment, wage advances in line with productivity increases, and a standard of health, education, and welfare commensurate with the need to maintain labor's reproductive powers and the

hegemony of the corporate liberal labor unions over the masses of industrial workers.

The second tributary runs parallel with, but runs faster and stronger than, the first, and flows from the same source—the development of modern technology. Corporate capital at home and abroad increasingly employs a capital-intensive technology, despite a surplus of unskilled labor, partly because of relative capital abundance in the advanced economies, and partly because of the ready supply of technical-administrative labor power. From the standpoint of large-scale capital, it is more rational to combine in production technical labor power with capital-intensive technology than to combine unskilled or semi-skilled labor power with labor-intensive technology. As we have seen, the fundamental reason is that many of the costs of training technical labor power are met by taxation falling on the working class as a whole.

Advanced capitalism thus creates a large and growing stratum of untrained, unskilled white, black and other Third-World workers that strictly speaking is not part of the industrial proletariat. The relative size of this stratum does not regulate the level of wages, because unskilled labor power does not compete with technical labor power in the context of capital-intensive technology. This stratum is not produced by economic recession and depression, but by prosperity; it does not constitute a reserve army of the unemployed for the economy as a whole. Unemployed, under-employed, and employed in menial jobs in declining sectors of the private economy (e.g., household servants), these workers increasingly depend on the state. "Make-work" state employment, health, welfare, and housing programs, and new agencies charged with the task of exercising social control (to substitute for the social discipline afforded by the wages system itself) proliferate. The expansion of the welfare rolls accompanies the expansion of employment. For the first time in history, the ruling class is beginning to recognize that welfare expenditures cannot be temporary expedients but rather must be permanent fea-

---

[7]James Weinstein, *The Corporate Ideal in the Liberal State* (Boston: Beacon Press, 1968), p. 22.

tures of the political economy: that poverty is integral to the capitalist system.

.   .   .

The second major cost of politically containing the proletariat at home and abroad (including the proletariat in the socialist world) consists of police and military expenditures required to suppress sections of the world proletariat in revolt. These expenditures place the single greatest drain on the state budget. A full analysis of these expenditures would require detailed development of the theory of imperialism, which cannot be undertaken here.

.   .   .

IV

In the preceding sections, we have attempted to analyze state expenditures in terms of the development of the forces and relations of production. We have seen that the increasingly social character of production requires the organization and distribution of production by the state. In effect, neo-capitalism fuses the "base" and "superstructure"—the economic and political systems—and thus places an enormous fiscal burden on the state budget.

5.4   *Capitalist Control of the State*

Our analysis of the state implies that the capitalist class benefits most from state activities. But we do not mean to suggest that all state activities benefit only the capitalist class. There are times when all classes may benefit from particular state actions; for example, medical research or community immunization programs may improve everyone's health possibilities.[1] Moreover, other programs (medicare, welfare) have clearly resulted from the demands and serve the needs of groups other than capitalists.[2] What we are asserting is that the capitalist state operates to regulate the society in such a way as to serve the capitalist class interest in maintaining capitalism as a system. As the most privileged class under capitalism, capitalists are the ones who benefit most from the continuation of the system.

But this analysis of the state raises the question: How are capitalists, admittedly a small minority of the population, able to get the state to serve their interests? This is an especially important question where (as in the United States) the people who run the state are chosen in democratic elections. How, then, does the capitalist class control the state? We turn to this question in the next two readings.

The so called "pluralist" theories of the state deny that capitalists are able

[1]Even here, class dimensions enter: for example, the bias of medical research toward investigation of cures for rare diseases rather than prevention of common ones (e.g., work-related hazards) disproportionately benefits rich people, who typically are not subject to workplace health hazards and can afford the exotic cures to less common maladies.

[2]Again the simple analysis must be qualified: welfare programs provide income to the poor, but they do so in such a demeaning way and in a manner that incurs such hostility from working people (for example, through exaggerated stories of "welfare chiselers") that they also help control the poor. Hence even here the particular manner of meeting others' needs and demands reflects capitalists' power.

to dominate state policy. The pluralists begin with the observation that there are many factions or interest groups in society that influence state decisions. For example, the two major political parties and occasionally minor ones compete for positions of power in the institutions of the state; also active are industry associations, church groups, taxpayer groups, public interest organizations, labor unions, and many others. These groups lobby, contribute money, and otherwise try to influence decision making. The pluralists conclude that historically no single group has been able to dominate the state, nor, given the crosscutting membership of these groups, are they likely to be able to do so in the future.

As William Domhoff shows in the next reading, pluralist theories are fundamentally wrong. Domhoff challenges the basic premise of the pluralist argument by investigating the role of the capitalist class (or, to use Domhoff's phrase, "ruling" class) in the formation of state policy.

Excerpted from "State and Ruling Class in Corporate America" by WILLIAM DOMHOFF, *Insurgent Sociologist*, 4, no. 3 (Spring 1974). Copyright © 1974 by *Insurgent Sociologist*. Reprinted by permission of the author.

On top of the gradually merging social layers of blue and white collar workers in the United States, there is a very small social upper class which comprises at most 1% of the population and has a very different life style from the rest of us. Members of this privileged class, according to sociological studies, live in secluded neighborhoods and well guarded apartment complexes, send their children to private schools, announce their teenage daughters to the world by means of debutante teas and debutante balls, collect expensive art and antiques, play backgammon and dominoes at their exclusive clubs, and travel all around the world on their numerous vacations and junkets.

There is also in America, an extremely distorted distribution of wealth and income. Throughout the twentieth century, the top 1% or so of wealthholders have owned 25–30% of all wealth and 55–65% of wealth that really counts, corporate stock in major businesses and banks. But even that is not the whole story, for a mere .1% have at least 19% of all the wealth in the country—190 times as much as they would have if everyone had an equal share. As for income, well, the maldistribution is not quite as bad. But one recent study argues that if income from capital gains is included, the top 1.5% of wealthholders receive 24% of yearly national income. And, as all studies on matters of wealth and income are quick to point out, these estimates are conservative.

It is not hard for most of us to imagine that the social upper class uncovered in sociological research is made up of the top wealthholders revealed in wealth and income studies. However, it is not necessary to rely on our imaginations, for it is possible to do empirical studies linking the one group to the other. The first systematic studies along this line were reported by sociologist E. Digby Baltzell, but there have been others since.

In most countries, and in most times past in our own country, it would be taken for granted that an upper class with a highly disproportionate amount of wealth and income is a ruling class with domination over the government. How else, it would have been argued, could a tiny group possess so much if it didn't have its hooks into government? But not so in the United States of today. This nation is different, we are assured. It has no social classes, at least not in the traditional European sense, and anyhow there is social mobility—new millionaires are created daily. Besides, many different groups, including organized labor, organized farmers, consumers, and experts, have a hand in political decisions—at least since the New Deal. There is no such thing as a ruling class in America.

In this paper I am going to suggest that in fact a ruling class does dominate this country, a suggestion which not only flies in the face of prevailing academic wisdom, but raises problems for political activists as well. To support this suggestion, I will describe four processes through which the wealthy few who are the ruling class dominate government. Let me begin by defining two terms, "ruling class" and "power elite." By a ruling class, I mean a clearly demarcated social upper class which

a. has a disproportionate amount of wealth and income:

b. generally fares better than other social groups on a variety of well-being statistics ranging from infant mortality rates to educational attainments to feelings of happiness to health and longevity;

c. controls the major economic institutions of the country; and

d. dominates the governmental processes of the country.

By a power elite I mean the "operating arm" or "leadership group" or "establishment" of the ruling class. This power elite is made up of active, working members of the upper class and high level employees in institutions controlled by members of the upper class.

Both of these concepts, I contend, are important in a careful conceptualization of how America is ruled. The distinction between ruling class and power elite allows us to deal with the everyday observation, which is also the first objection raised by critics of ruling class theory, that some members of the ruling class are not involved in ruling, and that some rulers are not members of the upper class. Which is no problem at all, in reality. There always have been many members of ruling classes who spent most of their time playing polo, riding to hounds, or leading a worldwide social life. And there always have been carefully groomed and carefully selected employees, such as Dean Rusk of the Rockefeller Founda-

tion, Robert McNamara of Ford Motor Company, Henry Kissinger of the Council on Foreign Relations, and Herb Stein of the Committee for Economic Development, who have been placed in positions of importance in government.

Now, many other criticisms have been raised about ruling-class theory, and many different kinds of evidence have been put forth to deal with these criticisms. One typical criticism is that the ruling class is never specified in a way that it can be studied empirically. But this argument can be met by reputational, positional, and statistical studies which show that certain social registers, blue books, prep schools, and exclusive clubs are good indicators of upper class standing.

Another usual comment is that there is no reason to believe the alleged ruling class is "cohesive" or "class conscious," a criticism which can be countered by pointing to systematic evidence on interregional private school attendance, overlapping club memberships, interlocking corporate directorships, and nationwide attendance at annual upper-class retreats like the Bohemian Grove and the Ranchero Visitadores.

Then there is the assertion that members of the upper class have lost control of corporations and banks to middle class managers and technocrats, which flies in the face of facts on corporate ownership, on the social backgrounds of corporate directors, and on the motives and goals of corporate managers.

Perhaps the most important criticism, however, is that championed by political scientists, who say proponents of ruling-class theory do not spell out the mechanisms by which the ruling-class supposedly dominates government. Not content to infer power from such indicators as wealth and well being statistics, they want the case for governmental domination by a ruling class demonstrated in its own right, without appeal to statistics on wealth, income, health, and happiness.

My first attempt to satisfy the political science fraternity on this score was to show that members of the power elite hold important governmental positions, especially in the executive branch of the federal government, which I assume everyone now agrees is the most important part of American government. But critics were not satisfied by a sociology-of-leadership approach, which infers "power" to be present when a disproportionate number of people from a given class, ethnic, racial, or religious group appear in positions of responsibility in a given institution.

. . .

Such critics often argue that members of the power elite may not act in the interests of the ruling class while in governmental positions. Instead, they may act in the "national interest," a claim that probably strikes many people as a little empty when they contemplate oil industry tax favors, subsidies to corporations and rich farmers, defense contract overruns, loans to failing corporations, and the general social science finding that most human beings rarely if ever transcend their class, religious and/or ethnic background in viewing the world.

. . .

I have a new way of thinking about the problem of ruling class and government that may put things in a new light. Simply put, I think there are four general processes through which economically and politically active members of the ruling class, operating as the leaders of the power elite, involve themselves in government at all levels. I call these four processes:

1. the special-interest process, which has to do with the various means utilized by wealthy individuals, specific corporations, and specific sectors of the economy to satisfy their narrow, short-run needs;

2. the policy-planning process, which has to do with the development and implementation of general policies that are important to the interests of the ruling class as a whole;

3. the candidate-selection process, which has to do with the ways in which members of the ruling class insure that they have "access" to the politicians who are elected to office; and

4. the ideology process, which has to do with the formation, dissemination, and enforcement of attitudes and assumptions which permit the continued existence of policies and politicians favorable to the wealth, income, status, and privileges of members of the ruling class.

Let me now turn to each of these processes to show their role in ruling class domination of the government. Although my focus will be on the federal government in Washington, I believe the general schema can be applied, with slight modifications, to state and local governments.

The special-interest process, as noted, comprises the several means by which specific individuals, corporations, or business sectors get the tax breaks, favors, subsidies, and procedural rulings which are beneficial to their short-run interests. This is the world of lobbyists, Washington super-lawyers, trade associations, and advisory committees to governmental departments and agencies. This is the process most often described by journalists and social scientists in their exposés and case studies concerning Congressional committees, regulatory agencies, and governmental departments. This process also has been the target of the excellent investigations by Ralph Nader and his colleagues.

. . .

The information in these [and other similar] studies might seem on its face to be impressive evidence for ruling-class theory. After all, it shows that members of the ruling class are able to realize their will on innumerable issues of concern to them. They can gain tax breaks, receive subsidies, subvert safety laws, and dominate regulatory agencies, among other things. However, in the eyes of most political scientists this is not adequate evidence, for it does not show that the various "interests" are "coordinated" in their efforts. Moreover, it does not show directly that they dominate policy on "big issues," or that they control either of the political parties.

In order to deal with this argument it is necessary to consider next the policy-formation process, the process by which policy on "large issues" is formulated, for it is in the policy process that the various special interests join together to forge general policies which will benefit them as a whole. The central units in the policy network are such organizations as the Council on Foreign Relations, the Committee for Economic Development, the Business Council, the American Assembly, and the National Municipal League, which are best categorized as policy planning and consensus seeking organizations of the power elite. I will not repeat here the information on the financing and leadership of these organizations which shows beyond a doubt that they are underwritten and directed by the same upper class men who control the major corporations, banks, foundations, and law firms. More important for our purpose is what goes on in the off-the-record meetings of these organizations.

The policy planning organizations bring together, in groups large and small, members of the power elite from all over the country to discuss general problems—e.g., overseas aid, the use of nuclear weapons, tax problems, or the population question. They provide a setting in which differences on various issues can be thrashed out and the opinions of various experts can be heard. In addition to the group settings, these organizations also encourage general dialogue within the power elite by means of luncheon and dinner speeches, special written reports, and position statements in journals and books.

It was in groups such as these that the framework for a capital-labor detente was worked out at the turn of the century, that the bill for a Federal Trade Commission was drafted, that the plans for social security were created, that the ideas behind the Marshall Plan were developed, that national goals for the 1960's were projected, and the "population problem" was invented.

· · · ·

Let me summarize the policy-planning network by means of the diagram on page 197, and list some of the most important functions of [the policy-making organizations].

1. They provide a setting wherein members of the power elite can familiarize themselves with general issues.

2. They provide a setting where conflicts within the power elite can be discussed and compromised.

3. They provide a setting wherein members of the power elite can hear the ideas and findings of their hired experts.

4. They provide a "training ground" for new leadership within the ruling class. It is in these organizations that big bussinessmen can determine which of their peers are best suited for service in the government.

5. They provide a framework for commissioned studies by experts on important issues.

6. Through such avenues as books, journals, policy statements, press releases and speakers, they can greatly influence the "climate of opinion" both in Washington and the country at

These are several points for political scientists and other critics of ruling-class theory to consider in contemplating the policy-planning network. First, it provides evidence that businessmen, bankers, and lawyers concern themselves with more than their specific business interests. Second, it shows that leaders from various sectors of the economy do get together to discuss the problems of the system as a whole. Third, it suggests that members of the power elite who are appointed to government are equipped with a general issue-orientation gained from power-elite organizations that are explicitly policy oriented. Fourth, it reveals that the upper-middle-class experts thought by some to be our real rulers are in fact busily dispensing their advice to those who hire them.

If I am right that members of the ruling class gain their narrow interests through the well-known devices of the special-interest process and their general interests through the little-studied policy-planning process, then the question immediately arises: how is all this possible when we have a government elected by the people? Shouldn't we expect elected officials to have policy views of their own that generally reflect the wishes of the voters who sent them to office? There is certainly one group of political scientists who believe this to be the case—they have developed a detailed argument to suggest that the deep-seated political ambitions of individuals and parties lead them to take the policy stands which will get them a majority of the vote, thereby insuring that the policy views of politicians will reflect more or less the views of the people.

To answer questions about our elected officials, we must examine the political parties and the candidates they nominate. When it comes to the parties, political scientists have suggested that a fully developed political party fulfills four functions: (1) integrating conflicting regional, ethnic, and class identifications; (2) selecting candidates to fill offices; (3) political education; and (4) policy making. In the United States, however, the parties have little or nothing to do with political education or policy making: "Particularly in our own century," writes political scientist Walter Dean Burnham, "American political parties have been largely restricted in functional scope to the realm of the constituent [integrative function] and to the tasks of filling political offices."[1] Another observer, the executive director of the National Committee for an Effective Congress, puts the matter even more strongly.

> For all intents and purposes, the Democratic and Republican parties don't exist. There are only individuals [candidates] and professionals [consultants, pollsters, media advisers].[2]

It is because American politics is restricted largely to office-filling functions that I prefer to talk about the candidate-selection process rather than the political process. The term political process gives the impression that more is going on in our electoral system than is really the case. And it is precisely because the candidate-selection process is so individualistic and issueless that it can be in good part dominated by means of campaign contributions from members of the ruling class. In the guise of fat cats, the same men who direct corporations and take part in the policy groups play a central role in the careers of most politicians who advance beyond the local or state legislature level in states of any size and consequence. To quote again from Walter Dean Burnham: "Recuitment of elective elites remains closely associated, especially for the more important offices and in the larger states, with the candidates' wealth or access to large campaign contributions."[3]

The fat cats, of course, are by and large hard to distinguish in their socio-economic outlook whatever their political party. Indeed, most corporations, banks, and law firms try to have personnel who are important donors to both parties. Then too, many of the fattest cats of the opposing parties join together as leaders of such policy-planning groups as the Council on Foreign Relations and Committee for Economic Development. For example, in 1968 there were 144 members of the Council on Foreign Relations who gave $500 or more to the Republicans, 56 who contributed $500 or more to the Democrats. One hundred twenty-six members of the National Council of the Foreign Policy Association donated sums of $500 or more to Republicans, 71 gave to Democrats. At the Committee for Economic Development, there were 95 Republican donors and 16 Democratic donors. Although well-connected in both parties, we can see a power elite preference for the Republican Party, at least in 1968. There is one other difference among fat cats worth nothing—Southern and Jewish members of the upper class are more likely to be Democrats than are their WASPy counterparts.[4]

What kind of politicians emerge from this individualistically-oriented electoral politics that has to curry favor with large contributors? The answer is available from several studies. Politicians are first of all people from

[1]Walter Dean Burnham, "Party Systems and the Political Process," p. 279. In *The American Party Systems*, William Chambers and Walter Dean Burnham, eds. (Oxford University Press, 1967).

[2]John S. Saloma III and Frederick H. Sontag, *Parties* (Alfred A. Knopf, 1972), p. 295.

[3]Burnham, op. cit., p. 277.

[4]G. William Domhoff, *Fat Cats and Democrats* (Prentice-Hall, 1972), for the information in this paragraph.

The power elite policy-making process.

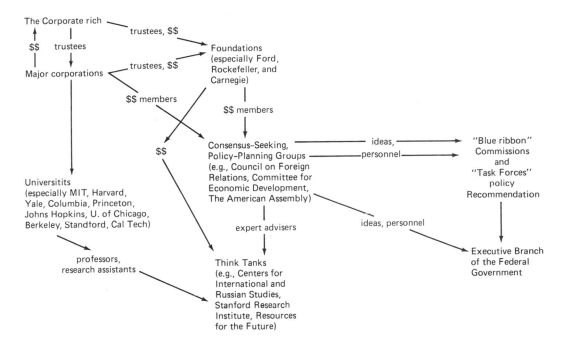

the higher levels of the social ladder: "The wealthiest one-fifth of the American families contribute about nine of every ten of the elite of the political economy."[5] They are secondly, at least among those who wish to go beyond local and state politics, quite ambitious men who are constantly striving for bigger and better things. They are thirdly people who are by and large without strong ideological inclinations; the exceptions to this statement are well known precisely because they are so unusual. Finally, with the exception of the local level, where businessmen are most likely to sit on city councils, they are in good part lawyers, an occupational grouping that by training and career needs produces ideal go-betweens and compromisers. The result of the candidate selection process, in short, is (1) men who know how to go along to get along, and (2) men who have few strong policy positions of their own, and are thus open to the suggestions put

forth to them by the fat cats and experts who have been legitimated as serious leaders within the framework of the policy-planning network.

When we consider the interaction between the policy process and the political process, it is not surprising that there is a considerable continuity of policy between Republican and Democratic administrations. As columnist Joseph Kraft wrote about the Council on Foreign Relations, "The Council plays a special part in helping to bridge the gap between the two parties, affording unofficially a measure of continuity when the guard changes in Washington."[6] Nor is it surprising that Hubert Humphrey would reveal in early 1973 that he had asked Henry Kissinger before the election in 1968 to serve as *his* foreign policy adviser should he win the Presidency. But David Halberstam's *The Best and the Brightest* best reveals the degree to which politicians defer to representatives of the policy process. After

[5]Kenneth Prewitt and Alan Stone, *The Ruling Elites* (Harper & Row, 1973), p.137.

[6]Joseph Kraft, "School for Statesmen," *Harper's Magazine*, July, 1958, p. 68.

winning an election based upon "new frontiers" and nonexistent missile gaps, President-elect John F. Kennedy called in Republican Robert Lovett, a Wall Street financier who hadn't even voted for him, and asked him for his advice as to whom should be appointed to important government positions. Kennedy did this because he only knew mere politicians, not the kind of "serious men" who were expert enough to run a government:

> He had spent the last five years, he said ruefully, running for office, and he did not know any real public officials, people to run a government, serious men. The only ones he knew, he admitted, were politicians, and if this seemed a denigration of his own kind, it was not altogether displeasing to the older man. Politicians did need men to serve, to run the government.[7]

Among Lovett's suggestions were Dean Rusk of the Rockefeller Foundation, Robert McNamara of Ford Motor Company, and Douglas Dillon of Dillon, Read, who, as we all know, ended up as Kennedy's choices to head the state, defense, and treasury departments.

So politics in America has little to do with issues and public policy. It is an exercise in image-building, name-calling, and rumor mongering, a kind of carnival or psychological safety valve. Thus, a Richard M. Nixon can unctuously claim he is dealing with the issues in the 1972 campaign, when in fact even the *Wall Street Journal* has to admit that all he does is wave the flag and accuse people who disagree with him of being traitors.[8] And at about the same time he is pretending to discuss the issues, he can quietly tell his campaign strategists not to worry about what the platform says because. "Who the hell ever read a platform?"[9]

. . .

I conclude that the notion of public policy being influenced to any great extent by the will of the people due to the competition between the two political parties is misguided. "Politics" is for selecting ambitious, relatively issueless middle-and upper-middle-class lawyers who know how to advance themselves by finding the rhetoric and the rationalizations to implement both the narrow and general policies of the bi-partisan power elite.

At this point I can hear the reader protesting that there is more to American politics than this. And so there is. I admit there are serious-minded liberals who fight the good fight on many issues, ecologically oriented politicians who remain true to their cause, and honest people of every political stripe who are not beholden to any wealthy people. But there are not enough of them, for there is also a seniority system dominated by ruling class-oriented politicians who have a way of keeping the insurgents off the important committees and out of the centers of power. There is in addition a Southern Democratic delegation which retains its stranglehold on Congress despite all the claims of the mid-Sixties that its star was about to fade. Then there are the machine Democrats who aid the Southerners in crucial ways even while they maintain a liberal voting record. And finally, there are the myriad lobbyists and lawyers who are constantly pressuring those who would resist the blandishments of the power elite. As former Congressman Abner Mikva once said, the system has a way of grinding you down:

> The biggest single disappointment to a new man is the intransigence of the system. You talk to people and they say, "You're absolutely right, something ought to be done about this." And yet, somehow, we go right on ducking the hard issues. We slide off the necessary confrontations. This place has a way of grinding you down.[10]

In short, even though there is more to American politics than fat cats and their polit-

[7]David Halberstam, *The Best and the Brightest* (Random House, 1972), p. 4.

[8]James P. Gannon, "Is GOP Campaign Rhetoric Too Hot?," *Wall Street Journal*, Sept. 8, 1972, p. 8.

[9]"Republicans: Cloth-Coat Convention," *Newsweek*, August 7, 1972, p. 23.

[10]Robert Sherrill, "92nd Congress: Eulogy and Evasion," *The Nation*, February 15, 1971.

ical friends, the "more" cannot win other than headlines, delays, and an occasional battle. The candidate-selection process produces too many politicians who are friendly to the wealthy few.

Contemplation of the ways in which the special-interest, policy-planning, and candidate-selection processes operate brings us to the $64 question: Why do we, the general public, acquiesce in this state of affairs? Why is it, as Marx warned, that the ruling ideas of any age are the ideas of the ruling class? Why does the ruling class have what the Italian Marxist Antonio Gramsci called "ideological hegemony," by which he meant that "the system's real strength does not lie in the violence of the ruling class or the coercive power of its state apparatus, but in the acceptance by the ruled of a 'conception of the world' which belongs to the rulers?"[11] Unfortunately, no one has given an adequate answer to these interrelated questions. Such an answer would involve insights from a variety of disciplines including history, anthropology, and psychology as well as political science and sociology, and would quickly lead to age-old problems concerning the origins of the state and the general nature of the relationship between leaders and led.

However, at the sociological level which concerns me in this paper, we certainly can see that members of the ruling class work very hard at helping us to accept their view of the world. Indeed, we can be sure from past experience that they will stop at nothing—despite their protestations of "democracy" and "liberalism"—to get their views across. Through the ideology process, they create, disseminate, and enforce a set of attitudes and "values" that tells us this is, for all its defects, the best of all possible worlds. At the fount of this process are the same foundations and policy-planning groups which operate in the policy process. For in addition to providing policy suggestions to government, these policy-planning organi-

zations also provide the new rationales which make the policies acceptable to the general public. Thus, in the case of the ideology process we must link these organizations not to the government, as in the policy process, but to a dissemination network which includes middle-class discussion groups, public relations firms, corporate-financed advertising councils, special university and foundation programs, books, speeches, and various efforts through the mass media.

The dissemination apparatus is most readily apparent in the all-important area of foreign policy. Perhaps most critical here is the Foreign Policy Association and its affiliate, the World Affairs Council. Tightly interlocked with the Council on Foreign Relations, the Foreign Policy Association provides literature and discussion groups for the "attentive public" of upper-middle-class professionals, academics, and students. For local elites, the Council on Foreign Relations sponsors Committees on Foreign Relations in over 30 cities around the country. These committees meet about once a month during the nonsummer months to hear speakers provided by the Council on Foreign Relations or the government. The aim of this program is to provide local elites with information and legitimacy so they may function as "opinion leaders" on foreign policy issues. In addition to the Foreign Policy Association and the Committees on Foreign Relations, there are numerous foreign affairs institutes at major universities which provide students and the general public with the perspectives of the power elite on foreign policy. Then too, political leaders often play an intermediary role in carrying foreign policy positions to the general public.

The enforcement of the ideological consensus if carried out in a multitude of ways that include pressure, intimidation and violence as well as the more gentle methods of persuasion and monetary inducement. Those who are outspoken in their challenge to one or another of the main tenets of the American ideology may be passed over for promotions, left out of junkets, or fired from their jobs. They may be

[11]Giuseppe Fiori, *Antonio Gramsci: Life of a Revolutionary* (NLB, London, 1970), p. 238.

The flow of foreign policy ideology to the general public: Political leaders play an intermediary role

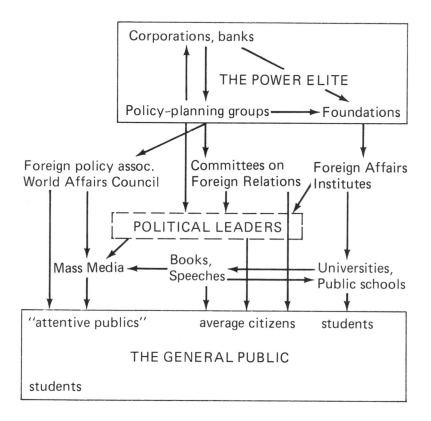

excluded from groups or criticized in the mass media. If they get too far outside the consensus, they are enmeshed in the governmental law enforcement apparatus which is shaped in the policy-formation process with a special assist from the ruling-class dominated American Bar Association and its affiliated institutes and committees. But I do not think we need to spend much time considering the bitter details of ideology enforcement, for they are all too fresh in our minds after years of struggle over civil liberties and the war in Southeast Asia.

5.5 *Liberal Democracy, Political Parties and the Capitalist State*

Government in capitalist society is not class-neutral. As Domhoff argued in the previous reading, the notion of class neutrality is belied by the class origins of those who have political influence and resources, by the class orientations of most high officials, and by the class bias of formal and informal mechanisms for making public policy. These political facts of life contradict the pluralist view that there are many within-class and cross-class special interest groups, equally and freely competing for policy influence and public power, and that class represents only one basis (out of many) on which such interest groups form. Instead it appears that special interest politics represent only part of the political process, and interest groups tend in any case disproportionately to represent capitalist rather than other interests.

Yet we must go further to understand how a numerically insignificant capitalist class can dominate a nominally democratic state. In the following reading Michael Reich and Richard Edwards begin by noting the important pro-capitalist constraints that capitalist organization of the economy places upon any government.

Reich and Edwards go on to investigate the operation and evolution of the American system of party politics. Their analysis emphasizes the class character of capitalist society, including the dominant position of the capitalist class, and they interpret the history of party politics as the history of class struggle in the political sphere. The electoral system produces the public acquiescence to (if not outright support of) state policy, but, they argue, voting and elections also create an important arena for class struggle.

This essay was written by MICHAEL REICH and RICHARD C. EDWARDS for this book. Copyright © 1986 by Michael Reich and Richard C. Edwards. We thank John Judis for letting us draw on his unpublished notes in this article.

Do democratic governments in capitalist countries represent the people or do they instead reflect the *class* nature of those societies. Both Marx and Lenin identified the state unequivocally with the capitalist class; in Marx's (and Engels') words:

> The bourgeoisie has at last, since the establishment of modern industry and of the world market, conquered for itself, in the modern representative state, exclusive political sway. The executive of the modern state is but a committee for managing the common affairs of the whole bourgeoisie.[1]

Both stressed the capitalist use of the state as a "special repressive force" against working class and peasant insurgency.[2] In many third-world countries—for instance, Chile, Iran, or

Indonesia—the capitalist class relies principally on force and terror to retain the support (or acquiescence) of other classes.

But the U.S. state has functioned largely through the consent of the governed rather than through recourse to its repressive apparatus. And the political process in the United States—the struggle that determines government policies and officials—is formally democratic and includes participation by wage-workers, farmers, and small business people as well as large capitalists. Is it then valid to describe the U.S. state as "but a committee for managing the common affairs of the whole bourgeoisie"?

Our intention here is to answer this question by examining the operation and evolution of American party politics. We argue that, while capitalists have historically dominated the American government, changes in capitalism itself have made their control both more crucial and more uncertain. The most important challenge to capitalists' domination of the state comes from the political power of the working class.

[1] Karl Marx and Frederick Engels, *The Communist Manifesto*.

[2] See Vladimir Lenin, *State and Revolution, Selected Works*, vol. 2 (Moscow: 1960).

Our argument proceeds as follows. First, we review how the capitalist economy imposes objective constraints on the state, regardless of what party gets elected or who the high government officials are. This context biases the political system in favor of capitalists and constitutes the most fundamental source of the capitalists' power over the state. Second, we look at how the two major political parties operate. Capitalists have dominated both parties, and Democratic and Republican programs can be seen as alternative strategies for advancing capitalist interests. On the other hand, working-class groups in this century have been able to gain some significant leverage in the Democratic Party. As a result, certain reforms have been won that extend democracy and that present capitalist rule with a potentially serious challenge. Third, we argue that in response to this growing challenge capitalists have sought to restructure the state so that, while its democratic form is maintained, its democratic content is reduced. In the present period, the operation of the state reflects a growing conflict between capitalism and democracy.

I. CAPITALIST CONSTRAINTS ON THE STATE

We begin by examining the economic context in which state policies are fashioned. This context—that is, capitalist relations of production—places severe constraints upon what the state can and cannot do. Investment decisions and the production of goods and services (and therefore also the level of economic activity and the number of jobs in the economy) are determined primarily by capitalists seeking to make profits. Consequently, the state cannot execute public policies that lower substantially the rate of capitalists' profit without jeopardizing the "health" of the economy. For example, if the state taxes profits too much or allows unions too much power, capitalists will reduce their investments. Similarly, state policies that undermine the work incentive, redistribute income and wealth, or otherwise interfere with

the capitalist mode of production create economic problems. Even the prospect of such policies in the future is enough to erode "business confidence," send the stock market down, and encourage the outflow of funds eroding the national currency's exchange rate. When lowered profit prospects affect enough investors, reduced investment produces an economic downturn, a balance of payments problem, and a fiscal crisis for the state.

Hence, state policies are constrained by the imperatives of the capitalist economy *regardless of who runs the state or what their intentions may be.* Even if a pro–working-class government is elected, its power to make changes is fundamentally constrained to the extent that capitalists control investment.[3] The capitalist class is thus able to achieve without direct control a relative dominance over the "democratic" state simply because that state exists in the larger context of capitalist society.

In the United States, because capitalists dominate the political process, the state typically tends to promote capitalists' interests.

The concept of capitalist dominance over the state must be qualified in two important ways. First, the state must operate for the general capitalist interest, but not necessarily for the interest of any individual capitalist. Since capitalists compete with each other for profits, state policies that are in the common interest of the whole capitalist class may actually conflict with particular interests of specific capitalists. For example, an individual capitalist may wish to see a tariff for his product erected against foreign competition. Most capitalists, however, benefit from access to overseas markets, and a specific tariff may bring retaliation by foreign governments against U.S. exports. In this case, for the state to pursue capitalists' classwide interests it must oppose certain capi-

---

[3]In many advanced capitalist countries today much investment is undertaken by the state. This fact is not by itself evidence that the capitalist class has "lost control" of that investment; see O'Connor, Section 5.3, p. 185. On the other hand, the growth of this state investment may ease the constraints on a pro–working-class government.

talists' particular interests. Thus, the state operates with some autonomy from the pressures of individual capitalists.[4]

Indeed, since capitalists are busy making their individual profits, they do not always have a classwide outlook of their interests. While the capitalist class agrees on fundamental issues of property, it is often divided on others—such as foreign policy and welfare and labor legislation. Their divisions may be expressed in public political struggle, or a consensus may be built through the policy formation process.[5] In either case it is the state that executes the policies that best fit the capitalists' classwide interests. The state may even see that a certain policy is in the long-term common interests of capital before many capitalists so perceive it. This was the case, for example, when Keynesians pushed the idea of state deficit spending to stimulate the economy—a policy the capitalist class later came to support.

Second, the capitalist class's dominance over the state is relative rather than absolute. For much of the post-World War II era, government policies in advanced capitalist nations have been subject to another important influence: the working class, which has grown not only numerically but also in its organizational strength and political power. In the United States the political influence of organized labor unions and federations of unions, particularly in the Democratic Party, has restricted the range of options available to the state. For example, the state cannot attempt to reduce inflation by creating the extremely high levels of unemployment that existed in the 1930s. Thus, by seeking to implement programs in their interests, labor unions, black groups, women's groups, organizations of poor people, and so on push the state in directions that are often opposite to those desired by cap-

italists. So while capitalists dominate the state, they are not unopposed and their control is far from complete. We now turn to the contradictions that are created by these pressures.

II. THE EXTENSION OF DEMOCRACY

From the capitalists' standpoint, the electoral process serves to legitimize their control, yet it also threatens it. In the long run, the state's effectiveness in legitimizing capitalist dominance depends upon the state's *appearing* neutral in the class struggle. Hence, it must be open to all interests and politics. This can and does lead to a parade of special interests, representing parts of the working class as well as parts of the capitalist class. These special interests often threaten policies important for capital accumulation. Another and more serious problem is that the electoral system provides an opening for a working-class movement to contest for the right to govern. Given universal suffrage in a society in which the working class far outnumbers capitalists, the capitalist class must take this potential threat seriously.

The early ruling classes were aware of the potential contradictions of representative government. They were concerned with creating a balanced coalition of various propertied interests (Southern slaveholders and Northern merchants and manufacturers). They established forms of government that allowed only for indirect representation of the (relatively) propertyless workers, small farmers, and artisans.[6] The president was to be chosen by an electoral college. Senators were originally elected by legislative houses. In many states, only white male property-owners could participate in electing these legislators. An elaborate system of checks and balances among the judicial, legislative, and executive branches was designed to prevent propertyless groups or

---

[4]This perspective explains the often expressed grumblings of business against state policy and helps us avoid the mistaken conclusion that the state is acting in a generally anticapitalist manner.

[5]See Domhoff, Section 5.4, p. 191.

[6]Slaves and Indians were to be kept in place largely through force and terror.

any single section of the propertied classes from running roughshod over the others. In this way, the Founding Fathers insulated the chief public offices from worker and farmer control and balanced competing propertied interests.

The present American electoral system, which allows for universal adult suffrage and direct election of senators, was only achieved through the struggles of women, small farmers, workers, and blacks and other minorities. Like the economic reforms won by the working class, these democratic reforms have created new opportunities for previously excluded groups to influence state policy.

Capitalists and the Political Parties

With the expanded franchise and direct election of office-holders, electoral activity came to be organized through the mechanism of political parties. Capitalists have been active in the affairs of both major parties, but in this century consistent political differences have existed between the parties. The Republican Party today represents both "moderate" corporate capitalists (the "liberal" or "Eastern establishment" wing) and small business and the more conservative and reactionary big-business elements (the party's right wing). Republican programs tend to rely more directly and immediately on repression ("law and order") to maintain capitalist rule, and Republicans see little merit in policies (e.g., welfare, mass higher education, and so on) that serve to legitimize capitalism and to co-opt working-class dissent. Instead, the Republican Party is openly for high profits, rapid capital accumulation, and the policies that would promote them: lower business taxes, restrictions on unions, reducing those government payments to the poor which interfere with work incentives, higher unemployment to replenish the reserve supply of workers, and so on.

In contrast, those big-business capitalists who favor a strategy of "corporate liberalism" operate within the Democratic Party. These capitalists are also primarily concerned about profits and accumulation. But, in contrast to the Republicans, the corporate liberal strategy to achieve accumulation makes them more favorable to reform policies, such as welfare, aid to education, accommodation with labor unions, maintaining low levels of unemployment through deficit spending. Such reforms, although costly perhaps in the short run, may alleviate serious class conflicts that would be even more costly to capitalists.[7]

Yet the two parties tend to develop a symbiotic relationship. Republican policies to promote accumulation, such as those of the 1950s and the 1980s, succeed until sufficient resentment among workers gathers to necessitate reforms, including full employment, social security and welfare improvements, extension of public services, and enforcement of anti-discrimination laws. The Republican accumulation strategy thus becomes outmoded because it provokes too much dissent. Democrats are able to exploit these grievances to create a winning electoral coalition. Once in power, as in the 1960s, they begin to increase social service spending, stimulate the economy, and undertake other reforms or legitimation programs. Eventually, however, the costs of these efforts (in higher taxes, inflation, the "burden" of regulation, more militant workers, and so on) tends to mobilize capitalists, small business people, homeowners, tax-payers, and other groups into resisting further programs—that is, the Democratic accumulation strategy becomes obsolete. Once again the guard changes.

Workers and the Democratic Party

The working class is usually more attracted to the Democratic Party, which offers some

---

[7]Although their primary allegiance is to "moderate Republicanism" (i.e., some mixture of legitimation policies and repression), corporate capitalists are financially more able, and hence more willing, to support reform programs than are small capitalists, who are directly threatened by higher taxes, the costs of regulation, etc. Thus, some corporate capitalists (especially investment bankers and corporate lawyers) are Democrats.

concessions and reforms, than to the Republican Party, which offers workers lower taxes and less inflation. In the twentieth century the working class has been able to use its electoral power to increase its influence within the Democratic Party. It has affected candidate selection and legislative action, and Democratic administrations have been forced to include representatives of working-class and minority interests. In some local and state races, anti-capitalist working-class candidates have been able to win Democratic nominations and sometimes the election itself.

By 1900, the American working class was becoming the majority class in America. But its members were not organized politically. The American Federation of Labor (AFL), whose members primarily were skilled workers, followed pressure-group tactics, pressuring both parties and supporting neither officially. In 1901, the Socialist Party was formed, and it was able to build a growing working-class constituency until the end of World War I, when it was permanently weakened by internal splits and by government repression.

After World War I, the march of the working class into the Democratic Party began, first with the white urban ethnic minorities (many of whom had been Democrats earlier), and then with the industrial unions and blacks in the 1930s and 1940s. By the late 1940s, the Democratic Party had become the "party of the working class." The key event was the open support of Roosevelt by leaders of the Congress of Industrial Organizations (CIO) in 1936. (In fact, the CIO was Roosevelt's single largest campaign contributor in 1936.) Open CIO support broke the AFL tradition. It was based on an understanding of the importance of political action for the success of the industrial union's organizing drive.

In return for their organized support, Democratic officials supported legislation favored by working-class interests and appointed representatives from the labor unions and black organizations to administration positions within the federal, state, and local bureaucracies. Through these positions, labor and black representatives were able to fight on behalf of their respective interests within administrations.

But while the Democratic Party is the party of the working class, it is not a working-class party. As we indicate below, capitalist interests hold key positions of power in the party through their financial role. The party's programs and candidates come out of a complex process of maneuver and compromise that involves interests of small and large capitalists as well as working-class interests. And the dominant ideology and practice within the Democratic Party sees labor and business as interest groups, whose contending claims it seeks to balance, rather than as conflicting classes. As a consequence, the party has successfully transformed potentially autonomous working-class power into a subordinated interest group. While the results express working-class interests, they also express the predominance of capitalist interests within the party. In this sense, the Democratic Party, like the state itself, is an arena of class struggle. Compared to the Republican Party, it is a much more favorable arena of struggle for the working class, and that is why working-class groups flocked into it in the 1930s. But it expresses nonetheless the relative dominance of the American capitalist class over other contenders for political power.

During the 1930s, the growing working-class movement demanded and finally obtained unemployment compensation, social security, welfare programs, public housing, and government support for collective bargaining. Without this pressure, the government would never have acted. But the final results of the legislation only emerged after intense struggles among capitalists and between capital and labor, and they ultimately reflected the predominance of capital interests. Social security, for instance, was largely financed through workers' incomes; capitalist pressure was able to eliminate the redistributive aspects of the proposals for social security that were supported by many working people. The Wagner Act of 1935, putting unions and collective bargaining on a legal basis, was passed over considerable opposition from capitalists who saw labor unionism as a threat to their rates of profit and eventually to their control over the means of production.

But over the next twenty years, capitalists were able to blunt the impact of labor unionism. The anti-capitalist elements were driven out of the labor movement and McCarthyist repression was used to decimate the Left. For most of the postwar period, monopoly corporations were able to grant wage increases while maintaining or increasing their rates of profit. And labor leaders themselves were brought into a political consensus around capitalist goals in a pro-capitalist and anti-communist Cold War liberalism that was centered in the Democratic Party. Although the party has struggled against some sections of the capitalist class and small business, it has never opposed the entire capitalist class on any important issue.

So the Democratic Party itself tends to mirror the contradictions of the entire electoral system. Possibilities exist for working-class victories, including important reforms. The larger context in which politics occurs, however, tends both to restrict the nature of reforms and to limit the probability of their being enacted. Moreover, capitalists have attempted to retain control of the state by restructuring the political system.

III. THE ATTACK ON DEMOCRACY

As the public electoral process has been opened up, the capitalist class has moved to prevent working-class and small business interests from taking full advantage of their new opportunities. First, capitalists have tried to limit the effect of the electoral process on state policy by isolating decision-making in governmental bodies that are far removed from democratic accountability. Second, capitalists have sought to control the parties themselves through financial means and through their control over the media and the ideological apparatus. Finally, they have attempted, when necessary, to destroy third parties and to preserve the present two-party system.

Like other capitalist measures, these actions were not taken consciously by a united capitalist class, but instead were instituted by fractions of that class acting in concert with politicians who shared their interests. But their net effect was to limit, at least temporarily, the challenge posed by the democratic reforms of the electoral system.

Isolating "Democratic" Government from the People

Throughout the twentieth century power has been shifted from elected and hence democratically accountable government institutions to appointed, non-accountable bodies. As a result, party politics, citizen voting, and the entire electoral process have come to have less and less effect on government policy.

In part this shift reflects the dramatic decline of the Congress (and state legislatures and town meetings) as real governing bodies; more, it reflects the rapidly growing power of the bureaucracies, "public authorities," regulatory bodies, state commissions, the courts, "expert" or "professional" bodies, and so on. The Congress, legislatures, and the like are all popularly elected, of course, while the latter groups (the bureaucracy, courts, etc.) are appointive. Moreover, while officials in popularly accountable bodies tend to serve fairly short terms (two to four years generally, excepting the Senate), the non-accountable agencies are run by officials enjoying, as an additional protection from popular will, extremely long terms (five or seven or ten years or even life).

The most salient and crucial case of this shift in power away from democratic accountability has emerged with the expansion of executive power. The American president was originally likened to a monarch. Like a monarch, the president would be aware of popular needs and interests, but would be accountable only to his propertied peers. He would be able to make decisions that were unpopular to the public at large but that were necessary for preserving or extending capitalism. Like that of monarchs, the power of the president was to be checked by feudal barons in the legislative and judicial branches. Today, participation in the electoral process is broader and presidents are elected directly by universal suffrage. Monopoly capitalists have become the dominant propertied interest; and monopoly capitalism's economic contradictions demand a greater role for the federal government in the economy. Presidents, facing popular movements and having to follow unpopular policies but moving with capitalist support, have created a new and greater realm of decision-making and planning for themselves: the national security apparatus and the Executive Office of the President.

The purpose of creating this new realm was to insulate an area of decision-making and planning from popular pressure—which in the first instance meant shielding it from congressional influence (and since cabinet members are partially responsible to congressional scrutiny, it meant shielding it from even cabinet influence).[8] The expanded power taken by the executive has consequently occurred at the expense of Congress. There have been four significant steps on this path in the twentieth century. In the early decades of this century, Theodore Roosevelt and Woodrow Wilson began framing their own legislation and sending it to Congress rather than leaving this initiative to Congress. In 1939, having begun to draw back from the second phase of New Deal programs under capitalist pressure and also having begun to plan for war with Germany, Franklin Roosevelt created the Executive Office of the President. Among other things, he moved the Bureau of the Budget from the Treasury Department to the Executive Offices; this meant that appointees were not subject to congressional approval, and that its operations were shielded from public influence.[9]

In 1946, Harry Truman, about to launch the Cold War in the face of possible public resistance, made the Council of Economic Advisors, the National Security Council, and the Central Intelligence Agency part of the Executive Offices. Finally, Richard Nixon moved even more drastically to enlarge the Executive Offices. Some of his innovations succeeded, such as the Office of Management and Budget; others, such as the attempt to create a domestic counterintelligence agency within the Executive Offices, were abandoned during the Watergate scandals.[10]

The development of capitalist-sponsored policy formation groups, such as the Council for Foreign Relations and the Committee for Economic Development, accompanied the enlargement of executive power and the creation of the Executive Office. These corporate capitalist groups have contributed both their members and their ideas to the president's executive councils.

As with the Executive Offices, so in state and local governments and in other areas of the federal government, power and decision-making have been transferred out of institutions (e.g., Congress) that are somewhat sensitive to popular opinion (even if imperfectly so) and into other institutions that retain nearly no democratic content. The National Security Council, the Federal Reserve Board, the New York Port Authority, state bureaucracies, licensing commissions, and so on have become the anti-democratic form of modern "democratic" government. In this way, the main area of state policy formation has been subject to direct capitalist influence, while it has been relatively isolated from the electoral process and from working-class pressures. This has limited the effect of the electoral process on American policy.

---

[8]Of all federal government officials, members of the House of Representatives, elected locally every two years, are most likely to represent special interests—often, the special interests of the working class and minorities—in conflict with interests of the capitalist class.

[9]See William E. Leuchtenberg, *Franklin D. Roosevelt and the New Deal* (New York: 1963), pp. 327–28.

[10]See Rowland Evans, Jr., and Robert D. Novak, *Nixon in the White House* (New York: 1972), pp. 237–41.

Controlling the Republicans and Democrats by the Purse Strings

The American political parties are decentralized coalitions of state and local parties that come together, every four years, to nominate a presidential candidate. Neither the Republicans nor the Democrats are explicitly tied to one class's interests, as is for example the British Labor Party. They are both multiclass coalitions.

The capitalist class maintains tremendous influence within the two parties largely through its major responsibility for campaign finances. The scope of these contributions has come into better focus recently with the disclosure of widespread and massive contributions by corporations directly out of their corporate coffers. Gulf Oil alone, for example, has admitted to having dispensed millions of dollars during the 1960s and 1970s.[11] These legal and illegal contributions, often hidden in the books as "business expenses" and hence used to reduce the corporation's taxes, supplemented the vast above-board (and legal) giving by wealthy individuals. No candidate can expect to be nominated or elected without enormous contributions, especially as the scope of the campaign widens from city to nation.

Most political scientists concede that the Republican Party depends on capitalist support. It reportedly commands the allegiance of 80 to 90 percent of American capitalists. But the Democrats also depend on capitalist financing. In a study of the Democrats, William Domhoff estimates that Democratic candidates receive 45 to 65 percent of their funds from capitalist donors, while labor unions contribute at most 20 to 25 percent, "little people" about 15 percent, and racketeers, in some areas, up to 15 percent. Domhoff shows how capitalist interests are able to use their financial power to weed out overtly anti-capitalist candidates at the primary level, especially in state and federal races.[12]

[11]*New York Times,* March 5, 1976, p. 1.

[12]See William Domhoff, *Fat Cats and Democrats* (Englewood Cliffs, N.J.: Prentice-Hall, 1972); see also David Nichols, *Financing Elections* (New York, 1974).

Capitalist financial influence has not led to political uniformity. The Democrats remain a party more influenced by working-class interests than the Republicans. But what financial influence does ensure is that the candidates of both parties fall within a generally acceptable spectrum of political views, neither too far to the left nor to the right. Given capitalist influence, neither party will nominate candidates for state or national office who oppose capitalist property relations, or who advocate, on the other side, race war or the abrogation of bourgeois democracy. When a person who has strayed too far to the left or right has gained a presidential nomination—for instance, Goldwater in 1964 or McGovern in 1972—capitalists have almost universally supported his opponent, with the result of a resounding defeat for the candidate and cries for moderation within the defeated party.

In 1971 and 1974, new campaign financing legislation was passed, ostensibly in order to expose and limit capitalist influence over the campaign financing process. But aside perhaps from limiting contributions to presidential campaigns, these laws do not in practice limit capitalist contributions; they only require new means of funneling them to candidates. For example, replacing the sub rosa corporate gifts is the open and systematic collection of contributions from corporate management under the (legal) rubric of corporate "political action committees." Similarly, although direct contributions to candidates are limited, wealthy individuals can undertake *independent* advertising campaigns to promote a candidate and spend any amount desired. Indeed, there is some evidence that the new rules may *increase* capitalist influence.

It would be a mistake, however, to view campaign financing as the only or even principal level of capitalist control over the political parties. In fact, a few rich individuals were *more* able to buy politicians in the nineteenth century than today. At least as important today is who the capitalist-controlled media are likely to promote as an attractive public personality—a required attribute for a candidate—and what the likely class orientation of such a person will be. Probably more important are how the two-party system defuses dissent, how the capitalist class has dealt with labor union leaders and other groups, and how serious challenges to capitalist rule are smashed.

Maintaining the Two-Party System

The American party system has evolved in such a way as to favor capitalist interests. The structure of the two-party system, with winner-take-all elections, single-member districts, and separate election of Congress and president, makes it difficult for third parties to arise that would unite the working class and small business people against capitalist interests. And when third parties have arisen, capitalists, along with political allies in the established parties, have been able to isolate them and absorb them back into the Democratic or Republican parties or repress and smash them.[13]

In some countries in Western Europe, officials are elected on a proportional system. Each party gains seats in local or national assemblies according to its proportion of the total vote. So parties that initially represent minority political positions or class interests can arise and still gain some victories on the basis of which to go forward. They can also influence the election of a head of government, who is chosen either by the majority party or, if there is no majority, by a coalition of parties.

In the United States, by contrast, election of a single representative from each district on the basis of a winner-take-all election is the universal form. In cities where proportional voting was tried, the success of anticapitalist candidates led to vigorous attempts to go back to the winner-take-all form.[14] At the beginning of this century, capitalist reformers eliminated the ward system of voting

in many cities, a system that—like the proportional one—had encouraged representation by minority interests.[15] American capitalists, aware of the importance and success of their political party system for preserving capitalist hegemony, encouraged its adoption by Germany and Japan after World War II.

This electoral system in the United States has given third parties an enormously difficult time in building a stable base of support, especially in national elections. Leaders of the Democrats and Republicans have been able to cast such parties in the role of spoilers, often by taking over one of the third party's main issues. The result is that the voters have to choose between the survival of the third party and their support for the party's issue. This happened to the Populist Party in 1896, which lost its distinctive character when the Democrats nominated William Jennings Bryan on a "free silver" platform. In the 1948 elections, the Progressive Party saw its base of support eroded by the Democratic Party because of Truman's earlier veto of the anti-labor Taft-Hartley bill (which became law anyway). A similar fate met the right-wing American Independence Party in 1972, when Nixon and the Republican Party were able to attract many of its supporters.

Recently, these older means of restricting electoral competition to the two major parties have been supplemented by new elements. Campaign financing "reform" makes public funds available, but almost all the money goes to Republicans and Democrats under the law's restrictive formula. Similarly, although the "equal time" laws mandate equal access to TV and radio broadcast time for all serious candidates, the major networks, with official connivance, regularly violate these laws. For example, the broadcast of the Carter-Ford debates evaded the law's strictures by a legal ruse: sponsorship of the debates by the League of Women Voters transformed them into "legitimate news events," which are not subject to equal time laws. Thus even as popular pres-

[13]E. E. Schattschneider, *Party Government*, chap. 4 (New York, 1942).

[14]Belle Zeller and Hugh A. Bone, "The Repeal of Proportional Representation in New York City," *American Political Science Review*, 42 (1948).

[15]James Weinstein, *The Corporate Ideal in the Liberal State* (Boston, 1968), chap. 4.

sure forces Congress to pass new laws opening up access to political resources, administrative and legal fiat transforms these reforms into new barriers protecting the monopoly of the two major parties.

If a third party's issues fall largely outside the range of capitalist acceptability, then different strategies are sometimes followed. During World War I, when the Socialist Party advocated a socialist transformation of society and opposition to American participation in the war, the Party was illegally and violently suppressed and its victorious candidates barred from holding office. Similarly, the Black Panther Party was subjected to terror tactics during the late 1960s. The Socialist Worker's Party through court action was able to force the FBI to disclose that for thirty-eight years it planted undercover agents within the party to disrupt its activities, ruin its finances, embarrass its candidates, and so forth.[16]

Democracy in Form but Not in Content

The isolation of government from the electoral system, the capitalists' financial weight with both parties, and the sterility of the present two-party system have wrung from American government much of its democratic content. Many civil liberties and personal freedoms remain, but the basic elements of democratic government—consent of the governed and control of the government by popular majority—have been seriously eroded.

Not only have old methods of making government accountable decayed, but new ones have been avoided. For example, although referenda on important issues were technically impossible (given the difficulty in communications) when the Constitution was written, in the electronics age they are technically trivial; yet fear of what the people might decide (as, for example, on war policy during the Vietnam era) prevents this most democratic of decision-making procedures from achieving a serious hearing.

So the average citizen's participation in "democratic government" is restricted to voting once every two or four years. Yet as we have seen, even voting has had less and less influence on how the government operates. These developments have not escaped the average citizen: modern "democracy," rather than fostering participation, has reduced the public's interest in elections. Despite what was widely perceived as a very close race, roughly 70 million eligible voters refused to vote in the 1976 presidential elections—a massive nonturnout accounting for nearly half of all qualified voters.[17] In the 1980 and 1981 presidential elections, the turnout was even lower. When a large 1976 sample was interviewed as to why they were not planning to vote, nonvoters declared that "candidates say one thing and then do another" (68 percent), "it doesn't make any difference who is elected" (55 percent), and "all candidates seem pretty much the same" (50 percent).[18]Although such attitudes are much deplored by defenders of the system, these citizens seem to understand their own increasing powerlessness.

IV. CONTEMPORARY CAPITALISM, THE STATE, AND CLASS CONFLICT

The state's activities have grown enormously in the twentieth century. This growth has been caused in part by the persistent tendency of the economic system to become more interdependent in character. In order to regulate the movement of the economy as a whole, the state has undertaken macroeconomic planning. Similarly, the state has taken on new responsibilities for planning transportation systems, energy development, training of the labor force, reorganizing the international monetary system, and so on.

The struggle of working-class groups to improve their living standards has been a second cause of the growth in state activities. The re-

---

[16]*New York Times,* September 15, 1976, p. 15.

[17]*New York Times,* November 4, 1976, p. 28.

[18]*Newsweek,* September 13, 1976, p. 16.

form struggles of the 1930s produced federal responsibility for social security, regulation of labor relations, unemployment compensation, etc. These struggles were extended in the 1960s and 1970s to obtain federal antidiscrimination statutes, state expenditures for education, pollution control, Medicare and Medicaid, legalization of collective bargaining rights for some state workers, health and safety regulations at workplaces, and product safety. Thus, the state has become more immediately and directly involved in the accumulation process.

For capitalists, this increasing intervention of the state in the economy makes control over state policies more crucial. How the state regulates industries, sets taxes, conducts macroeconomic policy, buys military hardware, etc. has an increasing impact on profits. The problem this creates for capitalists, as we have seen, is that their control over the state is far from complete. It is certainly less complete than their control over the means of production, and it becomes more uncertain with the continuing demise of small propertied interests and the expansion of an enfranchised working class. Led by Ronald Reagan, capitalists in the 1980s have sought to contain and even rollback the extent of state intervention precisely because of these contradictions.

At the same time, because of the growth of state activities, the working class and its associated social movements must also struggle over state policy to defend or advance their interests. Class struggle occurs not only in relation to individual employers, but more and more spills over into the political arena itself. This struggle includes, though is not limited to, elections and party politics.

We have seen how capitalists have responded to democratic political reforms by seeking to limit democracy and the role of government. The struggle to extend democracy consequently has become increasingly a struggle against capitalists and against the structural constraints that capitalist relations of production place upon the state. The struggle to extend democracy has become more than ever a struggle against the capitalist mode of production.

CHAPTER 6

CLASS AND INEQUALITY

CAPITALISM HAS GENERATED a tremendous increase in the productive capacity of the capitalist economies of North America, Western Europe, Japan, Australia, and New Zealand. Yet this tremendous growth in the forces of production has been accompanied by vast inequalities in the distribution of the fruits of that production. The disparity in income and wealth between the industrialized nations at the center of the world capitalist system and the underdeveloped areas on the periphery has been increasing continuously since the early days of colonial plunder. Moreover, *within* each capitalist nation tremendous fortunes coexist with indescribable poverty in spite of the growth of the modern "welfare state." And while inequalities in income and wealth reveal the primary dimension of inequality in a capitalist society, they also give rise to further inequalities—in power, political influence, occupational status, and privilege—which exist alongside and reinforce the inequalities in income and wealth.

It is no historical accident that great inequalities have always characterized capitalism. Quite the contrary: a significant degree of income inequality is inherent in the capitalist mode of production. The generation of an unequal distribution of income can be traced di-

rectly to the operation of the basic capitalist institutions described in Chapter 2.

THE NECESSITY OF INCOME INEQUALITY

The most fundamental characteristic of the distribution of income under capitalism is that it is tied directly to the production process. The only legitimate claims to income arise from possession of "factors of production" that are used to produce goods and services.[1] Factors of production can be divided into two basic categories: labor-power and the (physical) means of production. Labor-power includes all of the productive capacities of human beings, from the most elementary manual ability to the most sophisticated technical skills. The means of production include all forms of property devoted to productive purposes: land, natural resources, buildings, plant and equipment, and so on. The income received by any individual depends on how much labor-power and/or means of production he or she possesses and on how highly the factors are valued in the relevant market.

People who sell their own labor-power receive *labor income* in the form of wages or salaries; the amount of such income an individual receives depends on wage or salary rates established in the labor market. Although the nature of the work varies enormously from one job to another, people must do some work in order to receive labor income. People who own means of production are in a position to

[1]There are other sources of income from which some people do receive a limited amount of income in capitalist societies—welfare agencies, gifts, prizes, crime, and the like. However, such sources are always treated as exceptions to the normal capitalist rules of the game—exceptions that arise from unusually distressing or pathological circumstances.

receive *property income* without doing any work. People may own means of production directly (e.g., by owning a piece of land or a building) or indirectly (e.g., by owning stock that represents some fraction of the assets of a corporation). In either case, such ownership entitles the owner to a share of the surplus value that is realized when the means of production are combined with labor-power to produce output that is sold on the market. This surplus value is received as property income in the form of profits, interest, or rent.

The class structure of a capitalist society is reflected in the sources of people's incomes. Capitalists are those whose primary source of income is ownership of means of production. Capitalists may (and usually do) also hold jobs that provide them with labor income, but they are still capitalists as long as their property income is substantial enough to enable them to live without working if they chose to do so. Workers are those who own little or no means of production and who depend therefore on labor income for their livelihood. Some people—such as small-scale family farmers, independent professionals, and small business proprietors—receive income that represents a return on both their own labor-power and some means of production that they possess. It may be difficult to determine what proportion of their income is attributable to labor and what proportion is attributable to property. But with the continuing development of the capitalist mode of production such "intermediate" classes of people become less and less significant as a proportion of the total population.[2] Most of the income generated in an advanced capitalist economy can be identified clearly as labor income or property income, and most people can be classified unambiguously as workers or capitalists.

The most basic source of income inequality in a capitalist society is the vastly unequal distribution of property income that results from the capitalist-class monopoly of the means of production. Under capitalism a small minority of the population (the capitalists) own most of the means of production and a large majority (the workers) own virtually nothing productive other than their own labor-power.[3] Since income from property is dependent on ownership of property, this concentration ownership of the means of production results in a corresponding concentration in property income. In fact, it is generally true that the rate of return to productive property increases with the size of the property owned; thus the degree of inequality in the distribution of property income tends to be even greater than the degree of inequality in the distribution of property ownership.[4]

In advanced capitalist societies property income typically accounts for roughly 25 to 30 percent of total national income.[5] Even if labor income were distributed equally among the entire population, the large inequality in the distribution of property income would lead to a highly unequal distribution of total income. In fact, however, capitalism requires an unequal distribution of labor income as well as property income.

A high degree of inequality in the distribution of labor income arises necessarily from the alienated character of labor in a capitalist enterprise. Since workers under capitalism are deprived of control over the process and product of their work, they will rarely be motivated to work by intrinsic aspects of the work process or by any sense of dedication to the enterprise, the community, or the society as a whole. As long as work itself is perceived as a burden to be endured rather than a creative or a socially rewarding endeavor, workers must be motivated to work by extrinsic rewards such as income with which they can purchase material

---

[2]See Reich, Section 4.1, p. 122, for a discussion of long-term changes in the class structure of the United States.

[3]See Table 6-D, p. 220, for estimates of the distribution of ownership of the means of production (income-producing wealth) in the United States.

[4]See the afterword to Section 3.3, p. 83, for evidence that larger units of productive property tend to gain higher rates of return than smaller units.

[5]For evidence on this point, see Simon Kuznets, *Modern Economic Growth* (New Haven, Conn.: Yale University Press, 1966), pp. 167–86.

goods and services. For the same reasons people in a capitalist society generally require a monetary incentive such as a wage increase or a promotion to a higher paying job in order to be induced to acquire new skills and increase their productive abilities through education, job training, and so on.

In principle, nonmonetary status rewards could substitute for income rewards and provide an extrinsic psychic rather than material motivation for work. But capitalist ideology (promoted by powerful ideological institutions such as schools, the media, etc.) places so high a value on monetary success that significant status can rarely be achieved independently of income. Hence, status rewards unrelated to monetary success cannot be expected to play a significant motivational role under capitalism. Instead, material gain incentives are generally necessary to encourage the development of productive attributes and to call forth the energies of workers who do not control the work process.

In order for a material gain incentive system to operate effectively, there must be a highly differentiated hierarchy of jobs with correspondingly differentiated levels of pay. This is not to suggest that *no* work would be done in a capitalist society in the absence of significant labor income differentials. The point is rather that the capitalist mode of production, because it depends on alienated labor, is characterized by a serious conflict between income equality on the one hand and economic efficiency on the other. A high degree of income equality could be attained in a capitalist society only at a very high cost in productive efficiency. In order to remain economically viable, the capitalist mode of production therefore requires significant inequalities in the distribution of labor income.

If people with high property incomes received low labor incomes, and vice versa, then the inequality in the distribution of labor would offset to some extent the inequality in the distribution of property incomes. It is quite evident, however, that in the real world of capitalism the opposite is true. Inequalities in labor income tend to reinforce inequalities in property income because one form of income can be used to generate the other. Capitalists with substantial property income can use it to help themselves (and their children) enhance their labor skills and command higher salaries for their labor-power. Similarly, the relatively few privileged workers who manage to reach high-paying jobs can afford to invest some of their labor income in the acquisition of productive property. On the opposite end of the scale, those people with no property income find it much more difficult to raise their labor income, and vice versa.

For the reasons discussed in the preceding paragraphs, we can conclude that a substantial degree of inequality in the distribution of overall income is inherent in the nature of capitalist institutions. This means that only a complete transformation of the mode of production could eliminate income inequality in currently capitalist societies. Such a transformation would not only have to eliminate private ownership of the means of production; it would also have to develop a new system of work organization that did not rely on individual material gain incentives to motivate people to work.

THE DEGREE OF INCOME INEQUALITY

While a significant amount of inequality is inevitable, the actual degree of income inequality in any given capitalist society will depend on a number of variable factors. Particularly significant is the division of total income between property income and labor income, respectively. Property income is much more highly concentrated than labor income, since only a small minority of people own significant quantities of income-producing property while most people earn some amount of labor income. Moreover, there are limits beyond which salaries do not rise (even automobile executives and sports superstars in the United States today do not get salaries much higher than a million dollars a year), while there are no limits to the amount of income-producing property that a person can own. Therefore, the higher the share of property income in total national income, the more unequal the overall distribution of income is likely to be.

One of the most important determinants of the share of property income is the state of the class struggle between capitalists and workers. As long as capitalists maintain control of the means of production, they can assure that property income will persist, for they can pose the very real threat of withholding their property from production if they do not receive some income for it. However the share of property income in total income is variable within a certain range; it is likely to increase when workers as a class are weak and to fall when workers are strong. Capitalists obviously have a class interest in weakening the bargaining power of workers. One way in which they attempt to do this is by fostering antagonisms within the working class which undermine the potential for working class unity. Indeed, a differentiated hierarchy of jobs (described earlier as essential for a material gain incentive system) is often developed by capitalists to a much greater degree than is functionally necessary because it helps to weaken workers' bargaining power by segmenting the labor force.[6] But capitalists do not always succeed in dominating workers in such ways; there are circumstances in which workers are able to improve their bargaining power and increase their share of total income. Unless the resulting income gains are concentrated in a relatively privileged segment of the labor force, they will lead to a more equal overall distribution of income.

The exercise of economic and political power can affect the overall distribution of income in other ways as well. Without necessarily changing the relative shares of property and labor income, powerful classes or groups of people can use their power to change the distribution of property income or labor income in their own favor. We have seen in Chapter 4 how the capital accumulation process tends to increase the concentration of

ownership of means of production in the hands of the wealthy, as large companies jointly monopolize industries and increase their own profits. Similarly, people with relatively good educational backgrounds are generally able to assure themselves (and their children) of better opportunities to increase their earnings than people from less privileged classes. And in Chapters 9 and 10 we will see how discrimination against women and blacks reduces their income-earning capacity relative to men and whites.

Finally, the state plays an extremely important role in determining the final outcome of the income distributional process. This is not only because the pattern of government taxation and transfers affects the level of disposable income available to each individual. The government also profoundly affects the pre–tax and transfer income of individuals by its expenditure patterns (which firms and industries it chooses to purchase goods and services from), its subsidies (which industries are favored), its regulatory policies (what rates airlines, utilities, etc. can charge), its macroeconomic policies (what will be the rate of unemployment and inflation), its attitude toward the wage bargaining process (under what circumstances will strikes be tolerated), and—in general—its enforcement of the legal rules of the game under which the capitalist economy operates. Thus the current distribution of income depends to a considerable extent on the ability of different classes and groups to get the government to act on their behalf.

We have seen in Chapter 5 that wealthy capitalists are clearly in the strongest position to shape government policy. But there are also circumstances in which poorer groups may be able to mobilize enough power in the political arena to improve their economic position. On the one hand, organized workers may develop enough strength to use orthodox political methods (electing pro-labor representatives, for instance) to force the state to take some actions in their favor. On the other hand, various oppressed groups with little access to orthodox channels of power may take to the street in

[6]See Edwards, Section 6.2, p. 227.

protest demonstrations or riots, forcing the state to ameliorate their condition in the interest of preserving the stability of the society as a whole. Whatever the reasons for it, however, such income redistribution in favor of the poor would have to stop far short of equality because of the systemic capitalist need for an unequal distribution of income.

In the three readings in this chapter we will turn from these theoretical considerations to examine some of the salient facts about the generation and reproduction of class and inequality in our own society. The first reading documents the persistence of inequalities in the distribution of income and wealth in the United States. The second examines the fractions of the working class. The last reading shifts the focus from the *structure* of inequality to the *dynamics* of inequality; it analyzes why the American educational system, ostensibly an important means of equalizing opportunity, has in fact served primarily to perpetuate inequality by transmitting it from one generation to the next.

The persistence of inequality in the United States is clearly an important element in our critique of American capitalism. Whether it is also likely to give rise to contradictions that could threaten the future viability of the system is not clear. In the past, mounting protests by impoverished groups have often been warded off by judicious redistributional policies on the part of the government; for example, Franklin D. Roosevelt's New Deal policies helped to alleviate the problems of the poor and unemployed in the 1930s. More generally, the long-run growth of total income in the United States has made it possible for the *absolute* level of income of the poor to increase even without any change in their *relative* position in the overall distribution. These same processes may continue to contain protests against income inequality in the future. But as we shall see in Chapter 10, there is reason to believe that the long-run rate of growth of total income in the United States will slow down, and this could seriously exacerbate the tensions arising from the persistent inequalities we discuss in this and the following two chapters.

6.1   *Capitalism and Inequality in the United States*

In the following reading Frank Ackerman and Andrew Zimbalist present detailed information on the distribution of income and wealth in the United States. The importance of property ownership as a source of income inequality emerges clearly from their presentation, as does the role of government in maintaining the overall pattern of inequality.

In this essay we first document the extent of income and wealth inequality in the United States; we then consider the effect of taxes and government spending on the distribution of income and wealth: and, finally, we relate the observed inequalities in the United States to the class structure of the capitalist mode of production.

THE DISTRIBUTION OF INCOME AND WEALTH

Income

The best measure of ability to purchase goods and services is after-tax income. However, appropriate data exist only for the distribution of before-tax income, so we must look at that first and consider the tax structure separately. A good way to illustrate the income distribution is to rank the population by income and measure the percentage of total personal income received by the highest-income fifth of the population, the next fifth, and so on. The more income going to the top fifth and the less going to the bottom fifth, the more unequal is the distribution of income.

The Census Bureau collects income statistics separately for families of two or more people and for "unrelated individuals" not living in family units. In 1983, there were 62 million families and 29 million "unrelated individuals."[1] Tables 6-A and 6-B present the distribution of income for both groups.

Table 6-A shows that since World War II the poorest 20 percent of all families have consistently received less than 6 percent of total family income, while the richest 20 percent have gotten more than 40 percent. In 1983 the top 5 percent of all families received nearly 16 percent of total family income, more than three times as much as the entire bottom 20 percent.[2]

The income of individuals who don't live in families (Table 6-B) is more unequally distributed than that of families: in 1983 the top fifth got 48.3 percent of income among unrelated individuals, compared to 42.7 percent among families. But while the family distribution is quite stable over time, the individual distribution has been growing more equal. Between 1947 and 1983 the share of the top fifth dropped from 57 to 48 percent of individual income, with the gain distributed over all four other fifths. This is probably due to the rise of social security and private pension payments to retired people, who often do not live in family units. (In 1983, only 15 percent of family heads were 65 or older, compared to 29 percent of unrelated individuals, and 34 percent of the bottom four-fifths of unrelated individuals. So increased income for retired people should affect the unrelated individuals' distribution far more than the family distribution.)[3]

The growth in income equality among individuals is not likely to continue. The gains associated with large numbers of people starting to receive social security or pensions cannot be repeated because social security coverage is already widespread, and private pensions are no longer expanding rapidly. Furthermore, both social security and most private pension plans are running out of money[4] and may not be able to keep up their present levels of payments; the immediate prospects are for less, not more, real income transfers to retired people.

Tables 6-A and 6-B are based on the Census Bureau's definition of personal money income, which includes government and other transfers to individuals (unemployment insurance, welfare, social security, pensions, etc.) but excludes capital gains (that is, the increase in the value of assets such as corporate stocks). Because 60 percent of capital gains are tax-

[1]U.S. Census Bureau, *Current Population Reports*, Series P-60, no. 137, p. 3; no. 145, p.10.

[2]In 1983, the dollar incomes corresponding to the income groups shown in Tables 6-A and 6-B were as follows:

Bottom Income In:	Families	Unrelated Individuals
Poorest fifth	0	0
Second fifth	$11,629	$ 4,478
Middle fifth	20,060	8,000
Fourth fifth	29,204	13,025
Richest fifth	41,824	20,823
Richest 5%	67,326	36,000

Source: Same as Table 6-A.

[3]Ibid., pp. 69, 72, 81.

[4]See, for instance, *Dollars & Sense*, no. 8 (Summer 1975), p. 16, and no. 9 (1975), pp. 4–5. We thank Janet Corpus and Regina O'Grady for help in researching pension funds and social security.

TABLE 6-A   DISTRIBUTION OF BEFORE-TAX FAMILY INCOME

	1983	1977	1971	1965	1959	1953	1947
Poorest fifth	4.7%	5.2%	5.5%	5.2%	4.9%	4.7%	5.0%
Second fifth	11.1	11.6	12.0	12.2	12.3	12.5	11.9
Middle fifth	17.1	17.5	17.6	17.8	17.9	18.0	17.0
Fourth fifth	24.4	24.2	23.8	23.9	23.8	23.9	23.1
Richest fifth	42.7	41.5	41.1	40.9	41.1	40.9	43.0
Richest 5%	15.8	15.7	15.7	15.5	15.9	15.7	17.5

Source: U.S. Census Bureau, *Current Population Reports*, Series P-60, no. 137, p. 47; no. 145, p. 10.

TABLE 6-B   DISTRIBUTION OF BEFORE-TAX
INCOME AMONG UNRELATED
INDIVIDUALS

	1983	1965	1947
Poorest fifth	3.5%	2.9%	2.0%
Second fifth	8.9	7.6	6.2
Middle fifth	15.2	13.6	12.7
Fourth fifth	24.4	25.0	22.5
Richest fifth	48.2	50.9	56.6
Richest 5%	19.1	20.0	29.3

Source: U.S. Census Bureau, *Current Population Reports*, Series P-60, no. 137, p. 48; no. 145, p. 10.

exempt, stockholders generally prefer capital gains to dividends; corporations systematically retain earnings rather than pay them out in dividends, so capital gains are a customary source of income for many rich people. A complete picture of income distribution should include capital gains.

Table 6-C presents a rough adjustment of the share of the top 20 percent of families to include estimated capital gains.[5] When capital

[5]See Stephen Lehman, *Survey of Current Business* (December 1976), and Thae Park, *Survey of Current Business* (April 1983). Reported capital gains before 1978 were twice as great as taxable capital gains because federal laws considered only half of long-term capital gains as taxable income. Since 1978, reported capital gains are two and a half times as great as taxable capital gains, as federal laws were changed to consider only 40 percent of long-term capital gains as taxable income. Data on taxable capital gains are in Lehman and in Park. We are assuming that capital gains are long term and go to the richest 20 percent (which is approximately true), and that capital gains bear the same proportion to family as to individual income.

On the relation between Personal Income (used in Lehman and in Park) and Money Income (used in Tables 6-A, 6-B, and 6-E here), see U.S. Census Bureau, *Current Population Reports*, Series P-60, no. 137, p. 212.

gains are included, even the slight apparent decline in the income share of the top fifth of families vanishes. We conclude therefore that when capital gains are included, the distribution of family income has not essentially changed since World War II. (A similar adjustment in unrelated individual income would reduce but not eliminate the drop in the top fifth's share.)

Wealth

Income distribution is only part of the picture of the distribution of economic welfare. Two people with the same incomes but with different amounts of wealth are certainly not in the same position economically. We must consider, therefore, the distribution of wealth as well as income.

A person's wealth includes all of the property (or "assets") the person owns. It is important to distinguish between two major types of wealth: (1) income-producing wealth, such as stocks, bonds and real estate other than one's own home; and (2) property held for personal use, such as cars, homes, and checking account deposits. Property for personal use is relatively widely distributed throughout the population, corresponding in predictable ways to the income distribution (richer families are more likely to own their homes and to have a second car). And it has little direct effect on the distribution of income and power in the economy.

Income-producing wealth, on the other hand, is quite tightly concentrated in the hands of a small minority. Because it produces income, it reinforces the position of this group

TABLE 6-C   CAPITAL GAINS AND THE TOP FIFTH'S SHARE OF FAMILY INCOME

Year	Share of Top Fifth Without Capital Gains	Total Reported Net Capital Gains	Share of Top Fifth with Capital Gains
	(all figures are percent of total family income)		
1947	43.0%	2.4%	44.3%
1953	40.9	1.5	41.8
1959	41.1	3.4	43.0
1965	40.9	3.8	43.1
1971	41.1	3.1	42.9
1977	41.5	2.7	43.0
1981	41.9	3.0	43.6

Source: *Survey of Current Business*, December 1976; *Survey of Current Business*, April 1983.

TABLE 6-D   DISTRIBUTION OF WEALTH, 1962

Wealth Size	Households %	Households Cum. %	Total wealth %	Total wealth Cum. %	% Wealth Income-Producing[a]	Income-Producing Wealth[a] %	Income-Producing Wealth[a] Cum. %
Negative	1.7	1.7	—	—	—	—	—
Zero	8.1	9.8	—	—	—	—	—
$0–1,000	15.5	25.3	0.3	0.3	8	—[b]	—[b]
$1–5,000	18.6	43.9	2.4	2.7	10	0.4	0.4
$5–10,000	15.7	59.6	5.5	8.2	16	1.6	2.0
$10–25,000	23.0	82.6	17.6	25.8	23	7.1	9.1
$25–50,000	10.7	93.3	17.9	43.7	42	13.2	22.3
$50–100,000	4.3	97.6	14.1	57.8	62	15.4	37.7
$100–200,000	1.2	98.8	7.6	65.4	66	8.8	46.5
$200–500,000	0.9	99.7	12.9	78.3	83	18.8	65.3
$5000,000+	0.3	100.0	21.7	100.0	91	34.7	100.0

[a]All assets other than homes, automobiles, and noninterest-bearing accounts.

[b]Negligible quantity.

Source: Dorothy Projector and Gertrude Weiss, *Survey of Financial Characteristics of Consumers* (Federal Reserve Board, 1966), various tables.

at the top of the income distribution. And because ownership of stocks, one of the major forms of income-producing wealth, brings with it ownership of corporations, the minority of top wealth holders have tremendous power over the workings of the economy.[6] Our examination of wealth, then, must focus particularly on corporate stocks and other forms of income-producing wealth.

A 1966 survey of more than 2500 households provides useful data on the distribution of wealth.[7] Table 6-D presents some of its major findings. In 1962, households with under $200,000 of wealth, 98.8 percent of all households, owned only 65.4 percent of all wealth and only 46.5 percent of income-producing wealth. Households with over $200,000 in wealth, only 1.2 percent of all households, owned the rest—one-third of all wealth and one-half of income-producing wealth.

Corporate stock is even more concentrated than other forms of income-producing wealth.

[6]The very rich, as a group if not as individuals, own and control major corporations. For a review of recent debates on this subject, see Edward S. Herman, "Do Bankers Control Corporations?", *Monthly Review*, June 1973.

[7]Dorothy S. Projector and Gertrude Weiss, *Survey of Financial Characteristics of Consumers*, (Federal Reserve Board, 1966).

As shown in Table 6-E, in 1972 the wealthiest one-half of 1 percent of the population owned 49.3 percent of personally owned corporate stock, and the top 1 percent owned 56.5 percent. It is difficult to judge changes in the distribution of wealth over time, since the data are much more fragmentary than for income distribution. There have been some studies of time trends in the proportion of total personal wealth held by the wealthiest people at the top of the distribution, and the results of these studies are presented in Table 6-F. According to the figures in the table, the shares of both the top 1 percent and the top 0.5 percent of all wealth holders have decreased between 1922 and 1972. Virtually all of the change, however, appears to have occurred between 1939 and 1945 (i.e., during World War II). From 1922 to 1939 and from 1945 to 1972, there have been fluctuations but no significant trends one way or the other. Just as in the case of the distribution of income, there is no evidence for growing equality in the distribution of personal wealth since 1945.

Personally owned wealth does not tell the

TABLE 6-E   CONCENTRATION OF DIFFERENT FORMS OF PERSONAL WEALTH, 1972

	Percent of Total Held by	
	Top 0.5% of Wealth Holders	Top 1% of Wealth Holders
All assets	18.9%	24.1%
Real estate	10.1	15.1
Corporate stock	49.3	56.5
Bonds	52.2	60.0
Cash	8.5	13.5
Debt instruments	39.1	52.7
Life insurance	4.3	7.0
Trusts	80.8	89.9

Source: *Statistical Abstract of the United States, 1982–83*, table 742, p. 449.

whole story. For example, institutional owners—public and private pension funds, personal trusts, insurance companies, foundations, educational institutions, and mutual savings banks—held stock worth $358 billion, accounting for 34.4 percent of the outstanding shares in 1978. Private pension funds ($107.9 billion)

and personal trusts ($93.1 billion), the two biggest institutional categories, are usually managed by bank trust departments.[8]

To the extreme concentration of personally owned wealth, therefore, we must add the control by banks of another big chunk of institutionally owned wealth.

A View from the Bottom

Extensive poverty accompanies the great concentration of income and wealth. The most common estimates of poverty, published by the Social Security Administration (SSA), define it as an income below $9278 for a family of four in 1981 (with different income cutoffs for different family sizes and residences). In 1981, 31.8 million people, or 14 percent of the population, were living in poverty by these

TABLE 6-F   CONCENTRATION OF WEALTH, 1922–1972

	Percent of Total Wealth Held by	
Year	Top 0.5% of Wealth Holders	Top 1% of Wealth Holders
1922	29.8	31.6
1929	32.4	36.3
1933	25.2	28.3
1939	28.0	30.6
1945	20.9	23.3
1949	19.3	20.8
1953	22.0	27.5
1958	20.4	25.5
1962	20.7	26.2
1965	23.7	29.2
1969	19.9	24.9
1972	18.9	24.1

Source: 1922–1949: Robert J. Lampman, *The Share of Top Wealth-Holders in National Wealth, 1922–1956* (Princeton, N.J.: Princeton University Press, 1962), table 97, p. 209; 1953–1969: J. D. Smith and S. D. Franklin, "The Concentration of Personal Wealth, 1922–1969," *American Economic Review* (May 1974), table 1, p. 166; U.S. Congress, House Committee on the Budget, *Date on the Distribution of Wealth in the United States.*

[8]Edward S. Herman, *Corporate Control, Corporate Power* (New York: Cambridge University Press, 1981), table 4.4, p.138.

criteria. The SSA allows food expenditures of $2.12 per person per day, and assumes that food makes up one-third of the total household budget.[9] We reject poverty lines in the neighborhood of $9300, and thus most poverty figures published by government agencies, as implausibly low.

A more reasonable definition of poverty is the Bureau of Labor Statistics (BLS) subsistence budget for 1967. It totals $15,323 (in 1981 dollars) for an urban family of four. The BLS calculates its budget on a much more detailed and reasonable, basis than the SSA budget.[10] It assumes that of the $15,323, taxes and social security take $2632, leaving $12,691 after tax. Food, assumed to cost less than $3.12 per person per day (this requires very careful shopping and cooking and few meals away from home), takes $4545 for the year. The BLS assumes rent, heat, and utilities for an inexpensive five-room, one-bath apartment to be under $177 per month. House furnishings and household expenditures add another $703. Clothing and personal care together total $1316 for the family or $329 per person. Transportation, assumed to be by an eight-year-old used car except in cities with good public transportation, costs $1311. Medical care and medical insurance for the whole family costs $1436 (less than the cost of many family medical insurance plans or of a one-week stay in a hospital). Only $1236 remains for other expenses.[11]

Most people would agree that a family living on the BLS subsistence budget would feel quite poor, always worrying about making ends meet and constantly threatened with financial disaster in the event of an unexpected illness or job layoff. In 1981, 25 percent of families in the U.S. had incomes below the BLS subsistence budget, adjusted for family size.[12]

TAXATION AND GOVERNMENT SPENDING

Taxation

How do taxes affect the distribution of income? To answer this question we first examine specific taxes and then present evidence on their overall impact.

Table 6-G displays the major sources of government revenue at all levels (federal, state, and local combined). The largest is the individual income tax, almost all collected at the federal level. It is widely believed that the federal income tax is a progressive tax, taking a greater percentage of income from the rich than from the poor, and thereby equalizing the distribution of income. But this view is mistaken; the federal income tax has little, if any, redistributive effect.

It is important to distinguish between the nominal and effective rates of taxation. Nominal income tax rates are progressive, taking more from the rich than from the poor. But because of loopholes that benefit the rich more than the poor (such as taxation of only 40 percent of capital gains, tax-free interest on municipal and state bonds, tax breaks for homeowners but not tenants, income splitting, etc.), the effective rates are nearly proportional.

The second most important source of government revenue is the payroll tax, primarily the social security tax. In 1981, all wage and salary income up to $29,700 was taxed at the rate of 6.65 percent.[13] Wage and salary income above $29,700, and all unearned income, were not touched by social security.

---

[9]U.S. Census Bureau, *Current Population Reports*, Series P-60, no. 138, pp. 2, 3, 180.

[10]U.S. Department of Labor, Bureau of Labor Statistics, Press Release of April 16, 1982 (USDL 82-139).

[11]Ibid.

[12]Ibid. The Bureau of Labor Statistics subsistence budget is not given for a complete range of family sizes. Hence, to adjust the subsistence budget for family size, we used alternative poverty line figures by family size given in U.S. Department of Labor, Bureau of Labor Statistics, Press Release of May 25, 1983 (USDL 83-241). A breakdown of family size by income is in U.S. Census Bureau, *Current Population Reports*, Series P-60, no. 137, p. 86.

[13]From time to time the taxable income limit and the tax rate are raised, but as long as the basic procedure remains the same, the social security tax remains highly regressive.

This means someone making $10,000 a year, for instance, paid 6.65 percent of $10,000 or $665, while an executive with a $100,000 salary paid 6.6 percent only on the first $29,700 amounting to $1975, or 1.975 percent of total salary. And a landlord with no salary but $100,000 income from rents didn't pay a cent into social security.

While the federal income tax is nearly proportional in impact, the social security tax is clearly regressive, taking a higher percentage from the poor than from the rich. More than half of all taxpayers give more each year to the Social Security Administration than they do to the Internal Revenue Service.[14]

Sales taxes and similar charges are the third largest source of government income. Of the $111.9 billion collected in 1980, gasoline, alcohol, and tobacco taxes accounted for $29.3 billion, and general state and local sales taxes made up most of the rest.[15] Sales taxes are based only on what you spend, not on your entire income; since richer people save a higher percentage of their income and spend a lower percentage, they pay a lower percentage of income in sales taxes than do poor people. In particular, lower-income people undoubtedly spend a higher percentage of their income on the most heavily taxed goods—gasoline, alcohol, and tobacco—than do higher-income people.

Property taxes, the fourth largest form of government revenue, are also regressive. Landlords pass on property taxes to tenants in higher rents; and the richer you are, the less of your income you spend on rent. Similarly, if you are a homeowner, the richer you are, the smaller the proportion of your income you are likely to spend on home expenses and property tax.

Corporation income taxes, fifth in importance, have been growing more slowly than other taxes. In 1950 they accounted for 16.6 percent of all taxes; by 1982 they were only 6.4 percent. In theory, they are progressive: The *nominal* rates are 22 percent on the first $25,000 of a corporation's income, 26 percent for corporate income between $25,000 and $50,000, and 48 percent above $50,000. However, because of numerous loopholes, the *effective* overall corporate tax rate in 1981 was only 20.4 percent.[16]

At least three major loopholes reduce corporate taxes. First, industry is allowed to claim accelerated depreciation, which means padding the tax deductions for the costs of plants and machinery. Second, the investment tax credit enables companies to deduct 10 percent of the value of new investment from their tax payment (this is in addition to their normal depreciation deductions). Third, U.S.-based multinational corporations can take advantage of the foreign tax credit that allows them to subratct from U.S. taxes an amount equal to foreign taxes paid on income returned to the U.S. In addition, other write-off provisions

TABLE 6-G   GOVERNMENT REVENUE, ALL LEVELS, BY SOURCE

	1982	1965	1950
Total	100.0	100.0	100.0
Individual income taxes	37.6	26.1	24.7
Payroll taxes[a]	22.5	13.1	8.2
Sales, excise, customs taxes	13.8	16.2	19.5
Property taxes	9.3	11.2	10.9
Corporation income taxes	6.4	13.5	16.6
Estate and gift taxes	1.1	1.7	1.3
All other[b]	9.4	18.2	18.6

[a]Primarily social security; also includes government employee pension payments, unemployment taxes, and similar programs.

[b]Includes minor taxes, license fees, public utility and state liquor store income, and intergovernmental funds.

Source: U.S. Census Bureau, *Statistical Abstract of the United States, 1982–83,* p. 275, *1975,* pp. 252–253; *1966,* p. 418; *1952,* p. 358; Joseph A. Pechman, *Federal Tax Policy* (Washington, D.C.: Brookings Institution, 1983), table 1-1, p. 2.

[14]William K. Tabb, "Income Shares and Recovery," *The Nation,* October, 4, 1975, p. 301.

[15]U.S. Census Bureau, *Statistical Abstract of the United States,* 1982–83, p. 275.

[16]Joseph Pechman, *Federal Tax Policy* (Washington, D.C.: Brookings Institution, 1983), table 5-3, p. 144.

and accounting manipulations are possible to further reduce the corporate tax burden. It is also important to point out that corporate taxes are often paid indirectly by the consumer in the form of higher prices.

Taxes on wealth—estate and gift taxes—constitute less than 2 percent of government revenue and have very little impact on the distribution of wealth. Trust funds allow the estate tax to be skipped from one generation to the next. An estate left to a spouse is taxed at one-half the normal rate. Gift taxes can be avoided or greatly minimized by parcelling out gifts over several years or over several recipients. One recent study calculated the effective wealth tax rate for individuals with net worth over $500,000 to be a trifling one-half of 1 percent.[17]

When all taxes are considered together, there is little, if any, difference in the distribution of before- and after-tax income. A 1985 Brookings Institution study attempted to calculate the impact of the overall tax structure on the distribution of family income from 1966 to 1985.[18] Such calculations depend on certain assumptions about the extent to which businesses and landlords pass on taxes to consumers. Table 6-H reports the findings of this study for the "most progressive" and "least progressive" assumptions regarding the incidence of various taxes.

Under both the "most progressive" and "least progressive" assumptions there is basically no change between the before- and after-tax distributions of income. This study also found that the tax structure became less progressive between 1966 and 1985.

Government Spending

If taxes don't improve the income distribution, what about government spending? It's not much help either. The effect of government spending is largely to preserve the society's basic institutions that generated the inequality in the first place.

Table 6-I summarizes the components of government spending (federal, state, and local combined). The largest single item is the military budget. It goes in large part to cost-plus contractors. Profits are guaranteed and the

TABLE 6-H   DISTRIBUTION OF FAMILY INCOME BEFORE AND AFTER ALL TAXES, 1985

Fifths of All Families	Most Progressive Assumption		Least Progressive Assumption	
	Before Tax	After Tax	Before Tax	After Tax
Poorest 20%	4.2%	4.4%	4.2%	4.2%
Second 20%	10.0	10.2	10.0	10.0
Third 20%	15.8	15.8	15.9	15.6
Fourth 20%	23.3	22.4	22.5	22.2
Richest 20%	47.7	47.3	47.3	48.0

Source: Joseph A. Pechman, *Who Paid the Taxes, 1966–85* (Washington, D.C.: Brookings Institution, 1985), p. 74.

capital-intensive nature of military production assures that wage payments are a small portion of total costs. The same applies to space and technology outlays. And a major function of military and diplomatic activity is to maintain U.S. control and profitable investment opportunities for U.S. corporations in as much of the world as possible. Military and space spending, one-sixth of government spending in 1980, seems to benefit the rich, not the poor. Interest on debt is paid to owners of government bonds, who are usually very wealthy.

Police departments protect the property of businesses and affluent homes, while providing zero or negative benefits to poor neighborhoods. Natural resource spending is ambiguous in impact, but benefits many particular industries. Highways and the Postal Service are used at times by almost everyone, but disproportionately benefit business: automobile manufacturers, trucking firms, and related companies in the case of highways; nearly all advertisers in the case of the Postal Service.

Fire protection, sanitation, and sewers seem neutral in distributional impact. Housing and urban renewal may at times provide housing

[18]Joseph Pechman, *Who Paid the Taxes, 1966–85* (Washington, D.C.: Brookings Institution, 1985).

[17]James Wetzler, *"Studies on the American Distribution of Wealth,"* Ph.D thesis, Harvard University, 1973, p. 60.

TABLE 6-1   TOTAL GOVERNMENT SPENDING, BY
FUNCTION

	1980	1965	1950
Total	100.0	100.0	100.0
Military, State Department, space	15.6%	29.6 %	26.2 %
Interest on debt	7.9	5.5	7.0
Police	1.6	1.4	1.3
Natural resources	3.7	5.4	7.1
Highways	3.5	6.0	5.5
Postal Service	1.9	2.6	3.3
Fire protection, sanitation and sewerage	2.0	1.8	1.8
Housing and urban renewal	1.3	1.1	0.1
Education	15.0	14.4	13.7
Social security	15.6	8.1	1.0
Public employee pensions	3.0	1.7	0.1
Health and hospitals	4.5	3.7	4.0
Public welfare	6.9	3.1	4.3
Unemployment compensation	1.3	1.2	2.8
Veterans' benefits[a]	1.3	2.0	4.7
Local parks and recreation	0.1	0.05	0.04
All other[b]	14.2	12.0	15.6

[a]Excluding some benefits included in other categories.

[b]General administration, public utilities and liquor stores, and miscellaneous.

Source: U.S. Census Bureau, *Statistical Abstract of the United States: 1982–83*, p. 274; *1975*, p. 253.

for the poor but more frequently have subsidized private construction companies, and destroyed existing low-income neighborhoods to "renew" them for new business use.

The programs mentioned so far, amounting to a third of government spending in 1980, have a fairly clearly neutral or regressive effect on income distribution. The situation is more complex in the remaining cases, roughly speaking the "health education and welfare" programs.

Education is the only budget category in Table 6-1 rivaling the military in size. It is often viewed as a great equalizer, allowing the

poor to "get ahead." Yet, as many critics have shown,[19] the educational system usually tracks people into jobs corresponding in status to their parents' jobs and provides differentially greater opportunities to get ahead for those who already started ahead. While education provides an orderly channel for the upward mobility of some low-income individuals, there is little evidence that it raises the relative position of low-income people as a group.

Social security and pension payments have been a rapidly growing part of government spending, rising from 2 percent of the total in 1950 to 19 percent in 1980. As mentioned above, they are probably among the causes of the one observed instance of growing equality—the distribution of income of unrelated individuals. They are also, however, one of the areas most threatened with cutbacks in the next few years.

The remaining areas of health and welfare spending—health and hospitals, public welfare, unemployment compensation, and veterans' benefits—all surely provide greater benefit to the poor than to the rich. Like social security, many of these programs emerged from periods of crisis and popular struggle, from the 1930s to the present. But they are very partial victories: public hospitals and public welfare, for instance, provide notoriously inadequate services under degrading conditions.

It is extremely difficult, if not impossible, to assess precisely the overall distributive effects of all types of government spending. The programs of clearly greater benefit to the poor than to the rich amounted to less than a third of government spending in 1980 (social security, pensions, health and hospitals, welfare, unemployment compensation, veterans' benefits), and more than half of that amount was in social security and pensions. Over the years, as government spending has accounted for a larger and larger share of GNP, the distribution of family in-

[19]See Bowles, Section 6.3, p. 235, for an analysis of how and why the U.S. educational system does not promote greater equality.

come (covering 90 percent of the population) has not become more equal. It seems likely, therefore, that government spending serves not to redistribute resources to the poor but to maintain the existing unequal distribution of resources and the capitalist institutions that generate it.

CLASS AND INCOME DISTRIBUTION

There are many sources of income inequality in the United States. Race, sex, education, and regional differences all affect the distribution of income. The primary source of high incomes, however, is ownership of income-producing property. At the very top of the income pyramid are the big capitalists, supported primarily by their stocks and bonds. Just below the top there is a concentration of small business people, whose income arises both from their property and their labor. The rest of the people (roughly 80 percent) live mainly on wages and salaries, pensions, or welfare.

Table 6-J presents data from federal income tax returns on the sources of income by income bracket in 1979. We define "small business" income to include rent and income from unincorporated businesses and professions, farms, partnerships, and small business corporations. "Capitalist" income includes dividends, capital gains, and interest. Small business and capitalist income each amount to only 8 percent of all income, but they are concentrated in the hands of upper-income groups.

Taxpayers who reported under $25,000 in net taxable income, the vast majority, got 86 percent of their income from wages and salaries and only 7 percent from capitalist sources (including interest on savings accounts). At higher income levels, the share of wages and salaries falls steadily and that of capitalist income rises. Small business income is of greatest relative importance in the $50,000 to $100,000 bracket, but even there it is not the major form of income; above $100,000 it fades rapidly. The 3,600 taxpayers reporting over $1,000,000 in gross income (they averaged

over $2 million each) got three-quarters of their incomes from dividends, capital gains and interest and only one-seventh from salaries.

Moreover, the Internal Revenue Service data used in Table 6-J are biased to minimize the significance of property for the rich. Much of capitalist income, including all interest on state and municipal bonds, is tax-exempt and therefore not included in these figures. Exaggerated depreciation and depletion allowances are common. Tax-exempt charitable donations can be padded and overstated. True income figures, therefore, would show even greater concentrations of capitalist income in the hands of the very rich.

The argument that property ownership is a primary source of income inequality gains further support from a comparison of income distribution in capitalist and state socialist countries. An exhaustive study of international patterns of inequality found that out of seventy-two countries for which comparable data were available, the four Soviet bloc countries in the sample (East Germany, Czechoslovakia, Poland, and Hungary) had the four most equal income distributions.[20] Even the relatively egalitarian capitalist countries (New Zealand, Canada, the Scandinavian countries) had income distributions substantially more unequal than those of the four Soviet bloc countries. Another study found that in 1960 the ratio of the average income of the highest 10 percent of income earners to that of the lowest 10 percent was roughly 5 to 1 in the Soviet Union and 30 to 1 in the United States.[21] Such differences can be attributed to the absence of property income as well as the

---

[20]Jerry Lee Cromwell, *"Income Inequalities, Discrimination and Uneven Capitalist Development,"* Ph.D. thesis, Harvard University, 1974, pp. 234–237, 279–287.

[21]Murray Yanowitch, "The Soviet Income Revolution," reprinted in *The Soviet Economy,* ed. M. Bornstein and D. R. Fusfeld (Homewood, Ill.: Richard Irwin, 1966), p. 237. The presence of many free services (e.g., education, medicine) and many state-subsidized goods and services (e.g., house rent, transportation, basic food items) makes the actual distribution of income yet more equal in the Soviet bloc countries than these figures would indicate.

TABLE 6-J   INCOME BY SOURCE, 1979

Size of Gross Income ($)	Number of Tax Returns (thousands)	Total Income ($ billion)	Percent of Total Income		
			Wages and Salaries	Small Business	Capitalist
All sizes	92,152	1,475,264	83.2	5.7	9.4
1–25,000	74,826	786,915	86.1	3.2	6.9
25–50,000	14,985	490,610	86.9	5.3	6.9
50–100,000	1,890	123,200	66.8	16.8	16.3
100–500,000	438	69,721	53.9	15.9	29.0
500,000–1,000,000	9.9	6,572	30.4	10.8	55.5
1,000,000 and up	3.6	8,116	14.1	8.1	74.6

Source: U.S. Internal Revenue Service, *Statistics of Income 1979: Individual Income Tax Returns,* table 1.3, pp. 14–23. Some minor sources of income, included in total income, are not shown separately.

absence of unemployment in state socialist countries.

CONCLUSION

In this paper we have documented the extent of income and wealth inequality in the United States. The basic pattern of inequality has scarcely changed in the last thirty years, and appears to be unaltered by government taxation and spending policies. At the upper end of the distribution, property income accruing to the capitalist class is the primary source of inequality. The evidence available from international comparisons suggests that socialism leads to much more equality.

6.2 *The Fractions of the Working Class*

Although property ownership constitutes a major source of inequality in the United States, dividing workers and capitalists, a considerable amount of inequality among workers exists as well. In the following reading Richard Edwards addresses these inequalities and shows that divisions among workers are rooted in the character of the economic system.

Excerpted from RICHARD EDWARDS, *Contested Terrain: The Transformation of the Workplace in The Twentieth Century* (New York: Basic Books, 1979). Reprinted by permission of the author and Basic Books.

The development of twentieth-century American capitalism has fractured, rather than unified, the working class. Workers have been divided into separate groups, each with its distinct job experiences, distinct community cultures, and distinct consciousnesses. The inability of working class-based political movements to overcome these divisions has doomed all efforts at serious structural reform.

The mark of twentieth-century divisions in the working class is their enduring, deeply anchored, institutionalized nature. Employers have always attempted to exploit differences among workers, and their efforts often proved successful at crucial turning points in labor history. But such efforts were transitory, requiring new outbursts of nativism or anti-immigrant bias or antiblack hatred or anti-Catholicism to renew the divisions. It is an unfortunate truth about the American past that new divisive campaigns were never long absent, but they still must be understood as political and ideological efforts rather than the products of economic structure. They were indeed rooted in real differences in the living conditions of the laboring populations, but nineteenth-century capitalism, much as it profited from these differences, was busy eroding them.

Not so in this century, where the divisions have been made more permanent because they were rooted in the normal, everyday operation of economic institutions, in particular in the differing systems of control in the firm and their associated labor market segments. In the last chapter, these divisions were described in terms of distinctions among jobs, and it is true that the clearest and (in terms of change) the most powerful divisions have evolved in the job structure. Yet sharp divisions between groups of jobs tend to create discrete populations of job-holders as well. The tendency of segmented markets to divide the working class is especially strong since the differences among market segments include distinct career mobility patterns; that is, job-holders tend to experience these differences not just in current jobs but over their entire lifetimes.[1]

Before turning directly to the fractions of the working class, we must choose some compromise in the problem of terminology. One set of terms—"lower class," "working class," and "middle class"—derives from the popular media and from bourgeois sociology. Although they have the advantage of being well known and simple, these terms also have many disadvantages. They are imprecise ("middle class" includes both those within capital's employ and those outside it); they focus too exclusively on income rankings; and by making different fractions of the working class into distinct classes, they mask the real relations we want them to reveal. Terminology from classical Marxism does not precisely fit the fractions described here either, and it has the added disadvantage that its usage in a substantial literature has left it with multiple and sometimes contradictory meanings. In what follows, then, let us label the various fractions of the working class Fraction I, Fraction II, and Fraction III. Perhaps the closest descriptive titles for these respective segments would be the "working poor," the "traditional proletariat," and the "middle layers." These three groups roughly correspond to the three "classes" of bourgeois sociology, although it should be clear that they do not represent separate classes but instead are fractions of the working class; they are all composed of wage or salary workers dependent upon capital for employment.

FRACTION I: THE WORKING POOR

American society in the 1960s rediscovered its poor. More, we learned poverty's distinctive social markings, and it became clear that the poor constitute an identifiable and enduring subpopulation of society. Two-thirds of all poor persons in 1974 were either black, of Hispanic origin, elderly, or in families headed by women; some persons, or course, shared some or all of these characteristics. Whites comprise about 66 percent of all poor people, but the proportion of each population in poverty is much higher among blacks (31 percent) and Hispanics (23 percent) than among whites (9 percent). Similarly, slightly more than half of

[1]The evolution of economic life has tended to segment the working class, but the experience, "social practices," and political behavior of each fraction cannot be understood as simply an expression of these economic realities. Indeed, as recent historical scholarship has emphaszied so well, the working class creates for itself a complex and multifaceted reality in which culture, family patterns, ethnicity, and tradition all play central parts. This holds for class fractions as well as for the working class as a whole. This chapter focuses on the fractions' economic existences, and it therefore represents an incomplete (and beginning) analysis.

all poor persons come from families with a male present, but the proportion of female-headed households that are poor (31 percent) greatly exceeds those family groupings with a male present (8 percent). Most of the poor (86 percent) are less than sixty-five years of age, and indeed nearly half (42 percent) are younger than eighteen years old, but again the rate of poverty is higher among old people (16 percent) and the young (15 percent) than among those eighteen to sixty-five (9 percent).[2]

Moreover, poverty has a striking spatial dimension. Three-quarters of all poor people live either in rural areas or the central city, and the rates of poverty (14 percent for nonmetropolitan areas, 14 percent for the central city, 7 percent for the suburbs) reveal its geographical concentration. The rural poor are most likely to be residents of regions (such as Appalachia) where stagnating agriculture left a redundant population; the low density of settlement makes the social causes of poverty less immediately apparent. But in the cities, the poor are collected and pushed into highly visible, low-income ghettos; more than a third of the urban poor live in the officially defined poverty areas—neighborhoods in which 20 percent or more of the inhabitants have poverty-level incomes.[3]

For all these reasons, the poor, and especially the urban poor, became a recognizable group. Yet if American society rediscovered its poor in the 1960s, it only belatedly recognized that its biggest poverty population is the *working* poor. In 1974, for example, slightly over half of those families with income below the officially defined poverty level had family heads who worked; in fact, for a fifth of poor families, the head of the household worked full time. In less than one-third of the officially defined poverty families there are no income earners, and the members of these families are primarily old people. For poor families with

an adult male present, inability to find work is the third most important reason, after illness or disability and retirement, for the man's not working; for poor families headed by a female, inability to find work is again the third most important reason for unemployment, behind "keeping house" (two thirds of these families have two or more dependents) and illness or disability.[4] In short, most poor families are the working poor; the rest cannot work because of age, ill health, or the need to care for dependents, or because they cannot find work. And particularly among the able-bodied poor, the poor are poor because they are employed at low wages, are irregularly employed, or cannot find work at all.

There is a deep structural basis for the poverty of Fraction I: the working poor are in families where the principal wage-earner (male or female) or all wage-earners are employed in secondary-market jobs. The conditions of the secondary market (low wages, employment irregularity, lack of job security, and little benefit from greater seniority or education) establish the patterns for the employment experience of the working poor. The barriers to the primary markets—the lack of enough subordinate primary jobs; the craft restrictions, the educational requirements, and racial and sexual discrimination in independent primary jobs—set the limits for the employment possibilities of the working poor. Subject to secondary-market conditions and excluded (except toward the end of the boom) from primary markets, the working poor survive the ups and downs of the cycle as an enduring feature of American society.

The identity of Fraction I becomes clearer if we investigate the holders of secondary jobs. There seems little doubt that people who are black, Hispanic, female, teenage, or undocumented workers (illegal aliens) are heavily overrepresented. Again, caution is in order. Since the biggest single group in the labor force is white males, white males tend to show up in large numbers even in the secondary market. Nevertheless, several studies have

[2]U.S. Bureau of the Census, *Current Population Reports*, Series P-60, no. 102, Characteristics of the Population Below the Poverty Level: 1974, pp. 1, 2, 36, 38, 39.

[3]Ibid., pp. 36, 38, 46.

[4]Ibid., pp. 4, 92, 94, 108.

documented the heavy overrepresentation of blacks. Similarly, Samuel Rosenberg's study of the low-income areas of four major cities found high proportions of Hispanic workers in secondary jobs. But perhaps the most revealing estimates come from the very careful and useful study of low-wage employment by Barry Bluestone, William Murphy, and Mary Stevenson; more than three-quarters of all low-wage job-holders are black and/or female. Even here, however, the concentration among specific population groups is understated: Hispanics are not identified, the data come from census surveys that admittedly fail to count many black and brown workers, and undocumented workers are almost completely unrecorded.[5]

PROPORTION OF WORKING POOR BY SEX-RACE GROUPS

	Percent
White Males	22.4
White Females	26.3
Black Males	27.1
Black Females	24.2
	100.0

Source: Calculated from Barry Bluestone, William Murphy, and Mary Stevenson, *Low Wages and the Working Poor* (Ann Arbor, MI, 1973), pp. 51, 215.

The newest source of secondary-market workers has been the flood of undocumented or illegal migrants from Mexico, the Caribbean, and elsewhere. Estimates on the size of this influx range from 5 to 10 million, and since most such workers are immediate job-seekers (children and old people having been left at home), it is clear that this group now constitutes a critical component of the total low-wage labor pool.[6] Fleeing phenomenal rates of unemployment and superexploitative wages in their home countries, undocumented

workers arrive without rights or resources. They make ideal fodder for secondary-market employers, since their illegal status, the dangers of being discovered, and their inability to obtain unemployment compensation force them to become resigned to harsh discipline and low wages, with little or no protest. Thus are new recruits added to Fraction I.

We should note, however, that not all secondary workers can be properly analyzed as part of the working poor. Teenagers, for example, often accept secondary-market employment while still in school or on vacation. Many women are in low-wage jobs although, due to other family members' earnings, the family itself is not poor. White males, before settling on a primary-market career, frequently begin by working in secondary-market jobs. The non-work environment of community, homelife, and culture distinguish these workers from the working poor.

But for the rest—the working poor with their principal wage-earners rooted in secondary employment—capitalism's segmentation of the labor force becomes manifested in enduring poverty. The working poor thus come to constitute a permanent fraction of the working class, a population for whom, even in good times, the chief concern must be survival.

FRACTION II: THE TRADITIONAL PROLETARIAT

The second fraction of the working class, the traditional proletariat, is that portion of the producing population employed in subordinate primary-market jobs. These are production workers who form the most familiar image of working-class life. The males tend to be manual workers in industrial plants, and they frequently are union members. The females tend to be homemakers, clerical workers, or factory operatives. Their incomes (at least in good times) are sufficiently above poverty levels to permit some to own their own homes and nearly all to enjoy the consumption benefits associated with high-wage factory labor.

Fraction II is properly labeled "traditional," not because it conforms to the work-

[5]Samuel Rosenberg, *"The Dual Labor Market: Its Existence and Consequences,"* unpublished Ph.D. thesis. University of California, Berkeley, 1975. Barry Bluestone, William Murphy and Mary Stevenson, *Low Wages and the Working Poor* (Ann Arbor, MI, 1973).

[6]Michael J. Piore, *Birds of Passage* (New York: Basic Books, 1979).

ing-class stereotype prevalent in popular films or mainstream sociology but because it (collectively) has the longest experience as wage labor. Fraction II workers are the descendants of the first large concentrations of industrial workers in the United States, the semiskilled and unskilled proletariat created by the upsurge of capitalism between the Civil War and the First World War. That original "triumph of capitalism" revolutionized the production of steel, electrical goods, processed foods, machinery, autos, and other industrial products and brought into existence the railroads, communications networks, utilities, and other infrastructures to serve the new order. In the process, capitalist development also gave birth to the first large industrial proletariat in the United States; the traditional proletariat today continues that employment.

In many cases these workers are not only descended from the earlier factory proletariat in some collective sense; they can also individually trace their own ancestors. Thus, the major concentrations of ethnic workers today—Italians, Poles, Hungarians, Germans, Greeks, Irish, Slavs, and others—represent a continuing link to the great migrations that provided the first factory populations. Large numbers of these workers live in the blue-collar communities that either uneasily coexist with low-income ghettoes and luxury-housing enclaves or that have increasingly invaded the residential areas outside the central cities. These communities are too prosperous to be accurately labeled "ghettoes" (though they once served as such), and they now function as stable ethnic neighborhoods. More generally, the traditional proletariat lives in what have come to be (meaningfully) referred to as "working-class neighborhoods."

If this second fraction of the working class survives as the lineal descendant of nineteenth-century workers, it has nonetheless undergone extensive change. For one thing, blacks have entered subordinate primary employment in large numbers. In both the First and Second World Wars, rural blacks migrating to industrial employment found that wartime labor shortages opened job opportu-

nities that had been firmly closed to them. In the postwar period, their foothold has been secured on a more permanent basis. So, for example, Martin Carnoy and Russell Rumberger found that nearly half (47.3 percent) of the employed black males in their 1970 sample were subordinate primary workers. Similarly, Samuel Rosenberg found that between 60 and 74 percent of black males from four major cities were primary-market workers. Paul Osterman found that the proportion of black males in the subordinate primary market closely paralleled the representation of black males in his entire sample. If Osterman's sample can be taken as representative of the national male labor force—which it was weighted to be—then it would appear that blacks comprise some 8 to 10 percent of this segment. Whereas at one time blacks found industrial employment only during wars and strikes, they have now become a central and continuing source of factory labor.[7]

A second change concerns females. Most of the segmented-market studies have used samples consisting solely of male workers, so we are left with little solid information about the employment of women in subordinate primary jobs. It seems apparent, however, that some women workers have themselves moved into production or blue-collar subordinate primary jobs. This is part of the general increase in female industrial employment. Between 1959 and 1974, for example, the number of female workers on manufacturing payrolls jumped by nearly a million, an increase of over 55 percent. But female manufacturing workers are more likely to be employed as secondary workers than as subordinate primary workers (nearly 60 percent of all women in manufacturing are employed in textiles or related products, where secondary-market patterns prevail), so the increase in female manu-

[7]Martin Carnoy and Russell Rumberger, *Segmented Labor Markets: Some Empirical Forays* (Palo Alto, Calif.: Center for Economic Studies, 1975) table 2; Rosenberg "The Dual Labor Market," table 3-4; Paul Osterman, "An Empirical Study of Labor Market Segmentation," *Industrial and Labor Relations Review*, 1975 table 2.

facturing workers overstates the move into subordinate primary-type production jobs. Much more significant numerically for women is nonproduction or white-collar employment—comprising the other large group of subordinate primary workers. Female clerical and sales workers numbered less than half a million in 1900; by 1940 this group had increased to about 3½ million. Between 1940 and 1974 employment of women in sales and clerical work added another 10 million to the total. Much of this increase, like the increase in female production workers, undoubtedly took place in secondary-type jobs, but a substantial amount (much of the nonproduction personnel added by the core firms) has been in subordinate primary jobs. Thus, just as the subordinate primary market has incorporated blacks, so has it come to embrace ever-larger numbers of women.[8]

The increase in female subordinate primary workers—indeed, the increase in employment for both subordinate primary- and secondary-market women—has worked a substantial change in the typical family of Fraction II. The most representative traditional proletariat family is fast coming to depend upon two income earners: the husband is a blue-collar machine operative in the subordinate primary market, while the wife works as a clerical or operative herself, either in the subordinate primary market or (more likely) in the secondary market. Their combined income is what decisively lifts them out of poverty status, and especially for younger families, the loss of either job threatens to move them back to the margin of poverty.

Unionization constitutes the third great change in the move from the nineteenth-century industrial proletariat to the Fraction II of today. Most industrial workers before the 1930s had few job protections; employed as casual labor, they experienced conditions much like secondary workers today. Unionization, however, brought the establishment of seniority protections, pensions, internal job bidding, and other job rights, that is, precisely those characteristics that changed the employment pattern to subordinate primary.

Thus, the traditional proletariat has come to form the second distinct fraction of the working class. It has attained a relatively high standard of living because of high and (with seniority) rising wages for unionized males and because of most families' reliance on having two income earners. In boom times such as the 1960s, the job security and good wages, combined with the routinized, machine-paced nature of subordinate primary work, tend to lead to increasing conflict on the shop or office floor, as workers seek relief from degraded work. In hard times like the 1970s, the precariousness of Fraction II's prosperity reasserts itself, and blue-collar families must again battle the dangers of unemployment and inflation. Uncertain and eroding real income again becomes a central concern.

FRACTION III: THE MIDDLE LAYERS

Independent primary work supplies the jobs of the middle layers of employment, those workers who stand between all lower-level administrative and production workers, on the one side, and capitalists and the various echelons of high management, on the other. This group includes craft workers, technical and professional employees, and supervisors and middle-level administrative staff; public-sector employment constitutes a significant share.

Fraction III tends to be the preserve of white males. More than 70 percent of all independent primary workers are white males, and among craft workers (87 percent white males) and supervisory workers (79 percent white males), women and nonwhites are excluded almost altogether. Blacks hold less than 7 percent of these jobs; the only large instrusion into this segment has been achieved by white women in professional and technical jobs such as teaching, social work, and nursing. White males in independent primary jobs account for 48 percent of all white male workers.[9]

---

[8]See Introduction to Chapter 7, p. 249.

[9]Calculated from *Handbook of Women Workers*, 1975, table 19, and Census of Population, 1970, "Occupational Characteristics," table 2. The figures represent illustrative orders of magnitude rather than precise measurements.

Wages tend to be considerably higher among independent primary workers than among workers in the other two market segments, and higher incomes undoubtedly help create the many notable differences in life style. Fewer wives of independent primary males work, although, as for other segments, the proportion is rapidly rising; and more Fraction III families live either in the suburban rings around major cities or, when in the city, in neighborhoods isolated from the poor.[10]

Fraction III thus gives rise to the "new middle class" that has appeared during the last three decades or so. This group has replenished the badly depleted ranks of the old middle class and has usually been interpreted as simply its extension. But as several have observed, the new middle class is unlike the old in some fundamental respects. The old middle class (or petty bourgeoisie) achieved its position by remaining outside the accumulation process, that is, outside the relations of employment between capitalists and workers; shopkeepers, tradesmen, petty commodity producers, independent professionals, and other middle-class elements retained their autonomy, some even rising to the status of small-scale employers. But today's middle-layer workers have been transformed into employees (even if privileged ones) of capital, made crucial to continued accumulation given the present organization of industry, and hence they were brought within the relations of employment as workers. The typical Fraction III worker can continue to dream of being "one's own boss," but the real basis for any significant numbers of them being able to achieve that dream has evaporated.

The contrast between old and new could hardly be greater. Where the members of the old middle class were necessarily risk-takers, attempting to calculate the possible returns of one course of action versus those of another, middle-layer workers today find employment within large institutions, experiencing risk-taking as a corporate (not an individual) phenomenon, and seeing the gains and losses from risk accrue to the organization, not to the individual. Where the old middle class always confronted the prospect of ruin and dreamed of the chance of big success, middle-layer workers today face a range of possibilities limited downward by the employment guarantees of independent primary employment and upward by the inherent constraints of working for someone else's profit. Where the old middle class had command over its immediate conditions of work (often, as J. K. Galbraith has noted, choosing to exploit itself through exceptionally long hours), today's Fraction III work is organized and governed by the highly structured apparatus of bureaucratic control. Where members of the old middle class were constantly making decisions based on their own interests, middle-layer workers today are perpetually applying preestablished rules or other work criteria. The old middle-class situation produced the shrewd, petty, calculating, opportunistic, independent-minded, politically conservative but personally bold small entrepreneur, but today's Fraction III employment produces the organization person. As we saw in a previous chapter, the outstanding characteristics reinforced in bureaucratic employment are rules orientation, habits of predictability and dependability, and internalization of the enterprise's goals and values.

For middle-layer workers today, then, the loss of control over the labor process has been as complete as for other fractions of the working class. The new control imposed upon Fraction III workers takes a different form from that imposed on other workers, and Fraction III workers superficially have more autonomy. But their situation fails the test of true autonomy, since such workers cannot decide anything about either the product of their work or their labor process; control over these fundamentals passed out of their hands when they became wage (or salary) workers. Instead, bureaucratic methods foster indirect control or "self-control," for they function in the interest not of the worker but of his or her employer.

Thus the middle layers of employment have come to constitute the third fraction of the

[10]Ibid., "Occupational Characteristics," tables 29, 48; "Low Income Areas in Large Cities," table 4.

working class. Relatively high wages, secure employment, and a low rate of unemployment make the issue of survival less crucial, although in the 1970s this concern has become less remote than before. Specific groups have been threatened by depression in the stock brokerage business, the cancellation of military contracts (such as that for the B-1 bomber), and the decline in school enrollments, and all groups have been made more nervous by the deep recession starting in 1974. Despite these occasional reminders of their lack of independence, the concerns of Fraction III workers focus instead on inflation and taxes—threats to affluence developing from outside the workers' own employment situations.

THE CONTINUING DIVISIONS OF RACE AND SEX

Writing in *The Communist Manifesto*, Marx and Engels thought that the logic of capitalist accumulation would lead to the progressive erosion of all precapitalist distinctions among workers. Milton Friedman, in numerous forums with titles such as "Capitalism: The Cure to Racism," has propounded a similar thesis. Yet anyone familiar with the recent history of the American working class can but acknowledge the continuing reality of racial and sexual divisions.

How are we to account for such divisions? In part, of course, our analysis already provides an explanation for the positions of these groups. Blacks, Hispanics, and women entered the wage-labor force during the regime of monopoly capitalism. In contrast to nineteenth-century immigrants, who were pushed into direct competition with native white workers and often served as the unskilled phalanx that smashed the skills of native whites, the later groups entered during a period when developmental forces were pushing toward a segmented, rather than a homogeneous, workforce. They moved into secondary jobs because direct discrimination at the time of hiring prevented them from obtaining primary-market jobs. In addition, discrimi-

nation in schooling and other preemployment institutions further hindered their efforts to obtain entry to better jobs. As these and other forces produced segmented markets, segmented markets in turn tended to reproduce discrimination. Thus, blacks, Hispanics, and women are disadvantaged because they are crowded into the secondary-labor market. In this way, our analysis of market segmentation already accounts for part of the racial and sexual differences in income, unemployment, and other labor market outcomes.

Yet just as market segmentation partly explains racial and sexual divisions, so does it fail to explain them fully. Blacks and other minorities and women come to constitute yet further fractions of the working class, because racial and sexual relations continue to develop according to distinct processes of development or "separate dialectics." These various groups face very different circumstances, of course, and for most purposes to consider them together is misleading. They do, however, share the characeristic of having separate dialectics. Whereas the first set of fractions—the market-segment fractions—were derived from an analysis concerned solely with the capitalist accumulation process, such a procedure cannot be followed for blacks and females. The histories of racism and sexism, intimately linked though they are to that of capitalism, are not subsets of the latter. Accordingly, the dynamics of racial and sexual divisions require separate analyses.

· · ·

Blacks and women, then, came to constitute further fractions of the working class. For blacks, slavery, sharecropping, expulsion from the rural South, continuing discrimination, and residence in Harlem, Watts, the South Side, and other ghettoes—that is, the historical legacy and everyday manifestations of racism—shape a separate consciousness. For women, the double workload of wife-mother and worker, the demands and dangers of sexual objectification (from harassment to rape), the special responsibilities for children, the conflict between competence at home and ambition at work—in short, the consequences of sexism—also shape a separate consciousness. For members of both groups, their daily existence as workers is always conditioned by their special status.

The rise of technical and bureaucratic control inside the core corporations altered the way in which core firms recruit, direct, evaluate, motivate, and discipline their workforces. These two forms of control, and the residual simple control in firms of the competitive periphery, all give rise to distinct labor market processes; indeed, when combined with the economic manifestations of racism and sexism, these forces have led historically to the segmentation of labor markets. The institutional-ization of these various forces in the operation of segmented labor markets has in turn created the material basis for enduring divisions or fractions within the working class. This process has created, as distinct elements, the working poor, the traditional proletariat, and the middle layers. Enduring divisions by race and sex create further and overlapping fractions of black workers and female workers. Each of these groups remains subject to the yoke of capitalist employment, yet each also experiences that employment under different concrete conditions. Since these differences have been institutionalized in the economic structure of society, and more fundamentally since they serve the needs of capital accumulation, they persist.

6.3   *Schooling and Inequality*

In analyzing the distribution of income it is important to distinguish between equality of *income*, on the one hand, and equality of *opportunity*, on the other. Equality of income means that everyone receives the same income. Equality of opportunity means that everyone has the same chance to reach the top (or the bottom) of the prevailing income hierarchy, in the sense that a person's family background has no influence on a person's chances of economic success. Inequality of opportunity exists to the extent that economic success (or failure) is transmitted from parents to children.

We have seen that capitalist societies are characterized by a high degree of income inequality. A hierarchy of unequal incomes, based on the distinction between capitalists and workers and the hierarchical division of the labor force, is an essential feature of the capitalist mode of production. But does this inequality of income necessarily imply inequality of opportunity as well? Many defenders of the capitalist order concede that the distribution of income must be and will be unequal, but they argue that it is inequality of *opportunity* rather than inequality of *income* that really matters. This raises the question of whether it is possible to equalize opportunity within the unequal structure of a capitalist society.

One important source of unequal opportunity under capitalism is the intergenerational transmission of wealth. As long as income-producing property can be transferred from parents to children through inheritance, the children of the rich will have much greater chances of economic success than the children of the poor—if only because they can count on a steady flow of property income. It would require a drastic curtailment of the rights of inheritance to prevent such intergenerational transmission of wealth; but to interfere seriously with these rights would be as incompatible with the capitalist mode of production as to abolish private property altogether.

A second source of unequal opportunity in a capitalist society is the intergenerational transmission of the capacity to command labor income. Parents from high socioeconomic classes generally pass on to their children certain attitudes, skills, and privileges which give them better opportunities for success in the labor market than children from lower classes. Some of the economic advantages that are transmitted in this way can be purchased with parents' income (e.g., a first-rate education); others are associated with parents' social status (e.g., useful contacts).

For advocates of more equal economic opportunity within the framework of a capitalist society, it is this second source of unequal opportunity that has appeared to be the most amenable to change. In particular, reformers in the United States have looked to the expansion of the *educational* system as the most promising means of providing that equality of opportunity which has long been promised to all Americans. Indeed, it has been an important part of the prevailing American ideology that the school system can and does lead to greater equality of both income and opportunity.

Yet, as Samuel Bowles argues in the following reading, the American educational system is in fact instrumental in the legitimation of income inequality and in its transmission from one generation to the next. For one of the primary functions of schools in a capitalist society is to *reproduce* the hierarchical division of labor that is such an essential feature of the capitalist mode of production.

The argument that schooling cannot be expected to reduce inequality in the United States derives additional support from some recent evidence on trends in educational attainment and labor income.[1] Since World War II, the degree of inequality in years of schooling attained by Americans has been significantly reduced, as more and more students finish their high school education. Yet in the same period the distribution of labor income has actually become more unequal. So even when efforts are made to equalize access to education, the impact on the structure of economic rewards is minimal. The impact on the distribution of economic opportunity is likewise very limited, for inequality of both income and opportunity is deeply rooted in the capitalist system.

[1]See Samuel Bowles and Herbert Gintis, *Schooling in Capitalist America* (New York: Basic Books, 1976), pp. 33–34, for documentation of this point; the data cited by Bowles and Gintis refer only to men twenty-five years or older, but the same general pattern no doubt applies to women as well.

The following is excerpted from "Unequal Education and the Reproduction of the Social Division of Labor" by SAMUEL BOWLES. From *Schooling in a Corporate Society: The Political Economy of Education in America and the Alternatives Before Us*, edited by Martin Carnoy (New York: David McKay Co., 1972). Copyright © 1971 by Samuel Bowles. Reprinted by permission of the author. Updated tables provided by Michael Reich and S. William Segal.

The ideological defense of modern capitalist society rests heavily on the assertion that the equalizing effects of education can counter the disequalizing forces inherent in the free market system. That educational systems in capitalist societies have been highly unequal is generally admitted and widely condemned. Yet educational inequalities are taken as passing phenomena, holdovers from an earlier, less enlightened era, which are rapidly being eliminated.

The record of educational history in the U.S., and scrutiny of the present state of our colleges and schools, lend little support to this comforting optimism. Rather, the available data suggest an alternative interpretation. In what follows I will argue (1) that schools have evolved in the U.S. not as part of a pursuit of equality, but rather to meet the needs of capitalist employers for a disciplined and skilled labor force, and to provide a mechanism for social control in the interests of political stability; (2) that as the economic importance of skilled and well-educated labor has grown, inequalities in the school system have become increasingly important in reproducing the class structure from one generation to the next; (3) that the U.S. school system is pervaded by class inequalities, which have shown little sign of diminishing over the last half century; and (4) that the evidently unequal control over school boards and other decision-making bodies in education does not provide a sufficient explanation of the persistence and pervasiveness of inequalities in the school system. Although the unequal distribution of political power serves to maintain inequalities in education, their origins are to be found outside the political sphere, in the class structure itself and in the class subcultures typical of capitalist societies. Thus unequal education has its roots in the very class structure which it serves to legitimize and reproduce. Inequalities in education are a part of the web of capitalist society, and likely to persist as long as capitalism survives.

THE EVOLUTION OF CAPITALISM AND THE RISE OF MASS EDUCATION

In colonial America, and in most precapitalist societies of the past, the basic productive unit was the family. For the vast majority of male adults, work was self-directed, and was performed without direct supervision. Though constrained by poverty, ill health, the low level of technological development, and occasional interferences by the political authorities, a man had considerable leeway in choosing his working hours, what to produce, and how to produce it. While great inequalities in wealth, political power, and other aspects of status normally existed, differences in the degree of autonomy in work were relatively minor, particularly when compared with what was to come.

Transmitting the necessary productive skills to the children as they grew up proved to be a simple task, not because the work was devoid of skill, but because the quite substantial skills required were virtually unchanging from generation to generation, and because the transition to the world of work did not require that the child adapt to a wholly new set of social relationships. The child learned the concrete skills and adapted to the social relations of production through learning by doing within the family. Preparation for life in the larger community was facilitated by the child's experience with the extended family, which shaded off without distinct boundaries, through uncles and fourth cousins, into the community. Children learned early how to deal with complex relationships among adults other than their parents, and children other than their brothers and sisters.[1]

It was not required that children learn a complex set of political principles or ideologies, as political participation was limited and political authority unchallenged, at least in normal times. The only major socializing institution outside the family was the church, which sought to inculcate the accepted spiritual values and attitudes. In addition, a small number of children learned craft skills outside the family, as apprentices. The role of schools tended to be narrowly vocational, restricted to

---

[1]This account draws upon two important historical studies: P. Aries, *Centuries of Childhood* (New York: Random House, 1970); and B. Bailyn, *Education in the Forming of American Society* (New York: Random House, 1960).

preparation of children for a career in the church or the still inconsequential state bureaucracy. The curriculum of the few universities reflected the aristocratic penchant for conspicuous intellectual consumption.

The extension of capitalist production, and particularly the factory system, undermined the role of the family as the major unit of both socialization and production. Small peasant farmers were driven off the land or competed out of business. Cottage industry was destroyed. Ownership of the means of production became heavily concentrated in the hands of landlords and capitalists. Workers relinquished control over their labor in return for wages or salaries. Increasingly, production was carried on in large organizations in which a small management group directed the work activities of the entire labor force. The social relations of production—the authority structure, the prescribed types of behavior and response characteristic of the workplace—became increasingly distinct from those of the family.

The divorce of the worker from control over production—from control over his own labor— is particularly important in understanding the role of schooling in capitalist societies. The resulting hierarchical social division of labor— between controllers and controlled—is a crucial aspect of the class structure of capitalist societies, and will be seen to be an important barrier to the achievement of social class equality in schooling.

Rapid economic change in the capitalist period led to frequent shifts of the occupational distribution of the labor force, and constant changes in the skill requirements for jobs. The productive skills of the father were no longer adequate for the needs of the son during his lifetime. Skill training within the family became increasingly inappropriate.

And the family itself was changing. Increased geographic mobility of labor and the necessity for children to work outside the family spelled the demise of the extended family and greatly weakened even the nuclear family. Meanwhile, the authority of the church was questioned by the spread of secular rationalist thinking and the rise of powerful competing groups.

While undermining the main institutions of socialization, the rise of the capitalist system was accompanied by urbanization, labor migration, the spread of democratic ideologies, and a host of other developments which created an environment—both social and intellectual—which would ultimately challenge the political order.

An institutional crisis was at hand. The outcome, in virtually all capitalist countries, was the rise of mass education. In the U.S., the many advantages of schooling as a socialization process were quickly perceived. The early proponents of the rapid expansion of schooling argued that education could perform many of the socialization functions which earlier had been centered in the family and to a lesser extent, in the church. An ideal preparation for factory work was found in the social relations of the school: specifically, in its emphasis on discipline, punctuality, acceptance of authority outside the family, and individual accountability for one's work. The social relations of the school would replicate the social relations of the workplace, and thus help young people adapt to the social division of labor. Schools would further lead people to accept the authority of the state and its agents—the teachers—at a young age, in part by fostering the illusion of the benevolence of the government in its relations with citizens. Moreover, because schooling would ostensibly be open to all, one's position in the social division of labor could be portrayed as the result not of birth, but of one's own efforts and talents. And if the children's everyday experiences with the structure of schooling were insufficient to inculcate the correct views and attitudes, the curriculum itself would be made to embody the bourgeois ideology. Where precapitalist social institutions—particularly the church—remained strong or threatened the capitalist hegemony, schools sometimes served as a modernizing counter-institution.

The movement for public elementary and secondary education in the U.S. originated in the 19th century in states dominated by the burgeoning industrial capitalist class, most notably in Massachusetts. It spread rapidly to all parts of the country except the South. The fact that some working people's movements had demanded free instruction should not obscure the basically coercive nature of the extension of schooling. In many parts of the country, schools were literally imposed upon the workers.

The evolution of the economy in the 19th century gave rise to new socialization needs and continued to spur the growth of education. Agriculture continued to lose ground to manufacturing; simple manufacturing gave way to production involving complex interrelated processes; an increasing fraction of the labor force was employed in producing services rather than goods. Employers in the most rapidly growing sectors of the economy began to require more than obedience and punctuality in their workers; a change in motivational outlook was required. The new structure of production provided little built-in motivation. There were fewer jobs like farming and piece-rate work in manufacturing in which material reward was tied directly to effort. As work roles became more complicated and interrelated, the evaluation of the individual worker's performance became increasingly difficult. Employers began to look for workers who had internalized the production-related values of the firms' managers.

The continued expansion of education was pressed by many who saw schooling as a means of producing these new forms of motivation and discipline. Others, frightened by the growing labor militancy after the Civil War, found new urgency in the social control arguments popular among the proponents of education in the antebellum period.

A system of class stratification developed within this rapidly expanding educational system. Children of the social elite normally attended private schools. Because working class children tended to leave school early, the class composition of the public high schools was distinctly more elite than the public primary schools. And university education, catering mostly to the children of upper-class families,

ceased to be merely training for teaching or the divinity and became important in gaining access to the pinnacles of the business world.

Around the turn of the present century, large numbers of working class and particularly immigrant children began attending high schools. At the same time, a system of class stratification developed within secondary education. The older democratic ideology of the common school—that the same curriculum should be offered to all children—gave way to the "progressive" insistence that education should be tailored to the "needs of the child." In the interests of providing an education relevant to the later life of the students, vocational schools and tracks were developed for the children of working families. The academic curriculum was preserved for those who would later have the opportunity to make use of book learning, either in college or in white-collar employment. This and other educational reforms of the progressive education movement reflected an implicit assumption of the immutability of the class structure.[2]

The frankness with which students were channeled into curriculum tracks, on the basis of their social class background, raised serious doubts concerning the "openness" of the class structure. The relation between social class and a child's chances of promotion or tracking assignments was disguised—though not mitigated much—by another "progressive" reform: "objective" educational testing. Particularly after World War I, the capitulation of the schools to business values and concepts of efficiency led to the increased use of intelligence and scholastic achievement testing as an ostensibly unbiased means of measuring the product of schooling and classifying students. The complementary growth of the guidance counseling profession allowed much of the channeling to proceed from the students' "own" well-counselled-choices, thus adding an apparent element of voluntarism to the system.

[2] See D. Cohen and M. Lazerson, "Education and the Corporate Order," *Socialist Revolution 2*, No. 3 (May/June, 1971).

The class stratification of education during this period had proceeded hand in hand with the stratification of the labor force. As large bureaucratic corporations and public agencies employed an increasing fraction of all workers, a complicated segmentation of the labor force evolved, reflecting the hierarchical structure of the social relations of production.

The social division of labor had become a finely articulated system of work relations dominated at the top by a small group with control over work processes and a high degree of personal autonomy in their work activities, and proceeding by finely differentiated stages down the chain of bureaucratic command to workers who labored more as extensions of the machinery than as autonomous human beings.[3]

One's status, income, and personal autonomy came to depend in great measure on one's place in the hierarchy of work relations. And in turn, positions in the social division of labor came to be associated with educational credentials reflecting the number of years of schooling and the quality of education received. The increasing importance of schooling as a mechanism for allocating children to positions in the class structure, played a major part in legitimizing the structure itself.[4] But at the same time, it undermined the simple processes which in the past had preserved the position and privilege of the upper class families from generation to generation. In short, it undermined the processes serving to reproduce the social division of labor.

In pre-capitalist societies, direct inheritance of occupational position is common. Even in the early capitalist economy, prior to the segmentation of the labor force on the basis of differential skills and education, the class structure was reproduced generation after generation simply through the inheritance of physical capital by the offspring of the capitalist class. Now that the social division of labor is differentiated by types of competence and educational credentials as well as by the ownership of capital, the problem of inheritance is not nearly as simple. The crucial complication arises because education and skills are embedded in human beings, and—unlike physical capital—these assets cannot be passed on to one's children at death. In an advanced capitalist society in which education and skills play an important role in the hierarchy of production, then, laws guaranteeing inheritance are not enough to reproduce the social division of labor from generation to generation. Skills and educational credentials must somehow be passed on within the family. It is a fundamental theme of this paper that schools play an important part in reproducing and legitimizing this modern form of class structure.

CLASS INEQUALITIES IN U.S. SCHOOLS

Unequal schooling reproduces the hierarchical social division of labor. Children whose parents occupy positions at the top of the occupational hierarchy receive more years of schooling than working class children. Both the amount and the content of their education greatly facilitate their movement into positions similar to their parents'.

Because of the relative ease of measurement, inequalities in years of schooling are particularly evident. If we define social class standing by the income, occupation, and educational level of the parents, a child from the 90th percentile in the class distribution may expect on the average to achieve over four and a half more years of schooling than a child from the 10th percentile.[5] As can be seen in Table 6-K, social class inequalities in the number of years of schooling received arise in part because a disproportionate number of children from poorer families do not complete high school. Table 6-L indicates that these inequalities are

---

[3]See Reich, Section 4.1, p. 122.

[4]See S. Bowles, "Contradictions in U.S. Higher Education," in James H. Weaver, ed., *Modern Political Economy* (Boston: Allyn & Bacon, 1973).

[5]The data for this calculation refer to white males who were in 1962 aged 25–34. See S. Bowles, "Schooling and Inequality from Generation to Generation," *Journal of Political Economy*, 80 no. 3 (May/June 1972).

exacerbated by social class inequalities in college attendance among those children who did graduate from high school: even among those who had graduated from high school, children of families in the lowest socioeconomic quartile were over two and a half times less likely to attend college as were the children of families in the top quartile.[6]

Inequalities in schooling are not simply a matter of differences in years of schooling attained. Differences in the internal structure of schools themselves and in the content of schooling reflect the differences in the social class compositions of the student bodies. The social relations of the educational process ordinarily mirror the social relations of the work roles into which most students are likely to move. Differences in rules, expected modes of behavior, and opportunities for choice are most glaring when we compare levels of schooling. Note the wide range of choice over curriculum, life style, and allocation of time afforded to college students, compared with the obedience and respect for authority expected in high school. Differentiation occurs also within each level of schooling. One needs only to compare the social relations of a junior college with those of an elite four-year college, or those of a working class high school with those of a wealthy suburban high school, for verification of this point.

[6]For evidence on these points, see U.S. Bureau of the Census, *Current Population Reports,* Series P-20, nos. 185 and 183.

TABLE 6-K   PERCENTAGE OF CHILDREN AGED 16–17 ENROLLED IN PUBLIC SCHOOL, BY PARENTS' EDUCATION AND INCOME, 1970[a]

	Percent of Children Aged 16–17 Enrolled in Public School
1. Parents' Education Less than 8 Years	
Family income:	
less than $4,000	74.4
$4,000–9,999	78.2
$10,000 and over	81.1
2. Parents' Education 8–11 Years	
Family income:	
less than $4,000	81.6
$4,000–6,999	83.3
$7,000–9,999	86.6
$10,000 and over	88.3
3. Parents' Education 12 Years	
Family income:	
less than $4,000	88.8
$4,000–6,999	89.2
$7,000–9,999	91.4
$10,000 and over	93.1
4. Parents' Education over 12 Years (some college).	
Family income:	
less than $4,000	92.9
$4,000–9,999	93.0
$10,000–14,999	95.1
$15,000 and over	96.5

[a]Father's education is indicated if father is present; otherwise mother's education is indicated.

Source: Bureau of the Census, *Census of Population, 1970,* vol. PC(2)-5A, table 8.

TABLE 6-L   PROBABILITY OF COLLEGE ENTRY WITHIN FOUR YEARS OF HIGH
SCHOOL GRADUATION

	Probability of College Entry
1. Lowest ability quartile	
Lowest SES quartile	20.3
Middle SES quartiles	22.7
Highest SES quartile	46.2
2. Middle ability quartiles	
Lowest SES quartile	32.7
Middle SES quartiles	46.8
Highest SES quartile	75.8
3. Highest ability quartile	
Lowest SES quartile	62.6
Middle SES quartiles	73.0
Highest SES quartile	93.0
4. All ability quartiles	
Lowest SES quartile	30.7
Middle SES quartiles	46.8
Highest SES quartile	81.3

SES indicates socioeconomic status index, a composite measure including parental income, occupation, and schooling, and a household items index. The ability scale is a composite of tests measuring general academic aptitude.

Source: National Longitudinal Study of the High School Class of 1972 as reported in *National Center for Education Statistics,* "College Attainment Four Years after High School," Center for Educational Research and Evaluation, June 1981, p. 60.

The differential socialization patterns in schools attended by students of different social classes do not arise by accident. Rather, they stem from the fact that the educational objectives and expectations of both parents and teachers, and the responsiveness of students to various patterns of teaching and control, differ for students of different social classes.[7] Further, class inequalities in school socialization patterns are reinforced by the inequalities in financial resources. The paucity of financial support for the education of children from working class families not only leaves more resources to be devoted to the children of those with commanding roles in the economy; it forces upon the teachers and school administrators in the working class schools a type of social relations which fairly closely mirrors that of the factory. Thus financial considerations in poorly supported working class schools militate against small intimate classes, against a multiplicity of elective courses and specialized teachers (except disciplinary personnel), and preclude the amounts of free time for the teachers and free space required for a more open, flexible educational environment. The lack of financial support all but requires that students be treated as raw materials on a production line; it places a high premium on obedience and punctuality; there are few opportunities for independent, creative work or individualized attention by teachers. The well-financed schools attended by the children of the rich can offer much greater opportunities for the development of the capacity for sustained independent work and the other characteristics required for adequate job performance in the upper levels of the occupational hierarchy.

[7]That working class parents seem to favor more authoritarian educational methods is perhaps a reflection of their own work experiences, which have demonstrated that submission to authority is an essential ingredient in one's ability to get and hold a steady, well-paying job.

While much of the inequality in U.S. education exists between schools, even within a given school different children receive different educations. Class stratification within schools is achieved through tracking, differential participation in extracurricular activities, and in the attitudes of teachers and particularly guidance personnel who expect working class children to do poorly, to terminate schooling early, and to end up in jobs similar to their parents'.[8]

Not surprisingly, the results of schooling differ greatly for children of different social classes. The differing educational objectives implicit in the social relations of schools attended by children of different social classes has already been mentioned. Less important but more easily measured are differences in scholastic achievement. If we measure the output of schooling by scores on nationally standardized achievement tests, children whose parents were themselves highly educated outperform the children of parents with less education by a wide margin. A recent study revealed, for example, that among white high school seniors, those students whose parents were in the top education decile were on the average well over three grade levels ahead of those whose parents were in the bottom decile.[9] While a good part of this discrepancy is the result of unequal treatment in school and unequal educational resources, it will be suggested below that much of it is related to differences in the early socialization and home environment of the children.

Given the great social class differences in scholastic achievement, class inequalities in college attendance are to be expected. Thus one might be tempted to argue that the data in Table 6-L are simply a reflection of une-qual scholastic achievement in high school and do not reflect any *additional* social class inequalities peculiar to the process of college admission. This view is unsupported by the available data, some of which are also presented in Table 6-L. Access to a college education is highly unequal, even for children of the same measured "academic ability."

The social class inequalities in our school system and the role they play in the reproduction of the social division of labor are too evident to be denied. Defenders of the educational system are forced back on the assertion that things are getting better; the inequalities of the past far worse. Yet the available historical evidence lends little support to the idea that our schools are on the road to equality of educational opportunity. For example, data from a recent U.S. Census survey indicate that graduation from college has become increasingly dependent on one's class background. This is true despite the fact that the probability of high school graduation is becoming increasingly equal across social classes. On balance, the available data suggest that the number of years of schooling which the average child attains depends at least as much now upon the social class standing of his father as it did fifty years ago.[10]

The argument that our "egalitarian" education compensates for inequalities generated elsewhere in the capitalist system is patently fallacious. But the discrepancy between the ideology and the reality of the U.S. school system is far greater than would appear from a passing glance at the above data. In the first place, if education is to compensate for the social class immobility due to the inheritance of

[8]See P. Lauter and F. Howe, "How the School System is Rigged for Failure," *The New York Review of Books,* June 18, 1970.

[9]Calculation based on data in James S. Coleman et al., *Equality of Educational Opportunity*, vol. II (Washington, D.C.: U.S. Department of Health, Education and Welfare, Office of Education, 1966), and methods described in Bowles, "Schooling and Inequality from Generation to Generation."

[10]See P. M. Blau and O. D. Duncan, *The American Occupational Structure* (New York: Wiley, 1967). More recent data do not contradict the evidence of no trend towards equality. A 1967 census survey shows that among high school graduates in 1965, the probability of college attendance for those whose parents had attended college has continued to rise relative to the probability of college attendance for those whose parents had attended less than eight years of school. See U.S. Bureau of the Census, *Current Population Reports,* Series P-20, no. 185, July 11, 1969.

wealth and privilege, education must be structured so that the poor child receives not less, not even the same, but *more* than equal benefits from education. The school must compensate for the other disadvantages which the lower-class child suffers. Thus the liberal assertion that education compensates for inequalities in inherited wealth and privilege is falsified not so much by the extent of the social class inequalities in the school system as by their very existence, or, more correctly, by the absence of compensatory inequalities.

Second, considering the problem of inequality of income at a given moment, a similar argument applies. In a capitalist economy, the increasing importance of schooling in the economy will increase income inequality even in the absence of social class inequalities in quality and quantity of schooling. This is so simply because the labor force becomes differentiated by type of skill or schooling, and inequalities in labor earnings therefore contribute to total income inequality, augmenting the inequalities due to the concentration of capital. The disequalizing tendency will of course be intensified if the owners of capital also acquire a disproportionate amount of those types of education and training which confer access to high-paying jobs.

CLASS CULTURE AND CLASS POWER

The pervasive and persistent inequalities in U.S. education would seem to refute an interpretation of education which asserts its egalitarian functions. But the facts of inequality do not by themselves suggest an alternate explanation. Indeed, they pose serious problems of interpretation. If the costs of education borne by students and their families were very high, or if nepotism were rampant, or if formal segregation of pupils by social class were practiced, or educational decisions were made by a select few whom we might call the power elite, it would not be difficult to explain the continued inequalities in U.S. education. The problem of interpretation, however, is to reconcile

our society as we perceive them: public and virtually tuition-free education at all levels, few legal instruments for the direct implementation of class segregation, a limited role for "contacts" or nepotism in the achievement of high status or income, a commitment (at the rhetorical level at least) to equality of educational opportunity, and a system of control of education which if not particularly democratic, extends far beyond anything resembling a power elite. The attempt to reconcile these apparently discrepant facts leads us back to a consideration of the social division of labor, the associated class cultures, and the exercise of class power.

The social division of labor based on the hierarchical structure of production gives rise to distinct class subcultures. The values, personality traits, and expectations characteristic of each subculture are transmitted from generation to generation through class differences in family socialization and complementary differences in the type and amount of schooling ordinarily attained by children of various class positions. These class differences in schooling are maintained in large measure through the capacity of the upper class to control the basic principles of school finance, pupil evaluation, and educational objectives.

The social relations of production characteristic of advanced capitalist societies (any many socialist societies) are most clearly illustrated in the bureaucracy and hierarchy of the modern corporation. Occupational roles in the capitalist economy may be grouped according to the degree of independence and control exercised by the person holding the job. There is some evidence that the personality attributes associated with the adequate performance of jobs in occupational categories defined in this broad way differ considerably, some apparently requiring independence and internal discipline, and others emphasizing such traits as obedience, predictability, and willingness to subject oneself to external controls.

These personality attributes are developed primarily at a young age, both in the family and, to a lesser extent, in secondary socialization institutions such as schools. Because people tend to marry within their own class (in part because spouses often meet in our class-segregated schools), both parents are likely to have a similar set of these fundamental personality traits. Thus children of parents occupying a given position in the occupational hierarchy grow up in homes where childrearing methods and perhaps even the physical surroundings tend to develop personality characteristics appropriate to adequate job performance in the occupational roles of the parents. The children of managers and professionals are taught self-reliance within a broad set of constraints; the children of production line workers are taught obedience.

While this relation between parents' class position and child's personality attributes operates primarily in the home, it is reinforced by schools and other social institutions. Thus, to take an example introduced earlier, the authoritarian social relations of working class high schools complement the discipline-oriented early socialization patterns experienced by working class children. The relatively greater freedom of wealthy suburban schools extends and formalizes the early independence training characteristic of upper-class families.

The operation of the labor market translates differences in class culture into income inequalities and occupational hierarchies. The personality traits, values, and expectations characteristic of different class cultures play a major role in determining an individual's success in gaining a high income or prestigious occupation. The apparent contribution of schooling to occupational success and higher income seems to be explained primarily by the personality characteristics of those who have higher educational attainments.[11] Although the rewards to intellectual capacities are quite limited in the labor market (except for a small number of high level jobs), mental abilities are important in getting ahead in school. Grades, the probability of continuing to higher levels of schooling, and a host of other school success variables, are positively correlated with "objective" measures of intellectual capacities. Partly for this reason, one's experience in school reinforces the belief that promotion and rewards are distributed fairly. The close relationship between the amount of education attained and later occupational success thus provides a meritocratic appearance to mask the mechanisms which reproduce the class system from generation to generation.

Positions of control in the productive hierarchy tend to be associated with positions of political influence. Given the disproportionate share of political power held by the upper class and their capacity to determine the accepted patterns of behavior and procedures, to define the national interest, and in general to control the ideological and institutional context in which educational decisions are made, it is not surprising to find that resources are allocated unequally among school tracks, between schools serving different classes, and between levels of schooling. The same configuration of power results in curricula, methods of instruction, and criteria of selection and promotion which confer benefits disproportionately on the children of the upper class.

The power of the upper class exists in its capacity to define and maintain a set of rules of operation or decision criteria—"rules of the game"—which, though often seemingly innocuous and sometimes even egalitarian in their ostensible intent, have the effect of maintaining the unequal system.

The operation of two prominent examples of these "rules of the game" will serve to illustrate the point. The first important principle is that excellence in schooling should be rewarded. Given the capacity of the upper class to define excellence in terms on which upper-class children tend to excell (for example, scholastic achievement), adherence to this principle yields inegalitarian outcomes (for example, unequal access to higher education) while maintaining the appearance of fair treatment.[12] Thus the principle of rewarding

[11]This view is elaborated in H. Gintis, "Education, Technology, and Worker Productivity," *American Economic Association Papers & Proceedings*, May 1971.

[12]Those who would defend the "reward excellence" principle on the grounds of efficient selection to ensure the most efficient use of educational resources might ask

excellence serves to legitimize the unequal consequences of schooling by associating success with competence. At the same time, the institution of objectively administered tests of performance serves to allow a limited amount of upward mobility among exceptional children of the lower class, thus providing further legitimation of the operations of the social system by giving some credence to the myth of widespread mobility.

The second example is the principle that elementary and secondary schooling should be financed in very large measure from local revenues. This principle is supported on the grounds that it is necessary to preserve political liberty. Given the degree of residential segregation by income level, the effect of this principle is to produce an unequal distribution of school resources among children of different classes. Towns with a large tax base can spend large sums for the education of their disproportionately upper-class children even without suffering a higher than average tax rate. Because the main resource inequalities in schooling thus exist between rather than within school districts, and because there is no effective mechanism for redistribution of school funds among school districts, poor families lack a viable political strategy for correcting the inequality.

The above rules of the game—rewarding "excellence" and financing schools locally— illustrate the complementarity between the political and economic power of the upper class. Thus it appears that the consequences of an unequal distribution of political power

themselves this: Why should colleges admit those with the highest college entrance examination board scores? Why not the lowest, or the middle? The rational social objective of the college is to render the greatest *increment* in individual capacities ("value added" to the economist), not to produce the most illustrious graduating class ("gross output"). Yet if incremental gain is the objective, it is far from obvious that choosing from the top is the best policy. And because no one has even attempted to construct a compelling argument that choosing from the top is the policy which maximizes the increment of learning for students, we can infer that the practice is supported by considerations other than that of efficient allocation of resources in education.

among classes complement the results of class culture in maintaining an educational system which has thus far been capable of transmitting status from generation to generation, and capable in addition of political survival in the formally democratic and egalitarian environment of the contemporary United States.

THE LIMITS OF EDUCATIONAL REFORM

The role of the schools in reproducing and legitimizing the social division of labor has recently been challenged by popular egalitarian movements. At the same time, the educational system is showing signs of internal structural weakness.[13] These two developments suggest that fundamental change in the schooling process may soon be possible. Analysis of both the potential and the limits of educational change will be facilitated by drawing together and extending the strands of our argument.

·   ·   ·

I have argued that the structure of education reflects the social relations of production. For at least the past 150 years, expansion of education and changes in the forms of schooling have been responses to needs generated by the economic system. The sources of present inequality in American education were found in the mutual reinforcement of class subcultures and social-class biases in the operations of the school system itself. The analysis strongly suggests that educational inequalities are rooted in the basic institutions of our economy. Reconsideration of some of the basic mechanisms of educational inequality lends support to this proposition. First, the principle of rewarding academic excellence in educational promotion and selection serves not only to legitimize the process by which the social division of labor is reproduced. It is also a basic part of the process that socializes young people to work for external rewards and encourages them to develop motivational structures fit for the alienating work of the capitalist economy. Selecting

[13]See Bowles, "Contradictions in U.S. Higher Education."

students from the bottom or the middle of the achievement scale for promotion to higher levels of schooling would go a long way toward equalizing education, but it would also jeopardize the schools' capacity to train productive and well-adjusted workers.[14] Second, the way in which local financing of schools operates to maintain educational inequality is also rooted in the capitalist economy, in this case, in the existence of an unequal distribution of income, free markets in residential property, and the narrow limits of state power. It seems unwise to emphasize this aspect of the long-run problem of equality in education, however, for the inequalities in school resources resulting from the localization of finance may not be of crucial importance in maintaining inequalities in the effects of education. Moreover, a significant undermining of the principle of local finance may already be underway in response to pressures from the poorer states and school districts.

Of greater importance in the perpetuation of educational inequality are differential class subcultures. These class-based differences in personality, values, and expectations, I have argued, represent an adaptation to the different requirements of adequate work performance at various levels in the hierarchical social relations of production. Class subcultures, then, stem from the everyday experiences of workers in the structure of production characteristic of capitalist societies.

It should be clear by this point that educational equality cannot be achieved through changes in the school system alone. Nonetheless, attempts at educational reform may move us closer to that objective if, in their failure, they lay bare the unequal nature of our school system and destroy the illusion of unimpeded mobility through education. Successful educational reforms—reducing racial or class disparities in schooling, for example—may also serve the cause of equality of education, for it seems likely that equalizing access to schooling will challenge the system either to make good its promise of rewarding educational attainment or to find ways of coping with a mass disillusionment with the great panacea.[15]

Yet, if the record of the last 150 years of educational reforms is any guide, we should not expect radical change in education to result from the efforts of those confining their attention to the schools. The political victories of past reform movements have apparently resulted in little if any effective equalization. My interpretation of the educational consequences of class culture and class power suggests that these educational reform movements failed because they sought to eliminate educational inequalities without challenging the basic institutions of capitalism.

Efforts to equalize education through changes in government policy will at best scratch the surface of inequality. For much of the inequality in American education has its origin outside the limited sphere of state power, in the hierarchy of work relations and the associated differences in class culture. As long as jobs are defined so that some have power over many and others have power over none—as long as the social division of labor persists—educational inequality will be built into society in the United States.

---

[14]Consider what would happen to the internal discipline of schools if the students' objective were to end up at the bottom of the grade distribution!

[15]The failure of the educational programs of the War on Poverty to raise significantly the incomes of the poor is documented in T. I. Ribich, *Education and Poverty* (Washington, D.C.: Brookings Institution, 1968).

CHAPTER 7

MALE DOMINANCE

MODERN FEMINISM HAS TOUCHED, in one way or another, almost every person in the country.[1] Earlier feminists fought for the vote, for rights to education, and for married women's rights to own property. Today, campaigns fighting discrimination against women and gender inequality have begun to reach everywhere: the media, schools, sports, clubs, political parties, hospitals, churches, labor unions, government agencies, offices, factories, and, of course, families themselves. The feminist movement has begun to alert and to change the consciousness of women, and of men as well. It has exposed patterns and incidences of sexism that have always existed but were often ignored, patterns that women experienced but could not always label. Today, there is much more consciousness of and struggle against the reality that women do not have the same economic opportunities as men; that women still have the primary responsibility for parenting of children and for housework, whether or not they hold a paid job; that women are sexually assaulted by individual men—as in rape—and assaulted and stereotyped by male-dominated institutions—as in much advertising; that women, in other words, are subjected to a special and systematic oppression. We shall use the term male dominance to denote this systematic oppression of women.

From the perspective of what human relationships and human fulfillment *could* be, the system of male dominance distorts and warps interpersonal relationships for *both* sexes; it creates barriers between men and women as well as among women and among men, and it narrows the kinds of personal relationships and personal development available or allowable. For example, male dominance pressures men always to appear strong and tough and not to express their feelings and emotions; men thus limit their own personal development.

Male dominance does not oppress women and men equally, however. All men derive some privileges from it, and men are in many ways the agents of the oppression of women. Men are not likely to see all the ways in which women are oppressed, and they are unlikely to give up all their privileges willingly.

How can we account for the present status of women? How is that status affected by capitalism? What is the connection between the system of male dominance and the capitalist system? What sorts of changes are needed to eliminate male dominance from our society? In this chapter we shall take up these questions.

We begin by observing that, although there are important biological differences between the sexes, our understanding and experience of the concepts "male" and "female" are much more the product of social and cultural than of biological and physiological factors. Anthropologists, who live in and study different societies, find a wide variety of rituals, symbols and divisions of labor that serve to distinguish the sexes; these differences are so varied (and even

[1]This introduction and the entire chapter were prepared with the major assistance of Nancy Chodorow.

249

completely opposite from one society to another) that they could not possibly emerge directly from biology. Most societies, and certainly our own, go to truly astonishing lengths to differentiate males and females. Physiology does dictate that only women can bear and breast-feed infants, but the remaining aspects of parenting are all open to social arrangement. Their organization cannot be explained by biology alone. All societies contain a gender system, a social process that transforms the biological differences between the sexes into structured social relations of gender. All gender systems, anthropologists also tell us, have hitherto included some form of gender inequality, that is, women were subordinated to men in precapitalist societies, but again in varying ways and to varying degrees.

The gender system that prevailed in feudal, precapitalist Western Europe was based primarily on the patriarchal family of the time. In feudal society lords controlled the labor of their serfs, and a set of legal relations and religious beliefs supported this arrangement. Within the family, which was the basic production unit of feudal society, another serf-type relationship held: the father controlled the labor of women and children and exercised power over the capacity of the wife to bear children. Indeed, this unequal relationship provides our definition of patriarchy. The patriarchal authority structure was also accompanied by a set of legal relations that vested most property and legal rights with the father. Marriage essentially involved the exchange of women from one patriarchal family to another, as the father "gave away" the bride. Patriarchy was a self-reproducing system that bequeathed to men control over a major component of the means of production and reproduction.

The development of petty commodity and wage-labor systems of production at first strengthened this system of patriarchy. As a result, the relative status of women declined; for example, women in the United States had fewer property rights in the nineteenth century than they had in the eighteenth. Capitalist development at first reinforced patriarchy

simply by removing many production activities from the home to factories and thereby reducing the significance of women's labor in home production. A decline in women's status followed. But to see fully why patriarchy was strengthened, we must examine the important connections between the patriarchal family and the economy.

Most importantly, the patriarchal family provided a system of reproduction. Capitalism involves not only the accumulation of capital, but also the reproduction of labor-power. The physical and emotional labor of maintaining wage-workers and children—cooking, keeping house, caring for children—must be somehow organized if reproduction of wage-labor is to occur. The patriarchal family that already existed by the time the capitalist mode of production had emerged provided a ready-made system for these purposes. Men could work as wage workers in factories and leave to their wives the essential reproductive activities that continued to be carried out in the home. While young single women could expect to work for several years at wage labor outside the home, most married women could not, for reproductive work itself required many hours of labor over most of a wife's adult married life. Women who did want a career were rejecting the possibility of having a family. This alone kept many married women out of the wage-labor force and confined them to the home. In the United States, for example, at the end of the nineteenth century more than 95 percent of all married women stayed at home to do unpaid work in the household (the percentage was a little lower among black married women). As late as 1940 only 15 percent of married women were in the wage-labor force.

As long as the patriarchal family reproduced labor, capitalists did not have to bother to create a new institution of social reproduction. As long as they could get immigrant men from abroad and from rural areas, capitalists did not need to draw upon married women for wage-labor. At the same time, the general exclusion of married women from wage-labor perpetuated their economic dependence upon men. The sexual division of labor thus simultaneously reproduced the male wage-labor force for capital and the subordination of women.

Moreover, male dominance is very useful to capitalists who employ women as wageworkers.[2] Women who lack the economic support of a husband and women who are in the wage-labor force on only a temporary basis have always been an important source of easily exploitable labor for capitalists. Such subordinated women provide a significant portion of the marginal labor force needed by capitalists to draw upon during upswings in the business cycle and to release during downswings. And the divisions between men and women workers that result from gender inequality weaken labor's overall strength against capital.

Although capitalism at first reinforced patriarchy, in the longer run capitalism fundamentally undermined it. Today, it is no longer accurate to speak of the family as patriarchal in the full feudal sense of the term. But the result has not been equality for women. Instead, a system of male dominance has evolved, incorporated in the institutions of the capitalist system. And it is still accurate to speak of the contemporary family as generally male-dominant and embodying sexual inequality.[3] We must examine both how capitalism attacked patriarchy and how capitalism is an obstacle to the further elimination of male dominance.

The attack by capitalism on patriarchy occurred on both economic and ideological levels. At the economic level, the employment of women in industry, by giving women a potential source of economic independence, tended to undermine the power of husbands and fathers over women's labor. This tendency has become stronger in the present century, and particularly since World War II. The decline in the birth rate, the growth of mass schooling for children, the increase in life ex-

pectancy and the spread of productivity-increasing appliances within the home have reduced substantially the portion of a wife's labor time needed for social reproduction within the home. And the progressive exhaustion of reserve supplies of male immigrants and farmers has made all women and especially married women a more important source of wage labor for capitalists.

At the ideological level, bourgeois revolutions, such as in the United States in 1776 and in France in 1789, spread new ideas about the inalienable rights of individuals and the immorality of slavery. These ideals were not at first extended to women (or to slaves), but in the last half of the nineteenth century such ideas did support the struggles of feminist movements for full citizenship rights for women. Real advances were made by these movements, such as women's right to vote and to hold property when they were married. The legal inequality of women was still an issue in the 1970s, when feminists again made use of much proclaimed ideas about individual rights and the equality of individuals before the law to help win changes in laws concerning abortion, access to credit, employment, and the like.

But despite the undermining of patriarchy and advances in women's rights, male dominance has survived in contemporary capitalism. Although the economic and ideological bases of patriarchy have been much dissolved, capitalist development has maintained male dominance rather than eliminating it. To see why this is, we must further examine the relation between male dominance and capitalism in the current stage of contemporary capitalism.

To appreciate the role of the male-dominant family in contemporary capitalism, we must consider why much reproduction work is still located in the family. To begin with, many reproductive activities, especially the care of young children, are hard to standardize and require considerable labor time. As a result, it is difficult for capitalist firms to compete against the unpaid labor of women available in the household. One might think that

[2] A statistical appendix following this introduction provides a series of tables that document trends in the position of women in the wage-labor force.

[3] In principle, families could be egalitarian, but that is generally not the case today.

the capitalist state would provide substitutes, especially since this would free more labor for the wage-labor force. This has occurred to some extent in periods of labor scarcity; for example, government child-care centers were established during World War II and some income tax deductions are made available for child-care expenses today. But the degree of U.S. state expenditure on such activities has so far been quite minimal, because of the endurance of sexist beliefs about motherhood, and because working women with small children have somehow been able to make their own child-care arrangements, at their own expense.

The psychological factors in social reproduction have also ensured the survival of the male-dominant family and made it useful to capitalism. The labor performed by women in the family is more than purely physical work. Much of it is emotional work: building and maintaining interpersonal relationships and ensuring the emotional development and stability of children and men so that they can function in a capitalist society. This work is crucial for the reproduction of labor-power in capitalism, and it becomes even more important in contemporary capitalism. It is one of the principal functions that the modern family serves for capitalism, and it would be difficult for individual capitalists or the state to provide it so well.

At the same time, the male-dominant family is so organized as to ensure its own reproduction; this point is crucial for understanding the perpetuation of male dominance. As long as mothering is carried out primarily by women and not equally by men and women, little boys and girls develop emotionally in different ways. Girls tend to develop in ways that help prepare them for their future role as nurturant mothers; they sense themselves as more in personal connection with other people, and they tend to be more open to their emotions. Boys tend to develop in ways more adapted to becoming fathers and wage workers; they are more likely to repress their emotions and thereby be able to work responsibly and regularly at alienated labor outside the home; typ-ically, they are engaged very little in the emotional development of children.[4] The male-dominant family thus perpetuates sexism while benefiting capitalism.

Male dominance today is also based in the sexist operation of the labor market, in a manner that also benefits capitalism. It is still true that women who are trying to support themselves and their families or who are only temporarily in the wage-labor force provide an especially vulnerable and therefore exploitable labor supply for capitalists. Many of the lowest-paid jobs in the economy are filled by such women.

Since the turn of the century, women have been entering the U.S. wage-labor force in very large numbers, and many women are now wage-workers on a permanent and not at all marginal basis. But women have not entered wage-labor on an equal basis with men, and gender inequality has been perpetuated. By and large, women have entered already female occupations, such as nursing, or new occupations, such as office work, that became quickly feminized and were segmented from male jobs.[5] The effect of this sexual segregation has been to limit women's wages, to the benefit of capitalists. In turn, the lower wages received by women and the continued inequality inherent in their having responsibility for child care and housekeeping has perpetuated women's economic dependence upon men.

---

[4]This argument is further developed in Nancy Chodorow, *The Reproduction of Mothering: Psychoanalysis and the Sociology of Gender* (Berkeley: University of California Press, 1978); see also Beatrice Whiting and Carolyn Pope Edwards, "A Cross-Cultural Analysis of Sex Differences in the Behavior of Children Aged Three Through Eleven," *Journal of Social Psychology*, 91 (1973), 171–88.

[5]For more on the history of job segregation by sex, see Alice Kessler-Harris, "Stratifying by Sex: Understanding the History of Working Women," in R. Edwards, M. Reich, and D. Gordon, eds., *Labor Market Segmentation* (Lexington, Mass.: D.C. Heath, 1975); and Heidi Hartmann, "Capitalism, Patriarchy and Job Segregation by Sex," in M. Blaxall and B. Reagan, eds., *Women and the Workplace: The Implications of Occupational Segregation* (Chicago: University of Chicago Press, 1976), as well as the other essays in both of these volumes.

The long-term rise in real wages in this century has allowed more single women to subsist on their own (although at a lower standard of living than single men), but these wages are hardly sufficient for most women to support any children. The family thus continues to rest on an economic basis that is unequal for women and inherently sexist. Male dominance is now based not just in the family but also in a labor market that segregates jobs unequally by sex.

The modern family, however, does not fit perfectly the needs of contemporary capitalism. Largely through the input of women's labor, the family provides primary emotional relationships and a place to escape from alienated wage-labor. It therefore potentially contains an implicit critique of social relations based purely on exchange, and indicates, albeit in a sexist and distorted form, what society could be like if it were governed by criteria of human needs instead of the exchange relations of capitalism.

In recent decades women's lives have changed, and the status of women has undergone some evolution. For example, the development of contraceptive techniques and successful feminist struggles to legalize abortion have given women more control over sexuality and procreation. One of the most striking changes has been the increase in the number and proportion of married women and mothers who work at wage-labor.[6] In the United States, over half of all husbands who are wage-workers have wives who are also wage-workers, and both husband and wife are now wage-workers in nearly half of all husband-wife families with young children.

These wives, however, are still unequal wage-workers: the relative wages, degree of occupational segregation, and unequal responsibility of working wives for housework has remained relatively unchanged. Moreover, contradictory demands are increasingly being made upon women. Within the family

itself, women face contradictions between being good mothers (active, nurturant, and caring for the welfare of their children) and being good wives (passive and submissive to their husbands seeking escape from the alienated work world). Women wage-workers are expected to be good wives, filling their household responsibilities when they come home, resuscitating their husbands for the following day, and expected to be good wageworkers without themselves receiving the same kind of support. At the same time, a society that pressures women to become mothers and provides practically no alternate child-care arrangements expects these same mothers to be full-time wage-workers. These contradictions have been intensifying, producing a growing feminist consciousness, and a consciousness that male dominance is incorporated in the capitalist system.

Statistical Appendix: Women in the U.S. Wage-Labor Force

Three major themes stand out when we look at the place of women in the U.S. wage-labor force. First, an enormous increase has taken place in the number and proportion of women who work outside the home; second, there is a marked tendency for occupations and jobs to be segregated by gender, and the degree of such segregation has not diminished over the years; and third, the increase in wage-labor participation of women has been accompanied by a *continuing* income differential between men and women, with women continuing to receive lower pay than men. In the following paragraphs we examine briefly the data that exhibit these themes.

PARTICIPATION IN WAGE-LABOR

Figure 7-A and Tables 7-A and 7-B indicate, from a variety of viewpoints, the long-run trends in the numbers and proportion of women who are wage and salary workers. In

[6]See the statistical appendix.

FIGURE 7-A   WOMEN WORKERS IN THE LABOR
FORCE.

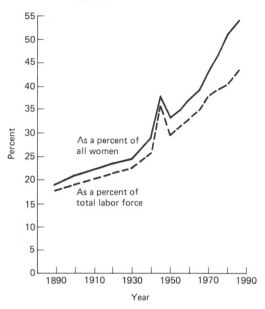

1890–1930: Persons 14 years and older in the total labor force.

1940–1980: Persons 16 years and older in the civilian labor force.

Source: U.S. Department of Labor, Women's Bureau, *1975 Handbook on Women Workers*, Bulletin 297 (Washington, D.C.: U.S. Government Printing Office, 1975), table 2; U.S. Bureau of the Census, *Statistical Abstract of the United States, 1985* (Washington, D.C.: U.S. Government Printing Office, 1985), p. 398.

Figure 7-A we see that the percentage of women who are wage-workers increased from 18.2 percent in 1890 to 53.2 percent in 1984.[1] In the same period women workers rose from 17 percent to 43.3 percent of the wage-labor

[1]We are using the term "wage-workers" for those who receive a wage or salary for their work and the term "wage-labor force" to refer to all those who are working for a wage or salary or presently searching for such a job. The official government statistics that we are using also count the self-employed (e.g., small business people, independent professionals, farmers) in the labor force category. We will ignore this group in our discussion; their importance has declined markedly in recent decades (see Reich, Section 4.1, p. 122), and the proportion of the self-employed in the labor force is much lower among women than among men.

force. As one might expect, such a massive increase in the number of women workers has resulted in a substantial change in the characteristics of women entering the wage-labor force. This shift can be seen by comparing the female wage-labor force of 1890 with that of the present.

In 1890, most women workers were young— over half were under 25—and single—70 percent had never married. Only 13 percent of all working women were married and living with their husbands. Most women workers dropped out of the wage-labor force, never to return, once they were married; in 1890, only 4.5 percent of married women (with husbands present) were wage-workers. Adult women who were not supported economically by men— women who were divorced, separated, or wid-

TABLE 7-A   MARITAL STATUS OF WOMEN IN THE
LABOR FORCE

Year	Married, Husband Present	Never Married	Widowed, Separated, Divorced	All Women in Labor Force
1890	13.9%	68.2%	17.9%	100%
1940	30.3	48.5	21.2	100
1950	48.0	31.6	20.4	100
1960	54.4	24.0	21.6	100
1970	58.8	22.3	18.9	100
1980	55.4	25.0	19.6	100
1984	54.6	25.5	19.9	100

Sources: U.S. Bureau of the Census, *Historical Statistics of the United States, Colonial Times to 1970*, p. 133; *Statistical Abstract of the U.S., 1985*, p. 398; *1975 Handbook on Women Workers*, table 4.

owed—were more likely to be in the wage-labor force; their participation rate in 1890 was 29 percent. Black women were also more likely to be wage-workers—37.7 percent in 1890 compared to only 15.8 percent of white women.[2]

Tables 7-A and 7-B show the shifts in the marital and family status of women workers that have taken place since 1890. Since that time the largest increase in women workers

[2]U.S. Bureau of the Census, *Historical Statistics of the United States, From Colonial Times to 1957*, p. 72.

has occurred among married women with husbands present (see Table 7-A); such women now comprise over half of all women workers.

In 1947, among families with both spouses present, there were 29.9 million husbands who were employed, and only 6.5 million employed wives. By 1981 the comparable figures were 39.7 million working husbands (an increase of 33 percent over 1947) and 23.6 million working wives (an increase of 263 percent).[3] More recently, the increase in working women has been particularly marked among married women with children. The increase in the number of working wives has been especially rapid since World War II, as Table 7-B shows. Today, nearly two-thirds of all married women with school-age children are wage-workers, as are over half of married women with preschool-age children. The highest wage-labor force participation rates today are still found among women who provide the primary economic support for their children: of mothers with children under 18 who were widowed, divorced, or separated, 69.4 percent were wage-workers in 1980.[4] The wage-labor

participation rates of both white and minority-race women have increased since 1890, but a greater increase has occurred among white women, so that the racial differences in participation rates are much smaller today than in 1890: 53.6 percent among minority-race women in 1981, compared to 51.9 percent among white women.[5]

The above trends indicate that women in the United States are increasingly in the wage-labor force on a permanent basis. The life cycle of women has changed, with fewer years spent in pregnancy and raising children, and more years devoted to participation in wage-labor.

Despite this increase in the participation of women in wage-labor outside the home, the amount of time that women spend working in the home is still substantial. Table 7-C shows the results of a survey of husband-wife families who kept detailed records on the time they spent on shopping, food preparation, and after-meal cleanup, care of family members, care of clothing, house, yard and car, and household management and recordkeeping. The amount of time spent on household work

[3]U.S. Department of Labor, *Manpower Report of the President, 1974*, table B-1; U.S. Department of Labor, Women's Bureau, *1975 Handbook on Women Workers*, Bulletin 297; *Statistical Abstract of the United States, 1982-83, p. 383.*

[4]U.S. Bureau of Labor Statistics, press release of December 9, 1980 (USDL-767), table 4.

[5]*1975 Handbook on Women Workers*, table 15: in this report, minority race denotes blacks, American Indians, Japanese, Chinese, Filipinos, and Koreans; U.S. Bureau of the Census, *Statistical Abstract of the United States, 1982-83*, p. 377.

TABLE 7-B   LABOR FORCE PARTICIPATION RATES OF WOMEN, BY MARITAL AND CHILD STATUS

		Married, Husband Present			
Year	Total Number: Married, Husband Present	With Children 6–17 Only	With Children 0–6	Never Married	Widowed, Separated, Divorced
1890	4.5%	—	—	36.9%	28.6%
1940	14.7	—	—	48.1	36.2
1950	23.8	28.3	11.9	50.5	37.8
1960	30.5	39.0	18.6	44.1	40.0
1970	40.8	49.2	30.3	53.0	39.1
1980	50.1	61.7	45.1	61.5	44.0
1984	52.8	65.4	51.8	63.3	44.9

Sources: *Manpower Report of the President, 1975; 1975 Handbook on Women Workers; Historical Statistics of the United States*; U.S. Bureau of the Census, *Statistical Abstract of the United States, 1985*, pp. 398, 399.

TABLE 7-C   AVERAGE DAILY TIME SPENT ON HOUSEHOLD WORK

Number of Children	Age of Wife or Youngest Child	Nonemployed-Wife Families		Employed-Wife Families	
(1)	(2)	(3a)	(3b)	(4a)	(4b)
	Wife	*Wife*	*Husband*	*Wife*	*Husband*
	Under 25	5.1	0.9	3.5	1.4
None	25–39	5.9	1.2	3.6	1.4
	40–54	6.2	1.5	4.3	1.8
	55 and over	5.4	2.0	4.3	1.1
	Youngest Child				
	12–17	7.1	1.7	4.8	1.7
Two	6–11	7.4	1.6	5.4	1.5
	2–5	8.2	1.6	6.2	1.7
	1	8.8	1.7	6.2	3.5
	Under 1	9.5	1.5	7.7	1.6

How to read this table:

Take, for example, a family with no children (col. 1) where the wife is between 25 and 39 years of age (col. 2 and row 2). If the wife is not employed (col. 3) she does an average of 5.9 hours per day (col. 3a) while her husband does an average of 1.2 hours per day (col. 3b). Even if the wife in this family works (col. 4) she still does 3.6 hours of housework (col. 4a) per day while her husband does an average of 1.4 hours per day (col. 4b).

Source: *1975 Handbook on Women Workers*, p. 174; based on a sample of 1378 families in upstate New York in 1967–1968 and 1971.

varied with the number and age of children, and with whether the wife worked outside the home. The average time spent on household work ranged from four to eight hours daily for women who were also wage-workers, and from five to twelve hours daily for those who were not. The time spent by husbands on household work was considerably less. A comparison of these results with a similar survey from the 1920s indicated that neither the proliferation of household appliances nor the increase in the number of women who are wage-workers had resulted in significantly less time spent in housework. The average working wife today puts in a 66- to 75-hour week at combined wage-labor and household jobs.

OCCUPATIONAL SEGREGATION

Despite the growth in the numbers and proportion of women in the wage-labor force, the occupational segregation between "men's work" and "women's work" that was apparent at the end of the nineteenth century has not diminished in intensity.

The sectors that accounted in 1870 for almost all of women's wage employment were agriculture, domestic servants, and textile apparel industries: of nonfarm women wage-workers in 1870, 70 percent were domestic servants, and 24 percent worked in textiles and apparel.[6] Women had always played a major role in the labor force in textiles, the first major factory-based industry to emerge in the United States, but they never moved from clothing into other manufacturing industries in significant numbers. The rapid growth of manufacturing in the nineteenth century did not lead to comparable increases in the employment of women in those industries. At the same time the decline in the importance of maids and servants and agricultural employees reduced the significance of these occupations for working women (see Table 7-D). As recently as 1981, only a fifth of employed women worked in professional or managerial occupations.

[6]U.S. Bureau of the Census, *Comparative Occupational Statistics, 1870-1940.*

The areas in which female employment have grown most rapidly are the newly expanding occupations that have for long been seen as "women's work"; office and retail sales workers, nurses, schoolteachers, cooks, and waitresses. These occupations alone accounted for nearly half of all employed women in 1981. As Table 7-E shows, these occupations are predominantly female in composition.

One major attribute of the occupations in which women are concentrated is that they are relatively low-paying compared to occupations that contain a very small proportion of women. This pattern extends also to the industries that employ large numbers of blue-collar women: in general, the higher the pro-

TABLE 7-D   MAJOR OCCUPATIONAL GROUPS OF EMPLOYED WOMEN

	1900	1940	1981
Professional and technical	8.1%	12.8%	14.9%
Managers and administrators	7.3	4.5	6.4
Clerical and sales	8.2	28.8	40.4
Craft workers	1.5	1.1	2.0
Operatives	23.8	19.5	12.8
Nonfarm laborers	2.6	1.1	1.4
Service workers	35.5	29.4	20.4
Private household	28.8	18.1	4.0
Other service	6.7	11.3	16.4
Farm workers	13.1	2.8	1.6
Total	100.0	100.0	100.0

Sources: *Historical Statistics of the United States; 1975 Handbook on Women Workers; Statistical Abstract of the United States, 1982–83*, pp. 388–390.

portion of women, the lower the average wages in the industry.

This association between low wages and high concentrations of women workers is not accidental. On the one hand, the most rapidly expanding job sectors have been low-wage jobs and women have been drawn into the wage labor force to meet the expanded demand for labor. On the other hand, the restriction of women to female-sex-typed occupations has the effect of overcrowding those occupations, holding down pay rates in them

TABLE 7-E   PERCENTAGE FEMALE IN SELECTED OCCUPATIONS, 1981

All employed persons	42.8
Professional and technical	44.6
Computer specialists	27.1
Librarians	82.8
Physicians	13.7
Registered nurses	96.8
Teachers, college and university	35.2
Teachers, elementary school	83.6
Managers and administrators	27.5
Salesworkers	45.4
Insurance agents	23.9
Salesclerks, retail trade	71.2
Clerical workers	80.5
Bookkeepers	91.1
Computer operators	63.8
Keypunch operators	93.5
Postal clerks	37.9
Secretaries	99.1
Shipping clerks	22.5
Telephone operators	92.9
Craft workers	6.3
Operatives	32.1
Nonfarm laborers	11.5
Service workers	62.1
Private household	96.5
Other	59.2
Farm workers	15.9

Source: *Statistical Abstract of the United States, 1982–83*, pp. 388–390.

and thereby contributing to women's lower earnings.

WAGES

The trends in money earnings of men and women from 1939 to 1983 are shown in Table 7-F. For year-round, full-time workers, the ratio of female to male earnings has remained stable, at .64 in 1955 and .64 in 1983. It is often said that women's wages are lower than men's because they are more likely to move in and out of the labor force and therefore have less job experience than men. But several studies have examined earnings differences be-

TABLE 7-F   MEDIAN EARNINGS OF MALES AND FEMALES[a]

| | All Wage and Salary Earners | | | % Full Time[b] | | Full-Time Workers | | |
Year	Male	Female	F/M	Male	Female	Male	Female	F/M
1939	$ 939	$ 555	.59	—	—	—	—	—
1950	2,670	1,203	.45	—	—	—	—	—
1955	3,552	1,363	.38	67.2	39.5	4,252	2,719	.64
1960	4,392	1,695	.39	63.8	36.9	5,368	3,257	.61
1965	5,194	2,098	.40	66.3	39.8	6,375	3,823	.60
1970	7,152	2,730	.38	64.3	39.8	8,966	5,323	.59
1975	9,674	3,953	.41	62.9	40.6	12,758	7,504	.59
1980	14,011	6,624	.47	64.7	44.4	18,612	11,197	.60
1983	16,072	8,230	.51	63.7	47.4	21,881	13,915	.64

[a]Income in current prices of civilians 14 years or older; for 1980 and 1983, 15 years or older.
[b]Year-round full-time workers—that is, those working at least 35 hours per week and 50 weeks per year.
Sources: U.S. Department of Commerce, Bureau of the Census, *Current Population Reports*, Series P-60, annual issues.

TABLE 7-G   MEDIAN WEEKLY EARNINGS OF FULL-TIME MEN AND WOMEN
WORKERS, 15 YEARS OLD AND OVER, BY OCCUPATION, MARCH 1981

	Women	Men	Ratio of Women's to Men's Earnings
Professional and technical	$294	$443	.66
Managers and administrators	249	453	.55
Sales	187	383	.49
Clerical	211	351	.60
Operatives	182	302	.60
All occupations	215	358	.60

Source: *Statistical Abstract of the United States, 1982–83*, p. 403.

tween men and women who have the same years of job experience, age, education, hours worked per year, and so on. These studies consistently find that more than half of the total earnings gap between men and women can *not* be attributed to such factors.[7]

Women received substantially lower earnings than men in the same broadly classified occupations, as Table 7-G indicates. Much of this difference is due to the fact that women and men have different jobs within these occupational groups. Of professional and technical workers in 1981, for example, about 44.6 percent were women. But within this group, over three-fourths of elementary school teachers, librarians, and nurses were women, while four-fifths of doctors, lawyers, and electrical engineers were men. This sexual segregation tends to occur as well within detailed occupational classifications. The economic consequence of this segregation is lower average wages for women than for men.

[7]There are two excellent recent surveys of such studies: D. Treiman and H. Hartmann, *Women, Work and Wages* (Washington, D.C.: National Academy Press, 1981); and F. Blau, "Labor Market Discrimination Against Women: A Survey" in W. Darity, ed., *Labor Economics: Modern Views* (Boston: Kluwer-Nijhoff, 1984).

7.1 *Patriarchy and Capitalism*

The nature of the relationships among the family system, the property and class system, and the state provides the central focus of much thinking about the sources of male dominance in a capitalist society. In the following reading Heidi Hartmann examines these relationships by looking at internal family conflicts as well as conflicts between the family and outside institutions. The family has a dual character: interdependence among family members creates a basis for internal family unity, while the unequal power relations within the family create the basis for conflict among family members. This duality permeates the relationship of the family to the economy and the state.

Excerpted from HEIDI HARTMANN, "The Family as the Locus of Gender, Class, and Political Struggle," *Signs*, 6, 3, (Spring 1981). © 1981 by The University of Chicago Press. Reprinted by permission of the author and the publisher.

In this essay I suggest that the underlying concept of the family as an active agent with unified interests is erroneous, and I offer an alternative concept of the family as a locus of *struggle*. In my view, the family cannot be understood solely, or even primarily, as a unit shaped by affect or kinship, but must be seen as a *location* where production and redistribution take place. As such, it is a location where people with different activities and interests in these processes often come into conflict with one another. I do not wish to deny that families also encompass strong emotional ties, are extremely important in our psychic life, and establish ideological norms. But in developing a Marxist-feminist analysis of the family, I wish to identify and explore the material aspects of gender relations within family units. Therefore, I concentrate on the nature of the work people do in the family and their control over the products of their labor.

In a Marxist-feminist view, the organization of production both within and outside the family is shaped by patriarchy and capitalism. Our present social structure rests upon an unequal division of labor by class and by gender which generates tension, conflict, and change. These underlying patriarchal and capitalist relations among people, rather than familial relations themselves, are the sources of dyna-

mism in our society. The particular forms familial relations take largely reflect these underlying social forces. For example, the redistribution that occurs within the family between wage earners and non–wage earners is necessitated by the division of labor inherent in the patriarchal and capitalistic organization of production. In order to provide a schema for understanding the underlying economic structure of the family form prevalent in modern Western society—the heterosexual nuclear family living together in one household—I do not address in this essay the many real differences in the ways people of different periods, regions, races, or ethnic groups structure and experience family life. I limit my focus in order to emphasize the potential for differing rather than harmonious interests among family members, especially between women and men.

. . . This essay explains the family's role as a location for production and redistribution and speculates about the interaction between the family and the state and about changes in family-state relations. . . . Since, as I argue, members of families frequently have different interests, it may be misleading to hold, as family historians often do, that "the family" as a unit resists or embraces capitalism, industrialization, or the state. Rather, people—men and/or women, adults and/or children—use familial forms in various ways. While they may use their "familial" connections or kin groups and their locations in families in any number of projects—to find jobs, to build labor unions, to wage community struggles, to buy houses, to borrow cars, or to share child care—they are not acting only as family members but also as members of gender categories with particular relations to the division of labor organized by capitalism and patriarchy.

Yet tensions between households and the world outside them have been documented by family historians and others, and these suggest that households do act as entities with unified interests, set in opposition to other entities. This seeming paradox comes about because, although family members have distinct interests arising out of their relations to production and redistribution, those same relations also ensure their mutual dependence. Both the wife who does not work for wages and the husband who does, for example, have a joint interest in the size of his paycheck, the efficiency of her cooking facilities, or the quality of their children's education. However, the same historical processes that created households in opposition to (but also in partnership with) the state also augmented the power of men in households, as they became their household heads, and exacerbated tensions within households.

Examples of tensions and conflicts that involve the family in struggle are presented in Table 7-H. The family can be a locus of internal struggle over matters related to production or redistribution (housework and paychecks, respectively). It can also provide a basis for struggle by its members against larger institutions such as corporations or the state. Will cooking continue to be done at home or be taken over largely by fast-food chains? Will child care continue to be the responsibility of parents or will it be provided by the state outside the home? Such questions signal tensions over the location of production. Tax protest, revolving as it does around the issue of who will make decisions for the family about the redistribution of its resources, can be viewed as an example of struggle between

families and the state over redistribution. In this essay I intend to discuss only one source of conflict in any depth—housework—and merely touch upon some of the issues raised by tensions in other arenas. As with most typologies, the categories offered here are in reality not rigidly bounded or easily separable. Rather they represent different aspects of the same phenomena; production and redistribution are interrelated just as are struggles within and beyond households.

PRODUCTION, REDISTRIBUTION, AND THE HOUSEHOLD

Let me begin with a quote from Engels that has become deservedly familiar: "According to the materialistic conception, the determining factor in history is, in the final instance, the production and reproduction of immediate life. This, again, is of a twofold character: on the one side, the production of the means of existence, of food, clothing and shelter and the tools necessary for that production; on the other side, the production of human beings themselves, the propagation of the species. The social organization under which the people of a particular historical epoch live is determined by both kinds of production."[1]

Engels and later Marxists failed to follow through on this dual project. The concept of production ought to encompass both the production of "things," or material needs, and the "production" of people or, more accurately, the production of people who have particular attributes, such as gender. The Marxist development of the concept of production, however, has focused primarily on the production of things. Gayle Rubin has vastly increased our understanding of how people are produced by identifying the "sex/gender system" as a "set of arrangements by which a society transforms biological sexuality into products of human activity, and in which these transformed sex-

[1] Frederick Engels, *The Origin of the Family, Private Property and the State*, ed. with an introduction by Eleanor Leacock (New York: International Publishers, 1972), "Preface to the First Edition," pp. 71–72.

TABLE 7-H   CONFLICTS INVOLVING THE FAMILY

Sources of Conflict	Conflicts Within the Household	Conflicts Between Households and Larger Institutions
Production issues	*Housework*: Who does it? How? According to which standards? Should women work for wages outside the home or for men inside the home?	*Household production versus production organized by capital and the state*: Fast-food or home-cooked meals? Parent cooperative child care or state regulated child-care centers?
Redistribution issues	*Paycheck(s)* How should the money be spent? Who decides? Should the husband's paycheck be spent on luxuries for him or on household needs?	*Taxes*: Who will make the decisions about how to use the family's resources? Family members or representatives of the state apparatus?

ual needs are satisfied."[2] This set of arrangements, which reproduces the species—and gender as well—is fundamentally social. The biological fact of sex differences is interpreted in many different ways by different groups; biology is always mediated by society.

From an economic perspective, the creation of gender can be thought of as the creation of a division of labor between the sexes, the creation of two categories of workers who need each other. In our society, the division of labor between the sexes involves men primarily in wage labor beyond the household and women primarily in production within the household; men and women, living together in households, pool their resources. The form of the family as we know it, with men in a more advantageous position than women in its hierarchy of gender relations, is simply one possible structuring of this human activity that creates gender; many other arrangements have been known.

Although recent feminist psychoanalytic theory has emphasized the relations between children, mothers, and fathers in typical nuclear families, and the way these relations fundamentally shape personality along gender lines and perpetuate hierarchical gender rela-

tions, the pervasiveness of gender relations in all aspects of social life must be recognized.[3] In particular, the creation and perpetuation of hierarchical gender relations depends not only on family life but crucially on the organization of economic production, the production of the material needs of which Engels spoke. While a child's personality is partly shaped by who his or her mother is and her relations to others, her relations to others are products of all our social arrangements, not simply those evident within the household. Such arrangements are collectively generated and collectively maintained. "Dependence" is simultaneously a psychological and political-economic relationship. Male-dominated trade unions and professional associations, for example, have excluded women from skilled employment and reduced their opportunities to support themselves. The denial of abortions to women similarly reinforces women's dependence on men. In these and other ways, many of them similarly institutionalized, men as a group are able to maintain control of women's labor

[2]Gayle Rubin, "The Traffic in Women: Notes on the 'Political Economy' of Sex," in *Toward an Anthropology of Women*, ed. Rayna Rapp Reiter (New York: Monthly Review Press, 1975), p. 159.

[3]In addition to Rubin, see Nancy Chodorow, *The Reproduction of Mothering: Psychoanalysis and the Sociology of Gender* (Berkeley and Los Angeles: University of California Press, 1978): Dorothy Dinnerstein, *The Mermaid and the Minotaur: Sexual Arrangements and Human Malaise* (New York: Harper Colophon Books, 1977); and Jane Flax, "The Conflict between Nurturance and Autonomy in Mother-Daughter Relationships and within Feminism," *Feminist Studies* 4, no. 2 (June 1978): 171–89.

power and thus perpetuate their dominance. Their control of women's labor power is the lever that allows men to benefit from women's provision of personal and household services, including relief from child rearing and many unpleasant tasks both within and beyond households, and the arrangement of the nuclear family, based on monogamous and heterosexual marriage, is one institutional form that seems to enhance this control.[4] Patriarchy's material base is men's control of women's labor; both in the household and in the labor market, the division of labor by gender tends to benefit men.

In a capitalist system the production of material needs takes place largely outside households, in large-scale enterprises where the productive resources are owned by capitalists. Most people, having no productive resources of their own, have no alternative but to offer their labor power in exchange for wages. Capitalists appropriate the surplus value the workers create above and beyond the value of their wages. One of the fundamental dynamics in our society is that which flows from this production process: wage earners seek to retain as much control as possible over both the conditions and products of their labor, and capitalists, driven by competition and the needs of the accumulation process, seek to wrest control away from the workers in order to increase the amount of surplus value. With the wages they receive, people buy the commodities that they need for their survival. Once in the home these commodities are then transformed to become usable in producing and reproducing people. In our society, which is organized by patriarchy as well as by capitalism, the sexual division of labor by gender makes men primarily responsible for wage labor and women primarily responsible for household production. That portion of household production called housework consists largely in purchasing commodities and transforming them into usable forms. Sheets, for example, must be bought, put on beds, rearranged after every sleep, and washed, just as food must be bought, cleaned, cooked, and served to become a meal. Household production also encompasses the biological reproduction of people and the shaping of their gender, as well as their maintenance through housework. In the labor process of producing and reproducing people, household production gives rise to another of the fundamental dynamics of our society. The system of production in which we live cannot be understood without reference to the production and reproduction both of commodities—whether in factories, service centers, or offices—and of people, in households. Although neither type of production can be self-reproducing, together they create and recreate our existence.

This patriarchal and capitalist arrangement of production necessitates a means of redistribution. Because of the class and gender division of labor not everyone has direct access to the economic means of survival. A schematic view of the development of capitalism in Western societies suggests that capitalism generally took root in societies where production and redistribution had taken place largely in households and villages; even though capitalism shifted much production beyond the household, it did not destroy all the traditional ways in which production and redistribution were organized. In preindustrial households, people not only carried on production but also shared their output among themselves (after external obligations such as feudal dues were met), according to established patriarchal relations of authority. In the period of capitalist primitive accumulation, capitalists had to alienate the productive resources that people previously attached to the land had controlled in order to establish the capitalist mode of production based on "free" wage labor. Laborers became "free" to work for capitalists because they had no other means of subsistence and therefore required wages to buy from the capitalists what they had formerly produced in

[4]Heidi I. Hartmann, "The Unhappy Marriage of Marxism and Feminism: Towards a More Progressive Union," *Capital and Class* 8 (Summer 1979): 1–33. See also extensions and critiques in Lydia Sargent, ed., *Women and Revolution* (Boston: South End Press, 1981).

households and villages and exchanged with each other.

With the development of the capitalist mode of production, the old, the young, and women of childbearing age participated less in economic production and became dependent on the wage earners, increasingly adult men. People continued to live in households, however, to reproduce the species and to redistribute resources. Households became primarily income-pooling units rather than income-producing units.[5] The previously established patriarchal division of labor, in which men benefited from women's labor, was perpetuated in a capitalist setting where the men became primarily wage laborers but retained the personal services of their wives, as women became primarily "housewives."[6] The interdependence of men and women that arises out of the division of labor by gender was also maintained. The need for the household in capitalism to be an income-pooling unit, a place where redistribution occurs between men and women, arises fundamentally from the patriarchal division of labor. Yet it is income pooling that enables the household to be perceived as a unit with unitary interests, despite the very different relationships to production of its separate members. Because of the division of labor among family members, disunity is thus inherent in the "unity" of the family.

Recent, often speculative, anthropological and historical research, by focusing on the development of households and their role in political arenas, has contributed to my understanding of the family as an embodiment of both unity and disunity. Briefly, this research suggests that women's status has declined as

political institutions have been elaborated into state apparata, although the mechanisms that connect these two phenomena are not well understood.[7] One possible connection is that the process of state formation enhanced the power of men as they became heads of "their" households. The state's interest in promoting households as political units stemmed from its need to undermine prior political apparata based on kinship. In prestate societies, kinship groups made fundamental political and economic decisions—how to share resources to provide for everyone's welfare, how to redistribute land periodically, how to settle disputes, how to build new settlements. States gradually absorbed these functions.

For instance, in the process of state formation that took place in England and Wales roughly between the eighth and fifteenth centuries, Viana Muller suggests, emerging rulers attempted to consolidate their power against kin groups by winning the allegiance of men away from their kin. One means of doing this may have been allowing men to usurp some of the kin group's authority, particularly over land and women and children.[8] In this view, the household, with its male head, can be seen

[5]See Heidi Hartmann and Ellen Ross, "The Origins of Modern Marriage" (paper delivered at the Scholar and the Feminist Conference, III, Barnard College, April 10, 1976). Batya Weinbaum, "Women in Transition to Socialism: Perspectives on the Chinese Case," *Review of Radical Political Economies* 8, no. 1 (Spring 1976): 34–58, shows that the family is also an income-pooling unit in China under socialism.

[6]See Heidi Hartmann, "Capitalism, Patriarchy, and Job Segregation by Sex," *Signs: Journal of Women in Culture and Society* 1, no. 3, pt. 2 (Spring 1976): 137–69, for how this came about.

[7]See Rayna Rapp, "Gender and Class: An Archaeology of Knowledge concerning the Origin of the State," *Dialectical Anthropology* 2 (December 1977): 309–16; Christine Gailey, "Gender Hierarchy and Class Formation: The Origins of the State in Tonga," unpublished paper (New York: New School for Social Research, 1979); Ruby Rohrlich, "Women in Transition: Crete and Sumer," in *Becoming Visible: Women in European History,* ed. Renate Bridenthal and Claudia Koonz (Boston: Houghton Mifflin Co., 1977); Ruby Rohrlich, "State Formation in Sumer and the Subjugation of Women," *Feminist Studies* 6 (Spring 1980): 76–102; and a symposium in *Feminist Studies,* vol. 4 (October 1978), including Anne Barstow, "The Uses of Archaeology for Women's History: James Mellart's Work on the Neolithic Goddess at Çatal Hüyük," pp. 7–18; Sherry B. Orther, "The Virgin and the State," pp. 19–36; and Irene Silverblatt, "Andean Women in the Inca Empire," pp. 37–61.

[8]Viana Muller, "The Formation of the State and the Oppression of Women: Some Theoretical Considerations and a Case Study in England and Wales," *Review of Radical Political Economics* 9 (Fall 1977): 7–21. Muller bases her account on the work of Tacitus, Bede, Seebohm, Phillpotts, F. M. Stenton, Whitelock, Homans, and McNamara and Wemple.

to be a "creation" of the state. George Duby reports that by 1250 the household was everywhere the basis of taxation in Western society.[9] Lawrence Stone argues that the state's interests were served by an authoritarian household structure, for it was generally believed that deference shown to the head of household would be transferred to the king: "The power of kings and of heads of households grew in parallel with one another in the sixteenth century. The state was as supportive of the patriarchal nuclear family as it was hostile to the kin-oriented family; the one was a buttress and the other a threat to its own increasing power."[10]

As Elizabeth Fox-Genovese points out, the authoritarianism of the new nation-state was incompatible with developing capitalism, and Locke's concept of authority as derivative from the individual helped to establish a new legitimating ideology for the state: it serves with the consent of the propertied individuals. To put forward his theory with logical coherence, Locke had to assert the authority of all individuals, including women and children. But by removing the family from the political sphere, ideologically at least, later theorists solved the contradiction between the elevation of women to the status of individuals and the maintenance of patriarchal authority. The family became private, of no moment in conducting the politics of social interchange, and the head of the family came to represent its

interests in the world.[11] The ideology of individualism, by increasing the political importance of men beyond their households, strengthened patriarchy at home; it completed the legitimation of male public power begun during the process of state elaboration.

Yet even as the household, and particularly the man within it, became in this view an agent of the state against collectivities organized by kinship, the household also remained the last repository of kin ties. Even the nuclear household continues to tie its members to others through the processes of marriage, childbirth, and the establishment of kinship. These ties to others beyond the household (though much more limited than in the past) coupled with the interdependence of household members stemming from their different relations to production continue to give members of households a basis for common interests vis-à-vis the state or other outside forces. Household members continue to make decisions about pooling incomes, caring for dependent members, engaging in wage work, and having children, but it is important to remember that within the household as well as outside it men have more power. Therefore, viewing the household as a unit which jointly chooses, for example, to deploy its available labor power to maximize the interests of *all* its members (the implicit approach of those historians who discuss family strategies and adaptations and the explicit approach of others) obscures the reality of both the capitalist and patriarchal relations of production in which households are enmeshed.[12] Mutual depen-

[9]George Duby, "Peasants and the Agricultural Revolution," in *The Other Side of Western Civilization,* ed. Stanley Chodorow (New York: Harcourt Brace Jovanovich, 1979), p. 90, reprinted from *Rural Economy and Country Life in the Medieval West,* trans. Cynthia Poston (Columbia: University of South Carolina Press, 1968).

[10]Lawrence Stone, "The Rise of the Nuclear Family in Early Modern England: The Patriarchal Stage," in *The Family in History,* ed. Charles E. Rosenberg (Philadelphia: University of Pennsylvania Press, 1975), p. 55. Also see Ellen Ross, "Women and Family," in "Examining Family History," by Rayna Rapp, Ellen Ross, and Renate Bridenthal, *Feminist Studies* 5, no. 1 (Spring 1979): 174–200, who discusses the transition from kin to nuclear family in more detail than I do here and offers a number of useful criticisms of family history.

[11]Elizabeth Fox-Genovese, "Property and Patriarchy in Classical Bourgeois Political Theory," *Radical History Review* 4 (Spring/Summer 1977): 36–59. See also Robert A. Nisbet, *The Sociological Tradition* (New York: Basic Books, 1966).

[12]Joan Scott and Louise Tilly, "Women's Work and the Family in Nineteenth-Century Europe," *Comparative Studies in Society and History* 17, no. 1 (January 1975): 36–64, use the concepts of choice and adaptation. Louise Tilly, "Individual Lives and Family Strategies in the French Proletariat," *Journal of Family History* 4, no. 2 (Summer 1979): 137–52, employs the concept of family strategies but incorporates an understanding of potential intrafamily conflict. Jane Humphries, "The Working Class

dence by no means precludes the possibility of coercion. Women and men are no less mutually dependent in the household than are

Family, Women's Liberation, and Class Struggle: The Case of Nineteenth Century British History," *Review of Radical Political Economics* 9, no. 3 (Fall 1977): 25–41, makes explicit use of the concept of family unity.

workers and capitalists or slaves and slave-owners. In environments that are fundamentally coercive (such as patriarchy and capitalism) concepts of choice and adaptation are inevitably flawed—as is the belief that workers and capitalists or men and women have unified interests. This is not to say that such unity can *never* exist.

7.2   *Women: From Home Production to Wage Labor*

The growth since 1900 in the participation of women in the wage-labor force has had profound consequences both for male-female relationships and the structure of the economy. In the following reading Marilyn Power examines the causes and consequences of this historic shift.

Excerpted from MARILYN POWER, "From Home Production to Wage Labor: Women as a Reserve Army of Labor," *Review of Radical Political Economics*, 15, 1 (Spring 1983). © 1983 by The Review of Radical Political Economics. Reprinted by permission of the author and the Union for Radical Political Economics.

One striking and important change in women's economic role in the twentieth century has been the proletarianization of ever-increasing numbers of married women; to understand women's work under capitalism, we must be able to explain this movement of married women into the *wage* labor force. Further, any understanding of women's economic roles requires an examination of their work in the labor force, their work in the home, and the interrelationships between these two spheres. The purpose of this paper is to develop an analytic framework for understanding why married women have entered the wage labor force, especially in the latter half of the twentieth century, by looking at change in their work in the home which made them available for wage labor, and the development of capitalism which created wage jobs for them. In brief, capitalism's invasion of women's work in the home over the course of the nineteenth and early twentieth centuries gradually changed women's home work from predominantly *production* to predominantly *maintenance*,

thereby eliminating women's ability to provide for the support of themselves and their families through work outside the sphere of capitalist production. Married women became a *latent* reserve army of labor, to be drawn into wage labor with the development of the capitalist economy.

This argument builds upon feminist theoretical writings of the past decade, and at the same time takes issue with some of the theoretical directions that have been taken in recent years. In specific, this analysis will take issue with the concept of women as a *permanent* marginal labor force under capitalism; stress the importance of understanding *changes* as well as *continuities* in women's work in the home; suggest that the existence of the "family wage" was always more ideological than actual; and emphasize the importance of *contradictions* rather than mutual accommodation between capitalism and patriarchy.

In order to develop the argument that married women became a latent reserve army of labor in the twentieth century United States, this paper ... first will discuss the historical transformation of women's work in the home from predominantly production to predominantly maintenance, and explain the implications of this change for women's economic role, their transformation into a latent reserve of labor. The second [section] will describe the movement of this latent reserve into the active labor force in the course of capitalist development, particularly the expansion of the clerical and service sectors. Finally, the paper will elaborate upon the theoretical implications of this analysis for feminist political economy. Before beginning this discussion, however, it is necessary to summarize the data on the movement of married women into the wage labor force.

THE ISSUE: MARRIED WOMEN IN THE LABOR FORCE

The movement of married women into the labor force in the twentieth century has been steady and dramatic, particularly since World War II, and perhaps most strikingly in the last ten to fifteen years. Labor force participation rates of married women rose from an estimated 5% in 1890 (for paid work *outside* the home) to 21.6% in 1950, 30.6% in 1960, and 49.4% in 1979. By 1960 the majority (57%) of women workers were married with husbands present.[1] Even among women with preschool children, 44% are in the labor force (this group, historically the last group of women to enter the labor force, has entered wage labor particularly rapidly in the past decade). In short, it is now "normal" for married women to participate in wage labor, and increasingly fewer of them are taking time out even when their children are small.

This movement into the wage labor force constituted a significant change in the economic role of married women. It has frequently been pointed out that the methods

used to measure labor force participation undercounted women's economic contributions through work for pay in the home, especially before 1940.[2] A great deal of the paper will in fact be focused on a discussion of the nature and significance of these contributions. It is important, however, to distinguish them from women's participation in the labor force, for two reasons. First, women's labor force participation as conventionally measured takes place *outside of* and *separate from* the home and family. Thus the growth in the labor force participation of married women is likely to have considerable effects on relations within the family. And second, while their economic contributions in the home were often *outside* or only *peripherally* connected to capitalist production, married women's entrance into the labor force constitutes, for the vast majority, a complete integration into capitalist wage labor.

This paper will argue that we can understand this movement of married women into wage labor as a result of capitalist development which first transformed them into a latent reserve army of labor, and has gradually incorporated them into the active labor force in the twentieth century.

. . .

CHANGES IN THE CONTEXT OF HOUSEWORK: THE "FREEING" OF WOMEN

The expansion of capitalist production changed the content of women's work in the home over the course of the nineteenth and early twentieth centuries. This change occurred unevenly and at varied rates: in addition to race and class, residence in a rural or urban area, occupation (especially farm or non-farm), and geographic area or residence (e.g. West vs. East) all affected the speed with

---

[1]Robert W. Smuts, *Women and Work in America*, (New York: Schocken, 1971), p. 23; U.S. Department of Labor, Bureau of Labor Statistics Bulletin 2080, *Perspectives on Working Women: A Databook*, October 1980, p. 22.

[2]Census takers in 1920, for example, were instructed to *exclude* boarders as a form of employment, unless it was the principal means of support. See Joan Jensen, "Cloth, Butter and Boarders: Women's Household Production for the Market," *Review of Radical Political Economics*, 12, 2 (Summer 1980), p. 15.

which capitalism invaded and changed women's work in the home. Nonetheless, the content of that work did change for virtually all women over the course of this period, with profound implications for women's economic roles. We can most usefully explain the changes in women's work in the home by examining two aspects: the change in the content of the work from predominantly *production* to predominantly *maintenance*; and the elimination of production for *exchange* for the home.

Production involves the transforming of raw or unfinished materials into finished goods (e.g. growing food, preserving, weaving cloth, sewing clothes); maintenance involves the care and maintaining of the family and its possessions (e.g. caring for the ill, house cleaning, laundry, shopping for household goods). Both production and maintenance have historically been aspects of women's work in the home, included in the general category "housework," but over time the mix has changed, with increasing emphasis on maintenance work and a corresponding limiting of women's ability to contribute to family support through their work in the home. That is, production housework provided goods for the support of the family *outside of and independent from* capitalist production. Maintenance housework does not provide such support and may, in fact, increase the family's dependence on wage labor, as cash income is required to provide the appliances and other products used in maintenance. This is not to say that maintenance housework is unimportant for subsistence (reproduction of labor power)—keeping the house clean and family members healthy are necessary to reproduction (and the socially-determined level of subsistence includes the possession of a certain quantity of commodities, which need to be purchased and maintained)—but maintenance housework provides no means of support separate from capitalist production.

In the pre-industrial U.S., women's work time was largely taken up with production housework. They grew much of the food consumed by the family, as well as gathering wild foods and herbs, and caring for chickens and other domestic livestock. They dried, salted, pickled, and preserved food for winter use, and made soap and candles. They were responsible for the production of clothing, starting, in many cases, with raising the sheep or growing the flax to use for the yarn. Women performed these tasks with the aid of their children and often servants; an affluent woman may have spent most of her time supervising the production work of servants. Further, the amount of household manufacture was probably less in towns, especially trading towns, than it was in rural areas, since towns had access to cloth and other finished goods from Great Britain. Nevertheless, even town women had kitchen gardens, chickens, and often cows; all engaged of necessity in the preserving of food for the winter; and spinning, knitting, and sewing were performed by town as well as rural women.[3]

Through their production, women contributed significantly to the support of the family, both in towns and in the countryside; it was hardly possible, especially, for a farm to survive without the labor of a woman, and her children as well. Further, women contributed to the household's small but necessary cash income, through such activities as selling extra butter and eggs, and by spinning and weaving cloth for sale.

As industrial capitalism developed, it increasingly eliminated spheres of petty commodity production and production for use in the home; the forces of competition and accumulation meant that capitalism gradually incorporated (and continues to incorporate) any production that could be made to produce profit. Petty commodity production was eliminated because the capitalist organization of production in factories substantially cheapened the production of commodities; petty commodity producers in the home were immediately affected by this process. For example, textile production was incorporated into the capitalist sector in the first wave of indus-

---

[3]Since no time-use studies exist for pre-industrial women's work, we must piece together an image of their work days, largely through diaries, letters and household inventories.

trialization. The price of factory cloth was substantially lower than that of hand-woven cloth, and women gradually lost their market for home-produced textiles; (one off-shoot of industrialization of this aspect of home production was the movement of many young, single women into the textile mills). By the Civil War, according to Jensen, few women did any spinning or weaving except on the frontier.

Production for *use* also tended to be removed from the home through this cheapening of commodities by capitalist production. That is, a woman could choose to continue producing cloth (for example) for her family's use at home, despite the fact that factory cloth was more efficiently produced and cheaper. However, this activity no longer made sense as a *survival strategy* for herself and her family. In addition, as the price of land rose and industrialization increased urban density, fewer families, especially of the working class, had access to the most important means of home production, land. Families turned increasingly to the market for goods that women had previously produced at home.

However, this transformation occurred only gradually: textile production moved out of the home very early, but capitalist penetration of other areas of home production developed over the entire course of the nineteenth century. Home production was replaced by capitalist production in urban areas more quickly than in rural areas, and in more "settled" parts of the country before less (e.g. the East before the West); both access to land and accessibility to capitalist markets played a role in determining the rate of change. There is some evidence that working class households turned to the market somewhat before petit bourgeois households, which often had more land, a less urgent need for married women to work *outside* the home, and, often, servants to aid in the work of home production.

The gradual nature of this transition from home production to capitalist production must be stressed. Home production for use and for exchange continued to contribute significantly to family support into the twentieth century

even in urban areas. A study by the U.S. Commissioner of Labor of 2,500 families living in the principal coal, iron, and steel regions in 1890 shows that about half the families had livestock, poultry, vegetable gardens, or all three. Nearly 30% purchased no vegetables during the year except potatoes.[4]

A common pattern for working class households by the late 1800's was for men to engage in wage labor in the factories while the women engaged in domestic production, producing much of the family's food. Thus families continued for a long time to cushion their dependence on wage income; in times of layoffs or strikes, they could at least partially subsist from their garden plots, allowing them a modicum of independence for capital.

By the 1920's, use of market substitutes for home production was widespread; the era of the "mass market" had begun. Urbanization and the expansion of capitalist production of food and clothing had effectively eliminated women's ability to provide direct support through domestic production. For example, U.S. Dept. of Agriculture figures show an increase in the apparent annual consumption of canned vegetables from 15 pounds per person in 1909 to 21 pounds in 1921 and 26 pounds in 1931.[5] The Lynds, in their 1929 study of a small midwestern city, found that 70% of the city's bread was commercially baked, compared with 25% in 1890. Backyards were shrinking, and vegetable gardens were disappearing; a Middletown seed store proprietor estimated that not over 40 to 50% of families had even small vegetable gardens, compared with at least 75 to 80% in 1890, and the gardens in 1890 had been considerably larger.[6] With the demise of the backyard garden went the decline of canning and preserving; by 1929 only low income families in Middletown did much canning, and that was probably

[4]U.S. Commissioner of Labor, *Sixth Annual Report*, Washington, D.C., 1891, cited in Smuts, *Women and Work*, p. 11.
[5]Cited in Carolyn Shaw Bell, *Consumer Choice in the American Economy*, (New York: Random House, 1967), pp. 18-19.
[6]Robert S. and Helen Merrell Lynd, *Middletown*, (New York: Harcourt Brace, 1929), pp. 95, 155.

predominantly of produce purchased, not grown at home.

Production for exchange was also gradually eliminated from women's work in the home. As described above, women in the preindustrial U.S. contributed to the family's small cash income through selling such products as surplus butter and eggs, cloth, and clothing sewn at home. Although capitalism invaded textile and clothing production early, limitations on transportation and storage facilities meant that markets for home-produced butter, eggs, and other fresh produce continued for most of the nineteenth century, except in major urban areas. In rural areas these markets were not penetrated by capitalist production until the early twentieth century. Jensen cites a study in Texas in 1928-30 which found that between one-fourth and one-third of farm women engaged in domestic production for exchange.

In urban areas many women (especially but not exclusively immigrant women) did piece work at home, performing such tasks as finishing sewing on factory made clothing, making artificial flowers, rolling cigars; their children in many cases worked along side them. But urban women also engaged in home production *outside* the capitalist sector. They did laundry and sewing for their neighbors and, especially, took in boarders. Taking in boarders was extremely common in late nineteenth and early twentieth century working class households, and often contributed significantly to household income (taking in boarders entailed cooking for them, cleaning up after them, and possibly doing their laundry as well). Jensen offers the example of a study of urban areas in 1892 which found that 27% of the women took in boarders, and that this income from boarders averaged 42.65% as much as their husbands' incomes. After the 1920's boarding was gradually eliminated as a source of income, however, largely through the curtailment of immigration.

In sum, by the 1920's, the expansion of capitalist production had eliminated most direct production for exchange and direct production for use from the home. Some production

housework remains—for example, food preparation involves the transformation of unfinished into finished products for use and thus is a production task. However, most production housework, as we have seen, was removed from the home to the capitalist sector, and even the content of tasks such as food preparation [was] changed and reduced. Such activities as grinding flour, preserving foods, and baking bread have essentially been removed from the home (although they do retain residual presence as hobbies), while cooking involves far less use of raw foods produced by the woman and her family, and far more putting the finishing touches on processed foods purchased from the capitalist sphere.

We can see a reflection of this trend if we contrast data from one of the earliest studies of time-use in housework, done by Maude Wilson in Oregon in 1926-27 with a time-use study by Kathryn Walker in Syracuse, N.Y. in 1967-68. Farm women in Wilson's study spent an average of 3.3 hours per day on food preparation, compared with Walker's results of 2.3 hours per day by women not employed outside the home and 1.6 hours by women who were employed outside the home. Wilson noted that one reason for the quantity of time spent by farm women in her study on food preparation was that 53% of them baked all or most of their own bread. It is true that 1926-27 is late for our purposes, since capitalist development was widespread by this time. Nevertheless, these farm women in Oregon lived in an area where capitalist markets were not as pervasive as in more industrialized areas, and thus may have retained many of the production tasks of an earlier era. It may be indicative that 43% of the households had neither electricity nor plumbing.[7]

[7]Maud Wilson, *Use of Time by Oregon Farm Homemakers*, (Portland, Oregon: Agricultural Experiment Station Bulletin 256, November 1929), pp. 14, 36, 68; Kathryn Walker and Margaret E. Woods, *Time Use: A Measure of Household Production of Family Goods and Services* (Washington, D.C.: Center for the Family of the American Home Economics Association, 1976), pp. 50-51.

Those few production tasks which *have* remained in the home do not contribute in any significant way to the family's support. Further, women are no longer able to produce goods within the home for exchange. Women's ability, then, to contribute directly to the *support* of themselves and their families through their work at home was gradually eliminated by the expansion of the sphere of capitalist production over the course of the nineteenth and early twentieth centuries. During the Depression of the 1930's there was some indication of a return to home production, as women attempted to supplement the family's diminishing cash income, but in general the 1920's and 1930's mark the transition of women from household production to wage labor: lacking the ability to provide support for their families through their production in the home, married women increasingly began entering the wage labor force.

Capitalism gradually eliminated women's production work at home; however, this does not mean that capitalism eliminated *housework*, or that women's role in the production and reproduction of the labor force became less significant. As production work left the home it was replaced by maintenance housework; women became responsible for the households' greatly expanding consumption of commodities (many of which the women had produced themselves in the past); they became "purchasing agents" for the family. Further, the family's gradually expanding stock of possessions required care and maintenance. In short, as production housework left the home, it was replaced by consumption and maintenance, and housework continued to require long hours.

We can illustrate this transition from production to maintenance housework by once again referring to the Wilson and Walker studies. The Oregon farm women averaged 7.4 hours per day on housework; to this they added 1.6 hours per day of farm work for a total work day of 9.0 hours. Urban women in Wilson's study spent 7.3 hours per day on housework while women in Walker's 1967-68 study who were not employed outside the

home spent 8.0 hours per day on housework. Hours spent on housework had actually *increased* somewhat over the forty year period. Further, the mix of tasks had changed (see Table 7-I) with, as we have discussed, a decrease in food activities but an increase in maintenance tasks of house and clothing care, in performing and recording the family's purchases, and in care of family members.[8]

This transformation of the content of women's work in the home from predominantly production to predominantly maintenance tied the family far more closely into capitalist production. Maintenance housework may be seen as a substitute for the purchase of services, but it cannot provide a source of use-values, for the support of the household separate from capitalist production (maintenance involves the preserving of existing use-values, not the creation of *new* use-values). Further, ... the *means* of household production have increasingly become commodities (i.e., purchased from the capitalist sector). This is true of both production and maintenance work; to the extent that women still engage in production tasks such as canning and sewing, the raw materials they transform are frequently purchased as commodities, while increasing maintenance work requires the purchase of appliances, cleaning fluids and powders, and even automobiles. Thus, the transformation of housework from predominantly production to predominantly maintenance reflected an increasing dependence of the household on the capitalist market both for the acquisition of use-values and for their maintenance.

Women continued to perform housework in the home, but with a crucial difference: they

[8]This last category requires more explanation. Family care largely consists of child care, and was divided by these studies into physical care (including bathing, feeding, dressing, etc.) and nonphysical care (including helping children with lessons, chauffeuring children and other family members, etc.). Thus the sharp increase in the time spent on family care could indicate more children per household in the Walker study or, more likely, a rise in the standards for child care, as an urban environment and new child rearing philosophies require women to spend more time supervising and chauffeuring their children.

TABLE 7-I   TIME-USE IN HOUSEWORK ACTIVITIES: FARM WOMEN AND URBAN
WOMEN IN OREGON IN 1926-27; AND FULL-TIME HOUSEWORKERS
IN SYRACUSE, N.Y. IN 1967-68: HOURS PER DAY.

| Activity | 1926-27 | | 1967-68 |
	farm (n = 288)	urban (n = 154)	(n = 979)
All housework[a]	7.4	7.3	8.0
food activities	3.3	2.8	2.3
care of house	1.2	1.3	1.6
care of family members	0.5	1.2	1.8
marketing and record keeping[b]	0.1	0.4	1.0

[a]for 1926-27 farm women, includes tasks not listed separately.

[b]for 1926-27 farm women, category is entitled "purchasing for Household."

Sources: Wilson 1929:68; Walker and Woods 1967:50.

could no longer contribute directly to family support through this work, probably for the first time in history. They could of course turn their attention to economizing, and thereby make the "breadwinner's" pay check stretch further—but they could no longer *themselves* provide bread. For women of the petite bourgeoisie this dependence began in the mid-1800's, but for most women, as we have seen, the early twentieth century marks the final step in the transition to economic dependence which began with industrialization.

To summarize, the expansion of capitalist production gradually changed the content of women's work in the home from production to maintenance work, and at the same time removed production for exchange from the home. These changes had the result that women lost their ability to contribute to the support of themselves and their families through their work in the home. In Marxist terminology, they had become a latent reserve army of labor.

THE MOVEMENT OF MARRIED WOMEN INTO WAGE LABOR

There is no one answer to the question of why married women had not entered the wage labor market force earlier in the nineteenth century; a complex of factors, both economic and ideological, are involved. The ideology of the nineteenth and early twentieth century was emphatic that women's true sphere was home and family. Further, there were legal barriers to women's access to many jobs. Hartmann suggests that protective legislation, demanded by the patriarchal male working class (who wanted to guarantee their control over women's labor at home) was an important force, as it effectively excluded women from many important sectors of industrial wage labor.[9] Sen argues that the role of patriarchy, while important, is overstressed in Hartmann's analysis. The difficulty women faced in combining their responsibilities for household production and child care with industrial labor, particularly given the long hours of nineteenth century factory work, were likely to discourage women from entering wage labor unless they were economically desperate[10]:

The contradictions between wage labor, infant care, and domestic work provided a strong enough impetus for mothers to stay at home, quite apart from their husbands' patriarchal drives.

[9]Heidi I. Hartmann, "Capitalism, Patriarchy and Job Segregation by Sex," in Zillah Eisenstein, ed., *Capitalist Patriarchy and the Case for Socialist Feminism* (New York: Monthly Review Press, 1979).

[10]Gita Sen, "The Sexual Division of Labor and the Working-Class Family: Towards a Conceptual Synthesis of Class Relations and the Subordination of Women," *Review of Radical Political Economics* 12, 2 (Summer 1980), p. 83.

My analysis suggests an additional factor encouraging married women to remain at home: their work in the home contributed significantly to the support of the family. They didn't need to enter wage labor as long as their home production provided sufficient goods for use and exchange.

By the beginning of the twentieth century, as we have seen, the expansion of capitalist production had essentially eliminated women's precapitalist economic roles in the home; married women began the transition from home production to wage labor. Of course this transition was a gradual process, and there was no dramatic and sudden surge of women into the labor force. In fact, there were a number of forces which tended to keep married women in the home despite economic dependence. First, as in the nineteenth century, ideology was unambiguous that married women belonged at home; patriarchal attitudes of husbands and fathers no doubt reinforced this message on a personal level. Second, although the birth rate was dropping, women continued to have total responsibility for child care and housework, with few alternative services offered by the society. Third, protective legislation and blatant discrimination severely limited the pool of jobs available to women; in 1900 almost 29% of all women in the labor force were private household workers.[11] Fourth, to the extent that male workers had won pay increases to achieve a "family wage" (i.e. enough to support a family on one pay check), married women weren't *forced* into the labor force by economic necessity (women who could not depend on a male wage, of course, were forced into paid labor). There is reason to question, however, the extent to which male workers *had* achieved the family wage: Hartmann suggests that it had largely been won by them by the early twentieth century, but some writers argue that for many workers it was never more than an ideological myth.[12]

Finally, it is precisely in the nature of the latent reserve army to *remain* latent until the growth of capital requires a new pool of labor. Women were not likely to enter the labor force en masse as long as the demand for their labor was limited. What was needed for their labor force participation to be actualized was a sharp increase in the demand for labor—and more particularly in the demand for labor in *female* occupations. Occupational segregation by sex has a long history in the U.S.; it predates industrialization, but was rigidified and reinforced during the 1800's through the actions of both capital and organized labor.[13] An increase in the demand for women's labor, then, could come in one of three ways: through a growth in occupations already defined as female, through the creation of new female occupations, or through the redefinition of a previously male occupation as female.

The movement of women into the labor force largely coincided with the latter creation of demand: clerical work, in particular, which had in the nineteenth century been a rela-

[12]Fox cites budget studies from the turn of the century through the 1960's which indicate that for most of the period a majority of families could not live in "health and decency" on the earnings of a male wage or salary earner alone. When women could not provide through work at home (as was increasingly the case, as we have seen), *children* were the main providers of supplementary income from paid work in the labor force in the first half of the twentieth century. By the 1950's, children were spending more time in school and less in the labor force, and increasing numbers of married women were working for pay. The percentage of households in the U.S. with three or more wage earners remained essentially the same between 1930 and 1970; the percentage with two or more wage earners remained the same from 1930 to 1950, after which it has increased. See Bonnie Fox, "Women's Double Work Day: Twentieth-Century Changes in the Reproduction of Daily Life," in B. Fox, ed., *Hidden in the Household*, (Toronto, Canada: The Women's Press, 1980), p. 202; Michele Barrett and Mary McIntosh, "The 'Family Wage': Some Problems for Socialists and Feminists," *Capital and Class* 11 (Summer 1980).

[13]The question of how / why occupational segregation by sex has remained embedded in U.S. capitalism is important, but discussion of it would lead us far astray from the major arguments in this paper. For the present purpose, I will simply take occupational segregation as a given.

[11]Valerie Kincade Oppenheimer, *The Female Labor Force in the United States*, Population Monograph Series, no. 5 (Westport, Conn.: Greenwood Press, 1976), p. 220.

tively small and characteristically male occupation, became redefined as a female occupation in the twentieth century at the same time that it began a process of phenomenal growth. The rapid growth in the demand for clerical workers has been associated with the increasing concentration of capital. Davies suggests[14]:

> As business operations became more complex, there was a large increase in correspondence, record-keeping, and office work in general. This expansion created a demand for an expanded labor force.

The growth in demand for clerical workers and the characterization of clerical work as a female occupation were both striking and coordinated: the 1880 Census reported a total of 5,000 stenographers and typists, of whom 40.0% were female; by 1900 there were 112,600 stenographers and typists, 76.7% female (the usual definition of a female occupation is one which is at least 70% female); by 1930 there were 811,200 stenographers and typists, of whom 95.6% were female. The period since 1930 has seen yet more phenomenal growth in employment in secretarial and other clerical work, which has continued since that period to be an essentially all-female occupation: in 1979, the roughly comparable category of secretaries and typists employed about 4.7 million workers, of whom 98.6% were women. Beside clerical work, women are also concentrated in service work, another occupational category which has expanded rapidly, particularly in the post-war period. In 1979 clerical and service occupations together accounted for 52% of all employed women.[15]

Thus the demand for women workers increased, and increased sharply, quickly outrunning the supply of young, unmarried women who had constituted the female labor force in the nineteenth and early twentieth centuries. The pool of single women aged 18 to 34 had actually *declined* by 2.8 million, or 46%, between 1940 and 1960[16] due to a combination of the low birth rate during the Depression and the high marriage rate in the post-war period. Where, then, were to be found the "great masses of (wo)men" to be thrown "on the decisive points without injury to the scale of production in other areas"[17]? Obviously, from among the latent pool of married women.

It would be an oversimplification, however, to attribute the increased labor force participation of married women solely to the removal of production housework and production for exchange from the home and the increase in demand for women workers. Clearly, other factors played a role, including, perhaps, an increased need for money income among families involved in the post-war rush to purchase homes, cars, appliances, and other consumer goods. Demographic factors were probably also significant: women finished bearing children earlier than they had in the past, so they completed their child raising well before old age. Many of the married women in the labor force in the 1950's and 1960's had reentered paid work after children were grown.

Whatever other factors were involved, however, it seems clear that one important component of married women's movement into the labor force was the change in their work in the home, which made them a latent reserve army, ready to be drawn into the labor force as the need arose.

IMPLICATIONS OF THE ANALYSIS FOR FEMINIST POLITICAL ECONOMY

A number of implications arise from this argument, perhaps the most important being that women have become part of the *permanent* labor force. Many feminists (including myself in

---

[14]Margery Davies, "Woman's Place is at the Typewriter: the Feminization of the Clerical Labor Force," *Radical America* (July-August 1974), p. 150.

[15]Ibid., p. 155; Bureau of Labor Statistics, *Perspectives on Working Women*, pp. 9, 10.

[16]Oppenheimer, *The Female Labor Force*, p. 17.

[17]Karl Marx, *Capital*, vol. 1 (New York: International Publishers, 1967), p. 638.

an early paper) have argued that women serve as a marginal labor force for capitalism, to be taken into wage labor when needed, sent back to their primary role in the home when no longer required. However, the removal of women's work for production and exchange from the home make this a much less viable alternative for capitalism. Economic stagnation or worse in the 1980's may fuel the "new right" rhetoric that women should go back to the home, and non-enforcement of affirmative action and anti-discrimination legislation may severely hamper women's ability to improve (or even maintain) their economic position, but the fact is that women's production work in the home is no longer available for them to do. They can be unemployed, of course, or employed temporarily or sporadically, but they cannot, in any meaningful numbers, just be sent "home"—the latent reserve army, once it has been activated, can never become *latent* once again.

Failure to distinguish between production and maintenance housework masks this reality. Anthias, for example, argues that women cannot be seen as a latent pool of labor because housework can't be analyzed as task specific, and because women continue to produce use-values in the home once they are in the labor force.[18] In this argument (and it is unclear why she sees housework as not task-specific; this seems a mystification of what is, in fact, a concrete series of tasks), by pooling all of housework as the production of "use-values," Anthias fails to recognize the historic invasion of the production of subsistence by capitalism. The implication is that the "use-values" remain at home for women to perform; if they are removed from the labor force they can simply increase production of domestic use-values. As I have argued, this option is not open to women, not because there is a lack of *work* to be done in the home, but because that work does not provide an alternative source of support for the family. A return to

home production is not feasible, because of a lack of access to land and because goods can be produced more cheaply in the capitalist sector. Maintenance housework can economize the household's need for commodities, by making them last longer; however, these savings are not an adequate substitute for women's earnings, especially as women continue to perform maintenance tasks *even when* they work for pay. In addition, maintenance work itself requires commodities (appliances, detergents, etc.), which increase the household's need for money. Maintenance work in the home is not a meaningful alternative to wage labor for women.

This argument has a number of implications for our understanding of the dynamic of capitalist development as it relates to the economic oppression of women. In particular it points to the possibility of contradictions between capitalism and patriarchy. One school of feminist thought, represented in particular by Heidi Hartmann and Zillah Eisenstein, argues that there exists a "partnership," a "mutual accommodation," or a "mutual dependence" between capitalism and men.[19] In brief, men control women's labor within the home and, through their demands for household services, limit women's ability to seek market work. Capitalism hires women only for

---

[18]Floya Anthias, "Women and the Reserve Army of Labour: a Critique of Veronica Beechey," *Capital and Class* 10 (Spring 1980), p. 59.

[19]Eisenstein labels this view "socialist feminism," in distinction from Marxist and radical feminist analyses. According to Eisenstein, a socialist feminist analysis views the oppression of women as affected by both capitalism and patriarchy, systems with *separate* and at least partially *independent* material bases. Hartmann's analysis also begins with this basic premise, although she describes herself as a "Marxist-feminist," and differs from Eisenstein on a variety of issues (including, possibly, the saliency of class in an analysis of the oppression of women). There is considerable analytic debate in the feminist literature about the relationship between capitalism and patriarchy: the relative importance of the two systems in determining the oppression of women; the dynamics of the interaction between capitalism and patriarchy; whether it is analytically correct to posit a separate material base for patriarchy; and even whether it is appropriate to use the term patriarchy at all, in describing the transhistorical and transcultural subordination of women to men. This is a very important debate, and it forms the context for the questions examined in this paper, A detailed discussion of the debate cannot be included here; however, the histori-

sex-segregated, low paid, dead end work (and, perhaps, pays women less than the value of their labor power). Thus, even when women do work for pay, they remain economically dependent upon men—essentially, are forced by economic pressure to marry and, once married, to provide household services for their husbands. This provision of services for the husbands also benefits capitalism, since it insures that women will continue to produce and reproduce the labor force within the home. Further, patriarchal relations within the home reproduce hierarchical gender identities, useful to capitalism in its super-exploitation of women.

While the description of this dynamic illuminates the dual pressure faced by women under patriarchal capitalism, there are two problems which tend to arise from this approach. First, there is a tendency for such an analysis to be static, posed in terms of an historic struggle perhaps, which developed the partnership; but once the partnership was established, it is seen as abiding. The possibility of contradiction between capitalism and patriarchy may be acknowledged, but the analysis seems to lead, not into an investigation of the possibility of contradiction but into an assumption that such contradictions, if they exist, can't be sufficiently fundamental to threaten the partnership. Thus, an area of what I believe is crucial investigation is in effect closed off.

Second, and closely related to this first tendency, the analysis tends to deemphasize women's labor force participation as a determinant of their condition, arguing that the low wages paid to women, combined with their continued responsibility for housework and child care, mean that patriarchal relations within the home remain the key determinant

even when women work for pay. The focus of the analysis, therefore, tends to remain on the family, with less attention paid to the possibility that changes in women's labor force experience may effect changes in their overall experience, and in the dynamic between capitalism and patriarchy.

For example, Hartmann points out that even though married women have entered the labor force in large numbers, they are occupationally segregated into specific low status, low wage jobs, largely in clerical and service occupations. Women continue to earn less than 60% of male earnings for full time full year work. It is this occupational segregation and pay differential, Hartmann argues, which maintain patriarchy even while families come to depend on two earners for their support:[20]

> The 'ideal' of the family wage—that a man can earn enough to support an entire family—may be giving way to a new ideal that both men and women contribute through wage earning to the cash income of the family. The wage differential, then, will become increasingly necessary in perpetuating patriarchy, the male control of women's labor power. The wage differential will aid in *defining* women's work as secondary to men's at the same time as it necessitates women's actual continued economic dependence on men. The sexual division of labor in the labor market and elsewhere should be understood as a manifestation of patriarchy which serves to perpetuate it. (emphasis in original)

Yet surely there is a difference in the possibility of forcing women to submit to patriarchal authority in the home between a situation in which women were directly dependent upon men for survival (as when women were not legally entitled to own farm land, and thus were essentially forced to marry in order to gain access to the means of survival—or to work sweatshop jobs at below subsistence pay), and a situation in which women work as wage laborers for capitalism, earning money

cal argument of this paper suggests that the dynamic between capitalism and patriarchy is contradictory as well as complementary, that economic forces play a crucial role in determining the sex-gender system, and that, insofar as patriarchy ever had a material base separate from capitalism, that material base has been continuously and substantially eroded by the expansion of capitalist relations of production.

[20]Heidi I. Hartmann, "The Unhappy Marriage of Marxism and Feminism: Toward a More Progressive Union," in L. Sargent, ed., *Women and Revolution*, (Boston: South End Press, 1981), p. 40.

separate from and *independent of* their husbands. Obviously, many women still cannot earn enough to survive, even poorly, outside of marriage. This is especially true of unskilled workers in blue collar and service work, many of whom are nonwhite. This reality is reflected in the poverty of families in the U.S. maintained by women. In 1978, one-third were poor by official government standards, and many of the rest were just above the poverty line. By contrast, one in eighteen families with a male present were below the poverty line.[21]

Nevertheless, the movement of married women into wage labor has created the *possibility* of supporting themselves outside of marriage. The option of leaving an oppressive marriage (or choosing not to make one) is far greater because of women's labor force participation; the option of refusing to be coerced into providing unequal amounts of labor and remaining subservient in the home exists to an unprecedented extent because much of women's productive labor takes place outside of and independent from the home. Thus, by forcing married women into wage labor, capitalism may be undermining the material basis of men's ability to enforce patriarchy in the home, *even though* it relegates women to low-paid "women's work" in the labor market. This is not to deny that patriarchy retains a powerful *ideological* presence even in households where material coercion is no longer a factor; patriarchy is deeply embedded in our ideological structure.

A further implication of this argument may be that the family wage never had an extensive actual (as opposed to ideological) existence. Certainly it is apparent that few working class families lived solely from the earnings of one male wage worker at least before the early part of this century. However, as married women began losing their ability to provide subsistence and cash at home, they began gradually entering the labor force, so that the family wage may perhaps at best be seen as a

temporary or transitional phenomenon. Hartmann suggests that[22]:

> ... the expropriation of production from the home was followed by a social adjustment process creating the social norm of the family wage ... (T)his process occurred in the U.S. in the early 20th century ... The 'family wage' resolution has probably been undermined in the post World War II period.

In this sense, the family wage may be seen as an almost meaningless concept, encompassing *at most* forty years of precarious existence (and remember the contribution of children to family income was important through most of this period as well). However the concept has had a powerful ideological life; it has been used historically to justify unequal pay, occupational segregation, preferential hiring of men, and to discourage women from identifying themselves as workers (since their paid work was "temporary" and "supplementary"—not their "true" role)—as well as, presumably, to keep male workers under control because of their responsibilities as "breadwinners." Hartmann argues that this ideological message continues unabated[23]:

> Yet whatever the *actual* situation today or earlier in the century, we would argue that the social norm *was* and *is* that men should earn enough to support their families. (emphasis in original).

This norm is upheld, in Hartmann's view, by occupational segregation and the extreme wage differentials between men and women. I would suggest that the reality of economic conditions over the past decade appears to have resulted in increasing awareness that the family wage no longer exists for most families. Certainly labor force participation is no longer seen as aberrant for married women; it is generally recognized as an economic necessity. This does not mean that it is seen as good or desirable, however; it is important to distin-

[21]National Advisory Council on Economic Opportunity, twelfth report, *Critical Choices for the 1980s* (Washington, D.C.: U.S. Government Printing Office, 1980), pp. 17-18.

[22]Hartmann, "Unhappy Marriage," pp. 30, 39.
[23]Ibid.

guish between a *norm* and an *ideal*. Whether many Americans still cling to an ideal of man/breadwinner and woman/housewife is difficult to guess, but it does seem possible to argue that its ideological power is weakening.

CONCLUSION

In sum, this paper argues that the rapid and steady increase in the participation of married women in wage labor in the latter half of the twentieth century can be understood as the result of the invasion of their traditional production for use and exchange in the home by capitalist production, coupled with a rising demand for clerical and service workers in the capitalist sector. Women were "freed" into the latent reserve army of labor, and have been gradually incorporated into active wage labor as capitalism has expanded.

This argument has implications for our understanding of women's historic economic roles, of the dynamic interaction between capitalism and patriarchy, and of the concept of the family wage. Women have always contributed significantly to the economic support of themselves and their families, but the source of that support has changed over time from production for use and exchange within the home to wage labor. Thus the expansion of capitalist production may be undermining the material base of patriarchy within the home; by separating home from work, gradually removing production work from the home, and finally incorporating women into the wage labor force, capitalism has "tended to whittle away at the economic and ideological basis of patriarchy."[24]

Understanding women's wage labor as an extension in another form of their historic economic contribution to the family, we can place women's current economic experience in historic perspective. Working class families have rarely been able to live from the earnings of only one person; women (and children) provided support first through home production and later through wage labor. Because home production is no longer an option for women, the trend toward wage work is irreversible. Despite occupational segregation, and cutbacks in affirmative action and the enforcement of antidiscrimination legislation, and despite the conservative calls for a return to the (mythical) family of man-the-provider and woman-the-receiver, working class women have no choice but to continue to seek paid work. They may be discriminated against, they may face severe and prolonged unemployment and an unending struggle to make ends meet, but they cannot just be sent "home."

This argument has implications for capitalism, and for the interaction between capitalism and patriarchy. Capitalism may find women a less flexible segment of the labor force than in the past. Forced by economic necessity to seek wage work, and to stay in the labor force for most of their adult lives, women are increasingly coming to define themselves as workers and to act in opposition to low pay and occupational segregation. Since wage work will continue to be an objective necessity for women, their consciousness of the problem of inequality, and their opposition to it, is likely to continue to exert pressure on the economic system.

This paper has argued that capitalism has eroded the material basis of patriarchy in the family. Further, by incorporating women into the permanent labor force, capitalism has fostered their increasing definition of themselves as workers, and hence their increasing opposition to economic inequality by sex. Does this mean that capitalism has set the stage for the destruction of patriarchy? No, I don't believe this is the case. There is no evidence that inequality in the labor force is decreasing, and inequality between men and women clearly continues in the family as well: for example, women continue to perform the vast majority of housework, whether or not they also perform wage labor. Whatever its historical origins (and whether or not patriarchy at one time had a separate material base), the op-

[24]Sheila Rowbotham, *Woman's Consciousness, Man's World* (Middlesex, England: Penguin Books, 1973), p. 119.

pression of women has become incorporated into the dynamics of capitalism, in a complex and contradictory interaction. It is the task of feminist political economy to investigate the nature of this interaction.

7.3   *Woman's Consciousness, Man's World*

Many feminist writers believe that capitalism has eroded much of the basis for patriarchy, while yet maintaining the subordination of women as a group. In the following reading Sheila Rowbotham makes such an argument, further examining the relationship between capitalism and male dominance. She concludes that an effective feminist movement must struggle against capitalism as well as against male dominance.

Excerpted from *Woman's Consciousness, Man's World* (Pelican Books, 1973), by SHEILA ROWBOTHAM. © 1973 by Sheila Rowbotham. Reprinted by permission of Penguin Books Ltd.

The predicament of being born a woman in capitalism is specific. The social situation of women and the way in which we learn to be feminine is peculiar to us. Men do not share it, consequently we cannot be simply included under the general heading of "mankind." The only claim that this word has to be general comes from the dominance of men in society. As the rulers they presume to define others by their own criteria.

Women are not the same as other oppressed groups. Unlike the working class, who have no need for the capitalist under socialism, the liberation of women does not mean that men will be eliminated. Sex and class are not the same. Similarly people from oppressed races have a memory of a cultural alternative somewhere in the past. Women have only myths made by men.

We have to recognize our biological distinctness but this does not mean that we should become involved in an illusory hunt for our lost "nature." There are so many social accretions round our biology. All conceptions of female "nature" are formed in cultures dominated by men, and like all abstract ideas of human nature are invariably used to deter the oppressed from organizing effectively against that most unnatural of systems, capitalism.

The oppression of women differs too from class and race because it has not come out of capitalism and imperialism. The sexual division of labour and the possession of women by men predates capitalism. Patriarchal authority is based on male control over the woman's productive capacity, and over her person. This control existed before the development of capitalist commodity production. It belonged to a society in which the persons of human beings were owned by others. Patriarchy, however, is contradicted by the dominant mode of production in capitalism because in capitalism the owner of capital owns and controls the labour power but not the persons of his labourers.

. . . .

In order to understand the traces of patriarchy which have persisted into the present, it is essential to see what part patriarchy played in precapitalist society. The dominance of men over women in the past was more clearly a property relation than it is now. We usually think of property as things. However, animals and people can also be possessions. The word "stock" still covers the breeding of animals and people as well as assets on the stock exchange. But women are no longer so clearly means of production owned by men. When a man married in a society in which production was only marginally beyond subsistence, he married a "yoke-fellow" whose labour was crucial if he were to prosper. Her procreative capacity was important not only because of the high infant mortality rate but also because children meant more hands to labour. The wife's role in production was much greater because although tasks were already sexually divided many more goods were produced in the household. Women who were too high up in the social scale to work with their own hands supervised household production.

The family was a collective working group. The father was its hand, but for survival the labour of wife and children was necessary. Notions of leisure were necessarily restricted in a situation of scarcity when the surplus produced was very small. Consequently, the economic and social cohesion of the family was more important than what individuals in the family might want or regard as their right. Indeed the notion that women and children had individual interests which could not be included in those of the father is a modern concept that belongs to capitalism. It would have seemed bizarre, atomistic and socially destructive in earlier times. The productive forces of capital thus made the concept of individual development possible even though it was still confined in practice to the lives of those who belonged to the dominant class.

The introduction of individual wages and the end of the ownership of people in serfdom did not dissolve the economic and social control of men over women. The man remained the head of the family unit of production and he retained control over the ownership of property through primogeniture. Both his wife's capacity to labour and her capacity to bear his children were still part of his stock in the world. Moreover, the notion that this was part of the order of things was firmly embedded in all political, religious and educational institutions.

Although capitalism temporarily strengthened the control over women by the middle- and upper-class men in the nineteenth century by removing them from production, it has tended to whittle away at the economic and ideological basis of patriarchy. As wage labour become general and the idea spread in society that it was unjust to own other people, although the exploitation of their labour power was perfectly fair, the position of the daughter and the wife appeared increasingly anomalous. Ironically, middle-class women came to the conviction that their dependence on men and the protection of patriarchal authority were intolerable precisely at a time when the separation of work from home was shattering the economic basis of patriarchy among the working class. The factories meant that the economic hold of men over women in the working-class family was weakened. Machinery meant that tasks formerly done by men could be done by women. The woman's wage packet gave her some independence. Ideologically, however, men's hold persisted among the workers and was nurtured by the male ruling class.

Subsequently by continually reducing the scope of production, by developing the separation between home and work, and by reducing the time spent in procreation, a great army of women workers has been "freed" for exploitation in the commodity system. This integration of married women into the labour market has been especially noticeable in the advanced capitalist countries since the Second World War and testifies to the tendency for capital to seek new reserves of labour. The result in terms of women's consciousness at work is only now beginning to be felt. While the dissolution of the extended kinship networks has produced in the nuclear family a streamlined unit suitable for modern capitalism, it has forced an examination of the relationships of man to woman and parent to child.

The struggle of the early feminist movement for legal and political equality and the assumptions it has bequeathed to women now, despite the degeneration of its radical impulse, have strained the hold of patriarchy in the capitalist state, though without dislodging it. The power of the working class within capitalism and the growth of new kinds of political movements recently, particularly for black liberation, have touched the consciousness of women and brought many of us to question the domination of men over women. This has taken a political shape, in the new feminism of women's liberation.

The development of contraceptive technology in capitalism means that the idea of sexual liberation can begin to be realized. The fact that sexual pleasure now need not necessarily result in procreation means a new dimension of liberation in the relation of men and women to nature is possible. It also removes some of patriarchy's most important sanctions against rebellion. The right to determine our own sexuality, to control when or if we want to give birth, and to choose who and how we want to love are central in both women's liberation and in gay liberation. All these are most subversive to patriarchy.

However, although capitalism has itself eroded patriarchy and has brought into being movements and ideas which are both anti-capitalist and anti-patriarchal, it still maintains the subordination of women as a group. Patriarchy has continued in capitalism as an ever present prop in time of need. Although women are not literally the property of men, the continuation of female production in the family means that women have not yet even won the right to be exploited equally. The wage system is capitalism has continued to be structured according to the assumption that women's labour is worth half that of men on the market. Behind this is the idea that women are somehow owned by men who should support them. Women are thus seen as economic attachments to men, not quite as free labourers. Their wage is still seen as supplementary. If a woman has no man she is seen as a sexual failure and the inference is often that she is a slut as well. She also has to struggle to bring up a family alone, on half a man's income. This very simple economic fact about the position of women in capitalism acts as a bribe to keep women with men: it has no regard for feeling or suffering and makes a mockery of any notion of choice or control over how we live. It also means that women make up a convenient reserve army which will work at half pay and can be reabsorbed back into the family if there is unemployment.

Our sexual conditioning means that we submit more readily than men to this intolerable state of affairs. We are brought up to think not only that it is just that the private owner of capital can extract profit from the surplus we produce but also that it is legitimate for the capitalist to return to us in the form of wages about half the sum he has to pay a man. Equal pay is obviously only the beginning of an answer to this. . . . The inequality of women at work is built into the structure of capitalist production and the division of labour in industry and in the family. The equality of women to men, even the equal *exploitation* of women in capitalism, would require such fundamental changes in work and at home that it is very hard to imagine how they could be effected while capitalism survives.

Our labour in the family goes unrecognized except as an excuse to keep us out of the better jobs in industry and accuse us of absenteeism and unreliability. This separation between home and work, together with the responsibility of women for housework and child care, serves to perpetuate inequality. Women, as a group in the labour force, are badly paid and underprivileged. This is not only economically profitable to capitalism, it has proved a useful political safety valve. There are many aspects of women's consciousness which have never fully come to terms with the capitalist mode of production. There is no reason why these should not take a radical and critical form in the context of a movement for liberation but in the past they have been used against women and against the working class. It is quite handy for capitalism if wives can be persuaded to oppose their husbands on strike, or if men console themselves for their lack of control at work with the right to be master in their own home. When this happens patriarchy is earning its keep. Similarly, when men and women do not support each other at work both patriarchy and capitalism are strengthened.

Because production in the family differs from commodity production we learn to feel that it is not quite work. This undermines our resentment and makes it harder to stress that it should be eliminated as much as possible not only by technology but by new styles of living, new buildings, and new forms of social care for the young, the sick and the old.

In capitalism housework and child care are lumped together. In fact they are completely different. Housework is drudgery which is best reduced by mechanizing and socializing it, except for cookery, which can be shared. Caring for small children is important and absorbing work, which does not mean that one person should have to do it all the time. But we are taught to think there is something wrong with us if we seek any alternative. The lack of nurseries and of other facilities for children and the rigid structuring of work and the division of labour between the sexes again makes choice impossible.

Propaganda about our feminine role helps to make us accept this state of affairs. Values linger on after the social structures which conceived them. Our ideas of what is "feminine" are a strange bundle of assumptions, some of which belong to the Victorian middle class and others which simply rationalize the form patriarchy assumes in capitalism now. Either way the notion of "femininity" is a convenient means of making us believe submission is somehow natural. When we get angry we are called hysterical.

Thus, although capitalism has eroded the forms of production and property ownership which were the basis of patriarchy, it has still retained the domination of men over women in society. This domination continues to pervade economic, legal, social and sexual life.

It is not enough to struggle for particular reforms, important as these are. Unless we understand the relationship of the various elements within the structure of male-dominated capitalism, we will find the improvements we achieve are twisted against us, or serve one group at the expense of the rest. For example, the wider dissemination of contraceptive information and the weakening of guilt about our sexuality have meant a major improvement in the lives of many women. However, the removal of fear alone is not enough because relations between the sexes are based on the ownership of property, property consisting not only of the woman's labour in procreation, but also of her body. Therefore, while class, race and sex domination remains a constituent element of relations between men and women, women and women, and men and men, these relations will continue to be distorted. Sexual liberation in capitalism can thus continue to be defined by men and also continue to be competitive. The only difference between this and the old set-up is that when patriarchy was secure men measured their virility by the number of children they produced, now they can apply more suitable means of assessing masculinity in a use-and-throw-away society and simply notch up sexual conquests.

. . . .

Capitalism is not based on the organization of production for people but simply on the need to secure maximum profit. It is naïve to expect that it will make exceptions of women. It is impossible now to predict whether capitalism could accommodate itself to the complete elimination of all earlier forms of property and production and specifically to the abolition of patriarchy. But it is certain that the kind of accommodation it could make would provide no real solution for women when we are unable to labour in commodity production because we are pregnant: socially helpless people protected in capitalism are not only treated as parasites who are expected to show gratitude but are under the direct power of the bourgeois state. Also class and race cut across sexual oppression. A feminist movement which is confined to the specific oppression of women cannot, in isolation, end exploitation and imperialism.

We have to keep struggling to go beyond our own situation. This means recognizing that the emphases which have come out of women's liberation are important not only to ourselves. The capacity to bring into conscious combination the unorganizable, those who distrust one another, who have been taught to despise themselves, and the connection which comes out of our practice between work and home, personal and political, are of vital significance to other movements in advanced capitalism. Similarly, the comprehension in women's liberation of the delicate mechanism of communication between the structures of capitalist society and the most hidden part of our secret selves is too important not to become part of the general theory and practice of the Left. Women's liberation has mounted an attack on precisely those areas where so-cialists have been slow to resist capitalism: authoritarian social relationships, sexuality and the family. "Personal" relations within capitalism, where the labour force is reproduced, are becoming increasingly crucial in the modern organization of industry. We have to struggle for control not merely over the means of production but over the conditions of reproduction.

CHAPTER 8

RACISM

IN THE 1980S THE RELATIVE ECONOMIC position of racial minorities in the United States has been deteriorating. Incomes of blacks have fallen farther behind those of whites, and joblessness among blacks has risen sharply, averaging more than 40 percent among teenagers in the years 1980–1983. The federal government, once a strong advocate of racial equality, now moves to dismantle programs that aid blacks. The earlier gains made by blacks and other racial minorities stand in substantial jeopardy.

How can we understand the persistence of racism and racial inequality in our society, where equal opportunity for all is a strongly shared value and South African–type apartheid is morally repugnant? Our concern in this chapter will be to analyze the nature of modern racism in the United States, and to try to comprehend its development and persistence within a capitalist system.

Modern racism has been defined as the "predication of decisions and policies on considerations of race for the purpose of subordinating a racial group and maintaining control over that group," or as "the systematized oppression of one race by another."[1] Such systematic racial oppression is not an age-old form of domination that has existed in all human societies. Racial factors played a minor role in the earlier slave systems of ancient Greece and Rome, and the casual racial prejudices and ethnocentrism that Europeans held against people of color in the fifteenth and early sixteenth centuries was qualitatively different from modern racism. Nothing like the systematic racial oppression of modern slavery existed in these societies, where it was commonly possible for people of different ethnic and racial groups to attain high social positions.

Modern racism began with the European colonization of the rest of the world and the subsequent systematic class domination of people of color. Race became a central justification of the colonial system ("the white man's burden") and the basis for the formation of classes in the colonies. In North America, the clearing away of the native "Indian" population and the enslavement of Africans for plantation labor led to the transformation of previously casual racial prejudices into a systematized and codified ideology and practice of racial subordination.[2]

Racism can take two different forms: *individual racism*, the overtly discriminatory ideas,

---

[1] These definitions are presented in Stokely Carmichael and Charles Hamilton, *Black Power* (New York: Random House, 1967); and James and Grace Boggs, *Racism and the Class Struggle* (New York: Monthly Review Press, 1970).

[2] Race itself became more a social than a scientific biological category. A person with one-eighth African ancestry and seven-eighths European ancestry was considered black, while whites were required to be pure European; such logic has no scientific justification. It is estimated that more than 70 percent of blacks in the United States are part-European. See Lerone Bennett, *Before the Mayflower* (Baltimore: Penguin Books, 1966), p. 273. The evolution of systematic racism in the seventeenth century is described in Winthrop Jordan, *White over Black* (Baltimore: Penguin, 1968).

attitudes, and practices of individual whites against blacks and other racial minorities;[3] and *institutional racism*, the functioning of institutions according to operating rules that may seem fair and unbiased on the surface, but result nonetheless, sometimes without conscious intent, in the subordination of blacks and other racial minorities. A substantial degree of both individual and institutional racism is evident in the United States, having permeated every sphere of social life. Blacks and other racial minorities face discrimination in employment, housing, schooling, and just about everywhere else. And racial stereotypes, cultural oppression, police harassment, and so on abound.

The effects of racism in the United States include differentials in income, occupational status, infant mortality rates, and many other measures. For example, nonwhites continue to lag far behind whites in income. Data on the relative income of nonwhites and whites (see Table 8-A) show only a small upward trend between 1950 and 1968 and have not improved since; median nonwhite family incomes now fluctuate around an average level of about 62 percent of white family incomes. Nonwhite incomes rise relative to white incomes during years of economic boom when labor shortages reduce nonwhite unemployment and open new employment areas for nonwhites. But the gains are mostly eliminated during recessions; no permanent improvement in the relative income position of blacks and other racial minority groups has occurred since the late 1960s.

Moreover, occupational statistics indicate that whites have maintained their relative advantage in occupational status over people of color since at least 1890. An examination of U.S. Census data from 1890 to 1970 showed

TABLE 8-A   RATIO OF NONWHITE TO WHITE MEDIAN INCOME, UNITED STATES, 1950–1983

Years	Families	Males	Females
1950	.54	.54	.49
1951	.53	.55	.46
1952	.57	.55	n.a.
1953	.56	.55	.59
1954	.56	.50	.55
1955	.55	.53	.54
1956	.53	.52	.58
1957	.54	.53	.58
1958	.51	.50	.59
1959	.52	.47	.62
1960	.55	.53	.70
1961	.53	.52	.67
1962	.53	.49	.67
1963	.53	.52	.67
1964	.56	.57	.70
1965	.55	.54	.73
1966	.60	.55	.76
1967	.62	.59	.78
1968	.63	.61	.79
1969	.63	.59	.85
1970	.64	.60	.92
1971	.63	.61	.90
1972	.62	.62	.95
1973	.60	.63	.93
1974	.64	.63	.92
1975	.65	.63	.92
1976	.63	.63	.95
1977	.61	.61	.88
1978	.64	.64	.92
1979	.61	.65	.94
1980	.63	.63	.96
1981	.62	.63	.92
1982	.62	.64	.92
1983	.62	.63	.90

Source: U.S. Bureau of the Census, *Income of Families and Persons in the United States*, Current Population Reports, Series P-60, various years (Washington, D.C.: U.S. Government Printing Office).

that, although the overall occupational distribution shifted markedly during the seventy-year period, the relative concentration of black males in the lowest-paid occupations changed very little.[4] Noneconomic indices dis-

[3]In addition to blacks, the other racial minorities numerous enough to be recognized and counted by the U.S. Census are Indians, Japanese, Chinese, Filipinos, Koreans, and Hawaiians. These groups together constitute the census category "nonwhite," of which blacks account for about 90 percent. The census also counts persons of Spanish origin (Mexican, Puerto Rican, Cuban, etc.) as a separate but not racial category.

[4]Michael Reich, *Racial Inequality: A Political-Economic Analysis* (Princeton, N.J.: Princeton University Press, 1981), p. 26.

play the same pattern of racial disadvantage. For example, in 1981, the infant mortality rate was 10.5 per 1,000 white births compared to 20.0 per 1000 black births.[5]

There have been some areas of improvement. In recent years, blacks have been elected mayors of several large cities, and the number of blacks in managerial and professional positions has increased. And the differences between blacks and whites in schooling, while still substantial, are not as great today as in 1900. Young black males aged 25 to 29 years old in 1900 had completed a median of 3.7 years of school, compared to 8.2 years for white males in the same age group; the comparable figures in 1980 were 12.6 (black) and 12.9 (white).[6] Moreover, black women, who used to work primarily as domestic servants and farm laborers, have moved in large numbers into the same low-level clerical and nonhousehold service jobs held by many white women; as a result the income differential between black and white women has narrowed, as shown in Table 8-A.[7]

But these improvements are surprisingly small when measured against the struggles and protests of blacks, as in the civil rights movement in the 1950s and 1960s and the antidiscriminatory legislation and widely publicized affirmative action programs of the 1970s. Racial inequality has persisted despite

these efforts, and despite the tremendous transformation that has taken place in the economic role of blacks since 1930. In that year 53.8 percent of blacks lived in the rural South, most as farm laborers, tenants, or small independent farmers.[8] The rural South was the poorest area of the nation, and the area with the greatest relative income gap between whites and blacks. With the subsequent mechanization of southern agriculture and demand for black labor in urban-centered capitalist industry and services, tens of millions of blacks moved out of the rural South. By 1980, 85.2 percent of the black population was located in urban centers, and concentrated in racial ghettos; most employed blacks today have wage-labor jobs in manufacturing, transportation, and services.[9] Since this massive migration has been toward areas of higher wages and narrower racial income differentials, the persistence of the gap between black and white incomes is quite remarkable.

The continuing income inequality indicates that the transition for blacks from a farming people to incorporation into the urban working class has occurred in ways that have reproduced rather than eliminated racism. As a result, blacks have made very little progress in overcoming racial inequality *within* many urban areas: indeed, as Table 8-B indicates, the income of nonwhites relative to whites within many major urban areas showed no improvement between the 1950 and 1980 censuses. The inequalities of the agricultural South have been transferred to urban factories and ghettos.

Besides blacks, the other racial minorities in the United States—Chicanos, Puerto Ricans, American Indians, and people of Asian origin—also experience racism. Each of these groups has its own specific history of incorporation into the American working class; they share with blacks and each other the experience of having been incorporated into the low-

---

[5]*Statistical Abstract of the United States, 1985*, p. 73.

[6]Based on U.S. Census of Population, 1940 to 1980. Figures for females are nearly identical to those for males.

[7]Much of this narrowing, however, is due to the decline in white women's earnings relative to men described in Chapter 7; also Table 8-A understates the gap between black and white women because black women are more likely to be the sole support of a family and on the average work more hours per year than white women.

Notice that the relative improvement for nonwhite women shown in column 3 of Table 8-A did not have much of an effect on the relative position of nonwhite families; this is because the rate of increase in labor-force participation has been greater among white women than nonwhite women and because the number of families with no male wage-earner present has grown faster among blacks than among whites. Both of these trends work to maintain the greater income of white families.

[8]Daniel Price, *Changing Characteristics of the Negro Population* (Washington, D.C.: U.S. Government Printing Office, 1966).

[9]U.S. Bureau of the Census, *Census of Population*, 1980.

TABLE 8-B   RATIO OF NONWHITE TO WHITE MALE MEDIAN INCOME IN SELECTED
CITIES, 1949–1979

	1949[a]	1969[a]	1979[b]	Percent Change 1949–1979
SMSAs in North and West				
Chicago	.714	.713	.642	–10.1
Cleveland	.702	.718	.668	– 4.8
Detroit	.808	.738	.629	–22.1
Los Angeles	.704	.726	.781	10.9
New York	.678	.712	.682	0.6
Philadelphia	.686	.689	.607	–11.5
Pittsburgh	.729	.638	.615	–15.6
San Francisco	.712	.686	.665	– 6.6
St. Louis	.632	.583	.563	–10.9
Average	.707	.689	.650	–8.1
SMSAs in South				
Atlanta	.520	.531	.571	9.8
Baltimore	.630	.631	.580	– 7.9
Birmingham	.581	.515	.532	– 8.4
Dallas	.505	.550	.608	20.4
Houston	.554	.551	.640	15.5
Memphis	.484	.583	.491	1.4
New Orleans	.557	.507	.535	– 3.9
Washington, D.C.	.627	.610	.594	– 5.3
Average	.557	.560	.569	2.1

[a]14 years and older.   [b]15 years and older.

Sources: 1949 data are for the Standard Metropolitan Area (SMA); calculated from the U.S.
Census of Population, 1950, *Characteristics of the Population*, table 185. 1969 and 1979 data are for
Standard Metropolitan Statistical Area (SMSA). 1969 data are calculated from the U.S. Census
of Population, 1970, state volumes, table 192. 1979 data are calculated from the U.S. Census of
Population, 1980, *General Social and Economic Characteristics*, tables 59, 130, 136, 142, 148, 154.
Nonblack Hispanics are included among whites to provide comparability with previous years.

est-paid segments of the American working class. The numbers of people of Asian and Spanish origin in the labor force has especially increased in the 1970s and 1980s, filling an ever-larger percentage of the lowest-paying jobs at the bottom of the occupational hierarchy, and in highly competitive and labor-intensive firms. Racial factors thus continue to be prominent in American life.[10]

[10]At the same time, to fill their need for cheap labor the European capitalist countries have drawn upon foreign labor, much of it people of darker complexion and races from North Africa, Italy, Portugal, Greece, Turkey and Yugoslavia. The racial and ethnic heterogeneity and hierarchy of the American working class have thus become reproduced in Europe as well.

Despite the above evidence, it is often argued that racism is an aberration in the United States, a legacy from the past that will gradually disappear in a democratic, capitalist society. Proponents of this view argue as follows: the capitalist drive to rationalize production, lower costs, and expand porfits is itself a strong force for the elimination of racial discrimination. Employers are trying to maximize their profits, and in organizing their work force they will be interested in a worker's productivity and potential contribution to profits and not in his or her skin color. The pressures from other firms competing for workers will overcome the resistance of racist employers who persist in discriminating. Similarly, purchasers of goods and services will be interested only in the product's price and its quality and not in the race of the workers who produce it. Thus, market forces, by allocating labor to its most efficient use, are themselves a strong stimulus for ending discrimination. And if market forces do not operate with sufficient speed or effectiveness, the government can be expected to pass and implement antidiscrimination legislation, create job-training and compensatory education programs, provide aid for ghetto economic development, and so on, for the purpose of hastening the eradication of racism. There was, in fact, much U.S. governmental activity along these lines in the 1970s.

Why, then, has racism proven so difficult to eradicate in the United States? We argue in this chapter that the conventional analysis in the preceding paragraph is not correct. Racism is not an aberration; it has persisted in the United States precisely because racial op-

pression is consistent with the logic of class divisions under capitalism and reinforces the interests of the capitalist class as a whole. By contributing to divisions and antagonisms among the population, thereby weakening hostility to the capitalist class, and by providing to whites a convenient scapegoat for social and economic oppression that is generated by capitalism itself, racism plays an important role in *stabilizing* a capitalist society. Whatever its origins—and we should keep in mind the historical importance for northern capitalism of the westward expansion against Indian opposition and the profits from black slavery—racism is likely to take firm root in a capitalist society. Racism is useful to capitalism; moreover, the hierarchical, materialistic, competitive, and individualistic environment of capitalism is not conducive to the elimination of racism. It is therefore extremely difficult to eradicate racism within the framework of a capitalist society.

8.1 *Racial and Class Dynamics in U.S. Industry*

Racism first emerged full-fledged in the United States as an essential aspect of slavery. But the breakup of slavery and the triumph of the North in 1865 did not result in the end of racism. Instead, racism continued to be an important feature of American life, both in the agricultural labor systems of the post–Civil War South and in the present era of contemporary capitalism. Throughout all these periods black labor played a central role in production, but the form of exploitation of black labor—and with it, the form that racism took—evolved with the different phases of capitalist development. In the following reading, Michael Reich analyzes this historical process and outlines how the current dynamics of race and class have developed.

Excerpted from MICHAEL REICH, *Racial Inequality: A Political-Economic Analysis* (Princeton, N.J.: Princeton University Press, 1981). Reprinted by permission of the author and the publisher.

In the decades following the Civil War, industrial development occurred at an impressive rate in the North. This industrial growth was expressed not just in quantitative terms of expansion, but in qualitative change as well. More and more industrial activity was concentrated in large factories, and mass-produc-

tion workers doing easily learned tasks increasingly supplanted artisans and their helpers as the main ingredient of the factory labor force. In short, an industrial working class was being created in the United States.

With capitalist development the workplace became more of an arena of conflict. In the latter third of the nineteenth century, strife between employers and workers became more frequent and involved more and more workers. As national competition among firms grew and prices fell, many employers attempted to institute wage cuts among their employees and to systematize the organization of work in greater detail. But, as the job conditions of the factory work forces became increasingly homogeneous, it became easier for workers to organize plant-wide and industry-wide collective actions to counter their employers. The result was an upsurge of what can only be called "class warfare."

In this context many employers began to experiment with different techniques to control their "labor problem," as they called it. In particular, employers sought consciously to organize work hierarchically and to institute divisions in their work force in order to preclude united organization among their workers. It took many years for employers to develop sophisticated bureaucratic personnel techniques to achieve these ends. In the interim, simpler methods were applied. These involved introducing moving assembly lines and other technologies to machine-pace workers, as well as cruder divide-and-conquer methods.

Many Northern employers adopted a technique that Southern industrialists had already worked out: the importation of black strikebreakers into an industry and the exploitation of the racism of white workers to help break strikes. Many Northern industries began to employ blacks for the first time in such circumstances. As in Southern industries, the most unskilled and demanding jobs would be assigned to black workers. The demand for black labor during the labor shortages of World War I and the subsequent reduction in foreign immigration in the 1920s would lead to further increases in black employment in manufacturing, but the already-developed patterns of racial inequality in industry would continue.

Racial discrimination by Northern employers and employees played only a partial role in excluding blacks from industry before 1914. Conditions in Southern agriculture also played a part. The tremendous demand for labor that came with the industrial expansion of the North after the Civil War was filled primarily by European immigrants and not by Southerners. Before 1915 very few Southern whites or blacks moved to the North to obtain jobs in the burgeoning industries. The low rate of migration out of the South seems remarkable when one considers the widening economic conditions between regions in this period. Certainly there were economic payoffs to migration.[1]

It might be thought that white or black Southerners, with their knowledge of the English language and familiarity with the American culture, would have been preferred by employers to the European immigrants. Indeed, much racial prejudice was expressed among Northerners after 1890, as the European immigration consisted increasingly of dark-complexioned peoples from southern and eastern Europe. But racial prejudice did not hinder the hiring of these workers.

Southern out-migration was low precisely because Southern farmers were kept in debt and could not accumulate the assets needed for a move out of the South.[2] In 1900 three-fourths of all blacks in the United States remained sharecropping farmers in the South. Blacks accounted for only 2.2 percent of non-agricultural employment outside the South in 1910, and the majority of these jobs were in household service. In 1910 over 70 percent of the black population still resided in the rural South.[3] The Southern sharecropping system thus kept most blacks out of the growing factory system of the North during this period.

Since World War I and the 1920s, but more especially since World War II, the Southern

[1] For a good discussion, see Gunnar Myrdal, *An American Dilemma*, (New York: Harper and Row, 1944), chapter 13, "Seeking Jobs Outside Agriculture."

[2] Roger Ransom and Richard Sutch, *One Kind of Freedom: The Economic Consequences of Emancipation* (New York: Cambridge University Press, 1977).

[3] Myrdal, *American Dilemma*, p. 285. In 1910 only one major Northern manufacturer, the McCormick Harvesting Company in Chicago, employed blacks in substantial numbers.

sharecropping system disintegrated, while the demand for labor in Northern industry continued to expand. Consequently large numbers of blacks have become incorporated in Northern industry. This dramatic shift has provided absolute economic and political gains for blacks as well as some advances relative to whites. But this incorporation has occurred in a manner that has reproduced many racial inequalities in the urban and industrial setting. We can understand these twentieth-century developments in relation to the changing demands for black labor and the changing dynamics of worker-capitalist class relations during this period.

THE 1919 STEEL STRIKE

Between 1910 and 1920 the number of black industrial workers almost doubled. By 1930 over 100,000 black workers were employed in Northern industry, most in blast furnaces, steel rolling mills, automobile factories, clothing industries, and slaughter and meat-packing houses.[4] Blacks entered most of these industries during strikes and were sometimes kept on after the strikes had ended. Myrdal concludes his detailed discussion of this period as follows: "Many of them wanted to keep their labor force heterogeneous so as to prevent unionization. Some of them even used Negroes as strikebreakers. This had happened several times before the first World War. In many of these cases Negro workers were dismissed when the labor conflict was ended. But sometimes, particularly between 1910 and 1930, they actually managed to gain a foothold in this way."[5]

A typical and significant example of this process occurred in 1904, during a midwestern meat-packing strike. Black strikebreakers were brought in by the employers and helped defeat the strike. Blacks stayed on afterward and became the largest group in the Chicago meat-packing industry by 1920.

Most blacks working in Northern industry were employed in the least-skilled occupations, a policy often formalized consciously by employers in racial terms. After World War I racial quotas were instituted deliberately in the Chicago meat-packing industry, in the steel industry, and in the farm equipment and automobile industries.[6] An employment manager of Calumet Steel explained the importance of quotas: "It isn't good to have all of one nationality; they will gang up on you. . . . We have Negroes and Mexicans in a sort of competition with each other."[7] In adopting racial quotas and deliberately inciting racial antagonisms, employers were following the examples set in Southern coal mining, iron and steel, and other industries. U.S. Steel, for example, adopted in Gary the policies of its Southern subsidiaries.

The incorporation of blacks into industry thus occurred with preexisting racial divisions continuing unabated. In this period these racial divisions proved costly to many union-organizing efforts. Nowhere were these effects more visible and more numerous than during the giant steel strike of 1919.

In 1919, a year of unprecedented strike activity throughout the United States (twenty-five urban race riots also occurred), over 360,000 workers went on strike throughout the iron and steel industry.[8] The strike, organized

---

[4]Ibid., p. 294. But blacks continued to be excluded from many Northern industries including textiles, sawmills, electrical machinery, bakeries, shoemaking, furniture, and utilities.

[5]Myrdal, *American Dilemma*, p. 293.

[6]Alma Herbst, *The Negro in the Slaughtering and Meat-packing Industry in Chicago* (Boston: Houghton Mifflin, 1932), pp. 103–108; B. J. Widick, *Detroit: City of Class and Race Violence* (Chicago: Quadrangle, 1972), p. ix; Robert Ozanne, *A Century of Labor-Management Relations at McCormick and International Harvester* (Madison: University of Wisconsin Press, 1967), pp. 184–185.

[7]Quoted in the excellent case study of Edward Greer, "Racial Employment Discrimination in the Gary Works, 1906–1974" (unpublished paper, Department of History, Roosevelt University, 1976), p. 12.

[8]For detailed accounts, see David Brody, *Steelworkers in America: the Nonunion Era* (Cambridge: Harvard University Press, 1960); David Brody, *Labor in Crisis: the Steel Strike of 1919* (Philadelphia: Lippincott, 1965).

by a broad coalition of unions representing both skilled and unskilled workers, became a crucial test of an important idea in the labor movement: to organize unions in factory-based industries on an industry-wide rather than occupational basis.

David Brody has chronicled in detail how the steel companies attempted to break the strike. Their main strategy was to exploit the divisions that separated native-born and English-speaking steelworkers, many of them skilled workers, from the thirty or more Eastern European immigrant groups among the steelworkers, most of them unskilled and not English-speaking. The steel companies deliberately hired "foreigners of different nationalities, in order that there would not be free-speaking discourse between them."[9] To the surprise of the companies as well as some labor leaders, the unskilled immigrant workers proved to be strong supporters of the strike, despite employers' attempts to exploit xenophobia among the "Americans."[10]

The weakest link in the workers' chain of solidarity appeared to be race. Although black employment in the steel mills had increased during the war, blacks were still excluded from the skilled workers' union, even during the union organizing drives of 1918–1919. Except in Cleveland and Wheeling, black steelworkers were not sympathetic to such discriminatory unions, nor were blacks outside the industry. The steel companies exploited this situation: in the sixth week of the strike, the steel companies imported over 30,000 black strikebreakers in a short period of time, to keep their plants operating. This key move turned the tide, and the strike was soon defeated.

The racism of the unions had broken the strike, and white as well as black workers paid a price: industrial unions did not arrive in the steel industry until the late 1930s. William Z. Foster, a leader of the strike, concluded that the mass production industries would not be unionized until white union leaders made

campaigning against racism a central and special priority of organizing efforts. This assessment proved to be correct, as both the employer offensives in the 1920s and labor's response in the turning point of the 1930s would demonstrate.

TURNING POINT: THE CIO IN THE 1930s AND 1940s

The experience of the Southern Populists, bituminous coal miners, New Orleans dock workers, and the steelworkers indicated that attempts were made to build biracial coalitions along class lines and that racism ultimately contributed to the breakup of these coalitions. The conservatism of the AFL, and its attempts to protect skilled craft workers from competition contributed significantly to the perpetuation of racial inequality in industry. But during the Great Depression, the AFL's racial practices were challenged decisively by the new industrial union movement of the 1930s.

Some black union leaders within the AFL had lobbied for decades to change the AFL's policy of countenancing racial exclusion practices among its affiliates. These efforts proved unsuccessful.[11] In 1935 the AFL opposed successfully the incorporation of an antidiscrimination clause in the Wagner Act, preferring to see the bill fail if the antidiscrimination clause were included.[12] The 1935 convention of the AFL not only rejected a proposal to organize industrial unions, but also explicitly rejected a proposal from black unionists to revoke the charters of unions that formally excluded blacks.[13] This action led black union leaders to break with the AFL and to support

[9]Brody, *Steelworkers in America*, p. 136.

[10]Brody, *Labor in Crisis*, p. 157.

[11]Philip Foner, *Organized Labor and the Black Worker, 1619-1973* (New York: Praeger, 1974), chapters 12 and 15.

[12]Ibid., p. 215; Raymond Wolters, "Closed Shop and White Shop: The Negro Response to Collective Bargaining. 1933–35," in Milton Cantor, ed., *Black Labor in America* (Westport: Negro Universities Press, 1970), p. 150.

[13]Foner, *Organized Labor and the Black Worker*, p. 213.

the formation of the Committee for Industrial Organization (CIO). Industrial unions seemed much more likely to meet the problems of racial discrimination.

By this point, black workers had become an important component of the mass-production work force in many industries, accounting for about 13 percent of workers at Ford's River Rouge Plant in Detroit, 8.5 percent of all steelworkers, and 17 percent of unskilled and semiskilled workers in the slaughter and packinghouse industry.[14] John L. Lewis, probably the most important figure in the early CIO, knew from the mine workers' experience the importance of organizing black workers. It would not be possible to organize industrial unions without the active support of black workers.

Recognizing this reality, the CIO paid special attention to black workers and to opposing racism among white workers. The CIO hired black organizers, built a strong working coalition with the NAACP, and worked actively to educate racist white workers. "Black and white, unite and fight" became one of the CIO's most important slogans in its organizing campaigns. In 1938 the Constitutional Convention of the CIO passed a resolution stating:

> *Whereas,* Employers constantly seek to split one group of workers from another, and thus to deprive them of their full economic strength, by arousing prejudices based on race, creed, color or nationality, and one of the most frequent weapons used by employers to accomplish this end is to create false contests between Negro and white workers; now therefore be it
>
> *Resolved,* That the C.I.O. hereby pledges itself to uncompromising opposition to any form of discrimination, whether political or economic, based on race, color, creed or nationality.[15]

To carry out its policies, the CIO created a special Committee to Abolish Racial Discrimination; by 1944 eighty-five such committees had been set up at the state and local levels.[16]

In its early years the CIO actively promoted racial equality. In contrast to the AFL, it prohibited constitutional exclusion clauses or segregation of blacks into separate locals. Unlike the AFL, the CIO sought to include black workers on an equal basis.

With this policy the CIO was able to overcome initial black skepticism of the labor movement, which had accumulated over decades of discrimination by white unions. Between 1936 and 1945 the CIO gained endorsements from the NAACP, the Urban League, and the black press.[17] The CIO succeeded in organizing hundreds of thousands of black and white workers in automobiles, electrical equipment, longshoring, meat-packing, the merchant marine, rubber, shipbuilding, steel, warehouses, and many other mass production industries. Consequently, although the black proportion of manufacturing employment declined from 7.3 percent in 1930 to 5.1 percent in 1940, the number of black members of national unions increased from approximately 56,000 members in 1930 (nearly half in the black Brotherhood of Sleeping Car Porters) to 150,000 in 1935 and over 500,000 by 1940. By the end of World War II, black union membership had risen to 1.25 million; black workers comprised over 7 percent of the CIO membership.[18]

CIO organization brought gains to both black and white workers, but especially to black workers. In each industry that the CIO organized, union bargaining committees negotiated contracts with employers that included significant wage gains, particularly for the unskilled segment of the labor force. Large num-

[14]Herbert Northrup, ed., *Negro Employment in Basic Industry: A Study of Racial Policy in Six Industries* (Philadelphia: University of Pennsylvania Press, 1970).

[15]Quoted in Foner, *Organized Labor and the Black Worker,* pp. 229–230.

[16]Robert Weaver, *Negro Labor—A National Problem* (New York: Harcourt, Brace and World, 1946), pp. 219–223.

[17]James Olson, "Race, Class, and Progress: Black Leadership and Industrial Unionism, 1936–1945," in Cantor, ed., *Black Labor in America,* p. 164.

[18]Ray Marshall, *Labor in the South* (Cambridge, Mass.: Harvard University Press, 1965), p. 49; Foner, *Organized Labor and the Black Worker,* p. 173.

bers of black workers, concentrated in unskilled occupations, were therefore among the main beneficiaries of these efforts.

By the end of 1937, for example, the Steel Workers Organizing Committee (SWOC, which later became the United Steel Workers of America) included 85,000 blacks among its 550,000 members and had been recognized by the major steel corporations.[19] SWOC had made special efforts to counter discrimination and to organize black steelworkers. When U.S. Steel recognized SWOC in March of 1937, it granted a general wage increase of 10 percent and an increase of 9 percent for unskilled workers. As a result, the earnings of black workers relative to those of whites rose from 79 percent in 1935 to 85 percent in 1938.[20] A similar story was repeated in many industries.

While the CIO brought gains to black workers already employed in mass production industries, it rarely succeeded in significantly changing discriminatory hiring, promotion, and layoff practices in these industries. Many basic industries remained virtually "lily-white" in 1940, and CIO organizing did little for blacks not already included in the industry. As a result, conflicts soon arose between CIO leaders and the black community.

A good example of this conflict occurred in the late 1930s in Harlem, where an estimated 80 percent of the labor force was either unemployed or on Works Progress Administration employment. Several black organizations had criticized the CIO-affiliated Transport Workers Union for not making the elimination of racial job barriers a condition of its negotiations. The bus companies had refused to hire blacks as drivers and mechanics, and the subway companies had refused to hire black conductors, motormen, or ticket agents, although many blacks worked as porters and cleaners in these companies. The union leadership was

hesitant to take on its more conservative, racist, and largely Irish membership.[21] The episode typified problems that the CIO failed to confront. Later, in the spring of 1941, the TWU cosponsored a bus boycott with Harlem organizations, with the result that the Fifth Avenue Coach Company agreed to employ blacks in 17 percent of its mechanics and driver positions. This, too, typified a smaller number of CIO advances.[22]

The CIO was best able to obtain "equal pay for equal work," thereby eliminating racial differentials paid to workers doing the same job. But black and white workers frequently were assigned to different jobs. Most of the 6,000 black workers at the giant Ford River Rouge plant in 1928 worked in unskilled, dirty, hot, and heavy jobs in the foundry, such as paint departments and rolling mills of the plant. Of about 4,000 black workers at Ford's Highland Park plant, only two were doing skilled work.[23] In the same year, at U.S. Steel's mammoth Gary Works, black and Mexican workers comprised nearly half of the unskilled workers, but only 2 percent of skilled workers; less than 5 percent of black workers held skilled jobs, as compared to nearly half of white workers.[24] Foner reports that in 1940, "General Motors still followed a rigid Jim Crow policy ranging from total exclusion of blacks at Fisher Body to the restriction of blacks to broom-pushers at Chevrolet or to foundry jobs at Buick."[25] "Equal pay for equal work" did not address black workers' problems in such situations.

The struggle for racial equality in CIO unions conflicted with another important CIO goal, the establishment of seniority rights.

[19]Ibid., p. 224.

[20]Greer, "Racial Employment Discrimination in the Gary Works," p. 18; Richard Rowan, "The Negro in the Steel Industry," in Northrup, ed., Negro Employment in Basic Industry, pp. 260–310.

[21]Mark Naison, "Harlem Communists and the Politics of Black Protest," Marxist Perspectives (Fall 1978).

[22]Ibid., p. 42.

[23]Sterling Spero and Abram Harris, The Black Worker (New York: Atheneum, 1968), p. 159.

[24]Greer, "Racial Employment Discrimination in the Gary Works," table 4.

[25]Foner, Organized Labor and the Black Worker, p. 232.

Both black and white workers in the CIO supported and had fought for formal seniority systems in order to curb the arbitrary power of supervisors and management in dictating work assignments, promotions, and layoff decisions. Black workers were the worst victims of the old system, but they continued at a disadvantage under the new one.

In both the South and the North segregated seniority rosters were common.[26] The seniority clause agreements contained in most contracts in effect institutionalized the disadvantages of black workers and maintained the difficulties blacks experienced in advancement into higher-skilled and higher-paid job titles. Often, these seniority rosters were organized on a departmental rather than plant-wide basis, providing a means to discriminate by race that could seem fair and nondiscriminatory in intent.

Moreover, while the CIO had been instrumental in creating integrated union locals throughout the South, an achievement unthinkable a few decades earlier, its principles barring discrimination and segregation were not always followed in practice. And many CIO unions did not confront successfully the racist attitudes and practices of their own members, particularly on issues that involved a community rather than workplace focus, such as segregated housing or schools. Consequently, the gains won by the CIO for black workers remained limited, no matter how much they contrasted with continuing exclusionary policies in the construction craft unions of the AFL.[27]

With notable exceptions, such as in shipyards around Baltimore, the racial barriers survived through World War II in most industries. Indeed, blacks began to be employed in significant numbers in war production only after a threatened mass protest march on Washington in 1941 persuaded President Roosevelt to issue a ban on discrimination in war industries and to create a Fair Employment Practices Commission. Black employment, which comprised only 2.5 to 3 percent of war production workers as late as March 1942, grew to over 8 percent by November 1944.[28]

THE POSTWAR PERIOD

After the war the demand for black labor diminished. The CIO initially attempted an organizing drive in the South, where it was still weak, but soon turned its attention to expelling leftists from its own ranks. In so doing it threw out the unions and union leaders that had been most militant in organizing and most committed to the advancement of racial equality.

After 1948 the labor movement failed to make further gains for racial equality; this stagnation paralleled and was directly related to the stagnation of the labor movement itself. By 1950 few CIO unions contained more than a token black among its elected leadership, and only one, the United Packinghouse Workers of America, actively pursued an antidiscrimination program. Throughout the South many CIO affiliates openly practiced Jim Crow segregation in their meeting halls.[29] The CIO's Southern organizing drive, begun in 1946, capitulated to racist practices and collapsed in ignominious defeat by 1952.

By the time of its merger with the AFL in 1955, the CIO no longer was working actively to eliminate racism in employer practices or racism among the AFL unions with which it was confederating.[30] On the eve of the mass protest era of the Southern civil rights movement (the Montgomery bus boycott demanding desegregation took place in 1956), the official House of Labor had given up its place at the cutting edge of the movement for racial equality in the United States.

[26]Marshall, *Negro Worker*, p. 271.

[27]Foner, *Organized Labor and the Black Worker*, pp. 233–235.

[28]Ibid., p. 243.

[29]Ibid., p. 292.

[30]Sumner Rosen, "The C.I.O. Era, 1935–55," in Jacobson, ed., *The Negro and the American Labor Movement*, pp. 190–194.

Accommodation to the racist status quo cost the CIO and white workers dearly. This effect can best be seen by looking not just at individual workplaces, but also at the broadest economic and political results. The failure to organize extensively in the South meant that North-South wage differentials would increase with union wage gains in the North, leading eventually to the relocation of Northern plants in Southern locales. Within the North the influx of blacks into industry in the postwar period would take place under conditions that reproduced enmity between black and white workers and weakened the union movement as a whole. The tensions that produced independent black worker organizations and black caucuses in many industrial unions in the 1960s bear witness to this problem.[31]

Furthermore, the accommodation to the racist status quo hampered labor's political program for liberal welfare-state reforms and for governmental commitments to full-employment policies. In the 1930s it was Southern politicians who blocked Federal relief and other programs that would "disturb the established patterns of segregation" or which would give Washington "the power to tell their states what aid levels they had to provide for Negroes."[32] These same interests opposed any liberal reforms that would have enhanced the mobility of Southern agricultural labor. As a result of the failure to institute the welfare-state agenda, United States workers in the postwar period have experienced higher unemployment rates and lower social welfare

benefits that workers in any other advanced capitalist country.

The most highly publicized aspect of postwar race relations concerns affirmative action and desegregation programs set up by governments, corporations, and unions. The effectiveness and magnitude of these programs has been the subject of some controversy. But it seems clear that the stagnation of the economy as a whole has more than offset any gains that blacks have obtained through these programs. Unionization of low-wage employment, especially in the South, and a greater commitment to full employment in government policy would have done more for the advancement of racial equality in the postwar period. Conversely, the incompleteness of welfare-state programs in the United States and the weak commitment to full-employment policies illustrate how racial inequality has held back the political programs of progressive labor-black-Democratic coalitions. Racial inequality has thus continued to hurt a broad spectrum of white workers in the United States.

CONCLUSION

The emancipation of slaves advanced an important freedom to blacks, but it did not eliminate the basis of racism. Blacks remained without independent economic means of support after the Civil War, while the antebellum slaveholding class maintained its dominant position in the South by virtue of its continuing ownership of plantation-belt land. Because of racism most blacks became tenant farmers or sharecroppers; only a few became small landowning farmers. The debt peonage system that developed in Southern agriculture inhibited innovation and the accumulation of capital, thus retarding economic development in the South. This system, together with overt racism, reproduced conditions of poverty for blacks for many decades.

The debt peonage system, which had been created because of racism, soon impoverished white farmers as well as black ones. Racism thus did not benefit most Southern whites in the decades following the Civil War. When

[31]See, for example, Dan Georgakas and Marvin Surkin, *Detroit: I Do Mind Dying, A Study in Urban Revolution* (New York: St. Martin's Press, 1975); James Geschwender, *Class, Race and Worker Insurgency: The League of Revolutionary Black Workers* (New York: Cambridge University Press, 1977).

[32]The quotations are taken from Fred Doolittle's study of the forces that shaped the ADC program in 1935: "Intergovernmental Relations in Federal Grant Programs: The Case of Aid for Families with Dependent Children" (Berkeley: Institute of Business and Economic Research, 1977), pp. 108, 111. For evidence on how Roosevelt was repeatedly forced to defer to Southern Democrats on racial issues, see Harvard Sitkoff, *A New Deal for Blacks* (New York: Oxford University Press, 1978).

poor black and white tenants and small farmers formed a People's Alliance in the 1880s and 1890s, Southern merchants and landowners were able to defeat this coalition, making use of racial divisions to do so. They then instituted state-enforced segregationist measures to prevent further interracial challenges from below. Once again, racism worked to benefit only the most privileged whites.

Southern industry developed after 1880. While blacks were largely excluded from industrial employment, interracial class alliances did develop in the major industries of the New South. Racism ultimately divided and helped defeat these working-class conditions, again to the detriment of most whites. An interracial alliance among bituminous coal miners was broken in 1908 by Jim Crow segregationist forces applied directly by the state of Alabama. This defeat postponed the effective formation of the United Mine Workers Union for decades. Events among the dock workers in New Orleans illustrate the same theme, illustrating as well how racism led white workers to struggle against black workers instead of against employers during economic downturns. The results again did not produce gains for the white workers.

Developments in the iron and steel industry in Alabama in this period illustrate how an exclusionary consciousness among skilled white craft workers resulted only in the ultimate deskilling of the craft occupations. The national iron and steel workers paid a price for this racism in the defeat of the 1919 steel strike, the first major attempt in the United States to organize manufacturing workers into an industrial union. The steel employers' use of overt divide-and-conquer techniques followed examples in the Southern textiles and other Southern industries and was frequently repeated throughout the North.

After the merger wave of 1897 to 1904 and the associated reorganization of much of American industry along oligopolistic lines, employers undertook an antiunion offensive, intensifying the use of divide-and-conquer techniques. Once again, racism worked to hurt white as well as black workers.

In the 1930s and 1940s the formation of interracial industrial unions on a massive and unprecedented scale ushered in a new era for American race relations. Interracial solidarity and the struggle against racism assumed a more central importance for labor organizing strategy than ever before. Industrial unionism and interracial cooperation advanced together as the Congress of Industrial Organizations organized six million white and black workers into unions between 1934 and 1946. The CIO unions countered, to a significant if partial extent, the divide-and-conquer patterns of the past. Both the average worker's wages and the relative wage of black workers came to depend partly on the degree of organization and militancy among black and white workers.

After the late 1940s the CIO no longer played a leading role in the struggle for racial equality, and the labor movement itself stagnated. Consequently, the divisive effects of racism have continued to operate in American industry, but in an institutionalized rather than an overt form.

Significant gains in race relations have occurred, nonetheless. The civil rights movement, allied with liberal forces in the North and in Washington, was able to achieve important advances in the field of political and civil rights for blacks. And the wartime demand for black labor, coupled with the collapse of the Southern debt peonage system, opened up employment opportunities in industry for blacks on a new scale. These advances eliminated major barriers to racial equality and promoted the basis for a renewed interracial alliance.

But the shift from excluding blacks from industry to incorporating them into the working class has not by itself resulted in racial equality. Racial inequality is now reproduced by bureaucratic structures in large modern corporations that organize jobs and workers hierarchically and by the farming out of a portion of production to small-scale low-wage employers in competitive market structures. The weaknesses of unions permitted employers to institute these hierarchical structures and to bypass unions with nonunion suppliers.

Racism has weakened the labor movement and hurt most white workers in the postwar period. Unionism remains weakest in the South because of the strength of racism in the region. The resultant low wages in the South have hurt white and black Southern workers directly. Northern workers have also suffered as a result. Wage gains by Northern workers have increased regional wage differentials, impelling many Northern employers to relocate their plants in the South.

The political weakness of progressive forces, due largely to racial divisions and to the continuing power of Southern conservatives in Congress, has also hurt blacks and most whites. These losses are most evident in the failure to achieve the welfare-state agenda that was instituted decades ago in most other developed capitalist countries. In the postwar era United States workers have experienced higher rates of unemployment and economic insecurity and receive a lower level of social-welfare benefits than workers in these other countries. Racism thus continues to hurt most workers, black as well as white.

8.2   *The Bases of Chicano Oppression*

Controversies over U.S. immigration policy have highlighted the recently growing role of Latinos in the United States. The U.S. Latino population has a long history, dating back to the annexation of Florida from Spain in 1819 and the usurpation of Texas from Mexico in the 1830s. The histories of Latinos and blacks in this country differ considerably; yet, as in the case of blacks, Latinos experience lower incomes and higher rates of unemployment. In the following reading Tomás Almaguer discusses the specific historical and contemporary bases of this oppression for one major part of the Latino population: Chicanos.

Excerpted from TOMÁS ALMAGUER, "The Historical Roots of Chicano Oppression," *Socialist Revolution*, 25 (July–September 1975). Reprinted by permission.

RACIAL AND CLASS domination form the principal basis of Chicano oppression. I will attempt to trace historically the development of both racial and class oppression in North America as it has affected Chicanos and our historical forefathers in Mexico. I will show that in the history of the colonization that has affected the Chicano people, class exploitation has taken on a very definite racial form. The racism and racial oppression faced by colonized people has been more than just part of an "ideological superstructure," for it has a very real structural basis in the organization of production.

. . .

In the colonial situation in Mexico, and in capitalist societies like the United States that have a history of colonial expansion *within* the continent, the class system has taken a marked racial form, and racial oppression has been mediated through the organization of class relations. In these societies class relations have given substance to and concretized racial domination.

In the United States, this class domination of racial minorities has shaped and conditioned their history of social oppression. In order to maintain the subordinate position of racial minorities within the class structure, an entire system of social control and political and cultural domination, as well as racial ideology, was developed. The effect of this "ideological superstructure" was not only to justify racial domination but also to maintain this subordination of racial minorities within the lowest strata of the working class.

. . . .

The colonization of the Indio-mestizo [largely the blood line of the Chicano] in the Southwest originated in a classic colonial conquest, but it did not follow the "classic" colonial form, in which the exploitative relationship is generally carried out between the metropolis and a spatially separated colony. Having soon become a numerical minority on their own land, and having had that land "annexed" to the American metropolis, Mexicanos found themselves members of an "internal colony."[1] The colonization of the Mexicano unfolded *within* the political boundaries of the metropolitan nation.

What is crucial in defining the colonial situation of Mexicanos within the United States was their use as a super-exploitable labor force. Unlike white wage-labor and like colonized laborers elsewhere, Chicanos were confined largely to employment sectors like agriculture and mining, and were often hired out by owners on a seasonal basis or were bound to contractors and used as gang laborers. Unlike white immigrants who worked within sectors of the economy based on free labor, Chicanos formed a sub-proletariat within the labor force of the United States.[2] This peonage-like status as contracted or gang laborers was justified by a view of Chicanos as an inferior mongrel race. Historically, this sub-proletarianization of Mexican labor played an important part in the development and stabilization of American capitalism.

First of all, the use of Mexican labor greatly helped transform the Southwest from a relatively underdeveloped area into an agricultural oasis. This development of agriculture in the West would not have been possible nor profitable without the super-exploitation of Mexican labor. Agriculture in the West, like cotton in the slave South, greatly contributed to the capital accumulation that made the transformation of these areas possible.

Testifying before congressional committees in the 'twenties, the principal employers of Mexican labor in the Southwest presented facts and figures showing that Mexicans had been a vital factor in the development of agricultural and industrial enterprises valued at $5,000,000,000. Starting with a scant production in 1900, the Southwest was by 1929 producing between 300,000 and 500,000 carloads of vegetables, fruits, and truck crops—forty percent of the nation's supply of these products. Most of this development took place in less than two decades and was directly based on the use of Mexican labor which constituted from sixty-five to eighty-five percent of the common labor used in the production of these crops.[3]

Second, the use of Chicano labor and technical skills provided for the development of the mining and railroad industry. Both of these sectors were crucial components of the "mineral-transport-communications" infrastructural base needed for future industrialization and modernization of the area. Chicano labor was used extensively both in the maintenance of the railroads at the turn of the century and in the development of mining in the Southwest. "From 1900 to 1940 Mexican workers constituted sixty percent of the common labor in the mines and from sixty to ninety percent of the section and extra gangs employed on eighteen western railroads.[4] By helping lay the foundation upon which the later industrial development of this region was built, Chicano labor played a central role in

---

[1]For discussions of the view that the Chicano is a colonized people see Tomás Almaguer, "Towards the Study of Chicano Colonialism," *Aztlán*, vol. 2, no. 1 (Spring 1971); Mario Barrera, Carlos Muñoz, and Charles Ornelas, "The Barrio as Internal Colony," in Harlan Hahn, ed., *Urban Politics and People: Urban Affairs Annual Reviews*, vol. 6, 1972; and Guillermo Flores, "Internal Colonialism and Racial Minorities in the U.S.: An Overview," in Frank Bonilla and Robert Girling, eds., *Structures of Dependency* (Palo Alto, Calif.: Stanford University Press, 1973).

[2]See Robert Blauner, *Racial Oppression in America* (New York: Harper & Row, 1972). The discussion here relies heavily on Blauner's chapter on "Colonized and Immigrant Minorities."

[3]Carey McWilliams, *North from Mexico* (New York: Greenwood Press, 1966), pp. 185–86.

[4]Ibid.

the development and spread of capitalism in the Southwest.

Third, as a largely mobile and seasonal work force, Chicano labor was used as an integral part of the "reserve army of labor." In times of intense labor needs Mexicanos have been actively recruited into the Southwest to work in agriculture, mining, the livestock industry, or the railroads (circa 1900–1940). Displaced by the Mexican Revolution at the turn of the century and by the intense United States foreign investment that hastened the break-up of traditional social and economic life in Mexico, thousands of Mexicanos became a highly exploitable work force that the American economy was able to draw upon. In times of economic and social crisis, the United States has been able to deport, repatriate, or simply disemploy this surplus labor with relative ease. In the depression years, for example, it is estimated by both Mexican and United States government officials that well over 415,000 Mexicanos were "repatriated" back to Mexico.[5] These wholesale deportations had no criminal offenses as a basis for cause; rather they were justified on the basis of "illegal entry." Similarly, during the economic downturn of the 1950s we witnessed the second major deportation of unwanted Mexican labor under the auspices of "Operation Wetback" (sic). From as far away as Chicago, St. Louis, and Kansas City, hundreds of thousands of Mexican workers were sent back to Mexico. This rising tide of deportations began to swell from 69,111 in 1945 to a high point of 1,108,000 in 1954.[6] From the mid-forties to the mid-fifties, the mass deportation of Mexican workers expelled no fewer than *four million*.

Today, we see a continuation of these same exploitative relationships and a reaffirmation of the use of the policy of widespread deportation of undocumented workers. As a result, the Chicano people have the dubious distinction of far outnumbering any other racial or ethnic minority in the number of forced repatriations or deportations from the territorial United States. Chicano labor has served as a "reserve army of labor" *par excellence*.

Finally, we have acted as "shock absorbers" for the class contradictions of society, i.e., any social or economic crisis that this society produces is generally felt most strongly and "absorbed" by third-world people within the United States.[7] As part of this community, the Chicano feels the force of the contradictions produced within this society. The class contradictions that Marx described as being endemic to this capitalist mode of production have largely manifested themselves as racial contradictions. The weight of social oppression and class contradictions of monopoly capitalism has fallen on the backs of people of color.

As the United States has developed industrially and as labor needs have increased and diversified, the American labor force has become increasingly segmented. Historically, as well as today, the racial form that the class structure in the United States has taken has been largely brought about through the occupational placement of racial and ethnic groups within the working class. Commenting on the role that race and colonized racial minorities have played in the organization of production in the United States, Robert Blauner has observed:

> *What has not been understood is the fact that racial realities have a material basis.* They are built into the economic structure as well as the culture of all colonial societies, including those capitalist nations which developed out of conquest and imported African slaves to meet labor needs.... From the very beginning race has been central to the social relations of production in America. The right to own property, the right not to become property, and the distribution of labor were all essentially matters of color. Southern slavery was a system of production based on race. But not only in the ante-bellum

[5]Abraham Hoffman, *Unwanted Mexican Americans in the Great Depression* (Tucson: University of Arizona Press, 1974), p. 126.

[6]Ernesto Galarza, *Merchants of Labor* (Charlotte, N.C.: McNally & Lofton, 1964), p. 59.

[7]This discussion is primarily based on a lecture given by Robert Allen, "The Illusions of Progress," University of California, Berkeley, 30 November 1973.

South, elsewhere and after, the racial principle continued to organize the structure of the labor force and the distribution of property. The free laborers, the factory proletariat, was largely recruited from white ethnic groups, whereas people of color (Mexicans, Asians, to a lesser degree Indians, and of course, Blacks) were employed in various unfree labor situations. The ethnic labor principle appears to be a universal element of the colonial situation and this is why race and racism are not simply aspects of cultural "superstructure," but cut through the entire social structure of colonial societies.[8]

By *"concentrating people of color in the most unskilled jobs, the least advanced sectors of the economy, and the most industrially backward regions of the nation,"*[9] the material basis of racism and racial oppression has become structurally incorporated into the organization of labor-systems in this society, and more concretely into the relation that workers (white and nonwhite) have to the means of production. In this society, the social relations of production have been largely cast in racial and ethnic terms. The racism and racial oppression that developed in the United States have been much more than a ploy on the part of the bourgeoisie to "divide the working class," for the real basis of racial contradictions is grounded in the different positions that white and nonwhite workers have held in the production process in the United States.

CHICANO LABOR AFTER 1940

Until 1940, Chicanos and other racial minorities were largely used in precapitalist employment sectors outside of urban, industrial centers. We were principally used as a superexploitable semifree labor force. After 1940, Chicanos and other racial minorities came increasingly to occupy the lowest parts of the working class. During and after World War II, the needs of defense industry combined with the introduction of technological innovations in agriculture caused the large-scale migration of Chicanos from the rural areas of the Southwest. For Chicanos, this movement into areas of urban industrial production did not bring with it the opportunity for social mobility that had been open to immigrant ethnic minorities in an earlier period. As the new colored migrant began to take over blue-collar jobs in the working class proper, the white sector of the working class increasingly moved into higher-paid white-collar and "new working class" jobs. The upgrading of racial minorities within the working class was to a great extent made possible through the automation of their old jobs and by entry into areas of production left open by the occupational upgrading of white workers. One social scientist has described this process in the following way:

During and after the Second World War blacks and browns from the rural backwaters of the South and Mexico came by the millions to northern and western industrial cities. But the era of increasing absorption of unskilled and semi-skilled labor into the industrial system, and thereby into the mainstream of class society, was rapidly drawing to a close. Blacks and browns were relegated to employment in the most technologically backward or labor-intensive sectors (menial services, construction labor, corporate agriculture) and to unemployment, the squalor of ghetto life, and welfare handouts. Today, the black, Chicano, and Puerto Rican colonies remain indispensable sources of cheap labor for the technologically backward and labor-intensive sectors. They also provide a servant class to relieve the affluent of the chores of ordinary living and to enhance their status and feeling of superiority. For the highly technological corporate and the rapidly expanding public sectors which require high skill levels, however, the minorities have become superfluous labor.[10]

These observations are confirmed when one examines the changes that have occurred in the placement of Chicanos in the occupational

---

[8]Robert Blauner, "Marxist Theory, Nationalism, and Colonialism," unpublished manuscript (emphasis in original).

[9]Robert Blauner, *Racial Oppression*, p. 62.

[10]Dale Johnson, "On Oppressed Classes," in Cockcroft, Frank, and Johnson, eds., *Dependence and Underdevelopment*, p. 286.

hierarchy. An examination of U.S. Census materials on Chicano occupational distribution shows that in the thirty-year period from 1930 to 1960, male Chicano workers moved from unskilled labor classifications (laborer and farm labor) into the operative and crafts area of production. Nearly 65 per cent of male Chicano workers in 1930 were employed in unskilled, manual laboring jobs. By 1960, this proportion had declined to 32 per cent while Chicano employment in the operative and crafts group rose from 16 per cent to 41 per cent (see Table 8-C). The decline in the use of Chicano labor as a largely unskilled cheap labor force was accompanied by the steady rise in our being used as semi-skilled and low-skilled urban workers. Table 8-C indicates a steady rise in the relative concentration of male Chicano workers in the crafts and operative occupations. While there has been a proportional increase of the Chicano labor force in these areas, many Chicano workers remain as farm and urban-based manual laborers.

More recent figures from March 1973 show a continued increase in Chicano workers in the crafts and operatives area, from 16.7 per cent and 24.1 per cent of the total male Chicano work force in 1960 to 20.0 per cent and 28.4 per cent respectively in 1973 (see Table 8-D). There has also been a recent increase in Chicanos employed as service workers (from 7.5 per cent in 1960 to 12.0 per cent in 1973). The other side of this increase is the dramatic decline in the proportion of Chicanos employed as farm workers (from 16.8 per cent in 1960 to 8.4 per cent in 1973). This trend is largely the result of the rapid automation of agriculture.

By 1973 over 83 per cent of Chicano males were in the non-white-collar areas of production (i.e., blue-collar, farm workers, and service workers occupations). This is to be contrasted with the 59.7 per cent figure for the total United States male employment in these areas for the same year. This of course means that over 40 per cent of the male labor force in

TABLE 8-C   OCCUPATIONAL DISTRIBUTION AND RELATIVE CONCENTRATION OF MEXICAN-AMERICAN MEN IN THE SOUTHWEST, 1930–60

Occupation	Percent Distribution			Relative Concentration*		
	1930	1950†	1960†	1930	1950	1960
Professional and technical	0.9	2.2	4.1	0.18	0.25	0.33
Managers and proprietors	2.8	4.4	4.6	.28	.35	.36
Sales	2.4	‡ 6.5	3.6	.29	‡ .48	.47
Clerical	1.0		4.8	.18		.69
Craft	6.8	13.1	16.7	.47	.67	.81
Operative	9.1	19.0	24.1	.92	1.16	1.35
Service	4.0	6.3	7.5	.68	.98	1.15
Laborer	28.2	18.7	15.2	2.50	2.22	2.12
Farm managers	9.8	5.1	2.4	.59	.65	.61
Farm labor	35.1	24.7	16.8	2.62	3.87	4.16

* The figures for these columns were obtained by dividing the proportion of Mexican-American men employed in each occupation for the years given by the corresponding proportion of all men in that occupation. Thus, the figure of 0.33 for the professional group in 1960 indicates that the fraction of Mexican-American employment which was in this category in 1960 was just one-third as large as the fraction for the total population.

† Computed on a base which omitted employed persons who did not report an occupation.

‡ The 1950 Census of Population combined the sales and clerical occupations into one category for the purpose of reporting occupations of persons with Spanish surname.

Source: Census of Population: 1930, 1950, 1960 (U.S. Bureau of the Census), as compiled by Walter Fogel, *Mexican-Americans in Southwest Labor Markets* (Los Angeles: University of California, Mexican-American Study Project, 1967).

TABLE 8-D   TOTAL EMPLOYED MEN 16 YEARS AND OVER BY MAJOR OCCUPATION
AND TOTAL MEXICAN ORIGIN FOR THE UNITED STATES: MARCH 1973

(Numbers in thousands)		
Occupation	Total Men, 16 Years Old and Over	Total Mexican Origin
Total employed	50,890	1,303
Percent	100	100
White-collar workers:		
Professional and technical	13.6	4.8
Managers and administrators, except farm	13.6	5.3
Sales	6.2	2.5
Clerical	6.8	4.1
Blue-collar workers:		
Craftsmen and kindred workers	20.9	20.0
Operatives, including transportation	18.9	28.4
Laborers, except farm	7.1	14.0
Farm workers:		
Farmers and farm managers	3.0	0.4
Farm laborers and foremen	1.6	8.4
Service workers:		
Service workers, except private household workers	8.2	12.0
Private household workers	—	0.1

— Represents zero or rounds to zero.

Source: U.S. Bureau of the Census, *Current Population Reports*, P-20, No. 26: *Persons of Spanish Origin in the United States: March 1973*. Adapted from Table H.

the United States was employed in white-collar jobs compared to only 16.7 per cent of Chicano males (see Table 8-D).

To make matters worse, one writer has recently noted that while Chicano employment in the crafts and operatives occupations has risen, these are two areas in which aggregate employment significance has actually *declined*.[11] "Far from being able to take advantage of the changing structure of employment opportunities, Chicanos seem to have increased their labor market handicaps by moving into occupations which face declining demand. By 1970, as a result of these adjustments [in the location of changing employment opportunities] fully 57.5 per cent of all Anglos were employed in expanding occupational groups but for Chicanos this figure was only 20.8 per cent."[12]

Thus, this shift in the composition of Chicano labor from a rural, unskilled labor force to the urban, blue-collar working class has not brought with it true social mobility nor a meaningful improvement in the condition of the Chicano people. Despite these changes in our areas of employment, Chicanos remain at the bottom of the working class, and in occupations that provide no real opportunity for group advancement. Moreover, the median income of Chicanos in the Southwest remains three-quarters that of their Anglo counterparts.[13] Even within the same occupations, Chicago workers earn less than Anglos.[14]

[11]Tim D. Kane, "Structural Change and Chicano Employment in the Southwest, 1950–70: Some Preliminary Observations," *Aztlán: Chicano Journal of the Social Sciences and Arts*, vol. 4, no. 2 (Fall 1973), p. 391.

[12]Ibid.
[13]Paul M. Ryscavage and Earl F. Mellor, "The Economic Situation of Spanish Americans," *Monthly Labor Review*, vol. 96, no. 4 (April 1973), p. 6.
[14]Ibid.

TABLE 8-E   INCOME IN 1972, CHICANO MEN AND WOMEN 16 YEARS OLD AND OVER, FOR THE UNITED STATES

Income	Male	Female
Total persons, 16 years old and over (thousands)	1,741	1,812
Persons with income (thousands)	1,604	1,029
Percent	100.0	100.0
$1 to $999 or loss	9.2	26.7
$1,000 to $1,999	7.6	21.8
$2,000 to $2,999	8.2	14.7
$3,000 to $3,999	10.5	12.1
$4,000 to $4,999	10.2	9.3
$5,000 to $6,999	17.1	9.3
$7,000 to $7,999	7.5	2.8
$8,000 to $9,999	12.2	1.7
$10,000 to $14,999	13.7	1.0
$15,000 to $24,999	2.7	0.1
$25,000 and over	0.3	—
Median income of persons with income	$5,489	$2,105

— Represents zero or rounds to zero.

Source: U.S. Bureau of the Census, *Current Population Reports*, P-20, No. 264; *Persons of Spanish Origin in the United States: March 1973.* Adapted from Table 11.

The position that Chicano workers occupy in the working class is clearly reflected in the income received by Chicano men and women. Table 8-E shows that in 1972 over 75 per cent of Chicana wage earners had an income of less than $4,000. In fact, nearly 50 per cent earned less than $2,000 for the entire year. Chicano workers on the other hand were largely concentrated in the $3,000 to $7,000 income bracket. Nearly 40 per cent of all Chicano workers were in this income range with our median individual income amounting to $5,489.

White workers, on the other hand, remained predominantly located in areas of production that enable them to benefit from changes in the occupational hierarchy. The implication here, of course, is that racism has in fact helped to maintain the subordination of Chicanos within the lowest level of the working class. Racism in the United States has not only provided benefits to the capitalist class but it has also provided real material advantages for the white working class. Along with providing important social and psychological benefits for Anglos, racism in the labor market

has provided a modicum of security and advantages in employment for white workers. Racism is in this sense more than just a trick used to "divide the working class" or a form of "false consciousness" imposed on white workers. Racism in the United States does in fact reflect the privileged position that some white workers have held over racial minorities within the working class.

Historically, changes in the form of this super-exploitation of racial minorities have caused shifts in the type of racial ideology that is used to justify and maintain their subordinate position.[15] Using Frantz Fanon's classic insight into the nature of racism we see how racial ideology has coincided and changed with shifts in this racial exploitation.

> The complexity of the means of production, the evolution of economic relations inevitably involving the evolution of ideologies, unbalance

[15]This point is made by both Guillermo Flores, "Race and Culture in the Internal Colony," and by Jeffrey Prager, "White Racial Privilege and Social Change: An Examination of Theories of Racism," *Berkeley Journal of Sociology,* vol. 17, 1972–73.

the system. Vulgar racism in its biological form corresponds to the period of crude exploitation of man's arms and legs. The perfecting of the means of production inevitably brings about the camouflage of techniques by which man is exploited, hence of the forms of racism.[16]

While as a group we toiled primarily with our hands, the type of racial oppression and exploitation we faced was physical in nature and forms of racism we confronted were based on biological premises. This is the period in which Chicanos labored primarily as captives of agricultural production and as exploited laborers in all facets of mining, the railroads, and the livestock industry.

In the period when the economy caused a large shift in the Chicano population from the fields into the cities, racial ideologies shifted from a biological to a cultural basis. As social contact between Anglos and Chicanos increased with this movement into the urban setting, Chicano "biological abnormalities" were increasingly replaced with "cultural" explanations for our backwardness. The reasons used to justify racist practices and poor living conditions were no longer merely that Chicanos had inherited "low-grade" biological traits but that our culture was "backward" or "traditional" and we were "culturally deprived."

Today, as the state has come to play an increasing role in dealing with racial minorities, racism is increasingly mediated by the state institutions—the educational system, the legal system, and the welfare system. Racism and racial exploitation are steadily being transformed from a biological racial ideology used to justify the widespread exploitation of colonial labor to an institutionally-mediated cultural ideology used to justify the subordination

[16]Frantz Fanon, *Towards the African Revolution* (New York: Grove Press, 1967), p. 35.

of Chicanos within the blue-collar working class.

From this it becomes clear that Chicano oppression in the United States has not been simply the outgrowth of a "culture conflict" between Anglos and Chicanos, nor merely the result of a vicious racist ideology. Rather, the many forms of social, political, and cultural oppression Chicanos have faced have ultimately been shaped by the material conditions of our labor. The racial oppression of the Chicano, and of other racial minorities, has largely stemmed from the place we occupy within the working class and from the fact that class exploitation in the United States has taken on a racial form. To do away with the class basis of this racial oppression, however, will not automatically ensure that racism will altogether disappear. For racial minorities, the end to class exploitation is not a panacea but merely an essential precondition for our true liberation and self-determination.

If meaningful political alliances between oppressed peoples are to take place then the left must face the fact that large sectors of the white working class do receive very real short-term benefits from racism. The question of how to convince these workers that they share overriding long-term interests with *all* sectors of the working class cannot be squarely faced if racism continues to be seen as merely a form of "false consciousness."

What is needed now is an honest appraisal of the many ways in which the working class has become segmented and divided. An assessment of racial minorities within the working class is but one step in this direction. It is only when oppressed peoples begin to seek out the commonalities—as well as differences—in their oppression that we can hope to build those political alliances that will be both meaningful and ultimately effective.

8.3 *The Political-Economic Effects of Racism*

In the introduction to this chapter we pointed out that racism is often seen as an aberration in the United States. According to conventional analyses of racial discrimination, employers hurt themselves financially by discriminating against blacks since the labor supply that employers draw upon is thereby restricted. On the other hand, white workers are said to benefit since discrimination reduces the competition from blacks for the jobs and wages of white workers.

In the following reading Michael Reich undertakes a statistical test of the effects of racism in the United States. Reich criticizes the conventional explanation of racism and concludes from his analysis that racism benefits white employers and other rich whites while it hurts poor whites and white employees. Thus racism is seen as a phenomenon of *capitalist* society. Racism is useful to capitalism because it obfuscates class interests and provides a convenient psychological outlet for worker frustration, thereby reinforcing the existing class structure.

It should be stressed that Reich argues not that racism is necessary to capitalism but that capitalism nurtures racist ideologies and practices that help to stabilize the capitalist system. Racism is likely to take firm root in a capitalist society.

The following essay was written for this book. Copyright © 1986 by Michael Reich.

In the early 1960s it seemed to many that the elimination of racism in the U.S. was proceeding without requiring a radical restructuring of the entire society. There was a growing civil rights movement, and hundreds of thousands of blacks were moving to Northern cities where discrimination was supposedly less severe than in the South. Government reports pointed to the rapid improvement in the levels of black schooling as blacks moved out of the South: in 1966 the gap between the median years of schooling of black males aged 25 to 29 and white males in the same age group had shrunk to one-quarter the size of the gap that had existed in 1960.[1]

In the 1980s, however, the optimism of earlier decades has vanished. Despite new civil rights laws, elaborate White House conferences, special government employment and training programs, the War on Poverty, and affirmative action in hiring, racism and the economic exploitation of blacks remain with us. During the past forty years racial discrimination has been made illegal, and most blacks live in urban areas, having left the oppressive agricultural sharecropping system of previous decades. But while blacks have won significant

civil rights, their economic position relative to whites has shown little permanent improvement. In recent years, median black incomes have been fluctuating at a level between 60 percent and 65 percent of median white incomes, the ratio rising during economic expansions and falling to previous low levels during recessions.[2] Segregation in schools and neighborhoods has been increasing in many cities, and the atmosphere of distrust between blacks and whites has been intensifying. Racism, instead of disappearing, seems to be permanent.

Besides systematically subjugating blacks so that their median income is 62 percent that of whites, racism is of profound importance for the distribution of income among white landowners, capitalists, and workers. For example, racism clearly benefits owners of housing in the ghetto where blacks have no choice but to pay higher rents there than is charged to whites for comparable housing elsewhere in the city. But more importantly, racism is a key mechanism for the stabilization of capitalism and the legitimization of inequality. We shall return to the question of who benefits from racism later, but first we shall review some of the economic mechanisms that subjugate blacks.

[1]U.S. Department of Labor, Bureau of Labor Statistics, Report No. 375, "The Social and Economic Status of Negroes in the United States, 1969," p. 50.

[2]The data refer to family incomes; see Table 8-A, p. 285.

THE PERVASIVENESS OF RACISM

Beginning in the first grade, blacks go to schools of inferior quality and obtain little of the basic training and skills needed in the labor market. Finding schools of little relevance, more in need of immediate income, and less able anyway to finance their way through school, black students still drop out at a lower grade than their 1983 white counterparts. In 1983, only 12.9 percent of blacks aged 25 to 29 were college graduates, compared to 23.0 percent of whites in the same age bracket.[3]

Exploitation really begins in earnest when the black youth enters the labor market. A black worker with the same number of years of schooling and the same scores on achievement tests as a white worker receives much less income. The black worker cannot get as good a job because the better-paying jobs are located too far from the ghetto or because he or she was turned down by racist personnel agencies and employers or because a union denied admittance or maybe because of an arrest record. In the 1980s, no matter what the level of schooling, disparities between black and white earnings still persist.[4] And the higher the average wage or salary of an occupation, the lower the percentage of workers in that occupation who are black.

The rate of unemployment among blacks is generally twice as high as among whites.[5] Layoffs and recessions hit blacks with twice the impact they hit whites, since blacks are the "last hired, first fired." The ratio of average black to white incomes follows the business cycle closely, buffering white workers from some of the impact of the recession.

Blacks pay higher rents for inferior housing, higher prices in ghetto stores, higher insurance premiums, higher interest rates in banks and lending companies, travel longer distances at greater expense to their jobs, suffer from inferior garbage collection and less access to public recreational facilities, and are assessed at higher property tax rates when they own housing. Beyond this, blacks are further harassed by police, the courts, and the prisons.

When conventional economists attempt to analyze racism they usually begin by trying to separate various forms of racial discrimination. For example, they define "pure wage discrimination" as the racial differential in wages paid to equivalent workers—that is, those with similar years and quality of schooling, skill training, previous employment experience and seniority, age, health, job attitudes, and a host of other factors. They presume that they can analyze the sources of "pure wage discrimination" without simultaneously analyzing the extent to which discrimination also affects the factors they hold constant.

But such a technique distorts reality. The various forms of discrimination are not separable in real life. Employers' hiring and promotion practices; resource allocation in city schools; the structure of transportation systems; residential segregation and housing quality; availability of decent health care; behavior of policemen and judges; foremen's prejudices; images of blacks presented in the media and the schools; price gouging in ghetto stores—these and the other forms of social and economic discrimination interact strongly with each other in determining the occupational status and annual income, and welfare, of black people. The processes are not simply additive but are mutually reinforcing. Often, a decrease in one narrow form of discrimination is accompanied by an increase in another form. Since all aspects of racism interact, an analysis of racism should incorporate all its aspects in a unified manner.

No single quantitative index could adequately measure racism in all its social, cultural, psychological, and economic dimensions. But while racism is far more than a narrow economic phenomenon, it does have very definite economic consequences: blacks have far lower incomes than whites. The ratio

[3] *Statistical Abstract of the United States, 1985,* pp. 134, 136.

[4] U.S. Bureau of the Census, Series P-60, "Income in Families and Persons in the United States."

[5] See, for example, U.S. Department of Labor, *Employment and Training Report of the President,* various years.

of median black to median white incomes thus provides a rough, but useful, quantitative index of the economic consequences of racism for blacks. We shall use this index statistically to analyze the causes of racism's persistence in the United States. While this approach overemphasizes the economic aspects of racism, it is nevertheless an improvement over the narrower approach taken by conventional economists.

COMPETING EXPLANATIONS OF RACISM

How is the historical persistence of racism in the United States to be explained? The most prominent analysis of discrimination among economists was formulated in 1957 by Gary Becker in his book, *The Economics of Discrimination.*[6] Racism, according to Becker, is fundamentally a problem of tastes and attitudes. Whites are defined to have a "taste for discrimination" if they are willing to forfeit income in order to be associated with other whites instead of blacks. Since white employers and employees prefer not to associate with blacks, they require a monetary compensation for the psychic cost of such association. In Becker's principal model, white employers have a taste for discrimination; marginal productivity analysis is invoked to show that white employers lose while white workers gain (in monetary terms) from discrimination against blacks.

Becker does not try to explain the source of white tastes for discrimination. For him, these attitudes are determined outside of the economic system. (Racism could presumably be ended simply by changing these attitudes, perhaps by appeal to whites on moral grounds.) According to Becker's analysis, employers would find the ending of racism to be in their economic self-interest, but white workers would not. The persistence of racism is thus implicitly laid at the door of white workers.

Becker suggests that long-run market forces will lead to the end of discrimination anyway: less discriminatory employers, with no "psychic costs" to enter in their accounts, will be able to operate at lower costs by hiring equivalent black workers at lower wages, thus bidding up the black wage rate and/or driving the more discriminatory employers out of business.

The approach to racism argued here is entirely different. Racism is viewed as rooted in the economic system and not in "exogenously determined" attitudes. Historically, the American Empire was founded on the racist extermination of American Indians, was financed in large part by profits from slavery, and was extended by a string of interventions, beginning with the Mexican War of the 1840s, which have been at least partly justified by white supremacist ideology.

Today, by tranferring white resentment toward blacks and away from capitalism, racism continues to reproduce rather than to undermine the capitalist system. Although some individual employers might gain by refusing to discriminate and hiring more blacks, thus raising the black wage rate, many employers would be worse off. It is not true that the capitalist class as a whole would benefit if racism were eliminated and labor were more efficiently allocated without regard to skin color. We will show below that the divisiveness of racism weakens workers' strength when bargaining with employers; the economic consequences of racism are not only lower incomes for blacks but also higher incomes for the capitalist class and lower incomes for white workers. Although capitalists may not have conspired consciously to create racism, and although capitalists may not be its principal perpetuators, nevertheless racism does support the continued viability of the American capitalist system.

We have, then, two alternative approaches to the analysis of racism. The first suggests that capitalists lose and white workers gain from racism. The second predicts the opposite—capitalists gain while workers lose. The first says that racist "tastes for discrimination"

---

[6]Gary Becker, *The Economics of Discrimination* (Chicago: University of Chicago Press, 1957).

are formed independently of the economic system; the second argues that racism interacts symbiotically with capitalistic economic institutions.

The very persistence of racism in the United States lends support to the second approach. So do repeated instances of employers using blacks as strikebreakers, as in the massive steel strike of 1919, and employer-instigated exacerbation of racial antagonisms during that strike and many others.[7] However, the particular virulence of racism among many blue- and white-collar workers and their families seems to refute our approach and support Becker.

SOME EMPIRICAL EVIDENCE

Which of the two models better explains reality? We have already mentioned that our approach predicts that capitalists gain and workers lose from racism, whereas the conventional Beckerian approach predicts precisely the opposite. In the latter approach racism has an equalizing effect on the white income distribution, whereas in the former racism has a disequalizing effect. The statistical relationship between the extent of racism and the degree of inequality among whites provides a simple yet clear test of the two approaches. This section describes that test and its results.

First, we need a measure of racism. The index we use, for reasons already mentioned, is the ratio of black median family income to white median family income (abbreviated as B/W). A low numerical value for this ratio indicates a high degree of racism. We have calculated values of this racism index, using data from both the 1960 and 1970 census, for each of the largest forty-eight metropolitan areas (boundaries are defined by the U.S. Census

Bureau, which uses the term standard metropolitan statistical areas—SMSA's). There is a great deal of variation from SMSA to SMSA in the B/W index of racism, even within the North; Southern SMSA's generally demonstrated a greater degree of racism. The statistical techniques used are based on this variation.

We also need measures of inequality among whites. Two convenient measures are: (1) the percentage share of all white income that is received by the top 1 percent of white families; and (2) the Gini coefficient of white incomes, a measure which captures inequality within as well as between social classes.[8]

Both of these inequality measures vary considerably among the SMSA's; there is also a substantial amount of variation in these within the subsample of Northern SMSA's. Therefore, it is very interesting to examine whether the pattern of variation of the inequality and racism variables can be explained by causal hypotheses. This is our first source of empirical evidence.

A systematic relationship across SMSA's between our measure of racism and either measure of white inequality does exist and is highly significant: where racism is greater, income inequality *among whites* is also greater.[9] This result is consistent with our model and is inconsistent with the predictions of Becker's model.

This evidence, however, should not be accepted too quickly. The correlations reported may not reflect actual causality since other independent forces may be simultaneously influencing both variables in the same way. As is the case with many other statistical analyses, the model must be expanded to control for such other factors. We know from previous in-

---

[7]See, for example, David Brody, *Steelworkers in America: the Nonunion Era* (Cambridge: Harvard University Press, 1966); Herbert Gutman, "The Negro and the United Mineworkers," in *The Negro and the American Labor Movement*, ed. J. Jacobson (New York: Anchor, 1968); S. Spero and H. Harris, *The Black Worker* (New York: Atheneum, 1968), *passim*.

[8]The Gini coefficient varies between 0 and 1, with 0 indicating perfect equality and 1 indicating perfect inequality. For a more complete exposition, see H. Miller, *Income Distribution in the United States* (Washington, D.C.: U.S. Government Printing Office, 1966).

[9]For example, the correlation coefficient between the B/W measure of racism and the Gini coefficient of white incomes is $r = -.47$. A similar calculation by S. Bowles, across states instead of SMSA's, resulted in an $r = -.58$.

ter-SMSA income distribution studies that the most important additional factors that should be introduced into our model are: (1) the industrial and occupational structure of the SMSA's; (2) the region in which the SMSA's are located; (3) the average income of the SMSA's; and (4) the proportion of the SMSA population that is black. These factors were introduced into the model by the technique of multiple regression analysis. Separate equations were estimated with the Gini index and the top 1 percent share as measures of white inequality.

All the equations showed strikingly uniform statistical results: racism as we have measured it was a significantly disequalizing force on the white income distribution, even when other factors were held constant. A 1 percent increase in the ratio of black to white median incomes (that is, a 1 percent decrease in racism) was associated with a .2 percent decrease in white inequality, as measured by the Gini coefficient. The corresponding effect on top 1 percent share of white income was two and a half times as large, indicating that most of the inequality among whites generated by racism was associated with increased income for the richest 1 percent of white families. Further statistical investigation reveals that increases in the racism variable had an insignificant effect on the share received by the poorest whites and resulted in a decrease in the income share of the whites in the middle income brackets.[10] This is true even when the Southern SMSA's are excluded.

Within our model, we can specify a number of mechanisms that further explain the statistical finding that racism increases inequality among whites. We shall consider two mechanisms here: (1) total wages of white labor are reduced by racial antagonisms, in part because union growth and labor militancy are inhibited; (2) the supply of public services, especially in education, available to low- and

middle-income whites is reduced as a result of racial antagonisms.

Wages of white labor are lessened by racism because the fear of a cheaper and underemployed black labor supply in the area is invoked by employers when labor presents its wage demands. Racial antagonisms on the shop floor deflect attention from labor grievances related to working conditions, permitting employers to cut costs. Racial divisions among labor prevent the development of united worker organizations both within the workplace and in the labor movement as a whole. As a result, union strength and union militancy will be less the greater the extent of racism. A historical example of this process is the already mentioned use of racial and ethnic divisions to destroy the solidarity of the 1919 steel strikers. By contrast, during the 1890s, black-white class solidarity greatly aided mine-workers in building militant unions among workers in Alabama, West Virginia, and other coalfield areas.[11]

The above argument and examples contradict the common belief that an exclusionary racial policy will strengthen rather than weaken the bargaining power of unions. Racial exclusion increases bargaining power only when entry into an occupation or industry can be effectively limited. Industrial-type unions are much less able to restrict entry than craft unions or organizations such as the American Medical Association. This is not to deny that much of organized labor is egregiously racist or that some skilled craft workers benefit from racism.[12] But it is important to distinguish actual discriminatory practice from the objective economic self-interest of most union members.

The second mechanism we shall consider concerns the allocation of expenditures for public services. The most important of these services is education. Racial antagonisms dilute both the desire and the ability of poor

[10]A more rigorous presentation of these and other variables and the statistical results is available in Michael Reich, *Racial Inequality: a Political-Economic Analysis* (Princeton, N.J.: Princeton University Press, 1981).

[11]See footnote 7.

[12]See, for example, H. Hill, "The Racial Practices of Organized Labor: The Contemporary Record," in *The Negro and the American Labor Movement*, ed. J. Jacobson (New York: Anchor, 1968).

white parents to improve educational opportunities for their children. Antagonisms between blacks and poor whites drive wedges between the two groups and reduce their ability to join in a united political movement pressing for improved and more equal education. Moreover, many poor whites recognize that however inferior their own schools, black schools are even worse. This provides some degree of satisfaction and identification with the status quo, reducing the desire of poor whites to press politically for better schools in their neighborhoods. Ghettos tend to be located near poor white neighborhoods more often than near rich white neighborhoods; racism thus reduces the potential tax base of school districts containing poor whites. Also, pressure by teachers' groups to improve all poor schools is reduced by racial antagonisms between predominantly white teaching staffs and black children and parents.[13]

The statistical validity of the above mechanisms can be tested in a causal model. The effect of racism on unionism is tested by estimating an equation in which the percentage of the SMSA labor force that is unionized is the dependent variable, with racism and the structural variables (such as the SMSA industrial structure) as the independent variables. The schooling mechanism is tested by estimating a similar equation in which the dependent variable is inequality in years of schooling completed among white males aged 25 to 29. Once again, the results of this statistical test strongly confirm the hypothesis of our model. The racism variable is statistically significant in all the equations and has the predicted sign: a greater degree of racism results in lower unionization rates and greater degree of schooling inequality among whites.

A further and in many ways more direct test of the hypothesis was then conducted using 1970 census and Internal Revenue Service

data. This test involved an examination of the relation across industries among profit rates, white workers' earnings, the extent of unionization among all workers, and the degree of racial inequality in earnings. As before, other control variables were introduced to isolate the separate effects of racism. The results—greater racial inequality in earnings within an industry were associated with lower unionization, lower average wages for white workers, and higher profit rates.[14] This empirical evidence again suggests that racism is in the economic interests of capitalists and other rich whites and against the economic interests of poor whites and white workers.

However, a full assessment of the importance of racism for capitalism would probably conclude that the primary significance of racism is not strictly economic. The simple economics of racism does not explain why many workers seem to be so vehemently racist, when racism is not in their economic self-interest. In noneconomic ways, racism helps to legitimize inequality, alienation, and powerlessness—legitimization that is necessary for the stability of the capitalist system as a whole. For example, many whites believe that welfare payments to blacks are a far more important factor in their taxes than is military spending. Through racism, poor whites come to believe that their poverty is caused by blacks who are willing to take away their jobs, and at lower wages, thus concealing the fact that a substantial amount of income inequality is inevitable in a capitalist society. Racism thus transfers the locus of whites' resentment towards blacks and away from capitalism.

Racism also provides some psychological benefits to poor and working-class whites. For example, the opportunity to participate in another's oppression compensates for one's own misery. Furthermore, not being at the bottom of the heap is some solace for an unsatisfying life; this argument was successfully used by the Southern oligarchy against poor whites al-

[13]In a similar fashion, racial antagonisms reduce the political pressure on governmental agencies to provide other public services that would have a pro-poor distributional impact. The two principal items in this category are public health services and welfare payments in the Aid to Families with Dependent Children program.

[14]For further details, see Reich, *Racial Inequality*, pp. 300–303.

lied with blacks in the interracial Populist movement of the late nineteenth century.

To conclude, racism is likely to take firm root in a society that breeds an individualistic and competitive ethos. In general, blacks provide a convenient and visible scapegoat for problems that actually derive from the institutions of capitalism. As long as struggling collectively against capitalism does not seem feasible to most whites, we can expect that identifiable and vulnerable scapegoats will prove functional to the status quo. These noneconomic factors thus dovetail with the economic aspects of racism discussed earlier.

CHAPTER 9

WASTE AND IRRATIONALITY

THE AVERAGE AMERICAN IS FAR RICHER than the average citizen of most other countries; but are we any happier? Nearly every year the productive capacity of the U.S. economy grows larger; but does this growth improve the quality of our lives? And why, with filthy cities and crumbling housing and rising crime, does the capitalist economy leave millions of ready and willing workers out of jobs?

The vast wealth and increasing productivity of the U.S. economy are everywhere evident. Almost every year new records of industrial output are set; even serious economic crises cause only a temporary halt in the growth of real output. News reporters approvingly quote the latest figures showing higher sales of new cars, travel services, television sets, cosmetics, pain relievers, cigarettes, health care, cameras, clothes, home appliances, and other consumer products. Agricultural productivity climbs, and now the average farm worker provides food and fiber for nearly sixty consumers. World trade, a large part of which is accounted for by U.S. exports and imports, routinely expands. The energies and resources of millions of people are devoted to the invention and promotion of new products for popular consumption.

Yet there remains the nagging feeling that all this activity is simply "running in place," that the potential of the economy has not been harnessed to serve people's real needs. We observe countless examples of productive capacity and individual effort devoted to activities that add nothing to human well-being and often impede the growth of human potentiali-

ties. In 1983, American firms spent $75 billion on advertising; drug firms alone spent $575 million on hard-sell network television commercials, probably creating more "nagging pain symptoms" than their products relieved. At a time of growing inadequacy in world food supplies, Craig Claiborne, food editor for the *New York Times*, took a friend to dinner in Paris; total cost of the "meal of the century": $4000. The bankruptcy of the Penn-Central Railroad, while it marked another collapse of rail transit for the heavily populated East Coast, nonetheless proved to be a bonanza for corporate lawyers; it was estimated that their fees would run in the tens of millions of dollars. The Bufferin commercial, Mr. Claiborne's Parisian paté, and railroad lawsuits all use society's scarce resources and count in the annual GNP.[1]

Thus are useless activities proliferated, and frivolous wants satisfied before serious ones. Moreover, the organization of economic activity and the choice of production techniques often lead to unnecessary and irreparable damage to the environment. No one needs to be reminded of the detergents, oils, and sludge that foul our streams, rivers, and seacoasts: the "deaths" of Lakes Erie and Ontario only foreshadow the future fates of the other Great Lakes. The massive scarring of the countryside

---

[1] *Statistical Abstract of the United States, 1985*, pp. 549, 550; *New York Times*, November 14, 1975, p. 1; *Forbes Magazine*, November 1, 1974. The paté, of course, counts negatively in the U.S. GNP, positively in the French. French visitors to Disney World increase the U.S. GNP.

from strip mining renders ugly and unusable what was formerly a precious natural heritage. Mountains of urban garbage, industrial trash, and the waste of radioactive power plants compound the damage. All this comes to a head in urban development that spreads mindlessly outward: between 1950 and 1975, Connecticut lost 70 percent of its farmland to "urban sprawl," while New Jersey lost nearly 40 percent.[2]

Nor is the public sector record more encouraging. The U.S. government channels billions of dollars into the production of modern weapons; by the mid-1970s, the annual defense budget had forever burst the $100 billion mark. Only forty-eight days after the $6 billion ABM missile complex in North Dakota became operational, the government decided to shut it down as obsolete.[3] More billions were poured into military aid for dictatorships around the world, from South Korea to Chile. At the same time day care, welfare programs, food stamps, public sector jobs and wages, legal aid, education, and other programs of direct benefit to people have been trimmed for lack of funds.

These topsy-turvy social priorities are aspects of the fundamental *irrationality* of capitalist production. Capitalist production is irrational because it wastes scarce economic resources on socially unnecessary or low-priority production while failing to meet many essential needs. The extent of the misordered priorities varies from one capitalist nation to another, and some misordering also arises in contemporary state socialist nations. Yet there are powerful forces arising directly from capitalism which serve to divorce production priorities from social needs.

The increasing conflict between people's needs and what capitalism produces creates growing contradictions within capitalism.

THE ORIGINS OF HUMAN NEEDS

What human beings want and need in any society is not simply god-given nor the result of "human nature"; instead, people's needs are a product of both their "fundamental needs" and their specific historical and social development. As Richard Lichtman put it

> Every society, in order merely to survive, must satisfy the basic subsistence needs of its members for food, shelter, clothing and human recognition. There is a level of productivity that must be achieved by any social group, for human beings have fundamental needs whose violation brings social disorganization or death. That is one half of the truth. The other is that human needs are satisfied through specific means of production that shape and alter the original needs and give rise to new needs whose satisfaction depends upon new technical instruments and new forms of social organization. Every society, therefore, in struggling to satisfy fundamental human needs, shapes these needs in distinctive ways and produces new needs which were not part of any original human nature."[4]

Capitalist society, like all societies, shapes people's "fundamental needs" even as it satisfies them. Thus, for example, people need food. In monopoly capitalist society the need for food is met through the production of food for profit by agribusiness. But in order to earn higher profits, agribusiness firms seek to fulfill not just the simple need for sustenance. After all, they are in business not to satisfy needs but rather to earn profits. So they try to encourage consumption of foods that are *profitable*. For example, they promote foods with much sugar and cholesterol because they are sensitive to profit, not to tooth decay or fatty heart tissue. They advertise foods containing additives, on which profit margins are higher, rather than nutritionally sound foods. Thus in all societies people must eat; but in capitalist society this fundamental need for food has been reshaped socially to appear as specific market demands

---

[2]*New York Times*, February 8, 1976, sect. 8, p. 1.

[3]*New York Times*, November 25, 1975, p. 1.

[4]Richard Lichtman, "Capitalism and Consumption," *Socialist Revolution*, 1, No. 3 (May/June 1970), 83.

for steroid-fed beef, nondairy creamers, oranges artificially dyed bright orange, sugar-soaked flakes, and sweetened granola bars.

CAPITALIST PRODUCTION VERSUS HUMAN NEEDS

In this chapter we argue that capitalist society is irrational in the way in which it shapes old needs and creates new ones and in the way in which it provides for the satisfaction of these needs. This irrationality is seen as a fundamental characteristic of capitalist society rather than, for example, the result of inadequate knowledge, of the "facts of life" or "necessary trade-offs," or of unfortunate "accidents"; capitalist production tends to generate such irrationalities *consistently* as part of its *normal* functioning.

Irrationality exists, for example, in the fact that capitalist society provides food products which, rather than providing nutrition, are detrimental to people's health. Food additives cause cancer, they may have disastrous genetic effects, and they appear to be linked to hyperactivity in children. Processing foods frequently eliminates nutrients, and fatty or sweet foods contribute to obesity, heart disease, and so on. People sooner or later rebel against these manipulations, as is evidenced by the popular interest in health foods, natural products, organic gardening, diets and nutrition, and consumerist efforts to ban Red Dye II, cyclamates, nitrites, and other dangerous additives. But such efforts by themselves do not solve the problem, because it derives fundamentally from the conflict between capitalist production priorities and human needs.

Firms in the food industry, and especially in recent years multinational agribusiness firms, have reorganized and developed food production on the basis of profitability and a wider market. This long historical process, revolutionizing the way food is produced, makes it no longer possible, for example, to easily retrace society's steps to an "organic" food supply. Most small local farmers have mostly been driven out of business, so eastern cities now depend on fruits and vegetables from Florida and California, meat from the Midwest, and so on. The truck farms have been paved over into suburbs and "industrial parks." Hence, the problem is not simply one of banning additives; it is instead the problem of reorganizing an entire food-production system that produces food far away from where it is consumed and therefore necessarily relies on taste enhancers, texturizers, preservatives, color restorers, and other additives. The food so produced is necessary to sustain life, yet eating it "may be hazardous to your health." Capitalist society, which has increased consumption levels, including the amount we eat, produces poisoned food.

What is it about the capitalist organization of production that generates these outcomes? The readings in this chapter explore this question in greater detail.[5] Here, however, we can point to the most basic source of social irrationality in capitalist production: the fact that firms produce for profit and only incidentally because the product is useful.

Production for profit means that only those social needs which appear as "dollar votes"—that is, market demands—will be met. Thus a carcinogenic additive and an "all-natural" ingredient are on an equal footing: each will be introduced into foodstuffs if and only if it is profitable, not because it improves the nutritional content of foods. Also, production for profit is biased in favor of those whose incomes afford them the greatest purchasing power. Hence the superficial wants of the rich take precedence over the basic needs of the poor.

Production for profit also establishes an exclusive concern for *private* benefits and costs while ignoring the *social* consequences of production. But as production becomes increasingly social in character, the social consequences become more important. For example, agribusiness capitalists deciding how to produce food tend to ignore the benefits that accrue to the whole society from having

[5]One of the greatest of capitalism's irrationalities, its unplanned and crisis-plagued character, is the subject of Chapter 10.

food with high nutritional value, because these benefits do not add to the profits of the firms. And the ecological damage and increased cancer caused by pesticide-polluted water tend to be ignored since they do not raise the firms' costs.

The terms "external economy" and "external diseconomy" have been used by economists to refer to those benefits and costs resulting from a private action that do not result in corresponding monetary gains or losses for the person or firm who took the action. External economies characterize the provision of almost all collective social services; the inadequacy of such services under capitalism can be attributed in large part to the inability of capitalists to realize profits corresponding to the social benefits provided.

Finally, production for profit creates great pressures for economic expansion, independent of the *need* for growth. But the more productive an economy becomes, the more questionable is the desirability of increasing production still further.

On the one hand, continual expansion exacerbates the problem of maintaining an ecological balance between human beings and our environment. The higher the rate of production, the faster natural resources are used up or destroyed and waste products are dumped back onto the land and into the water. Yet because capitalists continually seek new outlets for profitable reinvestment, continuous growth in productive capacity is inherent in capitalism and could not be restrained without a fundamental change in the mode of production.

On the other hand, continual expansion under capitalism gives rise to the problem of selling what is produced: how to dispose of the continually increasing surplus of production over the essential consumption requirements of the society. The problem is not a lack of human need; the unmet needs of the poor and the unsatisfied demand for public services remain. But in order for the surplus commodities to be absorbed, it is necessary that the *market demand* for goods and services keep pace with the expanding supply.

Of course capitalists do not wait for consumers to decide what their desires are; instead, firms take an active role in stimulating consumption demand. Their most obvious activity is the tremendous sales effort, exemplified by massive advertising. But marketing considerations have also penetrated into the production sphere, and many commodities are purposely designed and constructed to go out of fashion or wear out very quickly, ensuring that consumers will periodically have to buy a new model of the product. Automobiles are one of the most blatant examples of such planned obsolescence, but they are by no means atypical. In order to stimulate more sales, superfluous accessories are often attached to products such as automobiles and forced upon the consumer in need of the basic good. As the readings in this chapter argue, the need to expand sales has opened the way for wasteful forms of public expenditures, a massive advertising and sales effort, and an excessive emphasis on individualistic, private consumption.[6]

The emphasis on consumption complements the alienated nature of work under capitalism. Production is eliminated as an arena for the worker's expression and self-fulfillment; the principal incentive to work is wages—external to the work process and useful only during the nonwork part of the day or week. The alienation of the worker from production thus leaves only the sphere of consumption as an arena for expressing one's individuality, asserting one's humanity, and simply escaping the debilitating effects of one's job. At work one only "earns" a living; it is at home that one "lives."

The overall preoccupation of a capitalist society with production and consumption of commodities contributes to an increasing imbalance between the satisfaction of material and nonmaterial human needs. As it produces rising quantitative levels of material consumption, capitalism sets the stage for the relatively

[6]See Baran and Sweezy, Section 3.3, p. 78, for a discussion of the sales effort.

greater urgency of nonmaterial needs and desires—needs for community, for participation, for identity, for self-expression, for affectoin. In part these new demands are met by new "commodities"—massage parlors offer "affection," housing developers sell "community living," psychiatrists and sensitivity training centers release people from self-doubt for a fee. Yet, in general, nonmaterial needs cannot be satisfied with commodities that can be profitably marketed, so they remain unfulfilled. Nothing could be more illustrative of the fundamental irrationality of the capitalist system than the intensity with which capitalists seek to create and satisfy new material wants at the same time that other needs are both becoming more important and are ignored.

Thus the poisoning of our food grows with the profits of agribusiness; the satisfaction of our material needs is met with a more frantic sales effort; the depletion of our resources evokes not conservation but instead an intensified search for oil in the tundra; and the spoiling of our environment leads not to curbing wastes but instead to a new "growth industry" selling antipollution devices. Thus production becomes increasingly social in character but continues to be privately owned and controlled, and the contradictions of capitalism emerge.

In this chapter we investigate some of the ways in which capitalism causes production priorities to collide with human needs. We will argue that the process by which production decisions are made under capitalism progressively separates what people need to survive and develop from what they can obtain, and therefore capitalist production becomes wasteful and increasingly irrational.

9.1 *The Waste Economy*

Defenders of capitalism often claim that it maximizes efficiency in the allocation and productive utilization of scarce resources. Yet, according to Samuel Bowles, David M. Gordon, and Thomas E. Weisskopf, massive waste pervades our economy, and this waste is attributable precisely to the institutions of capitalism. In the following reading these authors discuss the sources and extent of this waste, which they estimate amounts to nearly half of the actual useful product.

Excerpted from SAMUEL BOWLES, DAVID M. GORDON and THOMAS E. WEISS-KOPF, *Beyond the Waste Land: A Democratic Alternative to Economic Decline* (New York: Anchor Doubleday, 1983). Reprinted by permisson of the publisher.

How do we measure the extent of waste in an advanced economy? How can we properly evaluate our claims about the size of the waste burden in the United States?

We have constructed for these purposes an *index of economic effectiveness* (IEE), a guide to the efficiency or wastefulness of any economic system. Figure 9-A provides a key to this index. It shows both the measure by which we judge the economy's effectiveness and the critical dimensions which determine its level of performance. The factors identified in Figure 9-A establish the guidelines for our estimation of the waste burden in the United States.

The IEE refers to *useful output per available labor hour*. It measures how many useful goods and services we produce from the basic labor resources available to contribute to production. We have previously analyzed productivity, or output per employed-labor hour. By focusing here on *useful* output, and not total output, we devote some attention to the *quality* of the goods and services we produce, not merely their quantities. And attention to *total available* labor time ensures that we gauge our ability to produce what we need and use with respect to *all* available labor resources, not just those of workers who have been lucky enough to find and keep a job.

Is available labor time being utilized? Are we wasting potential labor productivity? Is the economy *taut*—operating at or near its productive potential—or *slack*? As Figure 9-A shows, there are five critical factors which influence the IEE. The higher each of these ratios, the greater the useful output per available labor hour. Since the issue of unemployment and labor utilization is most familiar, we begin on the right-hand side of the equation and move from right to left.

Labor Utilization. Obviously we waste inputs if we don't use them. Our central resource is labor. Many workers now spend their time in such vital pursuits as clipping want ads, pounding the pavements in search of work, waiting on street corners for a glimmer of economic hope, considering the calculus of a new life of crime.

We measure labor utilization by the ratio of *total hours employed to available labor hours.* The higher this ratio, the more output we can potentially produce.

We should recognize, however, that there are both good ways and bad ways to increase this ratio. Providing employment opportunities for the millions of workers now unemployed is clearly a desirable way to increase labor utilization. But many workers now employed would rather work *fewer* hours, not more—enjoying shorter workweeks, longer vacations, and more leisure time. We do not want to endorse an increase in labor utilization achieved by cracking the whip, imposing compulsory overtime, inaugurating veritable work camps of enforced labor time.

We should judge our economy's performance, then, by its ability to promote increased choice in the amount of time worked. Everyone able to work should have the opportunity to make a productive contribution to the economy. Equally important, workers should have more choice about whether they would like to

FIGURE 9-A   A GUIDE TO ECONOMIC EFFECTIVENESS.

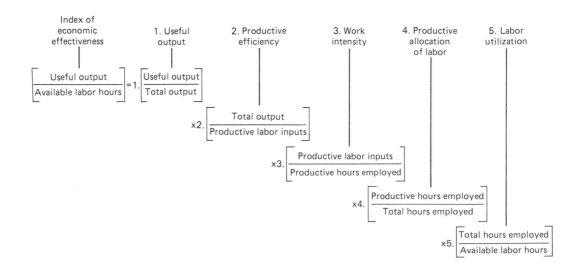

work more hours and consequently increase their incomes, or reduce their hours and enjoy more time for other pursuits. Our measure of waste due to a low rate of labor utilization should therefore reflect the absence of work opportunities for people ready and willing to work, not the reduced hours that some workers may voluntarily have obtained. This requires that we define and estimate "available labor hours" as the number of hours people would like to work if they had the opportunity.

Productive Allocation of Labor. . . . U.S. corporations dramatically expanded their bureaucratic battalions after World War II. Who would argue that all of these managers and supervisors perform useful economic tasks? Who would swear upon the managerial bible that every hour of supervisory time on the job contributes to our economic welfare? Do we really need nearly 13 million managers and supervisors to keep our economy in shape?[1]

To assess the productiveness of our allocation of labor, we measure the ratio of *productive-worker hours employed to total hours employed.* If we can eliminate redundant workers without lowering other dimensions of economic effectiveness, we can allocate our labor more productively and reduce the waste burden on our economy.

Work Intensity. It's not enough simply to hire labor. Workers must be committed to their tasks and motivated to work on the job. . . . (Workers may work more (or less) productively during any hour they spend on the job. They may toss monkey wrenches into the machines and work to rules. Or they may hum with the machines, helping figure out ways of making more effective use of their time spent on the job.

Work intensity refers to the ratio of *productive labor input to productive-worker hours employed.* How much effective worker effort do we get

with each hour of work in the production process? The higher this ratio, other things being equal, the more output we will enjoy at the end of the process of production.

We must be careful with this ratio, however, for an increase in it may have *either* benign *or* destructive effects. If "work intensity" increases because of dangerous speed-up or supervisory harassment, we may get more output but workers will be much worse off than they were before—limping off the job, paying their hospital bills, watching their blood pressure rise, working more and enjoying it less. If, on the other hand, productive labor effort increases because workers feel genuinely greater commitment to their jobs, if they work more effectively without jeopardizing either their health and safety or their psychic state, then we can unambiguously endorse this source of increasing economic effectiveness.

When we evaluate the ratio of productive labor inputs to employed labor time in the U.S. economy, therefore, we shall distinguish carefully between standards for comparison which would involve reduced workers' welfare and standards which would not. We are opposed to speed-up. We are opposed to supervisory harassment. But we shall show that there are many ways of increasing worker effort which would not have such disastrous effects. On balance, we shall demonstrate, workers could produce more per hour and also enjoy it more than they currently do. As a result we could *have* more or *work* less, or both.

Productive Efficiency. We may get more (or less) total output from the resources we use, depending on the efficiency of our productive system. Do we invest wisely? Does management make effective use of the capital and labor it employs? Do our productive enterprises clank and sputter, their engines clogged with the grime and dirt of inefficient production?

Productive efficiency refers to the ratio of *total output to productive labor input.* Given an hour of productive labor time, how many goods and services do we get in return? The greater the productive efficiency and the higher this ratio in Figure 9-A, the more effectively our economy will perform.

[1] This represents the sum, in 1980, of managers, clerical supervisors, and blue-collar supervisors (traditionally called foremen) in the census occupational tabulations. See U.S. Department of Labor, *Employment and Training Report,* 1981, pp. 152–53.

Usefulness of Output. Is all our output useful and necessary? Or does some of it serve no one's needs? If we devote large chunks of available resources to useless output, we're wasting our time. Do we need every missile we produce? Do we enjoy higher standards of living when expensive nuclear power plants lie idle because they are unsafe and too expensive to maintain?

This dimension of economic effectiveness involves the ratio of *useful output to total output.* We could begin to eliminate economic waste if we could increase this ratio, if we stopped devoting precious time and resources to the production of useless goods and services.

Before proceeding to apply our index of economic effectiveness, we should caution that the IEE is by no means a complete measure of economic welfare. It does not measure, for example, the fear, boredom, and anomie which accompany the destruction of community life. Nor the humiliation and harassment of sexism and racism on the job. Nor the long-term environmental destruction visited upon our land, air, and water by deadly chemicals and radioactivity. Nor the waste of talent and creativity from the mindless routine of many jobs.

Those dimensions of economic waste are crucial, but we have not sought . . . to assess everything that is important or relevant about the effectiveness of the economy. . . . We provide some conservative estimates of the waste burden in the following sections, summing them up in Table 9-A.

WHATEVER HAPPENED TO "FULL EMPLOYMENT"?

We begin our investigation with the issue of labor utilization, moving from right to left in Figure 9-A. Officially measured unemployment had risen by 1982 to more than 10 million. Some regard this as outrageous. Others sigh, practicing their staged regret, insisting that a "little" unemployment is necessary to lick inflation.

This conflict of views suggests two questions about high unemployment. The first

is obvious: Why is unemployment so high in the United States? The second follows from the first: If we were willing to change some of the rules of the postwar corporate system, what kind of "full-employment" goal would be attainable?

Our answer to the first question begins with a simple observation: in capitalist economies, the business of business is profits, not full employment. The historical record confirms this general view: during the first eight decades of the twentieth century, excluding the five years of peak wartime production during World Wars I and II, the U.S. economy averaged 6.9 percent unemployment—across both good times and bad.

    .   .   .

We can sharpen our answer with a comparative focus. Public policy in many European countries has pursued "full employment" much more insistently than in the United States. We can compare the U.S. unemployment experience since 1960 with that in West Germany and Sweden—two countries with notably more aggressive public support of full employment *and* with much more rapid economic growth.[2] (Unemployment rates are available for those countries which rely on definitions comparable to those in the standard U.S. unemployment series.) Between 1961 and 1980, the average annual unemployment rate in the United States was 5.7 percent. During those same years, unemployment averaged 1.4 percent of the labor force in Germany and 1.9 percent in Sweden. Despite the slower growth of the 1970s, unemployment has averaged under 2 percent in both of these countries over the past two decades and less than one third of the average levels of unemployment in the United States. Much full employment is possible, in short, even in capitalist economies. The governing coalitions in Germany and Sweden have consistently pursued policies which aim to smooth the cyclical fluctuations of market

[2]U.S. Bureau of Labor Statistics, "Statistical Supplement to International Comparisons of Unemployment," *Bulletin* No. 1979, June 1982.

economies, providing cushions for those who feel the sharpest jolts and reducing the inflationary pressures which full employment policies can sometimes generate.

Business in the United States has refused to consider such incursions on the unbridled reign of private profitability. Business leaders first mobilized their opposition during the post-World War II debate over the Employment Act of 1946. . . . They have sustained their opposition throughout the postwar period. . . . Unemployment has persisted and risen in the United States, in short, because the postwar corporate system imposed a particular set of priorities on economic policy. Suppose we shifted priorities and played by a different set of rules. How close to "full employment" could we realistically expect to move?

We propose a full-employment target of *2 percent* as a standard for measuring wasted labor resources in the United States. This standard seems to us quite reasonable. We achieved an even lower rate of unemployment during both World War I and the last three years of World War II; this rate of full employment was achieved during World War II with average inflation rates of only 2 percent. Comparable rates of full employment were achieved during the 1950s and 1960s in many other advanced countries—as we have already noted above—with comparably low levels of inflation.

How much additional output could we generate by achieving such a full-employment target? In order to arrive at a reasonable estimate of the additional labor resources we could tap if we had operated at 2 percent unemployment in 1980, we make four simple calculations:

- We assume that all those in 1980 who were unemployed in excess of 2 percent would have been employed.
- We assume that all those officially designated "discouraged workers" who were not in the labor force but who nonetheless said they "want a job now"—people who had given up in frustration or were hobbled by personal barriers which

any full-employment program could easily address—would also have been employed.

- We assume that those "involuntary part-time employees" who would prefer to work full time if they could find full-time jobs would also be able to satisfy their preferences, moving to full-time schedules.

- We also assume, finally, that many workers subjected to compulsory overtime in 1980 would have been free to determine their own hours and that some would have consequently *reduced* their working time.

Combining these four calculations, we estimate that the ratio of total employed hours to available labor hours could have been 8.9 percent higher than it actually was in 1980. An analogous calculation for 1982 would show that at least 11 percent more labor hours were available for utilization. . . .

WHO WORKS FOR WHOM AND WHY?

Continuing from right to left in Figure 9-A, we next encounter the problems of the productive allocation of labor and of work intensity. We discuss these two dimensions of economic performance together since they are intertwined. . . . Do we really need such top-heavy corporate bureaucracies? . . .

The Payoff to Worker Commitment

We argue that worker output per hour would be much higher in democratic enterprises than in capitalist firms. The key is worker commitment. You can give a worker a shovel and he may not use it. You can give a hotshot a computer and she may spend her time solving crossword puzzles. Labor effort varies . . . and economic waste results if workers have less commitment to their jobs in the present system than in some other plausible alternative.

Compare two workers. One of them works in a giant bureaucratic enterprise, surrounded by supervisors, constantly goaded to increase his or her effort in the service of corporate profits and owners' dividends. The other works in a democratic enterprise, owned or controlled by fellow employees, cooperatively managed, with year-end profits distributed equally to employees. Which worker is likely to feel more committed to productive activity on the job? Whose effort is likely to grow over the years?

We find it virtually self-evident that democratic enterprises would sustain much stronger worker commitment and effort than top-heavy bureaucracies with centralized power and supervision by command. A variety of experiences allows us to test this expectation. What happens when we compare similar enterprises which practice different systems of control? Are we correct that worker output increases in more democratic enterprises?

Researchers have studied the effects on worker productivity of systems providing greater job rotation, worker involvement in decision-making, and cooperative systems of coordination. These experiments have almost always found that workers' output per hour increases in response to greater variety in their work and increased control over their working conditions. While we should hardly find such results surprising, it is helpful to look at them a little more closely in order to assess the reasons for the observed effects. We rely for our summary on a particularly careful study of this experimental evidence conducted by three social psychologists in the mid-1970s and sponsored by the National Science Foundation[3]:

● The link between job change and productivity seem clearly to depend on worker *incentives* to change their work effort.

The key to have workers who are both satisfied and productive is *motivation*, i.e., arousing

and maintaining the desire and will to work effectively—having workers who are productive not because they are coerced but because they are committed.

● These responses cannot be easily bought, induced by distributing monogrammed tie clips or suggestion boxes. Experimental results suggest that performance will improve *if*

1. The changes in job content are sufficiently non-trivial to be perceptible to the workers, typically in terms of greater self-regulation, diversity, meaningfulness, challenge, and social responsibility . . . [and]
2. the changes in job content are part of a more pervasive program of improved working policies and practices, which include also as elements adequate pay and job security, proper resources and working conditions, increased mutual influence by people at all levels, and constructive labor-management relations.

● Higher productivity is also especially likely to result from changes in the control structure of an enterprise. Better worker performance seems to flow if and when employees obtain "greater over-all influence" and "greater voice in defining work goals, methods, and compensation at both the individual and group levels. . . ."

James O'Toole, writing in *Making America Work*, agrees about the critical importance of real control:

Significantly it has been where management has withheld full responsibility from workers that the rights of ownership have had no positive effects on behavior, morale, or productivity. . . . While workers are likely to reject responsibilities without accompanying rights, they are also likely to see rights without responsibilities as no less of a sham.[4]

Many readers might reasonably be skeptical about the implications of this experimental evidence on the grounds that workers enjoyed the novelty of the experiments. By their na-

[3]See Raymond A. Katzell and Daniel Yankelovich et at., *Work, Productivity, and Job Satisfaction: An Evaluation of Policy-Related Research* (New York: Harcourt Brace Jovanovich, 1975).

[4]James O'Toole, *Making America Work: Productivity and Responsibility* (New York: Continuum, 1981), p. 102.

ture, short-term experiments may not necessarily indicate longer-term effects.

There is another body of evidence which we believe carries more weight. Both at home and abroad, many worker-controlled enterprises have lasted long enough to permit actual—instead of experimental—comparisons of worker output in democratic and hierarchical workplaces.

In the United States, there are now roughly 1,000 firms that have some form of regular worker ownership and/or control. Although most of these firms are small, and therefore not fully representative of the entire U.S. economy, their experiences nonetheless are significant. The impact of worker ownership and control on worker effort has been evident. One recent review reports some comparative results:

> A study done in the 1950s found that worker-owned firms averaged 20–30 percent higher productivity than conventionally owned firms. A similar study done in the 1960s found an average of 30 percent higher productivity over conventionally owned firms.[5]

There have also been significant worker-controlled experiences throughout Europe, in Yugoslavia, in Israeli kibbutzim, in Chile under the Allende regime. Here, as well, the evidence clearly supports the view that worker productivity increases substantially in democratic enterprises. A recent compilation of careful studies on this workplace effect demonstrates clearly that both in the United States and abroad, greater worker participation in and control over their workplaces uniformly results in expanding labor productivity.[6]

The Advantages of Real Workplace Democracy

There is much in our preceding discussion with which many probusiness strategists would agree. Many of the experiments we have cited, indeed, resulted from management initiatives under the careful tutelage of business-school consultants. A Business Week team prescribing strategies for economic recovery, for instance, concludes that labor-management relations must change dramatically not only at the national and industrial levels, their first and second requirements, but also in direct administration of the production process itself:

> This is where the third level of the labor-management relationship—on the factory floor—assumes large importance. If rank-and-file workers can be given more responsibility and be drawn more deeply into the relationship (though not in a paternalistic way), a better understanding of the real constraints on bargaining may spread through the system. At the same time, redesigning jobs to allow greater worker participation in decision making can reduce alienation and give workers a sense of control over their work.[7]

If these probusiness strategists are so eager to involve rank-and-file workers in management decisions, why haven't corporate executives rushed to do so? What grounds might we have for assuming that workplace relations in 1980 were any less democratic than was institutionally and technologically possible?

The answer lies in a clearheaded analysis of the postwar corporate system. Large capitalist corporations pursued a particular path toward increased worker productivity in the postwar period. They built large and relatively inflexible structures for labor management, seeking wherever possible to remove autonomy and discretion from the shop and office floor. This produced a strong and persistent rigidity in postwar corporate hierarchies *and* in their poli-

[5]Karl Frieden, "Worker Ownership and Productivity," in R. Friedman and W. Schweke, eds., *Expanding the Opportunity to Produce: Revitalizing the American Economy Through New Enterprise Development* (Washington, D.C.: The Corporation for Enterprise Development, 1981), pp. 412–13.

[6]Derek C. Jones and Jan Svejnar, eds., *Participatory and Self-Managed Firms: Evaluating Economic Performance* (Lexington, Mass.: Lexington Books, 1982). See also Juan Espinosa and Andrew Zimbalist, *Economic Democracy: Workers' Participation in Chilean Industry 1970–1973* (New York: Academic Press, 1978), pp. 141–75.

[7]The Business Week Team, *The Reindustrialization of America* (New York: McGraw-Hill, 1982), pp. 91–92.

cies toward labor. Inflexibility is built into modern capitalist corporations, and nowhere has this inflexibility been more institutionalized than on questions of labor control. Top corporate management has recognized the need for greater worker motivation, to be sure, but top management has been equally determined to restore or enhance its leverage. While many called for more humane labor-management policies during the 1970s, most corporations pursued the microeconomics of the Great Repression—increasing the size of their supervisory apparatus, hiring management consultants to oust and prevent unions, threatening plant shutdowns in tough bargaining for work concessions. Better to stay at the helm of a foundering ship than to work alongside the crew!

These perceptions echo throughout the literature on corporate experiments at workplace reorganization.[8] Substantial increases in worker productivity, as we have already seen, require nontrivial changes in job content and work structures as well as adequate pay and job security. But management has found it extremely difficult, many conclude, to make non-trivial changes in workplace organization, resulting in improved worker effort, *without also ceding significant management prerogatives.* Corporations have shown all kinds of interest in improving worker motivation, but they have shown even greater interest in preserving their centralized power and privileges. Forced to choose, one gathers, most corporations have preferred to forgo greater worker effort rather than to give up any management control.

Some recent surveys of management attitudes lend at least partial support to this skeptical view. One comprehensive survey of management attitudes in the mid-1970s revealed a clear hierarchy of executive priorities.[9] A whopping 87 percent of the managers agreed that "there would be greater productivity . . . if workers were more satisfied with their jobs." But virtually none of them were prepared to abandon traditional top-down approaches to greater worker satisfaction. Asked to rate changes which they thought would be "very important in improving productivity in your organization," 65 percent cited "better planning" and "more effective management"; only 10 percent chose "greater participation by workers in decision-making," and only 6 percent chose "more democracy in the organization." The stakes are high and the corporations know it. As one research and training executive at General Motors concluded about quality-of-work-life experiments:

> What is really involved is politics, the conscious sharing of control and power. . . . [Workers participating in decisions about] rearranging the work area . . . may very well want to go on to topics of job assignment, the allocation of rewards, or even the selection of leadership.[10]

Perish the thought.

We conclude that the organization of production *could* have been much more democratic in 1980, but only if we had been able to change the rules of the game. And we further conclude that worker productivity could have been much higher than it was had there been greater workplace democracy.

Most working people seem to agree.[11] Among respondents in a 1975 survey, two thirds agreed that "people don't work as hard as they could because they aren't given enough say in decisions which affect their jobs." They were also asked the following question:

---

[8]See, for example, Richard Edwards, *Contested Terrain* (New York: Basic Books, 1979); Raymond Katzell, Daniel Yankelovich et al., *Worker Productivity Experiments in the United States* (New York: New York University Press, 1977); David Jenkins, *Job Power* (Baltimore: Penguin Books, 1974); and Charles Hecksher, "Worker Participation and Management Control," *Journal of Social Reconstruction*, January–March 1980.

[9]Based on Katzell and Yankelovich, *Work, Productivity, and Job Satisfaction*, pp. 114, 109–10.

[10]Quoted in Emma Rothschild, *Paradise Lost: The Decline of the Auto Industrial Age* (New York: Vintage Books, 1974), p. 163.

[11]Results from a poll by Peter D. Hart Research Associates, reported in Jeremy Rifkin, *Own Your Own Job* (New York: Bantam, 1975), pp. 137, 176.

Let us suppose that the people who worked in the companies selected the management, set policies, and shared in the profits. Do you think that this arrangement would improve the economic condition of the economy, make it worse, or not make much difference?

Of those expressing an opinion, 54 percent thought this form of worker management would "improve" our economic condition and only 15 percent thought it would make conditions "worse."

We conclude that hierarchial management of production is both wasteful and unpopular. How much waste resulted in 1980 from the burdens of top-heavy management and the denial of worker involvement in production decisions?

We return to the two related factors in Figure 9-A—the productive allocation of labor and work intensity. How much higher could our IEE have been in 1980 if we had organized production more democratically? We cannot make such estimates with any great precision, but it is possible to arrive at some reasonable (and conservative) approximations. Two likely effects of democratizing the workplace may be identified: a reduction in supervisory labor and an increase in the productivity of production workers.

With more democratic workplaces, we could eliminate many unproductive supervisory jobs because some supervisory functions would no longer be necessary and because productive workers themselves would perform many of the remaining necessary functions of those managers and supervisors. We are not the only observers to suspect that there is a great deal of waste resulting from the redundant managerial and supervisory personnel. Lester C. Thurow reports on widespread business views about the scale of corporate bureaucracies, reflecting that a "key to productivity improvements lies not on the factory floor, but in the office. . . . The problem is one we do not like to face. American government may be bureaucratic and inefficient, but American industry is just as bureaucratic and

inefficient."[12] A study by a corporate consulting firm reached similar conclusions after case studies of management practices in sixteen major manufacturing companies: Charles K. Rourke, president of SMC Hendrick, Inc., reported in 1982 on the firm's findings:

> While many manufacturing companies would point to the rising cost of materials, high interest rates, and other problems as the cause of their current business woes, a major factor appears to be this over-staffing in the middle and upper management levels. . . . This problem is not confined to any one industry, but is a pervasive condition in U.S. business.[13]

We have chosen a conservative estimate of the waste we could eliminate through more democratic coordination of the workplace. The ratio of supervisory to nonsupervisory employees grew rapidly during the 1950s and 1960s because U.S. corporations were building new and increasingly top-heavy empires to dominate their workers and their competition. "There has been," Rourke concludes from the consulting firm study, "30 to 40 years of excessive growth." Suppose that the supervisory and managerial apparatus were no larger in 1980, in relative terms, than it had been in 1948—when this growth in the administrative bureaucracy began to accelerate. Suppose further that all of those additional supervisory personnel performed productive tasks instead. The ratio of productive-worker hours employed to total hours employed, through more efficient use of this surplus supervisory labor, would have been 6.6 percent higher than it was.

Is this measure of the waste of top-heavy bureaucracy realistic? It is difficult to make international comparisons, but it is nonetheless possible to make a consistent comparison

---

[12]Lester C. Thurow, "Why Productivity Falls," *Newsweek*, August 24, 1981, p. 63.

[13]Survey results and quotes from Rourke (in both this and following paragraph) from Boston *Globe*, September 21, 1982, p. 63.

of the relative managerial burden in four advanced economies in 1980. In the United States in 1980, "administrative and managerial personnel" constituted 10.8 percent of total nonagricultural employment. In Germany this fraction was only 3.0 percent: in Sweden 2.4 percent; and in Japan, 4.4 percent.[14] Those three other economies were growing more rapidly than the United States by every available measure. A more productive allocation of labor surely didn't hurt.

As important as the savings to be made through the elimination of redundant supervisory jobs are the gains in the effectiveness of the production workers themselves. Suppose we had been able to achieve more democratic workplaces in 1980. How much more labor input per productive-worker hour employed—or how much greater work intensity—could we have achieved?

Available evidence on worker-managed or -controlled enterprises suggests that worker hourly output ranges from 15 to 30 percent higher in democratic workplaces, at a minimum, than in comparable bureaucratic enterprises.[15] We have chosen the bottom of this range for our estimate of the waste burden in the U.S. economy in 1980. We sacrificed a minimum of 15 percent of potential output, by this evidence, through our continued tolerance of undemocratic production systems.

We repeat that this waste estimate does not involve a call for speed-up and harassment in the workplace. Workers in more participatory workplaces are not only more productive but also much more satisfied with their jobs. We could apparently increase hourly output by at least 15 percent without pushing workers harder or exposing them to greater workplace hazards. This waste elimination would come

from great worker commitment, not speed-up. It would capitalize on all of the worker effort currently *wasted* in capitalist enterprises through working to rules, through slowdown, through plotting against the boss, through sabotage and shirking, through direct worker resistance. In hierarchical situations, worker resistance takes time and energy, diverting attention from the tasks at hand to the tasks of subversion. In democratic workplaces, this negative creativity can be translated into positive energy. If production workers controlled their own conditions of work, the returns in economic effectiveness would be enormous.

ARE COLD BATHS EFFICIENT?

The *productive efficiency* of the U.S. economy leaves much to be desired.... There have been two principal sources of sluggish productive efficiency in the United States in the 1970s, and both of them involve structural features of the postwar corporate system rather than attitudinal paralysis.

The first problem stems from the absence of any kind of long-term industrial planning; we have left such planning entirely to the corporations. If the steel companies chose to ignore necessary modernization for two decades, pity their workers. If the auto companies chose to postpone producing economical automobiles, pity their consumers. John DeLorean, former head of the Pontiac division at General Motors, recalls the thinking of GM during these critical years:

> When we should have been planning switches to smaller, more fuel-efficient, lighter cars in the late 1960s, in response to a growing demand in the marketplace, GM refused because "we make more money on big cars." It mattered not that customers wanted the smaller cars, or that a national balance of payments deficit was being built.... Refusal to enter the small car market when the profits were better on bigger cars, despite the needs of the public and

---

[14]These data comparisons are from consistent international data compilations provided in International Labor Organization, *Yearbook of Labor Statistics* (Geneva: International Labor Organization), 1981, Table II-c. The category included is that of "administrative and managerial employees."

[15]See summaries and studies in Jones and Svejnar, eds.

the national economy, was not an isolated case of corporate insensitivity. It was typical.[16]

The second structural problem results from corporate domination of macroeconomic priorities and the consequent pursuit of a "cold-bath" strategy of high unemployment [in order to discipline workers . . .] Capacity utilization and investment stagnated during the 1970s as a result of [such a cold bath]. . .

These two structural sources of inefficiency combine to force a single conclusion: There has been enormous productive inefficiency in the U.S. economy because the postwar corporate system imposed profitability over planning and steady growth. Inefficiency was rampant in the late 1970s because corporate priorities prevailed. Capacity utilization and capital intensity could have promoted much greater productive efficiency in 1980 than they did, we conclude, if we had been able to change the rules.

How much difference in our IEE would such rules changes have made? . . . Setting aside the longer-term problems of industrial planning, how much damage did the [cold bath of the 1970s] wreak? How much higher could productive efficiency have been in 1980 if we had been able to forsake the cold bath, eschewing corporate concerns for more stable growth? . . .

- Investment slowed after 1973. . . . Most of the sluggish growth in capital intensity can be attributed to the effects of fiscal restrictiveness—itself an effort to curb labor resistance. If this cold-bath effect had not chilled investment, the capital stock would have been much larger in 1980 and hourly output would have been significantly higher as a result. On the basis of our estimates . . . we conclude that the ratio of total output to productive labor inputs would have been 3.0 percent higher in 1980 if investment had not slowed from the cold-bath effects.

- Capacity utilization suffered similar refrigeration. If capacity utilization had not been

pushed down . . . hourly-output growth would also have been more rapid during the 1970s than it was. We estimate that hourly output would have been 1.7 percent higher in 1980 if the cold-bath effect had not slowed the economy and resulted in so much idle capacity.

Summing together these two results of the cold bath, we estimate that productive efficiency could have been 4.7 percent higher in 1980 than it was. Output per hour could have been that much higher as well. Escaping this wasteful legacy of the postwar corporate system would have benefited the vast majority of us through higher output or greater leisure time. And this estimate does not even include the potential gains from more effective industrial planning.

LET THEM EAT MISSILES!

People in the United States have grown more and more concerned about the social and economic costs of wasteful output. It is obvious, moving to the first right-hand term of Figure 9-A, that we could increase useful output per hour of available labor *if* we could transfer inputs from the production of some relatively useless commodities into production of more useful goods and services. Many goods and services currently produced in the United States add little or nothing to people's welfare. By eliminating this kind of waste, we could substantially increase our aggregate and individual welfare.

This is a sensitive issue. It is presumptuous for us to rank everything produced in the United States on some subjective scale of usefulness. How do we know what is healthy for children and other living things? Or enjoyable? In a democratic and egalitarian economy, these questions should be for people to decide for themselves through the market or the ballot box.

There are some cases where we think judgments can be made, however. We have chosen a few examples in this section in order to dramatize how much waste exists in our economy as a result of useless output. We have

[16]John Z. DeLorean with J. Patrick Wright, "How Moral Men Make Immoral Decisions—A Look Inside GM," in Mark Green and Robert Massie, Jr., eds., *The Big Business Reader* (New York: Pilgrim Press, 1980), p. 39.

identified these examples very selectively, ignoring many other obvious examples of waste. We have used conservative methods of estimating the amount of waste in each case. We have sought simply to provide a minimum and illustrative example of the waste burden imposed by misplaced production priorities. The magnitude of this waste, even by our conservative estimates, simply underscores the need to move away from the prodigality of the postwar corporate system.

Military Waste

We are not experts on military matters. We think there is good reason to believe, however, that we could achieve our legitimate defense objectives with far less expenditure than is now devoted to them. How much fat could we trim from the rows and columns of the Pentagon budget?

There are two principal sources of military waste: the inefficiency of U.S. defense policy and the inefficiency of military production.

Defense Policy. There have been two recent and systematic efforts to reexamine the relationship between defense policy and military expenditure.

One, through the initiative of Representative Ronald Dellums (D.-Cal.), proposes a reexamination of the entire range of "national-security" objectives, which would permit substantial attenuation of our arsenal of nuclear armaments. Based on careful review of Pentagon programs and appropriations, Dellums' security advisers estimate that more modest but fully adequate defense objectives could have resulted in a saving of $54 billion in fiscal year 1983.[17]

The Boston Study Group has prepared a somewhat more conservative estimate of potential reductions in military spending. They project continued security objectives of defending not only the United States but also Western Europe, Israel, and Japan. They also propose to maintain an invulnerable nuclear deterrent. Judging from these project objectives, they have examined the 1978 defense budget in detail. They have concluded that only $73 billion out of the total defense budget of $105.2 billion was necessary in that year to meet these consolidated military objectives—allowing for a reduction of $32.2 billion in the 1978 Pentagon budget.[18]

We choose the more conservative Boston Study Group study as the basis for our estimate of the necessary level of military expenditure—not because it is clearly superior but because it is the more conservative of the two. At 1980 prices, it would imply a total 1980 defense budget of $86.3 billion.

Military Production. Few would boast about the efficiency of military contracting and defense contractors' production. In the mid-1960s, the Pentagon under Robert McNamara estimated that procurement contracts cost at least 25 percent more if they are let through noncompetitive bidding, and yet, in 1981, roughly four fifths of all procurement contracts were still being secured through noncompetitive bids. With much more direct control over the wastefulness of military production—through either competitive bidding or direct public control of expenditures—we could apparently have saved nearly $5 billion in 1980 out of the defense expenditures necessary for the Boston Study Group's established security objectives.[19]

These two calculations combine to suggest that defense spending in 1980 could have been as little as $81.9 billion without forsaking a wide range of military objectives. Actual defense spending in 1980 was $131.7 billion. We could have saved $49.8 billion, or an amount equal to 1.9 percent of actual GNP in 1980.

[18]The Boston Study Group, *The Price of Defense: A New Strategy for Military Spending* (New York: New York Times Books, 1979).

[19]Study on waste through noncompetitive bidding reported in Mark Green, *Winning Back America* (New York: Bantam, 1982), p. 284. Data on procurement contracts in current defense budget from *Statistical Abstract*, 1981, p. 355.

[17]See Ronald Dellums, "Defense Sense," *The Nation*, August 21–28, 1982.

Energy Production

Energy policy in the United States has spawned waste on a monumental scale. We concentrate on only one dimension of the energy potlatch: the decision to pursue nuclear power in the 1950s and 1960s. . . . Corporations encouraged the development of nuclear power because of its high capital costs and potential returns on construction bonds. As was their wont, they ignored the potential inefficiencies and health hazards. When popular movements finally mobilized to block further nuclear power production and construction, we were stuck with a stockyard of white elephants—wasteful nuclear power plants, often idled, soaring costs, continual risks of radioactivity and explosion.

Suppose we had been able to block nuclear power construction during the 1960s and 1970s? Nuclear power provided only about 11 percent of total electricity in 1980. Let us assume that we had been able to meet these needs through a combination of more intense conservation efforts and through less capital-intensive coal production. We estimate very conservatively that net energy expenditures in 1980 would have been roughly $27.4 billion lower as a result of these savings on the capital costs of nuclear power construction. On the basis of this single dimension of a pervasively wasteful energy policy in the 1960s and 1970s, we estimate that we could have transferred 1 percent of actual GNP in 1980 to other, more useful output.

Food Production

Large food corporations gained control of the food business after World War II. This oligopolistic control has pushed food processing and distribution toward more and more expensive methods of packaging and advertising. It has also substantially increased the share of food expenditures devoted to transportation costs—the price of agribusiness centralization and long-haul shipping all across the country. As a result of these developments, the costs of "marketing" foods—the difference between the prices paid by consumers and the prices paid to farmers—rose from roughly half of all consumer expenditures on food to more than two thirds. Suppose this "marketing" bill had been no higher in 1980, as a proportion of food expenditures, than it was in 1948—when more accurate data on food costs first became available. We would have saved almost 14 percent of our food bill—for a total savings of $32 billion, or 1.2 percent of the actual 1980 GNP.

Health Care

The health-care system in the United States is a disgrace. We spend more and more on "health care" but the health of people in this country lags far behind that of other industrialized countries. We spend our health dollars on sophisticated and often useless equipment, top-heavy hospital bureaucracies, high-tech medical obsessions, bloated drug prices—and rarely on the kinds of preventive health care and nutritional education which would more effectively promote good health.

We pay more for health care than any other people, yet we get remarkably little out of it. We spent roughly $1,000 per person on health care in 1980—a higher level of per capita expenditures than that in any other country. But our health record—despite all that money thrown into the health-care system—compares poorly with most other industrialized countries.

This wastefulness in the health-care sector is typical of the postwar corporate system. The costs of health care have risen but the benefits of health-care expenditures have not followed along. We pour our money into an irrational and centralized system which operates more surely to increase suppliers' profits and practitioners' incomes than to prevent disease and promote good health. It aims its services at the highest bidder, leaving the wounds of the poor to fester and spread.

How much waste is built into our inefficient health-care system? We can compare our performance with that of the thirteen countries which outperformed us on infant mortality rates in 1974—the last year for which systematic comparative health expenditure data were available for the industrialized countries. Those thirteen countries spent, on average, only two thirds as much per capita on health expenditures as the United States. Applying that expenditure rate (per capita) to the United States in 1980, we would have saved 2.3 percent of the actual GNP in 1980—for a total savings of $61.1 billion in 1980.

Crime Control

Only garrison states spend as much money on criminal quarantines as we do. (There are more prisoners per one hundred people in the United States than in any other country save South Africa and the Soviet Union.)[20] There is substantial evidence that crime-control expenditures increase in the United States when problems of unemployment and social control become most threatening.[21] Total government expenditures on the crime-control establishment—on correctional, parole, and probation officers and the judiciary—began to accelerate, indeed, around 1966—exactly when the social instability induced by economic decline first began to spread.

All governments in the United States spent approximately $30 billion in 1980 on the "crime-control" system—on courts, parole, probation, and prisons (but not including police). Let us suppose that more rational economic policies had prevailed in the United States since the mid-1960s—pursuit of full employment instead of the Great Repression, economic equality instead of profiteering, community development instead of convict incarceration. If we had spent as little—in real dollars per capita—on corrections in 1980 as we had in 1966, at the beginning of economic decline, we would have saved $12.5 billion—or .5 percent of the actual 1980 GNP.

[20]*Statistical Abstract*, 1981, p. 695.

[21]This argument is most clearly formulated, although primarily in case-study form, in John Helmer, *Drugs and Minority Oppression* (New York: Seabury Press, 1975).

Advertising

Advertising has come to dominate much of our lives. Kids can sing commercial jingles before they can tie their shoes. Billboards dot the landscape. Television sales pitches shape our images of what's cool and uncool, acceptable and unacceptable, chic and ugly. Our city schools are decaying, but the talent and money devoted to ads for McDonald's and Burger King alone would be enough to support several school districts.

Advertising played a critical role in the postwar system—creating demand for products which might otherwise have suffered the fate of the Edsel. (Even heavy advertising couldn't save the Edsel!) By intensifying their advertising campaigns, many large companies diverted attention away from the need for cost reductions and quality improvements. You can't fool all of the people all of the time, of course, but many corporations hoped to tally the highest possible score. Did we need every ad?

It seems reasonable to assume that we could have survived in 1980 with the level of advertising expenditures per capita which prevailed before the frantic postwar scramble for product differentiation began. Companies devoted 2 percent of the GNP in 1980 to advertising expenditures. If they had spent as little—in real dollars per capita—as they did in 1948, we would have saved $30.7 billion—or 1.2 percent of actual 1980 GNP.

SUMMING UP THE COSTS OF CORPORATE POWER

Gross national product in 1980 was $2.6 trillion. Much of it was wasted. And much more could have been produced if we had been able to change the rules of the postwar corporate system.

We have presented a series of conservative estimates of the waste burden in the U.S. economy in 1980, relying on our index of economic effectiveness as a guide to the sources of waste. We compile the results of this exercise in Table 9-A. Each of the numbers in that table is based on the calculations reported in the text of this reading. . . . The third column in Table 9-A expresses all our estimates of waste as a percentage of *actual useful output* in 1980— that is, the actual GNP minus the wasted output estimated for category 5. We do this in order to measure potential useful output against that part of the actual output produced in 1980 which had some social value; this is the most relevant base for comparison.

Some of the individual sources of waste reported in Table 9-A seem relatively small. But they add up. According to the summary totals, useful output could have been $1.2 trillion higher in 1980 than it actually was. This means that useful output could have been 49.6 percent higher than its 1980 level.

Alternatively, suppose that we had been more interested in working fewer hours than in increasing our standards of living. The summary totals in Table 9-A provide a measure of potential leisure time as well. Translated from output into hours, they suggest that we could have enjoyed 1980 levels of useful consumption while working one third fewer hours in the aggregate, in order to produce that standard of living. Had the waste burden been lifted, the average workweek could have been reduced from 35 to 23 hours, with no loss of real consumption or investment.

The costs of corporate power in the 1980 U.S. economy were hardly negligible. We experienced a taut economy because we played by the rules of the postwar corporate system. But those rules were themselves responsible for an enormous amount of slack. We have provided conservative estimates of the resulting waste burden. If we could lift that waste burden off our shoulders, we could promote more consumption, more investment, and more free time. Any program which ignores this massive burden is accepting the straitjacket of our current economic practices.

TABLE 9-A   HOW LARGE A WASTE BURDEN IN 1980?

Components of Waste	Estimated Total Waste		
	Amount ($billions)	% of GNP	% of useful output
1. Labor utilization			
Unutilized labor hours	$ 234	8.9%	9.7%
2. Productive allocation of labor			
Surplus supervisory hours	174	6.6	7.2
3. Work intensity			
Wasted labor effort	455	17.3	18.8
4. Productive efficiency			
Utilization shortfall	45	1.7	1.8
Investment shortfall	79	3.0	3.3
5. Useful output			
Excess military spending	50	1.9	2.1
Excess energy expenditure	27	1.0	1.1
Excess food expenditure	32	1.2	1.3
Wasted health care spending	61	2.3	2.5
The crime control burden	13	0.5	0.5
Excess advertising	31	1.2	1.3
1980 Totals	$1,201	45.6%	49.6%

9.2 *The Irrational Attractions of Military Spending*

The immense military expenditures of the U.S. government—around $300 billion annually in the mid-1980s—constitute the most blatant and dangerous irrationality of capitalism. The armaments stockpiled (or used in Vietnam or elsewhere) not only represent resources wasted but more importantly threaten to annihilate rebellious peoples around the world and ultimately destroy humanity itself.

Yet military expenditures, because they are government expenditures, are often thought to result from particular *political* circumstances rather than from the institutional structure of capitalism. The high level of U.S. military expenditures is sometimes explained in terms of the external threat to national security or in terms of the quirks of domestic politics (e.g., the alliance of a few powerful southern congressmen with the Pentagon).

In response to these arguments, three points should be made. First, imperialism abroad is a natural consequence of capitalism at home, and that keeping the world open for capitalist penetration requires a substantial commitment of military strength. The threat to national security used to justify a high level of military expenditure is in part a direct consequence of the American capitalist system.

Second, military expenditures help to maintain aggregate demand. The close correlation between military expenditures and economic prosperity testifies to the importance of "defense" spending in the United States. While expenditures to maintain aggregate demand need not necessarily take the form of military expenditures, Michael Reich shows in the following reading that there are powerful forces in a capitalist system which favor such expenditures.

Finally, the military sector comprises the very heart of capitalist America. As Reich demonstrates, military expenditures benefit the largest and most powerful corporations, and their impact extends to many smaller companies as well. Thus, the role of "defense" spending is not to line the pockets of a few unscrupulous profiteers; instead, it is vital to the interests of many of the most powerful members of the U.S. capitalist class.

The following essay was written for this book by MICHAEL REICH. Copyright © 1986 by Michael Reich.

Since 1950 the U.S. government has spent well over two trillion dollars on the military, or about one-tenth of total economic output. Almost two-fifths of the federal budget feeds the "military-industrial complex." Nearly one-tenth of the labor force is engaged in military-related employment.

Why does this murderous and seemingly irrational allocation of resources occur? Why do we give the Pentagon $300 billion a year when so many basic social needs are ignored both in the United States and in the rest of the world? In this essay I will argue that the growth and persistence of a high level of military spending is a natural outcome in an advanced capitalist society that both suffers from the problem of inadequate private aggregate demand and plays a leading role in the preservation and expansion of the international capitalist system.

This perspective on military spending can best be understood by examining three more specific propositions:

Beginning in 1950, if not earlier, the United States economy was insufficiently sustained by private aggregate demand; some form of government expenditure was needed to maintain expansion.

The U.S. government turned to military spending to provide such expansion precisely because military spending provides the best means of stimulating the economy and simultaneously serving the interests of large corporations.

Federal expenditures on social welfare programs on a scale comparable to the military budget are not a feasible substitute.

Arguments in support of these propositions would advance the view that military spending is indispensable to the *domestic* economy. They would not touch on the other half of the argument—that militarism is a natural outgrowth of the international operations of American capitalism. I have not chosen to examine the second half of the argument in detail here because others have provided ample support.[1]

THE INADEQUACY OF PRIVATE DEMAND

The depression of the Thirties illustrated the incredible levels of unemployment and business lethargy the system would generate if left alone. The economy did not actually recover from the depression until World War II, when massive levels of government spending in defense created sufficient demand to alleviate unemployment. Since the war, the patterns have remained. An elaborate analysis of postwar investment demand by Bert Hickman, for example, showed that sluggish growth in the American economy from 1948 to 1963 could best be explained by a *downward* trend in business fixed investment as well as a full-employment surplus in the government budget.[2] Hickman showed, in other words, that private investment was tending to decline by itself and

that government *deficits* would be necessary to overcome these declines. Without the stimulus provided by government spending, economic growth in this period would have been substantially lower.

The government cannot supply this economic stimulation simply by lowering its taxes. While the economy can be stimulated for a time by reducing taxes and running larger deficits instead of increasing government expenditures, tax cuts cannot serve these purposes indefinitely. With government expenditures held constant, additional tax decreases have increasingly small effects on the economy. Eventually, taxes will reach such a low level that the stimulative effects of further decreases will be marginal.

So expenditures can and must play a role in stimulating the economy. Since 1950, military expenditures, averaging about 10 percent of GNP, have played this stimulative role. The fluctuation of military spending has been highly correlated with the cyclical pattern of the economy. This is largely because military expenditures play such a large role in the industries that produce capital goods—the sector of the economy that is most subject to cyclical fluctuations and is most affected by secular declines in business fixed investment. In that sector, military spending plays twice as great a role as in the economy as a whole.[3] And declines in military spending have been followed by declines in overall economic growth. This has been true at least partly because those sectors most heavily involved with the military, including the aerospace, communications, and electronics industries, have been among the fastest-growing industries in the economy in the postwar period. When military spending stagnates, the most dynamic industries will stagnate too.

[1]See MacEwan, Section 3.6, p. 107.

[2]Bert Hickman, *Investment Demand and U.S. Economic Growth* (Washington, D.C.: Brookings Institution, 1965).

[3]In 1958, 9.6 percent of total output in the economy was attributable to military spending, while in the metalworking industrial sectors (consisting of primary metals, nonelectrical machinery, electrical equipment and ordnance, and instruments and allied products) an unweighted average of 19.9 percent of output was attributable to military expenditures. See Table 9-C.

THE ATTRACTIONS
OF MILITARY SPENDING

The second proposition is that, given the necessity of some form of government expenditures, military spending provides the most convenient outlet for such expenditures. Military contracts are both easily expandable in the economy without confronting any corporate opposition and highly attractive to the firms that receive them.

Military spending is easily expandable because it adds to rather than competes with private demand. Military spending provides little competition for several reasons:

First, a convenient rationalization of the need for massive armaments expenditures exists. The ideology of anti-communism and the Cold War has been drummed into politicians and the public for thirty years and is a powerful force behind military spending. The U.S. government's role as global policeman for capitalism has reinforced this rationale.

Second, armaments are consumed rapidly or become obsolete very quickly. In southeast Asia, vast stocks of bombers were shot down, ammunition was used up or captured, and so on. The technology of advanced weapons systems becomes obsolete as fast as defense experts can think of "improvements" over existing weapons systems (or as soon as Soviet experts do). So the demand for weaponry is a bottomless pit. Moreover, the kind of machinery required for production is highly specific to particular armaments. Each time a new weapon is needed or a new process created, much existing production machinery must be scrapped. Extensive retooling involving vast new outlays is required. Since the technologies involved tend to be highly complex and exotic, much gold-plating (or rather titanium-plating) can occur; only specialists know how superfluous a particular frill is and whether a $1 billion missile would work as well as a $2 billion missile.

Third, there is no universally accepted yardstick for measuring how much defense we have or need. The public cannot recognize waste here as it would in, say, education or public housing. How do we know when an adequate level of military security is achieved? National security managers can always claim by some criteria that what we have is not enough. Terms like "missile gaps" and "nuclear parity" and "superiority" are easily juggled. Military men always have access to new "secret intelligence reports" not available to the general public. Since few people are willing to gamble with national defense, the expertise of the managers is readily accepted. Politicians and the general public have little way of adequately questioning their judgment.

These factors help explain why military spending can expand almost indefinitely. But what creates a strong preference for military spending in the first place?

To understand the sources of this pressure, we must first examine the role of defense contractors themselves. Military contracts are highly advantageous to the firms that receive them, and we can certainly expect that those corporations will push for more.

One hundred corporations receive nearly two-thirds of all prime contract awards each year, and thirty-three corporations receive 50 percent; the list of the top one hundred contractors has exhibited very little turnover in the last twenty years.[4] Prime contract awards are concentrated among just five industries: aircraft, electronics and telecommunications, shipbuilding and repairing, vehicles, and oil.[5] Moreover, subcontracts appear to be just as concentrated among the big firms.[6]

For these major beneficiaries of military spending, the rewards are high. Boondoggling

[4]W. Baldwin, *The Structure of the Defense Market, 1955-64* (Durham; Duke University Press, 1967), p. 9; *Aviation Week and Space Technology*, May 30, 1983, pp. 356–367.

[5]Research Analysis Corporation, "Economic Impact Analysis," in U.S. Congress, Joint Economic Committee, *Economic Effect of Vietnam Spending*, vol. II, 1967, p. 827; Jacques Gansler, *The Defense Industry* (Cambridge, Mass.: MIT Press, 1982), pp. 37, 40, 164.

[6]M. Peck and F. Scherer, *The Weapons Acquisition Process* (Boston: Harvard Business School, 1962), pp. 150–152; M. Weidenbaum, *The Modern Public Sector* (New York: Basic Books, 1969), p. 40.

and profiteering are endemic. Both the nature of the military "product" and the nature of the buyer-seller relationship in the military "market" foster this profiteering.

It has always been presumed that all armaments production should be carried on by private profit-seeking corporations as much as possible. Theoretically, the government, as sole buyer, would purchase from the most efficient, least-cost firms. But given the long lead times, inherent cost, and technological uncertainties in developing and producing complicated weapons systems, the government would find it difficult, to say the least, to identify in advance and reward the most efficient military contractors. In fact, of course, the Pentagon has rarely shown any interest in holding down costs or identifying efficient firms, since until recently it has not faced a real budget constraint of its own. The reality is that contractors and the Pentagon both follow the maxim of socialized risk but private profits—in C. Wright Mills' term, "socialism for the rich."

The profit incentives in military contracts reward boondoggling and waste. The Pentagon provides without charge much of the fixed and working capital for major military contracts, underwrites and subsidizes the costs of technological research and development for firms that engage in civilian as well as military production, and negotiates (and when necessary, renegotiates) cost-plus contracts that virtually guarantee the contractors against any losses. Military spending is supposed to take place competitively, but in fact it almost never does. Any number of excuses may justify the relaxation of competitive procedures. Of the Pentagon's contract dollars, 90 percent are negotiated under such "exceptions." That is why the Pentagon was discovered in 1984 to be paying $436 for a $7 hammer, $1.36 for a one cent washer.[7]

Because of the special relationship between the Pentagon and the defense corporations, cost overruns are permitted. Final costs average 320 percent of original cost estimates.[8] The average contractor, in other words, ends up charging the government over three times the cost estimate he initially submitted to "win" the contract. And because most contracts are on a cost-plus basis, his profits go up by 300 percent as well.

Companies do not lose their privileged status if their weapons do not meet specifications or perform properly. According to one study,[9] of thirteen major aircraft and missile programs since 1955 which cost $40 billion, only four (costing $5 billion) performed at as much as 75 percent of the design specifications. Yet the companies with the poorest performance records reported the highest profits.

As a result, in 1980 profits for defense work were higher than those in all but two other industries. And in 1984 the profit rates of the ten largest military contractors, according to a Census Bureau study, reached 25 percent, double the profit rate of all manufacturing corporations that year.[10] This is obscured by the Defense Department, which sometimes releases profits computed as a percentage of sales or costs. But, in the normal business world, profits are figured as a percentage of *investment*. Defense contractors invest very little of their own money, because in most cases the government provides most of the investment and working capital needed to set up plants and machinery and to buy the necessary materials and parts. The profits when measured against investment are often huge.

Murray Weidenbaum, formerly an economist for the Boeing Company and chair of the Council of Economic Advisors under President Reagan, studied a sample of large defense contractors. He found that in 1962 and 1963

[7]U.S. Congress, Joint Economic Committee Print, *The Economics of Military Procurement* (Washington, D.C.: U.S. Government Printing Office, 1969), p. 4; Gansler, p. 297; *Congressional Quarterly*, March 24, 1984, p. 671.

[8]Peck and Scherer, *The Weapons Acquisition Process*; Gansler, pp. 90–91.

[9]*The Economics of Military Procurement*, p. 1. See also Mary Kaldor, *The Baroque Arsenal* (New York: Hill and Wang, 1981).

[10]*Forbes*, 5 January 1981; New York Times, 4 April 1985.

they earned 17.5 percent on investment, compared to average civilian market earnings of 10.6 percent. And this probably understates the case. Many military contractors also sell in the civilian market. The machinery provided free by the Pentagon, the allocation of all overhead costs to military contracts, and the technological edge gained in cost-plus military contracts can be of enormous importance in increasing profits on civilian sales for firms doing some business with the Pentagon. In one of the most outrageous cases that has come to light, a tax count showed in 1962 that North American Aviation Company had realized profits of 612 percent and 802 percent on its investment in "military" contracts in two successive years.[11] With these profits and privileges, it seems clear, defense contractors have every reason to push for as much military spending as possible.

Yet the popular press sometimes conveys the view that defense firms are few—an economic enclave somehow isolated from the rest of the economy. And there is superficial evidence for the enclave view. As I noted above, fifty corporations receive 60 percent of prime contract awards. Prime contracts are concentrated in just five industries. Subcontracts appear to be just as concentrated among the big firms.

But this enclave image is highly misleading. First, a list of the top military contractors is virtually identical with a list of all the largest and most powerful industrial corporations in America (see Table 9-B). Nathanson estimates that of the 500 largest manufacturing corporations in 1964, at least 205 were significantly involved in military contracts, either in production or in research and development.[12] Among the top 100 firms, 65 are significantly involved in the military market. As Table 9-B

shows, all but five of the twenty-five largest industrial corporations in 1982 were among the 90 largest contractors for the Defense Department. Of these five, three are oil companies indirectly involved in military sales and one is a steel company also indirectly involved. It is difficult to think of these top corporations as constituting an "enclave."

Second, there are no self-contained enclaves in the American economy. As the study of input-output economics has revealed, the structure of American industry is highly interdependent. Focusing only on the prime contractors is like looking at only the visible part of an iceberg. This represents only the direct impact of the military budget. The indirect impact on subcontractors, on producers of intermediate goods and parts, and on suppliers of raw materials ties military spending into the heart of the economy.

Third, corporations in the civilian market have been competing to get a piece of the military action. A study of the years between 1959 and 1962 indicates that "manufacturing firms outside the defense sector purchased 137 companies in the defense sector (i.e., aircraft and parts, ships and boats, ordnance, electrical machinery, scientific instruments and computers)." By 1966, of the top 500 manufacturing firms 93 had diversified into the defense sector from a traditional nondefense base.[13]

Military spending is very important for a large number of manufacturing industries. As Table 9-C shows, about 11.5 percent of all manufacturing output as early as 1958 was attributable to military-related expenditures; the corresponding figure is 20 percent for the metalworking production sector, comprised of metals and metal products, nonelectrical machinery, electrical equipment and supplies, transportation equipment, ordnance, and instruments. The percentage of profits attributable to military spending is probably even higher, given that profit rates are higher on military contracts.

---

[11]Murray Weidenbaum, "Arms and the American Economy," *American Economic Review* (May 1968), p. 56. R. F. Kaufman, *The War Profiteers* (Indianapolis: Bobbs-Merrill, 1970).

[12]C. Nathanson, "The Militarization of the American Economy," in D. Horowitz, ed., *Corporations and the Cold War* (New York: Monthly Review Press, 1969), p. 231.

[13]Ibid., pp. 215–16.

TABLE 9-B   MILITARY CONTRACTORS IN THE AMERICAN ECONOMY, 1982

Top Pentagon Contractors (fiscal year 1982)		Top Industrial Corporations (1982)	
1. General Dynamics	(46)[a]	1. Exxon	(23)[b]
2. McDonnell Douglas	(43)	2. General Motors	(26)
3. United Technologies	(20)	3. Mobil	(64)
4. General Electric	(11)	4. Texaco	(88)
5. Lockheed	(56)	5. Ford Motor	(20)
6. Boeing	(34)	6. IBM	(17)
7. Hughes Aircraft	c	7. Standard Oil of California	(31)
8. Rockwell International	(42)	8. E. I. du Pont de Nemours	(50)
9. Raytheon	(58)	9. Gulf Oil	(71)
10. Martin Marietta	(108)	10. Standard Oil (Indiana)	(52)
11. Grumman	(177)	11. General Electric	(4)
12. Northrop	(158)	12. Atlantic Richfield	(62)
13. Westinghouse Electric	(31)	13. Shell Oil	(51)
14. FMC	(111)	14. U.S. Steel	—
15. Litton Industries	(68)	15. Occidental Petroleum	—
16. Honeywell	(59)	16. ITT	(40)
17. IBM	(6)	17. Phillips Petroleum	—
18. Sperry	(57)	18. Sun	(76)
19. RCA	(44)[d]	19. Tenneco	(22)
20. Ford Motor	(5)	20. United Technologies	(3)
21. TRW	(66)	21. Standard Oil (Ohio)	—
22. Tenneco	(19)	22. Western Electric (AT&T)	(25)[f]
23. Exxon	(1)	23. Procter & Gamble	—
24. Texas Instruments	(79)	24. Getty Oil	(90)
25. AT&T (Western Electric)	(22)[e]	25. R. V. Reynolds Industries	(59)

[a]Number in parentheses indicates rank in *Fortune* list of 500 largest corporations.

[b]Number in parentheses indicates rank among largest 100 Department of Defense contractors.

[c]Not included in *Fortune* 500 list because shares are not publicly traded on a stock exchange.

[d]Ranking from 1982 *Fortune* 500.

[e]Ranking for Western Electric, a wholly owned subsidiary of AT&T.

[f]Ranking for AT&T.

Sources: *Fortune Magazine*, May 2, 1983, and *Aviation Week and Space Technology*, May 30, 1983.

Another important feature is the increasing concentration produced by military spending within industry. Almost all of military spending goes to the most concentrated industries in the economy. The standard measure of concentration in an industry is the percentage of sales accounted for by the top four firms. Industries in which four firms monopolized over 50 percent of the sales accounted for about one-quarter of all sales by manufacturing industries in 1958. But 90 percent of all military contracts go to these most concentrated industries. Certainly, an expenditure program that

benefits 20 of the top 25 corporations and contributes to the concentration of economic power among the corporate giants is going to enjoy a political power base that lies deep in the heart of the U.S. economy.

Military spending has also created privileged interest groups within the occupational structure—an important factor that ties to government policy many professional people, university administrators, and labor union leaders. A large number of the most highly trained people in the economy owe their jobs to defense spending. For example, nearly half of all engineers and scientists employed in private industry are at work on military or space-related projects. Many of the scientists and engineers pursuing research in the universities receive money from the Pentagon.

The military industries generally employ a highly skilled work force. A 1962 Department of Labor study of the electronics industry showed that at military-space-oriented plants 59.2 percent of employees were highly paid engineers, executives, or skilled blue-collar craftsmen. In the consumer-oriented plants of the same electronics industry, in contrast, 70.2 percent of the employees were semiskilled and unskilled blue- and white-collar workers.[14] Professional and managerial workers comprise 22 percent of all private defense-related employment, but only 15 percent of all U.S. manufacturing employment.[15] Thus, a large proportion of the people in the most educated strata, many still university-based, are tied by military spending to a vested interest in existing national priorities. A large number of blue-collar workers are engaged in military-related work. The carrot the government can dangle in front of major union leaders has been a factor in their growing conservatism and endorsement of Cold War policies.

Military spending has a regressive impact on the distribution of income within the U.S. —that is, it benefits the rich and hurts the poor. This is suggested by the higher proportion of professional and skilled workers in defense-related work. Computations by economist Wassily Leontief show that one dollar of military spending generates half as many jobs, but 20 percent more in salaries, than does one dollar of civilian spending.[16] This means that tax money extracted from the whole population is paid out in such a way as to benefit high earners much more than low earners. Perhaps by accident, or perhaps by design, military spending is one of the mechanisms by which higher income groups use the government to prevent redistribution of income from taking place.

So military spending is easily expandable, is highly profitable, and benefits the major corporations in the economy. These factors combine to ensure that major corporations will push for military spending and that opponents will have little strength to resist its expansion. The same cannot be said for the nonmilitary sector.

TABLE 9-C   DIRECT AND INDIRECT DEPENDENCE OF INDUSTRIAL SECTORS ON MILITARY EXPENDITURES, 1958

Sector	Percent of Total Output Attributable to Military
1. Food and kindred products	1.6
2. Apparel and textile mill products	1.9
3. Leather products	3.1
4. Paper and allied products	7.0
5. Chemicals and allied products	5.3
6. Fuel and power	7.3
7. Rubber and rubber products	5.6
8. Lumber and wood products	3.9
9. Nonmetallic minerals and products	4.7
10. Primary metals	13.4
11. Fabricated metal products	8.0
12. Machinery, except electrical	5.2
13. Electrical equipment and supplies	20.8
14. Transportation equipment and ordnance	38.4
15. Instruments and allied products	20.0
16. Misc. manufacturing industries	2.8
17. Transportation	5.9
18. Construction	2.1
Average, metalworking industries (Sectors 10–15)	19.9
Average, all manufacturing (Sectors 1–16)	11.5
Average, (Sectors 1–18)	9.6

Source: Computed from Wassily Leontief and P. B. Hoffenberg, "The Economic Impact of Disarmament," *Scientific American* (April 1961).

[14]Bureau of Labor Statistics *Bulletin* (October 1963), p. 37.

[15]*Monthly Labor Review* (May 1964), p. 514. The same pattern was evident in the 1980s. See Robert DeGrasse, Jr., *Military Expansion, Economic Decline* (M. E. Sharpe, 1983).

[16]From W. Leontief and M. Hoffenberg, "The Economic Impact of Disarmament," *Scientific American*, 9 (April 1961); and Leontief et al., "The Economic Effect—Industrial and Regional—of an Arms Cut," *Review of Economics and Statistics* (August 1965).

THE OPPOSITION TO SOCIAL SERVICE EXPENDITURES

The last of my three major propositions was that federal spending on socially useful needs on a scale comparable to the military budget is not a feasible substitute. Social services spending is unlikely to be as profitable and expandable as is military spending. Social expenditures have never had the blank check that the military until recently has enjoyed.

Many kinds of social spending put the government in direct competition with particular industries and with the private sector as a whole. This goes against the logic of a capitalist economy. For example, government production of low-cost housing in large amounts would substantially reduce profits of private builders and landlords who own the existing housing stock. The supply of housing would be increased, and land would be taken away from private developers who want to use it for commercial gain. Similarly, building *effective* mass public transportation would compete with the automobile interests.

Any one of these interests taken by itself might not be sufficient to put insurmountable obstacles in the way of social spending. Most social service programs affect only one particular set of interests in the private economy. But there are so many forms of potential interference. Each of the vested interests is explicitly aware of this problem and each works to help the others. They adopt a general social ideology that says that too much social spending is dangerous and that governmental noninterference is good.

Furthermore, the capitalist system as a whole is threatened by massive governmental social spending because the very necessity of private ownership and control over production is inevitably called into question. The basic assumption in any capitalist society that goods and services should be produced by private enterprise according to criteria of market profitability thus also fuels the general ideology limiting social spending. This limits the satisfaction of collective needs, such as clean air and water and esthetic city planning, that cannot be expressed in market terms as demand for individually saleable commodities.

Massive social spending also tends to upset the labor market, one of the essential institutions of a capitalist economy. Public expenditures on an adequate welfare program would make it difficult for employers to get workers. If the government provided adequate nonwage income without stigma to recipients, many workers would drop out of the labor force rather than take low-paying and unpleasant jobs. Those who stayed at jobs would be less likely to put up with demeaning working conditions. The whole basis of the capitalist labor market is that workers have no legitimate income source other than the sale of their labor power, and capitalist ideology has long made it a cardinal rule that government should not interfere with this incentive to work. Powerful political forces thus operate to insure that direct income subsidization at adequate levels does not come into being.

Finally, good social services, since they have given people some security, comfort, and satisfaction—that is, have fulfilled real needs—interfere with the market in consumer goods. Corporations can only sell goods to people by playing on their unsatisfied needs and yearnings. New needs are constantly being artificially created: the need for a sporty new car to enhance one's status, the need for new cosmetics to build one's sex appeal, and so on. These needs are based on people's fears, anxieties and dissatisfactions that are continually pandered to by the commercial world. But if people's needs were being more adequately fulfilled by the public sector—if they had access to adequate housing, effective transportation, good schools, and good health care—they would be much less prey to the appeals of the commercial hucksters. These forms of collective consumption would have interfered with the demand for consumer products in the private market.

Military spending is acceptable to all corporate interests. It does not interfere with existing areas for profit-making, it does not undermine the labor market, it does not challenge the class structure, and it does not produce income redistribution. Social spending does all these things and thus faces obstacles for its own expansion.

I do not mean to imply by the above analysis that a capitalist economy has not and will not provide any basic social services through government expenditures. Some social overhead investment is obviously important and necessary for the smooth functioning of any economy, and the provision of local and national public goods has always been considered a proper activity for capitalist governments. For example, expenditures on education, highways, and transportation are obviously necessary to provide workers and to get them to the point of production; such expenditures are motivated by the needs of production and only incidentally to fill human needs. In fact, most state and local government expenditures have been directed to these basic infrastructural needs.

In recent decades production has become, as Marx put it, more social in character: the economy has become much more complex, more interdependent, more urbanized, more in need of educated labor. The recent increase in state and local expenditures can be explained by these increases in the social costs of production. Expenditures for such needs would be consistent with and are often necessary for private profitability.

Moreover, state and local expenditures are not motivated by the need to stimulate aggregate demand, for only the Federal government is concerned with maintaining aggregate demand. But nonmilitary federal purchases have barely, if at all, increased as a percentage of GNP since the thirties. Nonmilitary federal purchases of goods and services were only 2.4 percent of GNP in 1984. By contrast, nonmilitary federal purchases as a percent of GNP were 4.6 percent in 1938, 1.9 percent in 1954, and 2.5 percent in 1964.[17] Thus it cannot be said that the federal government has significantly turned to social services expenditures and away from military expenditures to meet the problem of inadequate aggregate demand.

In short, there are important obstacles to government spending for social needs. And the recent record reflects those obstacles; the government has not been spending money on those needs.

CONCLUSION

Is military spending really necessary to capitalism? I have framed the answer to this question in the following way. A capitalist economy with inadequate aggregate demand is much more likely to turn to military than social spending because military spending is more consistent with private profit and the social relations of production under capitalism. If this military outlet were blocked—by massive public opposition, for instance—it is certainly possible that a capitalist economy might be able to accommodate, transforming itself instead of commiting suicide. But that kind of reasoning misses the point. Military spending is favored by corporate powers and is likely to be defended with considerable vigor. As long as there are easy profits available through military spending, capitalists will turn to them.

---

[17]Calculated from *Economic Report of the President, 1985,* table B-1 (Washington D.C.: U.S. Government Printing Office, 1985).

9.3   *The Source of Militarism*

In the last reading we saw that military spending holds many attractions to corporations. But the military budget and the militaristic priorities of the United States stem from a variety of domestic and international sources. Tom Riddell surveys these in the following reading.

Excerpted from TOM RIDDELL, "Militarism: The Other Side of Supply," *Economic Forum*, Spring 1982. Reprinted by permission of the publisher.

Shortly after assuming the reins of the U.S. Government, the Reagan Administration unveiled its spending plans for one of the largest military buildups in U.S. history. In March of 1981, Secretary of Defense Caspar Weinberger outlined revisions in the defense budget for Fiscal Years 1981 and 1982, and the proposals for Fiscal Years 1983 to 1986. For this six year period, more than $1.6 trillion in total obligational authority was requested; while actual outlays for defense would amount to just under $1.5 trillion. The average annual increase in budget authority in real terms was projected to be 9.2 percent and the real annual growth rate for outlays was 8.4 percent. Department of Defense outlays as a percentage of GNP would increase from 5.7 percent to 7.1 percent. This massive outpouring of funds would finance a substantial increase in America's military forces—both conventional and strategic. Weapons procurement, research and development, and the salaries of military personnel will all expand. This means more aircraft, tanks and tactical missiles will be produced by U.S. military contractors. The Naval fleet is scheduled for a 33 percent expansion from 450 ships to 600 ships. The new Rapid Deployment Force will continue to be developed with forward supply bases in Oman, Kenya, Diego Garcia and possibly Somalia. In strategic forces, the Reagan Administration will produce neutron bombs, more cruise missiles and Pershing missiles for possible deployment in Europe. The Administration plans to fund accelerated research and development of a new manned bomber, an MX system, an improved Trident submarine and missile, and a renovated worldwide command and control system. There are also plans to add service personnel to the Army, Air Force and Navy.

This rearmament program raises several interesting questions which I will try to address in this paper: for example what is the political-economic context in which this buildup is taking place?; why is military spending so high in the U.S., or why is the U.S. militaristic?; what is the relationship between the Reagan economic recovery program and U.S. militarism, or why a buildup now?; are there inherent contradictions in this massive arms escalation, and what are they? and, finally, what are the political implications for progressive forces in the U.S.?

THE EVOLUTION AND LOGIC OF U.S. MILITARISM

From 1946 through 1979, the U.S. spent more than $2 trillion for national defense.[1] During that period of time, the Department of Defense (and the War Department before it) took responsibility for creating a worldwide military establishment and a vast conventional and nuclear arsenal. Following the post–World War II demobilization and the creation of a national security apparatus within the U.S. government, the U.S. embarked on a project to construct a permanent military establishment with centralized control under the direction of the Pentagon. This project consisted of a system of military contracting, military assistance programs, a conscription system, military bases all over the U.S. and the world, and occasionally the use of U.S. military forces in wars and armed interventions.

There are a variety of explanations for this massive arms buildup and each one of them has some merit. However, each one taken by itself is also insufficient as an explanation for

[1] In my discussions of military spending, I am using budgets for the Department of Defense. It is widely acknowledged that this figure understates the use of governmental resources for military purposes. For a more complete estimate, veterans' benefits, at least half the interest on the national debt (from past wars), the weapons portion of the Department of Energy budget, some forms of military assistance, etc., could be added. For more on this point see J.M. Cypher, "Capitalist Planning and Military Expenditures," *Review of Radical Political Economics 6* (Fall 1974), pp. 1–19.

the complex emergence, functioning and history of U.S. post-war militarism. Conservatives, while not usually calling it militarism, tend to reduce it to the "Soviet threat" and the need to preserve the "free world." Liberals also focus on the Soviet threat, but usually add that there is a need for power to protect human rights and democracy. Liberals are more likely to be concerned about limiting U.S. military power and demonstrate a sensitivity to its costs. What I want to concentrate on in the following discussion, however, are the more critical perspectives on U.S. militarism and its role in American capitalism. I will review four different theories of the high level of military spending in the U.S. since World War II. They have been developed by liberals, radicals and Marxists, for the most part, from positions outside of the National Security State. Two of the explanations focus on international political-military-economic considerations; the need to contain, deter and counter the Soviet Union and, secondly, the attempt to extend American dominance over the international trading and financial system. The other two focus on domestic considerations; military spending as a method of stabilizing the economy and the military-industrial complex's interests in, and benefits from military spending. I will argue that all four of these taken together provide a powerful framework for understanding and explaining the emergence, history and functioning of U.S. militarism. This perspective should then also help us to understand the current military buildup as part of the Reagan Administration's economic policies.

1. An Explanation of the Rise of U.S. Militarism in the Post–World War II Era

I have suggested above that four of the usual arguments offered to explain the existence of American militarism if taken together provide a powerful framework for understanding the emergence and history of sustained high levels of military spending. In this section I will demonstrate that the events of the immediate post–World War II period support my argument. In addition, I will refer to instances in which all of the arguments for increased military spending were utilized by policy-makers to justify the military buildup in the early 1950s. The principal point is that the militarization of American foreign policy following the Depression and World War II was perfectly consistent with the requirements for capital accumulation in American capitalism. I do not want to argue that U.S. militarism by itself would assure smooth capitalist growth. Nor do I suggest that the huge commitment of resources to the militarization of the U.S. was without contradiction. Rather, I want to argue that the emergence of an expanded military establishment here in the U.S. and abroad had a certain logic to it in support of the capital accumulation process in the late 1940s and early 1950s.

By the mid-twentieth century the U.S was an international economic, political and military power. It was involved all over the world in trade, mining and industrial production. It had also recently gone through the Great Depression. American capitalists and the U.S. Government were interested in protecting their international activities. They were also interested in the possibilities of expanding international activities—both in search of raw materials such as oil, and markets for U.S. goods. At home, the U.S. had just learned that militarism was a way out of depression. On the other hand, the power and the ambition of the Soviet Union posed a potential threat to existing and possible U.S. interests. In addition, the Soviet Union presented a social, political and economic reality as an alternative to capitalism; in fact, it preferred the alternative to the rest of the world. From this confluence of concerns, during the last 1940s and early 1950s, the U.S. progressively militarized its foreign policy in pursuit of its interests and goals in the world at large—in the Middle East, Western Europe, Asia, Latin America and Africa. Its military power at the end of the war had given it dominance in all of these spheres. Expanding and making permanent the American military establishment as a mechanism for preserving U.S. hegemony and its benefits was seen as necessary, and was eventually ratified in legislation. American militarism emerged in defense of American imperialism.

The articulation of these goals and interests and the development of policies directed toward their fulfillment can be seen forcefully in the history surrounding a National Security Council document produced in January 1950 called NSC-68.[2] This internal document was top secret and was first published in 1975 by the State Department. It focused on the increasing threat from the Soviet Union and the possible neutralization of Western Europe. It further suggested a host of policies to contain the Soviet Union and to retain Western Europe clearly in the U.S. orbit. In addition, NSC-68 recommended several tactics to be utilized in developing public opinion in support of its policy suggestions. Later that year the Korean War began. Within 18 months most of the recommendations of NSC-68 had been officially enacted through legislation. The military budget was increased dramatically. Some of the budget was allocated to finance the U.S. involvement in the Korean War. But it also financed the sending of almost 100,000 American troops to Western Europe and the creation of a Mutual Security Agency to administer increased and consolidated foreign and military aid to Western Europe. Jerry Sanders has concluded that NSC-68 and the decisions to expand the military in the early 1950s

> ... marked the transformation of the postwar policy of Containment from a 'balanced doctrine' projecting economic, political, and military power (in roughly that order), to one of

Containment Militarism, which called for the primacy of military force and the threat of its use to achieve the economic as well as the political goals of American foreign policy.[3]

In what follows, I will refer to some of the arguments used by those who drafted NSC-68 to illustrate their concerns and goals for U.S. foreign policy as well as their vision of the solutions to policy problems. In addition, I will also refer to the concerns of other administration officials in the formation of foreign and military policy outside of NSC-68. These will be organized into the four different arguments concerning the permanent militarization of American society. All were present in the policy debates at the time and were contained in the logic of increased militarization.

2. The Soviet Threat

The Soviet threat justifies large amounts of military spending in a variety of ways. The Soviet Union represents a hostile force and ideology to capitalism and Western notions of democracy. Given that it is perceived as an enemy, any time that it advances its own political interests or adds to its own military arsenal, then there is an argument that the U.S. needs to respond in kind or move to prevent the Soviet Union from going a step further. This is seen most powerfully in the arms race. In the early 1950s, the combination of Soviet influence in Eastern Europe, the detonation of its own atom bomb and finally, its involvement in the Korean War, provided ample ammunition for the use of the Soviet threat argument to bolster the defenses of the United States. Of course, there is also always room for exaggeration in interpreting the power and the influence of the Soviet Union. On the other hand, Soviet support for left politics in Europe and for liberation movements in other parts of the world has quite consistently worried American capitalists and foreign policymakers concerned about easy access to those areas. . . .

---

[2]Two recent treatments of this document and its history are: Fred Block, "Economic Instability and Military Strength: The Paradoxes of the 1950 Rearmament Decision," *Politics and Society 1* (1980), pp. 35–58; and Jerry Sanders, "Shaping the Cold War Consensus: The Soviet Threat, Interelite Conflict, and Mass Politics in the Korean War Era," *Berkeley Journal of Sociology 25* (1980), pp. 67–136.

[3]Sanders, "Shaping the Cold War Consensus," p. 73.

In this view, it is pretty clear that Americans are the "good guys," the Soviets are the "bad guys," and we need to be well armed to protect our way of life for ourselves and for others from the forces of evil. This perspective also found its way into the opening passages of NSC-68:

> ... the Soviet Union, unlike previous aspirants to hegemony, is animated by a new fanatic faith, antithetical to our own, and seeks to impose its absolute authority over the rest of the world. Conflict has, therefore, become endemic and is waged, on the part of the Soviet Union, by violent or non-violent methods in accordance with the dictates of expediency.... Any substantial further extension of the area under the domination of the Kremlin would raise the possibility that no coalition adequate to confront the Kremlin with greater strength could be assembled. It is in this context that this Republic and its citizens in the ascendancy of their strength stand in their greatest peril.[4]

In its conclusion, NSC-68 returns to this theme:

> The whole success of the proposed program hangs ultimately on the recognition by this Government, the American people, and all free people, that the cold war is in fact a real war in which the survival of the free world is at stake.[5]

In the late 1940s with the beginning of the Cold War, it was necessary, as Senator Vandenburg stated, to "scare the hell out of the country" in order to convince the American people that this somewhat apocalyptic view of the world was accurate.[6] Or as Acheson confessed concerning his efforts in 1950 to convince the public of the need for another round of military buildup:

> Qualification must give way to simplicity of statement, variety and nuance to bluntness, al-

most brutality in carrying home a point.... Points to be understandable had to be clear. If we made our points clearer than the truth, we could hardly do otherwise.[7]

Having made the threat "clearer than the truth," it was a simple step to suggest the remedy of increased militarization.

. . . .

3. Stabilizing the International Economy, Trade and Finance

American foreign and military policy in the post–World War II period was very much concerned with the health and stability of the international system—also known as the "free world"—and with American leadership of it. As William Appleman Williams has put it, American diplomacy in this century has always been based on the notion that "America's domestic well-being depends upon sustained, ever-increasing economic expansion."[8] Economic expansion has always been accompanied by and assisted by the development and the use of American power....

The economic logic behind the usurpation of worldwide political and military power and dominance at the time was suggested by then-Assistant Secretary of State Dean Acheson in 1944 to the Select Committee on Postwar Economic Policy and Planning:

> It seems clear that we are in for a very bad time, so far as the economic and social position of the country is concerned. We cannot go through another ten years like the ten years at the end of the twenties and the beginning of the thirties without having the most far-reaching consequences upon our economic and social system.... When we look at that problem we may say it is a problem of markets. You don't have a problem of production. The United States has unlimited creative energy. The important thing is markets. We have to see that what the country produces is used and is sold under financial arrangements which make its production possi-

---

[4]NSC-68 quoted in Block, "Economic Instability and Military Strength," p. 40.

[5]*Ibid.*, p. 40.

[6]Quoted in Borosage, "The Making of the National Security State," p. 45.

[7]*Ibid.*, p. 46.

[8]William Appleman Williams, *The Tragedy of American Diplomacy* (New York: Dell, 1959) p. 11.

ble.... You must look to foreign markets. The ... theory that I want to bring out is that we need these markets for the output of the United States. If I am wrong about that, then all the argument falls by the wayside, but my contention is that we cannot have full employment and prosperity in the United States without foreign markets.[9]

In other words, expansion is necessary, expansion into foreign markets is also necessary, and, if it is to be profitable, it must take place under favorable conditions. This concern was consistently pursued in the construction of numerous post war institutions directed toward creating a stable international environment with U.S. leadership (dominance). These institutions included the International Monetary Fund, the International Bank for Reconstruction and Development, the United Nations, the General Agreement on Trade and Tariffs, the North Atlantic Treaty Organization, among others.

Following the war, the U.S. was concerned about the economic health of Western Europe and its economic relationships with those countries. It was also concerned about the possibility of Europe assuming a neutralist stance between the U.S. and U.S.S.R. or even worse, the coming to political power of Socialist or Communist parties. The Marshall Plan of the late 1940s was directed toward rebuilding the capitalist economies of Western Europe, as well as providing direct business for American corporations through U.S. exports now that Europe had purchasing power, and more vigorous markets later on for industrial and consumer exports from the United States. To a marked degree, the Marshall Plan was successful. However, by 1949–1950, it became clear that the U.S. would have to supplement the Marshall Plan (due to expire in 1951) in order to address the dollar shortage in Europe, to prevent Europe from turning to the left or from pursuing neutralist policies, and to continue to build the hoped-for close integration

of the U.S. and Western European political-military-economic alliance. The solution to this problem was outlined in NSC-68 and involved a massive infusion of dollars into Europe in support of the mobilization of NATO—both for U.S. troops to be stationed in Europe and for military assistance to build up the arsenals of Western Europe. In the U.S., there was opposition to this strategy of financing the reconstruction of Europe throughout the postwar period from isolationists and from those who thought that the real danger was in Asia, not Europe. But the Soviet threat and the focus on the military solution won the day. As Fred Block suggested:

> Congressional resistance to what was widely perceived as a giveaway of U.S. dollars was only overcome through the deliberate creation and exaggeration of Cold War tensions by the Truman administration.[10]

In other words, the Soviet threat provided the justification of the military solution to the problem of holding on to Western Europe. The rearmament program of NSC-68, then, addressed both the Soviet threat and the desire to create an international system conducive to the capital accumulation needs of American capitalism. As NSC-68 put it:

> ... pressure [away from American hegemony] might come from our present allies, who will tend to seek other solutions unless they have confidence in our determination to accelerate our efforts to build a successfully functioning political and economic system in the free world.[11]

. . .

... The result was a continuing militarization of American foreign policy and an escalation of the Cold War rhetoric. In bureaucratic terms, it resulted in what former Secretary of Defense James Forrestal called:

> ... the formal legal coordination between the framers of foreign policy and the formulators

---

[9]Quoted in Block, "Economic Insecurity and Military Strength," pp. 38–39; and Borosage, "The Making of the National Security State," p. 4.

[10]Block, p. 43. Block's discussion of the economic concerns of the U.S. and the military policy solutions is excellent.

[11]Sanders, "Shaping the Cold War Consensus," pp. 77–78.

of military policy . . . and the thorough integration of our foreign policy with our military policy.[12]

It also produced the military buildup, in the form of a vast expansion of U.S. forces abroad and in the U.S. conventional and strategic forces, to allow the U.S. to pursue foreign policy objectives through what Acheson called "negotiation from strength." These international concerns, and their linkage to the health and power of the U.S., provided a powerful drive to U.S. militarism. But there were also some very direct connections made between military spending and the domestic economy.

4. Economic Stabilization and Military Spending

It was recognized by U.S. policy-makers that increased military spending at home and in Europe would have stimulative effects on Western economies. From the historical perspective of the Great Depression, this was not an unimportant result. And this position was included in NSC-68:

> . . . there are grounds for predicting that the United States and other free nations will within a period of a few years at most experience a decline in economic activity of serious proportions unless more positive governmental programs are developed than are now available. With a high level of economic activity, the United States could soon attain a GNP of $300 billion per year, as was pointed out in the President's Economic Report (January 1950). Progress in this direction would permit, and might itself be aided by, a build-up of the economic and military strength of the United States and the free world; furthermore, if a dynamic expansion of the economy were achieved, the necessary build-up could be accomplished without a decrease in the national standard of living because the required resources could be attained by siphoning off a part of the annual increment in the GNP.[13]

The principles of what has been called "military Keynesianism" had been noted by the Defense Department in its annual report in 1948: ". . . special measures were also taken to promote the President's program to stimulate industry in areas where unemployment exceeded 12 percent of the estimated labor force. The measures included the placement of military contracts in those areas wherever practicable."[14] With respect to the plans of NSC-68 for increased military spending by the U.S. for weapons produced in Europe, former Assistant Secretary of the Army and Committee on the Present Danger member, Tracy Voorhees, noted that: "Under the plan herein proposed, increased military production would also assist in sustaining the Western European economy by providing a market which it needs."[15]

The argument was not that military spending, per se, was necessary to prevent the recurrence of depression in the West, but rather that military spending would provide one convenient prop to aggregate demand in the context of an over-all commitment to stabilizing the economy. As we have seen, it was also not the only reason for increased military spending.

5. The Interests of the Military-Industrial Complex

It is obvious that some sectors of the economy, specific corporations and areas of the country, will stand to directly benefit from increased military spending. These institutions will tend to support militarization and a permanent military establishment. As H. L. Nieburg has written:

> . . . the increased flow of military expenditures into narrow areas of the economy tends to create a self-perpetuating coalition of vested interests. With vast public funds at hand, industries, geographical regions, labor unions, and the multitude of supporting enterprise band to-

[12]Forrestal quoted in Borosage, "The Making of the National Security State," p. 13.
[13]Quoted in Block, "Economic Insecurity and Military Strength," p. 47.

[14]Quoted in Borosage, "The Making of the National Security State," p. 31.
[15]Quoted in Sanders, "Shaping the Cold War Consensus," p. 77.

gether with enormous manpower, facilities, and Washington contacts to maintain and expand their stake.[16]

This is viewed as one of the fundamental aspects of the development of permanent military establishment by one of its key architects, James Forrestal:

> [The National Security Act of 1947] provides for the co-ordination of the three armed services, but what is to me even more important . . . , it provides for the integration of foreign policy with national policy, of our civilian economy with military requirements; it provides for . . . continual advances in the field of research and applied science.[17]

In 1944 Forrestal had created the National Security Industrial Association to make sure that "American business would stay close to the services."

Most of the large industrial corporations in the U.S. are, and were, involved in military production. As a result, they participated in the construction of the military establishment and in the debate surrounding its creation. As John Kenneth Galbraith has concluded, ". . . the industrial system helps win belief for the image of implacable confict that justifies its need."[18] This principle was also at work in the creation of the public support as well as the planning around the implementation of NSC-68. . . .

In this section, I have attempted to argue that there are a variety of reasons for the high level of military spending in the United States. It is a combination of the four reasons often cited—the Soviet threat, international expansion, military Keynesianism, and the military-industrial complex. Military spending is *one* support of the international and domestic requirements of capital accumulation: it is a necessary, but not sufficient, support. This view incorporates insights from each of the four usual arguments but is superior because each one by itself suffers from incompleteness. This perspective on American militarism should help us to understand its emergence and persistence. I think that it also sheds light on the current efforts to rekindle the Cold War and rearm American militarism.

MILITARISM, SUPPLY-SIDE ECONOMICS AND THE REAGAN RECOVERY PROGRAM—OR, WHY A BUILD-UP NOW?

The current military buildup takes place within a particular context—that of an economic crisis and efforts to deal with it. The rearmament program is a part of the overall attempt by the Reagan Administration to restore U.S. prosperity. As Casper Weinberger has said in presenting the military budget projections for the next five years to Congress, ". . . it is the second half of the Administration's program to revitalize America." In this section I will examine the ways in which a renewed military buildup is intended to revitalize U.S. capitalism.

Increased military spending will stimulate certain key sectors and areas of the economy—notably the high tech industry, as well as the traditional military sectors, and the Sunbelt. But, more importantly, the rekindling of the Cold War is an effort to regain the American political-economic-military power that was a key part of the success of U.S. post war prosperity. Containing and dominating the Soviet Union, Western Europe, Japan and the Third World "paid off." With the loss of U.S. power came increased difficulties for U.S. capitalism. Our allies were less cooperative and manipulable, the power of the Soviet Union and its assistance to national independence movements made the economic environment of the free world less certain; even Western access to the Middle Eastern oil field became questionable. With renewed power, presumably, the U.S. will not be bullied about, will be respected more, and will be able to get its way more often on favorable terms (i.e., to protect

[16]H. L. Nieburg, *In the Name of Science*, p. 193.
[17]Quoted in Borosage, "The Making of the National Security State," p. 10.
[18]John Kenneth Galbraith, *The New Industrial State*, p. 328.

its vital interests). Such power should pay off in direct and indirect terms it is argued; the free world was always America's oyster—there for the taking and encouraging the taking.

One clear example of the Reagan Administration's international intentions can be seen in the events surrounding the recent conference between the developed and the underdeveloped countries in Cancun, Mexico. Prior to attending, President Reagan gave several speeches in the U.S. defending a hardline position that the developed world was not responsible for the underdevelopment of the South. He rejected notions of increased aid from the wealthy nations or of a new international economic order, and instead he urged the poor countries to follow the "path of free enterprise" and the "magic of the marketplace." And, when he did agree, at Cancun, to a compromise position allowing the U.S. to participate in discussions about the international economic order, it was to be *only within* the existing international institutions of trade and finance—the IMF, the IBRD, the GATT, etc. These are the institutions that were created and dominated by the U.S. in the post war period. The goal of the Reagan Administration is a new international economic order just like the old one.

How is renewed militarization related to this general direction in foreign policy and how is it justified? Not surprisingly, we will find, a lot of the rhetoric has to do with the Soviet threat. This is connected with increased military spending by the Soviet Union and the decreased priority for military spending in the U.S. in the 1970s following the Viet Nam War. Defense spending decreased in real terms from 1970–1978, and it dropped from 7.5 percent of GNP to 4.6 percent in the same period. Actually, the new military buildup began in earnest during the Carter Administration with promises to increase the defense budget by three percent in real terms every year beginning in Fiscal Year 1979 (proposed in Carter's first budget). And, later on, in reaction to events in Iran and Afghanistan, the Carter proposals were increased. But the Reagan Administration wants to accelerate the

buildup even faster. Why? Let us allow them to explain it.

. . .

Statements explaining and justifying the policy goals of the Reagan Administration in foreign and military affairs from [former] Secretary of State Alexander Haig and Secretary of Defense Caspar Weinberger abound. Haig has stated "that our strength is the most important guarantee of our ability to maintain international peace and stability . . . to influence events and to make more effective use of the full range of our moral, political, scientific, economic and military resources in the pursuit of our interests. . . . The revised defense budget is designed to revitalize our Armed Forces and rebuild our capacity to defend our vital interest. . . ."[19] Reading into it only slightly, it is a program to reclaim American dominance in world political, economic and military affairs with respect to the Soviet Union, Western Europe and Japan and the Third World—in essence, a remilitarization of American foreign policy.

Secretary of Defense Caspar Weinberger has also spoken widely about the new "integrated" foreign and military policy. He has warned of "the threat to Western strategic interests posed by the growth and power projection of the Soviet armed forces" and has said that: "if we value our freedom, we must be able to defend ourselves in wars of any size and shape and in any region where we have vital interests. . . . The West's dependence on Persian Gulf oil means we must make sure we can respond effectively to threats in this region." And, specifically, on naval forces, he has said: "We have permitted our naval capacity to deteriorate, and now we must restore it. American commerce and industry and the sinews of the Western alliance depend on our ability to control the seas. We must have naval superiority. . . ."[20] It is a vision of a replen-

[19]All quotes here from the *Department of State Bulletin.* Volume 81, numbers 2049 and 2051.
[20]Caspar Weinberger quoted in *Department of State Bulletin; New York Times,* September 27, 1981; and *Business Week,* July 20, 1981.

ished worldwide and domestic military establishment in pursuit of "our vital interests."

An additional aspect of the current buildup
is one alluded to by Weinberger—the implications for the domestic economy. I have found
no direct statements by administration officials that the increased military spending is
designed to immediately stimulate a lackluster
economy. However, the infusion of concern for
the defense industrial base will have positive
effects on some corporations and some areas of
the economy. They will get more contracts for
production, research and development. And,
in the short run, increased contracting will
tend to dampen the current recession and is
intended to contribute to future activity directly and indirectly by creating a more positive international environment for American
capitalism. During the late Spring (1981)
when the Congress was engaged in debates
concerning domestic budget cuts and military
increases, the Department of Defense was
quick to seize the opportunity to disseminate
information on the impacts of increased military contracting on various regions in the
United States. Articles appeared in local papers detailing the local impact of increased
contracting for companies and communities.[21]

In this new military buildup we can see that
there is, once again, the appeal to militarization of American foreign policy in the service
of renewed prosperity and U.S. leadership in
the world—to counter the Soviet threat, to
protect our vital international interests and to
stimulate the domestic economy. Will it work?

• • •

CONCLUSION
AND POLITICAL IMPLICATIONS

The military buildup is a key part of the Reagan strategy to revitalize the U.S. economy.
The economic program is predicated on an attempt to get capitalism working again, and
the militarization of foreign policy is intended
to support that effort by restoring U.S. leadership in the world.

There is fertile ground for organizing
against both the Reagan economic program
and the military buildup. The budget cuts,
deregulation, tight money and the regressive
tax cuts all hurt most Americans. The military
buildup requires resources that could be put
to better use and has already required cuts in
domestic programs. In addition, the acceleration of the nuclear arms race has Americans
worried. Despite the supposed demise of the
"Vietnam syndrome," it seems that, in the
current environment, Americans would be unlikely to support armed intervention in the
Third World. There is already substantial resistance to U.S. involvement in El Salvador.
The possibilities for organizing people across
these concerns are plentiful—both against
Reaganomics and its priorities, but also
against an economic system that requires such
policies in order to promote growth. In the debates around these issues we must raise the alternative of an economy based on the priorities of the people and not on those of the rich
and the corporations.

[21]See Rachelle Patterson, "Reagan Budget Would Help
N.E. Defense Contractors," *Boston Globe* (April 5, 1981).
For excellent sources on defense contracting, see material
prepared by the Conversion Information Center of the

Council on Economic Priorities, 84 Fifth Avenue, New
York, NY 10011; and NARMIC, c/o American Friends
Service Committee, 1501 Cherry Street, Philadelphia, PA
19102.

9.4 *Nature and Its Largest Parasite*

The pollution and destruction of the natural environment reflect one way in
which the collective needs of society are ignored in capitalist production. Society at large has an immense stake in protecting our natural environment, but
this interest is not mirrored in the mechanisms that determine production priorities. Production organized for profit ignores the environmental costs of pro-

ducing goods and the environmental costs of disposing of goods; that is, these true costs to society do not help guide consumers in what to consume, nor are capitalists forced to pay for them. Production for private gain might have made sense in an earlier age characterized by open frontiers and an apparently limitless natural environment. In the present age, however, it is all too clear that we live within a closed system of limited natural and environmental resources. As a result, we must devote much greater attention to the quality of the world environment and restrain the unlimited exploitation of resources which fuels increases in the quantity of goods and services. The implications of this necessary change in orientation are profound.

In the following reading Michael Best and William Connolly explore some of the conflicts between the environment and production for profit. Best and Connolly go beyond simply pointing out that firms' profit calculations do not consider damage to the environment. Instead they provide a much more powerful analysis by investigating the conflict between social needs and the requirements for profit in the light of the vast power of monopoly corporations. This analysis shows that far from accepting the "inevitable" outcomes of market determination, corporations have actively intervened to counter, suppress, and eliminate ecologically more sound production. In part this power has been used directly to destroy technologies (mass transit, long-haul rail freight) which, while less destructive environmentally, threatened the profitability of the corporations' investments or markets. In part this power has been used to influence the state to guarantee corporate investments; for example, national energy policy, by focusing research and development on coal and oil rather than solar or geothermal energy, has guaranteed the profitability of massive corporate holdings of coal and oil.

This analysis indicates the enduring nature of the conflict between social priorities (in this case the need to preserve the environment) and production for profit. This conflict is not simply a *technical* problem susceptible of resolution through technical means.[1] Instead it reflects the profound irrationality of private control of social production.

[1]For example, conventional economists recommend a system of "compensatory" taxes and subsidies to make concern for the environment profitable.

Reprinted by permission of the publisher, from MICHAEL H. BEST and WILLIAM E. CONNOLLY, *The Politicized Economy* (Lexington, Mass.: D.C. Heath and Company, 1976).

Ecology deals with the balance between human beings and nature. The issues posed by such a relationship touch the very survival of humanity on the planet earth. We depend on nature for air to breathe, soil to grow food, water to drink and to sustain vegetation, fossil fuels to provide heat and to power the production system, metals to provide material for commodities. But if nature is our host we are its parasites. We abuse it unmercifully, robbing it of nonrenewable materials, straining its self-restorative capacities.

If some economic systems are more parasitical than others, the structural sources of that relationship must be confronted before the host collapses from the strain. The issue is particularly pertinent today. For as corporate capitalism, the ultimate eco-parasite on any measure of resource use or waste disposal, faces a new round of internal crises, ecology is apt to lose its popularity as a political issue. Such a lapse must be challenged because the current maladies of the system are partly rooted in a long-term debt to nature that is coming due.

In *The Social Costs of Private Enterprise*, published in 1950, K. William Kapp documents the

> destructive effects of air and water pollution ... [and] occupational diseases ..., the competitive exploitation of both self-renewable and exhaustible natural wealth such as wildlife, petroleum and coal reserves, soil fertility and forest resources ...; the diseconomies of the present transport system.[1]

These social costs have gone unnoted and untended, according to Kapp, because they "do not enter into the cost calculations of private firms." Air, water, and soil pollution have so far escaped the net of the market because the environmental effects of particular economic transactions are diffused over a wide population and, to some extent, projected onto future populations. Under such circumstances it is quite irrational for any individual producer or consumer to accept the higher costs involved in curtailing various assaults on the environment. Thus a company that purified the water used in production before disposing it into streams would add to its own costs, fail to benefit from the purified water flowing downstream, and weaken its competitive market position with respect to those companies unwilling to institute purification procedures. Since it is reasonable to assume that other companies in a market system will not voluntarily weaken their position in this way, it is irrational for any single company to choose to do so. The same logic applies to the consumer who assesses the rationality of, say, placing an

emission control device on his automobile exhaust system.

Thus a range of practices which are desirable from the vantage point of the public are irrational from the vantage point of any particular consumer or producer. And a range of policies which are rational from the vantage point of individual consumers and producers are destructive of the collective interest in preserving nonrenewable productive resources and in maintaining the environment's capacity to assimilate wastes. This is the "tragedy of the commons."[2]

PRODUCT ALTERNATIVES AND CORPORATE PRIORITIES

To specify the cause of a problem is to establish as well its appropriate remedy. We think the failure to consider the social costs of resource depletion and pollution grow out of the *power* of corporations to impose their priorities on *governments* and *markets* and that those priorities, in turn, flow from structural tendencies in corporate capitalism. We will start by exploring three related areas of production and consumption: transportation, energy, and petrochemical products.

Transportation

A national transportation system built around the private automobile, truck, and airplane uses fuel and metal resources extravagantly, imposes an enormous load on the self-purification capacities of the ecosystem, and increases the transportation costs of low income families. Assuming each vehicle to be half full, it takes ten gallons of gasoline per person to fly from Boston to New York, seven gallons per person by car, and only two gallons per person by train.[3]

If mass transit systems were introduced into our urban areas to replace commuting by au-

[1] K. William Kapp, *The Social Costs of Private Enterprise* (Cambridge: Harvard University Press, 1950), p. 229.

[2] This analysis is developed in Garret Hardin, "The Tragedy of the Commons," *Science* (1968), 1243–48.

[3] S. David Freeman, *Energy: The New Era* (New York: Vintage Books, 1974), p. 128.

tomobile, 50 percent of the fuel now consumed by automobile could be saved. And since it takes six times as much fuel to haul a ton of freight from Los Angeles to New York by truck as it does by rail, it is clear that the truck imposes similar strains on the fuel resources and waste absorption capacities of the environment.[4]

Why does the United States depend on such an irrational transportation system, then, and what stops us from shifting to more rational forms? A large part of the answer to these questions emerges when we explore the emergent hegemony of the automobile corporations in the first part of the twentieth century.

During the 1920s the United States had rather extensive trolley, transit, and rail systems and there was ample potential to expand these services to meet the needs of a growing industrial population. The dissolution of these systems is not sufficiently explained through reference to a history of informed consumer choices in a competitive economy, nor is such an explanation adequate to explain the contemporary pressure against the redevelopment of rail and transit systems.

As Bradford Snell has documented in a report of the Senate Judiciary Subcommittee on Antitrust and Monopoly,[5] the competitive situation of the twenties was short-lived. During the middle twenties General Motors, often in conjunction with Standard Oil of California and Firestone Tire, launched an investment program enabling it first to control and then to dismantle the electric trolley and transit systems of 44 urban areas in 16 states. Often operating through a holding company, National City Line, the three corporations acquired electric rail systems, uprooted the tracks, and substituted diesel-powered bus systems. After acquisition and conversion, the systems were sold back to local groups, but

only with a contractual clause which precluded the purchase of new equipment "using any fuel or means of propulsion other than gas."[6]

The life of a diesel bus is 28 percent shorter than that of its electric counterpart; its operating costs are 40 percent higher. Thus the typical result of the substitution of one system for the other was "higher operating costs, loss of patronage, and eventual bankruptcy."[7] General Motors pursued a similar program of acquisition and conversion with rail lines.

General Motors and its satellite companies benefited in two ways from this policy. First its profits from the sale of buses and diesel-powered locomotives are higher than from trolleys and electric trains. Second, the financial difficulties faced by these converted transportation systems encouraged consumers to buy more cars. General Motors' *incentive* to make cars and trucks the basic vehicles of American ground transportation is clear enough: Its gross revenues are 10 times greater if it sells cars rather than buses and 25 to 35 times greater if it sells trucks rather than locomotives.[8] Its expansion into mass transportation systems thereby enhanced its ability to make cars and trucks more attractive to consumers than alternative modes of ground transportation.

Its policy of acquiring, converting, selling, and strangling mass transportation systems—

---

[4]Barry Commoner, *The Closing Circle* (New York: Alfred Knopf, 1971), p. 169.

[5]*American Ground Transport: A Proposal for Restructuring the Automobile, Truck, Bus, and Rail Industries,* presented to the Subcommittee on Antitrust and Monopoly of the Committee of the Judiciary (U.S. Senate, Washington, D.C.: U.S. Government Printing Office, 1972).

[6]Ibid., p. 37.

[7]Ibid., p. 37.

[8]Ibid., p. 38. General Motors did, according to findings by the Interstate Commerce Commission, make cost claims for its diesel locomotives to potential buyers that were "erroneous," "inflated," and "manifestly absurd" (Ibid., p. 41), and corporate elites knew about the dangerous levels of pollution from cars and trucks as early as 1953. Nevertheless our argument leans less on an assessment of corporate *intent* formed in the twenties to dismantle trolley and train systems, and more on the identification of *policy tendencies* that emerge when a small group of corporations dominate all forms of ground transportation, some of which are more profitable than others. Moreover, consumer tastes and preferences are not strictly given, but are subject to the influence of advertising and all the other corporate resources devoted to shaping consumer demand.

in combination with the escalating pressure from the American Road Builders Association, American Trucking Association, and American Petroleum Association to launch massive state and federal highway construction programs—helped to make the truck and the automobile dominant vehicles for shipping and transportation in the country. Sandwiched between a private corporation with impressive market power over ground transportation and a governmental pressure system biased in favor of those organized corporate interests that pressed successfully for $156 billion in highway construction between 1945 and 1970, it was inevitable that mass transportation systems would eventually lose out to the "competition."

But as profitable as the operation was to the corporations involved, it was disastrous for the country. Besides the strain it imposes on our fuel resources, it has created cities crisscrossed with highways, straddled by distorted housing patterns, smothered in toxic emissions of carbon monoxide, lead, and other deadly chemical combinations from gasoline-powered vehicles.

It is absurd to argue that consumers have *chosen* cars and trucks over transit and rail systems after having considered each option in the light of its comparative costs and benefits, including the costs of highway construction and the effects on the environment. But rather a few corporations with effective market power, including control over information about the effects of alternative forms, helped to eliminate one mode of transportation as a viable consumer option and thereby stimulated consumer demand for the only option available. Thereafter market control in this area was further solidified as national patterns of employment (e.g., automobile factories, oil production, highway construction) and satellite entrepreneurial activities (e.g., motels, tourist businesses) developed around this system and established a vast constituency whose immediate interests are tied to the maintenance and expansion of an ecologically irrational transportation system.

Energy

Between October 17, 1973 and January 1, 1974 Americans became thoroughly aware of the nation's dependence on foreign energy supplies. On the first date Arab nations imposed a boycott on oil to industrial nations restricting energy use by American consumers; on the second, the Arabs doubled the price of crude oil, sending consumer prices skyward.

The energy crunch, it is often asserted, converted the recession of the mid-seventies into a near depression, one which took the form of high inflation and high unemployment. But this explanation stops where it should begin. Why has the United States become so dependent on Arab oil, thereby making boycotts and price increases effective, and what do our expanding energy needs forbode for the future?

The American economy cannot sustain full employment unless it achieves a rather high rate of growth. That growth in the past has been fueled by a large and cheap supply of energy, especially oil. Thus United States oil consumption increased from 2.4 to 6.4 billion barrels a year between 1950 and 1973. Between 1960 and 1972 alone, while our total energy consumption increased by 60 percent, no increase was made in our capacity to extract fuel from the earth. Instead we increasingly depended on cheap fuels from abroad. If present trends continue, that dependence will deepen:

> Before the Arab boycott we were importing one third of our oil supplies; if we return to a business as usual posture, we could well be importing one-half of our oil supplies by 1980.[9]

Moreover, the waste in our energy supply system is unbelievable. Only one-third of the oil discovered in any oil reservoir is actually lifted out. Fifty percent of the coal is left behind in deep coal mining. And conversion processes are equally wasteful. Only 20 percent of the energy potential of oil is employed in the automobile engine; 60 percent of energy po-

[9]Freeman, *Energy*, p. 119.

tential is lost in the conversion of coal into electricity. These figures only symbolize the immense amounts of energy lost in mining, distribution, and conversion processes. Electric rates are set by public authorities, but they offer the lowest rates to the biggest users, encouraging large users to substitute electricity for less wasteful forms of energy. Electric rates are also set on a cost-plus basis, discouraging managers from seeking ways to curb costs of materials and production.

While established energy resources are being rapidly depleted or subjected to the vagaries of international politics or both, the United States government has concentrated its research and development of energy alternatives in one area: nuclear energy. That policy promises to increase our dependence on a fuel with serious storage problems for radioactive wastes and increases the likelihood that the plutonium necessary for the construction of nuclear weapons will become widely available.

The energy crisis of the 1970s, then, was anchored in our increasing dependence on Arab oil; that dependency in turn was rooted in the growth imperatives of corporate capitalism as well as in the wasteful patterns of consumption predicated on cheap and plentiful fuel supplies. Finally, actions of the state tended to reinforce these patterns.

What has led us to this situation? Energy policy, as we have seen, results from both market processes and state actions. But the political and economic power of the energy industry complex insures that state activities, rather than serving the public's needs, will support the interests of the corporations.

Oil companies drill and refine oil for profit. Neither the oil industry nor any other agency is charged to ensure that the supply of oil in the United States matches its oil needs. As things stand, oil companies can be stimulated to meet oil needs only by market demands or governmental incentives that make it profitable for them to expand.

The increasing market power of the multinational energy firms has tightened their grip on energy policy. One important conse-

quence has been the decline in competition between alternative energy sources. Coal, which was a rather competitive industry, underwent a wave of mergers during the 1960s. By 1969 the thirteen largest coal producers accounted for 51 percent of coal production. Since part of the remaining coal production is in the hands of consuming companies, such as steel, this figure understates the extent of oligopoly. More importantly, the most significant mergers cut across the energy industries. In 1962 the oil industry accounted for 2 percent of coal production, but by 1969 it accounted for 25 percent. The oil companies have indeed diversified very effectively, for by 1969 the four largest firms had acquired holdings in gas, oil, shale, tar sands, and uranium. Such concentration decreases interfuel price competition and enables the oil industry to influence the type and supply of energy in its favor. As David Freeman, a student of energy resources in the United States, has concluded:

> One does not have to subscribe to a conspiracy theory to observe that a shortage of energy is a situation most favorable to the energy companies. Concentration within the industry makes it less likely that any producers will scramble to enlarge supplies unless profit margins are most attractive.[10]

The energy industry complex, led by oil, matches its market power with impressive leverage over governmental officials. Its huge contributions to presidential and congressional candidates, the secret and illegal political funds held by Gulf Oil and other oil companies, its favored policy treatment including the earlier oil depletion allowance and oil import quotas, all testify to the political power of energy corporations. It would take strong leadership by the President to launch needed new programs of energy research and development into the ecologically promising areas of solar energy, geothermal power, tides, wind power, and organic wastes. But no President has been eager to take on the oil companies; to do so

[10] Ibid., p. 155.

would be to write off immediately the electoral college votes of Texas and to unleash a well financed campaign of vilification against him. Any president who called for nationalization of energy would risk even more militant responses. The combined market and governmental power of the oil companies makes it exceedingly difficult to develop alternative energy forms *until* the energy problem itself attains crisis proportions.

Petrochemicals

The chemical revolution of the post–World War II period resulted in the systematic substitution of synthetic for organic substances in the production of innumerable commodities. Detergents replaced soap; synthetic fibres replaced cotton and wool; plastics substituted for leather, rubber, and wood; and massive infusions of synthetic fertilizers in intensive land cultivation replaced organic fertilizers tied to more extensive land use. Barry Commoner has demonstrated that such a substitution of synthetic for organic materials is almost always incompatible with ecological imperative, for the "chemical substances . . . which are absent from biological systems are, for that reason, frequently toxic and/or nonbiodegradable."[11] Typically, too, each synthetic material requires more energy for its production than does its organic counterpart.

Again, neither sovereign voters nor sovereign consumers can be said to have chosen these materials over their organic counterparts in the light of an informed assessment of the comparative utility of each option. In agriculture, once some farmers intensified the use of synthetic fertilizers, market competition required all farmers to do so; oligopolistic soap companies found that detergents were more profitable than soap—even though wastes from the latter are far less destructive of soil and waterways; and petrochemical companies generally found the production of synthetic alternatives to be more profitable to them in the

short run than the production and sale of organic materials.

In the areas of transportation, energy production and petrochemicals, then, product decisions with adverse environmental effects reflect the private priorities of corporations with massive market power. Another area where the needs of capitalist production and the environment collide is the workplace.

THE ENVIRONMENT AND THE WORKER

The work environment of the blue-collar worker is too often filled with deadly fumes, carcinogenic dust, high noise levels, and intense heat. Periodically a major mine disaster or a particularly harsh outbreak of cancer amongst workers handling deadly chemicals will arouse public awareness and mobilize support for reform of the work environment. But, just as typically, conditions gradually return to normal as public attention shifts elsewhere. One earlier incident, exceptional in the death and injury produced, exposes strikingly this cycle of brief uproar followed by a larger period of benign neglect.

In 1930, as the Depression was deepening, workers were too weak to insist on health standards and the public was easily kept ignorant about the most oppressive conditions of work. A subsidiary of Union Carbide began a hydroelectric project in the southern part of West Virginia, diverting water from two rivers through a tunnel to be constructed near the town of Gauley Bridge. The Gauley Bridge disaster, as it came to be known when finally it became a public issue five years after the fact, involved a group of mostly black, unskilled workers who dug the tunnel through silica rock.

Working for extremely low pay, breathing carbon monoxide fumes as they rode into the tunnel every day, the workers also inhaled the heavy clouds of silica dust created by rock blasting in the tunnel. Engineers wore masks inside the tunnel, for the adverse effects of silica dust inhalation were even then known to

[11]Commoner, *The Closing Circle*, p. 47.

health officials. But no masks were assigned to the workers. As increasing numbers of workers died from exposure to the dust, Rinehart Dennis, the subcontractor on the project, hired a local undertaker to bury the bodies at $55 per corpse.

When the U.S. Public Health Service probed the disaster in 1935, five years after its occurrence, it concluded that 476 men had died and 1,500 had been disabled. The case was eventually tried in the courts and congressional hearings were held, but the effective legal and legislative response was negligible. The settlements for survivors were extremely small; some defense lawyers were even caught accepting bribes from the company. The congressional hearings did not result in effective health regulations. And none of the companies involved—New Kanawha Power, Rinehart Dennis, and Union Carbide—ever faced official punitive action.

Despite recent legislation designed to protect the health and safety of workers, the classic cycle persists. Consider some of the facts about work and health in America today:

The Public Health Service estimates that *each year* prolonged exposure to toxic chemicals, dust, noise, heat, cold, and radiation kills 100,000 workers and disables 390,000 more.

A federally-sponsored, and more intensive, study of workers in a variety of factories and farms disclosed that 3 out of every 10 workers suffered occupationally related illnesses. Ninety percent of these illnesses were not reported through regular channels, suggesting that the Public Health estimates are seriously deflated.

While Congress, the President, and the federal courts were all moving to reduce the ability of the Occupational Safety and Health Administration (OSHA) to protect workers from job hazards, another study showed that one out of every four workers in a sample of small businesses incurred an occupationally-related disease. Eighty-nine percent of these were not reported to the Labor Department. The diseases included chronic respiratory disorders, loss of hearing, eye cataracts, and increased lead absorption in the blood.[12]

[12]*New York Times*, March 4, 1974, May 12, 1975, April 28, 1975.

Inside these global statistics are particular areas of extreme suffering and neglect:

Three million workers in fabricated metals, stone, clay, and glass products suffer a very high incidence of irreversible respiratory diseases such as silicosis, bysinosis, and emphysema.

The death rate among coal miners from respiratory diseases is five times higher than that of the general population.

Asbestos workers are disproportionately afflicted with asbestiosis, which is in turn linked to cancer of the lung, stomach, colon, and rectum.

Coke workers in steel factories assigned to the ovens for five years or more incur a risk of cancer 10 times greater than that of the general population.

One out of every six uranium miners will die of cancer within ten years.

Employees in petroleum-based mineral oils suffer a very high incidence of cancer.[13]

Passage of the Occupational Safety and Health Act of 1970 seemed to promise rectification of this miserable record of worker illness and death, but the effectiveness of its administrative and research arm, OSHA, has been severly limited. Of the half-million synthetic substances introduced into the work environment, threshold limits had been established for only 250 by 1974. Though the agency proposed new standards for a variety of toxic substances in 1971, including inorganic lead, carbon monoxide, arsenic, and sulphuric dioxide, the standards had not been enacted by time of printing. Indeed, the Nader Health Research Group contended in 1974 that Nixon campaign strategies used the promise of relaxed OSHA controls to gain large contributions from business elites during the 1972 campaign. And, indeed, a memorandum published by the Senate Watergate Committee quotes a Nixon official promising that "no

[13]These estimates, and others, are found in Frederick Wallick, *The American Worker: An Endangered Species.* (New York: Ballantine, 1972); Jean Stellman and Susan Daum, *Work is Dangerous to Your Health* (New York: Vintage, 1973); Special Task Force Report to the Department of Health, Education and Welfare, *Work in America* (Cambridge: M.I.T. Press, 1973).

highly controversial standards (i.e., cotton, dust, etc.) will be proposed by OSHA" during the next four Nixon years.[14]

By 1974 OSHA was hamstrung in a variety of ways: with less than 800 inspectors in the field, the average employer will see an inspector once every 66 years; after three years of operation only two firms had been convicted of criminal violations; and the average fine for OSHA violations is twenty-five dollars.[15]

Clearly the workplace is a major locus of ecological assault, but just as clearly corporate and business elites use the impressive resources at their disposal to hide the facts about worker disease, to deflect pressures for reform of the work environment into other channels, and to malign those who would convert the oppressive conditions of work into a public issue. The U.S. Chamber of Commerce reflected this orientation nicely when it told health officials, "The health of American industry is eroded every time a new standard is issued."[16]

---

[14]David Burnham, "Nader Group Says Labor Department Lagged on Health Rules to Spur Gifts," *New York Times,* July 16, 1974. The same memo goes on to emphasize "the great potential of OSHA as a sales point for fund raising."

[15]*Wall Street Journal,* August 9, 1974.

[16]Ibid.

CHAPTER 10

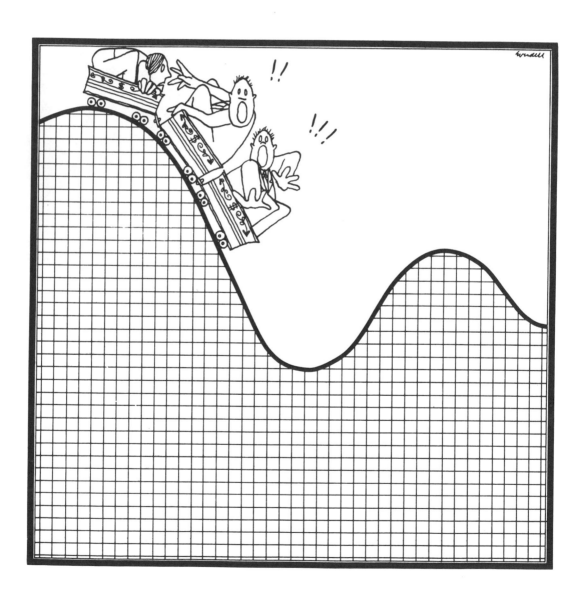

ECONOMIC CRISES

AFTER SEVERAL DECADES in which the term had rarely been mentioned in the United States, the reality of an "economic crisis" forced itself upon most Americans in the 1970s. Soaring rates of unemployment and inflation, declining levels of production and consumption, and widespread economic difficulties unmatched since the Great Depression of the 1930s shattered the prevailing myth that economic prosperity and stability could be taken for granted in a modern capitalist society. At first, many people thought the problems were temporary and would soon go away; but continuing economic difficulties in the 1980s suggest otherwise. Uncomfortable as it may be for the many economists and politicians who had predicted a more or less continuously prosperous future for the American economy, we are now all obliged to come to grips with the persistence of capitalist economic crises.

What exactly do we mean by an economic crisis? In its broadest sense, an economic crisis refers to a period of serious economic difficulties during which the viability of a socioeconomic system comes into question. A capitalist economic crisis marks an historical turning point for the capitalist system: heightened economic problems generate rising social and political tensions, which can lead either to a revolutionary break with the past or to major changes within the system which provide at least tempoary solutions to the problems raised.

During the history of capitalist development there have been a number of periods of eco-nomic crisis that have alternated with periods of general prosperity. In the first reading of this chapter, Eric Hobsbawm identifies three periods of generalized economic crisis for the world capitalist system during the past two centuries: from 1815 to 1848, from 1873 to 1896, and from 1917 to 1948. The economic difficulties of each of these periods led to a restructuring of the international capitalist economy that created the conditions for a subsequent period of economic expansion and prosperity. Although socialist revolutions have been successful in outlying parts of the world capitalist system, the industrialized center of the system—the capitalist metropolis—has thus far emerged from each crisis with renewed strength. Whether it can continue to do so after future crises remains an open question.

The period beginning in 1948 marked the most recent expansionary surge of the capitalist system. In a reformed world capitalist economy dominated by the economic and political power of the United States, the capitalist nations as a whole attained unprecedented rates of sustained economic growth.[1] U.S. hegemony guaranteed a stable international monetary system which encouraged the rapid growth of world trade, and it contributed to the availability of cheap supplies of energy and raw materials by enabling multinational corporations to obtain very favorable terms for

[1]The (unweighted) average annual rate of growth of total output in eight of the biggest capitalist nations was roughly 3 percent from 1865 to 1950 and 5 percent from 1950 to 1967.

the exploitation of natural resources in third world countries and territories. At the same time capitalist governments took on a greatly expanded role in managing the capitalist economies, and by applying Keynesian techniques of economic stabilization[2] they succeeded in staving off major economic downturns and assuring a more or less continuous upward trend in economic activity. Yet this latest period of relatively untroubled capitalist expansion lasted little more than two decades.

THE CRISIS OF THE 1970s and 1980s

Since the late 1960s, it has become apparent that the capitalist nations are again in serious economic difficulty. The 1970s and 1980s have marked another period of crisis for the capitalist system, and major changes will be necessary if the conditions for a renewed period of economic expansion and prosperity are to be restored within a capitalist framework.

The current crisis has appeared as a cluster of several different economic problems. These problems have affected virtually all of the nations within the world capitalist system simultaneously, and they have had a strong impact on the U.S. economy. First of all, the long-term trend rate of growth of real economic output (correcting for changes in the level of prices, and abstracting from cyclical fluctuations in the level of output) has slowed down. The rapid rate of expansion of the world capitalist economy in the 1950s and 1960s has not been matched in the 1970s and 1980s, nor is it likely to be matched well into the future. Even if estimates of gross national product do rise again as fast as they did in past decades, they will not reflect an equivalent rise in real material standards of living because of growing environmental costs of growth which escape the quantitative measures of total output.

[2]The British economist John Maynard Keynes, in *The General Theory of Employment, Interest and Money* (New York: Harcourt, Brace, 1936), developed the now orthodox theory of national income and output determination which underlies the macroeconomic stabilization policies of capitalist governments.

Second, the current crisis has been characterized by strong inflation pressures throughout the capitalist world. Moreover, these pressures have proven unusually resistant to orthodox capitalist antiinflationary policy. Until the late 1960s the rate of inflation became excessively high only at times when unemployment was very low. To reduce inflation to a tolerable level, it was sufficient to slow down economic activitiy and to cause a limited rise in the rate of unemployment. Such Keynesian techniques worked fairly well in maintaining overall price stability with moderate levels of unemployment. But since the late 1960s inflation has been more rapid than at any other time in the postwar period, and it has declined only under conditions of extremely high unemployment.

The third major element of the current crisis is a high rate of unemployment. The mid-1970s and the early 1980s witnessed the most severe cyclical economic downturns in the capitalist system since the Great Depression as levels of gross national product dropped sharply and rates of unemployment rose higher than at any other time since World War II. Long-term unemployment has become a more serious problem in most capitalist economies than it was in the earlier postwar period. In spite of a cyclical recovery in the early 1980s, the unemployment rate in the United States has remained near 7 percent; several European countries have experienced even higher rates.

SOURCES OF THE CRISIS

Like all capitalist economic crises, the current crisis grew out of certain contradictions that developed in the preceding period of expansion. The unprecedented postwar boom in the world capitalist economy had several significant consequences which ultimately put an end to the boom itself. In the following paragraphs, we discuss two of the most important contradictions that contributed to the crisis.

First of all, the postwar expansion of the world capitalist economy was dependent to a large extent on the hegemonic position of the United States. The U.S. government used its authority to establish and to maintain a system of international monetary arrangements conducive to the expansion of capitalist trade and foreign investment, and it used its power to guarantee favorable access to raw materials. While the United States gained special economic advantages by virtue of its dominant position in the world economy (for example, by having dollars join gold as the basic international currency), all of the advanced capitalist nations benefited from the general economic stability and cheap raw materials which U.S. hegemony provided. Yet the resulting economic expansion laid the basis for the ultimate erosion of the power relations upon which the expansion had been based.

On one side, the postwar boom enabled the advanced capitalist nations of Western Europe and Japan to build up their economic strength after the devastation of World War II; by the late 1960s they could successfully challenge the United States in markets that it had previously dominated. On the other side, the postwar expansion helped to strengthen the bargaining power of certain third world nations possessing key natural resources—especially the oil-producing states—because it increased their ability to play off rival industrial powers and corporations. The hegemonic position of the United States was further eroded by third world liberation movements, most notably in Indochina, which limited the American power to police the capitalist world. The growing economic strength of other advanced capitlist nations, the increased bargaining power of raw material exporters, and the rising military challenge from the third world combined to undermine the international monetary system that had prevailed for two decades. Stable international arrangements were needed for continued economic expansion, but by the early 1970s the United States was no longer powerful enough to impose such stability on the international capitalist system.[3]

The decline in U.S. hegemony has contributed to a slowdown in economic growth and to inflation throughout most of the capitalist world by causing general international instability and by helping to bring to an end the era of cheap energy and raw materials. The impact of these developments on the U.S. economy has been especially serious, because the United States has suffered not only from the generalized difficulties of the world capitalist economy but also from the loss of many of the special economic advantages that accrued to it by virtue of its dominant position. The decline in the ability of the U.S. government and U.S. corporations to obtain especially favorable terms for trade and investment in the rest of the world has led to some redistribution of the benefits of capitalist economic activity to rival capitalist powers and to those third world nations whose raw material export earnings have boomed—primarily the oil-producing states. But for most countries such redistributive gains have not made up for the losses attributable to the crisis as a whole.

The second important contradiction growing out of the postwar boom involved the ability of national capitalist governments to control their own domestic economies. The successful application of Keynesian stabilization policy to maintain relatively full employment with limited inflation in most of the advanced capitalist nations eventually created conditions that undermined the continued effectiveness of the policy. For the commitment of the capitalist state to maintain relatively high levels of employment has an increasingly inflationary impact on the economy, if only because it limits the application of the most reliable antiinflationary mechanism: a major downturn. With the prospect of a severe downturn ruled out, both capital and labor push harder for increases in prices and wages and resist more successfully any decreases.

[3]In principle, several strong nations could join forces to ensure the stability of the world capitalist economy and to defend the interests of the advanced capitalist nations. Thus far, however, international rivalries have made it impossible to substitute for the dominant role of a single state that was played by Great Britain for a long period in the nineteenth century and by the United States in the period following World War II.

Along with other developments in the advanced capitalist economies, such as the growing concentration of capital, this has contributed to increasing inflationary pressures at any given level of unemployment.

At the same time, the growing internationalization of the capitalist system as a whole has reduced the degree of control any individual government can exercise over domestic economic activity. Foreign investment by multinational corporations, international flows of short-term capital, overseas money markets, and similar activities have increased by leaps and bounds and blurred the lines between national economies. As a result, both inflation and economic downturns tend to become generalized throughout the world capitalist system. Differing conditions in different countries no longer tend to offset one another; instead, the problems are amplified by their simultaneous occurrence in many countries. Moreover, the ease with which commodities and money move from one country to another tends to frustrate the macroeconomic policies applied by any single capitalist state. This conflict between nationally based economic policies and an increasingly international economy is made worse by the decline in U.S. hegemony: the United States is now less able to coerce other capitalist governments into pursuing mutually needed but individually costly policies.

The contradictory consequences of the Keynesian strategy of economic stabilization, and the growing weakness of the standard tools of capitalist macroeconomic management, have been major contributing factors to the unprecedented combination of inflation and unemployment—stagflation—that has characterized the crisis in the 1970s. Inflation and unemployment can no longer be kept near tolerable limits simultaneously; to reduce one, it is necessary to increase the other to an unprecedented degree. The severity of the economic downturns of the mid-1970s and the early 1980s can be attributed in large part to the extraordinary extent to which the economy must now be slowed down in order to curb inflation.

PROSPECTS FOR THE FUTURE

If the history of capitalist crises can serve as a guide to the future, it is likely that the most recent crisis will last in one form or another for many years to come. Earlier crises of the capitalist system required several decades to be adequately resolved. It is hard to predict how long the crisis that began in the 1970s will last, but we can assert that major reforms in the capitalist system will be required if the world capitalist economy is to enter into a new period of prosperity and expansion.

The capitalist system clearly needs a new and effective international institutional framework to replace single-nation hegemony as a basis for managing the increasingly open and interdependent world economy. Such a framework might be built upon a supranational agency with broad powers to control the world economy, much as national governments have in the past controlled domestic economies. Alternatively, a new international framework might be based on some form of joint management by a closely cooperating group of major capitalist powers. But either of these solutions is fraught with difficulties and potential sources of tension, so that it remains highly uncertain whether the reestablishment of a strong international capitalist order can be accomplished very quickly.[4]

The capitalist system also clearly needs a new kind of domestic order to prevent the conflict between capital and labor from generating intolerable levels of unemployment and/or inflation. In effect, what is required is a "social contract" whereby labor would curtail its wage demands while capital would moderate its price increases and the age-old struggle over shares of the pie would be kept under close control. Such a contract could only be enforced by means of a greater degree of government intervention into the economy than

[4]See Fred Block, "Contradictions of Capitalism as a World System," *The Insurgent Sociologist*, 5, no. 2 (Winter 1975), for a thorough analysis of the difficulties faced by the advanced capitalist nations in restructuring the world capitalist economy after the decline of U.S. hegemony.

in the past: Keynesian techniques of (indirect) control would have to be replaced by a much more direct form of planning. While some advanced capitalist nations (e.g., Sweden) have already begun to move in this direction, there remain very substantial political and economic obstacles to its successful implementation.

The readings in this chapter pursue in much greater detail the issues raised in this introduction. The first reading defines the concept of a crisis and presents a broad historical account of past crises of the capitalist system as a whole. The remaining three readings focus on the crisis of the U.S. economy. The politics and economics of the crisis are explored from both international and domestic perspectives.

10.1 *Capitalist Crises in Historical Perspective*

To understand the nature of the economic crisis that has afflicted the world capitalist system since the 1970s, it is important to place the crisis in an appropriate historical perspective. In this first reading of the chapter, Eric Hobsbawm reviews the alternate periods of prosperity and crisis that have characterized the history of capitalist development since the Industrial Revolution in England. Hobsbawm's analysis represents an excellent example of the Marxist method of historical materialism (introduced in Chapter 2); he shows how each stage in the process of capitalist development generates certain contradictions, whose ultimate resolution paves the way for a new and more advanced stage of development.

Excerpted from "The Crisis of Capitalism in Historical Perspective" by ERIC HOBSBAWM. From *Marxism Today*, 19, no. 10 (October 1975). Reprinted by permission of the author.

Everyone has known for a long time that the operations of the capitalist economy generate various types of periodic disturbances which give it a sort of jerky rhythm. The best-known of these rhythms is the so-called trade-cycle, namely the slump,[1] which was discovered by radical and socialist economists from the 1830s on, and analysed by the orthodox from 1860 on. Sometimes it has been more dramatic than at other times, sometimes—and notably in the years since the Second World War—it has been so mild that people have seriously doubted whether it was still in operation. Certainly it has been much less visible and impor-

tant than ever before in capitalist history. However, though some of these slumps were catastrophic in their impact, both on business and on different classes of the people, with one exception none of them by themselves has looked like putting the capitalist system itself at risk on a world scale, nor possibly in any individual country. That exception is, of course, the slump of 1929 to 1933.

PERIODICAL FLUCTUATIONS

Once the rhythm of the trade-cycle was recognised, slumps were, for the best part of a century, regarded as inevitable but temporary interruptions, analogous to the less predictable, but certainly periodic cycle of harvests which dominated the lives of pre-industrial so-

[1]Editors' note: A "slump" is another word for a short-run cyclical economic downturn, which must be distinguished from the long-run crises discussed in this reading.

cieties. Capitalism lived with them, capitalism lived through them, capitalism survived them. However, perhaps it is less well known that there also appears to be a rather longer kind of periodical fluctuation in the course of capitalism, which the Russian economist, Kondratiev, tried to analyse in the 1920s, and which is still called by his name. Periods of 20 to 30 years or so—the exact length doesn't really matter—appear to alternate, marked until the present by the different movements of prices. Deflations succeeded inflations for fairly long periods. Then we may also detect a longer trend of this kind, a general tendency of prices to fall from the beginning of the 19th century, the end of the Napoleonic Wars, until almost the end, and a general trend of prices to rise, of which we are only too well aware—a longterm trend—since the beginning of the 20th century.

Periods of prosperity and capitalist expansion have thus alternated with periods of economic, and, as we shall see, with periods of political and social troubles.... From the beginning of the Industrial Revolution to the end of the Napoleonic Wars was one such period of long-term [upward] trend. It was followed until the middle or late 1840s, by a period of difficulties, though of rapid economic growth, and this in turn by the golden years of the mid-nineteenth century, the high point of capitalist, liberal, economics. From 1873 until almost the end of the century there was a period of difficulties called by contemporary business observers and also by some economic historians the "Great Depression," although, of course, it had only very small similarities with the Great Depression of the 1930s, which is what we know by this name. It was followed by another period of lengthy boom which lasted, I suppose, until the end of the First World War; thereafter came the depressed inter-war years which did not really end until after the Second World War, and lastly the greatest of all global booms in the 1950s, 1960s, and early 1970s, reaching its peak, as far as we can see, in 1973.

It looks as though we have now entered another period of general economic difficul-

ties.... [E]ach of these periods of troubles in the past was in some sense the result of the successes of the previous period. Each boom created the conditions which, as we now see, led inevitably to the subsequent difficulties. But I am also bound to point out that, until the present, each of these periods of trouble led to changes within the capitalist system which in turn provided solutions for the problems previously raised, and created the conditions for the subsequent secular boom.

Now the point I wish to make is that the times when the viability of the entire capitalist system could be questioned have occurred during these rather lengthy periods of trouble, between 1815 and 1848, betweeen 1873 and 1896, and between 1917 and 1948. It is during these periods that we can speak of a crisis of capitalism.

TYPES OF SOCIAL AND POLITICAL CONFLICTS

I have so far talked in what looks like entirely economic terms, but of course we are not talking about the economic mechanism in isolation, even on a world scale; we are talking about societies divided into classes and other social groups, organised in a system and a hierarchy of states with particular forms of political institutions. Moreover, we are not only concerned with the interaction within the international system, but with all these at a particular phase of history. For even if, from the Industrial Revolution on, we can speak of a world dominated by capitalism, we cannot yet speak of—in fact we can never speak of—a uniformly and homogeneously capitalist world. Capitalism, or bourgeois society, captured the world progressively, transformed its various parts which were in very different phases of their own development at various times, and what is more, progressed and still progresses at an uneven rate. This is true of the poor countries of the capitalist system, and of the so-called developed or industrialised countries of the West, and later Japan. All this is familiar. The Industrial Revolution before 1848 was virtually confined to Britain, Belgium and a few patches in Western Europe and the European seaboard. The Industrial Revolution in Germany and most of the US occurs after 1848, in Scandinavia even later, in Russia from the 1890s, and so on.

So what we are confronted with is a global, historical process, producing at least three types of social and political conflicts, in addition to, or rather in combination with, economic contradictions within capitalist development and complicated, moreover, by the unevenness of the transformation and timing in the various parts of the world. The first of these conflicts is the development, within the developed and developing countries, of a working class and its movements which are in conflict with the capitalists. The second is the resistance and developing rebellion of the dependent world, colonial and semi-colonial, against the domination of, or conquest by, the handful of developed countries. One might perhaps also add at this stage yet another contradiction—though it tends to be of a slightly different kind—the resistance of pre-capitalist strata such as the peasants and petit-bourgeoisie in the developed or semi-peripheral countries, to the process of capitalist development which destroyed their traditional economy and social order.

And finally there is the conflict between the [developed countries of the world, an international conflict involving the] various core states of capitalism themselves [and—since World War II—the USSR.]

THE AGE OF BRITISH POWER

I do not wish to suggest that these three conflicts exhaust the analysis, but for the sake of simplicity let us just concentrate on them. Now, until about the last quarter of the 19th century none of these three major conflicts could be expected to be acute on a global scale: industrialisation was only just beginning to produce massive proletariats, except in very few places such as Britain. Again, with certain exceptions, capitalism was only beginning to seize hold of the under-developed world from the middle of the 19th century on, and to engage in intensive capitalist investment there. Very little of the world was actually colonised, occupied and ruled from abroad, the major exceptions being India and what today is Indonesia. And since there was for more than half a century only one major industrial power, one workshop of the world and world trader, one power with a genuinely global policy and the means to exercise it—mainly through a global navy—the scope for major international conflict such as general, European or world war, was rather small. In world history this era, stretching from the defeat of Napoleon to the 1870s, perhaps to the end of the century if you like, may be described as the age of British power. It is this sort of world control of which the US has dreamed ever since 1941, and which it thought it had established in the 1950s and 1960s; but if the British era lasted little more than half a century, three-quarters perhaps, what the Americans call the American century turns out to have lasted little more than 25 years. But this is by the way. At all events, the moment when world capitalism was entirely successful, confident and secure, was comparatively brief, the mid-Victorian period, which may possibly be prolonged towards the end of the 19th century. In history this period is preceded by [an age] of revolution . . . from, say, 1776, the date of the American Revolt, to 1848, about 70 odd years. . . .

Why was it revolutionary? Because, as we see, looking back on it, it was a transition to the era of modern industrial capitalism, to bourgeois society; and what made it revolutionary was not only the attempt to break the fetters of earlier social and political orders which were believed to stand in its way, to construct an international system suited to the expansion of capitalism, but, I suggest, two further factors. First, the mobilisation of the common people which this revolutionary transition implied; that is why some phases of it have sometimes been called the age of democratic revolution; peasants, artisans, small shopkeepers, miscellaneous poor, were drawn into the drama of history as actors, rather than simply as crowd extras. Second, difficulties of developing industrial capitalism itself, which still found itself hampered by the very narrowness of the front on which it had broken through. It therefore . . . created . . . unusually acute social problems, unusual hardships for the emerging, exploited working class, a mass of people whom at this stage it was better at uprooting than at finding work, not even work at the modest wages then believed to be adequate. It also created difficulties for business. All this made the 1830s and the 1840s a period of unusually persistent and acute crisis; so much so that many—not least among the capitalists themselves—feared that the first stage of successful industrial capitalism might also be its last. The spectre of Communism haunted Europe.

Looking back we can see that this was not the end of capitalism but what today would be called in the jargon "teething troubles." But we can properly consider this as the first era of general capitalist crisis. From this crisis capitalism emerged in the 1850s, the years of railways, iron and free trade, and above all the era when the world as a whole was opened to capitalist development (which did not necessarily mean industrialisation), or the exploitation by the developed and developing industrial powers.

MID-NINETEENTH CENTURY BOOM

The giant and prolonged boom of the mid-nineteenth century was not based on a new technological breakthrough; by and large it utilised and acknowledged and developed the first Industrial Revolution, coal as a source of energy, the steam-engine as motor-power, iron rather than steel as the basic raw material for capital goods such as machinery and so on. But this technology was now used on a far greater scale internationally both in the countries which were now entering industrialisation, and also to create what is nowadays called an infrastructure in colonial and semi-colonial under-developed areas, railways, port installations—all that sort of thing. These allowed them to be integrated, mainly as suppliers of primary products into the capitalist world economy.

Hence the three major consequences of this boom: first, it replaced industrial world monopoly by Britain, by what you might call world industrial oligarchy by a handful of competing industrial powers among whom the USA and Germany were rapidly over-hauling Britain. We shall see that this situation has some parallels with the present. So long as the technology and methods of the first Industrial Revolution were very basic to industrialisation, this did not diminish the industrial role of Britain, but eventually it would do so. Second, in making possible through railways, steamships, etc., an economic trade in bulk goods from hitherto inaccessible areas, it created a number of potential mass exporters of primary products, generally specialising in one or two commodities—American and South Russian wheat, Argentinian and Australasian meat, South Asian tea, Latin American coffee, etc.—each dependent on the developed industrial world for their outlets. When these became actual rather than just potential mass exporters, the result would be a major disruption of agriculture, both in the exporting and importing countries, and also the development of dependent, mono-culture export economies like the banana and coffee republics of Latin America. . . .

Third, and in consequence of the first two developments, the boom enormously expanded imports and exports of both goods and capital. This world trading and payments system continued to hinge on Britain and in this respect the British economy continued to occupy a key position even after its industrial role began to diminish. However, the boom was particularly quick in getting under way because of two further factors: a rather large reserve of hitherto under-utilised resources, notably the labour which had been uprooted but was available for fairly short-term employment, and the discovery of vast supplies of precious metals, mostly gold, in California and Australia, but also silver in the USA.

The reserves of labour, although reinforced by a considerable degree of immigration from agriculture to industry and to the cities, were still only a small part of what was really available in the world. . . . The precious metals as well as the enormous expansion of the international market for goods, whose output may have somewhat lagged behind the demand, helped to create a moderate inflation of prices—it's the only period between 1850 and the end of the century when prices were not tending to drop—and, in short, there was no pressure on business profits. Quite the contrary. Except for greatly improved employment, the workers got little enough out of this boom, but on the whole conditions in developed countries improved after 1860 at least, and the prospects of capitalism looked extremely rosy.

LAST QUARTER
OF NINETEENTH CENTURY

As I have already implied, the great boom created its own troubles which became obvious in the last quarter of the 19th century. But, with some qualifications which I shall shortly be making, these troubles were, as we can see in retrospect, not fundamental. This is why most economic historians today take the phrase "The Great Depression," which was then widely used, with a very large pinch of salt, and many actually refuse to accept that it was a depression at all. What we find is not a general crisis of capitalism but a shift within it: from the technology of steam and iron and a limited knowledge of chemistry to electricity and oil, steel alloys and non-ferrous metals, turbines and internal-combustion engines; from competitive small firms to corporations, cartels and trusts; from free trade to protection and the partition of the world; from one industrial economy to several rival industrial economies; in short, from mid-19th century capitalism to imperialism or monopoly capitalism. Expansion in terms of output and trade continued faster than before, even during the period when businessmen complained

of the squeeze on profits and rate of interest. Probably agriculture rather than industry took the main brunt of the crisis, but incidentally the consequent rapid fall of the cost of living benefited a lot of workers, notably in Britain.

.   .   .

AFTER 1900

Now, even in a purely economic sense, capitalism seemed set for a long and untroubled future around 1900. Even British capitalism, which was by now lumbered with a lot of old-fashioned plants and methods, and both slowing down and falling behind the Germans and Americans, enjoyed the profits of being both the largest empire and increasingly the world's financier, shipper, insurance-broker, and in general the advantages of a world system which rested on the pound sterling. And, in fact, of the three major areas of conflict within the capitalist system, the one which had seemed most dangerous before 1848 now appeared to become quite manageable. During the so-called "Great Depression" mass trade union and labour movements developed in all industrial countries, even to a substantial extent in the USA, mostly socialist and indeed largely Marxist. But, in fact, though these Marxist mass movements continued to salute the flag of revolution every time their leaders opened their mouths in public, we know that they rapidly turned into harmless, social-democratic movements, though not, of course, in the illegal and marginal movements in the peripheral and under-developed countries such as Russia.

On the other hand, the two other types of conflict now became increasingly dangerous. The pressures of imperialism on parts of the colonial and semi-colonial world, including countries on the margins of capitalist development, such as Tsarist Russia, became intolerable. Between 1905 and 1914 a breaking-point was reached in three areas. One, the traditional structures of pre-capitalist empires in the Islamic world and Asia collapsed under the pressure of western penetration and conquest: Tsarist Russia, in so far as it belonged to this group, Persia, Turkey and, most significant of all in 1911, China.

Second, social revolution of peasants and workers broke out in Tsarist Russia, the first major social revolution of the 20th century. And, third, in Mexico in 1910 there occurred the first anti-imperialist social revolution in which the workers played no significant part because they did not form a significant part of the population.

These developments constitute the beginnings of the 20th century age of revolutions. At the same time the tensions of the state system led directly towards an era of international wars such as had not existed since the 18th and early 19th centuries. The first of these wars, expected, predicted, and in spite of great efforts not avoided, ended the era of triumphant confidence. After 1914 nothing would ever really be the same again. Then after 1917 one-sixth of the world's surface moved out of the capitalist economy and after the Second World War large regions of Europe and Asia joined this movement. Capitalism was not destroyed as a world system, but the First World War opened an era when all three of the main types of conflict became for a time apparently dominant and unmanageable.[2] The threat of social revolution dominated the politics of most of the highly developed capitalist states, though the operative factor at times was not so much the reality of this threat of social revolution as the fear of revolution in the minds of an uncertain, frightened, demoralized ruling class. This was particularly so in the period following the October Revolution and during the Great Depression. International conflict became endemic as a second and even greater world war

followed the first after barely 20 year's interval of a very uncertain peace. And the great empires into which the world had been divided at the end of the 19th century now lived on borrowed time. Their end could be predicted.

But what made this entire period so dramatic a crisis was the breakdown of the international capitalist economy which had, by and large, had such an astonishing run for its money—the money being the pound sterling—until 1914. The attempt to reconstruct this international liberal economy after the First World War in the 1920s failed. For one thing the keystone of the whole structure, Britain, was no longer in a position to bear its weight: the great slump of 1929 to 1933 showed just how unsuccessful this attempt had been, and brought the system close to actual collapse for a brief moment. To give you a single illustration: in 1938 world trade was little more than two-thirds of what it had been in 1913, and in 1948 European trade was about 15 percent below this modest level. There had been no setback of this kind since the beginning of the Industrial Revolution.

The period of depression, flanked on either side by war and revolution, remains to this day the only time when the future of the world capitalist system really looked as though it was in imminent danger. It did not seem unrealistic to speak in the words of a contemporary book-title of *This Final Crisis*. But, as we can see now, the immediate and urgent danger to capitalism was not due to the fact that the system had come to the end of its possibilities either economically or politically; it had merely come to the end of the possibilities of its 19th-century international structure and the assumptions on which its policy had then been based. The slump forced one country after another to abandon these, and Keynes—who you may remember set out to save rather than to undermine bourgeois society—provided the most familiar, theoretical reasoning behind this change. Actually, in all countries, even including Scandinavia, this change took place through a combination of experiment, accident and the discovery that even the slump of 1929 to 1933 ended of its own ac-

---

[2]Editors' note: The fact that the United States enjoyed a period of prosperity in the 1920s may appear inconsistent with the view that the entire period from 1917 to 1948 was one of crisis. But the U.S. economic boom was exceptional and short-lived. For almost all the other capitalist nations and for the world capitalist economy as a whole, the 1920s represented a period of political and economic instability which ushered in the all-encompassing Great Depression of the 1930s.

cord, and of course subsequently by the necessity of an economy of total war.

· · ·

THE NEW GREAT BOOM

The capitalist states of the new great boom moved back to some variant or other of an admittedly very much more bureaucratised and, so to speak, state-administered bourgeois parliamentarianism. We thought that declining capitalism would be unable to compete successfully with the rising rival socialist[3] economy, especially one so much larger than before. But the opposite happened. Capitalism outproduced socialism and even began to re-infiltrate and re-integrate socialist economy from outside by virtue of its technological superiority and greater wealth. And so on. So it is clear that the foundations of capitalism have not been fatally undermined by the era of crisis, profound though that crisis was. What happened is rather that capitalism abandoned the old assumption of a self-regulating, competitive market economy and changed its structure accordingly. In the first place the state expanded its economic function in all developed countries, including the USA, to the point where it deliberately planned and managed the economy to a large extent, including an enormous public sector, and in many countries, even a largely nationalized industry. In the second place, the developed economies abandoned the economies of cheap labour and market control of unemployment, thus incidentally making possible a vast extension of the market for consumer goods. In the third place, the concentration of capital created the phenomenon of the modern, super-giant, largely self-financing, independent-of-the-market, transnational corporation. The developed countries entered the era of state monopoly capitalism and welfare capitalism inasmuch as welfare is implicit in full employment

as a major government policy which automatically maintains workers' incomes.

I do not want to describe or analyse these far-reaching changes further; but I want just to point out that phrases like "state capitalism" or "state monopoly capitalism" obscure one very important aspect of this new relation between the state and the large corporations which increasingly and in all developed countries constitute the "private sector." The corporations both need the state—I mean the national state—and break its boundaries. They need it, and not only for various other purposes, but because it controls the conditions of political stability which makes the operation of the system possible in the post-1930 period, i.e., full employment and social security. These conditions depend on a constantly rising level of state expenditure. In the USA, for instance, it has risen from about 24 percent of GNP in 1948 to about 32 percent in 1969. And every time it drops, unemployment rises.

But at the same time the operations of the giant corporations become steadily more transnational, whatever their local base (which in most cases is American), and therefore to some extent they come into conflict with the interests of the economic policy of the national states; for instance, in the matter of the balance of payments. The fact that the United States has run an enormous deficit for many years—in the 1950s and 1960s—which in the end undermined the position of the dollar, was of considerable negative importance to the US Government, but it was an undoubted advantage to the American transnational corporations which used this fact to buy themselves into foreign economies. Hence, incidentally, the post-war international economy has not on the whole been one of mere mercantilism, as some Keynesians anticipated, but a sort of world restoration of free trade and free investent for the benefit of what is now, one might say, the major dynamic element in the capitalist economy, the large transnational corporations.

Given this restructuring of capitalism, its recovery was facilitated by the large reserve of unused resources, industrial capacity and la-

---

[3]Editors' note: In this essay Hobsbawm uses the term "socialist" to describe what we prefer to call the "state socialist" nations of the modern world: the USSR, the East European nations, China, etc.

bour available at the end of the war, and by the disproportion which had widened during the period of economic crisis, between the growing capacity to produce and the stagnation of world trade. It was also made possible by the systematic reconstruction, in which incidentally Keynes also took a leading part, of an international trade and payments system in the immediate post-war years. As I have already suggested, this system was in some respects a reversion to the mid-19th century order, only it rested on a US world monopoly instead of a British, on the dollar instead of on the pound sterling. But the unparalleled expansion of capitalism could not have occurred but for important changes in the level of the means of production, just as the previous expansions also occurred not simply by a widening of the market and changes in the structure, but also by changes in the means of production; changes comparable to cotton in the first Industrial Revolution, to railways and iron in the mid-19th century, to the new technology that I have sketched above of the early 20th century.

THREE KEY FACTORS

I would like to suggest three changes of this kind, not necessarily in order of importance. First, in addition to the generalisation of the internal combustion engine, the spread of the car from being virtually an American phenomenon to being a world phenomenon, there were the consequences of the technological revolution—in the field of light consumer goods—of electronics and plastics. Most of these, incidentally, like most of the technological revolutions which paid off in the later periods of boom, were made during the inter-war period, or at least during the period of crisis.

The technological revolution in light consumer goods, electronics and plastics, created an enormous number of new consumer goods, and increasingly cheapening consumer goods—you may observe that among the very few goods which still continue, even in the period of inflation, to become cheaper, are things like colour television sets. If we look at a coun-

try like Japan, the consumer society there is based much less on the car than on the camera and the television set. That was a devleopment in the fifties and sixties.

Second, there is something which perhaps made possible what I have just described, a really quite unprecedented development—at least unprecedented on this scale—an enormous, massive process of urbanisation of suburbanisation, the emptying of the countryside. In the 1950s and particularly in the 1960s, for the first time in Western and Central Europe, the old—not only Marxist—prediction of the disappearance of the peasant appeared to be coming true. . . . This phenomenon is not necessarily confined only to developed countries; urbanisation, suburbanisation, the consequent road-building and all the rest of it, also occurred in the peripheral and even in many of the underdeveloped countries, very notably in a region like Latin America.

Third, I think we have the systematic exploitation, again on quite an unprecedented scale, of ultra-cheap energy. This was not energy that had previously been unknown, because oil, after all, had been significant in the past. However, there was now exploitation of oil on a scale, particularly after the late fifties, which simply had no precedent. Alternative sources of energy were run down—coal mines, for instance, shut down, right, left and centre—in order to use the benefits, the advantages of this bonanza of ultra-cheap oil. We may also, however, note that capitalism began to do two things, one old and one new: first, unlike the inter-war periods, it once again relied very largely on immigrant labour, the abundant and cheap labour on its fringes. There were no longer such large reserves in central capitalist countries with full employment where the only unused labour capacity was that of married women—the percentage of employed married women shot up dramatically. Again there was no precedent for this post-war period rise in women's employment. We now find immigration, very notably controlled immigration in some instances, in Europe, from places as far away as Turkey, or Syria, in some instances, not to mention Asia and the West Indies. But we also find a new phenomenon: the export of the actual plant and industry to the areas where the reservoir of cheap labour was, to places like South Korea, Taiwan, Singapore. In the last ten years such transfers have taken place on a large scale, certainly in industries like electronics and cameras. In short, the exploitation of the under-developed world, both in labour and raw materials, by the developed world contributed to an important extent— and some would argue fundamentally—to the great boom of the 1950s and 1960s.

Now during this golden age of capitalism we may note that two out of the three main conflicts I have talked about ceased to be acute, at least for this period. After a few years of sharp confrontation, the USA and the USSR developed a stable *modus vivendi*, and in spite of bloody local wars an immediate world conflict has for several years appeared to be unlikely. Similarly the working class movements in the developed countries, whether under social-democratic or Marxist leadership, also established—there was little else to do—a *modus vivendi* with the existing system, which they screwed for all they were worth for the higher wages and better conditions which at that period the system was perfectly able to grant. . . .

Only the tension between the industrial and the under-developed countries remained alive, given the widening gap between the two and the role of exploitation in the world boom. But once again, with a few localised exceptions such as Cuba and Vietnam, we cannot really regard this conflict as unmanageable in the period, let us say, between 1950 and 1973.

INTERNAL CONTRADICTIONS

It is not my business to analyse the internal contradictions which led to the end of this golden age, though I will in passing point out three: first, the United States was incapable of maintaining its overwhelming economic and political supremacy, and consequently of maintaining the dollar in its position as the basis of the international payment system. That system, visibly shaken since 1968, is at present on the point of breakdown. The revival or rise of other capitalist economies, notably those in the EEC and Japan, puts the US today in a similar relationship to them as Britain was from the end of the 19th century in relation to Germany and the USA. It is no longer true to think of the USA as the overwhelmingly dominant, or even the technologically dominant, country. . . .

International rivalry and tensions, therefore, revived as American hegemony declined. Second, it is now clear that capitalism can choose either unemployment or inflation. However, while a moderate degree of inflation is rather good for business, an excessive amount produces, as we know too well, considerable social and economic political troubles. Moreover, it is possible . . . that the structure of capitalism has changed in such a way as to make it increasingly difficult to control either inflation by means of unemployment, or the other way round. Or rather that one would need an unpredictably greater amount of unemployment than was previously believed necessary to control inflation and the other way round.

And third, the now politically independent countries which happen to be sitting on scarce raw materials discovered how to turn the tables on the industrial world by using monopoly themselves, as in the oil crisis. In short, the era when capitalist corporations could operate at their will in a Third World of cheap resources was bound to end. And it did.

THE PRESENT PERIOD

So we are once again at the end of another bout of capitalist expansion. I do not say of capitalism, since, again speaking in purely economic and technical terms, the system has not exhausted its possibilities. For instance, it could quite easily extend the method of exporting industrialisation to the underdeveloped world, which it has already started to do, and it would then acquire a very large, cheap labour force once again, for a while. It can, and it almost certainly will, invest heavily in the search for new sources of energy, nuclear and other, and such a massive investment programme might well open up yet another phase of rapid development. Its immediate weaknesses are a combination of the economic and the political, and its vulnerability lies in this combination and not in the insolubility of any specific economic difficulties taken in isolation. Thus the reconstruction of the international monetary system has so far been prevented—and this is for at least four years—essentially by political frictions between the US and the European countries, with the socialist countries and the Third World countries intervening, since they also have their interests in this matter. The USA is no longer in the position it was at the end of the war to impose its own solution.

No one is able to impose a solution in a situation of tension between rival groups. We may take it that even if the control of inflation by unemployment were technically possible, which, as I have suggested, is not certain, a return to mass unemployment on the interwar scale is simply politically *not* on, both because governments in industrial countries fear the political consequences, and because the strength of organised labour movements in several of these countries makes such a course extremely difficult, if not impossible. If mass unemployment occurs again, it will not be the result of policy but of the breakdown of policy. The decline of the USA which has led to more freedom of action in smaller countries combined with the general atmosphere of uneasiness and fear—not least in the USA—has once again led to a much more explosive or potentially explosive international situation, from which once again major international conflicts may spring. The Vietnam War was terrible, but nobody seriously expected that it would widen into a world conflagration for more than the occasional moment. On the other hand, the Middle Eastern situation, particularly today and particularly in the last two years, is one which might well become a world crisis, into which the powers might quite well be drawn and from which they might not be able to escape. In this sense, once again, a period of economic difficulties and a period of political and international tensions combine and coincide.

.   .   .

How shall I end this historic survey? Marx showed that the basic contradiction of the system was between the social nature of production and private appropriation. Capitalism got as far as it could by uncontrolled private enterprise until, say, the end of the 19th century. Thereafter it entered a severe crisis. It emerged from this only by turning itself into a managed, monopolist, state capitalism, i.e., by involving as much social organisation as was compatible with it in the system, and by eliminating a large amount of the element of competition and of the market economy. Yet the contradiction remained. It remains within countries and, above all, on a global scale. It is clearly not impossible for capitalism to go yet further along the road of social organisation and planning of production, but while it remains capitalism there must be limits for this process, though at present it would be unwise to make a firm statement about what these limits are. The main strength of the system has evidently lain in the impressive viability and stability and, above all, the powers of recovery of a hard core of the old industrialised economies, Western and Central Europe, the USA and Japan. Let us not under-rate the blows that some of them have suffered; wars, slumps and so on, and from which they have so far recovered with one or two exceptions. . . . Its main weakness . . . has lain both in the peripheral countries, such as Tsarist Russia once was, and in its relation with the underdeveloped world. However, such breakaways from world capitalism, as there have been, have not so far destroyed the general dominance on a world scale of the capitalist economy. Its main vulnerability has lain in the combination of economic difficulties with internal and international political conflicts. All of these have tended, and perhaps increasingly tended, to combine during the periodic down-swings of the alternating long waves, and at the turning points between these long-term periods, which I sketched at the beginning of this [essay].

10.2   *The Politics of Long Economic Swings*

In the last reading Eric Hobsbawm discussed the long swings between times of prosperity and times of troubles that have characterized the world capitalist economy in the past two centuries. In Hobsbawm's view, the present period constitutes another long swing crisis. Historical patterns suggest both that this period of crisis will end only after major political and economic restructuring occurs and that a variety of restructuring outcomes are possible. In the following reading Samuel Bowles, David M. Gordon, and Thomas E. Weisskopf make a similar argument for the specific case of the United States.

Excerpted from SAMUEL BOWLES, DAVID M. GORDON, and THOMAS E. WEISSKOPF, *Beyond the Waste Land: A Democratic Alternative to Economic Decline* (New York: Anchor Doubleday, 1983). Reprinted by permission of the publisher.

After long periods of growth, the U.S. economy has experienced crises in the 1890s, the 1930s, and the recent period.

Table 10-A provides some partial evidence of this pattern of boom and bust in the U.S. macroeconomy. Where the data permit, we compare the years of expansion and of crisis during the three long swings in U.S. capitalism since the middle of the nineteenth century. The onset of each crisis—the late 1880s, the late 1920s, and the late 1960s—are included as the end of the boom rather than the first years of the crisis, for the major macroeconomic indicators (growth of output and investment) . . . generally decline only after the crisis is well under way. Each of the indicators in the table reveals the notable differences in economic vitality between the years of expansion and crisis.

• Accurate unemployment data are not available annually before the 1880s, but unemployment rates for the subsequent periods clearly alternate. Across the three long swings, unemployment during the periods of crisis has averaged two and a half times its levels during the booms.

• Aggregate output and gross investment also reflect the pendular swings. Growth rates slowed most dramatically during the 1930s, but they also slowed during the 1890s and the 1970s. Both rates averaged three times higher during the long booms than during the crises. By either

TABLE 10-A   BOOM AND CRISIS IN THE U.S. ECONOMY, 1873–1981

	I		II		III		Averages	
	Boom 1873-1892	Crisis 1892-1899	Boom 1899-1929	Crisis 1929-1937	Boom 1948-1973	Crisis 1973-1981	Boom	Crisis
Average unemployment rates	n.a.	11.8	4.9	18.3	4.8	6.9	4.8	12.3
Average annual growth in gross domestic nonfarm product	6.6	2.9	3.7	−0.5	3.9	2.2	4.7	1.5
Average annual growth in gross domestic private fixed nonresidential investment	8.0	1.3	2.4	−0.3	4.0	2.0	3.5	1.0

Source: *Historical Statistics of the United States* and U.S. Department of Commerce, *Long Term Economic Growth.* The dates for the crisis periods refer to the late years of accelerating decline; although we argue that economic decline began in 1966–73, the 1973–81 period is more comparable to the earlier periods of "late crisis."

measure, it seems evident that the economy sagged during these years of crisis.

If this is our third period of economic crisis, then, it is pertinent to examine the process by which the economy escaped from the earlier two crises and reestablished the basis for growth and expansion. We provide a condensed outline here in order to highlight the political dynamics of economic restructuring.

THE 1890s
AND THE BIG-BUSINESS COALITION

Entrepreneurial expansion after the Civil War began to fizzle for three related reasons.

First, the frontiers of the market did not extend forever. Once the national rail network was completed, transportation costs plummeted and price competition became more and more intense. With thousands and thousands of small enterprises pushing and tugging for a share of the new, larger national trade, there were no available mechanisms for blunting the razor's edge of capitalist competition. Andrew Carnegie aptly summarized the corporate view in 1889:

> Manufacturers have balanced their books year after year only to find their capital reduced at each successive balance.... It is in soil thus prepared that anything promising relief is gladly welcomed. The manufacturers are in the position of patients that have tried in vain every doctor of the regular school for years, and are now liable to become the victim of any quack that appears. Combinations, syndicates, trusts— they are willing to try anything.[1]

Second, firms had not yet succeeded in gaining effective control of either production or their workers. As prices fell, they naturally tried to reduce labor costs and increase productivity in order to protect their profits. They pulled at the levers, but neither wage-cutting nor speed-up had enough effect. As a result,

while prices continued to fall, unit labor costs rose, tightening the vise on firm profits.[2]

Third, agriculture had expanded rapidly along with the rest of the economy. Farmers had borrowed heavily to finance this expansion, plunging deeply into debt. As farm prices fell along with the general deflation, the incomes with which farmers could repay their debts slackened. Fixed debt obligations weighed more and more heavily upon declining money incomes. Farm prosperity soured, and the contribution of agriculture to the aggregate growth of the economy began to diminish.

These contradictions had combined by the late 1880s to produce both spreading economic crisis and increasingly frequent political eruptions. Popular reaction against business power was spreading on two horizons.

Farm protest focused on prices and credit. Farmers began to see bankers' faces behind every crop and a debt notice in every mail delivery. By the early 1890s, the National Farmers Alliance had hundreds of thousands of members. Its newspapers and magazines reached several million. Its chapters focused on some basic agrarian populist demands: easy money, increasingly linked to the demand for silver-backed currency; public control of the banks; and public ownership and control of the railroads and telegraph lines. Alliance members in the South, at least through the early 1890s, struggled to counter Dixie racism and establish political bonds among black and white farmers.[3]

On the urban front, working-class protest was episodic but nonetheless threatening. The Knights of Labor collapsed after the left-baiting which followed the Haymarket massacre in 1886. But local movements were beginning

---

[1]Quoted in Victor S. Clark, *History of Manufactures in the United States* (Washington, D.C.: Carnegie Institution, 1929), Vol. II, p. 175.

[2]See summary of evidence in David M. Gordon, Richard Edwards, and Michael Reich, *Segmented Work, Divided Workers: The Historical Transformation of Labor in the United States* (New York: Cambridge University Press, 1982), p. 234 and accompanying note.

[3]See Lawrence Goodwyn, *Democratic Promise: The Populist Movement in America* (New York: Oxford University Press, 1976); and C. Vann Woodward, *Tom Watson: Agrarian Rebel* (New York: Rinehart, 1955).

to escalate protest by 1890. Dockworkers organized a massive strike in New Orleans. Miners continued to rise against their working conditions in both the northern and the southern coal fields. In 1892, armed steelworkers fought a pitched battle against the Carnegie lockout at Homestead, Pennsylvania.

The election of 1892 was a watershed. The People's Party had formed officially in 1890. Although dominated by farming interests, the 1892 convention clearly signaled its intention to forge a close alliance between agrarian and urban working-class interests. The convention preamble advertised these political intentions in ringing language:

> The urban workmen are denied the right of organization for self-protection; imported pauperized labor beats down their wages; a hireling standing army . . . [is] established to shoot them down. . . . The fruits of the toil of millions are boldly stolen to build up colossal fortunes. . . . From the same prolific womb of governmental injustice we breed two classes—paupers and millionaires.[4]

To capitalists, the most threatening aspect of the emergent populism was its commitment to take democracy seriously. As Grant McConnell observes in his classic book *The Decline of Agrarian Democracy,*

> Yet, in 1892 . . . the farmer's movement was something more than a challenge to industrialism. There were economic demands, the class demands of agrarianism, to be sure. . . . But, equally, farmers demanded a graduated income tax, restraints on monopoly, education, the direct election of senators, the Australian ballot, the initiative, and the referendum. These were not narrow class demands. They were honest and genuine attempts to ensure the operations of democracy, to make certain that *no* group was excluded from sharing in the political process. . . .
> Even more important, the Alliance gave birth to a genuine political party. This implied that the agrarians were prepared to accept the

responsibility of building a majority, even if that majority included other than farmers. It implied a willingness to seek political solutions of a general character. This was the ultimate promise of agrarian democracy. . . .[5]

This promise seemed to be blossoming. In 1892, James Weaver, the People's Party candidate for president, won more than a million votes, nearly 9 percent of the total popular vote. The populists also took eight congressional seats, three governorships, and innumerable county offices.

The economy crashed in 1893, with unemployment climbing quickly to 18.4 percent in 1894, and protest seemed to spread even more rapidly. The Pullman strike captured national attention, building toward a dramatic confrontation between Eugene Debs' American Railway Union and federal troops; roughly fourteen thousand police, militia and troops were called upon to crush the strike, with hundreds arrested and at least thirty killed. Troops later routed Coxey's Army of unemployed marchers in Washington, D.C.

The emergent protest movement suddenly seemed momentous. As McConnell concludes: "Its onslaught shook to their foundations the structures of organizations and political alignment which had been long in building. Even more, it seemed to threaten the destruction of all the economic winnings of a capitalism so far everywhere victorious. For here was the fury of common men. . . ."[6]

Business interests rallied as if in a fire emergency. They concluded that agrarian and urban industrial interests must be split.[7] After two decades of inconsequential and essentially issue-free debate between the Democrats and the Republicans, the contest between the po-

---

[4]Quoted in Howard Zinn, *A People's History of the United States* (New York: Harper Colophon, 1980) p. 283.

[5]Grant McConnell, *The Decline of Agrarian Democracy* (Berkeley: University of California Press, 1959), pp. 5, 8–9 (emphasis in the original).

[6]McConnell, p. 3.

[7]For some evidence on business attitudes during this crucial period in the 1890s, see Samuel P. Hays, *The Response to Industrialism, 1885–1914* (Chicago: University of Chicago Press, 1957), Chapters 6–7; and Grant McConnell, *The Decline of Agrarian Democracy,* Chapters 1–2.

litical parties suddenly became a matter of life and death for northern industrialists. Beginning with the congressional elections of 1894, the wealthy mobilized their support behind the Republican Party, pouring millions into their campaigns. They concentrated on building an electoral alliance with industrial wage earners, seeking to forestall their potential coalition with populist farmers in the West. The Republicans promised tariffs, protecting industrial employment, and stable currencies, protecting the purchasing power of urban wages. When the Democrats won populist support behind the silver-currency candidacy of Bryan in 1896, the Republicans stepped up the pace. They outspent the Democrats by five to one, doubling the money they had poured into the 1892 campaign.[8] Mark Hanna and his monied circle virtually controlled the party and its campaign strategy, issuing directives to the compliant McKinley.

The strategy worked. While the Democrats carried the states where the People's Party had scored most substantially in 1892, McKinley won the election on the strength of his margins in the industrial states—New York, Pennsylvania, Ohio, and Illinois. The populists lost, soon to disappear from the political arena, and a new and powerful electoral coalition guided by big business had triumphed. The election returns of 1894 and 1896, as historian Samuel Hays concludes, produced "one of the greatest bloodless political realignments that this country has ever experienced."[9]

Big business moved quickly to consolidate its new political strength. The merger movement between 1898 and 1903 produced giant new industrial consolidations, accounting for as much as one third of total industrial assets in the United States.[10] Business groups began to promote foreign adventures; Teddy Roosevelt echoed their hopes when he wrote to

a friend in 1897, "I should welcome almost any war, for I think this country needs one."[11] The Spanish-American War provided them (and TR) exactly the opportunity they sought. The new industrial giants also increased their leverage over workers, pitting Poles against Germans, Italians against Irish, waging protracted battles against the IWW, the Socialist Party, and industrial union-organizing campaigns, perfecting what many called the "drive system" of labor management. They also planned for some government regulation to curb the excesses of continuing combination.

In building this new institutional strength, big business continued to fight two brush fires. One involved the resistance of small business, organized primarily through the National Association of Manufacturers. The other involved the socialist and revolutionary legatees of the earlier populist tradition. While big business fought a crafty battle, it sometimes relied on pure brute strength. It organized private militias to beat back unions, calling in federal troops whenever needed. It helped orchestrate the political purges during and after World War I, when thousands of radicals were jailed or deported as part of the "Red Scare." And it resisted to the end such popular reforms as the direct election of the U.S. Senate, hoping to keep its hands on as many political controls as possible.

At the same time, big business also found it necessary to respond to and eventually to court an important new political force: middle-class reform movements and their progressivism. These reformers helped ensure that big business would not engage in entirely unrestrained pursuit of profits, curbing some corporate excesses, such as child-labor abuse, and requiring some corporate attention to public opinion. Once Woodrow Wilson was finally able to shape a relatively successful integration of reform ambitions and corporate goals after 1913, the big-business coalition was complete. During and after World War I, more

[8]*Historical Statistics of the United States*, p. 1081.

[9]Samuel P. Hays, *The Response to Industrialism, 1885–1914,* p. 46.

[10]Ralph L. Nelson, *Merger Movements in American Industry, 1895–1956* (Princeton, NJ: Princeton University Press, 1959), p. 37.

[11]Quoted in Zinn, *A People's History of the United States,* p. 290.

and more middle-class voters felt comfortable supporting the new reign of profits.

In the end, the big-business coalition reshaped the U.S. economy. Four main institutional transformations promoted economic recovery. Business had itself helped resolve the anarchy of competition through merger and consolidation. It had gained additional leverage over workers through mechanization and the added strength which its more sophisticated and aggressive strategies helped provide. Through its new imperial adventures and favorable tariff policies, it had both won political and economic breathing space and begun to develop access to new markets for agricultural and industrial products. And it had helped to shape some carefully modulated government reforms coordinating the centralization and extension of its private domain.

These transformations emerged through political struggle. The populist challenge had initially spurred big business to organize and operate as a class. After the turn of the century, as the secretary of the principal big-business association, the National Civic Federation, observed, "our enemies are the Socialists among the labor people and the anarchists among the capitalists."[12] By winning both these battles, the big-business coalition secured a new basis for capitalist growth. The Roaring Twenties were its reward.

THE 1930s AND THE GROWTH COALITION

The Depression of the 1930s provides a more recent and more familiar example of the politics of economic restructuring.

The Depression had itself resulted from a complex combination of three important contradictions in the turn-of-the-century foundations for capitalist growth. First, imperialist rivalries among all the advanced powers led to continuing international instability which World War I failed to resolve; the 1920s therefore featured sharp swings in world prices

and trading relations, contributing to the vulnerability which the crash of the 1930s so bitterly exposed. Second, the very power of the big-business coalition led, during the 1920s, to a regressive distribution of income and wealth; this eventually led to slackening demand for consumption goods and an increased susceptibility of the economy to swings in the always volatile demand for investment goods.[13] Third, these surplus savings fed increasingly bullish financial speculation—whose unregulated bubble eventually burst in the 1929 crash.

As at the turn of the century, there were both a small-business backlash and a popular rebellion.

Small-business forces were inclined to ride out the crisis, hoping that the free market would quickly resolve the system's imbalances. Herbert Hoover's inaction during the first three years of the Depression reflected this faithful pursuit of the competition-as-usual response. Initial business opposition to political reforms such as the Wagner Act, legalizing unions and collective bargaining, equally reflected this knee-jerk preference for cure by the acid bath of the market.

Popular forces galvanized in the early 1930s. Tenant organizations and unemployed councils grew increasingly effective in 1931–32. The union movement spread like a prairie fire after 1935. Socialist and communist presidential candidates gained a combined total of a million votes in the 1932 election and, as before, third-party candidates won congressional and local elections. Much more significantly, the discontented were taking it to the streets, expressing their frustration not only with the economy but with the political mechanisms through which they were supposed to communicate their dissatisfaction.

Large corporations soon recognized that business as usual was suicidal. However well the turn-of-the-century institutions had worked

---

[12]Quoted in Zinn, p. 344.

[13]For detailed evidence on the swings in factors shares and the consumption-to-investment ratio, see Robert R. Keller, "Monopoly Capital and the Great Depression: Testing Baran and Sweezy's Hypothesis," *Review of Radical Political Economics*, Winter 1975, especially Tables 1, 3.

for a time, they were now clearly falling apart. There was strong and continuing business opposition to the New Deal, as might be expected, but growing numbers of business leaders recognized, as they had in the 1890s, the need for urgent action. One New Dealer recalled the growing receptiveness of corporate leaders to government reforms:

> The fact that people acted as they did, in violation of law and order, was itself a revolutionary act. . . . The industrialists who had some understanding recognized this right away. [Roosevelt] could not have done what he did without the support of important elements of the wealthy class. They did not sabotage the [New Deal] programs. Just the opposite.[14]

In moving toward coordinated action, the most forward-looking corporate leaders pursued three principal strategies:

● They accepted the need for even greater government regulation of excessive competition, supporting and helping chart the National Industrial Recovery Administration (NIRA), using it to help strengthen their monopoly leverage.

● They also began planning for dramatic extension of U.S. power overseas, aiming to overcome the slack demand for corporate products which had underlain the 1930s crunch. "The future of capitalism depends," as one government adviser concluded, "on increased foreign purchasing of our exports."[15]

● They also appreciated, however reluctantly, the need for compromise with the liberal and popular insurgencies against economic insecurity. Roosevelt aired some of their motivation midway through the New Deal effort: "The true conservative seeks to protect the system of private property and free enterprise," he concluded, "by correcting such injustices and inequalities as arise from it."[16] It was a proper measure of the strength of popular discontent that such widespread New Deal reforms proved necessary in order to "protect" that system.

But New Deal reforms were not enough. Business forces were unable to break the political stalemates which had emerged by the late 1930s. On one side, small-business forces had enough control over the conservative wing of the Republican Party to prevent the party from embracing the New Deal program. On the other side, popular discontent continued into and after World War II, exploding in strike waves immediately after the war.

Hot and cold war finally helped finish what the New Deal had begun. Wartime business strengthened large corporate control over its own markets and industrial wealth. The war itself produced a world economy in 1946 in which the United States accounted for half of all industrial output.[17] And postwar anticommunism provided the final weapon in the battle against radicals and insurgents, fostering the purges of "reds" from unions and popular movements, helping cement the bonds between large business and an increasingly cooperative organized-labor movement.

It was a powerful one-two punch. Government spending and international power fostered rapid economic growth, while anticommunism sealed an accord that further domestic conflict would be limited to the distribution of its rewards. Through that dynamic, a new political coalition, which political scientist Alan Wolfe calls the "growth coalition," was born. It was led by large corporations and included much of organized labor. Wolfe concludes that:

> This coalition advocated an overall expansion of the economy through macroeconomic policies made acceptable to the monopoly sector

---

[14]Studs Terkel, *Hard Times: An Oral History of the Great Depression* (New York: Pocket Books, 1970), p. 310.

[15]Quoted in Alan Wolfe, *The Limits of Legitimacy: Political Contradictions of Contemporary Capitalism* (New York: The Free Press, 1977), p. 130.

[16]Quoted in William A. Williams, *Americans in a Changing World* (New York: Harper and Row, 1978), p. 263.

[17]See William Ashworth, *A Short History of the International Economy Since 1850* (London: Longmans, Green, 1962), 2nd ed., p. 259.

of the economy.... Based upon the rapid expansion of the economy, it developed a foreign policy that combined a reorganization of the world under American economic hegemony with military power to ensure American influence.... The tasks established by the growth coalition were herculean, but anything seemed possible in an expanding economy. America had never before seen anything like this coalition, and it may never see anything like it again.[18]

Once again, large corporations had managed to resolve the crisis through a process which eventually restored and enhanced their economic power. Substantial institutional restructuring took place, resulting in the postwar corporate system we describe in [reading 10.3]. This system now seems to have been inevitable only because of the narrowness of retrospective vision. The postwar corporate system emerged not from the inevitability of history but from the dialectics of choice and compulsion, conflict and struggle, attack and counterresponse.

      .   .   .

[18]Alan Wolfe, *America's Impasse* (New York: Pantheon, 1982), pp. 22–23.

In each of the two previous crises, the wealthiest and most powerful business interests clearly contended with two alternative currents of political response. One, the more historically conservative, reflected small business interests and acted to protect the operations of the "free market." The other, reflecting sundry and shifting popular impulses, sought democratic control over the economy, hoping in often unspecified ways to shift economic priorities from profitability to popular needs.

In each case, as we have seen, large corporations triumphed against both tendencies, but the character of their triumph was somewhat different in the two successive episodes of institutional restructuring. In the first period after the turn of the century, they so successfully restored their economic and political power—particularly following their final victories against both unions and radicals after World War I—that they reigned virtually unchecked during the 1920s. After the second period of restructuring, in contrast, the postwar corporate system involved a much more complex balance of forces—with significant concessions to organized labor and substantial improvements in income security. Democratic forces had much greater effect on the second institutional transformation, in this respect, than they had on the first.

10.3   *The Rise and Demise of the Postwar Corporate System*

If the current crisis of capitalism represents an institutional crisis, it is important to identify both the specific institutions that made the great postwar boom possible and the mechanisms that eroded these institutions and broke up the boom. In the following reading, Samuel Bowles, David M. Gordon, and Thomas E. Weisskopf examine the rise and demise of three interlocking institutions that comprise what they call the postwar corporate system.

Excerpted from SAMUEL BOWLES, DAVID M. GORDON, and THOMAS E. WEISSKOPF, *Beyond the Waste Land: A Democratic Alternative to Economic Decline* (New York: Anchor Doubleday, 1983). Reprinted by permission of the publisher.

During the Great Depression and World War II, many U.S. corporate leaders wondered, as one business-magazine editor wrote in 1940, "whether the American capitalist system could continue to function."[1] Their fears proved to be short-lived. By the late 1950s, the Age of Affluence was upon us and the End of Ideology was at hand. The U.S. government and U.S. corporations now presided over a world trading system whose scope and fluidity was without historical precedent. The view from the top was resplendent. "World opinion? I don't believe in world opinion," financier and presidential adviser John J. McCloy announced in 1963. "The only thing that matters is power."[2]

This resurgence of U.S. corporate capitalism did not fall from the sky. It was nurtured through a profound alteration of the earlier capitalist order. The institutional changes which emerged after World War II created a new economic landscape. The U.S. economy was still capitalist, but it was a different kind of capitalism. Its institutional topography had changed.

.   .   .

We argue that the postwar corporate system rested upon not one but three principal buttresses of private power. Each involved a particular set of institutionalized power relations. One involved U.S. capital's dealings with foreign competitors and suppliers. A second featured new and much more structured relationships between corporations and a substantial segment of the work force in the United States. A third managed the continuing domestic conflicts between the business quest for profits and popular demands for the social accountability of business. Each of these three new institutional relations became structures of domination, ensuring for a while the unchallenged preeminence of private corporate power and privilege. Each worked, as well, to moderate

the tensions which hierarchical systems always produce. The success of each of these three institutional compromises contributed, in the end, to high rates of corporate profit and a rapid growth of hourly income. The postwar corporate edifice worked as long as each of its institutional buttresses held firm.

These structures of domination did not hold forever, however. Challenges to the power of U.S. corporations soon emerged along each of the three institutional dimensions. These challenges led to a realignment of political and economic power. This realignment reduced the effectiveness of U.S. corporate power, raising the real costs of imported materials and labor for U.S. corporations, reducing their ability to burden the domestic citizenry with the social costs of private capitalist development and slowing the rate of productivity growth. With this realignment, U.S. corporations suffered a sharp reverse on the front that most concerns them: their profitability fell.

Capitalism had not collapsed, to be sure; large corporations still held enormous power. But the particular structure of domination which had permitted rapid growth for twenty years had begun to erode. It no longer worked smoothly or effectively. Although worker, Third World, and popular resistance to business offensives now seem muted, they played a crucial role in the early erosion of the postwar corporate system. The resulting institutional disintegration produced economic decline.

.   .   .

THE LOGIC OF THE POSTWAR CORPORATE SYSTEM

Postwar Structure I: Pax Americana

.   .   .

The United States emerged from World War II as the world's dominant economic and military power. No European ally, much less the defeated Germans and Japanese, could challenge the preeminence of the United States. U.S. economic dominance was formalized by the Bretton Woods agreement, which established the new rules of the game for the

[1]Quoted in William Appleman Williams, *Americans in a Changing World* (New York: Harper & Row, 1978), p. 339.

[2]Quoted in Alan Wolfe, *The Limits of Legitimacy: Political Contradictions of Contemporary Capitalism* (New York: The Free Press, 1977), p. 176.

capitalist world economy. The dollar was king, Wall Street replaced the City of London as the world's financial center, and the International Monetary Fund and the World Bank set up shop within a stone's throw of the White House.

In subsequent years, the United States assured a stable climate within which capitalist trade, investment, and output could grow rapidly throughout much of the world. Insistent U.S. leadership helped to lower tariffs and other barriers to trade. Marshall Plan aid to devastated European economies facilitated their economic recovery. U.S. direct private investment abroad contributed as well to the reconstruction and development of capitalist enterprise in many parts of the world.

Altruism and self-interest worked hand in hand. The dollars pumped into the world system by U.S. investment and foreign aid quickly returned through growing demand for U.S. exports. Booming foreign markets and stable world market conditions raised both corporate profits and private business expectations; this stimulated high rates of U.S. capital investment at home as well as abroad. Domestically, U.S. corporate leverage in international markets helped promote high rates of growth and capacity utilization in key industries such as steel and auto. Internationally, the real value of U.S. direct long-term investments abroad grew at a blistering 8.8 percent average annual rate from 1948 to 1966, well over twice the rate of growth of U.S. gross domestic product.[3] The main features of this world economic dominion reinforced each other.

Two additional benefits flowed to U.S. corporations:

• U.S. capital gained access to foreign raw material and energy supplies on increasingly favorable terms. The real cost of imported raw materials—that is, their price relative to the prices received by U.S. producers of finished goods—fell until the mid-1960s.[4] Cheap energy helped to promote the spread of automobiles

and suburban housing throughout the postwar boom.

• U.S. sellers sold in a seller's market and U.S. buyers bought in a buyer's market. Between 1951 and 1966, the U.S. terms of trade—the average price of exports relative to the average price of imports—improved by 24 percent.[5]

None of these advantages emerged through private initiatives alone. The U.S. decisively abandoned isolationism to adopt an increasingly interventionist international stance. As with other empires, private gains—from international trade, the mobility of U.S. capital, and the central world financial role of Wall Street—were based on a confluence of economic and military power. U.S. ascendancy rested on two pillars. U.S. technology—the impressive machinery with which U.S. workers turned out products "made in America"—and the huge productivity advantages of U.S. workers combined to form the first. Aggressive political support of foreign investment and imposing military power joined to provide the second.

One of the most important government supports of foreign investment resulted from tax-code revisions. U.S. corporations were allowed to credit, rather than deduct, foreign tax payments against their domestic income tax obligations. They were also permitted to postpone tax payment until actual repatriation of profits earned overseas. All the while, they could juggle their internal accounts to take advantage of international differences in business-tax rates; this practice has been dubbed *transfer pricing*. By 1972, as a result of these numerous tax advantages on overseas invest-

---

[4]Although there is no single price index reflecting the cost of imported raw materials, the trend in their cost relative to domestic finished goods can be inferred from two available series: (1) the price of imports relative to gross domestic product (GDP) and (2) the price of nonagricultural crude materials relative to GDP. Series (1) declined from 1.28 in 1948 to 1.03 in 1966 and then increased to 1.51 in 1979 (calculated from data in *Economic Report of the President*, 1982, Table B-3); series 2 fell from 1.38 in 1948 to 1.08 in 1966 and rose to 1.78 in 1979.

[3]*Historical Statistics of the United States*, pp. 868–69.

[5]*Economic Report*, 1982, Table B-3.

ment, U.S. corporations paid only $1.2 billion in taxes on foreign earnings of $24 billion—an effective tax rate of just 5 percent.[6]

Military expansion was at least as important. The U.S. military had demobilized after World War I, but no such dismantling followed World War II. Ten years after the Treaty of Versailles in 1919, the combined Navy and War Departments' budgets constituted three quarters of 1 percent of U.S. GNP, an amount equal to only 8 percent of gross private fixed nonresidential investment. In 1955, military expenditures represented 10 percent of U.S. GNP, an amount actually greater than gross private fixed nonresidential investment.[7] Military expenditures have continued to constitute a significant fraction of GNP ever since.

Drawing from a varied tool kit, the U.S. government built the military, economic, and political machinery to police much of the world. Employing dollar diplomacy, CIA intervention, and occasional Marine landings, the United States blocked most challenges to the new order by populist, nationalist, and socialist movements.

. . .

Postwar Structure II: The Limited Capital-Labor Accord

International domination alone could not guarantee prosperity. The limited truce between corporations and labor was a second essential element of the postwar corporate system.

The capital-labor accord was not as formal as the Bretton Woods Agreement. It did not include all sectors of the U.S. labor force. But it did guide production in the postwar period, building upon a tacit agreement between corporate capitalists and the organized labor movement.

The accord required a purge of militant unionists from leadership positions in the late 1940s, and the passage of legislation, especially the Taft-Hartley Act of 1947, which limited union actions. Weakened by both McCarthyism and restrictive legislation, unions moved toward a clear *quid pro quo* with large corporations. Corporations would retain absolute control over the essential decisions governing enterprise operations—decisions involving production, technology, plant location, investment, and marketing. This set of corporate prerogatives was codified in the "management rights" clauses of most collective bargaining agreements. In return, unions were accepted as legitimate representatives of workers' interests. They were expected to bargain on behalf of labor's immediate economic interests, but not to challenge employer control of enterprises (much less the legitimacy of the capitalist system itself). Unions would help maintain an orderly and disciplined labor force while corporations would reward workers with a share of the income gains made possible by rising productivity, with greater employment security, and with improved working conditions.

There *were* productivity gains, and they were shared. The real value of the spendable hourly earnings of production workers rose at an annual average of 2.1 percent from 1948 to 1966—fast enough to double once every generation if the pace had continued. Job security also improved; the aggregate unemployment rate dropped to 3.8 percent by 1966, roughly one quarter of its average levels during the 1930s. Working conditions also improved; the industrial accident rate declined by nearly one third from 1948 through the early 1960s.[8]

If these realized promises were the carrot inducing labor accommodation, the continuing threat of cyclical unemployment was the stick sustaining capital's take-it-or-leave-it offer. Four cyclical downturns between the late 1940s and the early 1960s periodically boosted unemployment rates and reminded workers

[6]Barry Bluestone and Bennett Harrison, *The Deindustrialization of America* (New York: Basic Books, 1982), p. 132.

[7]*Economic Report*, 1982, B-1, B-15; *Historical Statistics*, pp. 1114, 229.

[8]*Handbook of Labor Statistics*, 1978, pp. 323, 175; and *Historical Statistics*, p. 182.

that they should be grateful to have a job.

Carrots and sticks combined to effect a steady movement toward labor cooperation. Negotiated union contracts, as in both steel and auto, were increasingly likely to include clauses restricting or prohibiting strikes. Strike activity itself dropped sharply: the proportion of work time idled because of strikes fell from an average of .54 percent in the first postwar business cycle (1946–48) to .22 percent in the next four cycles (1949–66).[9]

Corporations had agreed to cooperate with the unions they had battled only fifteen years before, and they reaped the dividends of restored control over production. As *Fortune* magazine noted about the first "productivity bargaining" agreements between General Motors and the United Automobile Workers Union in 1948 and 1950, "GM may have paid a billion for peace [but] it got a bargain. General Motors has regained control over . . . the crucial management functions."[10]

In order to take full advantage of this restored control, corporations dramatically expanded their supervisory apparatus. They developed systems of closely monitored bureaucratic control, applying sophisticated new methods for keeping track of employees' output, screening for favorable personality characteristics, and inducing worker effort through differentiated incentives, promotional rewards, and wage supplements. All of this took personnel—the managers and supervisors who watched over this system of bureaucratic control. One of the most rapidly expanding occupations between 1950 and 1970 was a relatively new category called labor-relations personnel. Overall, the resources devoted to managerial and supervisory personnel climbed significantly. Between 1948 and 1966, for example, the ratio of supervisory to nonsupervisory employees in the private business sector increased by nearly 75 percent—from roughly thirteen supervisory employees per one hundred nonsupervisory employees to

more than twenty-two. By the late 1960s, nearly twenty cents of every dollar of revenue paid to the private business sector covered the salaries of managerial and supervisory personnel.[11] Some of these employees were designated as supervisory workers simply in order to exclude them from collective bargaining units and narrow unions' base of operations. But most had real managerial and supervisory functions. Both tendencies resulted in an expanding bureaucracy beyond production workers' control. The internal costs of the postwar corporate system rose steadily.

While the accord benefited some workers, it excluded others. Unorganized workers, women, and minorities could not easily gain access to the bountiful garden of productivity dividends. The wages of workers in the "core" sector of industry outstripped those of workers on its periphery. Income inequality among wage and salary earners increased through the 1960s.[12] This growing segmentation of labor helped divide labor and strengthen corporate bargaining leverage. The limited capital-labor accord worked as long as these divisions remained firm. When the excluded began to knock at the garden gate, the terms of the accord would be jeopardized.

Postwar Structure III:
The Capitalist-Citizen Accord

. . .

The Depression generated more than labor struggles. Millions also battled for tenants' rights and public housing, for social security and public assistance, for protection against the vagaries of life in capitalist economies.

---

[9]*Historical Statistics*, 1978, pp. 508–9.

[10]Quoted in William Serrin, *The Company and the Union* (New York: Vintage, 1974), p. 170.

[11]*Employment and Training Report*, 1981, p. 212; and data for production and nonproduction workers' share of total employee compensation developed by David M. Gordon, based on *Employment and Training Report* and *Economic Report*, 1981, p. 247.

[12]See David M. Gordon, Richard Edwards, and Michael Reich, *Segmented Work, Divided Workers: The Historical Transformation of Labor in the United States* (New York: Cambridge University Press, 1982), Chapter 5; and Peter Henle, "Exploring the Distribution of Income," *Monthly Labor Review*, December 1972.

These demands were hardly new, but the state had not heeded them in earlier periods of crisis and instability. The "free-enterprise" system had forced people and businesses to fend for themselves. The government had kept its hands off, refusing to cushion the jolts of the roller-coaster ride.

But now these demands were at least partly accommodated. The state began trying to smooth the rough edges of the market economy without compromising the reign of profits as a guide to social priorities. The Social Security Act of 1935 and the Employment Act of 1946 represented two important milestones along the way.

Three aspects of the expanded state role were crucial.

First, the government sought to reduce macroeconomic instability, hoping to avoid the kind of economic downturn which had threatened the survival of all the leading capitalist economies in the 1930s. The government did not move in practice to eliminate the capitalist business cycle altogether, much less to provide for continuous full employment, since periodic contractions help to limit the power of labor and to purge the economy of weak and inefficient firms. (The former concern motivated the ferocious business opposition to the original ambitious, truly full-employment versions of the Employment Act of 1946). Macropolicy eventually sought much more modestly to moderate and guide the cycle, not to eliminate it, in the interests of political stability and profitability.

From the late 1940s to the mid-1960s, this effort succeeded. This was due partly to deliberate government stabilization policy and partly to the "automatic stabilizers" built into the postwar U.S. economy. (These latter include the progressive income tax and unemployment insurance, which tend automatically to reduce aggregate demand when the economy heats up and to stimulate demand when it cools.) The huge military buildup in the early 1950s also provided a fortuitous boost to aggregate demand after the initial postwar expansion ran out of steam in 1949, and high levels of military spending subsequently pro-

vided a solid base of demand stimulus that would help to prevent any recession from developing into a major downturn. The results were felicitous: the first five postwar business-cycle recessions were more than two thirds less severe—measured by the magnitude of their average-output slowdown—than business cycles during the comparable period of expansion after the turn of the century.[13]

Second, direct public expenditures supporting business increased substantially at all levels of government—federal, state, and local. Government contracts provided guaranteed markets for many major corporations, especially in military production, while government subsidies favored many private businesses, particularly in nuclear power and agriculture. Even more important, government expenditures on transportation, communications, and other infrastructural facilities, as well as on education and research, lowered the costs of business for almost all private firms. Some of the resulting economic benefits were passed on to consumers through lower prices, but firms also profited from this public largess.

Finally, the state committed itself to at least a margin of economic security for all Americans, whether aged, unemployed, or simply poor. As with the case of the "full-employment" objective, the social-insurance objective was tempered in practice by the need to preserve the effective disciplinary force of competition in low-wage labor markets. Yet over most of the postwar period, up to 1966, unemployment insurance coverage grew, the size of the weekly unemployment check relative to workers' take-home pay increased slightly, and the sum of social-insurance programs, education, health, and general assistance inched upward as a fraction of gross national product. These programs provided real benefits to many people but were nonetheless contained within the larger framework of capitalist priorities. For example, the distress of unemploy-

[13]Based on data in Jeffrey Sachs, "The Changing Cyclical Behavior of Wages and Prices," *American Economic Review*, March 1980, Table 2.

ment was reduced only by limited cash transfers to those who lost their jobs, not by structural changes guaranteeing everyone a job on a continuous basis. The plight of the elderly was addressed not by programs integrating them into useful social roles, but only by cash transfers to enable them to survive in the market economy.

This part of the capitalist-citizen accord, in short, involved a delicate dynamic. The new state role was constrained not to compromise the basic profitability of corporations while creating a new and significant relationship between the state and its citizens. "The emergence of the welfare state was a momentous development in American history," as social-welfare analysts Frances Fox Piven and Richard A. Cloward conclude. "It meant that people could turn to government to shield them from the insecurities and hardships of an unrestrained market economy."[14] The balancing act worked through the early 1960s, and the stability and legitimacy of the capitalist regime was bolstered as a result.

THE EROSION OF THE POSTWAR CORPORATE SYSTEM

These institutional foundations of corporate power and privilege promoted prosperity for twenty years. They worked because they secured the dominance of a private profit-making, capital-accumulating logic over the economy as a whole. They worked, but they were also vulnerable. Conflicts eventually emerged from *within* each of these three relations of power and privilege, challenges rooted in the spreading refusal by foreigners, U.S. workers, and U.S. citizens to accept the subordination required by the structure of the postwar corporate system.

Erosion I: The Decline of U.S. International Domination

U.S. corporations faced growing challenges in both the First and the Third worlds. These challenges substantially weakened the international position of U.S. capital. By the mid-1960s, the structure of Pax Americana was tottering.

One of the guiding principles of the postwar system had been the economic reconstruction and revival of war-torn Europe and Japan. U.S. aid for this purpose seemed necessary both to reverse the spread of anticapitalist movements abroad and to stimulate demand for U.S. exports. The phenomenal economic success of postwar Japan and most of Europe clearly helped pull the rug out from under left-wing labor movements in these countries, but Japanese and European economic growth also created a major competitive challenge to the United States in the world market and eventually led to a massive penetration of U.S. domestic markets.

In 1955, U.S. merchandise exports accounted for 32 percent of the merchandise exports of the major capitalist economies. By 1971, the U.S. share had fallen to 18 percent. Imports had remained a low and constant or declining share of gross domestic product over most of the postwar era. Around the mid-1960s, import penetration suddenly escalated. Between 1960 and 1970, imports rose from 4 percent to 17 percent of the U.S. market in autos, from 4 to 31 percent in consumer electronics, from 5 to 36 percent in calculating and adding machines, and from less than 1 percent to 5 percent in electrical components.[15] . . .

Aggregate import penetration began to increase precisely in 1965, and it accelerated in the 1970s.

---

[14]Frances Fox Piven and Richard A. Cloward, *The New Class War: Reagan's Attack on the Welfare State and Its Consequences* (New York: Pantheon, 1982), p. ix.

[15]The shares of U.S. exports in the exports of the advanced nations are calculated from OECD, *National Accounts* using current exchange rates (from the same source). The industry data are from *Business Week*, June 30, 1980, p. 60, based on Commerce Department data.

It seems likely that the decline in U.S. competitive strength was attributable, at least in part, to the size and relative importance of the U.S. military machine. The military role of the United States was indispensable in helping to police the postwar international system, but it also constituted an enormous drain on the productive capacity of the United States.... Among the four major economic units of the advanced capitalist world system during the 1960s—the United States, Great Britain, the Common Market countries, and Japan—there was an almost perfectly negative correlation between the growth of export shares and the rate of military spending during the decade of the 1960s. Because the United States and the United Kingdom were devoting substantially higher proportions of aggregate domestic product to military spending, they had significantly less available to devote to productive capital formation.

Could this drain have been avoided? In retrospect we can see that the Bretton Woods system required *both* a strong U.S. economy *and* a strong U.S. military—the former to reinforce the dollar's role as key currency, and the latter to stabilize the political relationships necessary to enforce U.S. access to foreign markets and secure the uninterrupted flow of dollars around the globe. But these requirements turned out to be as much competing as complementary, with military spending eventually sapping the economy's strength. When this contradiction became acute, by the mid-1960s, monetary stability began to unravel. There had been a growing glut of U.S. dollars on world money markets—beginning with the declining demand for U.S. exports and exploding from the burgeoning costs of the Vietnam War. Other nations hesitated to accumulate more dollars. Gold began to pour out of Fort Knox. When Nixon took to the television cameras in 1971, renouncing the dollar-based system of fixed exchange rates, the foundations of international monetary stability were shattered.

Challenges from the Third World also began to undermine U.S. international domination in the 1960s. For centuries, people in the "Third World" had been struggling to free themselves from colonial domination. It was hardly surprising that these liberation movements aimed increasingly at the United States. The U.S. government had provided most of the military aid to procapitalist governments and—where necessary—intervened by force or orchestrated coups to promote favorable foreign access for private capital. U.S.-based multinational corporations had led the penetration of Third World societies, scooping up resources and overturning traditional societies. More and more, the U.S. government and U.S.-based multinationals drew the sights of liberation rifles—whether fired for purely nationalist or explicitly socialist purposes.

The U.S. government initially had little difficulty suppressing such challenges; the ousters of Mossadegh [from Iran in 1953] and Arbenz [from Guatemala in 1954] came easily. But the failure of the Kennedy administration to overthrow Castro in the 1961 Bay of Pigs invasion, and especially the long and humiliating failure to stem the revolutionary tide in South Vietnam, marked a significant and escalating erosion of the U.S. government's capacity to "keep the world safe" for private enterprise. The United States could no longer throw its weight around so effectively.

A final significant challenge in the world economy came from exporters of raw materials, primarily in Third World nations. This development did not involve a direct political challenge to the reign of private corporate power. It reflected a narrower economic demand for greater national control over natural resources and for a larger share of the global economic pie.

By the late 1960s, the time for such demands was ripe: rivalry among the advanced countries had increased, U.S. military capacities were strained while countervailing Soviet power had grown, and pressure on worldwide resource supplies had begun to increase. The economic bargaining power of some of the Third World raw-materials-exporting nations increased substantially. The OPEC cartel was the most visible and important example. In conjunction with multinational petroleum companies, it succeeded in shifting the terms of the oil trade sharply against the oil-importing nations, first in 1973 and then again in 1979.

All three of these international challenges—from the advanced economies, from Third World rebellions, from raw-materials exporters—combined to diminish U.S. international power. One of the best indicators of this effect is the U.S. terms of trade, or the ratio of prices of U.S. exports to prices of U.S. imports. The higher the terms of trade, the greater the quantity of goods and services that can be purchased abroad by a unit of real output produced in the U.S. economy.... After an initial decline to 1951, the U.S. terms of trade improved steadily until the late 1960s—a clear summary indicator of the fruits of Pax Americana. The terms of trade reached their peak in 1969. They then turned sharply downward in the 1970s, notably before the impact of the OPEC price hike in 1973. This decline in the terms of trade was felt acutely in the domestic economy, as we shall see when we turn to our more quantitative analysis, and it contributed significantly both to declining profits and to the productivity showdown.

Erosion II: The Demise of the Capital-Labor Accord

The postwar corporate system rested upon a domestic political coalition which political scientist Alan Wolfe has dubbed the "growth coalition."[16] It was united around the principles of profit-led growth, the priority of profitability in establishing social objectives, and a mutual nonaggression pact in the distribution of economic bounty. (This last principle essentially involved a freeze of the distributive shares with which coalition members began, continuing the distribution of the dividends of growth in those relative proportions.)

This political coalition worked well because it united two powerful partners: multinational business and organized labor. Its politics

turned out to be complex, however, because it included neither *all* capital nor *all* labor. The coalition was broad enough to be electable and narrow enough to allow significant spoils to its constituent members—often at the expense of excluded elements in the United States. But its limited scope continually risked the rebellion of the excluded.

Through the 1960s, the exclusion of small capital was both obvious and effective. Small business had been lukewarm, at best, to the initial terms of the accord—particularly toward its accommodation of labor. But these constituent groups, like the left in the labor movement, suffered serious political defeats in the immediate postwar period: the Republican Party rejected isolationism (in favor of free trade), traditional conservatism (in favor of the accord with labor), and Robert Taft (in favor of Dwight D. Eisenhower and the Eastern, liberal wing of the party which supported him). The ideological and programmatic centers of the business community shifted to the Council on Foreign Relations and the Committee on Economic Development, which was an early pro-Keynesian advocate, and away from the National Association of Manufacturers. Small business continued to grow weaker economically, as both corporate concentration and the rate of small-business failures increased. Small enterprises were hardly in a position to challenge the central powers of the coalition.

The exclusion of many workers proved much more problematic, much earlier. While nonunion labor benefited substantially from the spillover effects of union political and economic victories, they were clearly not part of the coalition. Their exclusion had two critical consequences—for organized labor and eventually for the postwar accord itself.

From the side of organized labor, its narrow scope ultimately proved its undoing. Close to 40 percent of the wage-labor force worked in what many economists call "secondary jobs," which provided much less favorable opportunities for wage gains and stable employment than primary jobs. Women, minority, and younger workers disproportionately filled

---

[16]Wolfe, *America's Impasse*, pp. 22–23 and passim.

these secondary jobs. As a result of the effectiveness of the accord between large corporations and organized labor, the wage gap between "core" and "peripheral" sectors— between those industries most and least benefiting from the accord—widened steadily through the postwar period, increasing (according to our estimates) by 15 percent from 1948 to 1966. This resulted in widening income inequality by race and sex. . . . Unemployment disadvantages by race and by sex also widened significantly.[17]

The net effect for the labor movement was a significant narrowing of its reach. Labor-union membership, which had soared from the mid-1930s through the late 1940s and early 1950s, fell dramatically from its postwar peaks, dropping from 35 percent of the nonagricultural labor force at the time of the AFL–CIO merger in 1954 to only 28 percent in 1966.[18] Eventually, organized labor felt the effects of this decline through erosion of its bargaining power.

The consequences for the postwar accord were just as serious, beginning to backfire in the late 1950s and early 1960s. Protest against the racism, sexism, and distributive injustice of the growth coalition emerged through four different but effective movements: the civil rights movement, the welfare rights movement, the organization of the elderly, and the women's movement. These movements all led to government efforts at accommodation, cumulating with accelerating force in the mid-1960s through Medicare and Medicaid, the Great Society legislation producing the Voting Rights Act and the poverty program, the expansion of public assistance, and spreading attention to affirmative action and equal rights. Many of these programs cost money, and their growing costs reflected the mounting and increasingly expensive requirements of containing resistance to an unequal distribution of

power and privilege. These were real economic gains won by mass movements, and they tended increasingly, as we shall see throughout these chapters, to undermine the structure of the postwar corporate system.

These represented challenges from *outside* the capital-labor accord. Yet the accord began to encounter increasingly serious resistance from the predominantly unionized workers *within* the coalition as well. Several factors contributed to the growth of discontent and recalcitrance among these "primary" workers.

The first involves an apparent shift in attitudes and focus. Rising real wages, heightened job security, and improved working conditions were increasingly taken for granted—as memories of the Depression receded and young workers replaced those who had struggled through the 1930s. This decline in *material* insecurity apparently led to greater concern about occupational health-and-safety issues, influence over workplace decisions, and opportunities for meaningful and creatively challenging work. These spreading concerns could conceivably have been accommodated, but they tended to run up against the vast apparatus of bureaucratic control. The increasing intensity of supervision worked well for those workers who understood and still believed in the terms of the initial bargain, but it was less and less likely to remain effective when it confronted a labor force which—by age, education, and temperament—was increasingly resistant to arbitrary authority. Even among blue-collar workers, rank-and-file movements in the United Auto Workers, the United Steel Workers, the United Mine Workers, the Teamsters and several other important unions all challenged authoritarian and business-oriented leadership, often seeking to bring the issues of union democracy, racism, and job safety to the fore.

These sources of erosion were complemented by another and clearly critical problem for capital: the declining effectiveness of the traditional source of capitalist leverage over the work force, the threat of unemployment. This threat is based on two simple facts of life in a capitalist economy: workers depend

[17]Gordon, Edwards, and Reich, *Segmented Work, Divided Workers*, Figure 5.1A; Table 5.6.

[18]*Handbook of Labor Statistics*, p. 412.

on getting jobs in order to live, and a significant number of workers at any time are stuck without a job.

Two developments in the postwar period reduced the effectiveness of this threat. First, the unemployment rate was relatively low, by historical standards, throughout the period, and it fell to unusually low levels in the mid-1960s. Second, the social programs won by popular struggles in the 1930s—social insurance, unemployment compensation, and others—were gradually extended during the 1940s and 1950s and then, under the pressure of the initiatives of the "excluded," they were greatly expanded and augmented by new programs such as Medicaid, Medicare, food stamps, and Aid to Families with Dependent Children (AFDC). The combined effect of all these programs was to provide some cushion for those laid off from work.

To document this phenomenon and to assess its relative impact, we have combined the two effects—lower unemployment and the cushion provided by social programs—into a single measure of the "cost of losing your job." Our measure represents the average number of weeks' worth of overall income lost by a worker who is laid off. It varies with both the likelihood of remaining without a job for a long time—as when unemployment rises—and with the relative income lost when a worker is unemployed. The higher this measure, the greater the cost of job termination and the greater the potential corporate leverage over their workers.

· · ·

Measured by the cost to workers of losing their job, employers' leverage over workers declined by more than a quarter from the boom period to the first phase of crisis.

· · ·

This erosion of corporate leverage was bound to reduce employers' ability to push for greater work intensity and to hold down wages. When real output per worker-hour does not grow as rapidly as real compensation per hour, the real cost of labor to capital begins to rise. And this will tend, in turn, to increase the share of labor and reduce the share of capital in overall income. If the capital-labor accord was beginning to erode after 1966, we would expect it to have contributed to a simultaneous decline in corporate profitability. And this, as we show in the last section of this chapter, is exactly what happened.

Erosion III: Challenges to the Logic of Profitability

The postwar corporate system rested centrally on the premise "If it's profitable it must be desirable." The third critical fracture in the postwar edifice resulted from a widespread challenge to this principle.

At the beginning of the postwar period, the major decisions of economic life—concerning technology, product design, industrial location, occupational safety and health, and environmental balance—had been relegated to the market. Despite the more active intervention of the state, its economic intrusions did not affect the basic logic of profitability in the private sector. When Eisenhower's secretary of defense, Charles Wilson, suggested, "What is good for General Motors is good for the country," most people thought Wilson to be merely impolitic, not wrong.

But the bottom line was not to continue unchallenged for long. Beginning with occupational health-and-safety campaigns in the Oil, Chemical, and Atomic Workers Union and in the United Mine Workers, and equally with Ralph Nader's effective public mobilization around issues of consumer safety and product design, fueled by the notorious Pinto exploding-gas-tank scandal, sustained by Love Canal and the periodic burning of the Cuyahoga River, a wide variety of movements emerged to challenge the hallowed identity of private greed and public virtue. The oldest of these movements—conservation—enjoyed a veritable rebirth and transformation in the late 1960s and early 1970s, sparking a series of popular and often militant campaigns demanding environmental protection, alternative energy sources, and a halt to nuclear power.

Although these movements were largely disconnected and focused on single issues, they had the combined effect of challenging the basic logic of capitalist profitability. On issue after issue, they raised doubts about the primacy of private profitability in determining resource allocation and economic decision-making.

By the early 1970s, these several insurgencies had won a series of major legislative and legal victories, creating a sequence of agencies with major responsibility for corporate regulation—the National Highway Traffic Safety Commission (1970), the Occupational Safety and Health Administration (1970), the Environmental Protection Administration (1970), the Consumer Product Safety Commission (1972), the Mine Enforcement and Safety Administration (1973), and several others. Later in the decade, the environmental movement made further advances through its challenge to the safety hazards of nuclear power generation.

Though new social mores were important in this process, these movements did not arise solely or even primarily through changes in people's values. In many cases, they resulted much more simply from defensive and protective reactions against the rising and increasingly serious hazards of life in the postwar regime: the spread of lethal products on the market, urban air pollution, the threat of radioactive pollution, increasingly hazardous working conditions. In manufacturing, for example, the accident rate began to rise sharply

after 1963–65, having fallen from its wartime highs through the 1950s; by the early 1970s, it had surpassed its early postwar levels and by the late 1970s it had risen substantially above even its World War II peaks.[19] The Mine Safety Act of 1969 was passed in the wake of the terrible 1968 Mannington Mine disaster, which that year brought coal-mine fatalities (per million man-hours worked) to a postwar peak.[20] Faced with these threats, people had no choice but to react.

One of the clearest consequences of these challenges to profitability was the rapidly rising costs of "nature-based inputs"—agricultural products, fuels, and other raw materials. Many have attributed these rising costs to a "running out of nature," an issue about which we remain agnostic. It is much more likely, we think, that the rapid increases in various crude-materials prices after the mid-1960s were the result of a wide variety of contradictions within the postwar corporate system—due both to declining U.S. international domination and to spreading challenges to the logic of profitability.

[19]Michele I. Naples and David M. Gordon, "The Industrial Accident Rate: Creating a Consistent Time Series," Institute for Labor Education and Research, December 1981. See also David M. Gordon and Michele I. Naples, "More Injuries on the Job," New York *Times*, December 13, 1981.

[20]*Historical Statistics*, p. 607.

10.4 *World Capitalism and the Current Economic Crisis*

The previous reading discussed three dimensions of the rise and demise of the postwar corporate system. In the following reading Arthur MacEwan elaborates the international aspects of this transformation.

> Excerpted from "Changes in World Capitalism and the Current Crisis of the U.S. Economy" by ARTHUR MACEWAN. From *Radical America*, 9, no. 1, January–February 1975 (P.O. Box B, N. Cambridge, MA 02140). Reprinted with minor revisions by permission of Arthur MacEwan and *Radical America*.

The period since World War II has been characterized by a continuous increase in the integration of the world capitalist system. However, throughout the period, forces have been building towards the destruction of the stability of that system. By the beginning of the 1970s, those forces had come into their own, and the basis for stability—U.S. hegemony—had been eliminated.

The simultaneous *integration* and *destabilization* of the world capitalist system constitutes an important contradiction that has far-reaching implications. In particular, the operation of this contradiction has put the U.S. economy in a precarious position.

In this essay, I intend to describe some central features of the operation of world capitalism during the post–World War II period and to explain how the very success of those years was creating the conditions for the disruption of the system. I will then be in a position to relate the current crisis of the U.S. economy to the important changes in world capitalism and show how international affairs have played a central role in the development, precipitation and continuation of the crisis.

CREATION OF U.S. HEGEMONY

At the end of World War II, the United States was in a particularly fortunate position. While the economies of the other advanced nations—victors and vanquished alike—had been devastated by the war, the U.S. economy had flourished. Consequently, in 1945, the U.S. held a position of unique and unchallenged political-military and economic power among capitalist nations.

An era of U.S. hegemony had begun. The U.S. government was able to dictate economic and political policies within the world capitalist system.[1] Accordingly, it was possible to reestablish an international order which had been lacking for over half a century—since the time when other nations had begun to seriously challenge Britain's pre-eminence.

The new era of U.S. hegemony expressed itself in several new institutional arrangements. Most frequently noted are the set of monetary arrangements imposed on the other capitalist nations in 1944 at the Bretton Woods Conference. In the earlier periods of colonial expansion, each colonial power had imposed its currency—pound, franc, mark—within its empire. Now, after World War II, the U.S. established the dollar as the principal reserve currency throughout the capitalist world.

The role of the dollar was closely connected to the rapid international growth of U.S. business. The expansion of U.S. banking abroad highlights the general picture. In Europe, for example, U.S. banks had only 20 to 30 branches in the 1920s, and during the 1930s and the War most of these were closed down. The 1950s and the 1960s saw a steady advance to the point where by 1968 U.S. banks had 326 branches in Europe.[2]

The largest industrial corporations were central actors in the post-War overseas expansion. In 1950 General Motors was annually producing less than 200,000 vehicles abroad. By 1952 it had expanded production to approximately 600,000 units. In another year, with European production being supplemented by Australian and Brazilian expansion, GM was producing over one million vehicles in its foreign plants. And the boom continued on into the 1960s: between 1963 and 1964 GM's overseas production grew by a quarter of a million.[3]

Aggregate data show the same general picture of rapid growth of U.S. foreign investment in the 1950s and 1960s. The value of all U.S. direct investment abroad stood at roughly $11 billion in 1950; by 1960 the total had risen to over $30 billion; and in 1970 the figure was over $70 billion.[4]

---

[1]The ability of the U.S. government to dictate was, of course, limited in the ways that the power of any dictator is limited. A dictator must compromise sometimes, must cajole reluctant followers, and must smash rebellions. But as long as he is successful in maintaining the foundation of his power, the dictator remains a dictator.

[2]See J. P. Koszul, "American Banks in Europe," in C. P. Kindleberger, ed., *The International Corporation* (Cambridge, Mass.: MIT Press, 1970), pp. 274–75.

[3]See J. W. Sundelson, "U.S. Automotive Investment Abroad," in C. P. Kindleberger, ed., *The International Corporation*, p. 256.

[4]See Table 3-F, p. 103.

The absolute growth of U.S. business interests abroad is impressive, but it should be seen in the context of the establishment of overwhelming U.S. dominance in the international capitalist economy. In Latin America, for example, just prior to World War I, only 18 percent of foreign private investment and less than 5 percent of public debt was held by U.S. interests. British interests held 47 percent of private investment and 70 percent of public debt. In the early 1950s, direct investment in Latin America from sources other than the U.S. was negligible, and in the early 1960s the U.S. still accounted for roughly 70 percent of new foreign investment in Latin America. As to foreign public debt, the U.S. was supplying about 70 percent in the early 1950s and still more than 50 percent in the early 1960s.[5]

Not only has the U.S. replaced the European nations as the leading economic power operating in the Third World, but the post-War years saw a substantial penetration of the European economies by U.S. business. The value of direct U.S. investment in Europe tripled between 1950 and 1959 (from $1.7 billion to $5.3 billion), then quadrupled (to $21.6 billion) by 1969, and doubled again to $44.5 billion by the end of 1974.[6]

On the political and military level, U.S. expansion kept pace with economic interests. Economic aid, military aid, and the establishment of overseas military bases helped provide a political environment conducive to corporate penetration. Throughout the European colonial world, the U.S. ambassadors began to replace the European colonial administrators as the dominant political figures. And in line with the new world order European colonies were transformed to independent nations under the aegis of U.S. neocolonialism. More and more, the British and French military networks were replaced by U.S. centered "alliances" such as SEATO and CENTO.

The U.S. took on the role of maintaining an international police force to maintain "law and order" throughout the capitalist world. Moreover, it became the organizer and chief participant in the general effort of capitalist nations to contain and harass the socialist bloc.

BENEFITS OF HEGEMONY

This hegemony had its distinct advantages for U.S. business. To begin with, foreign activity has been a significant and growing source of direct profits. As a proportion of after tax profits of U.S. corporations, profits from abroad rose steadily from less than 10 percent in 1950 to about 25 percent at the beginning of the 1970s.[7] Moreover, these profits accrue disproportionately to the very large firms in the U.S. economy.[8] . . .

In addition to these direct benefits of international activity, the maintenance of an open and stable international capitalist system under U.S. hegemony has provided important elements in the structural foundations of the post–World War II expansion of the U.S. economy.

It has been generally recognized that having the dollar as the central currency of world capitalism assured that U.S. businesses would always have ample funds to undertake foreign activity. With the dollar-based monetary system, businesses in other nations had an increasing need for dollars in order to carry out their own international transactions. In the 1960s for example, the growth of dollars held outside the U.S. averaged about $2 billion a year. As a result, U.S. business could make purchases abroad with dollars without having all of those dollars redeemed by equivalent purchases by foreigners in the U.S. The rest of the world was effectively extending credit, to

---

[5]See United Nations Economic Commission for Latin America, *External Financing in Latin America*, 1965, pp. 16–17, 147–48.

[6]These figures can be derived from Table 3-F, p. 103.

[7]See Table 3-G, p. 104.

[8]For documentation, see MacEwan, Section 3.6, p. 107, and Table 3-I, p. 106.

the tune of $2 billion more each year of the 1960s, to U.S. business.[9]

Monetary matters are, however, only the beginning of the story. The story continues with the impact of international activity on domestic power relations and with the importance of access to and control over resources and markets.

Manufacturing has been the most rapidly growing sector of U.S. foreign investment.[10] Foreign expansion of manufacturing has been motivated by the dual goals of obtaining a foothold in foreign markets and exploiting cheaper labor. The process has a structural impact on power relations that goes far beyond its direct impact on corporate profits. The ability of capital to move abroad greatly strengthens its hand in disputes with labor. Labor, whether demanding higher wages or better working conditions, is threatened by the possibility that management will choose to close shop and relocate abroad (or simply cease domestic expansion). The effectiveness of the threat has been demonstrated by the extensive expansion of overseas operations by U.S. manufacturers. And that extensive expansion has been greatly facilitated by U.S. hegemony.

Consequently, we may say that one of the elements establishing labor discipline in the domestic economy is the international mobility of manufacturing capital. The labor discipline—or the power relations between capital and labor which it represents—has been a central element upon which the successful domestic expansion of the U.S. economy has been based.[11]

Another structural basis for economic growth has been provided by foreign investment based on natural resources. While not as rapidly growing as manufacturing investment, resource-based foreign investment has by no means been stagnant.[12] The central issue in assessing the importance of natural resource based investment is *control*. In the first place, as recent experience with oil makes clear, natural resource prices—of copper, bauxite, and so forth, as well as oil—are determined within a fairly wide range by power relationships. The low prices of certain resources which have been important to the post-War growth of the U.S. economy can now be seen to have rested on the combined economic and political power of U.S. corporations in the context of U.S. hegemony.

A second factor explaining the importance of natural resource control is that control provides a basis for security, for both the nations and companies involved. The U.S. military apparatus is dependent on several imported strategic raw materials, e.g., nickel and chromium.[13] Thus, the position of the military and all that it implies is tied to the control of cer-

[9]For more on this, see F. Ackerman and A. MacEwan, "Inflation, Recession and Crisis," *Review of Radical Political Economics*, 4, No. 4 (August 1972). By holding dollars as reserves, foreigners were allowing the dollar to be overvalued (i.e., the demand for dollars as reserves pushed the price of the dollar above what it would have been as a result simply of the demand for U.S. goods and services); foreign assets were accordingly cheaper to U.S. firms than they otherwise would have been.

[10]The value of manufacturing assets abroad rose from 33 percent of the total in 1950 to 43 percent of the total in 1974.

[11]The argument here should be distinguished from another argument sometimes put forth by opponents of the

runaway shop—to wit, that capital mobility means a slower overall growth of jobs in the U.S. economy. It is not at all clear that in the aggregate and over time capital mobility means fewer jobs. Of course, workers immediately affected by a runaway shop are thrown out of work. But the overall effect of foreign investment is to increase the surplus available for investment within the U.S. In any given year, profits returned from former foreign investment exceed the outflow of new foreign investment and, accordingly, contribute to the expansion of the U.S. economy including the aggregate expansion of jobs. However, regardless of the aggregate long-run impact of foreign investment, at any point in time the existence of options for capital weakens labor because the threat of joblessness for a particular group of workers at a particular time means it is less able to make effective demands on capital. Moreover, the sector of labor most immediately affected tends to be the most thoroughly organized, for it is in those cases relatively more advantageous for capital to move abroad.

[12]The value of foreign assets in petroleum and mining and smelting tripled between 1950 and 1959 (from $4.5 billion to $13.3 billion) and had almost tripled again by 1974 (to $36.3 billion).

[13]See Harry Magdoff, *The Age of Imperialism* (New York: Monthly Review Press, 1969), pp. 45–54.

tain natural resources. From the point of view of the corporations, control of resource supplies provides security for their monopoly positions, both domestically and internationally. In oil, in aluminum, in copper, the major companies have used "vertical integration"— i.e., involvement in all phases of the industry from crude material production to sales of final products—as a basis for their power.

In numerous other types of industries as well, international activity is bound up with monopoly power. Domestic monopoly power provides the basis for successful international expansion, and the international expansion further enhances size and power which secure the original monopoly position. A description of the drug industry's activities has been provided by no less a source than Senator Russell Long, speaking in 1966: "For more than a dozen years, American drug companies have been involved in a world wide cartel to fix the prices of 'wonder drugs' . . . the conspirators have embarked on an extensive campaign to destroy their competitors."[14]

All of these benefits that have been obtained by U.S. business during the era of U.S. hegemony in world capitalism have not, of course, been theirs alone. Other advanced capitalist nations have participated in and their businesses have gained from the international stability. The U.S. may have led, but the followers have done well for themselves. And therein lies one of the problems.

CONTRADICTIONS IN THE SYSTEM

The good times for U.S. business could not last because the successful operation of the system was, from the outset, leading towards its own destruction. Simply insofar as the U.S. used its power to maintain stability, it allowed the reconstruction of the other capitalist nations. Success for the U.S. meant stability, but

stability would allow its competitors to reestablish themselves.

In fact, the U.S. did far more than simply maintain stability. For both economic and political reasons, the success of the U.S. required that it take an active role in rebuilding the war-torn areas of the capitalist system. Economically, U.S. business needed the strong trading partners and investment opportunities that only reconstruction could provide. Politically, the U.S. needed strong allies in its developing confrontations with the Soviet Union and China.

Consequently, throughout the post-World War II period, the other capitalist nations were able to move toward a position where they could challenge the U.S., both economically and politically. As early as the late 1950s and early 1960s, it was becoming clear that Japanese and European goods were beginning to compete effectively with U.S. products. And other nations began to grumble about the costs of supporting a world monetary system based on the dollar. It was only a matter of time before the economic challenge would become serious, and the other nations would no longer allow the U.S. to dictate the rules and policies for the operation of international capitalism.

Still, "a matter of time" can be a long time or a short time. If the only challenge had been that from the expansion of other advanced capitalist nations, the U.S. might have maintained its position of hegemony for many more years. That was not, however, the only challenge.

The successful extension of capitalism into new geographic areas is—especially in the era of the rise of socialism—a process involving considerable conflict. In providing the police force for world capitalism, the U.S. government has been obliged to engage in numerous direct and indirect military encounters. Greece, Iran, Guatemala, Lebanon, the Dominican Republic only begin the list of nations that have felt the effect of U.S. coercion. In many cases, the overwhelming military capacity of the U.S. was sufficient to prevent serious military conflict from developing.

[14]Quoted by Richard Barnet and Ronald Müller, *Global Reach* (New York: Simon & Schuster, 1975), p. 187, from the *Congressional Record—Senate*, February 10, 1966, 2886–94.

Indochina, however, presented a different story. The liberation forces in Vietnam were not so easily contained, and the U.S. became more and more deeply involved. A particular dialectic was thus created which had far-reaching implications. On the one hand, unable to win in Vietnam, the U.S. was forced to act in a way that undermined its economic strength. On the other hand, as its economic position deteriorated, the U.S. government was less able to pursue a successful military policy in Vietnam.

This dialectical process combined the contradiction between the U.S. and other advanced capitalist nations and the contradiction between the U.S. (as the central power among the advanced nations) and the periphery of the system (i.e., the Third World). The combined operation of these contradictions has ended the era of U.S. hegemony in a manner that will be shortly described.

First, however, it should be pointed out that the operation of these two contradictions established the foundation for the operation of still another contradiction. Success in the era of U.S. hegemony meant the integration of world capitalism, the creation of a system in which business was less and less constrained by national boundaries, a system in which capital could move freely. Consequently, a general interdependence has developed within world capitalism. The continued operation of a system of interdependence requires stability and coordination. Without U.S. hegemony the basis for stability and coordination no longer exists. The resulting contradiction between an integrated capitalist system and a capitalist system that has destroyed its basis for stability plays a central role in the crisis of the 1970s.

. . . .

The new situation of the 1970s was marked by both political and economic disruption of U.S. world power. Politically, the experience in Vietnam has demonstrated the inability of the U.S. to effectively police the world. Economically, the shift in the balance of U.S. international trade brought the new reality into stark relief. In the period 1960 through 1965, U.S. power had been reflected in large trade

surpluses, averaging $5.8 billion. The trade surplus began to decline in 1966, and for the 1966 to 1971 period averaged only $1.4 billion. In 1971, 1972 and 1973 the U.S. ran trade deficits of $2.7 billion, $6.9 billion, and $0.7 billion, respectively.[15]

The challenge from Europe and Japan, which had been on the horizon in the early 1960s, had now arrived. Its coming was greatly hastened by the economic problems which the U.S. economy suffered as a consequence of the Vietnam War. In this sense, the two contradictions of international capitalism had come together to effect an alteration of the system. The formal alteration of international capitalism came with Nixon's declaration in 1971 of the New Economic Policy,[16] the devaluation of the dollar, and the destruction of capitalism's international monetary system.

. . . .

In concluding this paper it is useful to take particular note of the complications that international instability combined with integration creates for the formulation of government monetary and fiscal policy. Quite simply, under the present circumstances the implications of any particular policy are at best unclear.

Most obvious are the difficulties in formulating monetary policy. When in 1971 the U.S. lowered its interest rates relative to those in Europe, a huge, unprecedented outflow of capital took place. That experience showed the degree to which capital markets have become integrated and the speed at which money managers respond to interest rate variations. The situation would seem at least as sensitive today with the large amount of "oil money" moving around the system. Accordingly, it makes little sense for the U.S. or any other major nation to formulate monetary policy and adjust interest rates on its own. In 1974 all of the major nations did, in fact, act in the same manner, maintaining high interest

[15]From the *Economic Report of the President, 1974* (Washington: U.S. Government Printing Office, 1974).
[16]Editors' note: The New Economic Policy involved a set of domestic wage and price controls accompanying the devaluation of the dollar.

rates and tight money policies. There is, however, no reason to believe that in the absence of coordination they will continue to choose the same policies; different governments will face different circumstances and will act differently. Yet it is not clear how any coordinated policy would be developed.

The problems for fiscal policy are only slightly less immediate. It is at least a possibility that in carrying out expansionary programs designed to encourage investment, the U.S. government will find itself competing with the other advanced nations to see which can provide the most favorable investment climate. The result could be a substantial expansion of overseas investment, lacking any substantial direct and immediate impact on the U.S. economy.

Moreover, under conditions of international integration and instability, the impact of any policy is difficult to predict. When the time comes again for counter-inflationary actions, a deceleration of the economy could lead to a much greater cutback of investment than the government would be aiming for. If other governments were not following similar deflationary policies, overseas options might attract an unexpectedly large amount of U.S. capital. The results of the U.S. action could then be inflation-exacerbating shortages and the development of another round of recession.

The list of uncertainties and possible problems could be continued. Different nations may attempt to solve their own problems by raising tariffs; other nations might follow suit and a serious disruption of trade patterns could occur. Alternatively, a series of competitive devaluations may take place, or some nations might impose more stringent foreign exchange controls. Each such action would present new problems for the U.S. economy.

The governments of the leading capitalist nations are not unaware of the dangers in the current situation, but awareness and ability to cope are not the same thing. In his much publicized *Business Week* interview, Kissinger put the problem simply: "One interesting feature of our recent discussions with both the Europeans and Japanese has been the emphasis on the need for economic coordination. . . . How you, in fact, coordinate policies is yet an unresolved problem."[17]

Thus, international instability of an integrated world capitalism will continue to plague the U.S. economy for some time to come. Policy problems, trade and monetary instability, price shocks, and other unforeseeables will all be part of the new agenda.

[17]*Business Week*, January 13, 1975, p. 76.

CHAPTER 11

FROM CAPITALISM
TO SOCIALISM

THUS FAR IN THIS BOOK we have developed a critical analysis of the capitalist system, focusing especially on its operation in the United States. Our analysis is bound to raise some basic questions about alternatives to capitalism. What would a truly desirable society look like? How would it work? And how is it possible for us to get from here to there?

In this final chapter we will attempt to provide an initial basis for developing answers to these crucial questions. We will not try to provide definitive and comprehensive answers, for they do not yet exist. Instead, we urge you—our readers—to pursue these questions yourselves with the help of the readings in this chapter,[1] your own experience and imagination, and an open mind.

A VISION OF A SOCIALIST ALTERNATIVE

What kind of society might replace capitalism? What is our vision of a more decent and humane society?

We cannot present a blueprint or an exact specification of such a future society; nor should we attempt to do so, since constructing imaginary utopias bears little relation to the actual task of building a decent society. Any

[1]For additional literature on the subject of alternatives to the capitalist mode of production, we recommend very strongly that you consult *Socialist Alternatives for America: A Bibliography*, selected, structured, and annotated, with an introductory essay, by Jim Campen (New York: The Union for Radical Political Economics, 1974).

real alternatives to capitalism will be historically linked to the forces and movements that are successful in overcoming capitalist society itself. New institutions that liberate rather than oppress can only be created by real people confronting concrete problems in their lives and developing new means to overcome oppression. The political movements arising in opposition to capitalism therefore constitute the only means for society to move from its present condition to a new and more decent form, and only out of these movements will humane as well as practical new institutions be generated.

We can, however, explain what values would characterize a truly decent society and what goals should motivate the political movement for it. In a sense, the values underlying a decent society have been implicit throughout our analysis of capitalism. Our alternative society would be characterized by equality; equality rather than hierarchy in making social decisions; equality in sharing the material benefits of the society; and equality in society's encouragement to develop one's full potential. Work must cease to be a means of "making one's living" and become nonalienated, a part of one's living. Arbitrary distinctions by sex and race (or language or eye color) would cease to be criteria for particular forms of oppression or for tracking people into limited opportunities. The irrationality of production for profits would be transformed into the rationality of production to satisfy people's needs, and the unequal relations of imperialism would be replaced by a cooperative ethic recognizing people's responsibility to each other.

We call our vision of an alternative society *socialism*, because we identify with the humane values that have inspired generations of men and women to struggle for a socialist alternative to capitalism. But we wish to stress that our conception of a relevant and desirable socialist alternative to capitalism differs in certain important ways from most of the contemporary societies that are commonly referred to as socialist.[2]

For us, socialism is more than a set of humane values, and it is more than the substitution of public for private ownership of the means of production. We have in mind a socialism which means democratic, decentralized and *participatory* control for the individual: it means having a say in the decisions that affect one's life. Such a participatory form of socialism certainly requires equal access for all to material and cultural resources, which in turn requires the abolition of private ownership of capital and the redistribution of wealth. But it also calls for socialist men and women to eliminate alienating, destructive forms of production, consumption, education, and community and family life. Participatory socialism requires the elimination of corporate bureaucracies and all such hierarchical forms and their replacement, not by new state or party bureaucracies, but by a self-governing and self-managing people with directly chosen representatives subject to recall and replacement. Participatory socialism entails a sense of egalitarian cooperation, of solidarity of people with one another; but at the same time it respects individual and group differences and guarantees individual rights. It affords to all individuals the freedom to exercise human rights and civil liberties that are not mere abstractions but have concrete day-to-day meaning.

Our vision of a participatory socialist society is not one in which all problems miraculously disappear. Antisocial behavior, natural disasters, and necessary trade-offs (e.g., between production and the environment) will undoubtedly continue. But participatory socialism should provide a way of life and a set of social institutions that *encourage* cooperative, egalitarian, and decent relations among people—quite a contrast to capitalist organization, which fosters their opposites. And over time, as people live and experience the new society, they themselves will likely be changed. Greed, alienation, racism, and other forms of antisocial behavior, which grow so naturally in capitalist society, will become like exotic hothouse flowers transplanted outdoors; no longer matched to their environment, they will wither and die. To achieve this kind of participatory or democratic socialism clearly requires a radical transformation of the existing capitalist mode of production.

GETTING FROM HERE TO THERE

How is it possible to bring about the kind of fundamental social change that alone can lead to participatory socialism? In the first place, this requires a growing democratic socialist movement that can become strong enough to resist and overcome the power of the capitalist class to maintain the capitalist system from which it benefits. As the class that comprises the great majority of the people in any capitalist society, and which stands to benefit most clearly from the transformation of capitalism, the working class must necessarily be in the forefront of a successful movement for participatory socialism. The entire working class, defined in its broadest sense, has the potential, when allied with associated popular social movements, to become more powerful than the capitalist class in the United States.

But unless this diverse working class becomes fully more unified and more conscious of the source of its oppression, and aware of both the necessity and the realistic possibility of transforming the capitalist mode of produc-

[2]In the introduction to this book, we described briefly the relationship between our vision of socialism and various kinds of socialism currently in existence. See also the first part of Lerner, Section 11.3, p. 414.

tion, a movement for participatory socialism cannot be expected to grow. In this matter there has recently been much pessimism among socialists in the United States. Yet one can point to many signs resulting from popular opposition to the various forms of social oppression that capitalism generates and perpetuates. Indeed, U.S. history is replete with examples of mass, popular movements that have waged successful struggles for greater democracy, freedom and justice. Victims of alienation, inequality, sexism, racism, irrationality, economic crises, and imperialism are engaging in struggles to overcome their oppression. They are finding that capitalism is one of their principal enemies.

Outside the United States, socialist movements have already won important victories. In some parts of the underdeveloped world, capitalist domination has been successfully overthrown; in other parts, capitalism has been put in a defensive position. And in many advanced capitalist nations socialist movements have substantial strength. The very existence of such challenges suggests that capitalism is neither a smoothly operating system in which little protest is heard nor a system unsusceptible to any change. On the contrary, the entire history of the capitalist era has been marked by resistance from those whom capitalism has sought to subordinate.

Still, social systems do not fall simply because they are oppressive or considered by many to be unjust; the capitalist system has survived for a long time like this. There are countless examples of protests and rebellions that have not succeeded in transforming capitalism because they were self-destructive, they struck at the wrong targets, or they became co-opted and commercialized as part of the capitalist system itself. Fundamental social change will occur only if a self-conscious movement engages in organized political struggle in such a way as to challenge the basic capitalist relations of production. Moreover, the struggle must be carried out with an understanding of when, where, and why the capitalist system is relatively weak and vulnerable.

Dynamic forces within capitalist society ensure that some social change will always be occurring; yet this social change will not necessarily or inevitably take the form of a fundamental transformation of the capitalist mode of production. Capitalism can be radically transformed only if and when it produces progressive social forces that weaken the power of the capitalist class and encourage the growth of revolutionary opposition. A strategy for radical social change must begin with an understanding of the *contradictions* at work in a capitalist society.[3]

A contradiction of capitalism results when the very process of capitalist development produces simultaneously the conditions needed to transform it fundamentally; that is, when the successes of capitalist development create situations that are fundamentally antagonistic to capitalism itself. In this book we have discussed various kinds of contradictions which appear to be arising from the development of contemporary capitalism. Such contradictions cannot be resolved within the existing socioeconomic framework. Each contradiction creates dissatisfaction and tension among those people who are most directly and adversely affected by it, and it may become the locus around which opposition to capitalism can develop.

A radical transformation of capitalism into a better society can occur if men and women understand the historical and social forces at work in a capitalist society and intervene actively and collectively in a conscious attempt to direct and control those forces and turn them to desired humane ends.

The readings in this chapter are intended to develop further our conception of a participatory socialist society, and to discuss some of the issues involved in trying to bring it about. The basic goals of participatory socialism are restated at the beginning of the first reading, and an effort to describe its operation in much greater detail is undertaken in the

---

[3]The concept of a contradiction is a fundamental element of the Marxist method of historical materialism; see the introduction to Chapter 2, p. 7.

third reading. The first reading also reviews some of the principal contradictions arising in advanced capitalist societies and the second reading explores the contradiction between capitalism and democracy.

11.1   *Democratic Socialism in the United States: Goals and Means*

A socialist movement must have goals; it must have reason to believe that it can succeed; and it must have a strategy to achieve success. In this first reading, Samuel Bowles and Herbert Gintis address themselves to these preconditions for democratic socialism in the United States by discussing the goals of socialism, the contradictions of capitalism, and strategies for social change.

> Excerpted from *Schooling in Capitalist America: Educational Reform and the Contradictions of Economic Life* by SAMUEL BOWLES and HERBERT GINTIS. Copyright © 1976 by Basic Books. Reprinted by permission of Basic Books, Inc.

THE GOALS OF SOCIALISM

The goals of . . . socialism go beyond the achievement of the Soviet Union and countries of Eastern Europe. These countries have abolished private ownership of the means of production, while replicating the relationships of economic control, dominance, and subordination characteristic of capitalism. While the abolition of private property in the means of production has been associated with a significant reduction in economic inequality, it has failed to address [many] other problems. . . . The socialism to which we aspire goes beyond the legal question of property to the concrete social question of economic democracy as a set of egalitarian and participatory power relationships. While we may learn much about the process of building a socialist society from the experiences of the Soviet, Cuban, Chinese, and other socialist peoples—and indeed, may find some aspects of their work downright inspiring—there is no foreign model for the economic transformation we seek. Socialism in the United States will be a distinctly American product growing out of our history, culture, and struggle for a better life.

What would socialism in the United States look like? Socialism is not an event; it is a process. Socialism is a system of economic and political democracy in which individuals have the right and obligation to structure their work lives through direct participatory control. Our vision of socialism does not require as a precondition that we all be altruistic, selfless people. Rather, the social and economic conditions of socialism will facilitate the full development of human capacities. These capacities are for cooperative, democratic, equal, and participatory human relationships; for cultural, emotional, and sensual fulfillment. We can ascribe to a prospective U.S. socialism no fixed form, nor is socialism a solution to all the problems we have discussed here. Socialism directly solves many social problems, but, in many respects, it is merely a more auspicious arena in which to carry on the struggle for personal and social growth. Its form will be determined by practical activity more than abstract theorizing. Nevertheless, some reasonable aspects of socialism in the United States of direct relevance to the transformation of our society can be suggested.

The core of a socialist society is the development of an alternative to the wage-labor system. This involves the progressive democratization of the workplace, thus freeing the educational system to foster a more felicitous pattern of human development and social interaction. The ironclad relationship between the division of labor and the division of social product must also be broken: Individuals must possess, as a basic social right, an adequate income and equal access to food, shelter, medical care, and social services independent of their economic position. Conversely, with the whip of material necessity no longer forcing participation in economic life, a more balanced pattern of material, symbolic, and collective incentives can, indeed must be developed. Essential in this respect is the legal obligation of all to share equitably in performing those socially necessary jobs which are, on balance, personally unrewarding and would not be voluntarily filled. An educational system thus freed from the legitimation of privilege could turn its energies toward rendering the development of work skills a pleasant and desirable complement to an individual's life plans.

The object of these changes in the social division of labor is not abstract equality, but the elimination of relationships of dominance and subordinacy in the economic sphere. There will certainly always be individual differences in ability, talent, creativity, and initiative, and all should be encouraged to develop these capacities to their fullest. But in a socialist system, they need not translate into power and subordinacy in control of economic resources. For similar reasons, historical patterns of racial, sexual, and ethnic discrimination must be actively redressed as socially divisive and unjust. What is now called household work will also be deemed, at least in part, socially necessary labor. This work, whether done in collective units or individual homes, must be equitably shared by all individuals.

Another central goal of socialism in the United States must be the progressive democratization of political life. From production planning, the organization of social services, and the determination of consumption needs at the local level right up to national economic planning and other aspects of national policy, decisions will be made in bodies consisting of or delegated by those affected by the result. We envisage a significant role for the national government: assuring regional economic equality; integrating and rationalizing local production, service and consumption plans; and, directly implementing other social and economic policies which are infeasible at the local level. The egalitarian and democratic nature of economic life should vastly increase the responsiveness and flexibility of governmental institutions. While mediating disputes between groups and regions will remain a central political function, economic equality will eliminate the need of the state to pander to interests and powers of a small minority who control production. Though political activity will not be a major preoccupation of most, the process of participation in work and community should dramatically increase the political sophistication, participation, and knowledgeability of citizens. Indeed, we venture to suggest that all of the glaring inadequacies of political democracy in the United States are attributable to the private ownership of the means of production and the lack of a real economic democracy.

It is a tenet of liberal thought that social equality can be purchased only at the expense of economic efficiency. Yet the evidence is less than persuasive. Democratic social relationships in production lead to highly motivated and productive workers, who will turn their creative powers toward the improvement of work and the satisfaction of consumer needs rather than profit. Moreover, democratic control of work can reorient technology toward the elimination of brutalizing jobs, toward a progressive expansion of the opportunity of attaining skills through on-the-job and recurrent education, and toward a breakdown of the division between mental and physical labor. The elimination of racial and sexual discriminations would liberate a vast pool of relatively untapped talents, abilities, and human resources for productive purposes. Comprehensive and rational economic planning leads to heightened efficiency through elimination of wasteful competition and redundancy in the provision of services (e.g., insurance, banking, and finance), the elimination of unemployment, rational programs of research and development, and a balanced policy of resource development with environmental stability.

The increased efficiency of socialist economic life should quickly reduce the workweek devoted to the production of social necessities, thus freeing individuals for creative leisure and more informal production. Indeed, this aspect of individual development in U.S. socialism will represent one of its most central successes—a veritable new stage in the history of humankind. Under capitalism, a true dedication to the fostering of individual capacities for creative leisure and craft production is incompatible with generating a properly subservient labor force. We expect the creative production and consumption of social amenities to form an ever-increasing portion of economic activity in socialist society. Thus, there must be a stress on the development of a vital craft and artistic sector in production as a voluntary supplement to socially necessary work. It can be organized on a master-apprentice or group-control line and open to all individuals. Far from being a neglected afterthought in socialist society, this sector will be a major instrument in channeling the creative energies unleashed by liberated education and unalienated work toward socially beneficial ends.

To those of us who envision economic equality and a social system dedicated to fostering personal growth, democratic and participatory socialism is clearly desirable. But is such a system of economic democracy feasible? The conventional wisdom in academic social science supports a negative reply. Yet ... the cynicism bred by modern mainstream economics, sociology, and political science is based on a series of myths: that inequality is due to unequal abilities; that hierarchical authority is necessitated by modern technology; that capitalism is already meritocratic; and that the existing situation corresponds to people's needs and is the product of their wills.

Just as the philosophers of ancient Greece could not conceive of society without master and slave and the Scholastics of medieval times without lord and serf, so, today, many cannot conceive of society without a controlling managerial hierarchy and a subservient working class. Yet neither technology nor human nature bar the way to democratic socialism as the next stage in the process of civilization. Unalienated work and an equal distribution of its products is neither romantic nostalgia nor postindustrial Luddism. The means of achieving social justice and of rendering work personally meaningful and compatible with healthy personal development are as American as apple pie: democracy and equality.

.   .   .

THE CONTRADICTIONS OF CAPITALISM

We have argued both the desirability and the feasibility of a socialist society. But is it possible to get from here to there? And if so, what form might a democratic socialist revolution take?

.   .   .

A revolutionary transformation of ... economic life in the United States is possible because the advanced capitalist society cannot solve the problems it creates. A social system which generates or awakens needs in people which it cannot fulfill is surely vulnerable to social upheaval. This is all the more true when the means to the satisfaction of people's felt needs are clearly available. Capitalism in the U.S. is indeed such a system. It both awakens and thwarts people's needs—needs for economic security, for mutual respect, and for control over one's life. Capitalism has, at the same time, developed a technological and material base which could successfully address these needs, though under a radically different social order. . . . [Yet] while capitalism vigorously promotes the development of production, its basic social institutions are not geared to translating this development into balanced social development for fostering general human fulfillment and growth.

· · ·

The uneven development of social progress results from the inability of the social relationships of economic life in U.S. capitalism to harness for social ends the productive forces to which it gives rise. This contradiction between the forces and social relations of production under advanced capitalism not only renders democratic socialism a progressive transformation of social life, but gives rise to some of the basic preconditions of such a transformation. We believe that the political and social upheavals of the 1960s—including the black and women's movements, radical student revolts, rank-and-file unrest in the labor movement, the rise of the counterculture, and a new mood of equality among youth—have ushered in a growing consciousness directed against the power relationships of the U.S. society. These are but manifestations of the contradictions that inevitably arise out of the system's own successes—contradictions that lead to social dislocation and require structural change in the social relations of production for the further development of the social system.

· · ·

First, the legitimacy of the capitalist system has been historically based, in no small part, on its proven ability to satisfy people's consumption needs. The ever-increasing mass of consumer goods and services seemed to promise constant improvement in levels of well-being for all. Yet the very success of the process has undermined the urgency of consumer wants. Other needs—for community, for security, for a more integral and self-initiated work and social life—are coming to the fore and indeed are the product of U.S. society's very failures. These needs are unified by a common characteristic: They cannot be met simply by producing more consumer goods and services. On the contrary, the economic foundations of

capital accumulation are set firmly in the destruction of the social basis for the satisfaction of these needs. Thus through economic development itself, needs are generated that the advanced capitalist system is not geared to satisfy. The legitimacy of the capitalist order must increasingly be handled by other social mechanisms, of which the educational system is a major element. It is not clear that the latter can bear this strain.

Second, the concentration of capital and the continuing separation of workers—white-collar and professional as well as manual—from control over the production process have reduced the natural defenders of the capitalist order to a small minority. Two hundred years ago, over three-fourths of white families owned land, tools, or other productive property; this figure has fallen to about a third and, even among this group, a tiny minority owns the lion's share of all productive property. Similarly, two hundred years ago, most white male workers were their own bosses. The demise of the family farm, the artisan shop, and the small store plus the rise of the modern corporation has reduced the figure to less than 10 percent. Even for the relatively well-off, white, male American worker, the capitalist system has come to mean what it has meant all along for most women, blacks, and other oppressed peoples: someone else's right to profits, someone else's right to work unbossed and in pursuit of one's own objectives. The decline of groups outside the wage-labor system—farmer, artisan, entrepreneur, and independent professional—has eliminated a ballast of capitalist support, leaving the legitimation system alone to divide workers against one another.

Third, developments in technology and work organization have begun to undermine a main line of defense of the capitalist system; namely, the idea that the capitalist relations of production—private property and the hierarchical organization of work—are the most conducive to the rapid expansion of productivity. We have suggested[1] that in those complex

---

[1]Editors' note: See Bowles and Gintis, Section 4.4, p. 141.

work tasks that increasingly dominate modern production, participatory control by workers is a more productive form of work organization. The boredom and stultification of the production line and the steno pool, the shackled creativity of technical workers and teachers, the personal frustration of the bureaucratic office routine increasingly lose their claim as the price of material comfort. The ensuing attacks on bureaucratic oppression go hand in hand with demystification of the system as a whole. Support for capitalist institutions—once firmly rooted in their superiority in meeting urgent consumption needs and squarely based on a broad mass of property-owning independent workers—is thus weakened by the process of capitalist development itself. At the same time, powerful anticapitalist forces are brought into being. The accumulation of capital—the engine of growth under capitalism—has as its necessary companion the proletarianization of labor, and the constant increase in the size of the working class.

Fourth, the international expansion of capital has fueled nationalist and anticapitalist movements in many of the poor countries. The strains associated with the worldwide integration of the capitalist system are manifested in heightened divisions and competition among the capitalist powers, in the resistance of the people of Vietnam, in the socialist revolutions in China and Cuba, and in the political instability and guerrilla movements in Asia, Africa, and Latin America. The U.S. role in opposition to wars of national liberation—particularly in Vietnam—has brought part of the struggle back home and exacerbated many of the domestic contradictions of advanced capitalism.

Fifth, and cutting across all of the above, with the return of comparatively smooth capitalist development in the United States in the mid-1950s after the tumultuous decades of the 1930s and 1940s, the impact of far-reaching cumulative changes in the class structure is increasingly reflected in crises of public consciousness. The corporatization of agriculture and reduction of the farm population has particularly affected blacks; they are subjugated to the painful process of forceful integration into the urban wage-labor system. The resulting political instabilities are not unlike those following the vast wave of immigrants in the early decades of the century. Changes in the technology of household production and the increase in female labor in the service industries also portend a radically altered economic position for women. Finally, the large corporation and the state bureaucracies have replaced entrepreneurial, elite, white-collar, and independent professional jobs as the locus of middle-class economic activity. This effective proletarianization of white-collar labor marks the already advanced integration of these groups into the wage-labor system. In each case, the contradictions have arisen between the traditional consciousness of these groups and their new objective economic situations. This has provided much of the impetus for radical movements among blacks, women, students, and counterculture youth.

Sixth, even the vaunted material productivity of capitalism—its ability to deliver the goods—seems increasingly open to question. Inflation, commodity shortages, unemployed workers, and unmet social needs all attest to the growing inability of capitalism to meet people's needs for material comfort, economic security, and social amenity.

Lastly, in response to the unsolved—and we believe unsolvable—problems of capitalism, modern liberals have advocated, and won, significant extensions of the role of government in our society. . . . [T]he expansion of education is a prime example of this process. Increasingly, the government has taken responsibility for the attainment of social objectives unattainable within the capitalist economic framework: full employment, clean air, equality of opportunity, stable prices, and the elimination of poverty, to name only a few. The result: Social problems are increasingly politicized. People are increasingly coming both to understand the political origins of social and economic distress and to sense the possibility of political solution to these problems.

The assault on economic inequality and hierarchical control of work appears likely to intensify. Along with other social strains endemic to advanced capitalism, the growing tension between people's needs for self-realization and material welfare through work and the drive of capitalists and managers for profits opens up the possibility of powerful social movements dedicated to the construction of economic democracy.

STRATEGIES FOR SOCIAL CHANGE

. . .

How do we get there? This is the central question of political strategy. . . . We consider this a major task of socialists in the coming years—one to be dealt with in terms of both social theory and concrete political practice. In this section, we will restrict our remarks to [certain] aspects of socialist strategy [which we believe to be important].

Our analysis is inspired by three basic principles. First, socialism is the progressive strengthening and extending of the process of economic democracy, with its attendant continual transformation of the process of interpersonal relationships in work, community, education, and cultural life. Second, the nature of socialism will depend on the content of revolutionary struggle in this society. A socialist movement cannot subordinate means to ends and cannot manipulate and deceive to achieve success precisely because socialism is not an event. The consciousness developed in struggle is the very same consciousness which, for better or worse, will guide the process of socialist development itself. Thus a socialist movement while striving to obtain power, must do so through means which inexorably promote democracy, participation, and a sense of solidarity and equality. Third, a socialist movement must be based on the recognition of class struggle as its organizing principle. A revolution is a fundamental shift in the structure of power in the social system and, with it, a shift in those aspects of social life on which power is based and by means of which it is reproduced. A socialist revolution is the shift of control over the process of production

from the minority of capitalists, managers, and bureaucrats to the producers themselves. The move toward democratic and participatory economic relationships makes possible the breakdown of the hierarchical division of labor and the antagonistic relationships among groups of workers vying for positions in the stratification system (e.g., between blacks and whites, men and women, white- and blue-collar workers). It unleashes the possibility of turning technology and organization toward unalienated social relationships. By undermining the social subordination of working people, it allows the emergence of a truly democratic consciousness—both political and economic—of the citizenry. By removing the economic base of class oppression, it permits the construction of social institutions—such as schools—which foster rather than repress the individual's struggle for autonomy and personal development while providing the social framework for making this a truly cooperative struggle.

A revolutionary shift in power renders all this possible but not inevitable. A change which formally transfers power to workers but is not based on a spirit of socialist consciousness around the goals of economic democracy will merely reproduce the old power relationships in new forms. This is true also for the elimination of racism, sexism, and the fetishism of hierarchical authority.

A revolution may be violent or peaceful; it may succeed with the aid of existing political channels or in spite of them. Which characteristics predominate is of central strategic importance, but cannot be prejudged in one way or another as intrinsic to a revolutionary movement. Nevertheless, we must forcefully reject the notion that a revolution is a bloody putsch by a minority of political zealots. A socialist revolution in the United States cannot be a coup in which one small ruling minority replaces another. Nor can it be a result of the insurgency of a Messianic "vanguard." We have argued that those who will benefit from socialism are workers in all walks of life. We have also argued that, at the present time, the overwhelming majority of individuals are workers, and increasingly proletarianized workers at that. Hence, the new American revolution cannot succeed without being a truly democratic movement which ultimately captures the hearts of the majority of the people.

The question of violence, while clearly a weighty tactical consideration, must also be assigned to a position of secondary importance. A majoritarian revolution has no use for terrorism. The socialist alternative involves a struggle for power and the struggle will be bitter and hard-fought. It is almost inconceivable that a socialist revolution in the United States would not involve violence at some stage. But there is little reason to depend on violence as a basic strategic weapon. Rather, socialists must be prepared to counter violent measures taken against them; they must deploy all their resources to deflect and expose any such violent measures. Strong local and national victories, electoral or otherwise, by the socialist movement raise a strong probability that dominant elites will subvert the democratic process and attempt to draw on the might of the armed forces and the National Guard to restore order. This tactic can be countered only if military rank and file are on the side of the socialists and refuse to exercise a repressive role. The question of violence recedes into the background, for the only viable socialist strategy is to disable the military capacity of the capitalist class, rather than to develop the force to combat it on its own terms.

As we have suggested, the socialist movement is a social, not merely a political, movement as it deals with the transformation of daily life rather than the mere reorientation of political power. As such, the diversity of the U.S. working class lends a socialist movement immense potential for vitality and creativity. We expect socialist manual workers to use their extensive knowledge in reorganizing production and training others to do their share of manual work. We expect socialist women to be in the forefront of eliminating oppression in the home and demanding vital alternatives to traditional domestic patterns. We expect socialist artisans, architects, and planners to heighten the artistic and aesthetic powers of the rest of us in the process of pursuing their own struggles. We expect revolutionary health workers to open new horizons in health-care delivery, and revolutionary teachers to forge the liberating schools of tomorrow as major tactics in their struggles for power. Revolutionary athletes must teach us all to respect our bodies, and teachers our minds—all this and more the creative potential of the revolutionary movement derives from the diversity and resourcefulness of American workers.

The other side of the diversity of the U.S. working class is its lack of a unified consciousness. We [believe] that major aspects of U.S. society can best be understood in terms of the need of the dominant classes to fragment the work force and, by dividing, conquer [it]. The strategy is as old as civilization itself. In the United States today, the fragmention of consciousness is facilitated by racial, sexual, and socioeconomic antagonisms.

The overriding strategic goal of a socialist movement is the creation of working-class consciousness. Too frequently, this task is seen as simply making people aware of their oppression. Far from it! Most people are all too well aware of the fact of their oppression; what is lacking is a strategy to overcome it. The conviction that a change for the better is possible will arise only where the divisive and fragmented consciousness of U.S. working people is progressively replaced by an understanding that, beneath the all too real differences in needs, desires, and social prerogatives, all suffer oppression from the same source and stand to gain similarly from the socialist alternative. Toward the end, each group struggling for control over its conditions of production must deploy its forces to overcome immediate conflicts among the people. In part this can be done by each group extending its demands to embrace other potential allies and to protect their interests. Workers seeking higher pay and control of the enterprise must fight also to promote consumers' rights, to reduce pay differentials on the job, to eliminate the demeaning secondary-status jobs and discriminatory hiring, and to create free day-care centers for the children of employees. Pursuit of an integrated set of objectives broad enough to encompass most elements in the working class will of course require some form of coordination among popular groups. In the absence of a unified theoretical and programmatic framework, radical spontaneity may result in less rather than more unity among oppressed peoples.

. . .

A major strategic element of a socialist movement is the continual interjection of a broader vision of a socialist alternative into concrete struggles of all types. All too often, those with utopian visions of the Good Society have neither the capacity nor the inclination to engage in real social struggle. Conversely, those with an earthy sense of the arduous task of day-to-day struggle have either cynically or opportunistically buried their vision of the larger goals. Yet the propagation of a socialist vision in the context of down-to-earth politics is essential. Few in the United States will opt for a revolutionary change as a nothing-to-lose desperate assault on a literally unbearable status quo; life for most people is simply not that bad. People must choose, and choose to fight for, socialism as a positive alternative based on a serious, desirable, and feasible vision. This vision must develop in the course of struggle, but the struggle will not develop without it. Moreover, vague notions of socialism and economic democracy, however effective in producing change, will by no means insure that change will take desirable and ultimately progressive forms. As we are often reminded by our more conservative friends, revolutionary change can be a disaster, too—a disaster which

buries the fondest hopes of the strongest supporters. Only a vigorous and creative effort at defining the course of socialist development before its ultimate victory, however extensively this course must be altered through the practical experience of people involved in the struggle, can minimize this possibility. Finally, the fragmentation of consciousness of working people can be overcome only by offering an alternative in which the disparate objectives of different groups are simultaneously met.

The final strategic consideration we have in mind is the sober recognition that the preparatory phase of a revolutionary movement involves working in, and through, existing capitalist institutions. We cannot sit around and wait for a political cataclysm. We cannot rely solely on creating alternative institutions as ". . . little islands of socialism in a sea of capitalism." Rather, we must think in terms of building up working-class and popular power; creating arenas of social management and direct democracy in the major branches of production; conquering positions of strength in bodies such as unions, schools, the media, and government. In short, proper strategy requires what Rudi Dutschke called the ". . . long march through the institutions." This crucial aspect of movement strategy is necessary to prepare people for taking power in every area of their lives. It has two aims: (1) to weaken progressively the power of those who control economic life and undermine the functioning of oppressive capitalist institutions, and (2) to develop in people the facility for making cooperative decisions and for exercising power, an experience normally denied us in a capitalist society.

11.2   *Capitalism or Democracy?*

For many of its defenders, capitalism's virtues lie not just in its productive powers as an economic system but also in the association between capitalism as an economic system and liberal democracy as a political system. Many observers have noted that the political systems of most of the advanced capitalist countries are liberal democracies (but not all—consider the case of South Africa), while the countries that call themselves socialist hardly seem democratic. Capitalism seems to promote political democracy, goes the argument, while socialism does not.

Yet this understanding of the relationships among capitalism, socialism, and political democracy is fundamentally flawed. In most advanced capitalist countries, including the United States, the extension of civil liberties and the right to vote to all citizens—regardless of property holdings, race, or gender—involved long and arduous historical struggles by the disfranchised groups, often against the opposition of the capitalist class. Political democracy as we know it today arose through a popular historical process that cannot be attributed simply to the institutions of capitalism.

The relationship between socialism and democracy has also varied historically. In the nineteenth century socialism and democracy were seen as inextricably intertwined. Indeed, socialism was then understood as the further extension of democracy in the political, social, and economic spheres, and the modern phrase "democratic socialism" would have been seen as redundant. Today, many socialists in the advanced capitalist countries have returned to this tradition, criticizing the Eastern Bloc countries for their lack of democracy.

Recently, it is capitalism and democracy that seem to be coming increasingly into conflict with one another. In the Third World, where military dictatorships are not uncommon, it has long been true that capitalism has had little positive influence in the struggle for political democracy. More recently, the ending of the postwar capitalist boom has been attributed by capitalist-oriented observers to an "excess of democracy" in the advanced countries. The solution according to these observers, is to roll back democratic rights, to put profits before democracy. In the following reading, Richard Edwards examines this phenomenon. He asks whether we are approaching an era in which we may be forced to choose between capitalism and democracy.

Excerpted from RICHARD EDWARDS, *Contested Terrain: The Transformation of the Workplace in the Twentieth Century* (New York: Basic Books, 1979). Reprinted by permission of the author and publisher.

In the United States, capitalism and political democracy have developed together. Their symbiosis is by no means a necessary relationship, as the many capitalist and undemocratic regimes in the world remind us. Even in the democratic countries, the capitalist class's virtual monopoly on political resources has ensured that democratic rule is consistent with bourgeois hegemony. Capitalism's credit for fostering democratic rule is further qualified by the observation that the "lower orders" of society, in seeking to advance their position, have constituted the chief force pressing for the extension of democracy. In the United States, for example, nonproperty-holders, blacks, and women extended the franchise because they struggled for their own rights. Nonetheless, one cannot avoid the conclusion. The United States and the other nations that have sustained democratic rule (however imperfect) have been capitalist societies. In addition to the accumulated wealth that Marx saw as an essential prerequisite to socialism, capitalism has thus bequeathed us a second valuable legacy: democratic political traditions.

The central problem for our time is whether

this relationship will continue. The historical association between capitalism and democracy cannot be presumed to persist automatically, any more than we can expect capitalism's future to be like its past. Indeed, the real question now is whether the marriage between capitalism and political democracy was made in heaven and will therefore be eternal, or whether it is merely a marriage of convenience to be soon discarded. Capitalist ideology asserts that it is the former; twentieth-century political history (and even more, the events of the postwar period) suggest that the latter is true.

Throughout U.S. history and especially in this century, the relationship between capitalist economy and democratic government has been altered by two unfolding processes. One is the capitalists' increasing dependence upon the state to regulate, direct, and stimulate the economy. The other is the changing composition of the electorate, as the population becomes more dominated by the working class and suffrage has been won by women and blacks. The result is that while control over the state has become more essential for capitalists, it has also become more uncertain, and the further development of capitalism throws the future of democracy in doubt.

The first process of change is the growing economic role of government. In some cases capitalists have been forced to accept state intervention, in other cases they have independently sought it, but in all cases the state has been needed to resolve the contradictions of monopoly capitalism. In the transition to the new regime, anticorporate forces demanded regulation of the trusts, while corporate capitalists saw in regulation the possible means to police shared monopoly. During World War I, businessmen obtained first-hand knowledge of the largesse available through large-scale government planning. In the 1930s, labor turned to the state to recognize and enforce its right to organize, while capitalists (not without some internal opposition) began to rely on the state to stimulate and maintain the macroeconomy. In the postwar years, these groups have pushed upon the state responsi-

bility for educating and training the labor force, providing subsidies to specific industries, supporting research and development, monitoring workplace health and safety, financing the basic social insurance schemes, and arbitrating the bargaining disputes between capital and labor. In addition, the state collects an increasing proportion of national income through taxes and provides an increasing percentage of final demand through military contracts, social service spending, and so forth. Finally, a substantial portion of the total wage bill takes the form of a social wage, distributed as income and benefits paid by the state. In all these ways, the accumulation process has become increasingly politicized and the prospects for successful accumulation increasingly depend on state policies.

At the same time, the character of the democratic electorate has been changing. For one thing, the old middle classes—small-propertied groups like petty employers, self-employed persons, farmers, merchants, and independent craftsmen and tradesmen, who used to encompass a significant population and count even more heavily in political matters—have disappeared; at the turn of the century such groups represented about 30 percent of the labor force, but today they account for less than 10 percent. Correspondingly, there has been a steady expansion of the working class, from roughly 60 percent in 1900, to 75 percent in 1950, to 85 percent in 1975. Equally important, excluded groups have won the vote; property restrictions for voting have been eliminated, and women and blacks have successfully struggled to achieve the franchise. These new groups share one characteristic; almost uniformly they are wage or salary workers, and they do not own property that contributes critically to their way of earning a living. Thus the electorate has increasingly come to reflect the growing working-class majority in society.

These developments have brought the forces for capitalism and those for democracy into long-run conflict, and the conflict has been particularly intensified by the dynamics of class-fraction politics. By diverting working-class struggles from the economic sphere and increasingly focusing them in the state arena, the new form of politics makes control of government policy crucial. As the working poor achieve better social service benefits, an additional "social drag" on profits is imposed and the reserve army support for workplace discipline is weakened. As the traditional proletariat demands greater job security, better pensions, medical benefits, and occupational health and safety measures, employers lose prerogatives and possibilities for profit. As the middle layers demand consumer and environmental protection, they impose further costs on capitalists' operations. As blacks and women achieve antidiscrimination and affirmative action rights, they reduce employers' ability to divide and rule their labor forces. All this imposes increasingly severe strains and constraints on the profitability of capitalists' investment.

For capitalists, controlling the state has become both more essential and more precarious. It is understandable, then, that they should search for ways to restrict the democratic content of politics. They have not been unsuccessful; the central lesson of recent U.S. political history is that, as suffrage has been extended, the impact of elections on state policy has been reduced. Elected and democratically accountable government institutions have, in real power terms, been weakened throughout this century. The basic process at work here is the substitution of administrative power for power derived from the electorate. As a result, party politics, citizen voting, and the entire electoral process have come to have less and less effect on government policy.

In part, this shift is reflected in the dramatic decline of the Congress as a real governing body; even internally, with its committee system based on seniority, the Congress insulates itself from popular will. The shift is also seen in the rapidly growing power of the bureaucracies, public authorities, regulatory bodies, permanent commissions, courts, "expert" or "professional" bodies, and so on. As the Federal Reserve Board, National Security Council, and the various great federal departments

impose their will, they erode democratic power by replacing it with administrative power. Choices are removed from the political sphere, where they can be seen as products of clashing material interests, and instead are placed in the hands of administrators and technocrats, who can make decisions on the basis of technical or administrative criteria. The distinction is apparent even in their manner of selection: the Congress is popularly elected, of course, while the bureaucracy and court positions are appointive. Moreover, while officials in popularly accountable bodies tend to serve fairly short terms (two, four, or six years), the nonaccountable agencies are run by officials enjoying, as an additional protection from popular will, extremely long terms (five, seven, or ten years, or even life).

The shift to administrative power also grows out of the expansion of executive power. Although the president is elected, executive power has been increasingly institutionalized and insulated from popular influence. There have been several significant steps on this path in the twentieth century, including the Executive Branch's capture of the process of drafting legislation, its creation and expansion of the Executive Offices, and the establishment of the national security apparatus. These changes called for experts and bureaucrats to be in charge, with little or no provision for popular participation or accountability.

As with the federal government, so in state and local governments power and decision making have been transferred out of popularly accountable institutions (legislatures, city councils, town meetings) and into other institutions that retain only the most formal ties to democratic content. State bureaucracies, special bodies such as the New York Port Authority, regulatory and licensing commissions, and social welfare bureaucracies have become the antidemocratic form of modern state government.

In these developments we see the *substance* of democratic government being gutted, while the *form* is maintained. It is as though capitalists have applied to the state the lessons they learned in the workplace: institutionalized authority replaces more direct—and more directly challenged—rule. Until recently, one needed to infer this strategy from persuasive but nonetheless indirect evidence. However, the Trilateral Commission—that Rockefeller-financed international citizens' group claiming Jimmy Carter and Walter Mondale among its members—finally stated the obvious. In its report, *The Crisis of Democracy*, it warned of the social dangers deriving from what it perceived to be a growing "excess" of democracy. Too much democracy does not serve capital.

Except in a political crisis, the danger to democracy comes not from the coup, then, but from the incessant pressure to make democratic rule more modern, more efficient, more based on professional expertise, that is, more insulated from the demands of the working-class majority. Capitalists here, like "capitalist-roaders" in China, seek to put expertise instead of politics in command.

This analysis is no lament for some golden age of democracy; nineteenth-century democracy's great failure, aside from excluding blacks and women and others, was that it was restricted to a narrowly defined political sphere. Rather, the analysis challenges the mindless assertion that as capitalism develops, so does democracy. The marriage may have been over for some time, even though we, its children, are the last to know of it.

SOCIALISTS IN DEFENSE OF DEMOCRACY?

If capitalism and democracy have increasingly come into conflict, the best hope for democracy's survival appears to lie with socialism. But will (or can) the working class and socialists defend and extend democracy?

This question admits of no easy answer. For one thing, the American working class does not share a commitment to socialism. Decades of anticommunist propaganda and mistakes made by socialists have taken their toll, and explicitly socialist parties enjoy little support. Yet, while the name remains anathema, the social programs put forward by progressive

groups enjoy considerable support. Moreover, there has been a growing interest among workers, especially those in "rank-and-file" movements, in self-consciously socialist politics.

More directly relevant to the question is the fact that the so-called socialist countries have made little progress toward installing real democracy. And in the West, the left as a whole carries a terrible burden of antidemocratic theory and practice, deriving from the twin disillusionments of the Second International and contemporary Social Democratic parties. This collective past creates a presumptive and almost reflexlike bias against the "sham" of bourgeois democracy; more, it tends to give rise to a devaluation of the merits of democracy itself.

The problem is still more serious. No left party has constructed a satisfactory transition strategy that both defends (and utilizes) democratic government *and* provides for a transition to socialism. The difficulty is plain: as soon as a socialist party or coalition of parties nears power, a disastrous decline in "business confidence" sets in. Capitalists, who during the period when socialists are building an electoral majority still control investments, naturally stop investing, fearing expropriation. The fall-off in investment creates economic chaos, as foreign exchange reserves plummet, unemployment rises, inflation spurts up, capital flees, and hoarding begins. Socialist electoral victories thus tend to generate economic crisis, and as socialists succeed in the democratic arena, they are foiled by the capitalists' continuing economic power. Socialists then are confronted with an impossible choice: either back off from taking power or reassure capitalists that the socialist victory will not harm capital. In either event, the continuing extrademocratic power of capitalists defeats the democratic transition strategy.

These problems of history and strategy do not provide an auspicious background for the linking of socialism and democracy. Yet just as the relation between capitalism and democracy is undergoing change, so is the relation between socialists' program and democracy being revised. Most socialists acknowledge that previous formulations of strategy have failed to create revolution (or even strong revolutionary movements) anywhere in the advanced capitalist world, and increasing numbers see that their failure stems directly from the failure to take democracy seriously. So we find that in the most recent period, considerable progress has been made in reunifying the vision of industrial and political democracy. The commitment by the Western European Communist Parties—French, Italian, Spanish, and others—to a democratic program means that theoretical ideas will achieve their most severe and appropriate testing in the real practice of attempting a democratic transition. In the United States, a commitment to democracy by at least a significant share of the American left opens the way for new theory and practice here. The determination of these groups to find a program that is both democratic and thoroughly socialist promises much.

By such efforts, both the meaning and scope of democracy are being redefined, so the struggle involves extending democracy as well as retaining current democratic processes. The new programs declare that democracy must incorporate more than the choice of leaders through quadrennial or even biennial voting. Elections are not unimportant, but the content as well as the form of the political process must be democratized to expand popular participation; that is, to increase the extent to which decision-making processes allow for and encourage widespread discussion of issues, mobilizing of support, and expression of interests. From this perspective, democratic politics becomes not merely a device for recording preferences but also an organic process in which people can discuss and *formulate* their own attitudes and priorities. So too, the government must be more immediately responsible, to ensure that state policy is kept in line with the expressed real interests of the citizenry. More, democratic decision making must be extended to the range of social decisions currently beyond the reach of democratic rule, particularly those of economic and social life. Wide participation and close accountability would

seem to require decentralization wherever possible.

Whether this ambitious agenda can be accomplished remains uncertain, but there are at least some strong reasons to hope. Most importantly, the renewed interest in democracy among socialists rests not just on the ideas of socialists; instead, it builds upon more powerful forces operating in society. In particular, the division of the working class into class fractions and the shifting of class conflict into the political sphere imply two corollaries. First, there can be no immediate economic or social demands that unify the entire class; rather, a common program would necessarily incorporate a variety of such demands, each appropriate to the specific circumstances of one or other of the fractions. Second, just as the class is divided in the sphere of production, so the defense and extension of democracy potentially reunites the class in the political sphere; after all, the interests of all the fractions, as the overwhelming majority in society, can only be safeguarded in a system where majority rule is realized. The defense and extension of democracy thus becomes a *class* demand, and the taking up of this demand by socialists offers an avenue for reuniting the working class.

Interest in democracy is already evident in the struggle to democratize the large unions. Rank-and-file groups have waged courageous campaigns to open up the Steelworkers Union, to reclaim the Teamsters, to institute local initiative in the United Mine Workers, and to return power to the memberships in numerous other unions. These efforts suggest that broad segments of the working class appear ready to participate in the emerging struggle for democratic rule.

The defense of democracy thus entails a demand for its application at all levels and in all spheres of society. This is a crucial point, for here emerges the central theme of all socialist programs: the defense of political democracy is simply the logical corollary to the demand for democracy at the workplace and social control of the production process. Once workers raise a challenge to the existing system of control in the firm, they will through their experience be led to see the common content of these struggles. The defense and extension of democracy may ultimately rest, then, on the working class's effort to take possession of the means of production and to organize, through democratic rule, society's material resources for the benefit of all in society. Democracy thus becomes the rallying cry not only to unite various fractions of the working class, but also to unite the political and economic struggles of that class.

Whether a socialist and democratic society (and not just a democratic socialist program) can be constructed remains a further imponderable. Certainly our highly concentrated and increasingly undemocratic capitalism grows more intolerable daily. So, too, it seems inevitable that democratic socialism cannot be realized unless progressive forces everywhere struggle for both democracy and socialism. To do less shortchanges our future.

11.3   *After the Revolution*

Because a participatory socialist society can only be built by *all* of its participants, people who are struggling to make it possible are reluctant to go beyond the formulation of goals and principles and to spell out in detail what the system would look like. Yet, if only to motivate others to join the struggle, there is clearly a need to talk about participatory socialism in terms more specific than goals and principles. Therefore we will conclude this final chapter of our book with a more detailed account, by Michael Lerner, of how participatory socialism might actually operate in the United States.

What do we want? In a word, "socialism." Unfortunately, that word has been so misunderstood that it is often more confusing than illuminating to use it. We retain it because it is associated with a long history of human aspirations with which we essentially identify. But let us make clear what we mean by "socialism." Socialism is the ownership and control of the means of production, and, through that, the control of all areas of life, by the majority of people who work. So socialism is another way of saying "power to the people": power to control all the basic institutions that affect our lives. Socialism is radical democracy, democracy extended to every area of our collective lives.

.   .   .

DOES THE SOVIET UNION HAVE SOCIALISM?

We do not believe that socialism now exists in any country in the world. Socialism means ownership and *control* of the means of production, democratically by the people, rather than by a governmental bureaucracy. The critical element in our understanding of socialism is the democratization of the economy and of all areas of political and social life. In the Soviet Union, this does not exist. The Communist party runs everything, and the Party is not a democratic institution, but is dominated by a group of bureaucrats who in most respects fit the notion of a "new ruling class." The people are unable to organize any effective opposition elements, either inside or outside the Party, and hence have no effective way of making their will known, short of armed rebellion. Powerless to affect the decisions that affect their lives, the people in the Soviet Union are far from having socialism.

The Soviet Union does, however, have a high degree of welfare statism. And in this respect it is similar, though somewhat in advance of, Sweden and other countries that supply the minimum social welfare benefits all humans deserve. This feature should not be minimized. People in these countries are not deprived of medical attention because of the expense, people can get work to support themselves, their minds and bodies do not decay because they have too little money to buy food. These basic needs matter very much to those who cannot satisfy them, and in these respects the people in the Soviet Union are far better off than many people in America. But while it is a contingent fact that when socialism is established, all these basic human needs will be met, meeting these needs is not the defining essence of socialism. It is a necessary condition for people to be free and self-determining, but it is not a sufficient one. Slaves may be materially satisfied, but they are slaves nevertheless. Socialism is about power over one's life and circumstances; it is about freedom and self-determination, and these do not obtain in the Soviet Union. Nor is there any indication that the USSR is moving in that direction; the ruling class seems to have strengthened itself in the past decades sufficiently and to have retreated far enough from the ideals of socialism that it would be hard to envision anything short of a revolution establishing socialism in the Soviet Union. And, to the extent that other "socialist" countries are under the military or economic control of the Soviet Union, the same is true for them.

"But doesn't this show that revolution is no alternative, because a ruling class will always reemerge no matter what the original ideals of those who make the revolution?" No. This argument misses the historical context in which the revolutions in Russia, China, North Vietnam, Cuba, etc., developed. Marx predicted, accurately, that socialism would only be possible in an industrial society whose material base—the technology and factories and skilled workforce—was sufficiently advanced to make possible the elimination of scarcity. As Marx correctly saw, the advanced industrial societies had all the prerequisites necessary for abolishing forever the domination of man by irrational forces. But the countries that are now called socialist were all backward peasant countries, often prevented from developing by the capitalist countries that influenced their economic life. The main task of their "socialist" revolutions was to build up the industrial bases to the point where it was possible to talk about the elimination of scarcity. But in trying to industrialize, these countries faced a hostile capitalist world which would attempt to isolate and destroy them. In 1919, for example, the last remnants of the economic infrastructure of Russia were destroyed by the crippling civil war that was spurred by the United States, Britain, and France.

.   .   .

The great disservice done by the Communist parties around the world was to describe the Soviet Union, developing under extremely difficult circumstances that put industrialization, not socialism, on the agenda, as "socialist." This discredited socialism with people everywhere, especially in the Soviet Union and Eastern Europe. In taking the real for the ideal, in making a virtue out of necessity, the Communist parties helped undermine people's confidence in the ideal. Add to that the continued apologies for a regime whose paranoid excesses were inexcusable and you have all the ingredients for the widespread disillusionment experienced by so many good idealistic people of the 1930s. The same thing will happen again if the American Left tries to identify its aspirations with any existing state, whether China, North Vietnam, or Cuba. These states have much to recommend them: They have begun to deal with many of people's basic material needs, and unlike the Western nations during their period of capitalist industrialization, they have a real concern for the welfare of working people and a real interest in promoting liberation for women within the limits imposed by continued material scarcity. The rulers of these countries, unlike the ruling class of the Soviet Union, are not interested simply in self-aggrandizement and stabilization but are committed to building a socialist world eventually. Nevertheless, these countries do have "rulers," and these rulers are not elected representatives of the people. The people do not control the economy and are rarely consulted on crucial issues. These countries may be moving toward socialism, but it would be a critical mistake to say that they have achieved it. There is no socialism until there are substantial procedures through which the workers decide the basic questions facing them.

· · ·

WHAT WILL THE TRANSITION TO SOCIALISM BE LIKE IN THE UNITED STATES?

The situation in which socialism will come to the United States is totally different from that in which it emerged in Eastern Europe and in Asia. The United States is an advanced industrial society whose material base is adequate to meet all the material needs of its citizens and those of people around the world. Furthermore, the agent of revolutionary change in this country will be a highly diversified working class, literate and intelligent, that is capable of running things for itself and deciding on seemingly complex issues.

Immediately the socialists take control of the U.S. economy a high level of material prosperity will be possible in the United States and much of the rest of the world. Because we are so highly industrialized, it will be possible to decrease dramatically the amount of time the worker spends in work, at the same time producing adequate material goods for ourselves and helping to advance the underdeveloped parts of the world. The revolution will be experienced not as a new but goodhearted taskmaster, but as a liberation and freeing from much that is unpleasant in life. In this situation, it will be impossible for a new ruling class to emerge that encourages people to de-

lay gratification, while itself benefiting from the labor of the majority. Since the United States is the strongest military power in the world, with atomic weapons sufficient to destroy everyone else and hence sufficient to defend itself, no group will be able to argue that people must surrender their liberties or make other sacrifices in order to defend socialism from any "external threat."

The working class that will be part of the American revolution will have a high degree of intelligence and competence in running things. American workers have been heavily indoctrinated in anticommunism and hence are particularly sensitive to the mistakes created by a Stalinist direction. Moreover, one of their main motivating forces for making the revolution will be the desire to reclaim power over their lives; for many American workers, simple material scarcity is not a problem. Having fought for power in a real sense, having seen through strategies for "participation" and other cooptive schemes, such a working class will have developed the acuity not to be duped by a group of persuasive charlatans. To think otherwise is to believe that Americans are specially unintelligent—and I see no evidence of that. We must have enough faith in each other and our collective intelligence to believe that we can learn from the mistakes of the past and can transcend them.

· · ·

AFTER THE REVOLUTION

Those who are committed to the revolution have written almost nothing about what things will look like thereafter. And for a good reason. Socialism is the beginning of the epoch of human freedom and the end of the time when some men control all others. But once human beings are genuinely free, how can we know what they will choose to do? We can have some idea based on past behavior, but we cannot have a fixed blueprint. To the challenge, "What is your new society going to look like?" the first answer must be, "This is not *my* new society, but *our* new society, so what it will look like will in part depend on what you want it to look like." A liberal running for office may give a more satisfying answer; he will be able to make authoritative statements, since he is trying to put himself in a position where he will have power that others will not. But for the socialist revolutionary, the task is to build a society in which everyone together decides what it will be like.

Still, people have a good reason for asking the question. After all, if you are going to make sacrifices to build a new social order, you want to have some idea of what the order will be like. To say "We will all be free" is poetic, but contentless; people want to know *why* this freedom will produce desirable results for humanity. I cannot answer this question for everyone, but I can answer for myself, and I can tell you what I as one individual with one vote will argue for, and what kind of society I believe will be possible. I shall try to outline what will be possible after a fairly substantial period of control by the people, not what it will be like one or two years after the people have taken power, when the transition is still going on. So let me put forward one vision, among many, of what socialism could be like and would be like if others agree with me when we all get together to construct our new society.

POLITICAL AND ECONOMIC ORGANIZATION

Every important political question would be put directly to the people for their consideration and decision. We already have the technology to do this easily. Every home would have a very simple voting device, possibly attached to the phone or television receiver, which would send a message to a central computer in the city or area recording the vote. Prior to the vote, issues would be debated in newspapers and on television and in mass meetings in the community, with every major side given equal opportunity to present its position. At the local, regional, and national level there would be an elected body of delegates (each recallable to his district any time 10 percent of the voters signed a petition for a new election) whose responsibility would be to decide which issues would be put to the people and how to formulate them in the clearest possible way in order to maximize understanding and to bring out the potentially controversial aspects of the proposal under consideration. Any group that felt some key question was not being put to the electorate or that some key viewpoint was not being represented publicly on television, at mass meetings, or in newspapers, would circulate a petition stating its viewpoint. Signatures of 1 percent of the voting population in the relevant area would give the group the right to (1) write its own proposal to be put directly to the people, and (2) air its views on the media (it would be given more time than any single position normally is, on the grounds that its view had not previously been given exposure in the usual debates on relevant issues). The government would have an executive branch, most of the key positions of which would be filled by elections. But the executive would have little originating power, since the key decisions on policy would always be put to the people. Because of human fallibilities and weaknesses, important decisions, which should have been presented to the people, might occasionally be made under the guise of simple bureaucratic or administrative decisions. But rarely would such decisions have severe consequences, because they could always be challenged by those who were affected by them and brought directly to the people, and the official could simultaneously (if his fault was judged malicious) be recalled.

. . .

For the first hundred years, at least, the key decisions would probably remain in the area of production. Many economists argue that it would be possible to decentralize the economy without in the slightest decreasing its efficiency. But we would be in favor of decentralization even if it meant an additional cost. A decentralized economy would be easier to control and ecologically more sound. Regions of between 15 to 20 million people would be established to replace the present states, and those regions would themselves be composed of a variety of autonomous municipalities. In order to maximize the fulfillment of human needs and eliminate needless production, the economic area would be governed by a rational long-term plan developed every few years and approved by vote of the electorate. The plan would be developed from the bottom: each work unit and each consumer entity would submit its ideas and desires to a community board which would try to adjust them into a coherent whole, then resubmit the adjustments back to the populace for approval. Thereafter, they would be submitted to a regional board that took all the ideas and tried to develop a regional plan, which itself would be sent to a national board, which would try to adjust the regional plans. The last step would be to send that plan back to everyone for approval. Equally complex planning now takes place in the Department of Defense and other areas of the government, with one crucial difference: the people consulted are members of the boards of directors of large corporations instead of the people as a whole. Because the process would be complex, we would want two key qualifications on the procedure:

1. The plan would be voted on not only as a whole, but also with separable components (much as is the present budget before Congress) so that people who liked most of it could vote "yes" on the question of making the plan as a whole the basis of discussion, and could also vote against any section of which they disapproved.

2. Any plan would have to allocate a great deal of the social surplus to each locality, so that a significant part of the wealth created by each community was in its hands to use, hence avoiding a situation in which people from far away tell people who have worked to create wealth that they cannot use even part of it in ways in which they desire.

Every community must have enough resources to experiment with education, housing, creativity, etc. The regional and national plans should deal with the minimum necessary number of issues: e.g., where to build new cities, how to solve general ecological problems, how to arrange transportation between localities, foreign trade, taxation, and long-term financing. The regional and national plans would have as one key task the allocation and redistribution of resources in wuch a way as to guarantee that no one area suffers because it does not have adequate natural resources or because a main source of its economic strength (e.g., car manufacturing or mining) is shut down for reasons of preserving the ecology. But since the idea of giving each community a large sum initially for discretionary planning is key to this conception, the national plan is likely to be less complicated than the present federal budget in an unplanned economy, because so much that is now decided nationally will be decided at the local level.

The key unit in the plan is the local community, whose power and resources would be greatly expanded. The emphasis for each community will be on experimentation, and funds will be made available so that minorities and individuals within each community who do not like the drift of the majority can experiment on their own. Within each community, the key centers of power will be the workplaces. Each factory or office will be democratically controlled by those who work there. All decisions that primarily affect the workers (e.g., work conditions) will be totally under their control. On the other hand, we do not envision a society such as that developed in Yugoslavia, where workers' control of each factory was not balanced by community, regional, or national control of the economy. There, without central community planning, the workers in each factory and each area began to develop specialized interests and began to relate to other groups of workers as competitors. If an economy composed of factories, each run by the workers, is governed only by the free marketplace, it becomes nothing but a rerun of capitalism on a higher level. It would be unlikely, for example, that one group of workers would agree to shut down its factory because it was producing an unnecessary commodity; instead, the workers would try to convince people the commodity was necessary and even, perhaps, to conceal its harmful effects, if it had any. Only a larger regional and national framework can assure people that their talents will be used creatively and that they will never have to suffer want and hence will enable them to accept the closing of their workplace for the common good. So it is crucial that the productive life of a community be decided by a balance between the claims of the worker in the workplace, which are to be given much weight, and the interests of the community as a whole.

· · ·

The conditions of work will be decided collectively, and workplaces will be governed by those who work in them. Given the present level of technology, much less the probable advances of the period ahead, it will be possible immediately after the people take control of the economy to reduce substantially the number of work hours for the individual without in any way reducing real wages. One way in which this will be done is to employ the unemployed in the production of necessary goods. But the most important way will be to eliminate all wasteful production. Production will be geared to goods that last instead of goods that fall apart to satisfy the need for new markets. When the economy is no longer geared to the trash can, the same amount of labor will produce more lasting social goods, so the total amount of work hours required to fill social needs will be less. Advertising will be seriously curtailed, duplication of production reduced, and consequently needs for new kinds of goods will be seriously reduced. Once production is geared to human needs, and needs are not artificially created, there will be much less production time necessary. For instance, vast rapid transit systems, built on ecologically sound models, can replace the production of automobiles. Sales jobs, insurance jobs, promotion and advertising jobs, and many governmental jobs will be seen as socially useless labor, and billions of hours of office work and secretarial work will be eliminated. The elimination of this kind of work in a capitalist framework would be frightening—because the people involved would simply be put on the job market to compete with everyone else. But the elimination of all this useless

work in a socialist society would be coordinated as part of a plan for reemploying everyone, and reducing the total number of hours that all people had to work. Add to this the increase in automated work, which at this point would be welcomed rather than opposed by the workers (since automation would mean less work but not unemployment and economic insecurity), and it can be safely predicted that within a very short period of time, probably not more than twenty to thirty years, the average workday would be five hours and the workweek four days. And both would decrease progressively in the next period.

. . . In a socialist society, while the total amount of work will be greatly reduced, the work that remains will have to be shared by all. To a large extent work will seem much more meaningful because the work conditions are under the worker's control and he is working to serve his fellow human beings' needs, but some work will still be drudgery and some will be unpleasant. A just distribution of work will permit inequalities if, and only if, they improve the position of those who are worst off, and the offices and positions to which the inequalities attach are open to all. In general, this will mean that unpleasant labor and drudgery will be done by everyone in the community on a rotating basis. We do not, of course, want to call a doctor away from the operating table to collect garbage, but we do want to create enough medical schools and training programs so that, were a particular doctor unavailable, someone else would be able to take his place.

Not only the worst work, but also work in general, will be rotated to the greatest degree possible consistent with the wishes of the people doing it. This will involve two key societal changes:

1. Job categories will have to be much changed from the present, and many tasks that are now combined in the hands of a "professional" will be distributed to a number of trained personnel. For example, paramedical training could be given to a very large percentage of the popula-

tion so that most of the work of the average medical doctor could be competently handled by people with a more limited but still proficient training. Or, to put it another way, people whose present jobs require only menial work and limited use of their intelligence would be given broader training and jobs would be more broadly defined to give them opportunity to use their intelligence. So, for example, we might find that the design of a building was discussed and decided not merely by a group of architects, but also by the people who were involved in constructing it and the people who were going to use it. In some limited areas, special expertise and long training would still be called for. But every attempt would be made to share expertise, develop it widely, and to have the expert in a given area use at least part of his time to teach his talents to as many people as wanted to learn.

2. Job assignments would be rotated at given intervals, separated by vacation periods and periods to learn new skills and techniques. Rotation would allow people to experience several kinds of work in their lifetime, and the training periods would guarantee that they learned how to do different jobs well. Rotation would also ensure that new perspectives were brought to most assignments, to provide additional creativity in the work situation. Rotation would not operate merely in relation to similar kinds of jobs, but also to different ones: people would shift among managerial, labor, clerical, skilled, farm, and other work so that each person had a full variety of experiences.

To the greatest extent possible, consistent with getting all the necessary jobs filled, job allocation would be voluntary. People would choose the job they wanted to be rotated to, with the proviso that jobs with power over others (managerial, for instance) and jobs that were unpleasant could be held only for a limited number of years. In the case of the least pleasant jobs, there would have to be accompanying compensation so that people who did them even for a limited time had additional benefits, such as significantly short workweeks or longer vacation periods.

. . .

THE SOCIALIST COMMUNITY

. . .

Probably one of the first actions of a socialist government would be to make free such essential services as health care, transportation, utilities, and housing. All forms of cultural activity would be free, and one of the main tasks of local government or administration would be to provide plans for making cultural experimentation possible for everyone. As a beginning, of course, we want every neighborhood to be equipped with adequate musical supplies, sports supplies, painting supplies, sculpture supplies, knitting, embroidery, macrame, etc. Each neighborhood should have facilities for the development of film, and facilities for the presentation of concerts and plays, as well as printing presses for leaflets, poetry, books and community newspapers. One of the highest ideals of the socialist revolution is to liberate and actualize human creativity. That is why we can adopt the slogan that workers and students used in the 1968 French rebellions: All Power to the Imagination.

Education will be radically transformed in our socialist community. For one thing, schools for youngsters will no longer be prisons. While basic skills will be taught, the greatest energies will be placed on allowing students to develop their talents by exposing them to the greatest possible range of creative activities. There will be no grading, but comprehensive reports on each youngster's development. A key element will be helping young people learn how to work and act together, at the same time respecting each person's individuality and uniqueness. Particularly in the elementary school, there will be no pressure on people to learn isolated facts about the world: the main emphasis will be on learning how to play, how to create, how to be an individual, and how to live and work collectively. The course content in high school is likely to resemble that of today's best liberal arts colleges: an introduction to the full variety of human thought, science, art, music, literature, and history of the past, taught not as isolated subjects but from a point of view that integrates all these fields. It is only when this kind of basic appreciation of the achievements and disabilities of the past are fully assimilated that the student can begin to specialize. There is no reason that most of what is today taught in college cannot be learned as thoroughly and perceptively at an earlier age, providing the student has not gone through the systematically moronizing experience that now goes under the name of elementary and high school education. The next level is learning some series of skills, for one's first set of jobs, and this learning will be repeated periodically as jobs are rotated. Every time one learns a new skill, however, time will be allowed to pursue in-depth education in some other area of intellectual and artistic interest, so that one can use one's leisure more intelligently.

So far we have been talking about the structured periods in which education is the primary activity. But, after the socialist revolution, education will have a much broader role. Every community will begin to develop facilities for extensive educational opportunities in all areas of human intellectual life. Given that at least half of our day will be free, many of us will avail ourselves of this kind of opportunity, and education will become a permanent feature of life, not limited to the youthful period, or rotation intervals.

. . .

It should be clear that in our socialist community we place as one of our highest goals the full development of each person. And we understand that this is achieved only through the full development and liberation of all. Indeed, the one is inconceivable without the other, for one of the chief needs of each person will be that every other person be fulfilled and their potentialities developed to the greatest extent possible. People will be spurred to creativity and to invention, to the development of beauty and love, both because it is self-fulfilling and because it is a positive contribution to society. . . . We do not believe that collectivity should ever mean the sacrifice of one's talents or skills or the abandonment of one's individu-

ality and uniqueness. It is precisely these things that make each human being precious and which a socialist society seeks to maximize. Collective sharing, collective living, collective activity, and collective loving must develop out of an appreciation and love for each individual member of the collective, and not out of the sense that the collective itself has a transcendent worth unrelated and far superior to the sum of the worth of individuals that compose it.

. . .

The complete and permanent liberation of women will be a first priority of the transition period, and is likely to be accomplished within two to three generations of the revolution. In the transition every effort will be devoted to eliminating sex roles that have been developed for both men and women, in every area from jobs and education to personal relations. In that period it is not unlikely that a strong independent women's movement will still function at every level of society to check on the progress in the battle to eliminate sexism and chauvinism. But after a few generations, this will be unnecessary. At that point, women will not be thought of as having any "group" characteristics that distinguish them from men, and much of what goes under the name of "masculinity" will also be transcended by men. Housework and child rearing will be completely shared, not because men think they "ought to help out" but because no one will see the slightest reason for women to have any greater role in these areas than men. There will be no economic dependence on men, and no assumption that a woman must find a man or else be thought of as strange or as a failure. In the transition period, many collective living arrangements will be composed only of women or only of men, although this is likely to seem less important once sex roles have largely disappeared. Women's passivity will be completely dethroned, and women will as likely be initiators of sexual contact as men, or as likely to shape the lives of their men as vice versa. Since decent human relations will become one of the main foci of life, there will be a marked reduction in competition for the affection and love of other people. Once love becomes superabundant, competition for it makes much less sense.

. . .

One of the greatest beneficiaries of these possibilities will be children. No longer raised by parents who think of them as their own private property, children will have the opportunity to grow up in a more extended family where they come into contact with a variety of significant others, both adult and peer. Parents no longer will have the same need to make their children what they never could be, or to make their children feel and think like them. No longer will we be victimized by the desperate need of unhappy people to pretend that childhood is a utopian period full of innocence and free of frustration. It will thus be possible to see children for what they are. The mutual concern with love for children expressed by the whole collective at once will give the child much more support and much more room for uniqueness and self-development, since there will be less consensus on "the right" path for him. Once the notion that children are not possessions is taken seriously, a variety of ways for them to become self-governing will develop, allowing them to maximize their own autonomy and to develop at their own pace, without in any way sacrificing the context of love and support. On the contrary, if children's ability to be independent and to define their lives for themselves is not considered a threatening sign of disrespect or lack of love for parents, the parent can begin to take pleasure in the child's development without feeling anxiety or rejection.

In talking about human relations I have suggested one style of relating which is likely to become common. But it will not be the only one. It is perfectly conceivable and even likely that there will still be many couples who like the monogamous family situation, and who want to live by themselves. This preference will also be respected. But its content and meaning for the individuals involved will inevitably be different from what it is today. In a context where other forms of living and relating obtain, no one will be forced to remain in the monogamous family for lack of an alternative. Hence monogamy is likely to be a free choice that can always be reversed without the tremendous pain and complications that attend divorce in modern America. Just as in questions of dress, appearance, art forms, work forms, etc., there will be plurality of life styles, each of which will be acceptable as long as it does not depend on some structural position which allows one person to exploit another. . . .

The same kind of principle will govern the existence of minority communities. Ethnic, religious, cultural, aesthetic, national, and historical differences embedded in common customs and traditions will be respected and there will be no attempt to uproot or displace them from the outside. Internationalism and human solidarity do not imply homogeneity. This point must be stressed again and again, not only because the reactionaries try to portray socialism as an extension of the trend, so marked in capitalist society, toward the suppression of individual and group differences, but also because some people in the New Left have given the most vulgar interpretation to what it means to fight "individualism." In the transition period especially, it is quite likely that minorities oppressed under capitalism will cling strongly to their culture as they join the general societal battle to smash the remnants of racism and other forms of prejudice. But even after racism and other prejudices no longer play any role in the consciousness or institutions of the new society, it is both probable and desirable that people take what is best in their cultural inheritance and build on it, rather than try to assimilate into one large homogeneous culture.

At several points in this account I suggested forms of living, working, and community building that may not totally appeal to each reader of this [essay]. Hence, it is important to stress that what I have tried to do is to outline a vision of what could be and what *I* would probably vote for and try to influence others to want. But I will have one vote, just like everyone else, and I will not have any more access to instruments of influence and power than anyone else, so the view that will win out will be the one that succeeds in convincing the largest number of people. There is no guarantee that every decision made will be the best one, but there is a guarantee that the mistakes will be *our* mistakes, made in good faith, and rectifiable by *all of us* when we decide to do so. That kind of guarantee is a world of difference from a society in which decisions about what to do, insofar as they are not simply given by the structure, are made on the basis of the need of a small group to maximize their own wealth and power. In capitalist society, rationality and truth have no efficacy unless they happen to coincide with the needs of vested interests. In a socialist society, free conscious activity is finally possible for all of us: we become the masters of our own fate.

BIBLIOGRAPHY

THE FOLLOWING SELECTIVE BIBLIOGRAPHY is designed to refer both teachers and students to books that we recommend for further study. The sections of the bibliography correspond to each chapter of the book. In order to save space, we have not included here the sources from which we excerpted readings for this book; we do recommend that interested readers follow up those sources as well as the additional materials listed below.

Several excellent textbooks develop the viewpoint of radical political economics as a whole:

Bowles, Samuel, and Richard Edwards, *Understanding Capitalism: Competition, Command and Change in the U.S. Economy*. New York: Harper & Row, 1985.

Hunt, E. K., and Howard J. Sherman, *Economics: An Introduction to Traditional and Radical Views* (5th ed.). New York: Harper & Row, 1985.

Institute for Labor Education and Research, *What's Wrong with the U.S. Economy?* Boston: South End Press, 1982.

For more detailed bibliographies on a wide variety of topics in radical political economy, we recommend the *Reading Lists in Radical Social Science*, published periodically by the Union for Radical Political Economics (155 West 23rd Street, 12th floor, New York, NY 10011). We also recommend the following journals as particularly good sources of current work by radical political economists:

Cambridge Journal of Economics, published quarterly by Academic Press, Inc., 111 Fifth Avenue, New York, NY 10003.

Capital and Class, published three times a year by the Conference of Socialist Economists, 25 Horsell Road, London N5, England.

Monthly Review, published monthly by Monthly Review Foundation, 155 West 23rd Street, New York, NY 10011.

Review of Radical Political Economics, published quarterly by the Union for Radical Political Economics, 155 West 23rd Street, 12th floor, New York, NY 10011.

Finally, for a continuing topical review of current economic events from a socialist perspective, see *Dollars and Sense*, published monthly by the Economic Affairs Bureau, Inc., 38 Union Square, Room 14, Somerville, MA 02143.

CHAPTER 2

Gurley, John G., *Challengers to Capitalism,* (2nd ed.). New York: W. W. Norton, 1980.

Howard, M. C., and J. E. King, *The Political Economy of Marx* (2nd ed.). New York: Longman, 1985.

Mandel, Ernest, *Long Waves of Capitalist Development*. New York: Cambridge University Press, 1980.

Marglin, Steven, *Growth, Distribution and Prices*. Cambridge, Mass.: Harvard University Press, 1984.

Marx, Karl, *Capital,* 3 vols. New York: Random House, 1976–81.

Sweezy, Paul M., *The Theory of Capitalist Development*. New York: Monthly Review Press, 1968.

CHAPTER 3

Amin, Samir, *Unequal Delopment*. New York: Monthly Review Press, 1977.

Averitt, Robert, *The Dual Economy*. New York: W. W. Norton, 1968.

Barnet, Richard, and Ronald Muller, *Global Reach: The Power of Multinational Corporations*. New York: Simon & Schuster, 1974.

Dowd, Douglas, *The Twisted Dream: Capitalist Development in the United States Since 1776* (2nd ed.). Cambridge, Mass.: Winthrop, 1977.

Herman, Edward S., *Corporate Control, Corporate Power*. New York: Cambridge University Press, 1981.

Shepherd, William G., *The Economics of Industrial Organization* (2nd ed.). Englewood Cliffs, N.J.: Prentice-Hall, 1985.

CHAPTER 4

Braverman, Harry, *Labor and Monopoly Capital: The Degradation of Work in the Twentieth Century*. New York: Monthly Review Press, 1974.

Carnoy, Martin, and Derek Shearer, *Economic Democracy: The Challenge of the 1980s.* Armonk, N.Y. M. E. Sharpe, 1980.

Freeman, Richard B., and James L. Medoff, *What Do Unions Do?* New York: Basic Books, 1984.

Green, James R., *The World of the Worker: Labor in Twentieth-Century America.* New York: Hill and Wang, 1980.

Wachtel, Howard M., *Labor and the Economy.* Orlando, Fla.: Academic Press, 1984.

Zimbalist, Andrew, ed., *Case Studies on the Labor Process.* New York: Monthly Review Press, 1979.

CHAPTER 5

Carnoy, Martin, *The State and Political Theory.* Princeton, N.J.: Princeton University Press, 1984.

Domhoff, G. William, *Who Rules America Now? A View for the '80s.* Englewood Cliffs, N.J.: Prentice-Hall, 1983.

Ferguson, Thomas, and Joel Rogers, eds., *The Political Economy.* Armonk, N.Y.: M. E. Sharpe, 1984.

Jessop, Bob, *The Capitalist State.* New York: New York University Press, 1982.

Miliband, Ralph, *Marxism and Politics.* New York: Oxford University Press, 1977.

Piven, Frances Fox, and Richard Cloward, *The New Class War: Reagan's Attack on the Welfare State and Its Consequences.* New York: Pantheon, 1982.

CHAPTER 6

Blumberg, Paul, *Inequality in an Age of Decline.* New York: Oxford University Press, 1980.

Bowles, Samuel, and Herbert M. Gintis, *Schooling in Capitalist America.* New York: Basic Books, 1976.

Sabel, Charles F., *Work and Politics: The Division of Labor in Industry.* New York: Cambridge University Press, 1982.

Szymanski, Albert, *Class Structure: A Critical Perspective*. New York: Praeger, 1983.

Walker, Pat, ed., *Between Labor and Capital*. Boston: South End Press, 1979.

Wright, Erik O., *Class, Crisis and the State*. London: New Left Books, 1978.

CHAPTER 7

Chodorow, Nancy, *The Reproduction of Mothering: Psychoanalysis and the Sociology of Gender*. Berkeley: University of California Press, 1978.

Eisenstein, Zillah R., ed., *Capitalist Patriarchy and the Case for Socialist Feminism*. New York: Monthly Review Press, 1978.

Kessler-Harris, Alice, *Out to Work: A History of Wage-Earning Women in the United States*. New York: Oxford University Press, 1982.

Matthaei, Julie A., *An Economic History of Women in America*. New York: Schocken Books, 1982.

Sokoloff, Natalie J., *Between Money and Love: The Dialectics of Women's Home and Market Work*. New York: Praeger, 1980.

Treiman, Donald J., and Heidi I. Hartmann, eds., *Women, Work and Wages: Equal Pay for Jobs of Equal Value*. Washington, D.C.: National Academy Press, 1981.

CHAPTER 8

Barrera, Mario, *Race and Class in the Southwest*. South Bend, Ind.: Notre Dame University Press, 1979.

Bowser, Benjamin P., and Raymond G. Hunt, eds., *Impacts of Racism on White Americans*. Beverly Hills, Calif.: Sage Publications, 1981.

Davis, Angela, *Women, Race and Class*. New York: Random House, 1981.

Foner, Philip S., *Organized Labor and the Black Worker 1619–1973*. New York: International Publishers, 1974.

Fusfeld, Daniel R., and Timothy Bates, *The Political Economy of the Urban Ghetto*. Carbondale: Southern Illinois University Press, 1984.

Marable, Manning, *How Capitalism Underdeveloped Black America*. Boston: South End Press, 1983.

CHAPTER 9

Baran, Paul A., and Paul M. Sweezy, *Monopoly Capital*. New York: Monthy Review Press, 1966.

Gorz, Andre, *Ecology as Politics*. Boston, Mass.: South End Press, 1981.

Kaldor, Mary, *The Baroque Arsenal*. New York: Hill and Wang, 1981.

Kapp, K. William, *The Social Costs of Business Enterprise*. New York: Schocken Books, 1971.

Tabb, William K., and Larry Sawers, *Marxism and the Metropolis* (2nd ed.). New York: Oxford University Press, 1984.

Weisskopf, Walter, *Alienation and Economics*. New York: Dutton, 1971.

CHAPTER 10

Ackerman, Frank, *Hazardous to Our Wealth: Economic Policy in the 1980s*. Boston: South End Press, 1984.

Armstrong, Philip, Andrew Glyn, and John Harrison, *Capitalism Since World War II*. London: Fontana, 1984.

Block, Fred, *The Origins of International Economic Disorder*. Berkeley: University of California Press, 1977.

Bluestone, Barry, and Bennett Harrison, *The Deindustrialization of America*. New York: Basic Books, 1982.

Magdoff, Harry, and Paul M. Sweezy, *The Deepening Crisis of U.S. Capitalism*. New York: Monthly Review Press, 1982.

Sherman, Howard J., and Gary R. Evans, *Macro-Economics: Keynesian, Monetarist and Marxist Views*. New York: Harper & Row, 1984.

CHAPTER 11

Bowles, Samuel, David M. Gordon, and Thomas E. Weisskopf, *Beyond the Waste Land: A Democratic Alternative to Economic Decline*. New York: Anchor Doubleday, 1983.

Gurley, John G., *Challenges to Communism*. San Francisco: W. H. Freeman, 1983.

Hodgson, Geoff, *The Democratic Economy*. London: Penguin, 1984.

Horvat, Branko, *The Political Economy of Socialism*. Armonk, N.Y.: M. E. Sharpe, 1983.

Nove, Alec, *The Economics of Feasible Socialism*. Boston: Allen and Unwin, 1983.

Weinstein, James, *Ambiguous Legacy: The Left in American Politics*. New York: Franklin Watts, 1975.

Zimbalist, Andrew, and Howard J. Sherman, *Comparing Economic Systems: A Political-Economic Approach*. Orlando, Fla.: Academic Press, 1984.